P9-DGV-107

BRITISH WRITERS

BRITISH WRITERS

JAY PARINI
Editor

SUPPLEMENT X

CHARLES SCRIBNER'S SONS
An imprint of Thomson Gale, a part of The Thomson Corporation

Detroit • New York • San Francisco • San Diego • New Haven, Conn. • Waterville, Maine • London • Munich

British Writers Supplement X

Jay Parini, Editor in Chief

© 2004 Thomson Gale, a part of Thomson Corporation.

Thomson and Star Logo are trademarks and Gale and Charles Scribner's Sons are trademarks used herein under license.

For more information, contact
Thomson Gale
27500 Drake Rd.
Farmington Hills, MI 48331-3535
Or you can visit our Internet site at
http://www.gale.com

Permissions Department
Thomson Gale.
27500 Drake Rd.
Farmington Hills, MI 48331-3535
Permissions Hotline:
248 699-8006 or 800 877-4253, ext. 8006
Fax: 248 699-8074 or 800 762-4058

Since this page cannot legibly accommodate all copyright notices, the acknowledgments constitute an extension of the copyright notice.

LIBRARY OF CONGRESS CATALOGING-IN-PUBLICATION DATA

British Writers Supplement X / Jay Parini, editor.
  p. cm.
Includes bibliographical references and index.
  ISBN 0-684-31312-X (hardcover : alk. paper)
  1. English literature–20th century–Bio-bibliography. 2. English literature–20th century–History and criticism. 3. Commonwealth literature (English)–History and criticism. 4. Commonwealth literature (English)–Bio-bibliography. 5. Authors, Commonwealth–20th century–Biography. 6. Authors, English–20th century–Biography. I. Parini, Jay.
  PR85 .B688 Suppl. 10
  820.9'941–dc22
                              2004014730

Printed in the United States of America
10 9 8 7 6 5 4 3 2 1

Acknowledgments

Acknowledgment is gratefully made to those publishers and
individuals who permitted the use of the following materials in copyright:

DOUGLAS DUNN Dunn, Douglas. From *Barbarians*.
Faber and Faber, 1979. © Douglas Dunn, 1979. All
rights reserved. Reproduced by permission of Faber &
Faber Ltd. From *Dante's Drum-kit*. Faber and Faber,
1993. © Douglas Dunn, 1993. All rights reserved.
Reproduced by permission of Faber & Faber Ltd.
From *Elegies*. Faber and Faber, 1985. © Douglas
Dunn, 1985. All rights reserved. Reproduced by
permission of Faber & Faber Ltd. From *Love or Noth-
ing*. Faber & Faber, 1974. © 1974 by Douglas Dunn.
All rights reserved. Reproduced by permission of
Faber & Faber Ltd. From *Northlight*. Faber and Faber,
1988. © Douglas Dunn, 1988. All rights reserved.
Reproduced by permission of Faber & Faber Ltd.
From *Secret Villages*. Faber & Faber 1985. © 1985 by
Douglas Dunn. All rights reserved. Reproduced by
permission of Faber & Faber Ltd. From *St. Kilda's
Parliament*. Faber and Faber, 1981. © Douglas Dunn,
1981. All rights reserved. Reproduced by permission
of Faber & Faber Ltd. From *Terry Street*. Faber and
Faber, 1969. © Douglas Dunn, 1969. All rights
reserved. Reproduced by permission of Faber & Faber
Ltd. From *The Donkey's Ears: Politovsky's Letters
Home*. Faber and Faber, 2000. © Douglas Dunn, 2000.
All rights reserved. Reproduced by permission of
Faber & Faber Ltd. From *The Happier Life*. Chilmark
Press, 1972. © Douglas Dunn, 1972. All rights
reserved. Reproduced by permission of Faber & Faber
Ltd. From *The Year's Afternoon*. Faber and Faber,
2000. © Douglas Dunn, 2000. All rights reserved. All
reproduced by permission of Faber & Faber Ltd.
Haffenden, John. From *Viewpoints: Poets in Conversa-
tion*. Faber and Faber, 1981. © 1981 by John
Haffenden. Reproduced by permission of Faber &
Faber Ltd. *Verse*, no. 4, 1985 for "Douglas Dunn Talking with Robert Crawford" by Douglas Dunn. © 1985.
Copyright Douglas Dunn. Reproduced by permission
of PFD on behalf of Douglas Dunn.

ROMESH GUNESEKERA Gunesekera, Romesh. *London Review of Books*, v. 11, February 16, 1989 for
"Pigs". Reproduced by permission of the *London
Review of Books*. *Poetry Durham*, v. 11, winter, 1985
for "Circled by Circe"; "Going Home (A Letter to Colombo)"; "House Building"; "Indian Tree." All
reproduced by permission of Romesh Gunesekera.

Poetry Matters, v. 6, 1988 for "Frontliners" by
Romesh Gunesekera. Reproduced by permission of
the author. *The Pen*, no. 24, winter, 1988 for "Indefinite Exposure" by Romesh Gunesekera. Reproduced
by permission of the author.

JAN MORRIS Morris, Jan. From *Conundrum*, Revised
Edition. By Jan Morris. Faber and Faber, 2001.
Copyright 1974, 2001 by Jan Morris. Reproduced by
permission of Faber & Faber Ltd. From an Introduc-
tion in *Eothen*. Oxford University Press, 1982.
Reproduced by permission of A.P. Watt Ltd on behalf
of Jan Morris. Users must not reproduce, download,
store in any medium, distribute, transmit, retransmit
or manipulate any text contained in this. From
"Traveling Writer," in *The Writer on Her Work, Vol.
II*. Edited by Janet Sternberg. W. W. Norton &
Company, 1991. Copyright © Janet Sternberg. *Times
Literary Supplement*, August 12, 1960; January 11,
1974; © The Times Supplements Limited 1960, 1974.
Reproduced from *The Times Literary Supplement* by
permission.

ROBERT NYE Nye, Robert. From *A Collection of
Poems 1955-1988*. Hamish Hamilton, 1989. © 1989
Robert Nye. Reproduced by permission of Curtis
Brown Group Ltd., London on behalf of Robert Nye.
From *Collected Poems*. Sinclair-Stevenson, 1995.
Copyright © Robert Nye. Reproduced by permission
of Curtis Brown Group Ltd., London on behalf of
Robert Nye. From *Darker Ends*. Hill & Wang, 1969.
Copyright © 1969 by Robert Nye. All rights reserved.
Reproduced by permission of Hill & Wang, a division
of Farrar, Straus and Giroux, LLC. In the UK by
permission of Curtis Brown Group Ltd., London on
behalf of Robert Nye. From *Divisions on a Ground*.
Carcanet, 1976. © 1976 Robert Nye. Reproduced with
permission of Curtis Brown Group Ltd., London on
behalf of Robert Nye. From *Juvenilia 1*. Scorpion
Press, 1961. Reproduced by permission of Curtis
Brown Group Ltd., London on behalf of Robert Nye.
From *Juvenilia 2*. Scorpion Press, 1963. Reproduced
by permission of Curtis Brown Group Ltd., London
on behalf of Robert Nye. From *New and Selected
Poems*. Cecil Woolf. Copyright © Robert Nye.
Reproduced by permission of Curtis Brown Group
Ltd., London on behalf of Robert Nye.

ACKNOWLEDGEMENTS

DENNIS POTTER Potter, Dennis. From *Waiting for the Boat*. Faber and Faber, 1984. Reproduced by permission of Faber & Faber Ltd.

IAN RANKIN Pierce, J. Kingston. From "Ian Rankin: The Accidental Crime Writer," www.januarymagazine.com, February 23, 2004. Reproduced by permission of the author.

KEITH ROBERTS Roberts, Keith. From "Calais Encounter," in *A Heron Caught in Weeds*. Edited by Jim Goddard. Kerosina, 1987. Reproduced by permission of the author. From "Grainne," in *A Heron Caught in Weeds*. Edited by Jim Goddard. Kerosina, 1987. Reproduced by permission of the author. From "Home Thoughts from a Coach," in *A Heron Caught in Weeds*. Edited by Jim Goddard. Kerosina, 1987. Reproduced by permission of the author. From "Synth," in *New Writings in SF 8*. Edited by John Carnell. Dobson, 1966. Copyright © 1966 by John Carnell. Reproduced by permission of the author. From "The Grain Kings," in *The Grain Kings*, Hutchinson, 1976. Reproduced by permission of the author. From "Verulam," in *A Heron Caught in Weeds*. Edited by Jim Goddard. Kerosina, 1987. Reproduced by permission of the author. From "At Hellfire Corner" in *A Heron Caught in Weeds*. Edited by Jim Goddard. Kerosina, 1987. Reproduced by permission of the author.

VIKRAM SETH Seth, Vikram. From *All You Who Sleep Tonight*. Alfred A. Knopf, 1990. © 1990 by Vikram Seth. Reproduced by permission of Alfred A. Knopf, a division of Random House, Inc., and Curtis Brown Group Ltd., London on behalf of Vikram Seth. From *Arion and the Dolphin*. Phoenix House, 1994. Reproduced by permission of Curtis Brown Group Ltd., London on behalf of Vikram Seth. From *Mappings*. Writer's Workshop, 1981. Reproduced by permission of the author. *Indian Review of Books*, v. 2, 1993 for "A Conversation with Vikram Seth. Mixed Beasts and Cultural Products" by Makarand Paranjape. Reproduced by permission of the author.

JON STALLWORTHY Stallworthy, Jon. From *A Familiar Tree*. Chatto and Windus, 1978. Copyright © Jon Stallworthy and David Gentleman 1978. All rights reserved. Reproduced by permission of The Random House Group Limited. From *Anzac Sonata: New and Selected Poems*. W. W. Norton & Company, 1986. Copyright © 1986 Jon Stallworthy. All rights reserved. Reproduced by permission of W. W. Norton & Company, Inc. From *Hand in Hand*. Chatto and Windus with the Hogarth Press Ltd., 1974. Copyright © Jon Stallworthy 1974. All rights reserved. Reproduced by permission of The Random House Group Limited. From *Root and Branch*. Chatto and Windus with the Hogarth Press Ltd., 1969. Copyright © Jon Stallworthy 1969. Reproduced by permission of The Random House Group Limited. From *Skyhorse*. Thumbscrew Press, 2002. Reproduced by permission. From *The Almond Tree*. Turret Books, 1967. Copyright © Jon Stallworthy 1967. Reproduced by permission of The Random House Group Limited. From *The Guest from the Future*. Carcanet, Copyright © Jon Stallworthy 1995. All rights reserved. Reproduced by permission of Carcanet Press Limited. *Critical Quarterly*, v. 3, summer, 1961 for "Review of The Astronomy of Love" by Robin Skelton. Reproduced by permission of Blackwell Publishers. *London Review of Books*, v. 21, March 4, 1999 for "Untouched by Eliot" by Denis Donoghue. Reproduced by permission of the *London Review of Books*. *Ploughshares*, v. 17, spring, 1991 for "The Girl from Zlot" by Jon Stallworthy. Copyright © 1991 by Emersen College. Reproduced by permission of the author. *Times Literary Supplement* v. 8, January, 1999 for "Singing School: The Making of a Poet" by Peter McDonald. Copyright © The Times Supplements Limited 1999. Reproduced from *The Times Literary Supplement* by permission.

Editorial and Production Staff

Project Editors
LARRY TRUDEAU
MAIKUE VANG

Copyeditors
ROBERT E. JONES
LINDA SANDERS

Proofreader
ALLISON LEOPOLD

Indexer
SYNAPSE CORPORATION

Permission Researcher
JULIE VAN PELT

Composition Specialist
GARY LEACH

Buyer
RHONDA WILLIAMS

Publisher
FRANK MENCHACA

Contents

Introduction

"Reading is to the mind what exercise is to the body," wrote Richard Steele, the great English essayist from the eighteenth century. The articles in this collection point to a wealth of good exercise for the mind, treating a wide range of British authors, or authors who write in the tradition of British literature, often in a postcolonial setting. In Supplement X we present detailed, articulate introductions to authors, mostly contemporary, although some are from the recent past, and two—Richard Brome and James Hogg —belong to the distant past. In each case the articles have been written in a way designed to increase the reader's pleasure in the work of the subject, and to make the shape of that career, its evolution and influence, comprehensible.

As a whole, this series brings together a wide range of articles on British writers who have a considerable reputation in the literary world. As in previous volumes, the subjects have been chosen for their significant contribution to the traditions of literature, and each has influenced intellectual life in Britain in some way. Readers will find these essays lively and intelligent, designed to interest readers unfamiliar with their work and to assist those who know the work quite well by providing close readings of individual texts and a sense of the biographical, cultural, and critical context of that work. Detailed bibliographies of work by the given subject and work about this writer are included.

British Writers was originally an off–shoot of a series of monographs that appeared between 1959 and 1972, the *Minnesota Pamphlets on American Writers*. These pamphlets were incisively written and informative, treating ninety–seven American writers in a format and style that attracted a devoted following of readers. The series proved invaluable to a generation of students and teachers, who could depend on these reliable and interesting critiques of major figures. The idea of reprinting these essays occurred to Charles Scribner, Jr., an innovative publisher during the middle decades of the twentieth century. The series appeared in four volumes entitled *American Writers: A Collection of Literary Biographies* (1974). *British Writers* began with a series of essays originally published by the British Council, and regular supplements have followed. The goal of the supplements has been consistent with the original idea of the series: to provide clear, informative essays aimed at the general reader. These essays often rise to a high level of craft and critical vision, but they are meant to introduce a writer of some importance in the history of British or Anglophone literature, and to provide a sense of the scope and nature of the career under review.

The authors of these critical articles are mostly teachers, scholars, and writers. Most have published books and articles in their field, and several are well–known writers of poetry or fiction as well as critics. As anyone glancing through this volume will see, they have been held to the highest standards of clear writing and sound scholarship. Jargon and theoretical musings have been discouraged, except when strictly relevant. Each of the essays concludes with a select bibliography of works by the author under discussion and secondary works that might be useful to those who wish to pursue the subject further. Supplement X centers on contemporary writers from various genres and traditions who have had little sustained attention from critics, although most are well known. Ayi Kwei Armah, Douglas Dunn, Romesh Gunesekera, Alan Hollinghurst, Rohinton Mistry, Jan Morris, Robert Nye, Ian Rankin, Vikram Seth, and Jon Stallworthy have all been written about in the review pages of newspapers and magazines, often at considerable length, and their work has acquired a substantial following, but their careers have yet to attract significant scholarship. That will certainly follow, but the essays included in this volume constitute a beginning of sorts, an attempt to map out the particular universe of each writer.

INTRODUCTION

Four classic writers from the distant past included here are Richard Brome, James Hogg, Margaret Oliphant (usually known as Mrs. Oliphant), and Isabella Bird—important authors who, for one reason or another, have yet to be treated in this series. Some writers from the recent past, such as Vera Brittain, Nancy Mitford, Dennis Potter, and Keith Roberts, have attracted a following but not yet been considered in this series. All six deserve the quality of attention paid to them in this articles. These are well-known figures in the literary world, major voices, and it is time they were added to the series.

As ever, our purpose in presenting these critical and biographical essays is to bring readers back to the texts discussed, to help them in their reading. These are especially strong and stimulating essays, and they should enable students and general readers to enter into the world of these writers freshly, encouraging them on their intellectual journeys. They should help readers to appreciate the way things are said by these authors, thus enhancing their pleasure in the texts. Above all, these essays should lengthen the reading list of those wishing to exercise their minds.

—*Jay Parini*

Chronology

ca. 1342	John Trevisa born
1348	The Black Death (further outbreaks in 1361 and 1369)
ca. 1350	Boccaccio's *Decameron* Langland's *Piers Plowman*
1351	The Statute of Laborers pegs laborers' wages at rates in effect preceding the plague
1356	The Battle of Poitiers
1360	The Treaty of Brétigny: end of the first phase of the Hundred Years' War
1362	Pleadings in the law courts conducted in English Parliaments opened by speeches in English
1369	Chaucer's *The Book of the Duchess*, an elegy to Blanche of Lancaster, wife of John of Gaunt
1369–1377	Victorious French campaigns under du Guesclin
ca. 1370	John Lydgate born
1371	Sir John Mandeville's *Travels*
1372	Chaucer travels to Italy
1372–1382	Wycliffe active in Oxford
1373–1393	William of Wykeham founds Winchester College and New College, Oxford
ca. 1375–1400	*Sir Gawain and the Green Knight*
1376	Death of Edward the Black Prince
1377–1399	**Reign of Richard II**
ca. 1379	Gower's *Vox clamantis*
ca. 1380	Chaucer's *Troilus and Criseyde*
1381	The Peasants' Revolt
1386	Chaucer's *Canterbury Tales* begun Chaucer sits in Parliament Gower's *Confessio amantis*
1399–1413	**Reign of Henry IV**
ca. 1400	Death of William Langland
1400	Death of Geoffrey Chaucer
1408	Death of John Gower
1412–1420	Lydgate's *Troy Book*
1413–1422	**Reign of Henry V**
1415	The Battle of Agincourt
1420–1422	Lydgate's *Siege of Thebes*
1422–1461	**Reign of Henry VI**
1431	François Villon born Joan of Arc burned at Rouen
1440–1441	Henry VI founds Eton College and King's College, Cambridge
1444	Truce of Tours
1450	Jack Cade's rebellion
ca. 1451	Death of John Lydgate
1453	End of the Hundred Years' War The fall of Constantinople
1455–1485	The Wars of the Roses
ca. 1460	Births of William Dunbar and John Skelton
1461–1470	**Reign of Edward IV**
1470–1471	**Reign of Henry VI**
1471	Death of Sir Thomas Malory
1471–1483	**Reign of Edward IV**
1476–1483	Caxton's press set up: *The Canterbury Tales*, *Morte d'Arthur*, and *The Golden Legend* printed
1483–1485	**Reign of Richard III**
1485	The Battle of Bosworth Field; end of the Wars of the Roses
1485–1509	**Reign of Henry VII**
1486	Marriage of Henry VII and Elizabeth of York unites the rival houses of Lancaster and York Bartholomew Diaz rounds the Cape of Good Hope
1492	Columbus' first voyage to the New World
1493	Pope Alexander VI divides undiscovered territories between Spain and Portugal
1497–1498	John Cabot's voyages to Newfoundland and Labrador
1497–1499	Vasco da Gama's voyage to India
1499	Amerigo Vespucci's first voyage to America Erasmus' first visit to England
1503	Thomas Wyatt born
1505	John Colet appointed dean of St. Paul's: founds St. Paul's School
1509–1547	**Reign of Henry VIII**

CHRONOLOGY

CHRONOLOGY

1566   William Painter's *Palace of Pleasure*, a miscellany of prose stories, the source of many dramatists' plots

1567   Darnley murdered at Kirk o'Field
Mary Queen of Scots marries the earl of Bothwell

1569   Rebellion of the English northern earls suppressed

1570   Roger Ascham's *The Schoolmaster*

1571   Defeat of the Turkish fleet at Lepanto

ca. 1572   Ben Jonson born

1572   St. Bartholomew's Day massacre
John Donne born

1574   The earl of Leicester's theater company formed

1576   The Theater, the first permanent theater building in London, opened
The first Blackfriars Theater opened with performances by the Children of St. Paul's
John Marston born

1576–1578   Martin Frobisher's voyages to Labrador and the northwest

1577–1580   Sir Francis Drake sails around the world

1577   Holinshed's *Chronicles of England, Scotlande, and Irelande*

1579   John Lyly's *Euphues: The Anatomy of Wit*
Thomas North's translation of *Plutarch's Lives*

1581   The Levant Company founded
Seneca's *Ten Tragedies* translated

1582   Richard Hakluyt's *Divers Voyages Touching the Discoverie of America*

1584–1585   Sir John Davis' first voyage to Greenland

1585   First English settlement in America, the "Lost Colony" comprising 108 men under Ralph Lane, founded at Roanoke Island, off the coast of North Carolina

1586   Kyd's *Spanish Tragedy*
Marlowe's *Tamburlaine*
William Camden's *Britannia*
The Babington conspiracy against Queen Elizabeth
Death of Sir Philip Sidney

1587   Mary Queen of Scots executed

Birth of Virginia Dare, first English child born in America, at Roanoke Island

1588   Defeat of the Spanish Armada
Marlowe's *Dr. Faustus*

1590   Spenser's *The Faerie Queen*, Cantos 1–3
Richard Brome born

1592   Outbreak of plague in London; the theaters closed
Henry King born

1593   Death of Christopher Marlowe

1594   The Lord Chamberlain's Men, the company to which Shakespeare belonged, founded
The Swan Theater opened
Death of Thomas Kyd

1595   Ralegh's expedition to Guiana
Sidney's *Apology for Poetry*

1596   The earl of Essex's expedition captures Cadiz
The second Blackfriars Theater opened

ca. 1597   Death of George Peele

1597   Bacon's first collection of *Essays*

1598   Jonson's *Every Man in His Humor*

1598–1600   Richard Hakluyt's *Principal Navigations, Voyages, Traffics, and Discoveries of the English Nation*

1599   The Globe Theater opened
Death of Edmund Spenser

1600   Death of Richard Hooker

1601   Rebellion and execution of the earl of Essex

1602   The East India Company founded
The Bodleian Library reopened at Oxford

1603–1625   **Reign of James I**

1603   John Florio's translation of Montaigne's *Essays*
Cervantes' *Don Quixote* (Part 1)
The Gunpowder Plot
Thomas Browne born

1604   Shakespeare's *Othello*

ca. 1605   Shakespears's *King Lear*
Tourneur's *The Revenger's Tragedy*

1605   Bacon's *Advancement of Learning*

1606   Shakespeare's *Macbeth*
Jonson's *Volpone*
Death of John Lyly
Edmund Waller born

CHRONOLOGY

CHRONOLOGY

CHRONOLOGY

1656 Sir William Davenant produces *The Siege of Rhodes*, one of the first English operas

1657 Second Parliament of the Protectorate

Cromwell is offered and declines the throne

Death of Richard Lovelace

1658 Death of Oliver Cromwell

Richard Cromwell succeeds as Protector

1659 Conflict between Parliament and the army

1660 General Monck negotiates with Charles II

Charles II offers the conciliatory Declaration of Breda and accepts Parliament's invitation to return

Will's Coffee House established

Sir William Davenant and Thomas Killigrew licensed to set up two companies of players, the Duke of York's and the King's Servants, including actors and actresses

Pepys's *Diary* begun

1660–1685 Reign of Charles II

1661 Parliament passes the Act of Uniformity, enjoining the use of the Book of Common Prayer; many Puritan and dissenting clergy leave their livings

Anne Finch born

1662 Peace Treaty with Spain

King Charles II marries Catherine of Braganza

The Royal Society incorporated (founded in 1660)

1664 War against Holland

New Amsterdam captured and becomes New York

John Vanbrugh born

1665 The Great Plague

Newton discovers the binomial theorem and invents the integral and differential calculus, at Cambridge

1666 The Great Fire of London

Bunyan's *Grace Abounding*

London Gazette founded

1667 The Dutch fleet sails up the Medway and burns English ships

The war with Holland ended by the Treaty of Breda

Milton's *Paradise Lost*

Thomas Sprat's *History of the Royal Society*

Death of Abraham Cowley

1668 Sir Christopher Wren begins to rebuild St. Paul's Cathedral

Triple Alliance formed with Holland and Sweden against France

Dryden's *Essay of Dramatick Poesy*

1670 Alliance formed with France through the secret Treaty of Dover

Pascal's *Pensées*

The Hudson's Bay Company founded

William Congreve born

1671 Milton's *Samson Agonistes* and *Paradise Regained*

1672 War against Holland

Wycherley's *The Country Wife*

King Charles issues the Declaration of Indulgence, suspending penal laws against Nonconformists and Catholics

1673 Parliament passes the Test Act, making acceptance of the doctrines of the Church of England a condition for holding public office

1674 War with Holland ended by the Treaty of Westminster

Deaths of John Milton, Robert Herrick, and Thomas Traherne

1676 Etherege's *The Man of Mode*

1677 Baruch Spinoza's *Ethics*

Jean Racine's *Phèdre*

King Charles's niece, Mary, marries her cousin William of Orange

1678 Fabrication of the so-called popish plot by Titus Oates

Bunyan's *Pilgrim's Progress*

Dryden's *All for Love*

Death of Andrew Marvell

George Farquhar born

1679 Parliament passes the Habeas Corpus Act

Rochester's *A Satire Against Mankind*

1680 Death of John Wilmot, earl of Rochester

1681 Dryden's *Absalom and Achitophel* (Part 1)

CHRONOLOGY

1682 Dryden's *Absalom and Achitophel* (Part 2)
Thomas Otway's *Venice Preserv'd*
Philadelphia founded
Death of Sir Thomas Browne

1683 The Ashmolean Museum, the world's first public museum, opens at Oxford
Death of Izaak Walton

1685–1688 Reign of James II

1685 Rebellion and execution of James Scott, duke of Monmouth
John Gay born

1686 The first book of Newton's *Principia*—*De motu corporum*, containing his theory of gravitation—presented to the Royal Society

1687 James II issues the Declaration of Indulgence
Dryden's *The Hind and the Panther*
Death of Edmund Waller

1688 James II reissues the Declaration of Indulgence, renewing freedom of worship and suspending the provisions of the Test Act
Acquittal of the seven bishops imprisoned for protesting against the Declaration
William of Orange lands at Torbay, Devon
James II takes refuge in France
Death of John Bunyan
Alexander Pope born

1689–1702 Reign of William III

1689 Parliament formulates the Declaration of Rights
William and Mary accept the Declaration and the crown
The Grand Alliance concluded between the Holy Roman Empire, England, Holland, and Spain
War declared against France
King William's War, 1689–1697 (the first of the French and Indian wars)
Samuel Richardson born

1690 James II lands in Ireland with French support, but is defeated at the battle of the Boyne
John Locke's *Essay Concerning Human Understanding*

1692 Salem witchcraft trials

Death of Sir George Etherege

1694 George Fox's *Journal*
Voltaire (François Marie Arouet) born
Death of Mary II

1695 Congreve's *Love for Love*
Death of Henry Vaughan

1697 War with France ended by the Treaty of Ryswick
Vanbrugh's *The Relapse*

1698 Jeremy Collier's *A Short View of the Immorality and Profaneness of the English Stage*

1699 Fénelon's *Les Aventures de Télémaque*

1700 Congreve's *The Way of the World*
Defoe's *The True-Born Englishman*
Death of John Dryden
James Thomson born

1701 War of the Spanish Succession, 1701–1714 (Queen Anne's War in America, 1702–1713)
Death of Sir Charles Sedley

1702–1714 Reign of Queen Anne

1702 Clarendon's *History of the Rebellion* (1702–1704)
Defoe's *The Shortest Way with the Dissenters*

1703 Defoe is arrested, fined, and pilloried for writing *The Shortest Way*
Death of Samuel Pepys

1704 John Churchill, duke of Marlborough, and Prince Eugene of Savoy defeat the French at Blenheim
Capture of Gibraltar
Swift's *A Tale of a Tub* and *The Battle of the Books*
The Review founded (1704–1713)

1706 Farquhar's *The Recruiting Officer*
Deaths of John Evelyn and Charles Sackville, earl of Dorset

1707 Farquhar's *The Beaux' Stratagem*
Act of Union joining England and Scotland
Death of George Farquhar
Henry Fielding born

1709 The *Tatler* founded (1709–1711)
Nicholas Rowe's edition of Shakespeare
Samuel Johnson born

CHRONOLOGY

Marlborough defeats the French at Malplaquet

Charles XII of Sweden defeated at Poltava

1710 South Sea Company founded
First copyright act

1711 Swift's *The Conduct of the Allies*
The *Spectator* founded (1711–1712; 1714)
Marlborough dismissed
David Hume born

1712 Pope's *The Rape of the Lock* (Cantos 1–2)
Jean Jacques Rousseau born

1713 War with France ended by the Treaty of Utrecht
The *Guardian* founded
Swift becomes dean of St. Patrick's, Dublin
Addison's *Cato*
Laurence Sterne born

1714–1727 Reign of George I

1714 Pope's expended version of *The Rape of the Lock* (Cantos 1–5)

1715 The Jacobite rebellion in Scotland
Pope's translation of Homer's *Iliad* (1715–1720)
Death of Louis XIV

1716 Death of William Wycherley
Thomas Gray born

1717 Pope's *Eloisa to Abelard*
David Garrick born
Horace Walpole born

1718 Quadruple Alliance (Britain, France, the Netherlands, the German Empire) in war against Spain

1719 Defoe's *Robinson Crusoe*
Death of Joseph Addison

1720 Inoculation against smallpox introduced in Boston
War against Spain
The South Sea Bubble
Gilbert White born
Defoe's *Captain Singleton* and *Memoirs of a Cavalier*

1721 Tobias Smollett born
William Collins born

1722 Defoe's *Moll Flanders*, *Journal of the Plague Year*, and *Colonel Jack*

1724 Defoe's *Roxana*
Swift's *The Drapier's Letters*

1725 Pope's translation of Homer's *Odyssey* (1725–1726)

1726 Swift's *Gulliver's Travels*
Voltaire in England (1726–1729)
Death of Sir John Vanbrugh

1727–1760 Reign of George II

1728 Gay's *The Beggar's Opera*
Pope's *The Dunciad* (Books 1–2)
Oliver Goldsmith born

1729 Swift's *A Modest Proposal*
Edmund Burke born
Deaths of William Congreve and Sir Richard Steele

1731 Navigation improved by introduction of the quadrant
Pope's *Moral Essays* (1731–1735)
Death of Daniel Defoe
William Cowper born

1732 Death of John Gay

1733 Pope's *Essay on Man* (1733–1734)
Lewis Theobald's edition of Shakespeare

1734 Voltaire's *Lettres philosophiques*

1736 James Macpherson born

1737 Edward Gibbon born

1738 Johnson's *London*

1740 War of the Austrian Succession, 1740–1748 (King George's War in America, 1744–1748)
George Anson begins his circumnavigation of the world (1740–1744)
Frederick the Great becomes king of Prussia (1740–1786)
Richardson's *Pamela* (1740–1741)
James Boswell born

1742 Fielding's *Joseph Andrews*
Edward Young's *Night Thoughts* (1742–1745)
Pope's *The New Dunciad* (Book 4)

1744 Johnson's *Life of Mr. Richard Savage*
Death of Alexander Pope

1745 Second Jacobite rebellion, led by Charles Edward, the Young Pretender
Death of Jonathan Swift

1746 The Young Pretender defeated at Culloden
Collins' *Odes on Several Descriptive and Allegorical Subjects*

CHRONOLOGY

1747   Richardson's *Clarissa Harlowe* (1747–1748)
Franklin's experiments with electricity announced
Voltaire's *Essai sur les moeurs*

1748   War of the Austrian Succession ended by the Peace of Aix-la-Chapelle
Smollett's *Adventures of Roderick Random*
David Hume's *Enquiry Concerning Human Understanding*
Montesquieu's *L'Esprit des lois*

1749   Fielding's *Tom Jones*
Johnson's *The Vanity of Human Wishes*
Bolingbroke's *Idea of a Patriot King*

1750   The *Rambler* founded (1750–1752)

1751   Gray's *Elegy Written in a Country Churchyard*
Fielding's *Amelia*
Smollett's *Adventures of Peregrine Pickle*
Denis Diderot and Jean le Rond d'Alembert begin to publish the *Encyclopédie* (1751–1765)
Richard Brinsley Sheridan born

1752   Frances Burney and Thomas Chatterton born

1753   Richardson's *History of Sir Charles Grandison* (1753–1754)
Smollett's *The Adventures of Ferdinand Count Fathom*

1754   Hume's *History of England* (1754–1762)
Death of Henry Fielding
George Crabbe born

1755   Lisbon destroyed by earthquake
Fielding's *Journal of a Voyage to Lisbon* published posthumously
Johnson's *Dictionary of the English Language*

1756   The Seven Years' War against France, 1756–1763 (the French and Indian War in America, 1755–1760)
William Pitt the elder becomes prime minister
Johnson's proposal for an edition of Shakespeare

1757   Robert Clive wins the battle of Plassey, in India

Gray's "The Progress of Poesy" and "The Bard"
Burke's *Philosophical Enquiry into the Origin of Our Ideas of the Sublime and Beautiful*
Hume's *Natural History of Religion*
William Blake born

1758   The *Idler* founded (1758–1760)

1759   Capture of Quebec by General James Wolfe
Johnson's *History of Rasselas, Prince of Abyssinia*
Voltaire's *Candide*
The British Museum opens
Sterne's *The Life and Opinions of Tristram Shandy* (1759–1767)
Death of William Collins
Mary Wollstonecraft born
Robert Burns born

1760–1820 Reign of George III

1760   James Macpherson's *Fragments of Ancient Poetry Collected in the Highlands of Scotland*
William Beckford born

1761   Jean-Jacques Rousseau's *Julie, ou la nouvelle Héloïse*
Death of Samuel Richardson

1762   Rousseau's *Du Contrat social* and *Émile*
Catherine the Great becomes czarina of Russia (1762–1796)

1763   The Seven Years' War ended by the Peace of Paris
Smart's *A Song to David*

1764   James Hargreaves invents the spinning jenny

1765   Parliament passes the Stamp Act to tax the American colonies
Johnson's edition of Shakespeare
Walpole's *The Castle of Otranto*
Thomas Percy's *Reliques of Ancient English Poetry*
Blackstone's *Commentaries on the Laws of England* (1765–1769)

1766   The Stamp Act repealed
Swift's *Journal to Stella* first published in a collection of his letters
Goldsmith's *The Vicar of Wakefield*
Smollett's *Travels Through France and Italy*
Lessing's *Laokoon*
Rousseau in England (1766–1767)

CHRONOLOGY

1768   Sterne's *A Sentimental Journey Through France and Italy*
The Royal Academy founded by George III
First edition of the *Encyclopaedia Britannica*
Maria Edgeworth born
Death of Laurence Sterne

1769   David Garrick organizes the Shakespeare Jubilee at Stratford-upon-Avon
Sir Joshua Reynolds' *Discourses* (1769–1790)
Richard Arkwright invents the spinning water frame

1770   Boston Massacre
Burke's *Thoughts on the Cause of the Present Discontents*
Oliver Goldsmith's *The Deserted Village*
Death of Thomas Chatterton
William Wordsworth born
James Hogg born

1771   Arkwright's first spinning mill founded
Deaths of Thomas Gray and Tobias Smollett
Walter Scott born

1772   Samuel Taylor Coleridge born

1773   Boston Tea Party
Goldsmith's *She Stoops to Conquer*
Johann Wolfgang von Goethe's *Götz von Berlichingen*

1774   The first Continental Congress meets in Philadelphia
Goethe's *Sorrows of Young Werther*
Death of Oliver Goldsmith
Robert Southey born

1775   Burke's speech on American taxation
American War of Independence begins with the battles of Lexington and Concord
Samuel Johnson's *Journey to the Western Islands of Scotland*
Richard Brinsley Sheridan's *The Rivals* and *The Duenna*
Beaumarchais's *Le Barbier de Séville*
James Watt and Matthew Boulton begin building steam engines in England

     Births of Jane Austen, Charles Lamb, Walter Savage Landor, and Matthew Lewis

1776   American Declaration of Independence
Edward Gibbon's *Decline and Fall of the Roman Empire* (1776–1788)
Adam Smith's *Inquiry into the Nature & Causes of the Wealth of Nations*
Thomas Paine's *Common Sense*
Death of David Hume

1777   Maurice Morgann's *Essay on the Dramatic Character of Sir John Falstaff*
Sheridan's *The School for Scandal* first performed (published 1780)
General Burgoyne surrenders at Saratoga

1778   The American colonies allied with France
Britain and France at war
Captain James Cook discovers Hawaii
Death of William Pitt, first earl of Chatham
Deaths of Jean Jacques Rousseau and Voltaire
William Hazlitt born

1779   Johnson's *Prefaces to the Works of the English Poets* (1779–1781); reissued in 1781 as *The Lives of the Most Eminent English Poets*
Sheridan's *The Critic*
Samuel Crompton invents the spinning mule
Death of David Garrick

1780   The Gordon Riots in London
Charles Robert Maturin born

1781   Charles Cornwallis surrenders at Yorktown
Immanuel Kant's *Critique of Pure Reason*
Friedrich von Schiller's *Die Räuber*

1782   William Cowper's "The Journey of John Gilpin" published in the *Public Advertiser*
Choderlos de Laclos's *Les Liaisons dangereuses*
Rousseau's *Confessions* published posthumously

CHRONOLOGY

1783 American War of Independence
ended by the Definitive Treaty of
Peace, signed at Paris
William Blake's *Poetical Sketches*
George Crabbe's *The Village*
William Pitt the younger becomes
prime minister
Henri Beyle (Stendhal) born

1784 Beaumarchais's *Le Mariage de Figaro* first performed (published
1785)
Death of Samuel Johnson

1785 Warren Hastings returns to England
from India
James Boswell's *The Journey of a
Tour of the Hebrides, with Samuel
Johnson, LL.D.*
Cowper's *The Task*
Edmund Cartwright invents the
power loom
Thomas De Quincey born
Thomas Love Peacock born

1786 William Beckford's *Vathek* published in English (originally written
in French in 1782)
Robert Burns's *Poems Chiefly in
the Scottish Dialect*
Wolfgang Amadeus Mozart's *The
Marriage of Figaro*
Death of Frederick the Great

1787 The Committee for the Abolition of
the Slave Trade founded in England
The Constitutional Convention
meets at Philadelphia; the Constitution is signed

1788 The trial of Hastings begins on
charges of corruption of the government in India
The Estates-General of France summoned
U.S. Constitution is ratified
George Washington elected president of the United States
Giovanni Casanova's *Histoire de
ma fuite* (first manuscript of his
memoirs)
The *Daily Universal Register* becomes the *Times* (London)
George Gordon, Lord Byron born

1789 The Estates-General meets at Versailles

The National Assembly (Assemblée
Nationale) convened
The fall of the Bastille marks the
beginning of the French Revolution
The National Assembly draws up
the Declaration of Rights of Man
and of the Citizen
First U.S. Congress meets in New
York
Blake's *Songs of Innocence*
Jeremy Bentham's *Introduction to
the Principles of Morals and Legislation* introduces the theory of
utilitarianism
Gilbert White's *Natural History of
Selborne*

1790 Congress sets permanent capital
city site on the Potomac River
First U.S. Census
Burke's *Reflections on the Revolution in France*
Blake's *The Marriage of Heaven
and Hell*
Edmund Malone's edition of
Shakespeare
Wollstonecraft's *A Vindication of
the Rights of Man*
Death of Benjamin Franklin

1791 French royal family's flight from
Paris and capture at Varennes;
imprisonment in the Tuileries
Bill of Rights is ratified
Paine's *The Rights of Man* (1791–
1792)
Boswell's *The Life of Johnson*
Burns's *Tam o'Shanter*
The *Observer* founded

1792 The Prussians invade France and
are repulsed at Valmy September
massacres
The National Convention declares
royalty abolished in France
Washington reelected president of
the United States
New York Stock Exchange opens
Mary Wollstonecraft's *Vindication
of the Rights of Woman*
William Bligh's voyage to the South
Sea in H.M.S. *Bounty*
Percy Bysshe Shelley born

1793 Trial and execution of Louis XVI
and Marie-Antoinette

CHRONOLOGY

France declares war against Enggland

The Committee of Public Safety (Comité de Salut Public) established

Eli Whitney devises the cotton gin

William Godwin's *An Enquiry Concerning Political Justice*

Blake's *Visions of the Daughters of Albion and America*

Wordsworth's *An Evening Walk* and *Descriptive Sketches*

1794 Execution of Georges Danton and Maximilien de Robespierre

Paine's *The Age of Reason* (1794–1796)

Blake's *Songs of Experience*

Ann Radcliffe's *The Mysteries of Udolpho*

Death of Edward Gibbon

1795 The government of the Directory established (1795–1799)

Hastings acquitted

Landor's *Poems*

Death of James Boswell

John Keats born

Thomas Carlyle born

1796 Napoleon Bonaparte takes command in Italy

Matthew Lewis' *The Monk*

John Adams elected president of the United States

Death of Robert Burns

1797 The peace of Campo Formio: extinction of the Venetian Republic

XYZ Affair

Mutinies in the Royal Navy at Spithead and the Nore

Blake's *Vala, Or the Four Zoas* (first version)

Mary Shelley born

Deaths of Edmund Burke, Mary Wollstonecraft, and Horace Walpole

1798 Napoleon invades Egypt

Horatio Nelson wins the battle of the Nile

Wordsworth's and Coleridge's *Lyrical Ballads*

Landor's *Gebir*

Thomas Malthus' *Essay on the Principle of Population*

1799 Napoleon becomes first consul

Pitt introduces first income tax in Great Britain

Sheridan's *Pizarro*

Honoré de Balzac born

Thomas Hood born

Alexander Pushkin born

1800 Thomas Jefferson elected president of the United States

Alessandro Volta produces electricity from a cell

Library of Congress established

Death of William Cowper

Thomas Babington Macaulay born

1801 First census taken in England

1802 The Treaty of Amiens marks the end of the French Revolutionary War

The *Edinburgh Review* founded

1803 England's war with France renewed

The Louisiana Purchase

Robert Fulton propels a boat by steam power on the Seine

1804 Napoleon crowned emperor of the French

Jefferson reelected president of the United States

Blake's *Milton* (1804–1808) and *Jerusalem*

The Code Napoleon promulgated in France

Beethoven's *Eroica* Symphony

Schiller's *Wilhelm Tell*

Benjamin Disraeli born

1805 Napoleon plans the invasion of England

Battle of Trafalgar

Battle of Austerlitz

Beethoven's *Fidelio* first produced

Scott's *Lay of the Last Minstrel*

1806 Scott's *Marmion*

Death of William Pitt

Death of Charles James Fox

Elizabeth Barrett born

1807 France invades Portugal

Aaron Burr tried for treason and acquitted

Byron's *Hours of Idleness*

Charles and Mary Lamb's *Tales from Shakespeare*

Thomas Moore's *Irish Melodies*

Wordsworth's *Ode on the Intimations of Immortality*

CHRONOLOGY

1808   National uprising in Spain against the French invasion
The Peninsular War begins
James Madison elected president of the United States
Covent Garden theater burned down
Goethe's *Faust* (Part 1)
Beethoven's Fifth Symphony completed
Lamb's *Specimens of English Dramatic Poets*

1809   Drury Lane theater burned down and rebuilt
The *Quarterly Review* founded
Byron's *English Bards and Scotch Reviewers*
Byron sails for the Mediterranean
Goya's *Los Desastres de la guerra* (1809–1814)
Alfred Tennyson born
Edward Fitzgerald born

1810   Crabbe's *The Borough*
Scott's *The Lady of the Lake*
Elizabeth Gaskell born

1811–1820   **Regency of George IV**

1811   Luddite Riots begin
Coleridge's *Lectures on Shakespeare* (1811–1814)
Jane Austen's *Sense and Sensibility*
Shelley's *The Necessity of Atheism*
John Constable's *Dedham Vale*
William Makepeace Thackeray born

1812   Napoleon invades Russia; captures and retreats from Moscow
United States declares war against England
Henry Bell's steamship *Comet* is launched on the Clyde river
Madison reelected president of the United States
Byron's *Childe Harold* (Cantos 1–2)
The Brothers Grimm's *Fairy Tales* (1812–1815)
Hegel's *Science of Logic*
Robert Browning born
Charles Dickens born

1813   Wellington wins the battle of Vitoria and enters France
Jane Austen's *Pride and Prejudice*
Byron's *The Giaour* and *The Bride of Abydos*

Shelley's *Queen Mab*
Southey's *Life of Nelson*

1814   Napoleon abdicates and is exiled to Elba; Bourbon restoration with Louis XVIII
Treaty of Ghent ends the war between Britain and the United States
Jane Austen's *Mansfield Park*
Byron's *The Corsair* and *Lara*
Scott's *Waverley*
Wordsworth's *The Excursion*

1815   Napoleon returns to France (the Hundred Days); is defeated at Waterloo and exiled to St. Helena
U.S.S. *Fulton*, the first steam warship, built
Scott's *Guy Mannering*
Schlegel's *Lectures on Dramatic Art and Literature* translated
Wordsworth's *The White Doe of Rylstone*
Anthony Trollope born

1816   Byron leaves England permanently
The Elgin Marbles exhibited in the British Museum
James Monroe elected president of the United States
Jane Austen's *Emma*
Byron's *Childe Harold* (Canto 3)
Coleridge's *Christabel, Kubla Khan: A Vision, The Pains of Sleep*
Benjamin Constant's *Adolphe*
Goethe's *Italienische Reise*
Peacock's *Headlong Hall*
Scott's *The Antiquary*
Shelley's *Alastor*
Rossini's *Il Barbiere di Siviglia*
Death of Richard Brinsley Sheridan
Charlotte Brontë born

1817   *Blackwood's Edinburgh* magazine founded
Jane Austen's *Northanger Abbey* and *Persuasion*
Byron's *Manfred*
Coleridge's *Biographia Literaria*
Hazlitt's *The Characters of Shakespeare's Plays* and *The Round Table*
Keats's *Poems*
Peacock's *Melincourt*
David Ricardo's *Principles of Political Economy and Taxation*
Death of Jane Austen

CHRONOLOGY

Death of Mme de Staël
Branwell Brontë born
Henry David Thoreau born

1818 Byron's *Childe Harold* (Canto 4), and *Beppo*
Hazlitt's *Lectures on the English Poets*
Keats's *Endymion*
Peacock's *Nightmare Abbey*
Scott's *Rob Roy* and *The Heart of Mid-Lothian*
Mary Shelley's *Frankenstein*
Percy Shelley's *The Revolt of Islam*
Emily Brontë born
Karl Marx born
Ivan Sergeyevich Turgenev born

1819 The *Savannah* becomes the first steamship to cross the Atlantic (in 26 days)
Peterloo massacre in Manchester
Byron's *Don Juan* (1819–1824) and *Mazeppa*
Crabbe's *Tales of the Hall*
Géricault's *Raft of the Medusa*
Hazlitt's *Lectures on the English Comic Writers*
Arthur Schopenhauer's *Die Welt als Wille und Vorstellung (The World as Will and Idea)*
Scott's *The Bride of Lammermoor* and *A Legend of Montrose*
Shelley's *The Cenci*, "The Masque of Anarchy," and "Ode to the West Wind"
Wordsworth's *Peter Bell*
Queen Victoria born
George Eliot born

1820–1830 Reign of George IV

1820 Trial of Queen Caroline
Cato Street Conspiracy suppressed; Arthur Thistlewood hanged
Monroe reelected president of the United States
Missouri Compromise
The *London* magazine founded
Keats's *Lamia, Isabella, The Eve of St. Agnes, and Other Poems*
Hazlitt's *Lectures Chiefly on the Dramatic Literature of the Age of Elizabeth*
Charles Maturin's *Melmoth the Wanderer*

Scott's *Ivanhoe* and *The Monastery*
Shelley's *Prometheus Unbound*
Anne Brontë born

1821 Greek War of Independence begins
Liberia founded as a colony for freed slaves
Byron's *Cain, Marino Faliero, The Two Foscari*, and *Sardanapalus*
Hazlitt's *Table Talk* (1821–1822)
Scott's *Kenilworth*
Shelley's *Adonais* and *Epipsychidion*
Death of John Keats
Death of Napoleon
Charles Baudelaire born
Feodor Dostoyevsky born
Gustave Flaubert born

1822 The Massacres of Chios (Greeks rebel against Turkish rule)
Byron's *The Vision of Judgment*
De Quincey's *Confessions of an English Opium-Eater*
Peacock's *Maid Marian*
Scott's *Peveril of the Peak*
Shelley's *Hellas*
Death of Percy Bysshe Shelley
Matthew Arnold born

1823 Monroe Doctrine proclaimed
Byron's *The Age of Bronze* and *The Island*
Lamb's *Essays of Elia*
Scott's *Quentin Durward*

1824 The National Gallery opened in London
John Quincy Adams elected president of the United States
The *Westminster Review* founded
Beethoven's Ninth Symphony first performed
William (Wilkie) Collins born
James Hogg's *The Private Memoirs and Confessions of a Justified Sinner*
Landor's *Imaginary Conversations* (1824–1829)
Scott's *Redgauntlet*
Death of George Gordon, Lord Byron

CHRONOLOGY

CHRONOLOGY

Landor's *Pericles and Aspasia*

1837–1901   Reign of Queen Victoria

1837   Carlyle's *The French Revolution*
Dickens' *Oliver Twist* (1837–1838)
and *Pickwick Papers*
Disraeli's *Venetia* and *Henrietta Temple*

1838   Chartist movement in England
National Gallery in London opened
Elizabeth Barrett Browning's *The Seraphim and Other Poems*
Dickens' *Nicholas Nickleby* (1838–1839)

1839   Louis Daguerre perfects process for producing an image on a silver-coated copper plate Faraday's *Experimental Researches in Electricity* (1839–1855)
First Chartist riots
Opium War between Great Britain and China
Carlyle's *Chartism*

1840   Canadian Act of Union
Queen Victoria marries Prince Albert
Charles Barry begins construction of the Houses of Parliament (1840–1852)
William Henry Harrison elected president of the United States
Robert Browning's *Sordello*
Thomas Hardy born

1841   New Zealand proclaimed a British colony
James Clark Ross discovers the Antarctic continent
Punch founded
John Tyler succeeds to the presidency after the death of Harrison
Carlyle's *Heroes and Hero-Worship*
Dickens' *The Old Curiosity Shop*

1842   Chartist riots
Income tax revived in Great Britain
The Mines Act, forbidding work underground by women or by children under the age of ten
Charles Edward Mudie's Lending Library founded in London
Dickens visits America
Robert Browning's *Dramatic Lyrics*
Macaulay's *Lays of Ancient Rome*

Tennyson's *Poems*, including "Morte d'Arthur," "St. Simeon Stylites," and "Ulysses"
Wordsworth's *Poems*

1843   Marc Isambard Brunel's Thames tunnel opened
The Economist founded
Carlyle's *Past and Present*
Dickens' *A Christmas Carol*
John Stuart Mill's *Logic*
Macaulay's *Critical and Historical Essays*
John Ruskin's *Modern Painters* (1843–1860)

1844   Rochdale Society of Equitable Pioneers, one of the first consumers' cooperatives, founded by twenty-eight Lancashire weavers
James K. Polk elected president of the United States
Elizabeth Barrett Browning's *Poems*, including "The Cry of the Children"
Dickens' *Martin Chuzzlewit*
Disraeli's *Coningsby*
Turner's *Rain, Steam and Speed*
Gerard Manley Hopkins born

1845   The great potato famine in Ireland begins (1845–1849)
Disraeli's *Sybil*

1846   Repeal of the Corn Laws
The *Daily News* founded (edited by Dickens the first three weeks)
Standard-gauge railway introduced in Britain
The Brontës' pseudonymous *Poems by Currer, Ellis and Action Bell*
Lear's *Book of Nonsense*

1847   The Ten Hours Factory Act
James Simpson uses chloroform as an anesthetic
Anne Brontë's *Agnes Grey*
Charlotte Brontë's *Jane Eyre*
Emily Brontë's *Wuthering Heights*
Bram Stoker born
Tennyson's *The Princess*

1848   The year of revolutions in France, Germany, Italy, Hungary, Poland
Marx and Engels issue *The Communist Manifesto*
The Chartist Petition

CHRONOLOGY

The Pre-Raphaelite Brotherhood founded

Zachary Taylor elected president of the United States

Anne Brontë's *The Tenant of Wildfell Hall*

Dickens' *Dombey and Son*

Elizabeth Gaskell's *Mary Barton*

Macaulay's *History of England* (1848–1861)

Mill's *Principles of Political Economy*

Thackeray's *Vanity Fair*

Death of Emily Brontë

1849 Bedford College for women founded

Arnold's *The Strayed Reveller*

Charlotte Brontë's *Shirley*

Ruskin's *The Seven Lamps of Architecture*

Death of Anne Brontë

1850 The Public Libraries Act

First submarine telegraph cable laid between Dover and Calais

Millard Fillmore succeeds to the presidency after the death of Taylor

Elizabeth Barrett Browning's *Sonnets from the Portuguese*

Carlyle's *Latter-Day Pamphlets*

Dickens' *Household Words* (1850–1859) and *David Copperfield*

Charles Kingsley's *Alton Locke*

The Pre-Raphaelites publish the *Germ*

Tennyson's *In Memoriam*

Thackeray's *The History of Pendennis*

Wordsworth's *The Prelude* is published posthumously

1851 The Great Exhibition opens at the Crystal Palace in Hyde Park

Louis Napoleon seizes power in France

Gold strike in Victoria incites Australian gold rush

Elizabeth Gaskell's *Cranford* (1851–1853)

Meredith's *Poems*

Ruskin's *The Stones of Venice* (1851–1853)

1852 The Second Empire proclaimed with Napoleon III as emperor

David Livingstone begins to explore the Zambezi (1852–1856)

Franklin Pierce elected president of the United States

Arnold's *Empedocles on Etna*

Thackeray's *The History of Henry Esmond, Esq.*

1853 Crimean War (1853–1856)

Arnold's *Poems*, including "The Scholar Gypsy" and "Sohrab and Rustum"

Charlotte Brontë's *Villette*

Elizabeth Gaskell's *Crawford and Ruth*

1854 Frederick D. Maurice's Working Men's College founded in London with more than 130 pupils

Battle of Balaklava

Dickens' *Hard Times*

James George Frazer born

Theodor Mommsen's *History of Rome* (1854–1856)

Tennyson's "The Charge of the Light Brigade"

Florence Nightingale in the Crimea (1854–1856)

Oscar Wilde born

1855 David Livingstone discovers the Victoria Falls

Robert Browning's *Men and Women*

Elizabeth Gaskell's *North and South*

Olive Schreiner born

Tennyson's *Maud*

Thackeray's *The Newcomes*

Trollope's *The Warden*

Death of Charlotte Brontë

1856 The Treaty of Paris ends the Crimean War

Henry Bessemer's steel process invented

James Buchanan elected president of the United States

H. Rider Haggard born

1857 The Indian Mutiny begins; crushed in 1858

The Matrimonial Causes Act

Charlotte Brontë's *The Professor*

CHRONOLOGY

Elizabeth Barrett Browning's *Aurora Leigh*
Dickens' *Little Dorritt*
Elizabeth Gaskell's *The Life of Charlotte Brontë*
Thomas Hughes's *Tom Brown's School Days*
Trollope's *Barchester Towers*

1858 Carlyle's *History of Frederick the Great* (1858–1865)
George Eliot's *Scenes of Clerical Life*
Morris' *The Defense of Guinevere*
Trollope's *Dr. Thorne*

1859 Charles Darwin's *The Origin of Species*
Dickens' *A Tale of Two Cities*
Arthur Conan Doyle born
George Eliot's *Adam Bede*
Fitzgerald's *The Rubaiyat of Omar Khayyám*
Meredith's *The Ordeal of Richard Feverel*
Mill's *On Liberty*
Samuel Smiles's *Self-Help*
Tennyson's *Idylls of the King*

1860 Abraham Lincoln elected president of the United States
The *Cornhill* magazine founded with Thackeray as editor
James M. Barrie born
William Wilkie Collins' *The Woman in White*
George Eliot's *The Mill on the Floss*

1861 American Civil War begins
Louis Pasteur presents the germ theory of disease
Arnold's *Lectures on Translating Homer*
Dickens' *Great Expectations*
George Eliot's *Silas Marner*
Meredith's *Evan Harrington*
Francis Turner Palgrave's *The Golden Treasury*
Trollope's *Framley Parsonage*
Peacock's *Gryll Grange*
Death of Prince Albert

1862 George Eliot's *Romola*
Meredith's *Modern Love*
Christina Rossetti's *Goblin Market*
Ruskin's *Unto This Last*
Trollope's *Orley Farm*

1863 Thomas Huxley's *Man's Place in Nature*

1864 The Geneva Red Cross Convention signed by twelve nations
Lincoln reelected president of the United States
Robert Browning's *Dramatis Personae*
John Henry Newman's *Apologia pro vita sua*
Tennyson's *Enoch Arden*
Trollope's *The Small House at Allington*

1865 Assassination of Lincoln; Andrew Johnson succeeds to the presidency
Arnold's *Essays in Criticism* (1st ser.)
Carroll's *Alice's Adventures in Wonderland*
Dickens' *Our Mutual Friend*
Meredith's *Rhoda Fleming*
A. C. Swinburne's *Atalanta in Calydon*

1866 First successful transatlantic telegraph cable laid
George Eliot's *Felix Holt, the Radical*
Elizabeth Gaskell's *Wives and Daughters*
Beatrix Potter born
Swinburne's *Poems and Ballads*

1867 The second Reform Bill
Arnold's *New Poems*
Bagehot's *The English Constitution*
Carlyle's *Shooting Niagara*
Marx's *Das Kapital* (vol. 1)
Trollope's *The Last Chronicle of Barset*
George William Russell (AE) born

1868 Gladstone becomes prime minister (1868–1874)
Johnson impeached by House of Representatives; acquitted by Senate
Ulysses S. Grant elected president of the United States
Robert Browning's *The Ring and the Book* (1868–1869)
Collins' *The Moonstone*

1869 The Suez Canal opened
Girton College, Cambridge, founded

CHRONOLOGY

Arnold's *Culture and Anarchy*
Mill's *The Subjection of Women*
Trollope's *Phineas Finn*

1870 The Elementary Education Act establishes schools under the aegis of local boards
Dickens' *Edwin Drood*
Disraeli's *Lothair*
Morris' *The Earthly Paradise*
Dante Gabriel Rossetti's *Poems*
Saki [Hector Hugh Munro] born

1871 Trade unions legalized
Newnham College, Cambridge, founded for women students
Carroll's *Through the Looking Glass*
Darwin's *The Descent of Man*
Meredith's *The Adventures of Harry Richmond*
Swinburne's *Songs Before Sunrise*

1872 Max Beerbohm born
Samuel Butler's *Erewhon*
George Eliot's *Middlemarch*
Grant reelected president of the United States
Hardy's *Under the Greenwood Tree*

1873 Arnold's *Literature and Dogma*
Mill's *Autobiography*
Pater's *Studies in the History of the Renaissance*
Trollope's *The Eustace Diamonds*

1874 Disraeli becomes prime minister
Hardy's *Far from the Madding Crowd*
James Thomson's *The City of Dreadful Night*

1875 Britain buys Suez Canal shares
Trollope's *The Way We Live Now*
T. F. Powys born

1876 F. H. Bradley's *Ethical Studies*
George Eliot's *Daniel Deronda*
Henry James's *Roderick Hudson*
Meredith's *Beauchamp's Career*
Morris' *Sigurd the Volsung*
Trollope's *The Prime Minister*

1877 Rutherford B. Hayes elected president of the United States after Electoral Commission awards him disputed votes
Henry James's *The American*

1878 Electric street lighting introduced in London

Hardy's *The Return of the Native*
Swinburne's *Poems and Ballads* (2d ser.)
Births of A. E. Coppard and Edward Thomas

1879 Somerville College and Lady Margaret Hall opened at Oxford for women
The London telephone exchange built
Gladstone's Midlothian campaign (1879–1880)
Browning's *Dramatic Idyls*
Meredith's *The Egoist*

1880 Gladstone's second term as prime minister (1880–1885)
James A. Garfield elected president of the United States
Browning's *Dramatic Idyls Second Series*
Disraeli's *Endymion*
Radclyffe Hall born
Hardy's *The Trumpet-Major*
Lytton Strachey born

1881 Garfield assassinated; Chester A. Arthur succeeds to the presidency
Henry James's *The Portrait of a Lady* and *Washington Square*
D. G. Rossetti's *Ballads and Sonnets*
P. G. Wodehouse born

1882 Triple Alliance formed between German empire, Austrian empire, and Italy
Leslie Stephen begins to edit the *Dictionary of National Biography*
Married Women's Property Act passed in Britain
Britain occupies Egypt and the Sudan

1883 Uprising of the Mahdi: Britain evacuates the Sudan
Royal College of Music opens
T. H. Green's *Ethics*
T. E. Hulme born
Stevenson's *Treasure Island*

1884 The Mahdi captures Omdurman: General Gordon appointed to command the garrison of Khartoum
Grover Cleveland elected president of the United States

CHRONOLOGY

The *Oxford English Dictionary* begins publishing
The Fabian Society founded
Hiram Maxim's recoil-operated machine gun invented

1885   The Mahdi captures Khartoum: General Gordon killed
Haggard's *King Solomon's Mines*
Marx's *Das Kapital* (vol. 2)
Meredith's *Diana of the Crossways*
Pater's *Marius the Epicurean*

1886   The Canadian Pacific Railway completed
Gold discovered in the Transvaal
Births of Frances Cornford, Ronald Firbank, and Charles Stansby Walter Williams
Henry James's *The Bostonians* and *The Princess Casamassima*
Stevenson's *The Strange Case of Dr. Jekyll and Mr. Hyde*

1887   Queen Victoria's Golden Jubilee
Rupert Brooke born
Haggard's *Allan Quatermain* and *She*
Hardy's *The Woodlanders*
Edwin Muir born

1888   Benjamin Harrison elected president of the United States
Henry James's *The Aspern Papers*
Kipling's *Plain Tales from the Hills*
T. E. Lawrence born

1889   Yeats's *The Wanderings of Oisin*
Death of Robert Browning

1890   Morris founds the Kelmscott Press
Agatha Christie born
Frazer's *The Golden Bough* (1st ed.)
Henry James's *The Tragic Muse*
Morris' *News From Nowhere*
Jean Rhys born

1891   Gissing's *New Grub Street*
Hardy's *Tess of the d'Urbervilles*
Wilde's *The Picture of Dorian Gray*

1892   Grover Cleveland elected president of the United States
Conan Doyle's *The Adventures of Sherlock Holmes*
Shaw's *Widower's Houses*
J. R. R. Tolkien born
Rebecca West born
Wilde's *Lady Windermere's Fan*

1893   Wilde's *A Woman of No Importance* and *Salomé*
Vera Brittain born

1894   Kipling's *The Jungle Book*
Moore's *Esther Waters*
Marx's *Das Kapital* (vol. 3)
Audrey Beardsley's *The Yellow Book* begins to appear quarterly
Shaw's *Arms and the Man*

1895   Trial and imprisonment of Oscar Wilde
William Ramsay announces discovery of helium
The National Trust founded
Conrad's *Almayer's Folly*
Hardy's *Jude the Obscure*
Wells's *The Time Machine*
Wilde's *The Importance of Being Earnest*
Yeats's *Poems*

1896   William McKinley elected president of the United States
Failure of the Jameson Raid on the Transvaal
Housman's *A Shropshire Lad*

1897   Queen Victoria's Diamond Jubilee
Conrad's *The Nigger of the Narcissus*
Havelock Ellis' *Studies in the Psychology of Sex* begins publication
Henry James's *The Spoils of Poynton* and *What Maisie Knew*
Kipling's *Captains Courageous*
Shaw's *Candida*
Stoker's *Dracula*
Wells's *The Invisible Man*
Death of Margaret Oliphant

1898   Kitchener defeats the Mahdist forces at Omdurman: the Sudan reoccupied
Hardy's *Wessex Poems*
Henry James's *The Turn of the Screw*
C. S. Lewis born

Shaw's *Caesar and Cleopatra* and
You Never Can Tell
Alec Waugh born
Wells's *The War of the Worlds*
Wilde's *The Ballad of Reading Gaol*

1899 The Boer War begins
Elizabeth Bowen born
Noël Coward born
Elgar's *Enigma Variations*
Kipling's *Stalky and Co.*

1900 McKinley reelected president of the
United States
British Labour party founded
Boxer Rebellion in China
Reginald A. Fessenden transmits
speech by wireless
First Zeppelin trial flight
Max Planck presents his first paper
on the quantum theory
Conrad's *Lord Jim*
Elgar's *The Dream of Gerontius*
Sigmund Freud's *The Interpretation
of Dreams*
V. S. Pritchett born
William Butler Yeats's *The Shad-
owy Waters*

1901–1910 Reign of King Edward VII

1901 William McKinley assassinated;
Theodore Roosevelt succeeds to the
presidency
First transatlantic wireless telegraph
signal transmitted
Chekhov's *Three Sisters*
Freud's *Psychopathology of Every-
day Life*
Rudyard Kipling's *Kim*
Thomas Mann's *Buddenbrooks*
Potter's *The Tale of Peter Rabbit*
Shaw's *Captain Brassbound's Con-
version*
August Strindberg's *The Dance of
Death*

1902 Barrie's *The Admirable Crichton*
Arnold Bennett's *Anna of the Five
Towns*
Cézanne's *Le Lac D'Annecy*
Conrad's *Heart of Darkness*
Henry James's *The Wings of the
Dove*
William James's *The Varieties of
Religious Experience*
Kipling's *Just So Stories*

Maugham's *Mrs. Cradock*
Stevie Smith born
Times Literary Supplement begins
publishing

1903 At its London congress the Russian
Social Democratic Party divides
into Mensheviks, led by Plekhanov,
and Bolsheviks, led by Lenin
The treaty of Panama places the
Canal Zone in U.S. hands for a
nominal rent
Motor cars regulated in Britain to a
20-mile-per-hour limit
The Wright brothers make a suc-
cessful flight in the United States
Burlington magazine founded
Samuel Butler's *The Way of All
Flesh* published posthumously
Cyril Connolly born
George Gissing's *The Private Pa-
pers of Henry Ryecroft*
Thomas Hardy's *The Dynasts*
Henry James's *The Ambassadors*
Alan Paton born
Shaw's *Man and Superman*
Synge's *Riders to the Sea* produced
in Dublin
Yeats's *In the Seven Woods* and *On
Baile's Strand*

1904 Roosevelt elected president of the
United States
Russo-Japanese war (1904–1905)
Construction of the Panama Canal
begins
The ultraviolet lamp invented
The engineering firm of Rolls
Royce founded
Barrie's *Peter Pan* first performed
Births of Cecil Day Lewis and
Nancy Mitford
Chekhov's *The Cherry Orchard*
Conrad's *Nostromo*
Henry James's *The Golden Bowl*
Kipling's *Traffics and Discoveries*
Georges Rouault's *Head of a Tragic
Clown*
G. M. Trevelyan's *England Under
the Stuarts*
Puccini's *Madame Butterfly*
First Shaw-Granville Barker season
at the Royal Court Theatre

CHRONOLOGY

The Abbey Theatre founded in Dublin

Death of Isabella Bird

1905   Russian sailors on the battleship Potemkin mutiny
After riots and a general strike the czar concedes demands by the Duma for legislative powers, a wider franchise, and civil liberties
Albert Einstein publishes his first theory of relativity
The Austin Motor Company founded
Bennett's *Tales of the Five Towns*
Claude Debussy's *La Mer*
E. M. Forster's *Where Angels Fear to Tread*
Richard Strauss's *Salome*
H. G. Wells's *Kipps*
Oscar Wilde's *De Profundis*
Births of Norman Cameron, Henry Green, and Mary Renault

1906   Liberals win a landslide victory in the British general election
The Trades Disputes Act legitimizes peaceful picketing in Britain
Captain Dreyfus rehabilitated in France
J. J. Thomson begins research on gamma rays
The U.S. Pure Food and Drug Act passed
Churchill's *Lord Randolph Churchill*
William Empson born
Galsworthy's *The Man of Property*
Kipling's *Puck of Pook's Hill*
Shaw's *The Doctor's Dilemma*
Yeats's *Poems 1899–1905*

1907   Exhibition of cubist paintings in Paris
Henry Adams' *The Education of Henry Adams*
Henri Bergson's *Creative Evolution*
Conrad's *The Secret Agent*
Births of Barbara Comyns, Daphne du Maurier, and Christopher Fry
Forster's *The Longest Journey*
André Gide's *La Porte étroite*
Shaw's *John Bull's Other Island* and *Major Barbara*

Synge's *The Playboy of the Western World*
Trevelyan's *Garibaldi's Defence of the Roman Republic*
Christopher Caudwell (Christopher St. John Sprigg) born

1908   Herbert Asquith becomes prime minister
David Lloyd George becomes chancellor of the exchequer
William Howard Taft elected president of the United States
The Young Turks seize power in Istanbul
Henry Ford's Model T car produced
Bennett's *The Old Wives' Tale*
Pierre Bonnard's *Nude Against the Light*
Georges Braque's *House at L'Estaque*
Chesterton's *The Man Who Was Thursday*
Jacob Epstein's *Figures* erected in London
Forster's *A Room with a View*
Anatole France's *L'Ile des Pingouins*
Henri Matisse's *Bonheur de Vivre*
Elgar's First Symphony
Ford Madox Ford founds the *English Review*

1909   The Young Turks depose Sultan Abdul Hamid
The Anglo-Persian Oil Company formed
Louis Bleriot crosses the English Channel from France by monoplane
Admiral Robert Peary reaches the North Pole
Freud lectures at Clark University (Worcester, Mass.) on psychoanalysis
Serge Diaghilev's Ballets Russes opens in Paris
Galsworthy's *Strife*
Hardy's *Time's Laughingstocks*
Malcolm Lowry born
Claude Monet's *Water Lilies*
Stephen Spender born
Trevelyan's *Garibaldi and the Thousand*

CHRONOLOGY

Wells's *Tono-Bungay* first published (book form, 1909)

1910–1936   **Reign of King George V**

1910   The Liberals win the British general election

Marie Curie's *Treatise on Radiography*

Arthur Evans excavates Knossos

Edouard Manet and the first post-impressionist exhibition in London

Filippo Marinetti publishes "Manifesto of the Futurist Painters"

Norman Angell's *The Great Illusion*

Bennett's *Clayhanger*

Forster's *Howards End*

Galsworthy's *Justice* and *The Silver Box*

Kipling's *Rewards and Fairies*

Norman MacCaig born

Rimsky-Korsakov's *Le Coq d'or*

Stravinsky's *The Firebird*

Vaughan Williams' *A Sea Symphony*

Wells's *The History of Mr. Polly*

Wells's *The New Machiavelli* first published (in book form, 1911)

1911   Lloyd George introduces National Health Insurance Bill

Suffragette riots in Whitehall

Roald Amundsen reaches the South Pole

Bennett's *The Card*

Chagall's *Self Portrait with Seven Fingers*

Conrad's *Under Western Eyes*

D. H. Lawrence's *The White Peacock*

Katherine Mansfield's *In a German Pension*

Edward Marsh edits *Georgian Poetry*

Moore's *Hail and Farewell* (1911–1914)

Flann O'Brien born

Strauss's *Der Rosenkavalier*

Stravinsky's *Petrouchka*

Trevelyan's *Garibaldi and the Making of Italy*

Wells's *The New Machiavelli*

Mahler's *Das Lied von der Erde*

1912   Woodrow Wilson elected president of the United States

SS *Titanic* sinks on its maiden voyage

Five million Americans go to the movies daily; London has four hundred movie theaters

Second post-impressionist exhibition in London

Bennett's and Edward Knoblock's *Milestones*

Constantin Brancusi's *Maiastra*

Wassily Kandinsky's *Black Lines*

D. H. Lawrence's *The Trespasser*

1913   Second Balkan War begins

Henry Ford pioneers factory assembly technique through conveyor belts

Epstein's *Tomb of Oscar Wilde*

New York Armory Show introduces modern art to the world

Alain Fournier's *Le Grand Meaulnes*

Freud's *Totem and Tabu*

D. H. Lawrence's *Sons and Lovers*

Mann's *Death in Venice*

Proust's *Du Côté de chez Swann* (first volume of *À la recherche du temps perdu*, 1913–1922)

Barbara Pym born

Ravel's *Daphnis and Chloé*

1914   The Panama Canal opens (formal dedication on 12 July 1920)

Irish Home Rule Bill passed in the House of Commons

Archduke Franz Ferdinand assassinated at Sarajevo

World War I begins

Battles of the Marne, Masurian Lakes, and Falkland Islands

Joyce's *Dubliners*

Norman Nicholson born

Shaw's *Pygmalion* and *Androcles and the Lion*

Yeats's *Responsibilities*

Wyndham Lewis publishes *Blast* magazine and *The Vorticist Manifesto*

1915   The Dardanelles campaign begins

Britain and Germany begin naval and submarine blockades

The *Lusitania* is sunk

Hugo Junkers manufactures the first fighter aircraft

CHRONOLOGY

First Zeppelin raid in London
Brooke's *1914: Five Sonnets*
Norman Douglas' *Old Calabria*
D. W. Griffith's *The Birth of a Nation*
Gustav Holst's *The Planets*
D. H. Lawrence's *The Rainbow*
Wyndham Lewis's *The Crowd*
Maugham's *Of Human Bondage*
Pablo Picasso's *Harlequin*
Sibelius' Fifth Symphony
Denton Welch born

1916 Evacuation of Gallipoli and the Dardanelles
Battles of the Somme, Jutland, and Verdun
Britain introduces conscription
The Easter Rebellion in Dublin
Asquith resigns and David Lloyd George becomes prime minister
The Sykes-Picot agreement on the partition of Turkey
First military tanks used
Wilson reelected president president of the United States
Henri Barbusse's *Le Feu*
Griffith's *Intolerance*
Joyce's *Portrait of the Artist as a Young Man*
Jung's *Psychology of the Unconscious*
Moore's *The Brook Kerith*
Edith Sitwell edits *Wheels* (1916–1921)
Wells's *Mr. Britling Sees It Through*

1917 United States enters World War I
Czar Nicholas II abdicates
The Balfour Declaration on a Jewish national home in Palestine
The Bolshevik Revolution
Georges Clemenceau elected prime minister of France
Lenin appointed chief commissar; Trotsky appointed minister of foreign affairs
Conrad's *The Shadow-Line*
Douglas' *South Wind*
Eliot's *Prufrock and Other Observations*
Modigliani's *Nude with Necklace*
Sassoon's *The Old Huntsman*
Prokofiev's *Classical Symphony*

Yeats's *The Wild Swans at Coole*

1918 Wilson puts forward Fourteen Points for World Peace
Central Powers and Russia sign the Treaty of Brest-Litovsk
Execution of Czar Nicholas II and his family
Kaiser Wilhelm II abdicates
The Armistice signed
Women granted the vote at age thirty in Britain
Rupert Brooke's *Collected Poems*
Gerard Manley Hopkins' *Poems*
Joyce's *Exiles*
Lewis's *Tarr*
Sassoon's *Counter-Attack*
Oswald Spengler's *The Decline of the West*
Strachey's *Eminent Victorians*
Béla Bartók's *Bluebeard's Castle*
Charlie Chaplin's *Shoulder Arms*

1919 The Versailles Peace Treaty signed
J. W. Alcock and A. W. Brown make first transatlantic flight
Ross Smith flies from London to Australia
National Socialist party founded in Germany
Benito Mussolini founds the Fascist party in Italy
Sinn Fein Congress adopts declaration of independence in Dublin
Eamon De Valera elected president of Sinn Fein party
Communist Third International founded
Lady Astor elected first woman Member of Parliament
Prohibition in the United States
John Maynard Keynes's *The Economic Consequences of the Peace*
Eliot's *Poems*
Maugham's *The Moon and Sixpence*
Shaw's *Heartbreak House*
The Bauhaus school of design, building, and crafts founded by Walter Gropius
Amedeo Modigliani's *Self-Portrait*

1920 The League of Nations established
Warren G. Harding elected president of the United States

CHRONOLOGY

Senate votes against joining the League and rejects the Treaty of Versailles
The Nineteenth Amendment gives women the right to vote
White Russian forces of Denikin and Kolchak defeated by the Bolsheviks
Karel Čapek's *R.U.R.*
Galsworthy's *In Chancery* and *The Skin Game*
Sinclair Lewis' *Main Street*
Katherine Mansfield's *Bliss*
Matisse's *Odalisques* (1920–1925)
Ezra Pound's *Hugh Selwyn Mauberly*
Paul Valéry's *Le Cimetière Marin*
Yeats's *Michael Robartes and the Dancer*
Edwin Morgan born

1921   Britain signs peace with Ireland
First medium-wave radio broadcast in the United States
The British Broadcasting Corporation founded
Braque's *Still Life with Guitar*
Chaplin's *The Kid*
Aldous Huxley's *Crome Yellow*
Paul Klee's *The Fish*
D. H. Lawrence's *Women in Love*
John McTaggart's *The Nature of Existence* (vol. 1)
Moore's *Héloïse and Abélard*
Eugene O'Neill's *The Emperor Jones*
Luigi Pirandello's *Six Characters in Search of an Author*
Shaw's *Back to Methuselah*
Strachey's *Queen Victoria*
Births of George Mackay Brown and Brian Moore

1922   Lloyd George's Coalition government succeeded by Bonar Law's Conservative government
Benito Mussolini marches on Rome and forms a government
William Cosgrave elected president of the Irish Free State
The BBC begins broadcasting in London
Lord Carnarvon and Howard Carter discover Tutankhamen's tomb

The PEN club founded in London
The *Criterion* founded with T. S. Eliot as editor
Kingsley Amis born
Eliot's *The Waste Land*
A. E. Housman's *Last Poems*
Joyce's *Ulysses*
D. H. Lawrence's *Aaron's Rod* and *England, My England*
Sinclair Lewis's *Babbitt*
O'Neill's *Anna Christie*
Pirandello's *Henry IV*
Edith Sitwell's *Façade*
Virginia Woolf's *Jacob's Room*
Yeats's *The Trembling of the Veil*
Donald Davie born

1923   The Union of Soviet Socialist Republics established
French and Belgian troops occupy the Ruhr in consequence of Germany's failure to pay reparations
Mustafa Kemal (Ataturk) proclaims Turkey a republic and is elected president
Warren G. Harding dies; Calvin Coolidge becomes president
Stanley Baldwin succeeds Bonar Law as prime minister
Adolf Hitler's attempted coup in Munich fails
Time magazine begins publishing
E. N. da C. Andrade's *The Structure of the Atom*
Brendan Behan born
Bennett's *Riceyman Steps*
Churchill's *The World Crisis* (1923–1927)
J. E. Flecker's *Hassan* produced
Nadine Gordimer born
Paul Klee's *Magic Theatre*
Lawrence's *Kangaroo*
Rainer Maria Rilke's *Duino Elegies* and *Sonnets to Orpheus*
Sibelius' *Sixth Symphony*
Picasso's *Seated Woman*
William Walton's *Façade*

1924   Ramsay MacDonald forms first Labour government, loses general election, and is succeeded by Stanley Baldwin
Calvin Coolidge elected president of the United States

CHRONOLOGY

Noël Coward's *The Vortex*
Forster's *A Passage to India*
Mann's *The Magic Mountain*
Shaw's *St. Joan*

1925 Reza Khan becomes shah of Iran
First surrealist exhibition held in Paris
Alban Berg's *Wozzeck*
Chaplin's *The Gold Rush*
John Dos Passos' *Manhattan Transfer*
Theodore Dreiser's *An American Tragedy*
Sergei Eisenstein's *Battleship Potemkin*
F. Scott Fitzgerald's *The Great Gatsby*
André Gide's *Les Faux Monnayeurs*
Hardy's *Human Shows and Far Phantasies*
Huxley's *Those Barren Leaves*
Kafka's *The Trial*
O'Casey's *Juno and the Paycock*
Virginia Woolf's *Mrs. Dalloway* and *The Common Reader*
Brancusi's *Bird in Space*
Shostakovich's *First Symphony*
Sibelius' *Tapiola*

1926 Ford's *A Man Could Stand Up*
Gide's *Si le grain ne meurt*
Hemingway's *The Sun also Rises*
Kafka's *The Castle*
D. H. Lawrence's *The Plumed Serpent*
T. E. Lawrence's *Seven Pillars of Wisdom* privately circulated
Maugham's *The Casuarina Tree*
O'Casey's *The Plough and the Stars*
Puccini's *Turandot*
Jan Morris born

1927 General Chiang Kai-shek becomes prime minister in China
Trotsky expelled by the Communist party as a deviationist; Stalin becomes leader of the party and dictator of the Soviet Union
Charles Lindbergh flies from New York to Paris
J. W. Dunne's *An Experiment with Time*

Freud's *Autobiography* translated into English
Albert Giacometti's *Observing Head*
Ernest Hemingway's *Men Without Women*
Fritz Lang's *Metropolis*
Wyndham Lewis' *Time and Western Man*
F. W. Murnau's *Sunrise*
Proust's *Le Temps retrouvé* posthumously published
Stravinsky's *Oedipus Rex*
Virginia Woolf's *To the Lighthouse*

1928 The Kellogg-Briand Pact, outlawing war and providing for peaceful settlement of disputes, signed in Paris by sixty-two nations, including the Soviet Union
Herbert Hoover elected president of the United States
Women's suffrage granted at age twenty-one in Britain
Alexander Fleming discovers penicillin
Bertolt Brecht and Kurt Weill's *The Three-Penny Opera*
Eisenstein's *October*
Huxley's *Point Counter Point*
Christopher Isherwood's *All the Conspirators*
D. H. Lawrence's *Lady Chatterley's Lover*
Wyndham Lewis' *The Childermass*
Matisse's *Seated Odalisque*
Munch's *Girl on a Sofa*
Shaw's *Intelligent Woman's Guide to Socialism*
Virginia Woolf's *Orlando*
Yeats's *The Tower*
Iain Chrichton Smith born

1929 The Labour party wins British general election
Trotsky expelled from the Soviet Union
Museum of Modern Art opens in New York
Collapse of U.S. stock exchange begins world economic crisis
Robert Bridges's *The Testament of Beauty*

CHRONOLOGY

William Faulkner's *The Sound and the Fury*
Robert Graves's *Goodbye to All That*
Hemingway's *A Farewell to Arms*
Ernst Junger's *The Storm of Steel*
Hugo von Hoffmansthal's *Poems*
Henry Moore's *Reclining Figure*
J. B. Priestley's *The Good Companions*
Erich Maria Remarque's *All Quiet on the Western Front*
Shaw's *The Applecart*
R. C. Sheriff's *Journey's End*
Edith Sitwell's *Gold Coast Customs*
Thomas Wolfe's *Look Homeward, Angel*
Virginia Woolf's *A Room of One's Own*
Yeats's *The Winding Stair*
Second surrealist manifesto; Salvador Dali joins the surrealists
Epstein's *Night and Day*
Mondrian's *Composition with Yellow Blue*

1930 Allied occupation of the Rhineland ends
Mohandas Gandhi opens civil disobedience campaign in India
The *Daily Worker*, journal of the British Communist party, begins publishing
J. W. Reppe makes artificial fabrics from an acetylene base
John Arden born
Auden's *Poems*
Coward's *Private Lives*
Eliot's *Ash Wednesday*
Wyndham Lewis's *The Apes of God*
Maugham's *Cakes and Ale*
Ezra Pound's *XXX Cantos*
Evelyn Waugh's *Vile Bodies*
Ruth Rendell born

1931 The failure of the Credit Anstalt in Austria starts a financial collapse in Central Europe
Britain abandons the gold standard; the pound falls by twenty-five percent
Mutiny in the Royal Navy at Invergordon over pay cuts

Ramsay MacDonald resigns, splits the Cabinet, and is expelled by the Labour party; in the general election the National Government wins by a majority of five hundred seats
The Statute of Westminster defines dominion status
Ninette de Valois founds the Vic-Wells Ballet (eventually the Royal Ballet)
Coward's *Cavalcade*
Dali's The *Persistence of Memory*
John le Carré born
O'Neill's *Mourning Becomes Electra*
Anthony Powell's *Afternoon Men*
Antoine de Saint-Exupéry's *Vol de nuit*
Walton's *Belshazzar's Feast*
Virginia Woolf's *The Waves*
Caroline Blackwood born

1932 Franklin D. Roosevelt elected president of the United States
Paul von Hindenburg elected president of Germany; Franz von Papen elected chancellor
Sir Oswald Mosley founds British Union of Fascists
The BBC takes over development of television from J. L. Baird's company
Basic English of 850 words designed as a prospective international language
The Folger Library opens in Washington, D.C.
The Shakespeare Memorial Theatre opens in Stratford-upon-Avon
Faulkner's *Light in August*
Huxley's *Brave New World*
F. R. Leavis' *New Bearings in English Poetry*
Boris Pasternak's *Second Birth*
Ravel's *Concerto for Left Hand*
Peter Redgrove born
Rouault's *Christ Mocked by Soldiers*
Waugh's *Black Mischief*
Yeats's *Words for Music Perhaps*

1933 Roosevelt inaugurates the New Deal

CHRONOLOGY

Hitler becomes chancellor of Germany
The Reichstag set on fire
Hitler suspends civil liberties and freedom of the press; German trade unions suppressed
George Balanchine and Lincoln Kirstein found the School of American Ballet
Beryl Bainbridge born
Lowry's *Ultramarine*
André Malraux's *La Condition humaine*
Orwell's *Down and Out in Paris and London*
Gertrude Stein's *The Autobiography of Alice B. Toklas*
Anne Stevenson born

1934   The League Disarmament Conference ends in failure
The Soviet Union admitted to the League
Hitler becomes Führer
Civil war in Austria; Engelbert Dollfuss assassinated in attempted Nazi coup
Frédéric Joliot and Irene Joliot-Curie discover artificial (induced) radioactivity
Einstein's *My Philosophy*
Fitzgerald's *Tender Is the Night*
Graves's *I, Claudius* and *Claudius the God*
Toynbee's *A Study of History* begins publication (1934–1954)
Waugh's *A Handful of Dust*
Births of Alan Bennett, Christopher Wallace-Crabbe, and Alasdair Gray

1935   Grigori Zinoviev and other Soviet leaders convicted of treason
Stanley Baldwin becomes prime minister in National Government; National Government wins general election in Britain
Italy invades Abyssinia
Germany repudiates disarmament clauses of Treaty of Versailles
Germany reintroduces compulsory military service and outlaws the Jews
Robert Watson-Watt builds first practical radar equipment

Karl Jaspers' *Suffering and Existence*
Births of André Brink, **Dennis Potter, Keith Roberts, and Jon Stallworthy**
Ivy Compton-Burnett's *A House and Its Head*
Eliot's *Murder in the Cathedral*
Barbara Hepworth's *Three Forms*
George Gershwin's *Porgy and Bess*
Greene's *England Made Me*
Isherwood's *Mr. Norris Changes Trains*
Malraux's *Le Temps du mépris*
Yeats's *Dramatis Personae*
Klee's *Child Consecrated to Suffering*
Benedict Nicholson's *White Relief*

1936   Edward VII accedes to the throne in January; abdicates in December

1936–1952   Reign of George VI

1936   German troops occupy the Rhineland
Ninety-nine percent of German electorate vote for Nazi candidates
The Popular Front wins general election in France; Léon Blum becomes prime minister
Roosevelt reelected president of the United States
The Popular Front wins general election in Spain
Spanish Civil War begins
Italian troops occupy Addis Ababa; Abyssinia annexed by Italy
BBC begins television service from Alexandra Palace
Auden's *Look, Stranger!*
Auden and Isherwood's *The Ascent of F-6*
A. J. Ayer's *Language, Truth and Logic*
Chaplin's *Modern Times*
Greene's *A Gun for Sale*
Huxley's *Eyeless in Gaza*
Keynes's *General Theory of Employment*
F. R. Leavis' *Revaluation*
Mondrian's *Composition in Red and Blue*
Dylan Thomas' *Twenty-five Poems*

CHRONOLOGY

Wells's *The Shape of Things to Come* filmed

Reginald Hill born

1937 Trial of Karl Radek and other Soviet leaders

Neville Chamberlain succeeds Stanley Baldwin as prime minister

China and Japan at war

Frank Whittle designs jet engine

Picasso's *Guernica*

Shostakovich's Fifth Symphony

Magritte's *La Reproduction interdite*

Hemingway's *To Have and Have Not*

Malraux's *L'Espoir*

Orwell's *The Road to Wigan Pier*

Priestley's *Time and the Conways*

Virginia Woolf's *The Years*

Emma Tennant born

Death of Christopher Caudwell (Christopher St. John Sprigg)

1938 Trial of Nikolai Bukharin and other Soviet political leaders

Austria occupied by German troops and declared part of the Reich

Hitler states his determination to annex Sudetenland from Czechoslovakia

Britain, France, Germany, and Italy sign the Munich agreement

German troops occupy Sudetenland

Edward Hulton founds *Picture Post*

Cyril Connolly's *Enemies of Promise*

du Maurier's *Rebecca*

Faulkner's *The Unvanquished*

Graham Greene's *Brighton Rock*

Hindemith's *Mathis der Maler*

Jean Renoir's *La Grande Illusion*

Jean-Paul Sartre's *La Nausée*

Yeats's *New Poems*

Anthony Asquith's *Pygmalion* and Walt Disney's *Snow White*

Ngũgĩwa Thiong'o born

1939 German troops occupy Bohemia and Moravia; Czechoslovakia incorporated into Third Reich

Madrid surrenders to General Franco; the Spanish Civil War ends

Italy invades Albania

Spain joins Germany, Italy, and Japan in anti-Comintern Pact

Britain and France pledge support to Poland, Romania, and Greece

The Soviet Union proposes defensive alliance with Britain; British military mission visits Moscow

The Soviet Union and Germany sign nonaggression treaty, secretly providing for partition of Poland between them

Germany invades Poland; Britain, France, and Germany at war

The Soviet Union invades Finland

New York World's Fair opens

Eliot's *The Family Reunion*

Births of **Ayi Kwei Armah**, Seamus Heaney, Michael Longley and **Robert Nye**

Isherwood's *Good-bye to Berlin*

Joyce's *Finnegans Wake* (1922–1939)

MacNeice's *Autumn Journal*

Powell's *What's Become of Waring?*

1940 Churchill becomes prime minister

Italy declares war on France, Britain, and Greece

General de Gaulle founds Free French Movement

The Battle of Britain and the bombing of London

Roosevelt reelected president of the United States for third term

Betjeman's *Old Lights for New Chancels*

Angela Carter born

Chaplin's *The Great Dictator*

Bruce Chatwin born

J. M. Coetzee born

Disney's *Fantasia*

Greene's *The Power and the Glory*

Hemingway's *For Whom the Bell Tolls*

C. P. Snow's *Strangers and Brothers* (retitled *George Passant* in 1970, when entire sequence of ten novels, published 1940–1970, was entitled *Strangers and Brothers*)

1941 German forces occupy Yugoslavia, Greece, and Crete, and invade the Soviet Union

CHRONOLOGY

Lend-Lease agreement between the United States and Britain
President Roosevelt and Winston Churchill sign the Atlantic Charter
Japanese forces attack Pearl Harbor; United States declares war on Japan, Germany, Italy; Britain on Japan
Auden's *New Year Letter*
James Burnham's *The Managerial Revolution*
F. Scott Fitzgerald's *The Last Tycoon*
Huxley's *Grey Eminence*
Derek Mahon born
Shostakovich's *Seventh Symphony*
Tippett's *A Child of Our Time*
Orson Welles's *Citizen Kane*
Virginia Woolf's *Between the Acts*

1942   Japanese forces capture Singapore, Hong Kong, Bataan, Manila
German forces capture Tobruk
U.S. fleet defeats the Japanese in the Coral Sea, captures Guadalcanal
Battle of El Alamein
Allied forces land in French North Africa
Atom first split at University of Chicago
William Beveridge's *Social Insurance and Allied Services*
Albert Camus's *L'Étranger*
Joyce Cary's *To Be a Pilgrim*
Edith Sitwell's *Street Songs*
Waugh's *Put Out More Flags*
Douglas Dunn born

1943   German forces surrender at Stalingrad
German and Italian forces surrender in North Africa
Italy surrenders to Allies and declares war on Germany
Cairo conference between Roosevelt, Churchill, Chiang Kaishek
Teheran conference between Roosevelt, Churchill, Stalin
Eliot's *Four Quartets*
Henry Moore's *Madonna and Child*
Sartre's *Les Mouches*
Vaughan Williams' *Fifth Symphony*

1944   Allied forces land in Normandy and southern France
Allied forces enter Rome
Attempted assassination of Hitler fails
Liberation of Paris
U.S. forces land in Philippines
German offensive in the Ardennes halted
Roosevelt reelected president of the United States for fourth term
Education Act passed in Britain
Pay-as-You-Earn income tax introduced
Beveridge's *Full Employment in a Free Society*
Cary's *The Horse's Mouth*
Huxley's *Time Must Have a Stop*
Maugham's *The Razor's Edge*
Sartre's *Huis Clos*
Edith Sitwell's *Green Song and Other Poems*
Graham Sutherland's *Christ on the Cross*
Trevelyan's *English Social History*
W. G. Sebald born

1945   British and Indian forces open offensive in Burma
Yalta conference between Roosevelt, Churchill, Stalin
Mussolini executed by Italian partisans
Roosevelt dies; Harry S. Truman becomes president
Hitler commits suicide; German forces surrender
The Potsdam Peace Conference
The United Nations Charter ratified in San Francisco
The Labour Party wins British General Election
Atomic bombs dropped on Hiroshima and Nagasaki
Surrender of Japanese forces ends World War II
Trial of Nazi war criminals opens at Nuremberg
All-India Congress demands British withdrawal from India
De Gaulle elected president of French Provisional Government; resigns the next year

CHRONOLOGY

Betjeman's *New Bats in Old Belfries*
Britten's *Peter Grimes*
Orwell's *Animal Farm*
Russell's *History of Western Philosophy*
Sartre's *The Age of Reason*
Edith Sitwell's *The Song of the Cold*
Waugh's *Brideshead Revisited*
Births of Wendy Cope and Peter Reading

1946   Bills to nationalize railways, coal mines, and the Bank of England passed in Britain
Nuremberg Trials concluded
United Nations General Assembly meets in New York as its permanent headquarters
The Arab Council inaugurated in Britain
Frederick Ashton's *Symphonic Variations*
Britten's *The Rape of Lucretia*
David Lean's *Great Expectations*
O'Neill's *The Iceman Cometh*
Roberto Rosselini's *Paisà*
Dylan Thomas' *Deaths and Entrances*

1947   President Truman announces program of aid to Greece and Turkey and outlines the "Truman Doctrine"
Independence of India proclaimed; partition between India and Pakistan, and communal strife between Hindus and Moslems follows
General Marshall calls for a European recovery program
First supersonic air flight
Britain's first atomic pile at Harwell comes into operation
Edinburgh festival established
Discovery of the Dead Sea Scrolls in Palestine
Princess Elizabeth marries Philip Mountbatten, duke of Edinburgh
Auden's *Age of Anxiety*
Camus's *La Peste*
Chaplin's *Monsieur Verdoux*
Lowry's *Under the Volcano*
Priestley's *An Inspector Calls*
Edith Sitwell's *The Shadow of Cain*

Waugh's *Scott-King's Modern Europe*
Dermot Healy born

1948   Gandhi assassinated
Czech Communist Party seizes power
Pan-European movement (1948–1958) begins with the formation of the permanent Organization for European Economic Cooperation (OEEC)
Berlin airlift begins as the Soviet Union halts road and rail traffic to the city
British mandate in Palestine ends; Israeli provisional government formed
Yugoslavia expelled from Soviet bloc
Columbia Records introduces the long-playing record
Truman elected of the United States for second term
Greene's *The Heart of the Matter*
Huxley's *Ape and Essence*
Leavis' *The Great Tradition*
Pound's *Cantos*
Priestley's *The Linden Tree*
Waugh's *The Loved One*
Death of Denton Welch

1949   North Atlantic Treaty Organization established with headquarters in Brussels
Berlin blockade lifted
German Federal Republic recognized; capital established at Bonn
Konrad Adenauer becomes German chancellor
Mao Tse-tung becomes chairman of the People's Republic of China following Communist victory over the Nationalists
Peter Ackroyd born
Simone de Beauvoir's *The Second Sex*
Cary's *A Fearful Joy*
Arthur Miller's *Death of a Salesman*
Orwell's *Nineteen Eighty-four*

1950   Korean War breaks out
Nobel Prize for literature awarded to Bertrand Russell

CHRONOLOGY

R. H. S. Crossman's *The God That Failed*

T. S. Eliot's *The Cocktail Party*

Fry's *Venus Observed*

Doris Lessing's *The Grass Is Singing*

C. S. Lewis' *The Chronicles of Narnia* (1950–1956)

Wyndham Lewis' *Rude Assignment*

George Orwell's *Shooting an Elephant*

Carol Reed's *The Third Man*

Dylan Thomas' *Twenty-six Poems*

A. N. Wilson born

1951 Guy Burgess and Donald Maclean defect from Britain to the Soviet Union

The Conservative party under Winston Churchill wins British general election

The Festival of Britain celebrates both the centenary of the Crystal Palace Exhibition and British postwar recovery

Electric power is produced by atomic energy at Arcon, Idaho

W. H. Auden's *Nones*

Samuel Beckett's *Molloy* and *Malone Dies*

Benjamin Britten's *Billy Budd*

Greene's *The End of the Affair*

Akira Kurosawa's *Rashomon*

Wyndham Lewis' *Rotting Hill*

Anthony Powell's *A Question of Upbringing* (first volume of *A Dance to the Music of Time*, 1951–1975)

J. D. Salinger's *The Catcher in the Rye*

C. P. Snow's *The Masters*

Igor Stravinsky's *The Rake's Progress*

1952– Reign of Elizabeth II

At Eniwetok Atoll the United States detonates the first hydrogen bomb

The European Coal and Steel Community comes into being

Radiocarbon dating introduced to archaeology

Michael Ventris deciphers Linear B script

Dwight D. Eisenhower elected president of the United States

Beckett's *Waiting for Godot*

Charles Chaplin's *Limelight*

Ernest Hemingway's *The Old Man and the Sea*

Arthur Koestler's *Arrow in the Blue*

F. R. Leavis' *The Common Pursuit*

Lessing's *Martha Quest* (first volume of *The Children of Violence*, 1952–1965)

C. S. Lewis' *Mere Christianity*

Thomas' *Collected Poems*

Evelyn Waugh's *Men at Arms* (first volume of *Sword of Honour*, 1952–1961)

Angus Wilson's *Hemlock and After*

Births of Rohinton Mistry and Vikram Seth

1953 Constitution for a European political community drafted

Julius and Ethel Rosenberg executed for passing U.S. secrets to the Soviet Union

Cease-fire declared in Korea

Edmund Hillary and his Sherpa guide, Tenzing Norkay, scale Mt. Everest

Nobel Prize for literature awarded to Winston Churchill

General Mohammed Naguib proclaims Egypt a republic

Beckett's *Watt*

Joyce Cary's *Except the Lord*

Robert Graves's *Poems 1953*

Death of Norman Cameron

1954 First atomic submarine, *Nautilus,* is launched by the United States

Dien Bien Phu captured by the Vietminh

Geneva Conference ends French dominion over Indochina

U.S. Supreme Court declares racial segregation in schools unconstitutional

Nasser becomes president of Egypt

Nobel Prize for literature awarded to Ernest Hemingway

Kingsley Amis' *Lucky Jim*

John Betjeman's *A Few Late Chrysanthemums*

William Golding's *Lord of the Flies*

CHRONOLOGY

Christopher Isherwood's *The World in the Evening*
Koestler's *The Invisible Writing*
Iris Murdoch's *Under the Net*
C. P. Snow's *The New Men*
Thomas' *Under Milk Wood* published posthumously
Births of Romesh Gunesekera and Alan Hollinghurst

1955 Warsaw Pact signed
West Germany enters NATO as Allied occupation ends
The Conservative party under Anthony Eden wins British general election
Cary's *Not Honour More*
Greene's *The Quiet American*
Philip Larkin's *The Less Deceived*
F. R. Leavis' *D. H. Lawrence, Novelist*
Vladimir Nabokov's *Lolita*
Patrick White's *The Tree of Man*
Patrick McCabe born

1956 Nasser's nationalization of the Suez Canal leads to Israeli, British, and French armed intervention
Uprising in Hungary suppressed by Soviet troops
Khrushchev denounces Stalin at Twentieth Communist Party Congress
Eisenhower reelected president of the United States
Anthony Burgess' *Time for a Tiger*
Golding's *Pincher Martin*
Murdoch's *Flight from the Enchanter*
John Osborne's *Look Back in Anger*
Snow's *Homecomings*
Edmund Wilson's *Anglo-Saxon Attitudes*

1957 The Soviet Union launches the first artificial earth satellite, *Sputnik I*
Eden succeeded by Harold Macmillan
Suez Canal reopened
Eisenhower Doctrine formulated
Parliament receives the Wolfenden Report on Homosexuality and Prostitution
Nobel Prize for literature awarded to Albert Camus

Beckett's *Endgame* and *All That Fall*
Lawrence Durrell's *Justine* (first volume of *The Alexandria Quartet,* 1957–1960)
Ted Hughes's *The Hawk in the Rain*
Murdoch's *The Sandcastle*
V. S. Naipaul's *The Mystic Masseur*
Eugene O'Neill's *Long Day's Journey into Night*
Osborne's *The Entertainer*
Muriel Spark's *The Comforters*
White's *Voss*

1958 European Economic Community established
Khrushchev succeeds Bulganin as Soviet premier
Charles de Gaulle becomes head of France's newly constituted Fifth Republic
The United Arab Republic formed by Egypt and Syria
The United States sends troops into Lebanon
First U.S. satellite, *Explorer 1,* launched
Nobel Prize for literature awarded to Boris Pasternak
Beckett's *Krapp's Last Tape*
John Kenneth Galbraith's *The Affluent Society*
Greene's *Our Man in Havana*
Murdoch's *The Bell*
Pasternak's *Dr. Zhivago*
Snow's *The Conscience of the Rich*

1959 Fidel Castro assumes power in Cuba
St. Lawrence Seaway opens
The European Free Trade Association founded
Alaska and Hawaii become the forty-ninth and fiftieth states
The Conservative party under Harold Macmillan wins British general election
Brendan Behan's *The Hostage*
Golding's *Free Fall*
Graves's *Collected Poems*
Koestler's *The Sleepwalkers*
Harold Pinter's *The Birthday Party*
Snow's *The Two Cultures and the Scientific Revolution*

Spark's *Memento Mori*
1960　South Africa bans the African National Congress and Pan-African Congress
The Congo achieves independence
John F. Kennedy elected president of the United States
The U.S. bathyscaphe *Trieste* descends to 35,800 feet
Publication of the unexpurgated *Lady Chatterley's Lover* permitted by court
Auden's *Hommage to Clio*
Betjeman's *Summoned by Bells*
Pinter's *The Caretaker*
Snow's *The Affair*
David Storey's *This Sporting Life*
Ian Rankin born
1961　South Africa leaves the British Commonwealth
Sierra Leone and Tanganyika achieve independence
The Berlin Wall erected
The New English Bible published
Beckett's *How It Is*
Greene's *A Burnt-Out Case*
Koestler's *The Lotus and the Robot*
Murdoch's *A Severed Head*
Naipaul's *A House for Mr Biswas*
Osborne's *Luther*
Spark's *The Prime of Miss Jean Brodie*
White's *Riders in the Chariot*
1962　John Glenn becomes first U.S. astronaut to orbit earth
The United States launches the spacecraft *Mariner* to explore Venus
Algeria achieves independence
Cuban missile crisis ends in withdrawal of Soviet missiles from Cuba
Adolf Eichmann executed in Israel for Nazi war crimes
Second Vatican Council convened by Pope John XXIII
Nobel Prize for literature awarded to John Steinbeck
Edward Albee's *Who's Afraid of Virginia Woolf?*
Beckett's *Happy Days*
Anthony Burgess' *A Clockwork Orange* and *The Wanting Seed*

Aldous Huxley's *Island*
Isherwood's *Down There on a Visit*
Lessing's *The Golden Notebook*
Nabokov's *Pale Fire*
Aleksandr Solzhenitsyn's *One Day in the Life of Ivan Denisovich*
1963　Britain, the United States, and the Soviet Union sign a test-ban treaty
Birth of Simon Armitage
Britain refused entry to the European Economic Community
The Soviet Union puts into orbit the first woman astronaut, Valentina Tereshkova
Paul VI becomes pope
President Kennedy assassinated; Lyndon B. Johnson assumes office
Nobel Prize for literature awarded to George Seferis
Britten's *War Requiem*
John Fowles's *The Collector*
Murdoch's *The Unicorn*
Spark's *The Girls of Slender Means*
Storey's *Radcliffe*
John Updike's *The Centaur*
1964　Tonkin Gulf incident leads to retaliatory strikes by U.S. aircraft against North Vietnam
Greece and Turkey contend for control of Cyprus
Britain grants licenses to drill for oil in the North Sea
The Shakespeare Quatercentenary celebrated
Lyndon Johnson elected president of the United States
The Labour party under Harold Wilson wins British general election
Nobel Prize for literature awarded to Jean-Paul Sartre
Saul Bellow's *Herzog*
Burgess' *Nothing Like the Sun*
Golding's *The Spire*
Isherwood's *A Single Man*
Stanley Kubrick's *Dr. Strangelove*
Larkin's *The Whitsun Weddings*
Naipaul's *An Area of Darkness*
Peter Shaffer's *The Royal Hunt of the Sun*
Snow's *Corridors of Power*

CHRONOLOGY

1965   The first U.S. combat forces land in Vietnam
        The U.S. spacecraft Mariner transmits photographs of Mars
        British Petroleum Company finds oil in the North Sea
        War breaks out between India and Pakistan
        Rhodesia declares its independence
        Ontario power failure blacks out the Canadian and U.S. east coasts
        Nobel Prize for literature awarded to Mikhail Sholokhov
        Robert Lowell's *For the Union Dead*
        Norman Mailer's *An American Dream*
        Osborne's *Inadmissible Evidence*
        Pinter's *The Homecoming*
        Spark's *The Mandelbaum Gate*

1966   The Labour party under Harold Wilson wins British general election
        The Archbishop of Canterbury visits Pope Paul VI
        Florence, Italy, severely damaged by floods
        Paris exhibition celebrates Picasso's eighty-fifth birthday
        Fowles's *The Magus*
        Greene's *The Comedians*
        Osborne's *A Patriot for Me*
        Paul Scott's *The Jewel in the Crown* (first volume of *The Raj Quartet*, 1966–1975)
        White's *The Solid Mandala*

1967   Thurgood Marshall becomes first black U.S. Supreme Court justice
        Six-Day War pits Israel against Egypt and Syria
        Biafra's secession from Nigeria leads to civil war
        Francis Chichester completes solo circumnavigation of the globe
        Dr. Christiaan Barnard performs first heart transplant operation, in South Africa
        China explodes its first hydrogen bomb
        Golding's *The Pyramid*
        Hughes's *Wodwo*
        Isherwood's *A Meeting by the River*

        Naipaul's *The Mimic Men*
        Tom Stoppard's *Rosencrantz and Guildenstern Are Dead*
        Orson Welles's *Chimes at Midnight*
        Angus Wilson's *No Laughing Matter*

1968   Violent student protests erupt in France and West Germany
        Warsaw Pact troops occupy Czechoslovakia
        Violence in Northern Ireland causes Britain to send in troops
        Tet offensive by Communist forces launched against South Vietnam's cities
        Theater censorship ended in Britain
        Robert Kennedy and Martin Luther King Jr. assassinated
        Richard M. Nixon elected president of the United States
        Booker Prize for fiction established
        Durrell's *Tunc*
        Graves's *Poems 1965–1968*
        Osborne's *The Hotel in Amsterdam*
        Snow's *The Sleep of Reason*
        Solzhenitsyn's *The First Circle* and *Cancer Ward*
        Spark's *The Public Image*

1969   Humans set foot on the moon for the first time when astronauts descend to its surface in a landing vehicle from the U.S. spacecraft *Apollo 11*
        The Soviet unmanned spacecraft *Venus V* lands on Venus
        Capital punishment abolished in Britain
        Colonel Muammar Qaddafi seizes power in Libya
        Solzhenitsyn expelled from the Soviet Union
        Nobel Prize for literature awarded to Samuel Beckett
        Carter's *The Magic Toyshop*
        Fowles's *The French Lieutenant's Woman*
        Storey's *The Contractor*

1970   Civil war in Nigeria ends with Biafra's surrender
        U.S. planes bomb Cambodia

CHRONOLOGY

The Conservative party under Edward Heath wins British general election
Nobel Prize for literature awarded to Aleksandr Solzhenitsyn
Durrell's *Nunquam*
Hughes's *Crow*
F. R. Leavis and Q. D. Leavis' *Dickens the Novelist*
Snow's *Last Things*
Spark's *The Driver's Seat*
Death of Vera Brittain

1971 Communist China given Nationalist China's UN seat
Decimal currency introduced to Britain
Indira Gandhi becomes India's prime minister
Nobel Prize for literature awarded to Heinrich Böll
Bond's *The Pope's Wedding*
Naipaul's *In a Free State*
Pinter's *Old Times*
Spark's *Not to Disturb*
Birth of Sarah Kane

1972 The civil strife of "Bloody Sunday" causes Northern Ireland to come under the direct rule of Westminster
Nixon becomes the first U.S. president to visit Moscow and Beijing
The Watergate break-in precipitates scandal in the United States
Eleven Israeli athletes killed by terrorists at Munich Olympics
Nixon reelected president of the United States
Bond's *Lear*
Snow's *The Malcontents*
Stoppard's *Jumpers*

1973 Britain, Ireland, and Denmark enter European Economic Community
Egypt and Syria attack Israel in the Yom Kippur War
Energy crisis in Britain reduces production to a three-day week
Nobel Prize for literature awarded to Patrick White
Bond's *The Sea*
Greene's *The Honorary Consul*
Lessing's *The Summer Before the Dark*

Murdoch's *The Black Prince*
Shaffer's *Equus*
White's *The Eye of the Storm*

1974 Miners strike in Britain
Greece's military junta overthrown
Emperor Haile Selassie of Ethiopia deposed
President Makarios of Cyprus replaced by military coup
Nixon resigns as U.S. president and is succeeded by Gerald R. Ford
Betjeman's *A Nip in the Air*
Bond's *Bingo*
Durrell's *Monsieur* (first volume of *The Avignon Quintet*, 1974–1985)
Larkin's *The High Windows*
Solzhenitsyn's *The Gulag Archipelago*
Spark's *The Abbess of Crewe*
Death of Nancy Mitford

1975 The U.S. *Apollo* and Soviet *Soyuz* spacecrafts rendezvous in space
The Helsinki Accords on human rights signed
U.S. forces leave Vietnam
King Juan Carlos succeeds Franco as Spain's head of state
Nobel Prize for literature awarded to Eugenio Montale

1976 New U.S. copyright law goes into effect
Israeli commandos free hostages from hijacked plane at Entebbe, Uganda
British and French SST Concordes make first regularly scheduled commercial flights
The United States celebrates its bicentennial
Jimmy Carter elected president of the United States
Byron and Shelley manuscripts discovered in Barclay's Bank, Pall Mall
Hughes's *Seasons' Songs*
Koestler's *The Thirteenth Tribe*
Scott's *Staying On*
Spark's *The Take-over*
White's *A Fringe of Leaves*

1977 Silver jubilee of Queen Elizabeth II celebrated

CHRONOLOGY

Egyptian president Anwar el-Sadat visits Israel

"Gang of Four" expelled from Chinese Communist party

First woman ordained in the U.S. Episcopal church

After twenty-nine years in power, Israel's Labour party is defeated by the Likud party

Fowles's *Daniel Martin*

Hughes's *Gaudete*

1978   Treaty between Israel and Egypt negotiated at Camp David

Pope John Paul I dies a month after his coronation and is succeeded by Karol Cardinal Wojtyla, who takes the name John Paul II

Former Italian premier Aldo Moro murdered by left-wing terrorists

Nobel Prize for literature awarded to Isaac Bashevis Singer

Greene's *The Human Factor*

Hughes's *Cave Birds*

Murdoch's *The Sea, The Sea*

1979   The United States and China establish diplomatic relations

Ayatollah Khomeini takes power in Iran and his supporters hold U.S. embassy staff hostage in Teheran

Rhodesia becomes Zimbabwe

Earl Mountbatten assassinated

The Soviet Union invades Afghanistan

The Conservative party under Margaret Thatcher wins British general election

Nobel Prize for literature awarded to Odysseus Elytis

Golding's *Darkness Visible*

Hughes's *Moortown*

Lessing's *Shikasta* (first volume of *Canopus in Argos, Archives*)

Naipaul's *A Bend in the River*

Spark's *Territorial Rights*

White's *The Twyborn Affair*

1980   Iran-Iraq war begins

Strikes in Gdansk give rise to the Solidarity movement

Mt. St. Helen's erupts in Washington State

British steelworkers strike for the first time since 1926

More than fifty nations boycott Moscow Olympics

Ronald Reagan elected president of the United States

Burgess's *Earthly Powers*

Golding's *Rites of Passage*

Shaffer's *Amadeus*

Storey's *A Prodigal Child*

Angus Wilson's *Setting the World on Fire*

1981   Greece admitted to the European Economic Community

Iran hostage crisis ends with release of U.S. embassy staff

Twelve Labour MPs and nine peers found British Social Democratic party

Socialist party under François Mitterand wins French general election

Rupert Murdoch buys *The Times* of London

Turkish gunman wounds Pope John Paul II in assassination attempt

U.S. gunman wounds President Reagan in assassination attempt

President Sadat of Egypt assassinated

Nobel Prize for literature awarded to Elias Canetti

Spark's *Loitering with Intent*

1982   Britain drives Argentina's invasion force out of the Falkland Islands

U.S. space shuttle makes first successful trip

Yuri Andropov becomes general secretary of the Central Committee of the Soviet Communist party

Israel invades Lebanon

First artificial heart implanted at Salt Lake City hospital

Bellow's *The Dean's December*

Greene's *Monsignor Quixote*

1983   South Korean airliner with 269 aboard shot down after straying into Soviet airspace

U.S. forces invade Grenada following left-wing coup

Widespread protests erupt over placement of nuclear missiles in Europe

The £1 coin comes into circulation in Britain

CHRONOLOGY

Australia wins the America's Cup
Nobel Prize for literature awarded to William Golding
Hughes's *River*
Murdoch's *The Philosopher's Pupil*

1984 Konstantin Chernenko becomes general secretary of the Central Committee of the Soviet Communist party
Prime Minister Indira Gandhi of India assassinated by Sikh bodyguards
Reagan reelected president of the United States
Toxic gas leak at Bhopal, India, plant kills 2,000
British miners go on strike
Irish Republican Army attempts to kill Prime Minister Thatcher with bomb detonated at a Brighton hotel
World Court holds against U.S. mining of Nicaraguan harbors
Golding's *The Paper Men*
Lessing's *The Diary of Jane Somers*
Spark's *The Only Problem*

1985 United States deploys cruise missiles in Europe
Mikhail Gorbachev becomes general secretary of the Soviet Communist party following death of Konstantin Chernenko
Riots break out in Handsworth district (Birmingham) and Brixton
Republic of Ireland gains consultative role in Northern Ireland
State of emergency is declared in South Africa
Nobel Prize for literature awarded to Claude Simon
A. N. Wilson's *Gentlemen in England*
Lessing's *The Good Terrorist*
Murdoch's *The Good Apprentice*
Fowles's *A Maggot*

1986 U.S. space shuttle *Challenger* explodes
United States attacks Libya
Atomic power plant at Chernobyl destroyed in accident
Corazon Aquino becomes president of the Philippines

Giotto spacecraft encounters Comet Halley
Nobel Prize for literature awarded to Wole Soyinka
Final volume of *Oxford English Dictionary* supplement published
Amis's *The Old Devils*
Ishiguro's *An Artist of the Floating World*
A. N. Wilson's *Love Unknown*
Powell's *The Fisher King*

1987 Gorbachev begins reform of Communist party of the Soviet Union
Stock market collapses
Iran-contra affair reveals that Reagan administration used money from arms sales to Iran to fund Nicaraguan rebels
Palestinian uprising begins in Israeli-occupied territories
Nobel Prize for literature awarded to Joseph Brodsky
Golding's *Close Quarters*
Burgess's *Little Wilson and Big God*
Drabble's *The Radiant Way*

1988 Soviet Union begins withdrawing troops from Afghanistan
Iranian airliner shot down by U.S. Navy over Persian Gulf
War between Iran and Iraq ends
George Bush elected president of the United States
Pan American flight 103 destroyed over Lockerbie, Scotland
Nobel Prize for literature awarded to Naguib Mafouz
Greene's *The Captain and the Enemy*
Amis's *Difficulties with Girls*
Rushdie's *Satanic Verses*

1989 Ayatollah Khomeini pronounces death sentence on Salman Rushdie; Great Britain and Iran sever diplomatic relations
F. W. de Klerk becomes president of South Africa
Chinese government crushes student demonstration in Tiananmen Square

CHRONOLOGY

Communist regimes are weakened or abolished in Poland, Czechoslovakia, Hungary, East Germany, and Romania
Lithuania nullifies its inclusion in Soviet Union
Nobel Prize for literature awarded to José Cela
Second edition of *Oxford English Dictionary* published
Drabble's *A Natural Curiosity*
Murdoch's *The Message to the Planet*
Amis's *London Fields*
Ishiguro's *The Remains of the Day*
Death of Bruce Chatwin

1990 Communist monopoly ends in Bulgaria
Riots break out against community charge in England
First women ordained priests in Church of England
Civil war breaks out in Yugoslavia; Croatia and Slovenia declare independence
Bush and Gorbachev sign START agreement to reduce nuclear-weapons arsenals
President Jean-Baptiste Aristide overthrown by military in Haiti
Boris Yeltsin elected president of Russia
Dissolution of the Soviet Union
Nobel Prize for literature awarded to Nadine Gordimer

1992 U.N. Conference on Environment and Development (the "Earth Summit") meets in Rio de Janeiro
Prince and Princess of Wales separate
War in Bosnia-Herzegovina intensifies
Bill Clinton elected president of the United States in three-way race with Bush and independent candidate H. Ross Perot
Nobel Prize for literature awarded to Derek Walcott

1993 Czechoslovakia divides into the Czech Republic and Slovakia; playwright Vaclav Havel elected president of the Czech Republic

Britain ratifies Treaty on European Union (the "Maastricht Treaty")
U.S. troops provide humanitarian aid amid famine in Somalia
United States, Canada, and Mexico sign North American Free Trade Agreement
Nobel Prize for literature awarded to Toni Morrison

1994 Nelson Mandela elected president in South Africa's first post-apartheid election
Jean-Baptiste Aristide restored to presidency of Haiti
Clinton health care reforms rejected by Congress
Civil war in Rwanda
Republicans win control of both houses of Congress for first time in forty years
Prime Minister Albert Reynolds of Ireland meets with Gerry Adams, president of Sinn Fein
Nobel Prize for literature awarded to Kenzaburo Õe
Amis's *You Can't Do Both*
Naipaul's *A Way in the World*
Death of Dennis Potter

1995 Britain and Irish Republican Army engage in diplomatic talks
Barings Bank forced into bankruptcy as a result of a maverick bond trader's losses
United States restores full diplomatic relations with Vietnam
NATO initiates air strikes in Bosnia
Death of Stephen Spender
Israeli Prime Minister Yitzhak Rabin assassinated
Nobel Prize for literature awarded to Seamus Heaney

1996 IRA breaks cease-fire; Sein Fein representatives barred from Northern Ireland peace talks
Prince and Princess of Wales divorce
Cease-fire agreement in Chechnia; Russian forces begin to withdraw
Boris Yeltsin reelected president of Russia
Bill Clinton reelected president of the United States

CHRONOLOGY

Nobel Prize for literature awarded to Wislawa Szymborska

Death of Caroline Blackwood

1996　British government destroys around 100,000 cows suspected of infection with Creutzfeldt-Jakob, or "mad cow" disease

1997　Diana, Princess of Wales, dies in an automobile accident

Unveiling of first fully-cloned adult animal, a sheep named Dolly

Booker McConnell Prize for fiction awarded to Arundhati Roy

1998　United States renews bombing of Bagdad, Iraq

Independent legislature and Parliaments return to Scotland and Wales

Booker McConnell Prize for fiction awarded to Ian McEwan

Nobel Prize for literature awarded to Jose Saramago

1999　King Hussein of Jordan dies

United Nations responds militarily to Serbian President Slobodan Milosevic's escalation of crisis in Kosovo

Booker McConnell Prize for fiction awarded to J. M. Coetzee

Nobel Prize for literature awarded to Günter Grass

Deaths of Ted Hughes, Brian Moore, and Iain Chrichton Smith

2000　Penelope Fitzgerald dies

J. K. Rowling's *Harry Potter and the Goblet of Fire* sells more than 300,000 copies in its first day

Oil blockades by fuel haulers protesting high oil taxes bring much of Britain to a standstill

Slobodan Milosevic loses Serbian general election to Vojislav Kostunica

Death of Scotland's First Minister, Donald Dewar

Nobel Prize for literature awarded to Gao Xingjian

Booker McConnell Prize for fiction awarded to Margaret Atwood

George W. Bush, son of former president George Bush, becomes president of the United States after Supreme Court halts recount of closest election in history

Death of former Canadian Prime Minister Pierre Elliot Trudeau

Human Genome Project researchers announce that they have a complete map of the genetic code of a human chromosome

Vladimir Putin succeeds Boris Yeltsin as president of Russia

British Prime Minister Tony Blair's son Leo is born, making him the first child born to a sitting prime minister in 152 years

Death of Keith Roberts

2001　In Britain, the House of Lords passes legislation that legalizes the creation of cloned human embryos

British Prime Minister Tony Blair wins second term

Margaret Atwood's *The Blind Assassin* wins Booker McConnell Prize for fiction

Kazuo Ishiguro's *When We Were Orphans*

Trezza Azzopardi's *The Hiding Place*

Terrorists attack World Trade Center and Pentagon with hijacked airplanes, resulting in the collapse of the World Trade Center towers and the deaths of thousands. Passengers of a third hijacked plane thwart hijackers, resulting in a crash landing in Pennsylvania. The attacks are thought to be organized by Osama bin Laden, the leader of an international terrorist network known as al Qaeda

Ian McEwan's *An Atonement*

Salman Rushdie's *Fury*

Peter Carey's *True History of the Kelly Gang*

Deaths of Eudora Welty and W. G. Sebald

2002　Former U.S. President Jimmy Carter awarded the Nobel Peace Prize

Europe experiences its worst floods

in 100 years as floodwaters force thousands of people out of their homes

Wall Street Journal reporter Daniel Pearl kidnapped and killed in Karachi, Pakistan while researching a story about Pakistani militants and suspected shoe bomber Richard Reid. British-born Islamic militant Ahmad Omar Saeed Sheikh sentenced to death for the crime. Three accomplices receive life sentences.

Slobodan Milosevic goes on trial at the U.N. war crimes tribunal in The Hague on charges of masterminding ethnic cleansing in the former Yugoslavia.

Yann Martel's *Life of Pi* wins Booker McConnell Prize for fiction

Nobel Prize for literature awarded to Imre Kertész

2003 Ariel Sharon elected as Israeli prime minister

Venezuelan President Hugo Chavez forced to leave office after a nine week general strike calling for his resignation ends

U.S. presents to the United Nations its Iraq war rationale, citing its Weapons of Mass Destruction as imminent threat to world security

U.S. and Britain launch war against Iraq

Baghdad falls to U.S. troops

Official end to combat operations in Iraq is declared by the U.S.

Aung San Suu Kyi, Burmese opposition leader, placed under house arrest by military regime

NATO assumes control of peacekeeping force in Afghanistan

American troops capture Saddam Hussein

J.K. Rowling's *Harry Potter and the Order of the Phoenix*, the sixth installment in the wildly popular series, hit the shelves and rocketed up the best-seller lists

Nobel Prize for literature awarded to J. M. Coetzee

List of Contributors

FRED BILSON. Writer. Holds a bachelors in English and a masters in science. He has lectured in English, linguistics, and computer systems and works as a support tutor to university students with dyslexia. **Dennis Potter, Keith Roberts**

DAN BRAYTON. Professor of literature at Middlebury College in Vermont. Brayton received his doctorate in English from Cornell in 2001, having specialized in Renaissance drama, utopian literature, and literary and cultural theory. He is currently working on a book about Shakespeare and early modern geographical discourse. **Richard Brome**

CORNELIUS BROWNE. Cornelius Browne has written about literature and the environment. He is currently teaching at Oregon State University. **Isabella Bird**

SUSAN BUTTERWORTH. Adjunct professor of composition at Salem State College; freelance writer of journalism and creative nonfiction; contributor to *Oxford Encyclopedia of America Literature, Cyclopedia of Literary Places*, and other reference works and journals; producer of community workshops, lectures, and readings. **Vera Brittain**

SANDIE BYRNE. Fellow in English at Balliol College, Oxford. Her publications include works on eighteenth–and nineteenth–century fiction and twentieth–century poetry. **Jon Stallworthy**

GERRY CAMBRIDGE. Poet and Editor. Edits the Scottish–American poetry magazine, *The Dark Horse* (www.star.ac.uk/darkhorse.html). His own books of verse include *The Shell House* (Scottish Cultural Press, 1995), *Nothing but Heather!: Scottish Nature in Poems, Photographs and Prose* (Luath Press, 1999), illustrated with his own natural history photographs, and *Madame Fi Fi's Farewell and Other Poems* (Luath Press, 2003).

Cambridge was the 1997–1999 Brownsbank Writing Fellow, based at Hugh MacDiarmid's former home, Brownsbank Cottage, near Biggar in Scotland. **Douglas Dunn**

CLARE CONNORS. Lecturer in English language and literature at The Queen's College and Merton College, Oxford, where she teaches literature from 1740 to the present day. She has published widely on various aspects of literary theory and criticism, including an essay on the early Freud in Whitehead and Rossington, eds., *Between the Psyche and the Polis: Refiguring History* (Ashgate, 2000). She has lectured in both the United States and Japan. **Alan Hollinghurst**

PATRICK FLANERY. Patrick Flanery is a postgraduate student at St. Cross College, Oxford University. He has a special interest in British writers of the mid-twentieth century. **Nancy Mitford**

MICHELE GEMELOS. Michele Gemelos received her Bachelor of Arts degree from Skidmore College. She has an M.Phil. in English (1880 to the present day) from the University of Oxford, where she is currently completing her doctoral work on New York City in literature. She has contributed articles to the *Encyclopedia of British–American Relations* (2004) and *International Ford Madox Ford Studies* (2004). Her research and teaching interests include regional and ethnic American fiction and transatlantic literary relations. **Jan Morris**

GAUTAM KUNDU. Gautam Kundu is a professor of English at Georgia Southern University who has specialized in post–colonial literature, with a special interest in writers from India. **Romesh Gunesekera**

JOHN LENNARD. John Lennard teaches at Cambridge University in England and written a

CONTRIBUTORS

number of books and articles about modern literature. He has also published a well–known introduction to poetry. **Ian Rankin**

ANTONIA LOSANO. Professor of English at Middlebury College in Vermont. Losano teaches 19th century literature and women's studies. Her recent publications include an essay on women's exercise videos and an article on the Victorian travel writer Marianne North. She is currently at work on a book project on the intersections of women's writing and women's painting in the 19th century. **Margaret Oliphant**

HELENA NELSON. Writer and Lecturer. Born in Cheshire, England in 1953, Nelson holds a B.A. from the University of York and an M.A. in Eighteenth–Century literature from the University of Manchester. She has written romantic fiction and is a full–time lecturer in English and Communication Studies at Glenrothes College in Scotland. Nelson is the main writer and editor of the further education resource *Core.com 2002*. Her poetry collections include: *Mr and Mrs Philpott on Holiday at Auchterawe, Kettillonia 2001 and Starlight on Water*, Rialto Press, 2003. **Robert Nye**

YUMNA SIDDIQI. Yumna Siddiqi is an Assistant Professor of English at Middlebury College, where she specializes in postcolonial studies. She is completing a book entitled *Anxieties of Empire and the Fiction of Intrigue*, in which she investigates nineteenth– and twentieth–century British and South Asian fiction of intrigue, stories of detection, policing, and espionage. She has published articles in *Renaissance Drama, Cultural Critique, and Victorian Literature and Culture*. At Middlebury College, she has taught courses on postcolonial literature, South Asian literature and culture, and literary theory. **Rohinton Mistry**

ROBERT SULLIVAN. Writer. Sullivan has taught at Brown University, the University of Illinois, and was a Fulbright Professor at the University of Zagreb from 1997-2000. He is the author of *A Matter of Faith, Christopher Caudwell*, and numerous articles on modern and contemporary literature. Currently, he is engaged on various research projects, including participation in the *Modernist Journalist Project*. **Ayi Kwei Armah**

LES WILKINSON. Les Wilkinson is senior master at Nottingham High School, England, where he has taught English for twenty–five years and where he has directed a number of major dramatic productions. His interest in Scottish literature was awakened at St. Andrews University, where he studied in the early 1970s. He writes occasionally and continues to perform traditional and modern folk music and song. **James Hogg**

THOMAS WRIGHT. Writer. Editor of *Table Talk*, the first English language anthology of Oscar Wilde's spoken stories. He has published articles in numerous English periodicals and newspapers, including the *Daily Telegraph*, the *Independent on Sunday*, and the *Times Literary Supplement*. Wright has written articles on Peter Ackroyd for *British Writers Supplement VI*, Bruce Chatwin for *British Writers Supplement IX*, and Oscar Wilde for *British Writers Retrospective Supplement II*. **Vikram Seth**

BRITISH WRITERS

AYI KWEI ARMAH

(1939–)

Robert Sullivan

We're damned souls, aborted creatures suffering in hells created by white people to sustain their crass heaven. The central fact of our lives, the central statement in all of Fanon's work is simply this: we're slaves.

—Armah

AYI KWEI ARMAH is one of the most versatile and controversial West African writers of the past three decades. Although his output has not been vast—six novels and a few short stories in roughly twenty-eight years—the range and polemical nature of his work has drawn a considerable amount of criticism. The latter includes several book-length studies and a prodigious number of scholarly articles, some account of which is given in the "Critical Response" section toward the end of this essay. An extremely private person, Armah has given only one interview and has commented very little on his life or his work. However, his fiction traces in revealing ways Armah's own psychobiography and geographical wanderings, from the jaundiced depiction of postindependent Ghana under Kwame Nkrumah in *The Beautyful Ones Are Not Yet Born* (1968) to *Osiris Rising* (1995), published in Senegal, where Armah now resides. *Osiris Rising* is published by Per Ankh (ancient Egyptian for "The House of Life"), a press that Armah helped found and which is "committed to the emergence of a quality African book industry" (jacket blurb). This enterprise is further evidence of Armah's progressive cultural nationalism and his commitment to a pan-African vision, one that seeks to understand African culture as a totality rather than through the fragmented entities created by colonialism.

Such a vision informs his later fiction and is underscored by his decision to reside in various African countries—Algeria, Tanzania, Lesotho, Senegal, and his native Ghana—and his study of various African languages, including Egyptian hieroglyphics. Armah's anticolonial and antineocolonial stance has been nothing if not consistent: during a book tour of the United States in 2001, a publicity blurb stated that Armah would sign only the editions of his books published by Per Ankh, inferring that those published earlier in the African Writers series by Heinemann would be proscribed. Armah's hardened stance on colonialism's (and neocolonialism's) destruction of African culture and history becomes a major theme in his later fiction, and it has led some critics to accuse him of his own brand of "racial essentialism." His allegorization of how the black and white races (Africans and Europeans, and by extension Americans) are irreducibly historical, cultural, and ideological opposites, and how the white race can only be Africa's destroyer, begins in *Why Are We So Blest?* (1972) and gathers momentum in *Two Thousand Seasons* (1973) and *The Healers* (1978). *The Beautyful Ones* and *Fragments* (1970), the first two novels set in Armah's native Ghana, are concerned more with colonialism's immediate legacy and critique severely postindependent corruption and malaise, against which his central characters struggle to keep their integrity and sanity.

During the 1980s Armah published, in the journal *West Africa,* a series of polemical essays and a piece entitled "One Writer's Education" (1985), an essay that has helped commentators construct an account of his biography. He was born in 1939 in Sekondi-Takoradi, twin port cities west of Accra, in what was then the British colony of the Gold Coast. Armah was fortunate to get his secondary education (1953–1958) at the prestigious Achimota School just outside Accra, an elite institution set up by the colonists to train, predominantly, the indigenous middle class.

Such educational institutions, which could only help perpetuate a neocolonial presence, were to come in for criticism in Armah's third novel, *Why Are We So Blest?* Like the novel's hero, Modin Dofu, Armah won a scholarship enabling him to go to the United States, and in 1959, just two years after Ghana's independence, he went to the Groton School in Massachusetts and later to Harvard University, where he read sociology. In *Why Are We So Blest?* Modin abandons his studies at Harvard because of what he sees as various white strategies for maintaining a "slave mentality" among blacks, as well as his desire to leave the academic world in order to take up a more revolutionary posture.

After he left Harvard, Armah went to Algeria by way of Mexico (he had considered Cuba) and worked for a time as a translator for *Révolution africaine.* His experience in Algeria (he arrived in 1963, just a year after independence) must have been a great disappointment if his fictional account in *Why Are We So Blest?* is any guide. The novel in part recounts how the impetus of revolutionary movements can be arrested when they are hijacked by self-seeking bureaucrats and a new bourgeois elite. Such a state of affairs is fictionalized with more particular relevance to Ghana in the previous two novels, *The Beautyful Ones* and *Fragments.* Whether he was motivated to go to Algeria because of his reading of Frantz Fanon, the great theorist of colonialism and neocolonialism who lived and worked in Algeria, or whether Armah studied Fanon's writings during his sojourn in Algeria, there is no doubt about Fanon's influence on his writing. Indeed, Armah acknowledges a debt to Fanon in his essay "African Socialism: Utopian or Scientific?," published in *Présence africaine* (1967), and in another essay, "Fanon the Awakener," published in *Negro Digest* (1969).

However, even without the knowledge of these essays, it would be evident how Fanon's theories of revolution and postcolonial dependencies are dramatized in Armah's early work. Fanon, a psychiatrist by training, was as much interested in the incarceration of the colonized mind as he was in the chains that at times bound the colonized body. In texts such as *The Wretched of the Earth* and other works, he theorized how the colonized, always treated as inferior by their masters, retained this inferiority complex even after independence. This form of psychic dependency could perpetuate a slave mentality that would cripple any real freedom unless the oppressed could destroy their oppressors, who in many significant ways they had helped to create. Moreover, Fanon theorized the phenomenon of how national independence did not necessarily bring true economic and self-determining freedom; rather, he stressed how independence should be treated as the beginning of authentic social revolution and not its end. He showed how national independence led in most cases only to the perpetuation of the status quo under a new, elitist, African bourgeois class, and how this could lead to sterility and a concomitant endemic corruption. This is indeed exactly the state of affairs portrayed in Armah's first two novels. The third novel, *Why Are We So Blest?,* while still concerned with this theme of postindependence stagnation, introduces the now burgeoning theme of how multiple strategies on the part of the white race keep the African enslaved, a theme that rises to prominence in *Two Thousand Seasons* and *The Healers. Osiris Rising,* while advancing the theme of African enslavement, introduces complex contemporary issues and deserves separate treatment.

During his short stay in Algeria, Armah became ill, as does the main narrator, Solo, in *Why Are We So Blest?* Broken in spirit and body, Armah was hospitalized first in Algiers and then back in Boston, where he had come from. He returned to Ghana in 1964, and as he relates in the same autobiographical essay, he decided to "revert to writing." He worked for a time as a scriptwriter for Ghana Television, as does his character Baako in *Fragments,* but after the coup d'état that ousted the Nkrumah regime in 1966, Armah left Accra to teach in a secondary school at Navrongo in the remote north of Ghana. It is most likely that it was during this period of remoteness from the capital and the frustrations that he encountered there (his hero Baako is driven to distraction by ineptitude and corruption) that Armah began work on his first two novels, *The Beautyful Ones*

Are Not Yet Born and *Fragments*. Restless as ever, he left Ghana in 1967 and went to Paris, where for a time he worked on the journal *Jeune Afrique*. Whether to hone his creative writing skills or simply to spend more time in the United States, Armah left France in 1968 and studied for an M.F.A. in creative writing at Columbia University, which he had completed by 1970. He then went back to Africa, this time to teach at the College of National Education at Chamg'omge, Tanzania, where he stayed until 1976. It was during this sojourn that he published *Two Thousand Seasons* and *The Healers* under the imprint of the Eastern African Publishing House. Perhaps to widen his knowledge of postcolonial Africa, Armah then went to teach at the National University of Lesotho. For a short period in 1979 he worked as a visiting professor in the African Studies Department at the University of Wisconsin before returning to Africa to live and work in Senegal, where he still resides.

THE BEAUTYFUL ONES ARE NOT YET BORN *AND* FRAGMENTS

These two novels are set in Armah's native Ghana and deal with the immediate postcolonial maladies of that country. Both "the man" in *The Beautyful Ones* and Baako Onipa in *Fragments* share the same fate of being alienated not only from their society but from their families as well. They also share the paradoxical fate of believing themselves to be acting perversely because the environment they inhabit is so comprehensively corrupt that their integrity begins to seem like an eccentricity. Indeed, "the man"—as if to underscore his anonymity, he carries this appellation throughout the novel—bears an alienation so chronic that for a great deal of the novel he abides in an existential terrain bereft of any social comforts. Baako's alienation in *Fragments* leads eventually from exasperation through despair to breakdown, and he ends up in an asylum for the insane. Such are the vicissitudes of living in a Fanon-like postcolonial nightmare and trying to sustain some form of integrity.

When we meet "the man" in the first few pages of *The Beautyful Ones,* he has fallen asleep on a bus on his way to work, and although he does not see it, the reader is witness to the first act of ever-increasing corruption and its association with putrescence. As the bus conductor, unaware of the sleeping man, counts the money he has been able to swindle from his passengers, we read how he smells his ill-gotten gains: that the money is "so very rotten that the stench itself of it came with a curious, satisfying pleasure" (p. 3; Heinemann edition, 1988). This trope of contaminated, tainted money is part of a more complex figural plane in the novel that links postcolonial corruption with excrement. Seen here in its first miniscule appearance, this metaphoric representation of the decay and putrescence of a political and social system as human waste, this "excremental vision," gathers momentum throughout the text until it reaches its nauseating conclusion. So persuasive is this rank and squalid view of postcolonial Ghanaian society that even what could be termed "incidental" similes find their register in this vein, as when—to give one of many examples—a native Ghanaian attempting to speak like a colonist is described as being like "a constipated man, straining in his first minute on top of the lavatory seat" (p. 125).

The man, caught in the filthy mire of this corruption (his wife compares him to the chichidodo bird, which "hates excrement with all its soul" but must feed on the maggots that breed best in that environment), struggles daily to maintain a clean bill of mental and moral health (p. 45). Like Baako in *Fragments,* the man himself at times sees his behavior as perverse, as running against the living stream of "normal" life: "The foolish ones are those who cannot live life the way it is lived by all around them, those who will stand by the flowing river and disapprove of the current" (p. 108). This is certainly his wife's point of view, and it is at the conjunction of the personal and the social that we find the man's most intense feeling of alienation, what he terms the "hurt" or "reproach" of "the loved ones." In a very moving passage, we read that after his day's work the man feels "no hurry" because "at the other end there was only home, the land of the loved ones." And he is described most poignantly as walking "with the slowness of those whose desire has nowhere to go" (p. 35).

This remorse is particularly acute when the man and his wife, Oyo, are visiting his old classmate Koomson, now the ultimate "Party man," who has benefited greatly from his position and whose house is replete with things he has acquired for himself, his wife, and, most importantly for the man, for his children (p. 144). Oyo's desire to have nice things for her and her children causes friction between husband and wife, especially now seeing as she does the conspicuous affluence surrounding her husband's one-time fellow student. It is mainly because of these conflictful feelings that the man goes to see his old mentor, "Teacher," a character who functions as a kind of choric commentator, as does Ocran, Baako Onipa's mentor in *Fragments*. Looking for some kind of hope and reassurance, the man finds in his old friend only a cynical despair, a point of view that at times conjectures whether "the rot and the weakness were not after all the eternal curse of Africa itself" (p. 91). The man's interview with Teacher toward the end of chapter 5 and again at the beginning of chapter 7 is "interrupted" by the man's reflections as he surveys postwar Ghanaian history and his own childhood during this period, a rumination that makes up the long, discursive chapter 6. In this chapter, the protagonist describes how as a small boy he is witness to the injustices of colonial rule, a time when "there were tales of white men with huge dogs that ate more in single day than a human Gold Coast family got in a month" (pp. 66–67). But at least there was hope then, in the guise of a young new politician, perhaps one of the "beautiful ones" that would help lead the country from what many had come to believe was the "curse of its leaders." This "new man" (the historical Kwame Nkrumah) came to the people in all his honesty, but such promise did not last, and this new leader too succumbs to all the temptations that attend power.

Nkrumah was deposed in 1966, a historical event that was to afford Armah the dramatic closure to his novel. In the thirteenth chapter, the man is at work as usual when one of his junior colleagues arrives with the news that there has

been a coup "here in Ghana!" (p. 157). When he arrives home his wife is waiting for him with the news that Koomson, his erstwhile classmate, is hiding in the man's house in fear of his life now that the military regime has taken power. It is at this point in the novel that we see the central metaphor of an excremental environment reach its sickening crescendo. Koomson, by now soiling himself because of the fear of imminent arrest, must escape from the man's house (surrounded now by soldiers) through that very same latrine hole that in an earlier visit he had deemed too dirty for his own defecation: "'Push!,' the man shouted ... then there was a long sound as if he were vomiting down there. But the man pushed some more, and in a moment a rush of foul air coming up told him the Party man's head was out" (p. 168).

It now remains only for the fleeing Koomson to make his escape to the Ivory Coast by bribing his way onto the boat he has helped purchase with his ill-gotten gains. The man goes part of the way with him but eventually swims ashore. As he makes his way home, he comes across a police checkpoint at which a small bus waits its turn to pass. It is at this barrier, representative of the new order, that the man, unseen, witnesses the driver give the police officer a bribe. As the bus continues on its way, the man notices that it bears an emblem (most vehicles in Ghana of this type bear similar signs) that reads "The Beautiful Ones Are Not Yet Born," and in the same oval containing the inscription is the representation of "a single flower, solitary, unexplainable, and very beautiful." As he makes his way homeward, he ponders this "sign" and another, of a bird singing "over the school latrine," but these relatively optimistic tokens seem to be negated by the novel's ultimate closure, when the man thinks of home and "everything he was going back to" (p. 183).

Armah's second novel, *Fragments*, is to a large extent a continuation of the themes he had explored in his first. Again we are witness to a central protagonist's alienation from both family and social environment in a postcolonial Ghana rife with nepotism and political inertia. The novel tells the story (and given what we know of Armah's biography, it is a semiautobiographical story) of Baako Onipa, a young Ghanaian who has left Achimota School to study in the United States, and when the narrative begins he is returning after a five-year absence. We learn that, like Armah, he has had a mental breakdown while living abroad, brought about in part by insecurities concerning his writing but also because of his fear of "the return" to Ghana. The novel traces the attempts by Onipa (his name translates as "solitary" or "alone," as of course does "Solo" in *Why Are We So Blest?*) to contribute something constructive and creative to his society as well as his desire to bridge the gap of estrangement between him and his family. However, his efforts, both creative and familial, meet only with frustration and despair. Although he tries to come to terms with it, his family's bourgeois acquisitiveness drives him to distraction, and his creative enthusiasm meets only indifference or hostility. What begins in trepidation of "the return" modulates into anger and frustration at a social structure that seems concerned only with perpetuating the culture of its erstwhile white oppressors. This state of "dis-ease" eventually becomes one of acute alienation, bringing on Baako's old "sickness," and we leave him near the close of the narrative inside the walls of a mental asylum.

However, the narrative does not begin with Baako Onipa, nor does it end with him. As a way of framing Baako's story, Armah has his grandmother Naana (her name connotes wisdom and respect) reflect in the opening chapter on her grandson's departure and his imminent return. Naana fulfills the role of both blind "seer" and keeper of traditional beliefs, and in the opening incantatory chapter she tells the reader of how the traditional ways and rituals of African society have been undermined by neocolonial greed. She remembers especially the defilement of Baako's going-away ceremony, at which his Uncle Foli had been entrusted with the customary ritual of appeasing the spirits by pouring a libation: "when at last he began to pour it out he only let go of little miserly drops" so that he would have more for "his own dry mouth" (p. 7; Heinemann edition, 1974). It is a small enough example but a significant harbinger of how the acquisitive

society and family that celebrated Baako's going would also, only much more so, mark his return. This tainted ritual foreshadows a more tragic one when, against Baako's and his grandmother's wishes, Baako's mother, Efua, and sister, Araba, connive to have the ceremonial "outdooring" of Araba's new baby only five days after its birth, instead of waiting through the traditional time period, because this would coincide with a time of the month when guests would have more money to contribute. Left on show in the heat of the day while Araba and Efua elicit subscriptions for the child's "welfare," the baby succumbs to the chill produced by a powerful fan blowing over the crib. In the diminuendo-like concluding chapter, Naana prepares for her own death and ponders the events that have recently passed: how their fragmentary nature only serves to accentuate the breakdown (both psychic and social) of traditional African social and familial values; how "things [are] only broken and twisted against themselves." She is well aware of the psychic consequences of such fragmentation and of how the moral stand she and her grandson have taken (the symmetry of their names accentuating their alliance) has alienated them both from family and contemporary Ghanaian society

The psychic fragmentation Baako suffers takes place within the larger framework of a postcolonial Ghana that has lost its sense of identity and, as Fanon had theorized, suffers the kind of trauma associated with the legacy of colonialism. This theme is laid out in the second chapter, entitled "Edin" (all the chapters have titles in the Akan language), which roughly translates as "identity." It is here that we meet Juana, a psychiatrist who has come to Ghana from her native Puerto Rico with the idealistic purpose of helping in the "struggle." If in her introductory discourse Naana provides a kind of timeless and ancestral collective African consciousness that sets the stage for Baako's return, then Juana's reflections offer a much more densely textured introduction to the vicissitudes of living in contemporary Accra. Depressed by her work at Korle Bu hospital, she is compelled to "leave the whole aborted town ... to forget all the reminders of futility" (p. 17) by driving out along the coast and away from the city. We learn that this need is a recurrent one, a need that "was in some ways a cure for her own long unease, this leaving Accra to come out for air, with the used portion of the day behind her lined with the wrecked minds it was her job to try and repair" (p. 21). One of the "wrecked minds" she will meet is that of her eventual lover Baako Onipa. When Baako tells Juana in their first interview that he knows what he is "expected to be" but that it is not what he wants to be, she remarks that he is "going against a general current" and that he would need "a lot of strength" (p. 147). Eventually Baako's strength runs out. Like the "the man" in *The Beautyful Ones,* the conflict he faces is between his own moral steadfastness and the "things" his family desires, and like the hero of the previous novel, he ultimately comes to see his behavior as somehow "perverse."

Shortly before his ultimate crisis Baako engages himself in a comparative anthropological "study" of the "been-to" (the Ghanaian term for someone who has lived abroad and who is expected to return with the material evidence) and Melanesian cargo cults (religious belief centered on cargo worship). Had he himself conformed to the "traditional" profile of the been-to, it is more than likely his fate would have been different. Such a profile is provided for us by Henry Robert Hudson Brempong (the name betraying the caricature), whom Baako meets on the plane home. Brempong, who plays a similar role to Koomson in *The Beautyful Ones,* is a frequent traveler and a bringer of various kinds of "cargo" to his family members. Despite his caricatured portrayal, it is Brempong who warns Baako of the realities of life and work in Ghana. He says that Baako does not understand the need to "know people"; that if he were "a white man, it wouldn't matter," but with his "black face like their own" he will get "no respect" (p. 68). This proves to be so much the case that Baako eventually secures his post at Ghanavision only through the intervention of Ocran, his erstwhile mentor from Achimota School. Ocran's function in this novel is very similar to that of Teacher in *The Beautyful Ones.* He too has reached a cynical resignation with regard to the state of postcolo-

nial Ghana, and he warns Baako that the "place is run by this so-called elite of pompous asses trained to do nothing" (p. 116). When Ocran warns Baako that if he wants to do anything "serious" in Ghana he will have to work alone, it is a prediction that becomes painfully true. Late in the narrative, shortly before his final collapse, Baako burns his manuscripts and television treatments, and he reflects on the hope he once had for them and the indifference or animosity of their reception at Ghanavision. His telescripts "The Root" and "The Brand," both of which are allegories of colonialism, neocolonial corruption, and a concomitant slave mentality, foreshadow Armah's own scripting of such themes in *Two Thousand Seasons* and *The Healers.*

Fragments closes on an ambiguously optimistic note similar to that of *The Beautyful Ones.* In the penultimate chapter, entitled "Obra" (Life), which concludes the linear narrative (Naana's circumlocutory commentary has yet to come), Juana, always an advocate for perseverance and "life," goes home after visiting Baako in the asylum: "Walking around the house, she saw only lifeless things, till the idea came to her that she should prepare the unused room" (p. 277). A positive enough note, but it is Naana who has the last word. Her reflections on contemporary bourgeois materialism, the diminution of African values, and their linkage with slavery (pp. 283–284) sound a more ominous note, one that her creator will take up in his next novel and expand in those that follow.

WHY ARE WE SO BLEST?

Armah's third novel is a pivotal work in his oeuvre. Whereas the first two novels dwell for the most part on neocolonial corruption and the mediated "slavery" of the African elitist rulers, *Why Are We So Blest?* explores the origins and ideological forms of how such African intellectuals have become assimilated to Western ways and how this leads them to their destruction. "Destruction" is a key term in this narrative, and in this sense the novel looks forward to the two books that follow it: *Two Thousand Seasons* and *The Healers* are both allegorical epics that utilize the register of history and myth to depict the destructiveness of the European expansion into Africa. In *Why Are We So Blest?* this destructiveness remains as yet on a personal level in that the two major male African characters, Modin Dofu and Solo Nkonam, have their aspirations crushed by two women who serve allegorically as representatives of white colonialism. This novel, with its ideological distinctions between black and white—the irreconcilable differences between the wholly negative pole of destructive whiteness and the wholly positive pole of a benevolent and healing blackness—marks the beginning of a vision that burgeons into what some have called a fully-fledged "racist" ideology in the novels that follow.

The narrative of *Why Are We So Blest?* plunges us immediately into an alienated consciousness, an alienation that has both personal and political causes. Solo Nkonam, a would-be writer who hasn't yet written anything, opens the narrative by describing himself as a "ghost," a totally disillusioned outsider. Feeling himself a failure in the practice of revolution, he has come to Laccryville (a thinly disguised Algiers) in the hope of working for the political wing of the "Bureau of the People's Union of Congheria" but has met only with frustration and disappointment; when we meet him in the novel he has turned to translating articles for the periodical *Jeune nation*. Solo's embitterment and disillusion come about through both personal and political disappointment. Once, he tells us (p. 12), he had believed in love as a power that would transcend the differences between black and white, colonized and colonizer. But his Portuguese girlfriend Sylvia, during his time as a student in Lisbon, has to make a choice between him and "the pull of her race," and she chooses the latter. It is a reiteration of such a betrayal that Solo reads in(to) the narrative of Modin and his girlfriend, Aimèe, and which he extrapolates into a full-blown cultural and historical conspiracy of whiteness against blackness, of the destruction of Africa itself (pp. 207–209; Heinemann edition, 1981). The "story" of Modin Dofu and Aimèe Reitsch is related by Solo, who, we learn near the close of the novel, has been given both their journals by Aimèe after Modin's death. Solo's reading and retrospective analysis of the various entries in the notebooks are not presented to us chronologically; rather, the narrative is rendered in a mosaic way, with Modin's journal entries interleaved with those of Aimèe's, along with Solo's editorial chapters.

Modin Dofu, a Ghanaian student who has won a scholarship to Harvard, meets and becomes involved with a young American woman, Aimèe, who specializes in African studies and, it would seem from one journal entry (pp. 143–145), is a specialist in proffering sexual favors in the service of her research. Modin becomes more and more disturbed by what he sees as his privileged position, indeed his grooming to become one of the colonizer's clones who will return to Africa and perpetuate the colonial system. At one point in his reflections he compares himself to that of a "factor," the African middleman who served as negotiator between the white slavers and his own people. Modin is also presented as the academically privileged African and told time and time again how fortunate he is to be at Harvard. It is one of these occasions that serve as a catalyst in his decision to quit his studies. One of his fellow students expatiates on an article in the *New York Times,* occasioned by the advent of Thanksgiving, entitled "Why Are We So Blest?" which extols the advantages of living in America (p. 99). The debate surrounding this article makes Modin more aware of the attempts to assimilate him into Western culture at the cost of his African heritage, and it is this piece that gives the novel its ironic title. Tired of the Eurocentric curricula and driven by guilt to contribute in some practical way to Africa's freedom, Modin decides to go to Laccryville and offer his services to the Bureau of People's Union of Congheria. He is accompanied by Aimèe, whom he had met while earning money as a subject in a psychology experiment at Harvard. It is on their arrival at the bureau that they meet Solo Nkonam who, given his own embittered experience, is immediately suspect of their interracial relationship.

Solo tries to warn the couple that the possibility of their being recruited by the cynical cadres who run the bureau is unlikely. His prophecy is correct, and after waiting several weeks the couple set out for the southern frontier in the hope of joining up on their own with the revolutionary forces. After some time wandering on the periphery of the Sahara, Modin, fatigued in spirit and body, his revolutionary spirit simply withered away, wants to return to Laccryville. Indirectly due to Aimèe, they are eventually picked up by four French irregulars who drive them a small distance into the desert. There, in a bizarre danse macabre, both are sexually tortured, and Aimèe is eventually raped by the four men. Modin, who is naked and tied to the vehicle, is continuously aroused by the proximity of Aimèe's naked body, which the men hold against him. They eventually castrate him and leave him to die in the desert, but not before Aimèe has taken Modin's penis once more into her mouth, as if to suck the last drops of blood from his dying body. She makes her way back to Laccryville and entrusts both her own and Modin's notebooks to Solo, who, when she asks for them back, refuses to return them. It is from these journals, or notebooks, that Solo constructs their story and hence the novel *Why Are We So Blest?*

The bizarre scenario of the desert scene described above brings to a resounding crescendo the underlying politico-sexual allegorical plane of the novel, in which European (and by extension, American) women are figured as destroyers, leading their black partners to either literal (Modin) or symbolic (Solo) castration. After reading and synthesizing Modin's painful reflections, Solo summarizes what has become the central ideological thrust of the novel: through a continual process of assimilation and/or the concomitant loneliness that will result if it is resisted, Western white culture sucks the lifeblood out of the African, just as Aimèe had sucked the last drops of Modin's blood after he was castrated by the representatives of colonialism. In a rhetorical move reminiscent of Melville's story of Bartleby, Solo summarizes Modin's individual plight and equates it with the collective plight of Africa in an expression that approximates "Ah Modin, Ah Africa" (pp. 207–209). The closing of *Why Are We So Blest?* is sickening, if not entirely realistic. But it is this very difficulty in reading these

scenes of Modin's torture that moves the reader over, as it were, to the latent allegorical plane of the novel, and it points forward to Armah's new vision in *Two Thousand Seasons* and *The Healers,* novels that are less concerned with the destruction of any individual than they are with the drawn-out destruction of Africa itself.

TWO THOUSAND SEASONS *AND* THE HEALERS

One of Modin's diary entries in *Why Are We So Blest?* notes that if there is any hope for Africa and the African it lies in the kind of egalitarian society that existed before the European invasion, and that "war against the invader should be the educational process for creating new anti-European, anti-imperial, anti-elitist values" (p. 222). A little later in the narrative his alter ego, Solo, reflects that "only one issue is worth our time: how to end the oppression of the African, to kill the European beasts of prey" (p. 230). It is these twin sentiments that form the main narrative thrust of the two novels that follow. However, although the two later novels share and extensively advance this burgeoning vision of the white race as natural predator, Armah's readers could hardly have been prepared for the stylistic and narrative strategies he would choose to advance this vision. Unlike the complexly wrought and modernist mode of presentation in *Why Are We So Blest?*, Armah chose to adopt, or adapt, the mode of the oral historian for these two narratives. Indeed, both read less like novels than chronicles of an African past without division, reconstructing through myth, legend, and racial memory an Edenic time before the imperialist incursions of Arab and European expansionism. They depict a time of precolonial aggression and resistance, a time before the aggression and resistance brought by colonialism, of indigenous social formations premised on equality (especially gender equality), "reciprocity," and "connectedness"; what the plural narrative voice of *Two Thousand Seasons* calls "the way": "Our way is reciprocity. The way is wholeness. Our way knows no oppression. ... The way destroys only destruction" (p. 39; Heinemann edition, 1979).

It is just this social and ethical system, this "collectivity," that the European and Arab "marauders"—first as "guests," then as masters—pull asunder, destroying both the unity of the African continent and the African consciousness. The novel's italicized prologue utilizes the metaphor of the spring, the source, and its self-destructive flow to the desert: "Springwater flowing to the desert, where you flow there is no regeneration ... it is not in the nature of the desert to return anything but destruction" (p. xi). This metaphor then broadens into an analogue of Africa's death wish, as it at first embraces and then seeks a compromise with the destroyers who come from the North (the Islamic incursion) and the European imperialists who come from the sea. It is a prophet who forecasts the one thousand seasons wandering in the wilderness and another thousand seasons attempting to once again find "the way." This social structure resembles a kind of primitive communism based on equality and reciprocity, in which women play as significant a role as their male counterparts. An early section of the narrative relates how these women massacre the first "Arab predators" during their annual feast celebrating the end of Ramadan. There is a terrible excess in the descriptions of how these would-be enslavers die, some of them gasping their last breath as they lie in their own excrement and urine (pp. 20–30), betraying an awful hatred in this racial memoir, not to mention a defamation of the Islamic religion itself. After this initial success against "the destroyers," the narrative describes how the inauguration of chiefdoms allows the enemy to divide and conquer, utilizing those "factors" of whom Modin had spoken in *Why Are We So Blest?* The plural voice of the first four chapters (the narrational "we") recounts their exile and epic migrations in search of a homeland. The later chapters become less mythically diffuse and focus on the activities of a band of young male and female initiates as they seek a new homeland and a reestablishment of "the way." They are trained by various experts, of whom Isanusi (earlier driven into exile by the corrupt King Koranche) is the most versatile. It is he "whose vocation it was to keep the knowledge of

our way, the way, from destruction; to bring it back to an oblivious people" (p. 89). Isanusi, who teaches resistance but not revenge, dies in the struggle against the aggressors, but his younger followers carry on and achieve a victory of sorts. Anachronous as it may seem, it is they who are perhaps the "beautiful ones" who were not as yet born in Armah's first novel.

The fictional mode of *Two Thousand Seasons* was no doubt chosen by Armah to suit his subject matter—the depiction of the trials and tribulations of a legendary pan-African nation—but it is not entirely satisfactory. The plot, as in the novel that follows, is episodic, the characters are more tokens than conflicted beings, and the narrative is replete with anecdotal excess: "There is nothing white men will not do to satisfy their greed" (p. 78), for example. This is not, one believes, a diminution of Armah's powers as a novelist but rather an intentional choice of these fictive methods to suit his new vision. It is as if he is less interested in the aesthetics of the novel as such than in the delineation of an ideological premise: the ruination of a virtuous, Edenic Africa by the "white destroyer" in collusion with its sycophantic quisling collaborators, the chiefs and kings of a divided Africa.

Toward the end of *Two Thousand Seasons,* the anonymous narrator remarks on the "disintegration," the "bloody desolation the whites have stretched over this land!" and that the "destroyed fragments begin to call out for healing" now that the "destroyers cannot reach beyond these two thousand seasons" (pp. 202–206). If this novel dramatizes the loss of "the way" and the severing of the collectivity on which it was based, then *The Healers* seeks to tell the story of its attempted restoration. Although it bears the italicized subtitle "an historical novel," *The Healers* has a similar narrative mixture of myth and legend and a similar cast of unconflicted characters. It is "historical" in the sense that Armah sets the picaresque adventures of his epic heroes within the historical context of the fall of the great Ashanti empire and the consolidation of British imperialism in the territory that was to become the Gold Coast, later Ghana. The historical aspect of the novel moves through the Ashanti wars and employs "real" historical places and characters (even Queen Victoria gets a mention) and at times utilizes a detailed realism. But superimposed on this linear tale of adventure and quest—and, one imagines, intended to take precedence in Armah's narrative and ideological design—is that of a symbolic, or metaphoric, or visionary plane that seeks to explore the divisions that created the black diaspora and how these may be repaired. Consistent with Armah's vision of a once-unified African continent, the narrative associates the defeat of the Ashanti empire with the defeat of Africa itself. The blurb on the back cover of the novel describes this succinctly:

> A century ago one of Africa's great empires, Ashanti, fell. The root cause of that fall, symbolic of Africa's conquest, was not merely Europe's destructive strength. It was Africa's disunity: divisions among kindred societies; divisions within each society between aristocrats, commoners, slaves.

Two Thousand Seasons had documented this chronic disunity. *The Healers* sets out to describe how these numerous fissures in African society might be made whole again. Unlike the vatic voice that introduces us to the epic sweep of *Two Thousand Seasons,* the one that opens *The Healers* sounds more like that of the conventional novel: "In the twentieth year of his life, a young man found himself at the centre of strange, extraordinary events." The young man is Densu, and the "event" that starts the narrative on its detective-story-like course is the murder of his friendly rival, the young Prince Appia. Thus begins the linear or metonymic plane of the novel, as Densu sets out to clear his name and begins a series of episodic adventures that eventually lead him to the great healer Damfo, keeper of "the way." The metaphoric or symbolic plane of the text, reliant more on schematic dualisms ("the Manipulators" versus "the Inspirers," the evil Ababio versus the virtuous Densu), is less concerned with novelistic realism than with an aesthetic associated with myth. This strand of the novel explores the need for healing, both corporal and psychic, in an Africa riven by imperialist machinations. Damfo explains to his apprentice Densu that not only do individuals need the work of healers but also "a people can be diseased in the same way," that "sometimes a whole people needs healing work" (p. 82).

These healers, of whom Damfo is the most skillful, resemble proto-psychoanalysts in their work with individuals, and in their search for the restoration of an integral pan-African society based on reciprocity and equality they enact a program that is almost Fanon-like in its intentions. These twin responsibilities of the healers, that of offering individual therapy sessions as well as the restoration of pan-African spiritual health, come together in what is virtually the center of the novel, when Damfo tends to the troubled Ashanti general who will lead his forces against the British. Asamoa Nkwanta suffers from recurring dreams and nightmares brought about (Damfo explains) because of the split in his "soul" caused by his guilt in trying to serve Ashanti royalty at the cost of his peoples' welfare as a whole. It is during these analytical sessions with the emaciated and depressed general that we get the visionary and ideological center of the novel. Damfo addresses the general as follows: "If the past tells you the Akan and the black people were one in the past, perhaps it also tells you there is nothing eternal about our present divisions. We were one in the past. We may come together again in the future" (p. 176).

Damfo is aware that such a possibility may take "millennia," and the utter rout of Asamoa Nkwanta and his allies by the British forces (history records that General Wolseley ended his campaign successfully in less than two months, entering Kumasi in January 1874) would seem to confirm this pessimistic view. However, as if to bring the novel to a satisfactory, if ambiguous, close, the narrative allows for an ironic reunification of the kind the defeated healers had sought to achieve. Shortly after the victorious Wolseley sails from Cape Coast and the defeated peoples from all over Africa are assembled under the gaze of their rulers, Ama Nkroma, one of the female healers, remarks in the closing paragraphs of the novel, as follows:

> But look at all the black people the whites have brought here. Here we healers have been wondering about ways to bring our people together again. And

the whites want ways to drive us farther apart. Does it not amuse you, that in their wish to drive us apart the whites are actually bringing us work for the future? Look!

(p. 309)

History has defeated them, but their vision is unvanquished.

OSIRIS RISING

Armah's sixth novel and first fiction published under the imprint of his publishing collective in Popenguine, Senegal, has the following signature on the last page of text: "Mussuwam, 17 February 1984; Popenguine, 18 January 1994." It is difficult to believe that it took him some ten years to complete this novel, with its stereotypical cast of characters and straightforward narrative structure, and one assumes that he held it back until he had established Per Ankh, his African publishing company. He remarked in a rare interview that he had "not been publishing" [because] he did not want to give his books to "multinational companies" and that he would "keep his books in [his] drawer" until either a suitable "black publisher" came along or until he and his fellow writers could "get together and organize [their] own publishing house" (in Gurnah, p. 23). Given his choice of name for the new publishing company, it comes as no coincidence then that the plot of *Osiris Rising* centers around the renewal in modern Africa—and the suppression by governmental forces—of the ancient Egyptian collective known as the Ankh movement. The novel reflects Armah's burgeoning belief that ancient Egypt was a black civilization and that the peoples of West Africa can trace their origins to the Nile Valley, a thesis advanced by Cheikh Anta Diop, a thinker mentioned numerous times in Armah's nonfiction and lectures and who is invoked in *Osiris Rising.*

The society of the Ankh is reminiscent of the idealistic social structure promulgated in *The Healers,* and from the point of view of present-day authority in *Osiris Rising* "a dangerous secret society that tried at one time to destroy all existing social and political institutions here: monar-

chy, the aristocracy, slavery" (p. 35). As with Armah's previous two novels, the actual "story," or plotline, of *Osiris Rising* serves a didactic or parabolic purpose: it is an analogue of how truly democratic and progressive movements in Africa are undermined not only by neocolonial and imperialist influences but also by the machinations of a fifth column of corrupt and acquisitive indigenous men seeking power. And as the title from the Osiris myth suggests, the novel considers also the possibility of a regeneration, a resurrection, of the African unity that had existed before its various dismemberments. The vision is laudable, but the fictional carrier that delivers it is a strange mélange (some might say "hodgepodge") of genres and concerns. It is at once a satire of African Americans who "return" to Africa to seek their roots; a Bond-like thriller, with villains who house their sophisticated weapons of mass destruction in high-tech bunkers; a melodrama that opposes sacrificial virtue against corrupt and ruthless power mechanisms; and a classic depiction of triangular desire as played out between the three main characters, Ast, Asar, and the despicable Seth Spenser Soja.

The narrative begins with Ast, an assistant professor of African studies at Emerson University who was taught Egyptian hieroglyphics by her grandmother. She decides to relinquish her post and offer her teaching services in Africa because, as she explains later in the narrative, "in Africa, there could be a coming together of souls experiencing life as shared work and reward … instead of this brute competition between individuals and factions" (p. 70). Shortly before her departure she receives a communication from the secret society of the Ankh, and this piece of subversive literature is detected when she arrives at the fictitious African country of Hapi. She is taken into custody and is eventually interrogated by the deputy director of security himself, who, it turns out, was a contemporary at Emerson, as was Asar, the leader of the subversive and progressive movement she is to join. Asar, who fought in the liberation wars in the South and who eschews a brilliant career in order to teach at the provincial Teacher Training College at Manda, is goodness personified. Seth Spenser

Soja (SSS), the power-hungry deputy director and onetime school rival of Asar, is his ethical opposite. Such is the basic binary structure of the novel, but there are lesser examples as well, similar to the "Manipulators/Inspirers" model of *The Healers.*

After an unsuccessful attempt to win over Ast to his side, Soja attempts, rather unconvincingly, to rape her. It is unconvincing from the aesthetics of realism, but not from the novel's parabolic plane, as we witness the syphilitic Soja attempting to contaminate the pure and virtuous Ast (pp. 62–66). It is shortly after this that, while walking on the beach, Ast, as if by some cosmic plan of coincidence, sees Sheldon Tubman, a onetime civil rights activist now known as Ras Jomo Cinque Equiano and leader of a bizarre cult whose chosen names, ironically, had been "better left to rot in peace" (p. 96). He, his three wives (Ast rescues Jacqueline Brown, a possible fourth), and a motley crew of characters including the fake Ethiopian Prince Woosen—at one time a New York drug peddler and convicted felon—are introduced into the plot. The action of the novel and its ideological focus now moves to the college at Manda where Ast goes to join Asar in his struggle to reform the Eurocentric curriculum as well as his work to "turn [his] dismembered continent into a healing society, Africa" (p. 112). These pages of the novel include several "conversations" between Ast and Asar, the would-be lovers who betray Armah's recent predilection for writing fiction as thinly disguised political polemic. For example, the scene just before they make love for the first time (pp. 116–117) reads more like a monologic political speech than natural dialogue, but this is only one example of how the fictional apparatus is there only to carry a message. It is not that novels should not convey a critique of political systems or embody visionary ideals, but these can be handled in more artistically dramatic ways, as they are in *The Beautyful Ones* and *Fragments,* for example. As in those novels, there is much valid criticism in *Osiris Rising* of how supposedly "independent" African countries are still controlled by multinational corporations (Kaiserlever in this case), and how the African

elite, the "manipulators," are in turn bribed and manipulated by neocolonial interests. However, much of this critique is delivered in what is closer to a lecture format than the kind of dramatic representation rendered in the first two novels, and this latent tendency becomes manifest in the sections of the novel dealing with the "Proposals for a New Curriculum," where even the typography serves the didactic purpose (pp. 213–223).

Eventually it transpires that Ras Jomo, the fake Prince Woosen, and others have conspired with Seth Soja to plant weaponry in Asar's living quarters so that Soja might have a reason for killing his old rival. Symbolically enough, Asar dies trying to communicate with Ast as she approaches his little boat, held captive on Soja's Bond-like motor launch:

> She saw Asar raise his arms to cup his hands round his mouth, to repeat his query. The first bullet struck, giving him no time to register surprise. His body pivoted left. Other bullets reversed it. …
>
> Ast saw Asar totter upright in a flash, arms still in the communicant attitude of his last question. Then he exploded silently into fourteen starry fragments, and the pieces plunged into the peaceful water.
>
> (p. 305)

Climactic as it is, this is not the true closure of this morality tale. It is the execrable Seth Spenser Soja who brings it to its ambiguous ending when in the last sentence he whispers to Ast, the ultimate object of his desire, "When you are ready, come."

CRITICAL RESPONSE

There are literally scores of scholarly articles on Armah's first few novels alone, and several book-length studies take into account his fiction up to the publication of *The Healers.* A representative number of these are listed in the bibliography to this essay, but only a selected few can be addressed here. Since *The Beautyful Ones* burst upon the literary scene, there has never been any dispute concerning the originality and power of Armah's writing, although some have more recently suggested a waning of that early strength.

Most disagreements have concerned either the "Africanness" of his fiction (the early novels), or the ideology that imbues his later work, especially *Two Thousand Seasons* and *The Healers.* Generally speaking (and this is to generalize mercilessly), the early negative critiques centered on the lack of an "African" texture and vision in Armah's novels; such critiques accused him of adhering more to a Western sensibility and a vision wherein his protagonists seemed more like existentialist outsiders than indigenous Africans. Indeed, Charles Larson's (1978) seemingly incredible indictment, that there were "few Africanisms" in Armah's early work, prompted one of the few statements on his work by the author himself (see Armah, "Larsony, or Fiction as Criticism of Fiction," 1976).

Derek Wright, who has written extensively on Armah's work, has done us good service by bringing together twenty-two previously published articles in his *Critical Perspectives on Ayi Kwei Armah* (1992). These range from "general essays" to groups of essays centered on particular novels. In his brief introduction, Wright discusses some of the central issues brought to task in the individual essays, especially the early criticisms of Chinua Achebe and Kofi Awoonor, who formed in part (Wright colorfully suggests) a kind of "Un-African Activities Committee of the literary imagination" (p. 4) that called for a clearly recognizable style of documentary realism. Wright also suggests an intriguing correspondence between Armah's career to date with Frantz Fanon's "tripartite scheme for the decolorized writer" (p. 6). *The Beautyful Ones* corresponds to Fanon's "assimilation phase," whereas the next two novels fit into "the second phase of disturbance and painful liberation." The last two books (*Two Thousand Seasons* and *The Healers*) are then "fighting books" that "adopt the militant postures of Fanon's 'fighting phase'" (p. 6).

By the time Robert Fraser had completed his book-length study (1980), he had both the advantage of surveying the prodigious critical output on Armah's earlier work as well as being able to consider the radical shift marked by *Two Thousand Seasons* and *The Healers.* Noting Ar-

mah's somewhat eccentric publishing history, Fraser remarks on the tendency of critics to concentrate on the early books, especially *The Beautyful Ones,* "without any systematic attempt being made to place the asperity of that work within a broader picture of the writer's vision" (p. 1). This is exactly what Fraser sets out to do in the five chapters of his study, each of which is devoted to one of the first five novels. Importantly, Fraser attempts to link style with content as he examines the evolution of Armah's oeuvre, arguing that the complexity of form of the first few novels mirrored the subject of the alienated artist figure, whereas the protagonists of the later books—firmly ensconced in a community— ushered in the need for a communal voice as narrator. In his conclusion, Fraser asks whether or not Armah might have "paid too high a qualitative price for the dogmatic thrust he introduces into the more recent novels" (p. 106).

The above question is answered in two radically different ways in full-length studies of Armah by Neil Lazarus (1990) and Ode Ogede (2000). Lazarus' book, *Resistance in Postcolonial African Fiction,* is less concerned with narrative or stylistic strategies than it is with situating Armah within "postcolonial African intellectualism" (p. ix). This is a densely textured discourse on influences that shaped the ideological matrices of Armah's texts, both fictional and otherwise. It is at once a brilliant investigative study and a curiously lopsided one, with the late postrealist novels getting scant attention (around fifteen pages of text) and the novel *Why Are We So Blest?* alone taking up some sixty-seven pages. This is because Lazarus sees the latter as the marker of what could be called the "ideological break" in Armah's output, signaling a shift from an "ethics of resistance" in the first two novels to what is tantamount to a racist stance. Lazarus notes the beginnings of Armah's "manichean" vision in this text and condemns it as "both a racist and a poisonously misogynistic work" (p. 118). Although less emphatically condemnatory about *Two Thousand Seasons* and *The Healers,* Lazarus does note that "the essentialist language, in terms of which ideologies and social tendencies are cast as natural and viewed, accordingly, as unalterable, is reminiscent of that in *Why Are We So Blest?"* (p. 219).

By contrast, Ogede's book, far from being harshly critical, borders on hagiography. In his efforts to find no fault with Armah, Ogede is much too dismissive of earlier studies; indeed at times he seems to suggest that perhaps only an African critic can really come to terms with an African writer such as Armah. Ogede would seem to be in a position to offer such an analysis—he has significant things to say about African oral narratives and Armah's place within a specifically African literary context—but his characterization of earlier studies as "oversimplifications" proves to be somewhat ironic given some of his own readings. It seems astounding that, given the richness of Armah's earlier work, not to mention the wealth of other African literatures that deal with postcolonialism, Ogede can say of *Osiris Rising* that its "ambitiousness" is "stunning" and that the novel is "one of the most penetrating analyses of the African postcolonial situation ever presented in a creative work" (p. 132). And there is surely an unfortunate disabling irony in the statement "Armah interweaves [many] topics without reducing any one of them to a bland cliché" (p. 132), when in fact much of the novel is replete with stereotypical situations.

Ogede is too eager to forgive Armah any transgression, and this may ultimately stem from certain prejudices both writers seem to share. In the context of discussing how other African writers have used stereotypes to "underscore the superficial interactions between blacks and whites," Ogede remarks that despite the hope that these relations might change, "whites go on perpetuating their savage attacks and brutality on Africans whom they narrowly perceive through their cocoons of racial stereotypes" (p. 85). This is exactly the kind of generalization and racial essentialism for which Armah's later work has been held accountable.

In 2002, Armah published a novel entitled *KMT: In the House of Life* under the imprint of his publishing collective, Per Ankh, in Senegal, but at this time of writing the book was not widely available or reviewed. However, from the publicity that we have, it seems that this new fiction marks a continuation of Armah's earlier themes and concerns, particularly with those of *Osiris Rising*. In *KMT,* the narrator, Lindela, searches not only for self-fulfillment in Africa (as did Ast in *Osiris*), but also through her study of hieroglyphics she seeks the answers to why Africa, once so full of promise, has fallen into decay. Her investigations into what residual pan-African values might lie under the ruins of centuries of colonial expansion and exploitation mirror those of her creator Ayi Kwei Armah. His work over the past thirty years could be characterized as the fictional "excavation" of such possibilities.

Selected Bibliography

WORKS OF AYI KWEI ARMAH

NOVELS

The Beautyful Ones Are Not Yet Born. Boston: Houghton Mifflin, 1968; London: Heinemann, 1969, 1988.

Fragments. Boston: Houghton Mifflin, 1970; Nairobi: East African Publishing House, 1974; London: Heinemann, 1974.

Why Are We So Blest? New York: Doubleday, 1972; Nairobi: East African Publishing House, 1974; London: Heinemann, 1974, 1981.

Two Thousand Seasons. Nairobi: East African Publishing House, 1973; London: Heinemann, 1979; Chicago: Third World, 1979.

The Healers. Nairobi: East African Publishing House, 1978; London: Heinemann, 1979.

Osiris Rising: A Novel of Africa Past, Present, and Future. Popenguine, West Africa: Per Ankh, 1995.

KMT: In the House of Life. Popenguine, West Africa: Per Ankh, 2002. (Not widely available at this writing; for information contact www.perankhbookssentoo.sn.)

POETRY

"Speed." *West Africa,* February 13–19, 1989, p. 227.

"Aftermath." In *Messages: Poems from Ghana.* Edited by Kofi Awoonor and G. Adali-Mortty. London: Heinemann, 1970. Pp. 89–91.

SHORT FICTION

"The Ball." *Harvard Advocate* 98, no. 2:35–40 (1964).

"The Night Club Girl." *Drum,* January 1964, pp. 35–39. Reprinted as "The Offal Kind," *Harper's,* January 1969, pp. 79–84.

"Contact." *New African* 4:244–248 (December 1965).

"Asemka." *Okyeame* 3:28–32 (December 1966).

"Yaw Manu's Charm." *Atlantic Monthly,* May 1968, pp. 89–95.

"An African Fable." *Présence africaine* 68:192–196 (1968).

"Halfway to Nirvana." *West Africa,* 24 September 1984, pp. 1947–1948.

"Doctor Kamikaze." *Mother Jones,* October 1989, pp. 34–38, 46. Reprinted as "The Development Agent," *CODESRIA Bulletin* 4:11–14 (1990).

NONFICTION

"La mort passe sous les blancs." *L'Afrique littéraire et artistique* 3:21–28 (February 1960).

"Letter from Ghana." (Anonymous.) *New York Review of Books,* October 12, 1967, pp. 34–39.

"Pour les ibos, le régime de la haine silencieuse." *Jeune Afrique,* October 29, 1967, pp. 18–20.

"African Socialism: Utopian or Scientific?" *Présence africaine* 64:6–30 (1967).

"A Mystification: African Independence Revalued." *Pan-African Journal* 2:141–151 (spring 1969).

"Fanon: The Awakener." *Negro Digest,* October 1969, pp. 4–9, 29–43.

"Sundiata: An Epic of Old Mali." *Black World,* May 1974, pp. 51–52, 93–96.

"Chaka." *Black World,* February 1975, pp. 51–52, 84–90. Reprinted as "The Definitive Chaka," *Transition* 50:10–15 (1976).

"Larsony [sic], or Fiction as Criticism of Fiction." *Asemka* 4:1–14 (September 1976). Reprinted in *New Classic* 4:33–45 (November 1977).

"Masks and Marx: The Marxist Ethos vis-à-vis African Revolutionary Theory and Praxis." *Présence africaine* 131:35–65 (1984).

"Islam and 'Ceddo.'" *West Africa,* October 8, 1984, p. 2031.

"The View from PEN International." *West Africa,* November 26, 1984, pp. 2384–2385.

"The Oxygen of Translation." *West Africa,* February 11, 1985, pp. 262–263.

"The Lazy School of Literary Criticism." *West Africa,* February 25, 1985, pp. 355–356.

"The Caliban Complex." *West Africa,* March 18 and 25, 1985, pp. 521–522, 570–571.

"The Festival Syndrome." *West Africa,* April 15, 1985, pp. 726–727.

"Our Language Problem." *West Africa,* April 29, 1985, pp. 831–832.

"The Teaching of Creative Writing." *West Africa,* May 20, 1985, pp. 994–995.

"One Writer's Education." *West Africa,* August 26, 1985, pp. 1752–1753.

"Flood and Famine, Drought and Glut." *West Africa,* September 30, 1985, pp. 2011–2012.

"Africa and the Francophone Dream." *West Africa,* April 28, 1986, pp. 884–885.

"Dakar Hieroglyphs." *West Africa,* May 19, 1986, pp. 1043–1044.

"Writers as Professionals." *West Africa,* August 11, 1986, p. 1680.

"The Third World Hoax." *West Africa,* August 25, 1986, pp. 1781–1782.

"A Stream of Senegalese History." *West Africa,* March 9, 1987, pp. 471–473.

CRITICAL AND BIOGRAPHICAL STUDIES

Achebe, Chinua. "Africa and Her Writers." In his *Morning Yet on Creation Day.* London: Heinemann, 1975. Pp. 19–29.

Amuta, Chidi. "The Contemporary African Artist in Armah's Novels." *World Literature Written in English* 21:467–476 (autumn 1982).

Anyidoho, Kofi. "Literature and African Identity: The Example of Ayi Kwei Armah." *Bayreuth African Studies Series* 6:23–42 (1986).

Awoonor, Kofi. "Africa's Literature Beyond Politics." *Worldview* 15, no. 3:21–25 (1972).

Boafo, Y. S. "The Nature of Healing in Ayi Kwei Armah's *The Healers.*" *Komparatistische Hefte* 13:95–104 (1986).

Booth, James. "*Why Are We So Blest?* and the Limits of Metaphor." *Journal of Commonwealth Literature* 15:50–64 (August 1980).

Busia, Abena. "Parasites and Prophets: The Use of Women in Ayi Kwei Armah's Novels." In *Ngambika: Studies of Women in African Literature.* Edited by Carole Boyce Davies and Anne Adams Graves. Trenton, N.J.: Africa World, 1986. Pp. 89–114.

Collins, Harold. "The Ironic Imagery of Armah's *The Beautyful Ones Are Not Yet Born:* The Putrescent Vision." *World Literature Written in English* 20:37–50 (1971).

Colmer, Rosemary. "The Human and the Divine: *Fragments* and *Why Are We So Blest?*" *Kunapipi* 2, no. 2:77–90 (1980).

Dseagu, Samuel A. "Ayi Kwei Armah." In *Postcolonial Writers: A Bio-Bibliographical Critical Sourcebook.* Edited by Pushpa Naidu Parekh and Siga Fatima Jagne. Westport, Conn.: Greenwood Press, 1998. Pp. 45–51.

Fraser, Robert. *The Novels of Ayi Kwei Armah: A Study in Polemical Fiction.* London: Heinemann, 1980.

Griffiths, Gareth. "Structure and Image in Armah's *The Beautyful Ones Are Not Yet Born.*" *Studies in Black Literature* 2, no. 2:1–9 (1971).

Gurnah, Abdulrazak, ed. *Essays on African Writing.* Oxford: Heinemann Educational, 1993.

Izevbaye, D. S. "Ayi Kwei Armah and the 'I' of the Beholder." In *A Celebration of Black and African Writing*. Edited by Bruce King and Kolawole Ogungbesan. Oxford: Oxford University Press, 1975. Pp. 232–244.

Johnson, Joyce. "The Promethean 'Factor' in Ayi Kwei Armah's *Fragments* and *Why Are We So Blest?*" *World Literature Written in English* 21:497–510 (autumn 1982).

Kibera, Leonard. "Pessimism and the African Novelist: Ayi Kwei Armah's *The Beautyful Ones Are Not Yet Born.*" *Journal of Commonwealth Literature* 14:64–72 (August 1979).

Lazarus, Neil. *Resistance in Postcolonial African Fiction*. New Haven: Yale University Press, 1990.

Lindfors, Bernth. "Armah's Histories." *African Literature Today* 11:85–96 (1980).

Moore, Gerald. *Twelve African Writers*. London: Hutchinson, 1980.

Nkrumah, Kwame. *Class Struggle in Africa*. New York: International Publishers, 1979.

Ogede, Ode. *Ayi Kwei Armah: Radical Iconoclast*. Athens: Ohio University Press, 2000.

Okpewho, Isidore. "Myth and Modern Fiction: Armah's *Two Thousand Seasons.*" *African Literature Today* 13:1–23 (1983).

Owusu, Kwesi. "Armah's F-R-A-G-M-E-N-T-S: Madness as Artistic Paradigm." *Callaloo* 11, no. 2:361–370 (1988).

Soyinka, Wole. *Myth, Literature, and the African World*. Cambridge: Cambridge University Press, 1976.

Wright, Derek, ed. *Critical Perspectives on Ayi Kwei Armah*. Washington, D.C.: Three Continents, 1992. (Collects journal articles listed above by Amuta, Anyidoho, Boafo, Booth, Busia, Collins, Colmer, Griffiths, Izevbaye, Johnson, Kibera, Lindfors, and Okpewho.)

Wright, Derek. "Ayi Kwei Armah." *Dictionary of Literary Biography*. Vol. 117, *Twentieth-Century Caribbean and Black African Writers*. First series. Edited by Bernth Lindfors and Reinhard Sander. Detroit: Gale, 1992. Pp. 54–77.

Yankson, Kofi E. *Ayi Kwei Armah's Novels*. Accra, Ghana: [s.n], 1994.

ISABELLA BIRD

(1831–1904)

Cornelius Browne

IN THE EARLY twenty-first century, "adventure tourism" is mainly the province of Gore-Tex-clad, upper-middle-class Americans and western Europeans risking the wild in relative comfort, trekking through designated wilderness areas and national parks. But adventure tourism has its predecessors, and looking back to them can tell us much about ourselves as a culture. Granted, Isabella Bird traveled in far different circumstances than we do now, but she is strikingly similar at the same time. She possessed a powerful enthusiasm for the natural world; she also showed a deep respect for native cultures while at the same time voicing a condescending, national chauvinism that remains inherent in the very motivation many people have to visit less developed cultures. In other words, Bird could physically leave her culture, but, as is true for all of us, that culture was tenacious in its ability to shadow her all over the world, whether she welcomed it or not. Bird embodied the contradictions of the Victorian traveler, which we have inherited as we seek out other cultures for our own complex reasons. Her work rewards close study and remains valuable on one level for what it can tell us about Western attitudes toward the rest of the world as well as British attitudes toward the United States in the nineteenth century.

It would be a mistake, however, to reduce her and her work to a cultural comparison. Bird was many things, but primary among them is that she was a prose stylist of great beauty and vigor. In her work she is at her best describing the natural world and native peoples and in the narration of her many adventures and mishaps around the globe. She wrote travel books about Hawaii, the United States, Japan, Korea, the Malay peninsula, China, and the Middle East. In Colorado she traveled nearly 800 miles—from Estes Park to Colorado Springs, through South Park, and back to Estes Park via Denver and Longmont—alone on horseback during the winter through the Rocky Mountains in the 1870s, a trip few of even the heartiest adventure tourists would attempt today clad in wool and leather. Before she rode into Colorado Springs, she changed from her riding outfit to a black silken gown and switched to a sidesaddle for propriety's sake.

She is often credited with saying, after her marriage to John Bishop, that although she would like to travel to New Guinea, it was hardly a place to bring a man. Bird to a large extent created an identity for herself through writing about her travels, and it seems that this identity required that she not be in the company of an overshadowing male. In *A Lady's Life in the Rocky Mountains* (1879) she writes, "This is no region for tourists and women, only for a few elk and bear hunters at times, and its unprofaned freshness gives me new life" (p. 73). Of course, she—a woman—is there, but this is no place for women as constructed by her culture. Competent to thrive in the most difficult environments, Bird indeed created for herself a new life, a new definition of what it meant to her to be a "lady."

It is not clear whether Bird actually made the quip about bringing her husband to New Guinea. But it remains part of the legend surrounding her and seems indeed like something she might have said during her travels, though not at home in England, where she behaved as a different person from the woman abroad in the world. For the most part she was physically ill while in England and healthy when traveling. She seems also to have suffered guilt for enjoying herself so much and for making money through the wide sale of her travel books. Profiting from one's pleasure was not something a "lady" did in the British Isles. Given her class and religious background, such gain was inappropriate, yet she continued to travel and write about her travels into her old age. In order to get a grasp on this contradictory, complex, fascinating, and infuriating woman, this essay will tell her story alongside the examination of her most important books.

EARLY LIFE

Isabella Lucy Bird was born to Edward and Dora Bird on October 15, 1831, in Boroughbridge, Yorkshire. Two years later her sister, Henrietta, was born. Edward Bird was an evangelical minister in the Church of England, and his family moved several times to different parishes. Edward Bird often took his elder daughter along with him on visits to his parishioners, and early in her life she came to love the landscape of northern England. It seems that her father's influence—he often quizzed her on flora, fauna, and crops—disposed her from an early age to develop the keen eye for fine detail that permeates her writing.

She also had some interesting relatives, foremost among them her cousin William Wilberforce, famous for his leading role in the abolition of slavery in England. This abhorrence of slavery, of the maltreatment of native peoples and the abuse of arbitrary power, is apparent in Bird's writing, although that critique is sometimes muted in contrast to the comments she makes in her letters, from which many of her most important narratives are largely drawn. This is not to say that she ever fully lost her belief in British superiority to the rest of the world. That belief was, however, often tested.

The Bird family found itself periodically tested at home as well. Edward Bird was a straight-spined evangelist who insisted on the observance of the Sabbath. During her early years Isabella and her family lived in the rural village of Tattenhall in northern England. Because of her father's unbending conviction that the Sabbath be honored, he began to lose parishioners. Of course, telling farmers not to milk their cows on Sundays is absurd—cows have to be milked—but Edward Bird persisted despite the farmers' pleas to reason. He insisted that God's law took prece-

dence over any other laws; however, no one could convince the cows of this. Farmers continued to milk, Bird continued to rebuke them, and eventually he was asked to leave the parish.

Helped by his relative the bishop of Chester, Edward Bird was reassigned to a large parish in Birmingham in 1843. His living fell significantly, but the Birds had other significant means of income. Birmingham, one of the most industrialized of British cities in a time of rapid, unchecked industrialism, was an enormous change for Isabella. Just a few years earlier as many as two hundred thousand citizens rallied in Birmingham in support of the Chartist movement, and industrial Britain buzzed with attempts at reform for workers, child laborers, the poor, and the destitute. The price of bread remained artificially inflated while workers went hungry, and the Anti-Corn League advocated for removal of tariffs on imported grain. Much of the unrest grew out of the depression of 1839–1842, one of the worst of the century. By 1843 the depression had ended and good harvests had returned, so much of the agitation in the city had abated, but it must have been an unsettling place for the conservative Bird family.

Isabella, however, was a precocious young woman who kept up with the politics of the time. She wrote a pamphlet on the question of workers' rights and the free market, and her father later had it privately published. According to Evelyn Kaye in her biography *Amazing Traveler: Isabella Bird,* the pamphlet was populated by characters such as "Chief Justice Common Sense, Baron Public Opinion, Mr. Humbug, and Mr. Mock Philanthropist" (pp. 28–29), showing clearly that Bird was already turning a sharp, skeptical, Dickensian eye toward the politics of her day.

Her father, it seems, was less attuned. In Birmingham he was at first a successful preacher, but his continued rigid insistence on the observation of the Sabbath once again placed him at odds with his parishioners. Two merchants in his parish consistently refused to close their shops on Sunday, and the elder Bird sought a police summons and personally delivered it. Understandably his arrogance alienated the community: he, after all, did not have to run a shop in order to feed his family. On his way home one afternoon he was accosted by angry community members who showered him with stones and mud.

His experience caused him to have an emotional collapse, and one can only surmise the effect her father's failure and humiliation had on Isabella, who revered him. He was thereafter reassigned to a parish at Wyton, near Cambridge, a rural place with only around 300 parishioners. Once again Isabella was close to the rural life she loved so well. But while living at Wyton she began to develop serious physical ailments. She suffered backache and headaches that were probably migraines. At eighteen she was diagnosed with a fibroid tumor on her spine, which was surgically removed. In 1849 this procedure must have been unspeakably painful. Though she recovered from the operation, she suffered with back problems and physical pain throughout her life.

Bird began to travel for her health, first to the Scottish Highlands, a landscape she heartily loved and to which she would often return. She also began to write articles about her travels, which began to be published in journals such as the *Family Treasury, Good Works,* and the *Sunday Magazine.* Clearly Bird must have been a wide reader of the periodical press of the time—how else would she have realized that travel writing was a popular outlet for women writers in the mid-nineteenth century? Raised in a social and religious atmosphere in which women were unquestionably subservient to men, she also would have read about schools opening for girls and the struggles for women to be admitted to the universities and for their right to enter the professions. Though Bird never would have considered herself a feminist, she surely chafed under the constraints her society placed on life options for women.

Although the sources of her illnesses were admittedly complex, certainly one reason for her painful symptoms and their accompanying depression was the absence of a meaningful outlet for her many talents. The lack of choices open to her in Victorian England seems very

likely to have made her sick. Often the cure prescribed for illness or psychological stress was a change of locale, and in her case a sea voyage was suggested. In 1854 she had relatives visiting from Canada, and her father granted her permission to join them on their return trip to Nova Scotia in June of that year, sailing from Liverpool for Halifax, from which point she began her first exploration of Canada and the United States. This trip ultimately took her through the Maritimes into New England, west to Ohio, Chicago, and Detroit, then to Niagara Falls, Montreal, down to New York City, back to Boston, then back to Halifax for the voyage home. At age twenty-three she had covered six thousand miles in North America.

BIRD IN AMERICA

Bird's first book, *The Englishwoman in America,* is drawn from the journals she kept on this trip. It was published in 1856 by John Murray, who went on to publish all of her major works. This book is, however, clearly that of a journeywoman. Her most powerful works, following *The Englishwoman in America* and drawn largely from Isabella's letters to her sister Henrietta before the latter's death in 1880, include *The Hawaiian Archipelago* (1875), *A Lady's Life in the Rocky Mountains* (1879), *Unbeaten Tracks in Japan* (1880), and *The Golden Chersonese* (1883). Although much of the immediacy of these books is apparent in *The Englishwoman in America,* it also abounds in outbursts of cultural superiority and even downright nonsense about the United States in the mid-1850s. She appears to have taken too many comments at face value. But that aside, the book is also peppered with wonderful vignettes of life in Canada and the United States at the time along with faithful descriptions of some of the hardships and ugliness of life she observed in North America. Bird is at her best when she is narrating her travels and describing local characters and scenes, but she is difficult to read when she moralizes, even if—or because— she seems too often unaware at this point in her career of her own moralizing. Perhaps she felt the need to construct a site of superiority from which to establish the authorial control she felt she needed.

Surely the young writer felt compelled to situate herself in a rather long line of British Victorian women writers reporting back from the United States. Just a few of the notable texts published prior to Bird's book are Frances Wright's *Views of Society and Manners in America* (1821); Frances Trollope's biting evaluation of U.S. culture, *Domestic Manners of the Americans* (1832); Harriet Martineau's *Society in America* (1837); and Lady Emmeline Stuart Wortley's *Travels in the United States, Etc., during 1849 and 1850* (1851). Bird worked (brilliantly by the end of her career) to create a distinctive place for herself in this line of women.

Along with this perceived need, however, came a good share of snobbery. In the prefatory remarks to *The Englishwoman in America,* Bird writes:

> With respect to the people of the United States, I have given those impressions which as a traveller I formed; if they are more favourable than those of some of my predecessors, the difference may arise from my having taken out many excellent introductions, which afforded me greater facilities of seeing the best society in the States than are usually possessed by those who travel merely to see the country.
>
> (p. 2)

She further maintains that "I went to the States with that amount of prejudice which seems the birthright of every English person, but I found that, under the knowledge of the Americans which can be attained by a traveller mixing in society in every grade, these prejudices gradually melted away" (p. 3). But however she qualifies her statements, the United States remains "a receptacle for the barbarous, the degraded, and the vicious of all other nations. It must never be forgotten that the noble, the learned, and the wealthy have shrunk from the United States" (p. 39). This of course is nonsense, but nonetheless Bird goes on to exclaim that given these circumstances, it is "rather surprising, that a traveller should meet with so little to annoy—so few obvious departures from the rules of propriety" (p. 4).

Her landing in Halifax is anything but decorous as she disembarks onto an unlighted, narrow, rickety wharf, along which a mob of passengers tries to scramble at the same time, only to be met head on with the mayhem of carts, trucks, wagons, and horses jostling for position to take on freight and passengers. Porters accost disembarking passengers to the point where they simply seize luggage from the travelers. The roads are ankle-deep in mud and strewn with fish heads, oyster shells, potato peelings and cabbage stalks. It is 93 degrees in the shade.

From Halifax, Bird goes on to visit relatives on Prince Edward Island. En route she catches her first glimpse of native peoples. She waxes eloquent on the Mic-Mac Indians, who, from "among the dark woods which then surrounded Halifax … worshipped the Great Spirit, and hunted the moose-deer. Their birch-bark wigwams peeped from among the trees, their squaws urged their light canoes over the broad deep harbour, and their wise men spoke to them of the 'happy hunting ground'" (p. 19). Bird, astoundingly, condemns the French for telling the Indians that the British were "the people who had crucified the Saviour" (p. 20) and then partially redeems herself as she goes on to admonish the Europeans for their destruction of the native peoples. But she is also careful to add that "frequently *we* arrived too late to save them as a race" (p. 20). The italicized *we* presumably signifies the British who came too late to save them from the degradations of the French Catholics. She only wishes that the British could have shared the gospel with them on their way to near-extinction.

A few interesting passages reveal the quality of Bird's actual knowledge of the plight of Native-American peoples: "The silence of the forest was so solemn, that, remembering the last of the Mohicans, we should not have been the least surprised if an Indian war-whoop had burst upon our startled ears" (p. 32); "The memory of Uncas and Magua rose before me, and I sighed over the degeneracy of the race" (p. 49). James Fenimore Cooper's novel seems to be the primary lens through which she perceived Indian life, and her responses are romanticized and sentimentalized to such a degree that it is difficult to discern the real level of her concern, though she does eventually voice doubt that Cooper drew his characters from life, at least not the noble ones like Uncas and Chingachgook. These passages reveal two difficult problems. First, they show to a disturbing degree the real difficulty the Victorian upper-class traveler had to overcome if he or she cared to even begin to perceive the reality of Indian life. Second, it is impossible to tell if Bird in her more romantic flights is speaking her mind or if she is an author savvy about her audience's expectations for literary representations of native peoples. The vexed problem of Bird's relationships to native peoples runs through all of her work: these relationships shift and her judgments become more thoughtful as she matures as a writer, a traveler, and a human being.

In this early text we see too the unsettled ideas toward African Americans in Bird's young mind. Clearly she is deeply disturbed by slavery, expressing the deep repugnance for it one would expect in light of her family's long and honorable history of antislavery. However, mixed in with her hatred of the institution is an evangelical agenda that works in this case to mitigate the evils of slavery in the perception of the reader: "It is indeed true that, in America only, more than three million free-born Africans wear the chains of servitude; but it is no less true that in many instances the Gospel has penetrated the shade of their Egyptian Darkness" (p. 174). In some perhaps barely conscious way, evangelical Christianity elides the evil of slavery in her mind. Also, as she does at times with the Indians, she has trouble seeing the very humanity of races other than hers. One can see, however, Bird struggling with a prejudice that she is beginning to become aware of and one that is beginning to disturb her greatly. For instance, she holds in her arms the child of a black servant who is seasick. (Interestingly, Bird also claims that this was the first time she ever held an infant of any kind, ever.) She feels it is better mannered than a white baby, "but the poor little black thing … lay very passively, every now and then turning its little monkey-face up to mine, with a look of understanding and confidence which quite conciliated my good will" (p. 175). Yet, just as she feels the humanity of the child and seems to connect with it on a basic human level, she finds "it was so awfully ugly, so much like a black ape, and so little like the young of the human species, that I was obliged while I held it to avert my eyes from it, lest in a sudden fit of foolish prejudice and disgust I should let it fall" (p. 175). In the next sentence she is saddened by the white mistress boxing the ears of her slaves, which is understandable. But although Bird is gentle with the baby, she is blind to the real humanity of African Americans. Once again we can see here a young woman only half aware of the cultural assumptions she holds but beginning to sense their destructive nature, and this tension is prevalent throughout her writing. Regardless of her cultural blinders she sees that, even in the rise of U.S. democracy, lodged in the institution of slavery are the seeds of decay for any nation that claims to dedicate itself to liberty.

On her journey from Canada through New England, Bird greatly admires the quality of the New England landscape, most likely because it reminds her so much of home. But she is more enthralled—almost luridly so—with western cities, as seen in this description of Cincinnati:

> Dark browed Mexicans, in *sombreras* [sic] and high slashed boots, dash about on small active horses with Mamelouk bits—rovers and adventurers from California and the Far West, with massive rings in their ears, swagger about in a manner which shows their country and calling, and females richly dressed are seen driving and walking about, from the fair-complexioned Europeans to the negress or mulatto.
>
> (p. 118)

She has a strong attraction to the wildness of the people, especially to the men who seem to have stepped outside the borders of society. In Chicago too,

> Mexicans and hunters dash down the crowded streets at full gallop on mettlesome steeds, with bits so powerful as to throw their horses on their haunches when they meet with any obstacle. They ride animals that look too proud to touch the earth, on high-peaked saddles, with pistols in the holsters, short stirrups, and long, cruel looking Spanish spurs. They wear scarlet caps or palmetto hats, and high

jack-boots. Knives are stuck into their belts, and light rifles are slung behind them.

(p. 156)

In these and other passages Bird, so often reserved in her attitude toward Americans, feels a strong interest, even attraction, to these wild men of the West. They perhaps represent for her a culture that is as far away as possible from the one she knows at home, and this attraction will show itself more powerfully in her later relationship with Rocky Mountain Jim, her guide in Colorado, who figures so prominently in *A Lady's Life in the Rocky Mountains*.

In contrast to the wildness of the West, when we travel with Bird back to the eastern cities, particularly New York City, we see a Europeanized scene: "As it is impossible to display the productions of the millinery art in a close carriage in a crowd, Broadway is the fashionable promenade; and the lightest French bonnets, the handsomest mantles, and the richest flounced silk dresses, with *jupons,* ribands, and laces to correspond, are there to be seen in the afternoon" (p. 363). This is far from the Chicago street scene mentioned above, and Bird also notices a difference in the vitality of the people: "But unfortunately a girl of twenty is too apt to look faded and haggard; and a woman who with us would be in her bloom at thirty, looks *passé,* wrinkled, and old" (p. 362). Americans, it seems, lose their vitality the farther they are removed from the frontier to the west and England to the east.

Bird in this book also points to some abiding features of U.S. culture, and in this sense she is uncannily prescient in recognizing what will come to be some of its most characteristic problems. For example, she notes that "As everyone who has one hundred yards to go drives or rides, rings are fastened to all the side walks in the town to tether the horses to" (p. 119). (Change "tethering rings" to "parking lots" and this could be a woefully apt description of every urban area in modern America.) Bird also notices differences in agriculture as it is practiced in England and in the United States. Hundreds of thousands of pigs arrive in Cincinnati to be slaughtered, and Bird comments that "The day on which a pig is killed in England constitutes an

era in the family history of the year, and squeals of a terrific description announce the event to the neighborhood" (p. 125). There, the killing of animals for food was still a family event, and people remained close to and aware of the sources of their food. But in the United States of this same period, "There is not time or opportunity for such a process … and the first notification which the inhabitants receive of the massacre are the thousand barrels of pork on the quays, ready to be conveyed to the Atlantic cities, for exportation to the European markets" (pp. 126–127). This is agriculture not for the nurturance of a family but agriculture for profit. Clearly there is a vast difference here that still manifests itself in our ongoing discussion about industrialized agriculture, the factory farming of produce and livestock.

SCOTLAND AND GOOD WORKS

On her return to England, Isabella Bird began to gather her notes from her trip into a book that she at first titled *The Car and the Steamboat* but which became *The Englishwoman in America*. The book met with critical and popular success, and Bird's name began to be known. She also earned money on her writing for the first time, which she used to buy boats for poor Scottish fishermen. In 1857 her ailments returned and another trip to America was prescribed. Once again she traveled around the United States, this time also visiting the South, where she encountered brutal examples of slavery. Her father was interested in the growth of evangelism in the United Sates and the flourishing of religion there, and she collected notes that were intended as research for the book her father was writing about religion in North America. Shortly after Isabella's return, however, Edward Bird fell ill. He died on May 14, 1858, within a month of his elder daughter's return.

It seems that Isabella felt some guilt about her father's death; she had sensed, wrongly, that as she traveled around North America, her father was languishing at home. On the heels of these feelings of guilt, she decided against further travel in favor of self-denial and the performance of good works. She worked her notes from her second trip into a book, but this time John Murray declined to publish the manuscript. It was the work her father had imagined, and it was finally published to little notice under the title *Aspects of Religion in the United States of America* in 1859. Frankly, this book deserves the oblivion to which it has been assigned.

Following the Reverend Bird's death, the family was forced to move from Wyton and relocated to Scotland. Isabella, now twenty-nine years old, along with Henrietta and their mother, moved to 3 Castle Terrace, Edinburgh. In the nineteenth century, Edinburgh was one of the thriving intellectual centers of Europe, and Isabella and Henrietta began to make new friends such as John Blackie, a classics professor, and his wife, Ella. Through them they also met Anna Stoddart, who became Isabella Bird's first biographer. Bird devoted herself to good works and to writing magazine articles that promoted religion or advocated for the poor.

All through Scotland and England during the nineteenth century, following enclosures of common lands, poor small farmers were being pushed off the land and forced to work in the cities, where they often suffered under deplorable conditions. New technology had disrupted traditional home industries, and around 1860 Bird organized a plan to help poor crofters emigrate from Scotland to Canada. Using her contacts in Canada and much of her own cash, she was finally successful in relocating a number of families. Also, Edinburgh at the time was becoming gentrified, and many of the poor were thoughtlessly displaced into slums. She wrote and lobbied on behalf of the Edinburgh poor, and although her words fell on deaf or uncaring ears for the most part, in 1869 she published *Notes on Old Edinburgh,* which contains some of these accounts.

On August 14, 1866, her mother, Dora Bird, died. Now the two sisters were left alone, and Isabella and Henrietta decided to set up house together, with Isabella writing and Henrietta keeping house. Or so the relationship has been frequently described. This widely circulated version leaves Henrietta as a flat character sitting at home and acting as her sister's muse while Isabella roams the world. However, in the introduction to her edition of Isabella's letters, *Letters to Henrietta,* Kay Chubbuck convincingly argues for a more complex Henrietta and one less completely devoted to her sister. Chubbuck urges us to see Henrietta as a real person rather than a romanticized figure. Among other things Chubbuck claims that Henrietta was a classical scholar, artist, writer, poet, and mathematician and that she too traveled extensively, but mostly within the British Isles (p. 99). It is important to note this so as not to perpetuate a false portrait of the sisters. They were both vibrant human beings, and while their connection was deeply felt, both chafed in extended proximity to one another and held petty jealousies, as even the closest siblings do.

In the years immediately following Dora Bird's death the two sisters lived together and periodically separated. Henrietta often visited the village of Tobermory on the Isle of Mull, and Isabella spent long periods in London. They lived together for a time in Edinburgh and then spent the summer of 1867 in Tobermory. In 1869 the sisters summered again in Tobermory, and when Henrietta left, Isabella fell ill. In 1872 Isabella and Henrietta finally decided to forgo their flat in Edinburgh, and Henrietta moved again to Tobermory, while Isabella remained in Edinburgh with her friend Emily Clayton.

Isabella's health steadily worsened during the twelve years following her father's death, and her deluded commitment to good works and self-abnegation did not provide an effective cure. It is not known how often Isabella journeyed outside of the British Isles during this period, but there is some evidence that she returned to Canada to visit the crofters she had helped relocate there. She also took a six-month cruise, crossing the Atlantic to New York City and then back to ports in Italy, Algeria, Spain, and Portugal. In a letter to Ella Blackie collected in *Letters to Henrietta,* she writes about this voyage that "at last I am in love, and desperately in love, and the old sea god has so stolen my heart and penetrated my soul that I seriously fear that hereafter though I must be elsewhere in body I must be with him in spirit" (p. 31). The lure of the sea and the stimulation of traveling had clearly reawakened her wanderlust, and considering the nature of her illnesses, this passage resonates with some awareness of the wholeness she felt when she was abroad and the destructive schism of mind and body that consistently occurred when she returned to the British Isles.

Inevitably her health did fail on her return to her claustrophobic social environment. Deeply depressed by conventional life, Bird needed a stronger outlet for her creativity than doing altruistic works. So, predictably, the cure prescribed was a long sea voyage, and Isabella, now thirty-nine years old, planned her next trip: to sail for Australia, New Zealand, Hawaii, and California, cross North America, and sail home. Basically she would travel around the world. From this trip would emerge *The Hawaiian Archipelago* and *A Lady's Life in the Rocky Mountains.*

HAWAII AND COLORADO

The Hawaiian Archipelago (1875) is dedicated to Henrietta, and as mentioned earlier, the book is drawn and reworked from the letters Isabella sent home to Henrietta, which gives it an immediacy that infuses the prose with the real excitement Bird derived from her travels. It is as if she had been freed from prison, emerging as a writer of powerful talents. There is far more energy here than in *The Englishwoman in America,* at least in part because it is not as cluttered with her sense of cultural superiority, although that trait by no means ever vanishes entirely from her writing. Right from the outset, we find evocative, graceful prose: "White, unwinking scintillating sun blazed down upon Auckland, New Zealand. Along the white glaring road from Onehunga, dusty trees and calla lilies drooped with the heat. Dusty thickets sheltered the cicada, whose triumphant din grated and rasped through the palpitating atmosphere" (p. 6). There is an ominous, oppressive note to these lines, a sense of uneasiness. That uneasiness is layered on when she sees the *Nevada,* the ship on which she is to sail for California, "in whose seams the pitch was melting": "Huge, airy, perfectly comfortable

as she is, not a passenger stepped on board without breathing a more earnest prayer than usual that the voyage might end propitiously" (p. 7). The shift in Bird's technique here is clear. She does more than report on her experiences, she narrates a tale of danger. From the very beginning she will have obstacles to overcome, the first of which is crossing the Pacific Ocean in an unseaworthy ship. This is the framework of a raucous adventure story, and in many ways that is what her narrative becomes.

Once upon the high seas, the worst appears in the form of a hurricane, and her description shows the vibrancy of her prose and her high sense of adventure. The passengers are huddled together in the deck house:

> In this deck-house the strainings, sunderings, and groanings were hardly audible, or rather were overpowered by a sound which, in thirteen months' experience of the sea in all weathers, I have never heard, and hope never to hear again, unless in a staunch ship, one loud, awful, undying shriek, mingled with a prolonged, relentless hiss. No gathering strength, no languid fainting into momentary lulls, but one protracted, gigantic scream. And this was not the whistle of wind through cordage, but the actual sound of air travelling with tremendous velocity, carrying with it minute particles of water. Nor was the sea running mountains high, for the hurricane kept it down. Indeed during those fierce hours no sea was visible, for the whole surface was caught up and carried furiously into the air, like snow-drift on the prairies, sibilant, relentless.
>
> (p. 9)

After the storm the ship enters the tropics, with dead calm and sweltering temperatures. The *Nevada* has sustained heavy damage, and there is general concern that the ship will not make the crossing, but in spite of all this (or because of it), Bird writes, "It has been so far a very pleasant voyage" (p. 11). She would have her readers believe that she actually enjoyed the danger at sea, and perhaps she enjoyed it very much.

On the voyage there is only one other woman, referred to by Bird as Mrs. Dexter, whose son becomes ill onboard ship. Apparently he has burst blood vessels in his lungs, and his only hope for survival is to be put ashore in Hawaii. Bird, at

ISABELLA BIRD

Mrs. Dexter's request, agrees to accompany her ashore, and on arriving in Pearl Harbor, Bird is once again amazed at the diversity of people she sees and the vivid colors of their dress: "without an exception the men and women wore wreaths and garlands of flowers, carmine, orange, or pure white, twined around their hats, and thrown carelessly round their throats, flowers unknown to me, but redolent of the tropics in fragrance and color" (p. 19). Again she feels enticed by the beautiful and the unknown, lured by the strong difference from her own culture and the freedom this difference seems to represent to her. She wonders, "But where were the hard, angular, careworn, sallow, passionate faces of men and women, such as form the majority of every crowd at home, as well as in America and Australia" (p. 19). Clearly here she feels released from convention.

She even notices the marvelous Mexican saddles on the Hawaiian horses, and along with the saddles she describes a far different form of female behavior than she was accustomed to seeing in Britain, the United States, and Australia: "Every now and then a flower-wreathed Hawaiian woman, in her full radiant garment, sprang on one of these animals astride, and dashed along the road at full gallop, sitting on her horse as square and easy as a hussar" (p. 20). In this passage, the figure of the Hawaiian woman stands in sharp contrast to the picture of "angular" and "careworn" Anglo-American women of Bird's class. The Hawaiian woman is draped in flowers, her garments—and by extension her person—are radiant, and she sits her horse astride, not sidesaddle, which allows her to freely gallop in comfort. Along with her feminine qualities, she assumes also the role of a man, a hussar. She is not, at least in this passage, constrained by her gender, but rather luxuriates within it. In this role she also possesses power: she is like a soldier, a hussar. Surely this image reveals Bird's perception of what is possible for a woman outside of her own culture.

On the other hand, in her letters to her sister she alternately addresses Henrietta as "my darling," "my pet," or "my ownest" and often signs her letters "Its Pet, ILBird, Sweetest little thing." There is something both conventional and a bit strange in these forms of salutation and signature. The salutation indicates a deep though conventional affection, but also a sense of ownership; "My Ownest" and the signature certainly reveal a disturbing level of objectification on Isabella's part. This relationship must at times have irked Henrietta, but the letters also suggest a deep desire on Isabella's part for a greater level of freedom for both women. Isabella writes in a letter to Henrietta, "My Pet, if we lived here, we should be rich residents" and goes on to describe how much more easily they could live in Hawaii than in England. Most tellingly she writes, "I should never bother any more with a woman servant. I would have a man cook who would wash up clean knives and boots trim the lamps …" (*Letters to Henrietta,* p. 98). Clearly Isabella wants to revise traditional gender roles. Henrietta even seemed to warm up to the idea of moving to Hawaii, but that would never do for Isabella, who, whether she realized it fully or not, needed Henrietta at home.

Bird's excitement with Hawaii is mixed in with social commentary, at times a bit chauvinistic but nowhere near the level of her previous book. She is unhappy about the strong influence of the United States on the islands, and indeed the U.S. delegates were pulling the political strings in Hawaii. She also reports some animosity toward New England missionaries who, "finding a people rejoicing in the innocence and simplicity of Eden, taught them the knowledge of evil, turned them into a nation of hypocrites, and with a mingling of fanaticism and selfishness, afflicted them with many woes calculated to accelerate their extinction, clothing among others" (p. 43). Isabella does not necessarily accept this verdict, but it seems that she does see a glimmer of truth in it.

She loves the freedom and sublime beauty of the place, and the book is peppered with colorful descriptions of native life (for example, when she marvels at the national sport of surfing). Bird also finds near-absolute freedom and newborn courage and health as she rides her Hawaiian pony all over the islands, fording streams, riding in storms, admiring the landscape and the beauty of the native people. By this time Isabella has become accustomed to riding astride, but she is not always entirely comfortable riding in this manner, and she is deeply self-conscious about the "Bloomer Suit" that she takes to wearing, which consists of flounced trousers tight at the ankle worn under a dress. In one instance, she comes across the Hawaiian king in the company of several American officers, among them a Colonel Schofield and a General Alexander. She writes in *Letters to Henrietta,* "when I saw these strangers and their well veiled stare I remembered that I was in a Bloomer Suit astride a horse and that probably they had never seen such a thing! I wished I were anywhere else" (p. 59). The passage is telling not only in how it reveals Isabella's self-consciousness in the presence of other Westerners, but also about how the U.S. officials make her wish she were anywhere else, even as she is coming to love the place so well that she wishes herself nowhere but in Hawaii. It is more than a bit telling that Colonel John McAllister Schofield and General B. S. Alexander, whose intentions seem "veiled," would eventually become the architects of the "bayonet constitution" that in 1887 gave Pearl Harbor to the United States and disenfranchised native Hawaiians.

By far her most memorable exploits on the islands are her ascents up to the volcanic craters. The climb to the crater on Kilauea is arduous, and once there Bird observes, "there were groanings, rumblings, and detonations, rushings, hissings, and splashings, and the crushing sound of breakers on the coast, but it was the surging of fiery waves upon a fiery shore" (p. 72). The lake of lava becomes even more sublime, and Bird's prose becomes more powerful as she becomes more entranced with the scene:

> On our arrival eleven fire fountains were playing joyously round the lakes, and sometimes the six of the nearer lake ran together in the centre to go wallowing down in one vortex, from which they reappeared bulging upwards, till they formed a huge cone, thirty feet high, which plunged downwards in a whirlpool only to reappear in exactly the previousnumber of fountains in different parts of the lake, high leaping, raging, flinging themselves upward.

(p. 73)

Together with these descriptions of natural wonders the book is filled with images of a happy people who live closer to the natural world than anything Bird could have imagined in her life to this point. Of course she occasionally bemoans their slippage from Christianity; but at the same time that she feels an imbedded religious rigidity within herself, she seems to feel that rigidity begin to soften in Hawaii. This is not to say that Bird desired to "go native"—far from it. But she has come to see the constraints of her own limited point of view and to appreciate cultures other than her own on a level she had not yet experienced. It is no wonder she hated to leave, but she could not resist the need to travel on. Maybe she feared the great attraction the islands of the Pacific held for her.

On August 6, 1873, Bird boarded a ship headed for San Francisco, and from San Francisco she traveled by rail to Colorado. It is from this time in Colorado that she drew her most compelling book, *A Lady's Life in the Rocky Mountains* (1879). She arrived in Colorado in September, spending time first in Greeley and Fort Collins. Bird disparages the flat plains towns as coarse and utterly devoted to the earning of a dollar. Her immediate goal in Colorado is Estes Park, and on the way she meets with a number of pioneer characters, most of whom she dislikes for their slovenly character and, ironically, their too-narrow religious beliefs. While staying in a Longmont hotel, Bird is introduced to two young men who are on their way to Estes Park, Platt Rogers (later mayor of Denver) and S. S. Downer (later a Boulder judge); but to read Bird's account of the young men, one would never guess that they ever could have prospered. They, for their part, are disappointed in Bird's physical appearance, but they agree to guide her to Estes Park. They ride up the St. Vrain Canyon and along a route through present-day Lyons and Allenspark, and at the entrance to Estes Park, then a place called Muggins Gulch, the travelers come across a cabin inhabited by the one-eyed trapper Jim Nugent, known locally as Rocky Mountain Jim. Nugent was a minor desperado, to a degree romanticized by Bird just as the characters on the streets of Cincinnati and Chicago were. But this time her tendencies to romanticize fell away like scales as she came to know the man and, as seems clear at this late date, to fall in love with him. He was arguably the one and only great love in Isabella Bird's life, but that love was also held firmly at bay. About Bird's sexual life we know nothing, but it seems safe to say that, however tempted, she was not one to shrug aside the traditions and protocol of her religion and culture, especially her religion. But she loved Jim Nugent just the same.

On an excursion up Fall River Canyon, Jim revealed his deep feelings for Bird and confessed the evils of his prior life. She was taken aback with strong emotion—even love—but in a letter to Henrietta she writes sadly, "For 5 minutes at the camping ground on Longs Peak his manner was such that for a moment I thought this possible, but I put it away as egregious vanity unpardonable in a woman of 40" (*Letters to Henrietta*, p. 176). In the published text she tempers the same moment, and once textualized, her love turns to pity: "My soul dissolved in pity for his dark, lost, self-ruined life" (p. 216). She goes on to say in *Letters to Henrietta* that "I told him that if all circumstances on both sides had been favourable and I had loved him with my whole heart I would not dare to trust my happiness to him because of whiskey" (p. 182). Whatever her reasons, whiskey or vanity, she clearly felt strongly about him, strongly enough to cloud her feelings in the published book, and although she later denied having loved him, she claimed that his ghost appeared to her the moment he died of a gunshot wound sustained not long after she left Colorado.

In the company of Nugent and the men who guided her to Estes Park, Bird became one of the earliest women to climb Long's Peak, which rises to 14,255 feet and dominates the landscape around Estes Park. She writes in *A Lady's Life in the Rocky Mountains*:

> From it come all storms of snow and wind, and the forked lightnings play round its head like a glory. It is one of the noblest of mountains, but in one's imagination it grows to be much more than a mountain. It becomes invested with a personality. In its caverns and abysses one comes to fancy that it generates and chains the strong winds, to let them loose in its fury. The thunder becomes its voice, and the lightnings do it homage.
>
> (pp. 101–102)

Her description is on one level a conventional personification of the mountain, an example of the nineteenth-century literary sublime, but she is also consistent in her animation of this landscape. When she climbs the peak, she sees and later writes of her terror when confronted with such inhospitable terrain. She is as awestruck and terrified as Thoreau was on the summit of Mt. Katahdin. But the mountain and the landscape around Estes Park remain for her ever alive, and also like Thoreau, she is vocal in her call to preserve a well-loved place and in her justified fear that the beautiful valley will be commercialized beyond recognition.

Bird has come around to seeing the landscape not only as a picture or example of an aesthetic category; she now sees it in a proto-ecological way, as an entity in itself that deserves respect for its inherent value. Also valuable are Bird's set pieces about life in Colorado at the time. She leaves Estes Park and, in an amazing solo journey, often difficult enough in November in an automobile, rides south from Longmont to Colorado Springs, over into South Park, and back down into Denver, a trip that covers hundreds of miles, throughout which she is struck by the magnificence of the mountain vistas and frightened by the icy glens. In many places she is recognized, for by this time she had achieved some level of international fame, and her story had been printed in the Denver newspapers. Somewhere outside of South Park she stops for the evening and her host, "in a good natured stage of intoxication," asks if she is "the English Lady written of in the Denver News" (p. 188). She also notes that she carries a Sharp's revolver in her pocket, bringing her up at least on par with some of the desperadoes she encounters—so she constructs herself as both an "English Lady" and a female Rocky Mountain desperado.

Bird had planned on leaving Colorado after her trip, but found the banks unable to honor her notes temporarily because of a depressed economy and fear of a run on the banks. Forced to return to Estes Park, she lodged again at Grif Evans's ranch, where she had stayed on her prior visit. When it came time for her to leave the Rockies, Jim Nugent accompanied her down out of the mountains. Their parting was emotional, with Bird urging him toward sobriety, but Rocky Mountain Jim claimed it was too late for him. On leaving, the two met a Mr. Haig (Mr. Fodder in the published text), who was an agent of the earl of Dunraven, who wanted to purchase and develop Estes Park. Ironically Haig would have a prominent role in the shooting of Rocky Mountain Jim, whom Haig may have perceived as standing in the way of the real estate deal. But on her parting, Bird could not foresee Jim's untimely death, and she comments that she did not realize until that moment that her Rocky Mountain life was ended: "not even when I saw 'Mountain Jim,' with his golden hair yellow in the sunshine, slowly leading the beautiful mare over the snowy Plains back to Estes Park, equipped with the saddle on which I had ridden 800 miles!" (p. 54).

JAPAN AND THE MALAY STATES

Isabella Bird returned to Edinburgh in January of 1874. Although she was not necessarily happy to be back in conventional society, she began to fall back easily into a routine life. Isabella and Henrietta rented a flat together, and Isabella worked preparing her book on Hawaii. Later in the year Henrietta rented a cottage in Tobermory, which became a favorite place of the sisters. On June 29, Rocky Mountain Jim was shot in Colorado, and he died on September 7, 1874. In February 1875, *The Hawaiian Archipelago* was published by John Murray to wide acclaim, and Bird was ensconced in the ranks of the foremost travel writers of her time. Seven more editions were published over the next decade and a half. The following year Henrietta completed studies in Greek at the University of Edinburgh and leased the cottage at Tobermory for six years; it was a place that Henrietta loved, but at times Isabella found it too relaxing and traveled around England, again dedicating herself to good works. In 1877 Isabella and Henrietta committed them-

selves to helping form a college for medical missionaries, and in the course of their endeavor they met Dr. John Bishop, who soon played an important role in both of their lives. Isabella had developed a newfound interest in science and had purchased a microscope, over which she and Dr. Bishop spent hours together examining specimens.

It seems at this time that Isabella and John Bishop had become very close, even possibly engaged for a very short time. But Isabella's health was beginning to flag again, and she kept busy writing up the Rocky Mountain letters, which also likely provided an impetus to further travel. Isabella even corresponded with Charles Darwin, seeking advice on selecting a new travel destination. She had her sights set on South America, but he dissuaded her. In 1878 "Letters from the Rocky Mountains" was published serially in the *Leisure Hour.* Also in 1878, Henrietta fell seriously ill, and John Bishop attended her. Isabella was reluctant to leave her stricken sister, but Bishop agreed to keep Henrietta under his diligent care. So, substituting the Far East for South America, Bird sailed in April for North America, traversed the continent yet again, and sailed for Japan from San Francisco.

In Japan, Bird was at first greatly disconcerted and disoriented. Traveling around Hawaii and the wilds of Colorado and the American West was surely difficult enough, but here Bird was confronted with a strange language, a new alphabet, and a non-Western culture that she had difficulty comprehending. She was greeted by the British consul, who helped her obtain papers and travel permits throughout all of Japan. It is important to recall that Japan had been closed to Western influence for two hundred years before American warships forcibly opened the country to trade in 1854, only twenty-four years before Bird's arrival. She traveled through Japan during the Meiji period, which began reforms around 1868. During this time there was movement toward a Western way of life in Japan, but this cultural shift also engendered a sense of high resentment. In the year Bird arrived, the military faction of the government had begun to resist Western influence and set its eyes instead on the continent of

Asia, which led to the Sino-Japanese war in 1894 and the continued militarization and industrialization of Japan that culminated in World War II. Clearly there lurked a strong anti-Western undercurrent in the culture while Bird was there, and she experienced it firsthand on the back roads of the country, especially at the hands of minor bureaucrats who harassed her continually for her papers. Yet regardless of the inconvenience and official harassment, it was the little-traveled regions of this rapidly changing society that Bird was most interested in seeing.

Although this book too contains many passages that celebrate the landscape and the people, Bird does not become enamored of Japan as she did Colorado and Hawaii. She is greatly disturbed by the rapid changes she sees taking place in the country, especially the loss of traditional culture, just as the culture she belongs to and professes superior is becoming the very agent of destroying what she sees as traditional native Japanese life. At the same time, she is not blind to the brutal poverty and ignorance that many of the people of the Japanese countryside live in.

Still, she sees great beauty in many traditional ways. When she visits Nikko, for example, she is struck by the clean lines and polished yet delicate beauty of her host Kanaya's house. She claims, "I almost wish that the rooms were a little less exquisite, for I am in constant dread of spilling the ink, indenting the mats, or tearing the paper windows" (p. 109). But once she penetrates deep into the rural areas things change: "The room was dark, dirty, vile, noisy, and poisoned by sewage odors, as rooms unfortunately are very apt to be" (p. 169). In her examination of the rural poor Bird does not shrink from what must have been a realistic description, and only rarely do we hear the kind of sentimental outburst she had made about the American Indians in *The Englishwoman in America*. The book also contains invaluable information about the lives of women in Japan at the time.

Much of the first half of the second volume of *Unbeaten Tracks in Japan* deals with Bird's visit to the northernmost islands of Japan and her visit with the Ainu, the native inhabitants of the Japanese archipelago. Here she finds great interest. The reader can see in the following passage just how far Bird seems to have come in her generosity of judgment, and though her rigidity still may strike a modern reader as ungenerous, she has evolved into an observer and writer striving to be fair, at least within the constraints of her own cultural parameters:

> The glamour which at first disguises the inherent barrenness of savage life has had time to pass away, and I see it in all its nakedness as a life not much raised above the necessities of animal existence, timid, monotonous, barren of good, dark, dull, "without hope, and without God in the world"; though at its lowest and worst considerably higher and better than that of many other aboriginal races, and, must I say it? Considerably higher and better than that of thousands of the lapsed masses of our own great cities, who are baptized into Christ's name, and are laid at last in holy ground, inasmuch as the Ainos are truthful, and, on the whole, chaste, hospitable, honest, reverent, and kind to the aged.
>
> (p. 75)

These are not the noble savages of Rousseau: the Ainu are judged here in a way that retains their dignity, and we also see here an important shift in Bird's attitude toward the native people she observes. They force her to look back on her own culture, and in this altered vantage point resides the great value of much travel writing and in fact the value of travel itself. Travel enables us to gain fresh perspectives on our own cultures when undertaken with an open and generous mind.

By all accounts Bird was not a woman to wrestle with the metaphysical complexities of faith and spirituality, but she did apparently make an honest attempt to come to terms with, at least to understand, Buddhism. In the end, however, she terms the religion idolatrous, perhaps resorting to that judgment out of the threat posed by a religion that promises not salvation as resurrection but a concept of peace as a lack of the need to strive, the beauty of stillness, which to a person like Bird, driven to achieve and spread her faith, would be anathema. But no religion can be sustained with much hope in the face of the rampant materialism that Bird decries. Interestingly she alludes to Wordsworth's "Tintern

Abbey," a poem evoking lost childhood, in her reference to Christ's "still, small voice": "The chill of an atheistic materialism rests upon the upper classes; an advancing education bids religion and morality stand aside, the clang of new material progress drowns the still, small voice of Christ, the old faiths are dying, the religious instincts are failing, and religious cravings scarcely exist" (p. 314). She reads in the material progress of the nation a loss of its innocence, echoed by the reference to the poem and the loss of Christ. Also, in this passage, especially with the word "cravings," one can readily see how Buddhism appalled her. It is of the highest good for her to "crave" Christ. It is the highest good for the Buddhist to crave nothing. She feels the perfection of Buddhism is utterly unattainable and surely feels the perfection of Christ is within her grasp. She bemoans the adoption of Western culture and its accompanying materialism untempered by the Christianity she feels goes along with that culture. She remains blind to the fact that the enforced intrusion of a spiritual structure is no less destructive than the military imposition of economic ones.

On her return trip from Japan, Bird sailed to Hong Kong and then for Singapore, stopping in Saigon. She spent two months in the Malay States, which she calls the Chersonese, a rather literary name for the area. From there she sailed to Ceylon and then to Cairo, where she made a pilgrimage to Sinai. On a side trip to the Chapel of the Burning Bush, she was incensed by the monks' continual haranguing for money. The book that emerged from the tail end of this trip is *The Golden Chersonese,* published in 1883. Her narrative of the trip through the Malay States encompasses a cast of characters that includes elephants, cobras, tigers, water buffalo, and harem women. All this, she writes, "was delightful; every hour adds to the fascination which this place has for me. I thought my tropic dreams were over, when seven years ago I saw the summit peaks of Oahu sink sunset-flushed into a golden sea, but I am dreaming it again" (p. 132). We have come full circle, but to a more mature writer who in this volume has a stronger grasp of

the politics of the place as well as a firm grip on her prose in her evocation of the natural beauty of the place. She is of course always on some level an apologist for the British empire, but as we have seen, she can also be a very incisive critic of it. In *The Golden Chersonese,* the love of horses and horsemanship we have seen in earlier volumes is taken a step farther as we see Bird astride an animal that tests her wits to their maximum—an elephant—who, when goaded, always reacts with "the uprearing and brandishing of the proboscis, and a sound of ungentle expostulation, which could be heard a mile off" (p. 298).

A DEATH AND A MARRIAGE

Isabella Bird arrived home in the British Isles on May 27, 1879. Shortly before her return she had picked up a case of typhoid fever, and when she arrived home she remained ill and weak. She returned to Tobermory with Henrietta, who nursed her back to health. In her convalescence, she began work on *Unbeaten Tracks in Japan,* and in October *A Lady's Life in the Rocky Mountains* was published to huge acclaim. *Unbeaten Tracks in Japan* appeared in 1880. In April of that year Henrietta came down with typhoid, and Isabella nursed her with the help of John Bishop. On June 5, perhaps the defining moment in Isabella's life arrived when Henrietta died of typhoid.

Her sister's death struck Isabella into deep despair. Certainly there were tensions between the sisters, which we cannot know much about because most of Henrietta's correspondence is lost. But that they loved and cared deeply for one another cannot be doubted. All of Bird's most powerful writing is derived from letters written to her sister. Even the letters written to friends from faraway places after Henrietta's death lack the luster of the work done while Henrietta was alive.

In October 1880 a still-saddened John Bishop proposed to Isabella, probably for the second time, and she reluctantly accepted. They married on March 8, 1881, with Isabella still in mourning and wearing all black during the ceremony. The color set the tone for the marriage. They apparently found comfort in each other's company and in their common devotion to their religion and the memory of Henrietta. One of the lights during this dark time was that Isabella began to be publicly honored for her work. The king of Hawaii awarded her the Hawaiian Literary Order, and she met Queen Victoria in 1882. Meanwhile she traveled around the British Isles and worked on the manuscript for *The Golden Chersonese,* the title her sister had suggested. By December both she and her husband were dangerously ill, and the following year *The Golden Chersonese* was published.

On March 6, 1886, after a long illness and an unsuccessful blood transfusion, for which the technology was young and imperfect, John Bishop died after having been married to Isabella for a bit short of five years. Bird had stopped traveling to distant places during her marriage; now she found herself completely without family responsibility and was determined to stew in her grief no longer. She derived a plan to return to the Far East and establish mission hospitals in memory of Henrietta and John Bishop. On February 15, 1889, at the age of fifty-seven, Bird boarded ship alone for India. Her trip lasted for two years, during which time she traveled in India and Tibet and from the Persian Gulf to the Black Sea. She traveled much of the route to the Black Sea without a European escort, which at the time was an act of daunting courage for a European woman nearing sixty. The books that contain Isabella Bird's later exploits, *Journeys in Persia and Kurdistan* (1891), *Korea and Her Neighbors* (1898), and *The Yangtze Valley and Beyond* (1899), are all interesting, and there are still within them some scenes of high adventure, but they lack the vitality of the earlier work and are more self-consciously ethnographic in nature. After Henrietta's death the verve left Isabella's writing, though she remained widely read in her time. Since the main concern of this essay is with Isabella Bird the writer, these books are of less interest to the reader except for their historical detail, which is unquestionably valuable. To the postcolonial critical eye they are beginning to become more important. Later in life Bird became a fair photographer, and she even published a book of photographs called *Chinese Pictures* (1901).

She returned home to England in 1890, by now a highly celebrated personage. Isabella was called to testify before the House of Commons in regard to the status of Armenian Christians and the persecutions they had endured, she dined with the Prime Minister William Gladstone, and in 1892 she became the first woman elected as a fellow of the Royal Geographical Society and was inducted into the Scottish Royal Geographical Society. In 1893 she was formally presented to Queen Victoria, and the following year she sailed again to the East, first to Japan, then Korea, China, Manchuria, and Vladivostok, in all spending about three years in the Far East.

Toward the end of her life Bird slowed down very little. She traveled to Morocco in 1901, which was to prove her final trip into the distant world that was no longer so distant to her, since she had made the world her home. In 1903 she become seriously ill with spinal tumors and heart trouble. On October 7, 1904, Isabella Bird died of heart disease just short of her seventy-fourth birthday.

Perhaps the most valuable thing that we can take from the figure of Isabella Bird is that the only truly vigorous cultural health we can achieve is the health in knowing that the world is wide and that however we might wish otherwise, we are all deeply involved in it, as it is involved in us. One century after her death, through the efforts of feminist and postcolonial critics and scholars, Bird, with all her contradictions and complexities, seems poised to come vibrantly back to life.

Selected Bibliography

WORKS OF ISABELLA BIRD

BOOKS AND ARTICLES
The Englishwoman in America. London: John Murray, 1856.
Aspects of Religion in the United States of America. London: Sampson Low, 1859.

Notes on Old Edinburgh. Edinburgh: Edmonston & Douglas, 1869.

The Hawaiian Archipelago: Six Months among the Palm Groves, Coral Reefs, and Volcanoes of the Sandwich Islands. London: John Murray, 1875.

"Australia Felix: Impressions of Victoria." *Leisure Hour* 10 (1877).

"Letters from the Rocky Mountains." *Leisure Hour* 27 (1878).

A Lady's Life in the Rocky Mountains. London: John Murray, 1879. Reprint, Ernest S. Bernard, ed. Norman: University of Oklahoma Press, 1999. (Excellent annotated edition of this often-reprinted book.)

Unbeaten Tracks in Japan: A Record of Travels in the Interior, including Visits to the Aborigines of Yezo and the Shrines of Nikkô and Isé. 2 vols. London: John Murray, 1880.

Hymns and Poems of the Late Henrietta A. Bird. With Biographical Sketch of the Author. Edited by Isabella Bird. Edinburgh: James Taylor, 1881.

The Golden Chersonese and the Way Thither. London: John Murray, 1883.

"The Visitation of Mountain Jim." In *Phantasms of the Living.* Edited by Edmund Gurney, Frederick Myers, and Frank Podmore. London: Rooms of the Society for Physical Research, 1886. Pp. 531–532.

"A Pilgrimage to Sinai." *Leisure Hour* 35 (1886).

Journeys in Persia and Kurdistan, including a Summer in the Upper Karun Region and a Visit to the Nestorian Rajans. 2 vols. London: John Murray, 1891.

"A Journey through Lesser Tibet." *Scottish Geographical Magazine,* 1892, pp. 513–528.

Heathen Claims and Christian Duty. London: Church Missionary Society, 1893.

"Among the Tibetans." *Leisure Hour* 42 (1893).

Among the Tibetans. London: Religious Tract Society, 1894.

Korea and Her Neighbors: A Narrative of Travel, with an Account of the Recent Vicissitudes and Present Position of the Country. London: John Murray, 1898.

The Yangtze Valley and Beyond: An Account of Journeys in China, Chiefly in the Province of Sze Chuan and among the Man-Tze of the Somo Territory. London: John Murray, 1899.

Chinese Pictures: Notes on Photographs Made in China. London: Cassell, 1900.

"Notes on Morocco." *Monthly Review* 5:89–102 (1901).

COLLECTIONS AND LETTERS

This Grand Beyond: The Travels of Isabella Bird Bishop. Edited by Cecily Palser Havely. London: Century, 1984.

Letters to Henrietta. Edited by Kay Chubbuck. London: John Murray, 2001; Boston: Northeastern University Press, 2003. (Chubbuck notes that most of these letters are drawn from the Isabella Bird Collection owned by John Murray.)

CRITICAL AND BIOGRAPHICAL STUDIES

Barr, Pat. *A Curious Life for a Lady: The Story of Isabella Bird.* London: John Murray, 1970.

Bach, Evelyn. "A Traveller in Skirts: Quest and Conquest in the Travel Narrative of Isabella Bird. *Canadian Review of Comparative Literature* 22:587–600 (September–December 1995).

Checkland, Olive. *Isabella Bird and "A Woman's Right to Do What She Can Do Well."* Aberdeen: Scottish Cultural Society, 1996.

Harper, Lila Marz. *Solitary Travelers: Nineteenth-Century Women's Travel Narratives and the Scientific Vocation.* Madison, N.J.: Fairleigh Dickinson University Press, 2001.

Horsley, Reginald. *Isabella Bird, The Famous Traveller.* London, 1912.

Kaye, Evelyn. *Amazing Traveler, Isabella Bird: The Biography of a Victorian Adventurer.* Boulder, Colo.: Blue Panda, 1994.

Kowalewski, Michael. "Quoting the Wicked Wit of the West: Frontier Reportage and Western Vernacular." In *Reading the West: New Essays on the Literature of the American West.* Edited by Michael Kowalewski. Cambridge and New York: Cambridge University Press, 1996. Pp. 82–98.

Morgan, Susan. *Place Matters: Gendered Geography in Victorian Women's Travel Books about Southeast Asia.* New Brunswick, N.J.: Rutgers University Press, 1996.

Moring, Karen M. "Narrating Imperial Adventure: Isabella Bird's Travels in the Nineteenth-Century American West." In *Western Places, American Myths: How We Think about the West.* Edited by Gary J. Hausladen. Reno: University of Nevada Press, 2003. Pp. 204–222.

Norwood, Vera. "Heroines of Nature: Four Women Respond to the American Landscape." In *The Ecocriticism Reader: Landmarks in Literary Ecology.* Edited by Cheryll Glotfelty and Harold Fromm. Athens: University of Georgia Press, 1996. Pp. 323–350.

Park, Jihang. "Land of the Morning Calm, Land of the Rising Sun: The East Asia Travel Writings of Isabella Bird and George Cuzon." *Modern Asia Studies* 36.3:513–534 (July 2002).

Stoddart, Anna. *The Life of Isabella Bird (Mrs. Bishop).* London: John Murray, 1906.

VERA BRITTAIN

(1893–1970)

Susan Butterworth

VERA BRITTAIN'S LIFE and work was driven by her intense commitment to principle and social action. Best known for her memoir of the First World War, *Testament of Youth* (1933), she pioneered an innovative approach to autobiography, seeing herself as a typical person of her generation and using her own life to illustrate the course of historical events. Brittain was an intelligent and articulate woman who was dedicated to interpreting history and events through literature, both in fiction and nonfiction, and from the public-speaking platform. Her feminist and particularly her pacifist principles, freely expressed in her writing, led first to public acclaim and popularity following the publication of *Testament of Youth* and later to public disgrace when she continued to hold fast to her pacifism throughout World War II. Brittain's integrity through this period of her life is admirable. Ultimately her principles were more important to her than fame and celebrity.

EARLY LIFE: "PROVINCIAL YOUNG LADYHOOD"

Vera Brittain was born December 29, 1893, in Newcastle, Staffordshire, England, the first child of Thomas Brittain and Edith Bervon, and was raised in a prosperous industrial family of paper manufacturers. The first chapters of *Testament of Youth* are a pitiless indictment of the narrowness of middle-class provincial life. According to Brittain, her family read nothing and discussed nothing but papermaking. She stressed the point that there were fewer than a dozen books in the household, and she described Buxton, her hometown, as utterly closed-minded and dull.

Brittain's biographers Hilary Bailey and Deborah Gorham both point out some advantages to this dull middle-class life. Brittain was healthy and secure; she had a strong sense of self-esteem, a solid bond with her mother, father, and younger brother, Edward, and an independent and intelligent nature. Much as she reviled her provincial upbringing, it provided her with a secure and comfortable background that allowed her to maneuver freely in her world, without financial worry. Even at her most radical, Brittain remained a product of her class.

As adolescents both Vera and her brother were sent to boarding schools. Vera was sent to St. Monica's School, where her aunt was headmistress. The school was not academically rigorous, but there were some freethinking and liberal teachers who encouraged critical thinking. She wrote in *Testament of Youth* that at St. Monica's she was introduced to good literature, some politics and economics, and to Olive Schreiner's *Women and Labour,* an early feminist book advocating meaningful work for women.

Edward Brittain, two years younger than Vera, was at Uppingham School, a public school for upper-middle-class boys, being prepared for Oxford. At age eighteen, after boarding school, Vera was expected to stay home and wait for a husband, a situation she loathed and later described in her novel *Not without Honour.* The bright and energetic young woman simply could not abide the narrow provincial life and the "marriage market" in Buxton. She wrote in *Testament of Youth:* "To me provincialism stood, and stands, for the sum total of all false values … [and that] contempt for intelligence, suspicion and fear of independent thought, appear to be necessary passports to provincial popularity" (p. 55).

This was the era of the women's suffrage movement. While young Vera Brittain was aware of the movement, her own natural feminism had a more individual focus. She was determined to expand her horizons beyond Buxton, to go to

Oxford and study English literature. Her younger brother supported her ambition, but her parents were opposed to the plan. Her father was reluctant to spend further money educating a young woman, and her mother was influenced by provincial Victorian mores. Nevertheless, Vera persisted. She attended a series of university extension lectures in Buxton, wrote essays that were noticed by the lecturer, and finally managed to persuade her parents to let her apply to Oxford.

The process of preparing for the entrance exams began. Throughout 1913, Brittain studied on her own and with the help of a classics tutor, attempting to remedy the gaps left in her education by the finishing school atmosphere of St. Monica's. Her hard work preparing for the exams paid off, and she won admittance and an "exhibition," a minor scholarship, to Somerville College, Oxford. She would enter in the fall of 1914, at the same time as Edward.

THE WATERSHED YEAR: 1914

Two momentous events occurred in 1914, one private and one public and world-shaking. In the spring of that year, Edward brought a school friend, Roland Leighton, home to Buxton for a visit. Vera and Roland found themselves compatible, sharing walks and talks about books and common interests. In July 1914 Brittain went with her mother to Uppingham Speech Day. There she met more of Edward's friends, and she and Roland began a blossoming romance. Twenty years later, in *Testament of Youth,* she would recall that day as: "the one perfect summer idyll that I ever experienced, as well as my last care free entertainment before the Flood. The lovely legacy of a vanished world, it is etched with minute precision on the tablets of my memory. Never again, for me and for my generation, was there to be any festival the joy of which no cloud would darken and no remembrance invalidate" (p. 91).

The prospect of Oxford became even more attractive and exciting for the happy young woman because Vera, Edward, and Roland would all be "going up" together for the fall term. She had just begun to dream of herself and Roland together at Oxford, enjoying a life of intellectual and romantic companionship, when the First World War broke out in August 1914, and the world shattered for Brittain and all her generation. Public events irrevocably intruded on private lives in a way she and her sheltered Edwardian middle-class contemporaries had never imagined. As she eloquently wrote in the opening line of *Testament of Youth:* "When the Great War broke out, it came to me not as a superlative tragedy, but as an interruption of the most exasperating kind to my personal plans."

Brittain went up to Oxford alone. Her brother and Roland Leighton, along with their friends from Uppingham, had enlisted and were getting ready to go overseas to France. Vera and Roland, perhaps pushed by the urgency of events, fell further in love and decided to marry. By March 1915, less than a year after Uppingham Speech Day, Roland was at the front. Oxford by this time had begun to seem irrelevant to the impetuous young Vera. Like most of her contemporaries at this point in the war, she was caught up in a patriotic fervor and was eager to "do her part" for the war effort. She left Oxford at the end of her first year determined to take up volunteer nursing.

WAR YEARS

Throughout the summer of 1915, Brittain trained as a Red Cross volunteer nurse at the local Buxton hospital. In the fall she began her V.A.D. (Volunteer Aid Detachment) nursing career at the First London General Hospital at Camberwell. The work and the living conditions were difficult, but she was strong and able and felt that she shared a common experience with Roland, who was in the trenches of France. The months passed in hard work and worrying about and writing to Roland. She was sustained by the anticipation of Roland's Christmas leave.

Then the worst happened. Roland was due to arrive at his family home on Christmas Day. Vera and Roland's family waited all day and all night for him. On Boxing Day, the day after Christmas, they received the telegram with the tragic news. On December 23, 1915, the day before his

VERA BRITTAIN

twenty-second birthday, just as he was about to go on leave, Roland was killed in France. Vera was of course devastated. Within a week, overcome by a grief from which she never fully recovered, she was back at the hospital, nursing. Her only comfort came from their mutual friends Victor Richardson, who had attended Uppingham with Roland and Edward and who had not yet been sent to the front, and Geoffrey Thurlow, who had been wounded and was in the hospital, where Vera visited him regularly. Then Edward too was wounded and sent to Camberwell. The men and their wounds and suffering became Vera's reality, along with the drudgery of nursing. The war was no longer glamorous; it seemed to have been going on forever, with no end in sight.

Brittain applied for a post overseas and was sent to Malta, where the nursing duties were lighter and the conditions more congenial than they had been in London. Edward was still in England, recovering from his wounds, so her mind was relatively at ease. She corresponded regularly with Victor and Geoffrey, and she began to regain her physical and mental health in the balmy climate.

Once again her relative peace was shattered. In close succession, Victor was seriously wounded and blinded and Geoffrey was killed. In a desperate moment Vera decided to return to England and marry Victor, to sacrifice herself and devote her life to caring for him. However, Victor died shortly after she arrived in London.

Then in June 1917 Edward was sent back to France, and Vera decided to go there to work with the possibility that she might be able to be close to him. She was assigned to a hospital at Etaples, France, not far from the front. There she did nursing under incredibly difficult circumstances, experiencing air raids and receiving frequent convoys of wounded, sometimes working alone in wards of seriously wounded men. By this time the unquestioning patriotism of the first year of the war had been replaced by weariness and questioning. She spent some time nursing German prisoners in Etaples, so she was well aware that "the Hun" consisted of scared boys who were dying the same horrible deaths as her friends.

Brittain had overcome her parents' provincial Victorian objections and insisted on going to Oxford. Then the war further loosened traditional social expectations and restrictions, and she was able to become engaged to Roland Leighton without the formal permissions and process that would have been considered necessary and proper even a few years earlier. She had gone into volunteer nursing, traveled unchaperoned, and seen much that would have been impossible for a young woman before the war. But while she was in France, she encountered a parental demand that she could not refuse.

Her parents had moved from Buxton to Kensington, outside London. Wartime deprivations and worry had taken a toll on civilians at home. Her mother went into a nursing home due to a rather vague, unspecified illness, and her father demanded that she, the only daughter, return home to take care of him and the Kensington flat. Every pair of hands was needed at the hospital at that time. Brittain the feminist wrote: "I knew that no one in France would believe a domestic difficulty to be so insoluble; if I were dead, or a male, it would have to be settled without me" (*Testament of Youth,* p. 422).

Edward had been transferred to the Austrian front in Italy, dashing Vera's hopes of being near him in France. Perhaps she was too weary of the war and its tragedies to fight with her father. Domestic family duty overcame her independent work outside the home, and in early 1918 Vera returned to England. She was miserable in Kensington, which reminded her of the narrow life she had escaped in Buxton. She did take the opportunity to pursue her literary ambition and prepare a volume of poetry, *Verses of a V.A.D.,* which was published in 1918. But in June 1918 the worst happened yet again. Another telegram brought the news that Edward Brittain had been killed in Italy.

In numbness and despair, Brittain returned to nursing in London and was there when the armistice was announced in November 1918. She was too weary and discouraged and depressed to celebrate: too late, was her feeling. All her contemporaries were dead. "The War was over; a new age was beginning; but the dead were dead and would never return" (p. 463).

The First World War, the definitive event of the early twentieth century, of her generation, left Vera Brittain utterly exhausted and deeply changed. She had lost her youth and her optimism and felt that her entire generation had been betrayed and wasted. The outcome of the war, the Treaty of Versailles, seemed to her to be unjust, vindictive, inconclusive. "I was beginning already to suspect that my generation had been deceived, its young courage cynically exploited, its idealism betrayed" (p. 470). The foundations of Brittain's lifelong pacifism were laid on her experience in World War I. War solved nothing; it only wasted promising young lives.

OXFORD AFTER THE WAR

In 1919 Brittain returned to Oxford "because college seemed the one thing left out of the utter wreckage of the past" (*Testimony of Youth*, p. 468). She decided to study history rather than English in an attempt to understand the events that had destroyed her generation and her peace of mind. Possibly through interpreting history, future war might be prevented. International relations became her special subject and her lifelong passion.

Brittain did not find postwar Oxford congenial to a woman who had spent the last four years experiencing the reality of the war. Most of the other students were younger and had not experienced the harsh realities that she had. They did not want to be reminded of the war. But Brittain could not forget those experiences. She did not feel that she was the same person who had been at Oxford before the war, and she had not yet established a postwar identity. She felt that she was an outsider. Further, she had intense, undiagnosed and unrecognized post-traumatic stress disorder. She experienced hallucinations, torturing dreams, and insomnia for the next eighteen months. She thought she was growing a beard and was tormented by mirrors. Having lost so many of those she loved as a young woman, she suffered from anxiety and a "habit of apprehension" that lasted throughout her life.

As she gradually regained her mental health, she regained her interest in the Oxford world. She began to write for the *Oxford Outlook* and the *Oxford Chronicle* and became an editor of *Oxford Poetry*. She became outspoken about the role of women at the university. Although women followed the degree program at Oxford, they were not actually granted degrees until 1920. In 1919, when she returned to college, Brittain became involved in the struggle for women's degrees at Oxford and thus for the first time became formally involved in politics and with the feminist movement.

FRIENDSHIP WITH WINIFRED HOLTBY

A turning point in Vera Brittain's life, a factor in her healing from the traumatic experiences of the First World War, and a new beginning, a second life, was her friendship with Winifred Holtby. Vera and Winifred met in 1919 at Oxford, where they shared a history tutor. Holtby was a few years younger than Brittain and had served in the Women's Auxiliary Corps during the war. She was from a Yorkshire family of yeoman farmers, so the two young women had a provincial background in common. From all accounts Holtby was a hardworking student and writer, a kind person, and a warm and loving friend.

The two women crossed swords at an Oxford debate. Vera, who was still alienated and bitter, proposed the motion "that four years' travel are a better education than four years at a university." Winifred's speech defended the university against Brittain's argument for experience. The judging was unanimously against Brittain. She was miserable, feeling certain that she would never fit in at college, and further, that Holtby had deliberately engineered the humiliating debate.

Holtby, on the other hand, recognized a suffering woman and went out of her way to be kind and helpful to Brittain. She became a friend on whom Brittain depended and grew to love. They had common ambitions as well as similar backgrounds. Both were determined to make a living as writers and journalists after college. In 1921 the two young women graduated from

Oxford. They took a post-graduation tour of Europe, visiting Edward's grave in Italy and Roland's grave in France, as well as Paris and Rome.

With her dead somewhat laid (for they would never be truly laid), Brittain was ready to begin the next phase of her life. She and Holtby moved together into a flat in London, a most adventurous and experimental move for their time, ready to fight their way into the world of London journalism and publishing.

POST-OXFORD LONDON

Social mores in the 1920s were not as restrictive as in the prewar years, yet still there were not many options available to young educated women. An academic teaching post would be one, and both women were offered and turned down instructorships. However, they both had decided that they did not want to teach. Brittain wanted time free to work on her first novel, already begun. The novel that would become *The Dark Tide* was set at Oxford and explored the roles and relationships of women at the university. Still, a living had to be earned.

After her experience in the war, Brittain was deeply committed to internationalism and the new League of Nations. She took some part-time work lecturing and teaching on international relations and began to lecture for the League of Nations Union. She still aspired to journalism, accumulating a growing pile of rejection slips. Her father gave his unconventional daughter some shares of the family business, not enough to live on but enough to allow her to devote more time to writing and politics and less time to teaching and lecturing.

Both women became involved in political causes: the League of Nations, the Labour Party, and the Six Point Group, founded by Lady Rhondda, who also published *Time and Tide,* a radical magazine written by women. Universal suffrage for women was one of the Six Points. Women over thirty had been granted the right to vote in 1918, but suffrage was not extended to women under thirty until 1928. The Six Points were all feminist causes, advocating equal rights

for women, emphasizing the importance of meaningful work for women, and especially promoting the possibility of careers for married women, combining work and marriage.

Brittain attended the League of Nations Assembly in Geneva in 1922, triumphant to have her first commission for an article, "Women at Geneva," for *Time and Tide*. In 1923 Brittain was the official representative of *Time and Tide* at the assembly. In 1924 she and Holtby toured central Europe together, gathering firsthand information on the effects of the war in that part of the world. Brittain had ample material for her journalism and became more focused on politics than ever, with a growing conviction that war aggravated international problems rather than solving them.

In 1923 Brittain and Holtby both published their first novels. Brittain's *The Dark Tide* was set in Oxford, a semiautobiographical tale of two women, loosely based on Vera and Winifred. One has an affair with her tutor but leaves the university and volunteers to train as a nurse; the other fails her exams and marries her tutor. The novel suffered many rejections before it was finally taken by the publisher Grant Richards, who considered Brittain fresh and promising. Reviews were lukewarm; the novel is considered melodramatic and overwritten. Holtby's *Anderby Wold,* on the other hand, was published while Brittain was still struggling to find a publisher for *The Dark Tide*. It is considered an impressive first novel by a very young woman. Since Holtby had been in Brittain's intellectual shadow at Oxford, this reversal was difficult for Brittain.

The relationship between the two young women was based on shared principles and goals and mutual devotion to work. One issue Brittain considered and wrote about during the early 1920s was that of the "superfluous" or "surplus" woman. Women of their age and class outnumbered the available men, since so many had been killed in the war. Approaching the age of thirty, Brittain essentially gave up the idea of marriage for herself and focused on the idea of autonomy and useful work for women. She and Holtby were able to support each other in their work and served as inspiration, first readers, and critics of each other's writing. The years of living and working together were mutually supportive and productive.

By 1924 both women had second novels ready for publication. Brittain's *Not without Honour* was based on her days as an unmarried daughter in Buxton. Her female protagonist successfully battles against the restrictions of provincial life. Brittain was beginning her lifelong purpose of turning her experiences into literature, exploring the role of the individual against the background of political and social events and developing a compromise between traditional female roles and intellectual and economic independence.

MARRIED CAREER WOMAN

Just as her career as a novelist, journalist, and lecturer was taking off and she had abandoned any idea of marriage, the unexpected happened. Brittain received a fan letter from an Oxford graduate who had read her novels and admired her from afar. George Gordon Catlin, a bright and promising young political scientist, wrote and asked to meet her. Brittain was traveling, on the road lecturing for the League of Nations, and by the time the letter caught up with her, Catlin (always referred to as "G." in her memoirs) had left to take a teaching post at Cornell University in America. The two corresponded during the 1923–1924 academic year. They seemed to share political ideals and even feminist values, the idea that a woman might marry and combine intellectual work with motherhood.

Brittain and Catlin met for the first time when Catlin returned from Cornell in June 1924. He had made it clear in his letters that he hoped to marry her. He seems to have admired Brittain for her mind, her ideas, her writing, her education, and her politics. That June they became engaged, deciding to marry the following June, 1925.

Meanwhile Brittain and Holtby took their planned trip to central Europe. In occupied Germany she concluded that the only hope to avoid another war lay in internationalism. By internationalism she meant both the opposite or absence of nationalism and also logical arbitration of disputes by an enlightened League of Nations.

Catlin shared her belief in internationalism. Since the two had corresponded extensively yet barely knew each other in person, their attraction seems to have been intellectual, confirmed by the actual meeting in the summer of 1924. A further impetus for marriage would have been Brittain's hope for future generations. She felt despair that the best of her own generation was dead, lost in the war, and that any hope for a peaceful, united Europe lay in a new generation, trained in new, creative solutions to world disputes. She must have children.

Brittain and Catlin discussed by letter how they could both combine marriage and career, how they could have children without giving up their intellectual and creative lives. She wrote in *Testament of Youth* that G. offered her a "free marriage" and recognized that she cared as much for work as she did for him. She was torn by her loyalty to dead Roland but decided to look forward and to seize life. She planned to go to America for a year with her husband, writing and possibly lecturing in America, and then to work out some kind of part-year living arrangement in England so she could continue to work in London.

Brittain and Catlin were married in London on June 27, 1925. While she set off for a honeymoon in eastern Europe, interviewing politicians and government officials with her "gifted interpreter of politics," Holtby left for a long lecture tour of South Africa.

Brittain was bitterly disappointed by life at Cornell University. While she was happy with her husband, she found life as a faculty wife in a small university town depressingly like life in provincial Buxton. While Catlin had a rich intellectual life in America, with a book on politics accepted for publication and teaching and research work, Brittain was increasingly discouraged by American publishers. She wrote a book but it did not sell, nor did she sell a single article or receive an offer to speak. She felt strongly that the work of speaking and writing on antiwar issues was her mission. With Catlin's agreement, she returned to London after a year and was rewarded with immediate success, selling article after article.

Brittain and Catlin struggled with their marriage, since clearly the concept of a free and equal marriage was easier than the reality. Brittain returned to Cornell to be with her husband for two months in the spring of 1927 and became pregnant. Ultimately Catlin arranged to teach only the spring semester at Cornell, and they established a three-way household in London with Winifred Holtby. Their first child, a son, John, was born in December 1927.

During this period when Brittain was experimenting with living a feminist marriage, she published two books, both of which reflect her concerns with meaningful work for women and combining marriage and career. *Women's Work in Modern England,* a handbook of job opportunities for women, was published in 1928. *Halcyon; or, The Future of Monogamy,* written after John's birth and published in 1929, is a utopian fantasy, written as if in retrospect from the twenty-first century. The book makes the case for Brittain's choice of "semi-detached" marriage.

Brittain and Catlin's daughter, Shirley, was born in 1930. The Brittain household in London by this time consisted of Vera and Winifred and the children, with Catlin joining them when he was not in America. The arrangement with Winifred Holtby was not as unusual as it might seem today, partly because the adults had been raised in the Victorian tradition of larger households and partly because women living together was not uncommon during the years when there were many single women—widows and women who would never marry—in Britain after the First World War. The three adults shared expenses, Catlin was away at his university job in America half the year, and Vera and Winifred had established a mutually supportive working relationship even before Vera's marriage. In some ways Winifred, who was devoted to the children, took the traditional role of Victorian spinster aunt, but her creative and intellectual life and publishing success certainly went beyond that stereotype.

It is sometimes implied that the relationship between Vera and Winifred was a lesbian one.

There is no direct evidence to support the idea that their relationship was physical or sexual. In fact, the evidence of Brittain's published writing suggests otherwise. She was a defender of Radclyffe Hall when Hall's lesbian novel *The Well of Loneliness* (1928) was condemned as obscene and later wrote a book about that case. While she is compassionate and sympathetic to lesbianism, Brittain refers to physical love between women as abnormal or "inverted." In *Halcyon; or, The Future of Monogamy,* she defends monogamous, heterosexual marriage. Writing about this period of her life in her memoir *Testament of Experience,* she makes it clear that she regards marriage and motherhood as natural and instinctive for women. She grapples with the question of how a wife and mother can keep working, but never with her sexual identity. What was modern and unusual about the lifestyle of the two women was their literary ambition and their relationship as working partners.

Vera Brittain struggled with her work, her marriage, and the demands of raising two young children through the early 1930s. There were pressures on her "semi-detached" marriage that she found it difficult to acknowledge. As a professional feminist she needed her marriage to Catlin to be a model, but the reality could not measure up to the ideal.

In her journalism, and in her life at its best, Brittain offered a vision of modern feminist motherhood, postulating that the primary role an educated professional woman ought to perform for her children was that of moral and intellectual guide. She advocated professional care for children in infancy, suggesting that motherhood is not instinctive and that rather than sacrificing oneself as an infant nurse, a woman would be a better mother if she were a fully developed, fulfilled, and productive member of society. Here she reveals her middle-class bias, as her solutions reflect a limited understanding of social and economic reality. Her solution, paid professional household help, was more useful to her own affluent class than to the working-class woman. She was an enthusiastic advocate of information for young mothers, crediting the Chelsea Babies'

Club and what she learned there with saving her son John's life when he did not thrive as a young infant.

Brittain was discouraged about her work, writing to Catlin that since her marriage all she had produced was journalism and two "glorified pamphlets." She hoped to write a serious book about her war experiences, but the demands of running a household and managing young children (even with paid household help) made it extremely difficult to write. Then Winifred collapsed from the mysterious illness, misdiagnosed as overwork or a nervous breakdown, that would later be diagnosed as Bright's disease, the kidney disease that would lead to her early death.

TESTAMENT OF YOUTH

By the early 1930s a series of "war books" had begun to appear in print. Brittain had tried to write a novel about her war experiences in the 1920s but had not achieved sufficient distance from the event or sufficient craft to succeed. Most likely, the major books about the war did not appear until ten years had passed because the participants needed time and perspective to come to terms with the horror of the experience and because the public needed time before it would be ready to hear how futile the war had been and that the great sacrifices had not improved the world.

Ernest Hemingway's *A Farewell to Arms,* E. M. Remarque's *All Quiet on the Western Front,* and Robert Graves's *Goodbye to All That,* among others, were written from the male point of view. Brittain was determined to write the story of the war from the woman's point of view and to emphasize the great loss and futility of the war.

Brittain worked on the long book that would become *Testament of Youth* for the next three years, taking material from her diaries and her correspondence with Roland, Edward, and their friends Victor and Geoffrey. The memoir is remarkable and innovative for several reasons. Essentially Brittain was working in a new form of autobiography. Up until Brittain's time autobiography was chiefly a form used to record the lives and times of the great, mostly men, and

significant affairs of state or letters. It had not been developed as an expression of the lives of ordinary individuals. Brittain conceived a new kind of autobiography that would record her own life as that of a typical witness to the events of her generation. Her training in history at Oxford served her well as she used her personal life to explore the course of historical events. She was inventive and original in her plan to relate the private life of an individual woman to the public events of her time.

Brittain also was original and deliberate in her technique, as she began to redefine her ideas about serious writing. While she had written a great deal of nonfiction, discussing politics and ideas in her journalism, she considered fiction the genre of serious writing. She had written two immature novels and had struggled with writing a serious novel about the war. With *Testament of Youth* she began to explore a new kind of writing. She wrote in *Testament of Experience:* "Then, suddenly illumination came. I too must record my memories as an autobiography; nothing else is stark enough, nothing else so direct. ... A new type of autobiography was coming into fashion, and I might, perhaps, speed its development. I meant to make my story as truthful as history but as readable as fiction, and in it I intended to speak, not for those in high places, but for my own generation of obscure young women" (p. 77). With *Testament of Youth,* Brittain found a voice more immediate and authentic than she was ever able to achieve in her fiction.

A major theme of the volume is its indictment of war. Brittain clearly shows how the upper-class youth of her generation was raised in a classical form of patriotism that believed it was noble to die for one's country. The young men of her class and generation were trained as junior officers at their public schools and thus were the first to volunteer and then to die in the deplorable and wasteful conditions of trench warfare. In the chapter titled "Piping for Peace," she goes beyond describing the sorrows of the war and puts forward her own internationalist views as she describes the work she did for the League of Nations Union. She offers solutions, possibilities for changing the nationalist war-oriented society that perpetrated the First World War. One solution was internationalism and an effective League of Nations. Another solution was more female participation in public affairs.

For *Testament of Youth* is not only a statement against war but also a feminist statement. Brittain's own natural feminism permeates her story, from her indictment of the woman's position in provincial society and her determination to go to Oxford, to her friendship and working relationship with Holtby and her life as a young, single career woman. The volume ends with her marriage to Catlin, with its stated hopes for an equal marriage.

Writing *Testament of Youth* fulfilled a vital personal purpose for Brittain. She had been suffering from the effects of the war for many years. She was at last able to publicly celebrate her dead young men, to exorcise her own pain, to lay the past to rest. She carries her story forward to a personal resurrection: her education in international relations, her work for peace, and her hopeful look forward to her marriage.

Testament of Youth represented a new height of craftsmanship for Brittain as a writer. Her early novels had been melodramatic in their plotting and overly blunt in presenting their themes. In *Testament of Youth* she achieved drama and suspense mellowed by poignancy and sorrow. Brittain breaks the reader's heart as she portrays the ignorance and self-involvement of the summer of 1914, with the image of Uppingham Speech Day as lost innocence. The book's strength is in its portrayal of grief, in the classic image of a woman mourning the husbands, sons, and lovers killed in war. Yet this is a woman who survives her grief in spite of its costs.

Brittain was able to achieve the feeling of immediacy because she had all her diaries from the war years as well as all of the letters to and from the young men and her parents. A comparison of the memoir with the published diaries and letters reveals the writer's technique and purpose, as the memoir focuses the ambiguity and shading of reality. Certainly the memoir is oversimplified. She must not show her affection for her mother or the warmth of her family life because her mother's role in the memoir is to represent the

narrowness of provincial life. She must not reveal ambiguity in her feelings for her brother, who is after all a dead hero. She must fall deeply and immediately in love with Roland Leighton, for he is the young lover tragically killed before he can blossom. Brittain was unwavering in her pursuit of moral purpose in *Testament of Youth,* and she succeeded admirably. The book has become a classic of World War I literature.

Testament of Youth, published in 1933, was an immediate success. The manuscript was accepted by the London publisher Victor Gollancz within a week of its submission and by Macmillan & Co. for publication in America immediately thereafter. It was a best-seller and made Brittain well-known and financially secure. She enjoyed a triumphant celebrity speaking tour of the United States in 1934. Oxford, where she had been an outcast since publishing *The Dark Tide,* with its controversial affair between a fictional female student and an Oxford don, welcomed her back. Another book of poetry, *Poems of the War and After,* was published in 1934. At her creative height, she planned an ambitious novel that would become her most successful work of fiction, *Honourable Estate.*

TWO DEATHS

Throughout her life, Vera Brittain was haunted by the death of those she loved. In 1935 her father, Thomas Brittain, committed suicide. He had had a tendency toward depression for years, especially since Edward's death, and had been in and out of nursing homes. Duty toward her parents was another theme in her life, as it was for Winifred Holtby and many single daughters in her time. Vera had gone on her 1934 lecture tour of the United States against her mother's will, in the aftermath of one of her father's episodes.

Winifred had also been extremely ill for several years, alternating between periods of enforced rest, periods of productive writing work, and periods of helping Vera with the children's care. Winifred had been largely responsible for the children for the three months that Vera had been in the United States, although the household had a housekeeper and nanny. Winifred knew she was dying, and Vera seems to have had difficulty facing the truth.

Vera took the children to France on holiday before her father's unexpected death. Kind and sensitive Winifred knew that ever since the war Vera had dreaded receiving bad news in telegrams. So Winifred crossed the channel to give Vera the news about her father in person while George stayed in London with her mother. Winifred crossed back to England with Vera, then returned to France to care for the children. George fell seriously ill after the funeral, and Winifred kept the children in France for the summer. This was typical of Winifred, who was described by family and friends as an angel. It was almost her last act of self-sacrificing friendship, since she died of kidney failure only a month after she returned from France.

Vera was devastated and overcome with guilt. She had loved Winifred and had shared a creative working relationship with her friend. But from the very beginning of their friendship, Winifred had made herself indispensable to Vera. She had been the giver, and Vera felt great remorse when she died.

Immediately after Winifred's death, George Catlin stood for parliament and was defeated. This was a low point for both Brittain and her husband. Catlin had left Cornell in 1934, partly on the strength of Brittain's increased earnings from *Testament of Youth,* and had hoped to obtain either a prestigious teaching position at the London School of Economics or a Labour seat in Parliament. When neither materialized, he felt himself a failure.

Holtby, a successful journalist, novelist, and social activist in her own right, made Brittain her literary executor. After Holtby's death Brittain worked on three important projects for her friend. She helped to administer a scholarship at Somerville College, Oxford, endowed by Holtby. She edited the manuscript of Holtby's final novel, *South Riding,* and prepared it for publication. And she began the biography and tribute to Holtby that would be published as *Testament of Friendship.* It would be several years before *Testament of Friendship* would be finished, partly

due to the careful work to be done with *South Riding,* partly because, as with *Testament of Youth,* some distance from the event was needed before the book could be properly written, and partly because Brittain was working on her own novel *Honourable Estate.*

HONOURABLE ESTATE

A complex and ambitious novel, *Honourable Estate* is Brittain's most successful work of fiction. The novel unites a number of autobiographical elements, social commentary, and some of the main themes of Brittain's life and work.

The plot of the novel is in three sections, describing the lives of three generations of provincial British families, loosely based on Brittain's own family and the family of her husband. The first section is a portrait of Janet Rutherston, whose character is based on George Catlin's mother. Janet is a woman before her time, educated and interested in social and political action. She is married very young to a conservative clergyman who cannot understand her progressive views of women's suffrage and lack of interest in traditional woman's roles. Their only son, Denis, watches as his mother suffers in a repressive marriage. The one bright spot in her life is her friendship with the playwright Gertrude Ellison Campbell, but tragically Gertrude rejects her when Janet attends an important suffragist demonstration rather than Gertrude's opening night. Janet finally leaves her husband, but it is too late. Her health and spirit are broken and she dies sad and alone.

The second section of the novel is the story of the prosperous provincial Alleyndene family. The daughter Ruth goes to Oxford, but when her brother is killed in the First World War she becomes a V.A.D. in France. Her brother's American friend Eugene Meury seeks her out to give her a last letter written by her brother the night before his death. Her brother had been discovered in a homosexual affair, and he tells Ruth that he intends to be sure that he dies in battle the next day rather than suffer the disgrace of a court-martial. Ruth and Eugene fall in love and become lovers. Eugene is later killed. While

Ruth is devastated, she is glad that she was able to offer him the experience of physical love before he died.

In the third section of the novel, Denis Rutherston, now a young university lecturer, and Ruth Alleyndene meet in Russia, where she is nursing during the typhoid epidemic and he is on a committee investigating famine. Denis is able to persuade weary and depressed Ruth to return to England and become active in political life. They marry. Ruth wants more than the life of a wife and mother of the time. Because Denis has witnessed his own mother's misery, he resolves never to restrict his wife or make her unhappy. They achieve a mutually satisfying marriage, have twin children, and Ruth is elected to a Labour seat in Parliament.

Brittain based several of her characters on people in her life, most specifically Janet Rutherston, modeled on Catlin's mother, whom she never knew but admired for her outspoken views and social action. The character of Eugene Meury has elements of Roland Leighton but also of George Brett of the Macmillan Company in New York, with whom she fell in love during her 1934 American speaking tour. The fact that Ruth sleeps with Eugene before he is killed may have helped Brittain work through some unresolved issues about Roland. Ruth's brother's homosexuality gives Brittain an opportunity to express a tolerance and sadness for that lifestyle and indicates an unspoken possibility that Edward Brittain may have been homosexual as well. Gertrude Ellison Campbell suffers great remorse after Janet Rutherston's death, and while the friendship between Janet and Gertrude was more likely modeled on a failed friendship between Brittain and the novelist Phyllis Bentley, the guilt and remorse after a friend's death may have been an expression of her remorse after Winifred Holtby's death.

The provincial Alleyndene parents never truly understand their progressive daughter, but they always treat her with affection and indulgence. Thus there is an element of reconciliation with her family in the novel that never appears in the autobiographical *Testament of Youth*. The characters in *Honourable Estate* are fictional, and composite, but writing the book during a period

of suffering in her own life may have helped Brittain work through some of her own grieving.

Themes in the novel mirror those that were most important to Brittain: feminism, the never-forgotten war, social action, and feminist marriage and motherhood. The form of the novel is traditional, realistic social commentary, far from the experimental forms of her contemporaries Virginia Woolf, James Joyce, or T. S. Eliot. Yet the sentiments of the novel are liberal, even radical, for 1936. From repressed Janet Rutherston to Ruth Alleyndene, member of Parliament and working mother, Brittain manages to illustrate the changes in women's lives from the Victorian 1880s to the contemporary 1930s.

Brittain wrote in the novel's preface: "I make no apology for dealing in a novel with social theories and political beliefs." Denis Rutherston's thoughts on Ruth Alleyndene might describe Brittain's own purpose and unwavering commitment to interpreting history and social action. "Ruth Alleyndene was intelligent and courageous and capable of great intensity of purpose, and those were the qualities needed by the political England of the nineteen-twenties" (p. 449). Her "job in life is to examine and interpret and persuade" (p. 450).

Brittain's commitment to public speaking, as important to her as her writing, is clear also. Denis comments: "What's needed to speed things up are men and women who'll make these issues dynamic and urgent from public platforms the world over … public speakers with the eloquence of Isaiah and the technique of Sarah Bernhardt" (pp. 451-452).

PEACE PLEDGE UNION

Vera Brittain was now a mature woman in her forties, her publishing career at its height, a politically active woman who had managed to combine marriage, motherhood, and work that was meaningful to her. She was acquainted with life's sorrows, a woman who would always be haunted by the First World War, by the premature deaths of her loved ones, and by the guilt and remorse associated with death. The period of soul-searching that ensued after Holtby's death left her ripe for another turning point in her life, which occurred in 1936.

Lecturing on the international situation, she found herself on a platform with Canon H. R. L. Sheppard, a Christian pacifist and founder of the Peace Pledge Union. Sheppard was a convincing, charismatic leader. Brittain had been temperamentally opposed to war for many years, a supporter of diplomatic solutions to disputes among nations. Now she became an unequivocal, deeply committed pacifist.

Brittain had seen and studied firsthand the distress of central and eastern Europe through the 1920s and early 1930s and the hardships of civilians in occupied Germany, and she had spoken out against the inequities of the Treaty of Versailles. In her view the common people paid the price in suffering for the mistakes of politicians and generals. Also in 1936, Brittain and Catlin visited Germany to witness Hitler's progress, gathering valuable first-person observations, speaking out against the injustice they witnessed. No one was more aware of the desperate situation than Brittain. To be a committed pacifist as Europe was rushing toward another war was not politically or socially popular.

In the three years since publishing *Testament of Youth* she had enjoyed outstanding success and popularity. When she joined the Peace Pledge Union, she knowingly exchanged this welcome celebrity for public disapproval. She entered a phase of her life defined by peace activism, unpopular and even dangerous during World War II, which continued after the war as she worked for reconciliation, social justice, and disarmament. She had treasured her public recognition and approval, but she followed her conscience even though she lost writing work and distinguished friends because of her convictions.

Meanwhile there was her biography of Winifred Holtby to be written and another U.S. lecture tour scheduled for 1937. She was a popular speaker in the States, intelligent, attractive and refined, interpreting the European political and literary scene to Americans. Through her work with the Peace Pledge Union she had acquired many contacts among American Quakers. She had the opportunity to meet and interview prominent American politicians, including Franklin and Eleanor Roosevelt. When she returned to England, she had contracts from Macmillan for both *Testament of Friendship* and a nonfiction book on the American scene, published as *Thrice a Stranger* in 1938.

Politics continued to intervene. In 1938 the threat of nazism seemed so close that Vera and George decided to take their children to America and safety. They had been outspoken about their observations of Hitler's policies and they both expected to be at risk if Germany succeeded in invading Britain. In fact, they did take the children to the United States, but the crisis of the moment passed and they returned to England.

She finished *Testament of Friendship,* which had taken three years to write and was published by Macmillan in 1940, feeling that she was racing against the outbreak of the impending war. *Testament of Friendship* is regarded by feminists as an important work for its celebration of women's friendship. While the book portrays loyalty and affection between women, it also reveals that Holtby was exploited by many, including Brittain, Holtby's mother and family, and Lady Rhondda of *Time and Tide*. Holtby was a generous woman, always willing to give to others time that she needed for her own work. In the final chapters, Brittain's remorse that she could have given more to Winifred is evident. Brittain ends on a note of apologizing for her own guilt rather than of celebrating Holtby's life, thus diluting her purpose and weakening the book.

WORLD WAR II: HUMILIATION WITH HONOR

In September 1939, war against Germany was declared. "Peace," Brittain wrote in *Testament of Experience,* "had become ... a disreputable word."

Now the true struggle of being a pacifist during wartime began. The Ministry of Information contacted Brittain, urging her to use her writing skills for war work. As the United States was neutral, Brittain hoped that by continuing to work on Anglo-American relations she might still somehow further the cause of peace. She scheduled another lecture tour of the United States for the spring of 1940 and, typically, fought intellectually for her ideas by writing and publishing a pacifist newsletter, distributed to nearly two thousand subscribers in twenty-five countries. Her *Letter to Peace-Lovers* was published biweekly from September 1939 until 1947 under the most difficult of wartime conditions.

After the lecture tour of the United States in early 1940, Brittain returned to England to find herself a "suspect," even possibly a traitor, because of her pacifist convictions. She was under police surveillance and limited in her movements. She was denied an exit visa to return to the United States later in 1940. When France fell and German invasion of England threatened, she and Catlin made the difficult decision to send the children, now aged twelve and nine, to friends in the United States.

Brittain found herself alone in London during the Blitz, as Catlin was in the United States lecturing on politics and trying to raise U.S. support for Britain. She might have gone to live with relatives in the country, but her conscience demanded that she stay. She felt her true war work was to document the circumstances of civilians in London and to write her newsletter from the center of events. She worked on a documentary book *England's Hour,* which appeared in 1941, going on night air-raid duty, touring bombed areas, and serving meals to bombed-out families in soup kitchens. Catlin, returning from America in December 1940, was torpedoed and spent eight hours in an open boat in the winter North Atlantic in his pajamas.

Throughout 1941 Brittain continued to write and to lecture, often in churches and Friends meeting houses in bombed English cities, pleading for peace, forgiveness, and compassion. In 1942 her pacifist book *Humiliation with Honour* was published, written in the form of letters to her son, John, pleading the cause of refugees, prisoners, and civilian victims of war. She worked on committees devoted to famine relief and bombing restriction in Europe.

The cause of self-determination in India became important to Brittain and, as she wrote, to "all men and women who cared for freedom."

She was invited to go as a delegate to the All-India Women's Conference in 1941 but again could not get an exit visa from Britain.

Still this active and committed woman found time to work on a novel. *Account Rendered,* published in 1945, told the story of a World War I veteran who committed murder while suffering flashbacks from the stress of being in the trenches. The murderer is eventually found guilty but insane. The novel is an early psychological study of post-traumatic stress syndrome and was quite popular.

America entered the war after the bombing of Pearl Harbor in December 1941, and the tide of the war began to turn with the Allied victories in North Africa in late 1942. German bombing of England continued, but the prospect of invasion became less likely and Brittain and Catlin were able to consider bringing the children home. John and Shirley returned, separately, through neutral Lisbon, in 1943.

Always, Brittain was writing and producing her peace letters and speaking to Quaker and church groups, arguing against the saturation bombing of Germany and for compassion for German civilians. Her stance against saturation bombing made her extremely unpopular in England and the United States, especially after the publication in 1944 of a controversial small book against widespread bombing titled *Seed of Chaos: What Mass Bombing Really Means.*

In May 1945 the war in Europe ended, followed by the end of the war with Japan in August of that year. Horrified by the atomic bombing of Hiroshima and Nagasaki, Brittain would be involved in the cause of nuclear disarmament for the rest of her life.

Through 1946 and 1947 Brittain traveled throughout Europe, always lecturing, to see firsthand the aftermath of the war. The Gestapo List, a list of names of those the Nazis would arrest immediately if they invaded England, was published and widely circulated. Both Vera Brittain's and George Catlin's names appeared on it, which helped vindicate her to the public. She was commissioned to write a book called *On Becoming a Writer* and began work on a new novel.

VERA BRITTAIN

BORN 1925: A NOVEL OF YOUTH

Born 1925 appeared in 1949. The novel connects the First World War with the Second and, like *Honourable Estate,* is enriched by autobiographical elements and composite fictionalized characters. The older central figure, modeled on her mentor Canon Sheppard, is Robert Carbury, a veteran of World War I who realizes the ultimate immorality of war and becomes a pacifist clergyman. His wife had lost the love of her life, her first husband, in the war immediately after their marriage, and once married to Carbury she struggles with the demands of combining her artistic career and her family. They have two children, much like Brittain's own John and Shirley. As the European situation worsens in the 1930s Carbury founds a pacifist organization which makes him very unpopular during the war. The children are evacuated to America, in a moving scene much like the actual evacuation of John and Shirley.

Clearly the pain of her separation from her own children is expressed in this section of the novel, as the children have adult experiences in America totally unknown to their parents, and their return to England, combined with the surliness of adolescence, is a difficult transition for all. Later, in *Testament of Experience,* Brittain wrote of the return of her own adolescent children with some dismay and regret as she struggled simultaneously with their adolescence, the clash of cultures they had experienced, the hardships of the war, and her own unpopularity due to her outspoken pacifism, with which the children were not entirely in sympathy.

Adrian, the adolescent son in the novel, rejects his father's pacifism and registers for the draft. The epilogue is set in bombed Cologne, Germany, in 1947, where Adrian experiences compassion for the Germans, realizes his father was right about bombing, and faces the task of rebuilding Germany. It is a good story that illustrates many of Brittain's typical themes and preoccupations. Perhaps the novel is dated when read today, out of the context of Brittain's life, but in 1949 the novel would have been quite contemporary.

LATER WORKS

Brittain never regained the popularity that had followed *Testament of Youth,* but she continued to be an active woman of letters and socially concerned lecturer for the rest of her life. She followed the emotionally draining work of her autobiographical novel with a historical biography of John Bunyan, *Valiant Pilgrim,* published in 1950. Her works of history and biography during this period reflected her conviction that the role of a historian is not only to record but also to interpret history.

In 1949 and 1950 she was able at last to travel to India. She was deeply inspired by the work of Mahatma Gandhi and passionately devoted to the cause of India's independence. In 1951 she published a record of her travels and a commentary on Indian politics and government, *Search after Sunrise: A Traveller's Story.* She continued to follow and write about Indian politics for the rest of her life.

Lady into Woman: A History of Women from Victoria to Elizabeth II appeared in 1953. This contribution to the feminist canon is a history of the women's movement from her mother's generation to her daughter's, the years that Brittain knew best. The book is dedicated to her daughter, Shirley, who was educated at Oxford along with her brother and became a member of Parliament for the Labour Party, to the great pride of her feminist, activist mother and her political scientist father. *Lady into Woman* goes beyond the sequence of historical events to discuss women engaged in work, politics, literature, war, and peace. The conviction that informed Brittain's life, that a feminist must be committed to social and political awareness and activism, permeates the book.

Testament of Experience brings her memoirs up to date from the end of *Testament of Youth,* when she married George Catlin in 1925, to their twenty-fifth anniversary in 1950. The book lacks the emotional power of *Testament of Youth* but provides an impressive overview of historical events and records the contributions of a woman of great achievement. As she discusses the turbulent years before, during, and after World War II, with herself and George Catlin in the thick of events, one cannot help but be impressed with the courage and integrity of these two people. *Testament of Experience* is a major autobiography of the 1950s, a valuable first-person commentary on the period by a writer trained in the study of international relations, solidifying Brittain's role as a voice of her generation.

More works of history and commentary followed in the last decade of Brittain's life. In *The Women at Oxford* (1960), she returns to her early interest in the struggle for women's degrees at Oxford and provides a commentary on the role of women at the university. *Envoy Extraordinary: A Study of Vijaya Lakshmi Pandit and Her Contribution to Modern India* appeared in 1965. *Radclyffe Hall: A Case of Obscenity?* (1968) was her last book, providing her recollection from the perspective of forty years after the notorious 1928 obscenity trial at which Brittain had been a witness for the defense. Vera Brittain died in London on March 29, 1970, survived by her husband, son and daughter.

CONTRIBUTIONS OF A LIFETIME
One definition of feminism is "taking women seriously." Vera Brittain took herself seriously, as a woman, as a writer, and as an activist. She was a modern woman with a passion for social justice and a model of dedication to equality for women and to peace activism. Her work for peace, disarmament, and justice for the oppressed grew directly from her belief that a feminist has a responsibility to be committed to full personhood and political awareness. The causes she embraced during her lifetime were equal rights feminism—equal opportunity for education and work, degrees for women at Oxford, access to birth control and information about childbirth and child-rearing, equality in marriage, and feminist friendship—and internationalism, expressed through activism for the League of Nations, pacifism and the Peace Pledge Union, nuclear disarmament, food and medical relief for victims of famine and war, the Labour party, and self-determination in India.

Brittain deeply desired to create a memorial to her dead young men in a form that would influence the generations of the future to take a clear look at the pain and futility of war. With *Testament of Youth* she succeeded. Her literary triumph is the new form of autobiography she achieved in this memoir, her chief contribution to literature, to feminism, and to the canon of the First World War. Presenting herself as "everywoman," her concept of weaving the personal events of her ordinary life with the historical events of the era to create a portrait of a generation is original and effective.

Her purpose when she returned to Oxford after the war was to learn what she could of history and international relations so that she would be in a position "to examine, and interpret and persuade" (*Honourable Estate,* p. 450). Taken together, *Testament of Youth,* the war diaries published as *Chronicle of Youth,* and the letters published as *Letters from a Lost Generation* present a complete and realistic picture of a woman's experience of World War I. Her body of work—fiction, memoir, and nonfiction—presents a full and complex picture of a woman's experience of the first half of the twentieth century. Vera Brittain's contribution was in her active life experience, which she examined and interpreted with the purpose of representing the voice of her generation.

Selected Bibliography

WORKS OF VERA BRITTAIN
The Vera Brittain archives are held at the McMaster University Library, Hamilton, Ontario, Canada.

NOVELS, AUTOBIOGRAPHY, NONFICTION
The Dark Tide. London: Grant Richards, 1923.
Not without Honour. London: Grant Richards, 1924.
Women's Work in Modern England. London: Noel Douglas, 1928.
Halcyon; or, The Future of Monogamy. London: Kegan Paul, 1929; New York: Dutton, 1929.
Testament of Youth: An Autobiographical Study of the Years 1900–1925. London: Gollancz, 1933; New York: Macmillan, 1933.

VERA BRITTAIN

Honourable Estate: A Novel of Transition. London: Gollancz, 1936; New York: Macmillan, 1936.

Thrice a Stranger. London: Gollancz, 1938; New York: Macmillan, 1938.

Testament of Friendship: The Story of Winifred Holtby. London and New York: Macmillan, 1940.

England's Hour. London: Macmillan, 1941.

Humiliation with Honour. London: Andrew Dakers, 1942; New York: Fellowship, 1943.

Seed of Chaos: What Mass Bombing Really Means. London: New Vision, 1944.

Account Rendered. London: Macmillan, 1945.

On Becoming a Writer. London: Hutchinson, 1947. Published as *On Being an Author.* New York: Macmillan, 1948.

Born 1925: A Novel of Youth. New York: Macmillan, 1949.

Valiant Pilgrim. New York: Macmillan, 1950. Published as *In the Steps of John Bunyan.* London: Rich and Cowan, 1950.

Search after Sunrise: A Traveller's Story. London: Macmillan, 1951.

Lady into Woman: A History of Women from Victoria to Elizabeth II. London: Andrew Dakers, 1953; New York: Macmillan, 1953.

Testament of Experience: An Autobiographical Story of the Years 1925–1960. London: Gollancz, 1957; New York: Macmillan, 1957.

The Women at Oxford: A Fragment of History. London: George Harrap, 1960.

Envoy Extraordinary: A Study of Vijaya Lakshmi Pandit and Her Contribution to Modern India. London: George Allen & Unwin, 1965; South Brunswick, N.J.: A. S. Barnes, 1966.

Radclyffe Hall: A Case of Obscenity? London: Femina Press, 1968. South Brunswick, N.J.: A. S. Barnes, 1969.

POETRY

Verses of a V.A.D. London: Erskine Macdonald, 1918.

Poems of the War and After. London: Gollancz, 1934; New York: Macmillan, 1934.

JOURNALS, LETTERS, MANUSCRIPTS, JOURNALISM

Selected Letters of Winifred Holtby and Vera Brittain, 1920–1935. Edited by Vera Brittain and Geoffrey Handley-Taylor. London: A Brown, 1960. (Limited edition.)

Chronicle of Youth: War Diary, 1913–1917. Edited by Alan Bishop with Terry Smart. London: Gollancz, 1981; New York: Morrow, 1982.

Testament of a Generation: The Journalism of Vera Brittain and Winifred Holtby. Edited by Paul Berry and Alan Bishop. London: Virago, 1985.

Chronicle of Friendship: Diary of the Thirties, 1932–1939. Edited by Alan Bishop. London: Gollancz, 1986.

Testament of a Peace Lover: Letters from Vera Brittain. Edited by Winifred and Alan Eden-Green. London: Virago, 1988.

Wartime Chronicle: Diary 1939–1945. Edited by Alan Bishop and Y. Aleksandra Bennett. London: Gollancz, 1989.

Letters from a Lost Generation: The First World War Letters of Vera Brittain and Four Friends, Roland Leighton, Edward Brittain, Victor Richardson, Geoffrey Thurlow. Edited by Alan Bishop and Mark Bostridge. Boston: Northeastern University Press, 1999.

CRITICAL AND BIOGRAPHICAL STUDIES

Anderson, Linda. *Women and Autobiography in the Twentieth Century: Remembered Futures.* London and New York: Prentice Hall, 1997.

Bailey, Hilary. *Vera Brittain.* Harmondsworth, Middlesex, England: Penguin, 1987. (Penguin Lives of Modern Women series.)

Berry, Paul and Mark Bostridge. *Vera Brittain: A Life.* London: Chatto & Windus, 1995.

Catlin, John. *Family Quartet.* London: Hamish Hamilton, 1987.

Gorham, Deborah. *Vera Brittain: A Feminist Life.* Cambridge, Mass.: Blackwell, 1996.

Heilbrun, Carolyn G. Introduction to *Testament of Friendship.* New York: Seaview, 1981. Pp. xv-xxxii. (Highly regarded essay on women's friendship and the friendship of Winifred Holtby and Vera Brittain.)

Kennard, Jean E. *Vera Brittain and Winifred Holtby: A Working Partnership.* Hanover, N.H.: University Press of New England, 1989.

Smith, Harold L., ed. *British Feminism in the Twentieth Century.* Amherst: University of Massachusetts Press, 1990. (Contains Deborah Gorham's essay "'Have We Really Rounded Seraglio Point?': Vera Brittain and Interwar Feminism." The reader will find the entire study useful in understanding the context of Brittain's feminist politics.)

FILM BASED ON THE WORK OF VERA BRITTAIN

Testament of Youth. BBC Television in association with London Film Productions, Ltd. Produced by Jonathan Powell. Directed by Moira Armstrong. Written by Elaine Morgan. Originally broadcast on BBC Television, 1979. Four videocassettes (fifty-five minutes each) released by A&E Home Video, New York, 1998.

RICHARD BROME

(c. 1590–1652)

Dan Brayton

RICHARD BROME, A playwright and poet of England's Caroline period (1625–1641), is not nearly as well known as he should be. Brome is generally considered a lesser dramatist coming at the end of a great age of drama. A playwright whose works were well received in a time when writers, and playwrights in particular, were numerous, Brome has never achieved the fame of contemporaries such as Ben Jonson, Francis Beaumont, John Fletcher, and John Webster. Brome is frequently described as the most prominent of the minor Stuart playwrights, and it is indisputable that his life and works remain in the shadow of both his mentor Ben Jonson (1573–1637), a towering literary figure, and the seventeenth-century English revolution that put an end to his career. Yet Brome's best works, such as *A Jovial Crew* and *The Antipodes,* are not only excellent examples of late Stuart comedy, they are also innovative, well-crafted, and entertaining snapshots of English cultural life in the Caroline period. It would be impossible to account for Brome's relative obscurity simply by reading his works and comparing them with those of his more famous contemporaries, as if fame were simply a matter of literary merit. It is not. Historical circumstances dictate a great deal of what posterity will think of any artist. Brome's reputation suffers from adverse historical circumstances, not from any lack of talent.

It was, more than anything else, history that relegated Brome to obscurity; specifically, the drastic historical events leading up to and initiating the seventeenth-century English Revolution. For the London stage was shut down during this era of warfare and social unrest, no longer just censored as it had been previously but banned altogether. In 1642, just when Brome was doing his best work, plays and playing-companies in England were suppressed. Brome's career was

over. He died a decade later, in 1652. Alexander Brome (no known relation), claimed of his namesake, "Poor he came into the world, and poor he went out" (in Hill, *Liberty against the Law,* p. 8). The closing of the London stage ended Brome's career as well as the greatest era of drama England had ever known. To understand Richard Brome, then, requires some knowledge of the literary, cultural, social, and even the political circumstances in which he worked and lived.

It is an amusing fact that Brome's name was occasionally spelled "Broome." References to him as "sweeping" by witty contemporaries such as Jonson inform us that his name was pronounced, like the household object, "broom." This is more than just an unimportant anecdote about pronunciation, however, for in a time when social status profoundly affected the opportunities available to the ambitious, Brome spent much of his early life as a servant. To be a servant was certainly not an insurmountable obstacle to an aspiring playwright, but it is especially significant that Brome worked in the shadow of his onetime master Ben Jonson, a towering figure in Jacobean drama whose works and reputation eclipsed those of his lesser-known servant and disciple. At the same time, Brome benefited greatly from his association with Jonson, and Brome's name will forever be associated in literary history with that of his more celebrated mentor. The careers of master and man were intertwined, and the reputation of the latter remains wrapped up in that of his social superior to this day.

LIFE AND CAREER

As is the case with many writers from the sixteenth and seventeenth centuries, we know relatively little about the life of Brome, and what we do know comes largely from the prefaces to his plays and anecdotes of other, often later, writers. The claim by Colley Cibber that Brome was educated at Eton is unreliable. So are many other bits of supposed data furnished by subsequent admirers of the era in which Brome wrote. But we do know that Brome got his start as a playwright by his association with Ben Jonson, one of the most important writers of the Jacobean period. Poet, playwright, classicist, and powerful personality, Jonson is one of the towering figures of Tudor and Stuart literature, second only to Shakespeare. Brome's association with such a figure is the defining feature of his career. For a writer whose greatest theme was the freedom of the simple life, Brome seems destined to have remained enslaved to his humble origins.

The first public notice taken of Richard Brome comes at the start of one of Jonson's best-known comedies. The induction to Jonson's *Bartholomew Fair* supplies us with the following humorous lines: "But for the whole play, will you have the truth on't?—I am looking lest the poet hear me, or his man, Master Brome, behind the arras—it is like to be a very conceited scurvy one, in plain English" (*The Alchemist and Other Plays,* p. 138). "The poet" in question is Jonson, who wrote the play. His "man," Brome, was clearly a close association. Moreover, this joking reference gives us a clue as to Brome's age. A young servant would be referred to as Jonson's "boy"; the fact that Brome is here called his "man" suggests that Brome must have been born well before the start of the seventeenth century. Scholars assume that he was born no later than 1590. Whatever his age, the fact that Brome was by 1614 sufficiently close to Ben Jonson to be associated with the well-known playwright on the stage, in the opening of one of Jonson's plays, suggests that master and man were both closely connected with the theater.

To be a servant in sixteenth and seventeenth century England could mean a number of things; servitude entailed a range of relationships, obligations, and issues of social status. Some servants, such as stewards who managed great estates, lived in privilege and were considered to hold relatively high social rank. Many stewards were

themselves gentlemen. Even aristocrats at court performed menial duties for their king. Others were little better than slaves, and the landscape of England in the first few decades of the seventeenth century was populated by large numbers of poor folk willing to do just about anything to get by. From apprentices to indentured servants to slaves, servants came in many varieties. Questions of belonging and of subordination were prominent in the social and political life of the time, as beggary, vagabondage, and masterlessness became increasingly pressing issues. At the same time that the poor were getting poorer and the rich richer, servitude began to take on new dimensions and a new importance in the cultural life of the English. For instance, in the reign of Charles I, when Brome wrote his plays, the monarch's household and retinue numbered in the thousands, a significant proportion of which was comprised of servants. This was an enormous increase over the number of people living at court only half a century earlier. Increasingly, disparities in social standing were coming under public scrutiny and contributing to the unrest that would lead to civil war.

Jonson's immense importance for Brome, both as a mentor and a literary model, can hardly be overstated. Jonson cultivated a number of friendships with younger men, many of them with literary ambitions nurtured by the association with such a literary lion. Jonson was known as a powerful personality and a dominant man, outgoing, learned, and given to carousing in taverns (he once killed a man in a duel and was briefly imprisoned for it). His young friends, some of whom can be accurately described as his disciples, were generally known (and still are) as the "Sons of Ben." In sixteenth- and seventeenth-century English culture, a young man who formed a close friendship with an older man, even if no blood-relation, was generally referred to as the older man's "son." While the Sons of Ben was a loosely affiliated group of friends and could not be described as an organized club, it was sufficiently cohesive to be something of a social phenomenon in literary history. Several of the Sons of Ben were at one time his servants. Brome's relationship to Jonson seems to have been one of the closest, and in 1623 a play called *A Fault in Friendship* (now lost) was licensed for performance at the Red Bull, a playing-house, naming Brome and "Young Jonson" as authors.

The truism that Tudor and Stuart plays were made "for the stage, not the page" is largely correct of English drama in the age of Shakespeare. The concept of authorship as it now exists and functions in the market and society was in an early state of development, and Brome's literary production makes sense only within the context of the London playing-companies, which were profitable business ventures. It was not until Jonson published the first folio edition of his *Works* in 1616 that authorship began to take the form that it has today. Before his monumental contribution to English letters, the relationship of a writer to his work did not entail the same notions of copyright and intellectual-property rights as are in place today, nor did writers of dramatic literature tend to oversee the publication of their own writings. Collaboration was commonplace and widely accepted in the production of plays. Publishers frequently pirated plays for a profit; then as now, selling books could be lucrative for a publisher. But then, unlike now, there was very little legal precedent or judicial apparatus in place for instituting and preserving the relationship between writer and text that nowadays constitutes authorship. Oftentimes one playwright would be hired to complete the unfinished work of another, and frequently a play written by one playwright, and belonging to a particular playing-company, would be modified by a different dramatist hired to augment the drama. Thomas Middleton, for instance, wrote a significant part of act 4 of Shakespeare's *Macbeth*.

Brome's plays, then, were written for the stage, not the page, and their author considered himself a playwright first and foremost. Brome's relationship to Jonson, which all evidence suggests was one of tutelage as well as servitude, can be seen as part and parcel of the culture of theater. Crucial for the popular and financial success of a playwright was the patronage of a prominent literary or public figure or an affiliation with a playing-company—an association of actors, playwrights, and what we would now call produc-ers working together to make plays as a commercial venture. Theater was a lucrative business, and many who participated in it did so for financial reasons. The playing-companies func-tioned within a system of patronage that defined players as servants to a powerful, generally aristocratic, figure, and association with success-ful players could mean the difference between survival and starvation.

The playing-companies were in fact considered by the aristocracy to be companies of servants, and they were named and treated accordingly. These companies took part in a system of patron-age in which actors and playwrights were known as the servants of great and powerful figures. Thus before 1603 Shakespeare's company was known as the Lord Chamberlain's Men and considered the servants of that powerful political figure. After 1603, with the death of Queen Elizabeth I and the coronation of James I, Shakespeare's playing company came under the patronage of the king himself and was known thenceforth as the King's Men or the King's Majesty His Servants. For a time in his profes-sional life as a playwright, Brome also wrote for the King's Men, with several of his plays being performed at the Globe and Blackfriars theaters, although he wrote for several other playing-companies as well. At the height of his career Brome wrote plays for Queen Henrietta's Men, of the Salisbury Court Theatre. Not only was he Jonson's "man": as an aspiring playwright and an associate of a highly successful one, Brome was a servant who moved from one realm of servitude to another.

For Brome to be Jonson's "man," then, meant a proximity and association with greatness that was both a form of subordination and a means of social and literary recognition. Brome's proxim-ity to Jonson suggests that the younger man fashioned himself on his mentor's model. Such is largely the case. Jonson made his name as a humorist and a humourist. The distinction is important. His first play, *Every Man in His Hu-mour* (1598), which included Shakespeare in the cast, satirized characters who are completely given to one mood or humour. The humours were black bile, yellow bile, phlegm, and blood, the bodily fluids that in medieval and early modern medical theory were believed to determine behavior and character type—choleric, melancholy, phlegmatic, or sanguinary. An imbalance of one humour inevitably led to excesses of certain types of behavior, nearly always bad. Like Jonson, Brome often created characters dominated by the humours. Jonson's avowed purpose in writing his plays, to point out and to discipline the vices of society, was partially Brome's as well, but Brome lacked his master's fearsome drive to expose immorality by caricaturing recognizable social types. It is fair to say that Brome's works tend to be lighter than Jonson's, and his representation of the humours tends to be used more for the sake of delighting than instructing.

Brome already had a foot in the door when he began his career because of his affiliation with Jonson, whose plays were performed by a number of playing-companies, including the King's Men. In February 1629, Brome's play *The Lovesick Maid* (now lost) was successfully performed by the King's Men, and he seems to have made a good deal of money from its positive reception. The fact that he was achieving theatrical success at a time when his onetime master, Jonson, was experiencing theatrical failure for his *New Inn* caused a falling-out of sorts between the two. An early draft of Jonson's "Ode to Himself" refers to Brome derogatorily: "Broomes sweepings doe as well / Thear as his Masters Meale" (quoted in Andrews, p. 7). Jonson, however, removed the specific mention of Brome for the published version of the poem. We do not know whether the two playwrights genuinely quarreled, only that Jonson was bitter about the success of his disciple when he himself had suffered a setback.

Whatever differences Jonson and Brome may have had were certainly rectified by 1632, when Jonson wrote commendatory verses for the preface of Brome's new play *The Northern Lasse*. The lines are dedicated "To my old Faithfull Seruant: and (by his continu'd Vertue) my louing Friend" (quoted in Andrews, p. 10). Jonson goes on in the same, warm language: "Now, you are got into a nearer roome, / Of Fellowship, professing my old Arts. / And you do doe them well,

with good applause, / Which you haue iustly gained from the Stage" (Andrews, p. 10). Clearly Jonson felt pride in the success of his "son." Brome's mentions of Jonson are similarly warm.

Following the success of *The Lovesick Maid,* Brome wrote plays for the Blackfriars, a popular indoor theater, and the Red Bull, an open-air theater. Starting in 1635 he contracted with a company known as the Salisbury Court Company, but his relations with that group were not always good. His play *The Sparagus Garden* brought considerable money to Salisbury Court and fame to Brome, and he contracted to write three plays a year for three years for the company. But the horrible outbreak of plague in 1636–1637 put an abrupt, if temporary, end to the success of both playing-companies and playwrights, and in 1640 legal proceedings transpired between Brome and Salisbury Court. These proceedings provide the merest glimpse into Brome's personal life. Brome had written for the playing-company Beeston's Boys, which he was legally forbidden to do according to the terms of his contract with the Salisbury Court players. But Salisbury Court had failed to pay him his contracted remuneration—no doubt as a means of belt-tightening in hard times. In the legal documents produced by the squabble between Brome and his employers, a family is mentioned as one reason for Brome's need to sell plays outside his contract. This fact, along with statements by contemporaries about Brome's poverty and humility suggest that our playwright, while a success, never achieved the financial independence of a dramatist like Shakespeare.

The last years of Brome's life were especially difficult ones for playwrights in general and for Brome in particular. In 1642, the group of religious and political reformers commonly known as the Puritans held sway in London. Suspicious of many forms of art and of plays in particular, they closed the theaters. Yet Brome continued to write plays. It has been suggested that he wrote *Juno in Arcadia* for the arrival in Oxford of the queen in 1643, although nothing is known for certain. Oxford during the Civil War remained for some time a loyalist stronghold, and numerous court poets and dramatists went there in hopes of continuing to ply their trade. The 1647 folio of the works of Beaumont and Fletcher contains commendatory verses by Brome, and in 1649 he edited a collection of elegiac poems on the death of Lord Hastings. But the London stage remained closed, and when it reopened with the restoration of the monarchy over a decade later, an entirely new age of theater was to begin.

Brome's surviving literary works comprise fifteen plays plus a coauthored one and a handful of poems. Only four of the plays were printed during Brome's lifetime, in quarto editions. A year after their author's death, in 1653, five more plays were printed together. In 1657 another Brome play was published in quarto, and in 1659 five more came out. The plague, consequent difficulties with the Salisbury Court Theatre, and the revolution clearly had an impact on the publication history of Brome's works.

Brome's skill as a dramatist lay in comedy, not tragedy, and his comedies owe a clear debt to Jonson in their attention to social vices such as pretentiousness and hypocrisy. But most of the plays are not slavishly derivative of Jonson. Where Jonson tends to be strongly, or even viciously, satirical, Brome tends to be lighthearted and whimsical. And while none of Brome's plays is particularly famous or canonical, several of them have gone through cycles of relative popularity. The plays are generally classed according to subgenres of comedy: comedies of manners, romantic comedies, and dramas of intrigue. But the generic distinctions assigned to these works by scholars are not as interesting as what ties them together: their plain language, social realism, and consistent scrutiny of the English social structure in a time of crisis.

In general Brome's works are characterized by their depiction of English characters as opposed to foreign ones (a great many Tudor and Stuart era plays are set in Mediterranean countries; Brome's generally are not) in familiar circumstances. Brome's characters frequently undergo some form of social experiment—a journey or a change in fortunes—by means of which Brome suggests the possibility of reform or social transformation. These works frequently contain a form of gentle social critique; they are thus of particular interest to anyone interested in seventeenth-century English social history, particularly the English Revolution. For Brome's plays examine the very vices and anxieties that precipitated the greatest social upheaval England had undergone since the Wars of the Roses.

THE ENGLISH REVOLUTION

The historical period known as the seventeenth-century English Revolution, or alternatively, the English Civil War, put an end to Brome's career and in all likelihood to his life. A brief account of the social and political forces that produced this conflict tells us much about the context in which Brome worked and the kind of world his works depict. For Caroline England was a nation in crisis, torn between an increasingly arrogant and entitled monarchy and aristocracy on the one hand and a burgeoning middle class on the other. As the English middle class became rapidly more wealthy and the landed aristocracy suffered financial losses, social antagonisms frequently manifested themselves in religious controversy. The middle classes were largely on the side of religious and political reform, while the upper classes were largely for the consolidation of wealth and power in the hands of the nation's hereditary rulers.

The cultural history of the period leading up to the conflict is revealing. Popular ballads about the legendary Robin Hood, who stole from the rich to give to the poor, were all the rage in England at the end of the sixteenth century and in the early decades of seventeenth. This fact tells us a good deal about the nature of the social woes afflicting England at the time, for the popularity of such tales is an index of the English public's yearning for social and economic change. As feudalism waned and capitalism came increasingly to the fore in economic life, the developing market economy transformed the rural landscape—and the social landscape—of the nation. A large and increasing number of displaced rural workers were being driven off the land by wealthy landowners intent on increasing the profits of their estates. Huge numbers of peasants, impoverished and unemployed, migrated from the country to the city, begging, stealing, and filling poorhouses to the bursting point. By the time Shakespeare and Jonson were writing for the stage, their audiences in and around London contained large numbers of recently relocated rural types, beggars, prostitutes, charlatans, apprentices, and other malcontents. Much of the subject matter of late Tudor and Stuart drama reflects the social condition of its audience, none more so than the works of Brome.

At the same time that the lower classes were suffering as never before, the upper and middle classes felt themselves to be in crisis as well. Numerous plays attest to the fact that the nobility's financial stability—traditionally based on land ownership—was decaying, largely because of the liquidity of wealth in a market economy. Meanwhile the burgeoning middle class had an increasingly large voice in national affairs, at least until an entitled and misguided monarch began to take steps to reduce the power of the bourgeoisie. When King Charles I dissolved Parliament in 1629, a mere four years after coming to the throne, the middle classes felt that their own political interests were being pointedly denied. The decade following the dissolution of Parliament was a period of brewing rebelliousness; it also happened to be the era in which Brome wrote most of his plays.

These were dangerous times. Dissent was dealt with harshly. For instance, the Puritan lawyer William Prynne was fined and had his ears cut off for his writings. The religious conflicts on the Continent, the result of the Protestant Reformation, had enormous repercussions in England. At the same time, famine, inflation, unemployment on a large scale, and rising rates of crime all threatened the stability of the social order. Discontent was on the rise generally, as were punitive measures directed at the socially down-and-out. The Puritans, who dominated the City of London, were largely hostile to the theater, which was frequently depicted as the Devil's work. Yet players and playwrights relied primarily upon paying audiences drawn from the city and the suburbs. The context in which Brome worked, then, was fraught with tension and the potential for danger—all the more so as civil war began to brew.

Rather than choosing to set his plays in historically or geographically far-removed lands in the manner of Shakespeare or Marlowe, Brome chose to write numerous plays about the vicissitudes of the seventeenth-century here and now. These plays are marked by a kind of social realism that is quite striking for the literary output of the period. Moreover, Brome dealt with the social antagonisms and political divisions of the day with remarkable directness. Accordingly we can look to Brome's plays for a sense of what the prerevolutionary period looked and sounded like, and we can see in his characters and plots an especially clear picture of many of the divisions and antagonisms of his era. His language, plain and unadorned in comparison with that of most of his contemporaries, and his settings and characters portray the world of seventeenth century England as vividly as any literature. Brome's works not only appeal to the historian for their depiction of seventeenth-century English life. They also appeal to the student of literature interested in how a plain, direct style of writing can achieve a kind of realism far before the advent of realism as a recognizable phenomenon in English literature. Brome represents a new kind of literary emergence, the playwright of social realism, which separates him from his Stuart era predecessors and from his Restoration era successors. For the representation of English life in the seventeenth century, Brome stands alone.

BROME AS POET

Before turning to Brome's plays, it would be well to take notice of his talents as a poet in order to get a sense of the distinctness of his style. Playwright and poet were not mutually exclusive occupations in Tudor and Stuart England, as the careers of Shakespeare, Jonson, and many other writers attest, but Brome resolutely defined himself as a playwright. This form of self-fashioning was a humble one: for the most part, Brome did not publish poems, as Shakespeare did, or try to make his name as a poet.

Nevertheless he wrote poetry, some of it excellent. The songs and poems within his plays display a great deal of intelligence, talent, and learning. In an age of baroque eloquence and metaphysical adornment, Brome's verse is notable for its elegance, restraint, and taut simplicity.

Many of Brome's plays contain poems of a high order. Consider "Humility," from *The Northern Lasse:*

Nor Love nor Fate dare I accuse
For that my love did me refuse,
But oh! Mine own unworthiness
That durst presume so mickle bliss.
It was too much for me to love
A man so like the gods above:
An angel's shape, a saint-like voice,
Are too divine for human choice.

Oh had I wisely given my heart
For to have loved him but in part;
Sought only to enjoy his face,
Or any one peculiar grace
Of foot, of hand, of lip, or eye—
I might have lived where now I die:
But I, presuming all to choose,
Am now condemned all to lose.

Written in rhymed couplets of iambic tetrameter, this poem uses a simple form to express a simple lament, voiced by a female persona who has fallen head-over-heels for a man she cannot have, but it does so with grace and elegance. The verse form matches the sentiment perfectly; nothing seems forced. The directness of the speaker's voice easily evokes the persona of the Northern Lass herself, a character much admired by Brome's contemporaries. While readers today frequently find themselves at a loss as to why such a character would be appealing (she lacks depth, is somewhat coarsely drawn, and tends toward caricature), such verses as those above demonstrate Brome's ability to create the effect of personhood—to "personate," in early modern terms, a complex emotional state in simple, well-crafted verses.

A Jovial Crew, which undoubtedly contains some of Brome's finest writing, has several lovely songs. These too are deceptively simple, seemingly straightforward expressions of joy when in fact they are sophisticated verse constructions. "The Merry Beggars," for example, captures the sentiment of freedom and delight in nature that runs through the play:

Come, come away! The spring,
By every bird that now can sing,
Or chirp a note, doth now invite
Us forth to taste of his delight,
In field, in grove, on hill, in dale;
But above all the nightingale,
Who in her sweetness strives t'outdo
The loudness of the hoarse cuckoo.
"Cuckoo," cries he; "Jug, jug, jug," sings she;
From bush to bush, from tree to tree:
Why in one place then tarry we?

Come away! Why do we stay?
We have no debt or rent to pay;
No bargains or accounts to make,
Nor land or lease to let or take:
Or if we had, should that remore us
When all the world's our own before us,
And where we pass and make resort,
It is our kingdom and our court?
"Cuckoo," cries he; "Jug, jug, jug," sings she;
From bush to bush, from tree to tree:
Why in one place then tarry we?

(1.1.473-492)

Again we are struck by the elegance and seeming simplicity of the lines and by the perfect match between poetic form and sentiment. Couplets in iambic tetrameter create an effect of minimalism, while the repetition of "come away" and of the three-line refrain creates the effect of an echo between the two stanzas. Like the songbirds about which he writes, Brome offers a tantalizingly graceful statement about the sense of freedom produced by the changing of the seasons. The poet seems to vie with the birds to find the perfect form of expression with which to call for an escape from care. Here and elsewhere Brome crafts subtly persuasive lines that appeal not by the force of complex rhetorical forms but by the perfect marriage of tone, verse form, and theme.

Not all of Brome's poetry is of such a high standard as the two poems quoted above. Some of his verse can be simplistic, and it frequently lacks the force and beauty of a Jonson or a

Shakespeare. Brome's writing has been called coarse; at times, this assessment is accurate. The plays, too, vary in quality, and their reception in his lifetime does not always accord with the judgment of today's readers. His most successful works were not necessarily his best. Accordingly the summaries that follow focus mainly on *A Jovial Crew* and *The Antipodes,* the two plays that are most frequently read nowadays and most worthy of representing Brome to modern readers.

A JOVIAL CREW

Brome's greatest play, *A Jovial Crew* is a work that reflects many of the most pressing issues affecting Britons at the outbreak of the seventeenth-century revolution. Issues of wealth, property, liberty, vagabondage, beggary, social class, and the sadness of the times pervade the play. Liberty versus constraint, wealth versus poverty, age versus youth, property versus the open road—these are the comedy's major themes. A delightful romp that playfully questions the values, institutions, and practices of the English landed gentry, *A Jovial Crew* is a celebration of life on the road, an investigation of social inequity, and a contribution to utopian literature.

The plot begins at the household of the character Oldrents, an aged squire and father of the two lead female characters, Rachel and Meriel. Oldrents is, as his name indicates, a wealthy landowner. He represents the positive attributes of the wealthy country gentry; for the era, he is surprisingly uncorrupted, not given to the ubiquitous practice of rent-racking. The phrase "old rents" referred at this time to the rental prices that predated an era of inflated living expenses; Oldrents himself is one who charges his tenants the same old rent that they have always paid and is revered by them in return. When we consider that rents rose more than threefold in the course of the seventeenth century, it is evident that Oldrents represents goodness because he refuses to participate in the new, get-rich-by-any-means culture of the period.

Oldrents also appears, at the start of the play, to represent an idealized past. The bearer of bygone values, he is a good-natured squire who treats others well. As his friend Hearty puts it,

Do you not live
Free, out of law, or grieving any man?
Are you not th'only rich man lives unenvied?
Have you not all the praises of the rich,
And prayers of the poor? Did ever any
Servant, or hireling, neighbor, kindred curse you,
Or wish one minute shorten'd of your life?
Have you one grudging tenant? Will they not all
Fight for you? Do they not teach their children
And make 'em, too, pray for you morn and evening,
And in their graces, too, as duly as
For king and realm? The innocent things would think
They ought not eat else.

(1.1.65–77)

Here, as elsewhere in the play, the blank verse (unrhymed lines of iambic pentameter) is direct and powerful. In cataloging the virtues of his friend, Hearty paints a picture of the moral and social ideal of the gentry. Clearly Oldrents exemplifies the kind of ideal moral standard that many in the Caroline era lamented as a thing of the past. His response to Hearty speaks of his faith in humanity and goodness of heart: he modesty replies, "'tis their goodness" (1.1.78). In other words, it is the goodness of his social subordinates that makes them think so well of him. In fact, as Hearty informs Oldrents, it is the squire's fair treatment of others and his refusal to see the profit motive as the highest goal in life that puts him in such high estimation by all.

But Oldrents is a melancholy old man rooted to one place, bound by his wealth and property and accounts. He also suffers under the belief, fostered by a prophet, that his two daughters will become beggars. In contrast, his steward Springlove, around whom the entire plot revolves, is a free-spirited yet competent household manager who longs, with the arrival of spring, to escape to the open road and live carefree with troops of beggars. The action quickly moves away from the Oldrents household when Springlove turns in his yearly accounts to his master and begs for permission to go on a lengthy summer vacation on the road.

Oldrents dislikes the idea of his steward living like a beggar, even temporarily, but he is too indulgent to prevent him from going. Springlove thus takes his leave and joins a troop of merry beggars. He is entirely at ease with the beggars because he has supported them with his own and Oldrents' charity. He speaks their language, called "canting," and enjoys their free and easy lifestyle. Springlove is a prince of beggars and readily identifiable with Brome himself. Like Brome, Springlove is both a servant and an accomplished professional, at home in both the world of servitude and the world of gentlemen. Like Brome, too, Springlove is a master of language and a kind of stage director who controls the plot of the play.

The theme of escaping from the constraints of wealth to enjoy the freedom of beggars develops when Oldrents' two daughters, Meriel and Rachel, and their suitors, Vincent and Hilliard, also decide to take a vacation from the life of the rural gentry by joining a band of beggars for a whimsical holiday. The four of them, along with Springlove, share a desire for liberty and the open road that puts them in opposition to the representatives of property, Oldrents and his friend Squire Hearty. In temporarily sharing the fate of the vagabonds they normally support with alms, they transgress boundaries of class and partake of a way of life that they would normally be expected to hold in disdain. For a time, then, much as in a Shakespearean romantic comedy, they move to a "green world"—the phrase used to describe plays that set up a sharp contrast between a "green world" of pure play and the politically determined life of the court and the city.

The play vacillates between scenes that depict the beggar's life as a utopia of freedom and ease with scenes that suggest its hardship and hazards. Hilliard enthuses, "Beggars! They are the only people can boast the benefit of a free state, in the full enjoyment of liberty, mirth, and ease, having all things in common and nothing wanting of nature's whole provision within the reach of their desires" (2.1.2–5). In a similar vein, Meriel later describes beggars as

The only free men of a commonwealth;
Free above scot-free; that observe no law,
Obey no governor, use no religion

But what they draw from their own ancient custom,
Or constitute themselves, yet are no rebels.
(2.1.172–176)

The theme of the commonwealth of beggars as a "free state" is echoed in a number of the songs sung by the beggars themselves. Springlove, for instance, is treated to the following song shortly after his taste for wandering has been whetted by the sound of a nightingale:

From hunger and cold, who lives more free,
    Or who more richly clad than we?
Our bellies are full; our flesh is warm;
    And, against pride, our rags are a charm.
Enough is our feast, and for tomorrow
Let rich men care; we feel no sorrow.
    No sorrow, no sorrow, no sorrow, no sorrow.
    Let rich men care; we feel no sorrow.
(1.1.340–346)

This little ditty, reminiscent of the songs in Shakespeare's comedies, neatly encapsulates the appeal of being a beggar for the likes of Springlove. Simplicity and lack of pretension are advanced as the ideal way of life. Yet the song seems to protest too much, for the words "no sorrow" are repeated six times, suggesting, perhaps, the opposite of what the beggars are claiming of their own condition. As ensuing action will demonstrate, a beggar's life is not all fun and carefree feasting.

Indeed, the freedom and felicity found by the out-of-caste young people are short-lived and equivocal, for Brome reveals that to have nothing in Caroline England can be quite uncomfortable. As the plot progresses, the play demonstrates that beggary entails a good deal more negative liberty than positive liberty: the beggars are *free from* many of the constraints of the landed gentry, but they are not *free to* partake of much in the way of food, clothing, or shelter. Various "gentle," or upper-class, characters try to take advantage of the beggars and would-be beggars, and we are shown scenes in which insult, assault, and attempted rape are directed at the poor by the more fortunate. As the eminent historian Christopher Hill has written of *A Jovial Crew*, "we are left with a vision of freedom from property-ownership as well as the satirical comparison between courtiers and beggars. The irony in the beggars' claim that lack of property was true freedom, coming at a time when Parliamentarians were insisting on the intimate connection between liberty and property, must be deliberate" (*Liberty against the Law,* p. 5). It is indeed possible to read the play as an extended critique of private property and the institutions and practices associated with it.

Beggary is not the only issue of social subordination that Brome writes into this play. Servitude also figures prominently, not only in the figure of Springlove but in numerous interactions. Gentlemen refer to themselves as the servants of those whom they challenge to duels; a young woman spurns her wealthy suitor and runs off with a household servant; in a comical scene in act 4, a gentleman calling on Oldrents is forced to bide his time as a series of household servants is introduced and their functions described. Clearly Brome takes seriously comedy's traditional function as an examination of social relations, particularly hierarchical ones. He makes us laugh at social distinctions. We cannot help but suspect that Brome's own status as a servant-turned-playwright had much to do with his choice of subject matter and intimate knowledge of the functions and psychology of servants.

But the plot has a richness that makes the play more than an oblique political or social commentary. A number of stock subplots, with scenes of courtship, a beggars' marriage, an elopement, an attempted rape, and a near-dual, are interwoven with the main plot concerning Springlove and the two couples that accompany him. Eventually these plots come together in a comedic ending that reunites families, friends, and the entire social order. These disparate elements of both propertied and begging society are ultimately reunited through theater, which Brome seems to suggest has the power to renew our acquaintance with one another and with ourselves.

The climax of *A Jovial Crew* is brought about by a play-within-a-play put on by the band of beggars, which includes Springlove, Meriel, Rachel, Vincent, and Hilliard. This band is characterized by downward social mobility, for its regular members consist of a former lawyer, soldier, poet, and courtiers as well as the beggar-priest Patrico. The poet proposes utopia as the theme for their play: "I would present a commonwealth: Utopia, / With all her branches and consistencies" (4.2.179–180). When Rachel volunteers to play Utopia and asks "who must be my branches," the poet replies, "The country, the city, the court, and the camp, epitomiz'd and personated by a gentleman, a merchant, a courtier, and a soldier" (4.2.182–184). It will be a play made for and by the beggars themselves. As it happens, the play depicts the opening of *A Jovial Crew* itself, complete with Oldrents, Springlove (played by himself), and the four wayward young people (also played by themselves).

In the end it is revealed that Springlove is Oldrents' son, and also that Oldrents is the legal heir to his estate through his mother's line as well as his father's—a lucky revelation since it turns out that his paternal grandfather had come by the land illicitly. All told, it is clear that the vice-ridden social order is dominated by people of "gentle" status in need of moral reform. Thus both theater and the commonwealth of beggars are presented as forms of utopia, alternative worlds that act as foils for social norms and by means of which Brome engages in pointed social critique. His detailed portrait of social and economic relations, and his in-depth depiction of the lives, histories, and language of everyday English types generally not represented on the stage, add much to the social realism of Caroline drama and make *A Jovial Crew* a highly original play.

THE ANTIPODES

The other of Brome's plays that is frequently read and taught is *The Antipodes,* written in 1636 for a new company of boy actors commonly known as "Beeston's Boys," who performed at the Cockpit Theatre. The conditions of this play's production seem to mark its subject matter. A particularly severe outbreak of plague devastated London between April 1636 and December 1637. This situation is referred to at the start of the play as "time's calamity" (1.1.4). These were difficult days for dramatists and players and particularly for Brome, whose weekly salary of fifteen pounds was cut off for some months. Perhaps such a context helps to account for the play's treatment of travel literature and a young man's obsessive curiosity about foreign locales, for surely many Londoners dreamed of escaping the hard realities of their lives for the wonders of the exotic.

Like *A Jovial Crew, The Antipodes* presents a topsy-turvy world, and again we encounter utopian themes and a critical commentary on the social order of Caroline England. Some of the subject matter of *The Antipodes* is strikingly modern, in particular its examination of what we could today call a psychological complex or neurosis and its medical treatment. *The Antipodes* contributes to the large and fascinating body of literature on madness produced in early modern England. Plays such as Shakespeare's *Hamlet,* John Webster's *The Duchess of Malfi,* and John Marston's *The Changeling* examine the nature and meanings of madness. Unlike these earlier works, *The Antipodes* takes up this theatrical scrutiny of madness and sanity as the material for comedy, not tragedy.

The plot revolves around a young man named Peregrine, who suffers from a peculiar affliction, "a most deep melancholy," in the words of his father, the character Joyless (1.2.14). Joyless, whose name tells us much about him and the rest of his family, seeks the help of Doctor Hughball, a physician renowned for his expertise in the "medicine of the mind" (1.1.24). The plot then follows the treatment of Peregrine and the rest of the Joyless family for their various mental problems. To follow the logic of Doctor Hughball's treatment, and to understand the nature of the Joyless family's afflictions, it is necessary to know something of melancholy in Renaissance England.

Melancholy, also called melancholia, was a popular affliction in Tudor and Stuart England. While it may seem strange to describe a mental problem as fashionable, such was the case, as numerous medical, pseudo-medical, and fictional works about melancholia attest. Shakespeare's Prince Hamlet, for instance, suffers from melancholy, as do many other protagonists of the London stage. Robert Burton's immense tome *The Anatomy of Melancholy* (1621), a voluminous compendium of lore that describes, anatomizes, and digresses at length on all matters related to the affliction, was popular reading among the learned in Brome's day. Several characters in *The Antipodes* suffer from symptoms—and receive treatment—in exactly the form described by Burton, and there can be no doubt that Burton's work influenced Brome considerably in the characterization and plot of the play.

Peregrine's particular form of melancholy has been caused by too much reading and a complete suspension of disbelief. As his father explains,

In tender years he always lov'd to read
Reports of travels and of voyages;
And when young boys like him would tire themselves
With sports and pastimes, and restore their spirits
Again by meat and sleep, he would whole days
And nights (sometimes by stealth) be on such books
As might convey his fancy round the world.

...

    When he grew up towards twenty,
His mind was all on fire to be abroad;
Nothing but travel still was all his aim;
There was no voyage or foreign expedition
Be said to be in hand, but he made suit
To be made one in it.

                    (1.2.34–40, 42–45)

Peregrine's love of travel literature has transformed itself into a wanderlust that his parents seek to cure by marrying him off to Martha. Unfortunately for both young people, Peregrine's condition prevents him from consummating the marriage, which in turn drives Martha to a form of madness. Such is the condition of double madness that Doctor Hughball is called upon to cure.

Hughball has read his Burton well and demonstrates a familiarity with the intricacies of melancholy. He agrees to cure the members of the Joyless family and immediately recognizes in Peregrine's obsessions with "monsters, / Pigmies, and giants, apes, and elephants, / Griffins, and crocodiles, men upon women, / And women upon men" a dangerous literary taste (1.3.7–10). Like *Don Quixote,* a work that it resembles in its depiction of folly and the consequences of an overindulgence in imaginative literature, *The Antipodes* is a work of metafiction—fiction about fiction. In the great novel by Cervantes (which clearly influenced the play), the protagonist has become delusional from too much exposure to a particular kind of literature. Unlike Quixote, who has read too many chivalric romances and, as a consequence, mistakes the everyday world of late-sixteenth-century Spain for the world of chivalry, Peregrine in *The Antipodes* suffers from an affinity for the influential travel writings of John Mandeville (1300–1372).

The Voyages and Travels of Sir John Mandeville, Knight (c. 1356) was an immensely popular work among readers in Brome's day, as it had been for over two centuries. At times read as travel literature, at times as a work of fanciful pseudo–travel literature, this text greatly influenced the European picture of the world outside of Europe. By depicting Peregrine as a man driven mad by an obsession with things exotic, Brome pokes fun at both Mandeville and those who believe his preposterous tales of exoticism by showing the course of the young man's treatment for madness.

The specific treatment used by Doctor Hughball and his wealthy patron Letoy, a "fantastic" gentleman of eccentric taste, is a play-within-a-play put on by Letoy's servants at his eccentric household. Peregrine and his wife Martha, along with several other characters, are invited to watch a play about the far side of the world. But Peregrine has no idea that he is watching a play and has been tricked into thinking that he has in fact made the voyage to the antipodes. Thus the audience is presented with the spectacle of characters who are themselves watching a play. The audience is invited to laugh at the uncritical commentary of these deluded or simpleminded theatergoers, and Brome lards the performance with references to current events in London.

The setting of the play-within-a-play, the opposite side of the world from England, is a place of inversion, where conventional social relations are turned on their heads. As the servant-turned-actor Quailpipe puts it, "certes, my lord, it is a most apt conceit, / The comedy being the world turn'd upside down" (2.1.11–12). The doctor takes pains to explain to Peregrine that "this, sir, is Anti-London. That's the Antipodes / To the grand city of our nation: / Just the same people, language, and religion, / But contrary manners" (2.4.39–41). The motif of the world turned upside-down, nearly a cultural obsession in the decades leading up to the English Revolution, operates on several levels in *The Antipodes*. First, Peregrine's obsession with the far side of the world introduces inversion as a theme, for he longs for a place where all is the opposite of the here and now. Next, Doctor Hughball describes the opposite side of the globe as an inverted Europe and gives Peregrine a chance to believe he has entered this world. Third, the festive atmosphere created by the play-within-a-play at Letoy's household allows for all kinds of social insubordination, with wives countermanding the wishes of their husbands and talking openly of cheating on them, servants talking back to their masters, and players and audience engaging each other in conversation.

For most of the second act and all of the third and fourth we are shown a series of exchanges between social types that invert conventional hierarchies. Thus, in the antipodes, women have sovereignty over men and assume the superior sexual position; lawyers are honest and refuse money for their services; poets are Puritans; working folk are learned and well-spoken; courtiers have the speech and manners of ruffians; the sick advise their physicians on matters of health; the old are unruly and addicted to low forms of entertainment while the young are morally upright; and cuckoldry is treated as a good thing. Peregrine, initially delighted by this state of affairs, makes himself king of the antipodes by staging something of a coup d'etat. He attacks the actors and takes the stage, joining the performance and entering the kingdom of his fantasy. Such is Hughball's plan.

This state of affairs lends itself to numerous comic gags, many of which rely upon the audience's knowledge of current events at court and in London. The rivalry between sedan-carriers and watermen, for instance, provides material for some jokes. The "after you my dear Alphonse" courtesy of the Waterman and the Sedanman in the fourth act would undoubtedly have been hilarious to a contemporary audience. By inverting conventional social hierarchies, with well-spoken menials and boorish aristocrats, the antipodean world allows Brome a perfect vehicle for satire. It also works as a tonic for Peregrine's mind, which begins to balk at the monstrosities in his newfound kingdom.

Most consistently, Brome exploits conventional notions of sex and gender to get laughs. In the upside-down world women beat up men on the street and make aggressive sexual advances that men coyly reject; a man-scold is ducked in water (as women were in Stuart England) for not holding his tongue. Brome makes the most of the latter episode, offering such humorous passages as the following spoken by the man-scold:

Was ever harmless creature so abus'd?
To be drenched under water, to learn dumbness
Amongst the fishes, as I were forbidden
To use the natural members I was born with,
And of them all the chief that man takes pleasure in,
The tongue! Oh me, accursed wretch!

(4.5.17–22)

Yet while Brome seems to revel in the traditional topics and tricks of comedy, he also takes every opportunity to scrutinize the shortcomings of Caroline England—its traditions, social structure, and fashions. This is comedy with an edge.

Gradually Hughball's treatment begins to work. Confronted with a preposterous series of social inversions, Peregrine asks, "Will you make me mad?" To this the good doctor replies, "We are sail'd, I hope, / Beyond the line of madness" (4.9.55–56). Eventually Peregrine rebels against a world of inversion and is assimilated into the normative world of Caroline London. So too with his father and the other afflicted characters: the chaotic situation at the house of Letoy and the medically prescribed theatrical set pieces therein bring all the characters to a better sense of themselves.

The extended playacting scenes also provide Brome with ample material for commentary on the institution of theater itself. The character Byplay is known as an improviser, and the improvisational nature of Doctor Hughball's theatrical cure relies upon the quick adaptation of lines and scenes to sustain Peregrine's illusions. It is by means of theater, Brome suggests, that we look awry at the world and see the difference between sanity and insanity. Good acting, and good theater, does more than simply entertain: it reforms the social order and institutes sanity. Brome's dramaturgy seems driven by a need to push the limits of conventional social and theatrical roles to the breaking point in order to make a strong distinction between sanity and convention.

THE NORTHERN LASSE

The romantic comedy *The Northern Lasse* was not the first play that Brome wrote, but it is the earliest one to survive. Printed in 1632 and 1635 while the author lived and again in 1663 after his death, this was Brome's most popular play, and it gave his career momentum. There is no space here to describe the play at length, and it holds less interest for modern readers than it had for Brome's contemporaries, largely because the eponymous lass has been superseded by any number of similar, lovelorn heroines. The playwrights Thomas Dekker (1572?–1632?) and John Ford (1586–1639?) found the heroine Constance admirable, but today she lacks the appeal she once had. Constance speaks with a heavily drawn northern accent, which in Brome's day meant a somewhat quaint and antiquated English that his London audiences would immediately have recognized as such. She is also a relatively undeveloped character, less appealing, for instance, that the characters in *A Jovial Crew*. Nonetheless, some of the poetry in the play is lovely, and Brome caught enough of the zeitgeist of his age with this play to launch his career.

THE SPARAGUS GARDEN

While not one of Brome's greatest plays, the comedy of manners *The Sparagus Garden* is interesting for the way it recalls the plays of Thomas Dekker, and for its comical treatment of contemporary English behavior and customs. Dekker wrote city comedy—plays that reveal much about life in the London in his era. *The Sparagus Garden*, too, tells us something about English customs of the era, and it does so with some of the spiritedness and realism of Dekker's works. The title describes the setting, a garden where asparagus is both grown and eaten (as was usual in the period). The inevitable modern tendency to find something phallic in such a title is borne out, in fact, by the historical fact that such gardens had become socially unsavory places, so to speak. As in most of Brome's works, several plot strands are woven together, including one in which two men attempt to bring an end to a long-standing grudge between two old men by marrying the daughter of one to the son of another. The scheme fails, and in the immediately ensuing scenes the two schemers try to make amends with the young man who has been instrumental in their plot. In another series of scenes, a young man from the country, ignorant of city ways, is given comical advice on how to play the part of a gentleman. Brome creates some genuinely funny moments in this plotline and reveals a lively wit. Once again, the play is most interesting for its vivid depiction of social practices in Stuart London, not for its great originality or poetic achievement.

THE CITY WITT

The City Witt; or, The Woman Wears the Breeches (1632) is a lively comedy of manners that appeals to modern readers because, unlike many of Brome's plays, it does not attempt to weave together disparate themes and plot strands. There is a cohesiveness to this play that is, generally speaking, uncharacteristic of Brome, and its lightheartedness makes for highly entertaining reading. These traits also made for pleasurable viewing for Brome's audiences, as the prologue written for a revival attests. The Jonsonian spirit of correcting social vice and hypocrisy is evident in this play.

The name of the play's protagonist, Mr. Crasy, misrepresents him, for his character is marked by kindness and affability. He is not so much crazy as a figure of folly in the classical, Erasmian sense. When times become difficult for him and

he appeals to his friends for help, they fail to come to his aid. He therefore decides to vanish and returns in disguise in order to hold his onetime friends to account for their behavior. The theme of contempt for the worldly pretensions of money and rank, so evident in *A Jovial Crew,* runs through this earlier play as well. Crasy is an honest man in dishonest times, a tradesman who scorns the newfangled ways of a market economy. His despicable mother-in-law, Mistress Pyannet Sneakup, represents all that he does not; she is the worst kind of social climber and a vicious shrew. Brome's celebration of Crasy's honesty and unpretentiousness make us sympathize with the protagonist throughout, and the tightness and care of the plotting, along with the surprising denouement, reveal a level of craftsmanship not shared by all of Brome's works.

THE ENGLISH MOOR

Originally published with four other plays in 1659, seven years after Brome's death, *The English Moor* was performed by Queen Henrietta's Men at Salisbury Court between 1637 and 1639—about the same time as *The Antipodes.* This is not a great play, but it contains a number of features that demonstrate Brome's shaping of the materials available to him. In particular, city comedy and court masques influence the form of this play, the former contributing to one of the plotlines and the latter to both a subplot and a play-within-a-play. *The English Moor* owes a clear debt to Thomas Middleton, whose city comedies mix sexual and financial exchanges in a characteristically cynical way. It also owes a debt to Jonson's play *Epicoene* and to his court masques, in particular *The Masque of Blackness.*

CONCLUSION

Among the many notable Stuart-era dramatists, Richard Brome stands out for his unadorned language, social realism, and playful comedic imagination. At his worst a rough imitator of Jonson, Brome was also, at his best, capable of writing highly original works characterized by a whimsy and utopian playfulness that Jonson never achieved. For the student of seventeenth-century English social or cultural history, and for anyone interested in the trajectory of Tudor and public drama from its inception in the 1570s to its abrupt end in the early 1640s, Brome's career represents a fascinating terminus. To some extent his work bridges the dramatic sensibility of the Stuart era with that of the Restoration; to an even greater extent it stands out for its direct commentary on quotidian life in early modern England. While Brome's works are largely neglected today, the best of them, *A Jovial Crew* and *The Antipodes,* deserve to be on syllabi in courses on Stuart drama, utopian literature, and the literature of social realism. As current scholars reassess the drama of early modern England, they would do well to recuperate Brome as a great but neglected writer. More space should be created for him in anthologies, and no doubt more will.

Selected Bibliography

WORKS OF RICHARD BROME

The Dramatic Works of Richard Brome Containing Fifteen Comedies Now First Collected in Three Volumes. 3 vols. London: John Pearson, 1873. Reprint, New York: AMS Press, 1966.

A Jovial Crew. Regents Renaissance Drama Series. Edited by Ann Haaker. London: Edward Arnold, 1968; Lincoln: University of Nebraska Press, 1968.

The Antipodes. Regents Renaissance Drama Series. Edited by Ann Haaker. London: Edward Arnold, 1968; Lincoln: University of Nebraska Press, 1966.

CRITICAL AND BIOGRAPHICAL STUDIES

Andrews, Clarence E. *Richard Brome: A Study of His Life and Works.* Yale Studies in English, vol. 46. New York: Henry Holt, 1913.

Bilot, Michel. "Alteration in a Commonwealth: Disturbing Voices in Caroline Drama." *Cahiers Elisabethains: Late Medieval and Renaissance Studies* 47:79–86 (April 1995).

Clark, Ira. *Professional Playwrights: Massinger, Ford, Shirley, and Brome.* Lexington: University Press of Kentucky, 1992.

Gaby, Rosemary. "Of Vagabonds and Commonwealths: *Beggar's Bush, A Jovial Crew,* and *The Sisters.*" *SEL: Studies in English Literature* 34:401–424 (spring 1994).

Haaker, Ann. "The Plague, the Theater, and the Poet." *Renaissance Drama* n.s. 1:283–306 (1968).

Ingram, R. W. "The Musical Art of Richard Brome's Comedies of Manners: A Re-Interpretation." Ph.D. dissertation, University of Wisconsin, 1955.

Kaufmann, Ralph J. *Richard Brome: Caroline Playwright.* New York: Columbia University Press, 1961.

Kiehl, Ellen Dutton. "The Comedy of Richard Brome: A Study of Comic Form and Function." Ph.D. dissertation, State University of New York at Albany, 1977.

Leslie, Marina. "Antipodal Anxieties: Joseph Hall, Richard Brome, Margaret Cavendish, and the Cartographies of Gender." *Genre: Forms of Discourse and Culture* 30:51–78 (spring–summer 1997).

Panek, Leroy L. "Asparagus and Brome's *The Sparagus Garden.*" *Modern Philology: A Journal Devoted to Research in Medieval and Modern Literature* 68:362–363 (1971).

Sanders, Julie. "Beggar's Commonwealths and the Pre–Civil War Stage: Suckling's *The Goblins,* Brome's *A Jovial Crew,* and Shirley's *The Sisters.*" *Modern Language Review* 97:1–14 (January 2002).

Shaw, Catherine. *Richard Brome.* Boston: Twayne, 1980.

Spivak, Charlotte. "Alienation and Illusion: The Play-within-a-Play on the Caroline Stage." *Medieval and Renaissance Drama in England: An Annual Gathering of Research, Criticism, and Reviews* 4:195–210 (1989).

Steggle, Matthew. "Richard Brome's First Patron." *Notes and Queries* 49 (247), no. 2:259–261 (June 2002).

———. "Redating *A Jovial Crew.*" *Review of English Studies* 53:365–372 (August 2002).

Swinburne, Algernon Charles. "Richard Brome." *Fortnightly* 304:500–507 (1892).

BACKGROUND

THEATER HISTORY

Aylmer, G. E. *The King's Servants: The Civil Service of Charles I, 1625–1642.* London: Routledge; New York: Columbia University Press, 1961.Bentley, Gerald Eades. *The Jacobean and Caroline Stage.* 7 vols. Oxford: Clarendon, 1941–1969.

———. *The Profession of Dramatist in Shakespeare's Time, 1590–1642.* Princeton, N.J.: Princeton University Press, 1971.

Evans, G. Blakemore, ed. *Elizabethan-Jacobean Drama: The Theatre in Its Time.* New York: New Amsterdam, 1990.

Davis, Joe Lee. *The Sons of Ben: Jonsonian Comedy in Caroline England.* Detroit: Wayne State University Press, 1967.

Chambers, E. K. *The Elizabethan Stage.* 4 vols. Oxford: Oxford University Press, 1923.

Greg, W. W. *A Bibliography of the English Printed Drama to the Restoration.* Vol. 2. London: Oxford University Press, 1951.

Gurr, Andrew. *Playgoing in Shakespeare's London.* Cambridge: Cambridge University Press, 1997.

Hill, Christopher. *The Century of Revolution, 1603–1714.* New York: Norton, 1961.

———. *God's Englishman: Oliver Cromwell and the English Revolution.* New York: Harper & Row, 1970.

———. *Liberty against the Law: Some Seventeenth-Century Controversies.* New York: Penguin, 1996.

Jonson, Benjamin. *The Alchemist and Other Plays.* Edited by Gordon Campbell. Oxford: Oxford University Press, 1995.

———. *Bartholomew Fair.* In *The Complete Plays of Ben Jonson.* Edited by G. A. Wilkes. Oxford: Oxford University Press, 1982.

———. *Ben Jonson's Plays and Masques.* Edited by Robert M. Adams. New York: Norton, 1979.

Stone, Lawrence. *The Causes of the English Revolution, 1529–1642.* London: Routledge, 1986.

Underdown, David. *Revel, Riot, and Rebellion: Popular Politics and Culture in England, 1603–1660.* Oxford: Clarendon Press, 1985.

RENAISSANCE ENGLISH LITERATURE AND CULTURE

Agnew, Jean-Christophe. *Worlds Apart: The Market and The Theater in Anglo-American Thought, 1550–1750.* Cambridge and New York: Cambridge University Press, 1986.

Foucault, Michel. *Madness and Civilization: A History of Insanity in the Age of Reason.* New York: Random House, 1988.

———. *The Order of Things: An Archaeology of the Human Sciences.* New York: Random House, 1990.

THE ENGLISH CIVIL WAR

Hill, Christopher. *The World Turned Upside Down: Radical Ideas During the English Revolution.* New York: Penguin, 1972.

———. *The English Bible and the Seventeenth Century Revolution.* New York: Penguin, 1993.

Manning, Roger B. *Village Revolts: Social Protest and Popular Disturbances in England, 1509–1640.* Oxford: Clarendon Press, 1988.

Richardson, R. C. *Town and Countryside in the English Revolution.* Manchester, U.K.: Manchester University Press, 1992.

Stone, Lawrence. *The Crisis of the Aristocracy.* London and New York: Oxford University Press, 1967.

DOUGLAS DUNN

(1942–)

Gerry Cambridge

IN THE UNSPOKEN hierarchy of living Scottish poets at the beginning of the twenty-first century, Douglas Dunn was the obvious successor to the octogenarian Edwin Morgan, Scotland's poetic elder statesman. The two writers were, however, markedly different. Morgan was, until his retirement, a lifelong academic whose literary career was conducted entirely from Scotland. Dunn was a librarian who left Scotland in his early twenties and pursued an education and literary career in England, where he was closely connected with Philip Larkin and the city of Hull, returning to Scotland only in his mid-forties. Morgan was an experimental modernist, albeit with a strong traditional streak, while Dunn, with complications, was a traditionalist whose literary genealogy can in part be traced back through writers such as Philip Larkin, Edward Thomas, and William Wordsworth. While Morgan was ineluctably associated with his home city, Glasgow, a place for which Dunn expressed distaste—he regarded its expansion as a threat to the rural surroundings of his childhood—the younger poet was a romantic pastoralist, an advocate of small-town and village Scotland. Yet he also had an often combative role in Scottish letters: a trenchant critic, he was a fierce attacker of, for instance, Hugh MacDiarmid's politics as well as a distinguished and rigorous editor, litterateur, and general mentor to younger writers. A compact and dapper man with a reputation for acerbic plain-speaking, he at times spoke out on political matters while confessing himself to be "by temperament ... a quasi-mystical nature poet." The work reflects these polarities.

LIFE

Douglas Eaglesham Dunn was born on October 23, 1942, in the Renfrewshire village of Inchin-nan, near the south bank of the river Clyde, some ten miles from Glasgow. Paisley, four miles distant, was the nearest large town. It was a rural environment (modern Inchinnan retains only a hint of its pastoral flavor), though with anomalies: Dunn's father, William, worked in the local India Tyres factory. His mother, Margaret, a woman of strongly Presbyterian background, worked as a housekeeper.

Dunn attended Inchinnan Primary and, later, the junior secondary school, Renfrew High, before going on to Camphill Senior Secondary School in Paisley where, as often happens, a gifted and enthusiastic teacher, Thomas MacCrossan, inspired and encouraged him. Dunn's early bookish instincts had already been nurtured by his grandfather on his mother's side, a baker from the nearby mining town of Hamilton who, in characteristic Scottish autodidact style, had a library. Politically the family background was socialist, though the older Dunn remembered communist uncles invoking Russia's Red Army with bayonets transforming Scotland. (Dunn's politics have remained on the left.) The youngster showed the born writer's characteristic aptitude for language and a lack of interest in science and math, which would later mean he did not "seriously consider" going to university: he didn't possess the compulsory entrance certificates in these subjects.

Dunn's early career, understandably enough for a bookish young man, was in librarianship; in 1962, after three years working for Renfrew County Library, he qualified precociously as an associate of the Library Association in the Scottish School of Librarianship in Glasgow and took up a position in that city's Royal College of Science and Technology's Andersonian Library. (The college is now Strathclyde University.)

In late 1964, Dunn married his companion, Lesley Balfour Wallace, whom he had met in 1961; less than a week later the newlyweds were living in Akron, Ohio, where Dunn had found employment as assistant librarian at the Akron Public Library. The couple stayed for fourteen months—a valuable period that introduced Dunn not only to American intellectual life (he developed a circle of literary friends) but enabled him to read more widely among contemporary American short-story writers and poets than he had been able to do in Scotland. Among the latter, the work of Louis Simpson, Robert Bly, and especially James Wright, born in Ohio, made a deep impression. Wright's poetry, with its frequent identification with the poor and the dispossessed and its disaffected tone, would prove a considerable early influence on the younger Scottish poet.

By January 1966, however, the couple was back in Scotland. In late 1965, not only had the two been involved in a serious and traumatizing car accident—it killed one close friend and critically injured another—but Dunn had been called up by the draft for the U.S. armed forces, for which he discovered he was liable, being on a five-year immigrant's visa. (He would later write about this experience, sardonically, in his poem "The Wealth.") As a Scot, he was unwilling on terms of principle to fight in Vietnam, and he and his wife returned home by ship, unable to afford the flights. Bizarrely Dunn, having taken the army medical, was classed as a deserter by the U.S. military, an experience that shook him.

If one happier result of Dunn's exposure to America, however, had been his wide reading in contemporary American literature, another was that he became ambitious for a university education. Yet his lack of science qualifications proved a stumbling block with Scottish universities. Some English universities proved more flexible in this regard and were willing to overlook his lack of certificates. In 1966, ironically while working in the Joseph Black Chemistry Library at Glasgow University, he was accepted by the University of Hull to read English.

The move to Hull, a coastal city of northeast England with a reputation for bleakness, would have long-lasting consequences. Not only did it

give Dunn a subject for his first book, *Terry Street,* but, in 1967, while working as an assistant in the Brynmor Jones Library headed by Philip Larkin, he met the older poet. A friendship developed when, in 1968, Dunn won an E. C. Gregory Award—an annual money prize administered by Britain's Society of Authors to promising poets under the age of thirty—and Larkin, one of the judges, and unaware that his sometime colleague even wrote poetry, congratulated Dunn. Larkin may have suggested the title for Dunn's first book, based on the unsalubrious district in Hull where the younger poet and his wife were living. He certainly advised on the ordering of poems in that first collection as well as encouraging Faber and Faber, his own publisher, to publish Dunn's work.

Terry Street, which won a Scottish Arts Council Book Award and was a Poetry Book Society Choice, appeared in 1969, also the year in which Dunn received a first in English from Hull. Dunn began working under Larkin at the Brynmor Jones Library, but as early as 1971, frustrated by Larkin's inflexible attitude toward the other poet on his staff—he found Larkin reluctant to give him time off to do readings, for instance—he resigned to become a freelance writer, first spending six months in France on a Somerset Maugham travel award. (Dunn, as his first wife was, was a noted Francophile.) Throughout the 1970s Dunn reviewed, wrote his own collections—a further three books of verse appeared in 1972, 1974, and 1979—and tutored extramural courses at Hull University. His wife, meanwhile, had been consolidating her own career. She was the senior keeper of the Ferens Art Gallery in Hull by 1978, the year in which she was diagnosed with cancer of the eye. She died in March 1981 at age thirty-seven.

This tragedy marked the beginning of the end of Dunn's close association with Hull. Although the couple had never lost contact with Scotland, frequently returning there for holidays, and Dunn's 1981 collection of poems, *St. Kilda's Parliament,* had been perhaps his most Scottish in reference and subject matter to date, Dunn's appointment as writer in residence at the University of Dundee from autumn 1981 to July 1982

DOUGLAS DUNN

helped consolidate his ambition to return to Scotland to live. By January 1984 he had sold his house in Hull and, with his new partner, Lesley Bathgate, whom Dunn had met in April 1982 when she was an arts student, had moved to Tayport, outside Dundee, overlooking the Tay Estuary. The couple married in August 1985, a year that saw a new fame for Dunn owing to the publication in April of his collection *Elegies,* for his first wife. Dunn was favorably compared by reviewers to Hardy and Tennyson; the volume went into several printings.

Throughout the second half of the 1980s Dunn worked as chief book reviewer for the Glasgow *Herald,* Scotland's major daily broadsheet, as well as a writer in residence. He also became a father in early middle age: to Robbie in 1987 and Lillias in 1990. Appointed professor of English literature at St. Andrews University in 1991 and later director of the St. Andrews Scottish Studies Institute (a position he demitted in the late 1990s), he also led the creative writing course at the university, having gathered around him an impressive array of younger Scottish writers, including John Burnside, Kathleen Jamie, and A. L. Kennedy, as tutors. Dunn and his second wife separated in 1997, and he moved to the relative rural isolation of a cottage in the little Fife village of Dairsie, some nine miles from St. Andrews. In 2003, not only was he an indisputably major figure in contemporary Scottish poetry, a view confirmed by his substantial *New Selected Poems 1964–2000,* which appeared in January of that year, but widely respected for an old-fashioned decency and integrity, qualities notable not only in the verse but in many of the characters in Dunn's two short-story collections. Beautifully written, they are full of wry evocations of Scottish small-town and village life.

PROSE

Although Dunn's critical essays, written with the scrupulous judiciousness one would expect of a poet of his caliber, have yet to be collected (at this writing the provisionally titled *Selected Essays* is in preparation), the short stories, many of which appeared for the first time in the *New Yorker,* are gathered in two volumes, *Secret Villages* (1985) and *Boyfriends and Girlfriends* (1995). Even though the books were published a decade apart, they share many qualities: an interest in provincial life, in particular those moments of conflict between individuals of different social standing; an unshowy quietness that brings out something of the extraordinariness of the everyday; and astute observation. Frequently they are lightly plotted vignettes, strongest for their atmosphere and delicate perceptions, shot through with droll comedy and a strong satirical streak. For instance, "Old Women without Gardens" in *Secret Villages* is a withering portrait of the narrowed existences of three old ladies, Mrs. Ellison, Miss Drewery, and Mrs. Sinclair, whose characters are briskly delineated in a deadpan tone: "A tramp staggering across the park with his supermarket bag stuffed with newspaper bedding," the narrator writes, "can excite [Mrs. Sinclair] into raising the disturbing subject of capital punishment" (p. 96). "The Canoes," meanwhile, portrays the true nature of canny locals toward tourist visitors in a Scottish Highland setting. Any romantic perception of the Highlanders is quickly subverted by this account of locals who tell the tourists that they "may light fires and pitch tents to their hearts' desire where gamekeepers and bailiffs are guaranteed to descend on them once it is dark and there will be no end of inconvenience in finding a legal spot for the night" (p. 25). The self-awareness and mordant humor of the Highlander is incisively portrayed: when the young couple in the same story is conveyed across a loch to the island of Incharn, where the two are to holiday, the watching narrator records: "I treated them to one of my lugubrious waves, which I am so good at that no one else is allowed to make one while I am there. How many times, after all, have the holiday types said to us, 'We will remember you forever?' It is a fine thing, to be remembered" (p. 27). The closing sentence expertly captures both a characteristic mellow Highland sardonicism and a typical sentence structure. The realistic narrator gently mocks the sentimental hyperbole of the visitors.

Dunn has a keen eye for human foibles and pretensions. "Twin Sets and Pickle Forks" is a charming piece set in Arnot's Tea Room, presided over by the indomitable and invulnerable Miss Frame, who favors special clients with the use of a silver pickle fork. When her illegitimate son suddenly visits her with his girlfriend, her closely guarded secret is revealed to her waitresses. Unaccustomedly vulnerable, Miss Frame implores the girls to keep secret the fact that she is a mother. They agree, on condition, as one of them, Maureen, stipulates, that Miss Frame gets rid of "the pickle fork that no' everybody gets to use. It bothers me." Dunn highlights a typically Scottish egalitarianism and dislike of hypocrisy in conflict with the trammeling desire for respectability. Miss Frame is assured by her waitresses that the revelation of her private life means she will now just be "one of the girls": in some ways it seems like a promotion.

Boyfriends and Girlfriends both consolidates and extends the range of Dunn's fiction. Pieces such as "Orr Mount," "Needlework," and "Postponing the Bungalow" are vintage Dunn: in the first, a fair-minded small-time builder and handyman, Monty Gault, renovates a house, "Orr Mount," for a perplexing and newly arrived couple with a blind son; in "Needlework," the wife of an upper-class childless couple, Mrs. Esmée Boyd-Porteous, decides to have a girl from the local orphanage stay for the summer; while "Postponing the Bungalow" is a wonderful vignette in which an upper-class widow and widower fallen on hard times use the authenticity of their gentility to provide guided tours of the local area. While the situations are relatively unexceptional, Dunn's unsentimental affection for many of his characters and deft evocation absorb the reader. The writer is thoroughly on the side of life: in "Mulwhevin," for instance, Joan Bolton, inveigled by her boyfriend into spending a meditative weekend at a country house, quickly finds herself in the middle of a sect devoted to a kind of pagan mystic, Thomas Drinkwater. Responding with admirable animosity to the sect's po-faced acceptance of Drinkwater and to her boyfriend's increasingly bizarre behavior, she leaves, hitchhiking back to sanity. A car stops, she runs toward it, and the story finishes with her wondering of its driver:

"What," she asked herself, "does he, or she, believe?"

"I'm going to Dumfries," the woman who drove the car said. "Is that any use to you?"

"It sounds lovely," Joan said.

(p. 177)

A reassuring, saving ordinariness is subtly evoked. The proper noun "Dumfries," a town in southwest Scotland on the river Nith, takes on a new resonance in this context.

Elsewhere, in "The Boy from Birnam," Dunn writes engagingly about adolescent camaraderie via the relationship between the seventeen-year-old daredevil Jack Hogg and his more cautious and slightly younger friend Norrie Lamont. The relationship is set against a backdrop of poaching, first visits to pubs, and teasing questions about girls. It is a charming portrait, full of braggadocio and gaucheness, not least pleasing for its superb account of the youngsters poaching the landed gentry's river and the unappealing portrait of the offended upper classes.

Though Dunn is perfectly capable of writing a comic-surreal narrative, "Hazards of the House," spoken by an intellectual French mouse with a liking for reading Proust who drives English holidaymakers to distraction, the title story of *Boyfriends and Girlfriends* is, more typically, a portrayal of small village clannishness and social ostracism. In "Native Heath," George Barr, once wrongly imprisoned for fourteen years for murdering a woman, returns to the town of Dellonburn, where his three incriminators live. He is back to settle his mother's will and encounters his accusers. The grimness of small-town Scotland is bleakly depicted. Barr believes he was accused on insufficient evidence because he was "skirt daft"—a lady's man—and blames Scottish repressiveness, observing:

Take a look at Dellonburn. Fourteen years on and it still looks like a town that's never been fucked in. … Look in Telford's shop. He's got a top shelf in there for solitaires. In a town this size! And he's the nerve to employ a girl to sell them.

(p. 94)

This depiction of a bleak urban reality is, however, relatively unusual in Dunn's stories.

Generally they seem quite outside that contemporary Scottish mainstream which tends to focus on the uglier aspects of the country's urban life. Wry and elegantly written, in their focus on the provincial and parochial minutiae of Scotland Dunn's stories are unemphatically contrarian and pleasingly idiosyncratic. Frequently charming, their depictions are both affectionate and unillusioned.

TERRY STREET (1969)

Dunn's first book of poems made an immediate impression. Critics were full of praise for its understated realism and scrutiny of English town life in the Hull street of the book's title. Even that severe poet-critic Ian Hamilton—editor of the *Review,* Britain's most contentious little poetry magazine, which had previously published four of the *Terry Street* poems—commended the volume for offering "more convincing sketches of at least the surfaces of humdrum urban living than one can find in any current poet except Philip Larkin." Among these, presumably, would be a four-line poem such as "After Closing Time," in which the narrator sees, or hears, what he calls somewhat primly, "the agents of rot": "The street tarts and their celebrating trawlermen, / Singing or smoking, carrying bottles, / In a staggered group ten minutes before snow" (p. 26).

This has a likable air of bawdy carnival, in which the characters are getting what happiness they can in the moment; technically the poem contains a nice ambiguity in that "staggered"— the group is both spread out along the street and staggered by the effects of alcohol—though the rest of the verse is plain as the scene itself. A neighboring poem, also of four lines, "Winter," memorably describes "Recalcitrant motorbikes; / Dog-shit under frost," in the early morning. Plain diction married to realist subject matter gave the volume an impressive individuality.

In Dunn's *Selected Poems 1964–1983* the poet inserted an envoi among the selection from *Terry Street* that chose to remember a more pastoral experience from that period and ended: "A curse

on me I did not write with joy." Yet it is the lack of joy or of any sense of romantic uplift in *Terry Street* that gives its poems their distinctiveness. The book is divided into two sections. The first part, eighteen poems set in Terry Street itself, attracted the most attention. The poems' narrator observes what seems to him the "lost tribe" of the street's inhabitants in an imagistically vivid verse tonally reminiscent of the work of James Wright. Dunn is the excluded observer, cut off from those he observes by window glass or by his inability to fit in—a Scotsman in an English street, a bookish intellectual among the unliterary—or simply by the sex of his subjects, such as the young women "obsessed by beauty" in "The Clothes Pit" and "Young Women in Rollers." The world of the poems tends to the gloomy and subdued: it is a place of old men, "Patricians" who hand-wash their own "grey unmentionables" to avoid embarrassment among the women at the launderette, or in which "the sleepless, smoking in the dark," "count the years of their marriages." But there are also moments of light and of rare comedy. In the vignette "On Roofs of Terry Street," when a builder repairing a leaking roof "kneels upright to rest his back, / His trowel catches the light and becomes precious," while the eleven-line "A Removal from Terry Street" is one of the few poems to escape what some might find the claustrophobic atmosphere of the sequence. The narrator records seeing a family moving its household effects, "the usual stuff":

> Her husband
> Follows, carrying on his shoulders the son
> Whose mischief we are glad to see removed,
> And pushing, of all things, a lawnmower.
> There is no grass in Terry Street. The worms
> Come up cracks in concrete yards in moonlight.
> That man, I wish him well. I wish him grass.
>
> (p. 20)

The anomaly of the lawnmower strikes a note of rare comedy. It becomes a symbol of hope. Grass is the pastoral, which translates for Dunn's narrator into something affirming and positive. The rumbustiousness of the "removal," or the "flitting" as it would have been called in Scotland, is a movement out of the situational stasis many of the *Terry Street* poems occupy. It is vibrant with the possibility of elsewhere.

Tonally the book's second half continues the style of the first except on a wider canvas, in, for example, "Close of Play," which is set in the suburbs. The second section also presages later developments in Dunn's writing. "Tribute of a Legs Lover" affirms Dunn's sympathy with the disenfranchised. His "dancing girls" are "the wasted lives, / The chorus girls who do not make good / … but find themselves stiff and rotten at fifty." Dunn's five-line "Love Poem," addressed to his first wife, is eerily premonitory. The couple are "two gardens haunted by each other." The poem ends:

Sometimes I cannot find you there,
There is only the swing creaking, that you have just
  left,
Or your favourite book beside the sundial.

(p. 48)

The most striking fact about the poem is the woman's absence; the swing creaks ominously, conjuring the surrounding silence, and the book, symbol of culturedness, is beside the symbol of mortality. This quiet little poem shimmers with portents.

"Landscape with One Figure" and "Ships," meanwhile, provide the book's only indication of the author's nationality. Both are set on the banks of the Clyde. In the former, Dunn expresses a wish to "wait here / Forever," as "An example of being a part of a place." Both poems are distinguished for their imagistic details; in the former, the Robert Bly–like "Waves fall from their small heights on river mud" and in the latter, "A fine rain attaches itself to the ship like skin." "Ships" depicts the crews of merchant ships who leave "restless boys without work in the river towns." The poem has a subdued bleakness, somewhat reminiscent tonally of a piece by James Wright such as "Autumn in Martins Ferry, Ohio."

Terry Street finishes, however, with "Cosmologist," a nine-line mouthful of praise for the interconnectivity of the cosmos. The narrator visualizes the back of his hand as "the underside of a leaf. / If water fell on me now / I think I would grow."

Dunn's first book occupies a curious place in his oeuvre. While distinguished, its most notable connection with the later writing is that the volume's most significant poems appear as an Anglicized version of what Dunn might have written, albeit with less sense of alienation perhaps, in a Scottish context. His development can be seen as largely a realization and consolidation, book by book, of the sensibility prompted by his Scottish roots.

THE HAPPIER LIFE *(1972)*

Though greeted with considerable praise by reviewers, Dunn's next two volumes were, in retrospect, transitional. *The Happier Life*, the problematic second book for a poet whose first had been well received, appeared just three years after its predecessor; significantly, Dunn chose to reprint only six of its thirty-nine poems in his 2003 collection *New Selected Poems 1964–2000*. The book showed evidence of hasty composition in some of the poems and, at times, of a lassitude of spirit: "A Faber Melancholy," addressed to Philip Larkin and Ian Hamilton, whose verse was also issued by Faber and Faber, the United Kingdom's foremost poetry publisher, affects a cliquey friendliness; lacking a real subject, it has a meditative self-indulgence. "At a Yorkshire Bus Stop," written in four-beat rhyming couplets, at times descends to doggerel, like Patrick Kavanagh at his late worst. Elsewhere, in "The Sportsmen," Dunn launches into a revenge fantasy about "scum" with "fast cars and money." Interestingly two related poems, "After the War" and "Guerrillas," Dunn has never collected, though their plain narrative tone and solid verse technique give them a distinction lacking in many of the volume's other pieces. Both are childhood memories set, it appears, in Dunn's native Renfrewshire. "After the War" recounts youngsters encountering soldiers on an exercise. The children are thrilled and intimidated, pretend to attack the men, and are indulged by the soldiers who "made booming noises from behind big rifles"—all except one child who, living alone with his mother in straitened circumstances, runs home. "He went inside just as the convoy

DOUGLAS DUNN

passed," the poem closes. The implication of genuine loss and its knowledge is set against the other children's untried bravado. The poem works because of its solid technique and images: pine-cones in the grass are, memorably, "like little hand grenades"; the possibility of biological growth is married subtly to a potential destructiveness. "Guerrillas," meanwhile, a poem with an autobiographical tone, sets the affluent landowning children of the narrator's childhood against his own disinherited resentments and envy. The narrator and his fellows begrudge the farmers' sons "the ownership of all the land we roved on." The poem closes:

Outlaws from dark woods and quarries,
We plundered all we envied and had not got,
As if the disinherited from farther back
Came to our blood like a knife to a hand.

(p. 52)

The poem predicts interestingly Dunn's later development in his book *Barbarians.*

LOVE OR NOTHING *(1974)*

Nine poems from this third volume's thirty-four pieces survived into *New Selected Poems;* the volume as a whole is influenced by the surrealism Dunn had picked up from his reading of French poets such as Jules Laforgue. (After this book Dunn said, "I felt I was going up a dead end. I decided I needed something more robust, more public—but public in a way that didn't debar the possibility of subtlety or irony.") For many readers the surrealism and apparent arbitrariness of image in, for instance, "The White Poet," subtitled "A Homage to Jules Laforgue," while aesthetically interesting as evidence of the poet's imaginative push against a "realism" for which he had received considerable praise, was less satisfying than Dunn's naturalistic-documentary mode, exemplified in *Love or Nothing* by pieces such as "The Competition," and "Boys with Coats." Both seem reminiscences of Dunn's own childhood and are again, surprisingly, omitted from the *New Selected.* Each begins with the documentary clause "When I was ten ..."; both detail experiences with other children

that show the young Dunn being inculcated into class consciousness. In "The Competition," the poem's narrator meets a boy with his mother on a Hamilton bus who has the same toy aeroplane, but who is dressed in a uniform "Brown as barrowloads from the blue-bottled byre," a complex image in which Dunn records—no doubt retrospectively—a certain disdain. The derisive simile implies that the privileged classes serve to fertilize and cultivate the working class like a crop for harvesting. Dunn's narrator recalls how he talked to the brown-blazered boy, telling him with childhood innocence that he, "too, had a Hurricane." The boy unexpectedly sulks and calls him "a poor boy, who should shut up"—an unexpected response to which the narrator responds: "I'd never thought of it like that." The piece closes:

Years later, running in a race, barefooted
As I'd trained my spikes to ruin, convinced
My best competitor was him, I ran into
The worst weathers of pain, determined to win,
But on the last lap, inches from the tape, was beaten
By someone from Shotts Miners' Welfare Harriers Club.

(p. 34)

Shotts is a grim Lanarkshire town of high unemployment. The poem ironically delineates the hierarchy of class and poverty. While it seems to suggest a somewhat simplistic inverse relationship between poverty and athletic ability, this is tempered by the note of autobiography, which cannot be gainsaid. Even in this relatively simple poem one can see Dunn's understated craft: how "barefooted" and "convinced," for instance, poised at line ends after their commas, emphasize the relative poverty and set-mindedness of the speaker, and the way in which the sudden piling up of four adjectives before the plain noun "Club" at the close adds a note of ironic comedy. The poem has a documentary tone that "Boys with Coats," a neighboring piece, reinforces. The ten-year-old Dunn gives "a boy with no coat in the sleet and rain" his pocket money and model Hurricane. He feels "radical" that these gifts seem to make no difference: the boy is still not allowed by the bus conductress to get on the bus.

71

BARBARIANS *(1979)*

It was with *Barbarians,* which had a five-year gestation, that Dunn reached his mature voice. Some of the technical uncertainties of the previous two volumes had been replaced with an impeccable technique, often (though not exclusively) formal, and one of Dunn's major themes could be seen in the ambiguity of the book's title. Asked by an interviewer "Who are the Barbarians?" Dunn responded, with characteristic tartness, "A more interesting question would be "Who are the civilised?" (*Verse,* p. 27). "Barbarians," he observed, "are people who contest the Establishment and the degeneration of the State" (p. 28). The volume is prefaced by a translated excerpt from the French writer Paul Nizan's *Antoine Bloyé,* describing a character who, in becoming middle-class, had grown "further and further away from the hardship and simplicity of the workers, from his childhood environment. … The truth of life was on the side of the men who returned to their poor houses, on the side of the men who had not 'made good.'" Living in England, writing French symbolist–influenced poems, having, to an extent, "made good," and being of Dunn's background, the poet plainly felt the need to reaffirm some of that background's putative authenticity, now lacking. (In an illuminating interview with John Haffenden in 1981, he quickly contradicts the interviewer when asked about his "background," calling it "foreground.")

Dunn has pointed out that the marriage of stylistic formality and dispossessed subject matter in *Barbarians* was intended as ironic, and the three-part volume opens with the ironically titled "Barbarian Pastorals," nine poems examining what Les Murray, another poet of the societal grudge, would call "relegation." The book opens with "The Come-on," a sort of manifesto headed by an epigraph by the French existentialist Albert Camus in which a king's son is keeping watch "over the gates of the garden in which I wanted to live." Here are Dunn's opening lines:

To have watched the soul of my people
  Fingered by the callous
Enlivens the bitter ooze from my grudge.
  Mere seepage from "background"

Takes over, blacking out what intellect
  Was nursed by scholar or book
Or had accrued by questioning the world.
  Enchanting, beloved texts
Searched in for a generous mandate for
  Believing what I am,
What I have lived and felt, might just as well
  Not exist when the vile
Come on with their "coals in the bath" stories
  Or mock at your accent.

(p. 13)

The poem's gritty, assertive tone is arresting, though like many grudges, the one here seems a little overstated to an outsider who does not share its grounds. It hardly seems the work of a poet supposedly influenced by Philip Larkin, who by 1979 was surely representative of that aesthetic and cultural centrality Dunn is antagonizing. The poem goes on to envisage a return of the repressed, in which the narrator imagines he and his like, too, are "king's sons and guardians." Though the reader could object that a true evolution of spirit would be when the narrator had no such aspiration, which represents a "buying in" to a preexistent hierarchy, the narrator's grudge grants the poem a verbal energy confirmed by subsequent pieces. "Here Be Dragons" mocks the Roman author Pomponius Mela's arrogant conversion of a misunderstanding of African culture, in his *Chorographia,* into a demonization of its otherness. The next poem, "Gardeners," in four impeccable ten-line rhyming stanzas, enacts a Lawrentian revenge fantasy. Where Richard Wilbur, one of Dunn's favorite poets, in his poem "A Summer Morning," has the big house's cook and gardener "possessing what the owners can but own" while the owners sleep off hangovers, Dunn's gardeners, in a socialist fantasy whose climax Dunn has called "Grand Guignol," burn down the landowner's house after a dispute and hang him in the untouched garden's "shade." The poem is set in "Loamshire, 1789": Dunn is aware of the anachronism of his impulse. He was too critical of the political extremities of, for instance, Hugh MacDiarmid to fall into similar extremism. The retrospective dating of the poem allows the poet to both indulge and escape his grudge. "Empires," meanwhile, examines the death of empire and its cost. Dunn's attitude to

DOUGLAS DUNN

empire contrasts sharply with the considerably more positive take on it by a poet who might be expected to be even more critical, Derek Walcott. "Empires" starkly divides "us" from "them," ruled from rulers:

They ruined us. They conquered continents.
We filled their uniforms. We cruised the seas.
We worked their mines and made their histories.
You work; we rule, they said. We worked; they ruled.
They fooled the tenements. All men were fooled.
It still persists. It will be so, always.
Listen. An out-of-work apprentice plays
God Save the Queen on an Edwardian flute.
He is, but does not know it, destitute.

(p. 26)

It is the sheer piling up of statement here that is arresting. Staccato sentences and parallelisms, the one-word sentence and imperative "Listen," all make this versified opinionating—Dunn sounds like a literary soapbox socialist—a world away from the cautious imagistic outsiderness of *Terry Street* or Dunn's French-influenced surrealism. There is a strong irony in that many of the poem's readers are unlikely to be classed among the "us," from most of whom, in a final irony, Dunn is now separated by dint of education. The poem's closing points up the curious tendency of the oppressed, exemplified by the unemployed apprentice, to accede to and confirm their own circumstances.

Barbarians was the first volume in which Dunn's Scottishness seemed to predominate. The book's second section contains several poems explicitly set in Dunn's "foreground." These include "Drowning," the ironic title of which indicates not just a childhood memory of a boy's drowning but the slower, later drowning by circumstance of his contemporaries who discovered him; as well as the political "Ballad of the Two Left Hands," about enforced unemployment caused by the decline of the once world-renowned Clyde Shipbuilding. A fine poem, "The Musician," meanwhile, amply fulfills Dunn's stated desire to write poems that are like "sung short stories." Set in Dunn's childhood Inchinnan, as he noted in interview, it recounts the story of the bachelor MacAuley, a carpenter and talented fiddle player famed locally for "his carpenter's

wrist on the fiddle-bow / Stitching like mad through jig time." After his death, both his fiddles are found lying "in their cases under the stairs / With the music we never knew he could read"— Beethoven and Bach. The poem closes:

Let them open your window frames, open your doors,
Think, as they sit on their mended chairs,
Of you their musician, and doctor to wood,
That no one has heard what you understood.

(p. 37)

A local, traditional art and the fiddler's aspirations for something "grander" are set side by side. The window frames and doors are MacAuley's not just because he made them, as a carpenter; they are conceptual too, representing the musician's unfulfilled aspiration, and the narrator calls upon the villagers to discover it by opening those windows and doors. The locals have not only not heard MacAuley's unplayed classical music—which, in any case, society may have encouraged them to believe was not for "the likes of them"—but also the carpenter-fiddler's unspoken message: his own subjugation by the expectations of the local culture. This subjugation, as well as the sheet music of unplayed Bach and Beethoven, is what he "understood." "The Musician" is finally an elegy. Its bouncy meter—predominantly anapestic and dactylic—and lively tone are themselves ironic. There is a ghost of a pun on "would" in that "wood": the musician attempted to heal himself out of the conditional tense implied, but he never made it.

In later books, Dunn was able to come into fuller possession—as Ted Hughes intimated was a major reason for writing poetry—of the facts of his own "foreground." This would seem especially true of *St. Kilda's Parliament,* perhaps his strongest book.

ST. KILDA'S PARLIAMENT *(1981)*

The parliament of the book's title was a democratic daily gathering—at least, of the men—of St. Kilda, the Outer Hebridean island evacuated in 1930. The "Parliament"—in which the island men decided what tasks they would do for the

DOUGLAS DUNN

day—becomes, as the poet announces in a back cover blurb, representative of many of the characters of Scottish life who people the volume's poems. Subtitled "The Photographer Re-visits His Picture," the title poem—which appends the dates 1879–1979—refers to a famous black and white photograph of the parliament (usually dated 1886) taken by the Scottish photographer George Washington Wilson; 1979 was the year of the famous Scottish Referendum, which found Scotland thwarted in having its own parliament by political sleight of hand from London (a London bias was built into the voting conditions). Dunn therefore seems to be making a political point, though his is a romantic politics of the imagined ideal. His speaker, Wilson, has returned to the island's "parliament" after wide travel and more dramatic events because it is as if the islanders he portrayed "have grown from / Affection scattered across my own eyes." He is fascinated "By those who never were contorted by / Hierarchies of cuisine and literacy."

Impressive throughout the book are Dunn's technical adroitness and singular confidence of poetic line. Present are most of his major themes: the matter of Scotland, an interest in the assumed authenticity of pastoral life, his empathy with the poor and dispossessed, and anger on behalf of the gifted or those with artistic aspirations amid small-town Scottish jealousy and condescension.

A central piece, "Remembering Lunch," points to future developments as well as shedding light upon other poems in the volume. Fluently written in a rangy, fast-moving free-verse line, buoyant in tone, it is spoken by a disenchanted litterateur no longer at home in the bibulous capital among his drinking cronies; he longs to resemble "a schoolmaster of some reading and sensibility / *Circa* 1930 and up to his eccentric weekend pursuits." He is looking forward to "a tweed-clad solitude."

Other poems confirm this desire for a greater meaningfulness of existence. A poem such as "Second Hand Clothes," neatly written in trim trimeter, describes the experience of visiting secondhand-clothes shops; it finishes: "There's nothing to be done / Save follow the lost shoes."

Dunn commented on his fascination for dispossession and poverty in the Haffenden interview:

I've seen [the social mud] all my life, and I've always been drawn to it … even in a kind of fin de siècle way, perhaps. My imagination is drawn to it, it's not a political choice or anything like that. I still have the belief that these people know truths that I don't know, and I'd like to know what they know.

(p. 22)

While a shallow judgment could dismiss this is a form of voyeurism, Dunn never condescends in the later poetry. If "Second Hand Clothes" reveals a desire to seek out the "truths" of the dispossessed by following in imagination those shoes, Dunn also persists in his sympathy for those who, like MacAuley in his previous volume, have aspirations beyond their station. In "Tannahill," he examines the case of the Scottish poet Robert Tannahill, from Paisley, who committed suicide at the age of thirty-six when his second volume of poems was refused publication. The poem is deepened by Dunn's imaginative identification with Tannahill, a writer from Dunn's home area whose example showed "that verse did not exclude / a local skill." The narrator blames for Tannahill's demise the "kent y'r faither" syndrome—it translates as "knew your father," a sort of Scottish put-down based on familiarity—which Dunn pointed out was still overly prevalent in Scottish life as recently as 1999. Dunn implies that the syndrome mocked the desperate poet who committed suicide in a local river, "the dish-cloth Cart" (though some sources state it was the nearby Candren Burn) at a spot once shown to Dunn by his secondary school teacher, Thomas MacCrossan. The poem closes:

By broom, by briar, by Craigie Wood,
Through Cart-side's river neighbourhood,
Your papers rotting on the mud,
    My Tannahill!
But the shelfie and the hawthorn bud
    You could not kill.

(p. 56)

The poet can kill himself and destroy his unpublished poems, but not the nature—a "shelfie" is

74

DOUGLAS DUNN

Scots for chaffinch, a small, dapper European passerine—that often inspired his poems, some of which are still sung today. The closing reference to the chaffinch can be read as linking, intriguingly, to the lines earlier in the poem in which Tannahill sings, "like a beginning finch," his "common heart." That common heart or spirit gave his writing its force but also, paradoxically, subjugated him, the poem implies, in the form of his mocking contemporaries. The closing has a rich irony.

Other outstanding poems include "Washing the Coins," a memory of "tattie-howking," gathering potatoes on a farm. The narrator is a Scottish boy among Irish immigrant laborers. The backbreaking work is vividly conveyed in a rhythmically energetic blank verse; at the day's end, the young narrator, Dunn, returns home with his wages—two florins, silver two-shilling coins in pre-decimal sterling, and "a dozen pennies of the realm," bronze. The poem concludes:

I tumbled all our coins upon our table.
My mother ran a basin of hot water.
We bathed my wages and we scrubbed them clean.
Once all that sediment was washed away,
That residue of field caked on my money,
I filled the basin to its brim with cold;
And when the water settled I could see
Two English Kings among their drowned Britannias.

(p. 25)

The poem is a sardonic elucidation of imperialism, revealed in retrospect through the image of the coins. The English kings, probably King George V or King George VI, are featured on the florins; the pennies feature Britannia, the Roman name given to England and Wales, later symbolized as a woman complete with trident. (With wonderful irony in the context of "Washing the Coins," "Rule, Britannia," the unofficial English national anthem, composed in the eighteenth century by the Scot James Thomson, has a refrain that goes: "Rule, Britannia! Britannia, rule the waves: / Britons never will be slaves.") Dunn's remarkable poem's closing works by its staccato, end-stopped sentences, which convey a brisk efficiency; only when clear of "that residue of field" can the truth be seen. Yet the closing line seems somewhat ambiguous. If the "Britannias" repre-

sent the outposts of empire, then they are "drowned" because they are doomed to oppression by the triumph of imperialism. (If, however, they represent the spirit of imperialism itself, then they are "doomed," the image suggests, by the inevitable failure of empire.) The English kings are silver florins; the outposts are mere pennies. Money becomes a metaphor for power, which grants added significance to the possessive tone—"our coins," "my wages," and "my money"—employed by the narrator.

The book closes with two poems that demonstrate the expansive, unbuttoned side of Dunn, which would be increasingly noticeable in later collections. They are the relatively amiable "Ode to a Paperclip," ironically titled and most notable for its lively anecdotes and quirky close-up take on the humble stationery item; and a praise poem for the culinary delights of "Ratatouille," a symbol for pacifism and emotional generosity. "Ratatouille" is full of the benison of the vegetable realm; its aroma almost rises from the page.

The expansive note had, however, already been severely challenged at *St. Kilda's Parliament*'s appearance by tragedy in the form of cancer contracted by Dunn's first wife, Lesley. Following his impressive sequence *Europa's Lover* (1982), published as a pamphlet and dealing with European history in a style variously surreal and documentary, the poet's next book, *Elegies*, in commemoration of Lesley Balfour Dunn, would be, ironically, his most popular.

ELEGIES (1985)

Lesley Dunn's terminal cancer—she died in March 1981—led to the poet's most personal book to date. It must have involved both personal and aesthetic risk: as he himself said, being a son of Scottish Presbyterianism, he was "highly schooled in reticence." The volume's thirty-nine poems, however, never offend the ultimate privacy of Dunn's relationship with his wife; intimacies are hinted at rather than explicitly rendered, and the volatility of grief is tightly controlled by Dunn's formal mastery. While the book's contents were compared to Thomas

DOUGLAS DUNN

Hardy's *Veteris vestigia flammae,* the 1912–1913 poems of elegy for his dead wife, and to Tennyson's *In Memoriam* sequence for Arthur Hallam, Dunn's book has neither the pervasive guilt of Hardy's sequence nor the at times ponderous sentimentality of Tennyson's. Three poems near the volume's opening—"Second Opinion," "Thirteen Steps and the Thirteenth of March" (which was the date of her death in 1981) and "Arrangements"—are explicit narratives dealing with his wife's illness and her funeral arrangements; most of the rest of the volume consists of elegies for her that depict Dunn's present reality, memories of the couple together in happier times, and attempts at happiness together in the period before her death when the fact of her terminal illness was implicit. The verses' formality imposes an artistic distance on the author's grief, and the final effect of the volume is a celebration of Lesley Dunn's life, most explicitly at the close of "Dining," a memory of her culinary gifts and good taste. In closing, it accords thanks to a friend who made soup for her:

Know that I shake with gratitude, as, Jenny, when
My Lesley ate your soup on her last night,
That image of her as she savoured rice and lemon
Refused all grief, but was alight
With nature, courage, friendship, appetite.

(p. 28)

The refusal of grief in such grievous circumstances paradoxically increases the grievousness; this seems to be emotion recollected not in tranquillity but in considerable sorrow. Yet Dunn is too much an artist to forget the art of the poem: the judicious placing of commas in the first quoted line precisely convey the speaker's choked up expression of thanks, and the affecting deliberation in the placing of those commas in the last line, which emphasize the qualities stated, seem the verbal equivalent of a man placing stones, one by one, on a cairn.

The simple documentary underpinning of *Elegies* would have granted it a respectful reception at the least. The volume received, however, almost unanimous praise. Dunn's experience, if not the poems he made from it, is a sort of absolute that makes criticism to some extent seem, as he implied of his own poems recording the ordeal, "messages beside the point." Not that readers thought this of the poems: *Elegies* was reprinted in the year of its publication and went through three reprints the following year. It won the prestigious Whitbread Prize for 1985.

Dunn chose to reprint just over half of the book's contents in his *New Selected Poems.* They tend to be those most documentary in style, often affecting memories in sonnet form—which Dunn had begun using extensively for the first time in this memorial volume—such as "France" and "Tursac." The latter, referring to a French village where Dunn had holidayed with his wife, closes with her advice to the bookish poet: "Write out of me, not out of what you read." "Empty Wardrobes" is a memory in which the poet recalls episodes of buying clothes for his wife, this being "a way of exercising love," and of a day in Paris in which he couldn't afford to, a recollection that troubles the poet. Five relatively plain anecdotal stanzas, more exactly rhymed, suddenly transmute to the closing stanza:

Now there is grief the couturier, and grief
The needlewoman mourning with her hands,
And grief the scattered finery of life,
The clothes she gave as keepsakes to her friends.

(p. 29)

Each repetition of the word "grief" is like a knife being twisted in a wound; grief is the resolution, in poem and in life, irrespective of whether or not the narrator could afford to buy his wife clothes. The loss of former happiness, though not the cause of guilt, is as grievous as the narrator's guilt at having been unable, "franc-less and husbandly," to spend money on his wife. This is announced in that leveling and abrupt "Now" that introduces the more elevated register of the final stanza in sharp contrast to the anecdotal intimacies of the previous five.

Though the collection has an affirming note, irony is never far away. "At the Edge of a Birchwood" contrasts his wife's death and childlessness with the fecundity of the natural world. It begins:

Beneath my feet, bones of a little bird
Snap in a twig-flutter. A hundred wings

76

DOUGLAS DUNN

Adore its memory, and it is heard
In the archival choirs now where it sings.

(p. 38)

"A hundred wings" are presumably the living birds in the wood; they "adore its memory" by flying. The birds singing "now" represent the dead bird's song stored in "the archival choirs"—genetic memory—that enable the living birds to sing. The poet buries the bird, and the last line of this sixteen-line poem of four quatrains, which is a complete sentence, states bluntly: "This year her death-date fell on mother's day." The childless woman's anniversary of death is on a day celebrating the fact of motherhood in living women. The statement avoids the likelihood of mawkishness, and the first and last time his wife is mentioned, simply by the possessive "her," places the rest of the poem in perspective. The effect of the closing is to remind the reader of the narrator's unspoken preoccupation with his bereavement, consolidated by the line's abruptness.

Elegies finishes with "Leaving Dundee," a poem of reconciliation in which the poet is "alive again." Dunn had been writer in residence at the university there beginning the autumn after his wife's death. He sees and hears the wild geese crying over the "autumnal Tay"; they are "Communal feathered scissors, cutting through / The grievous artifice that was my life." The poem, and book, close:

She spoke of what I might do "afterwards."
"Go, somewhere else." I went north to Dundee.
Tomorrow I won't live here anymore,
Nor leave alone. *My love, say you'll come with me.*

(p. 64)

While the poet-critic Dave Smith has assumed that the italicized closing sentence refers to Dunn's relationship with his new partner, it is powerfully ambiguous. To finish such a book by addressing a new lover may have been thought insensitive. It seems, more plausibly, to indicate Dunn, in thought, addressing the spirit of his dead wife. If so, it implies an attachment no longer linked to place but a purely spiritual connection that transcends and can accommodate—while taking due note of that delicate "Nor leave alone"—Dunn's new life.

NORTHLIGHT *(1988)*

By the time of his next book, that life had changed considerably. He had been married for three years to Lesley Bathgate, a wood engraver, and lived in a house overlooking the Tay Estuary; his son, Robbie, had been born. Whereas *Barbarians* and *St. Kilda's Parliament* contained poems written by an expatriate Scot, *Northlight* was written by a resident. A number of its poems—"At Falkland Palace," "Love Making by Candlelight," "Abernethy," "Memory and Imagination"—have a new and at times mannered lyricism, some of which can be explained by the effect of Dunn's new relationship and by his return to a more pastoral Scotland after the gritty urbanities of Hull. One has the feeling at times of the poet's coasting on his achieved style, and the register can be windily abstract—especially in, for instance, the six-page "Memory and Imagination"—or pastoral without the spark and bite of real human characters. "At Falkland Palace," a love poem for Lesley Bathgate, has an at times winning lyricism a little overdone by Dunn's reversion to an older diction. Addressing his wife, he tells her she "is loveliness / In your green, country dress / So fair this day." The echo from Burns in "So fair this day," while plainly deliberate, tends merely to underscore the anachronism of the unabashed lyric voice. Dunn also begins to indulge, on occasion, stylistic tics, typically an abstraction yoked together with a concrete noun—"amazement's bud" or "hereafter's solitary," though a new Scottishness of diction is also present.

After the focused grief of *Elegies, Northlight* has a diverse air. There is an elegy for Philip Larkin, "December's Door"; a jeu d'esprit about, and a paean to, pigeons as exemplified by a wartime mascot pigeon, "Winkie"; a piece about the ledgers kept by Edwin Muir when he worked as a clerk at Lobnitz's shipyard in Renfrewshire; and a monologue spoken by a woman about the coming of television to her farmhouse in "In the 1950s." In "The Dark Crossroads," Dunn halts a journey to Scotland for a pint in a faux-Georgian English pub and experiences hints of prejudice against his Scottish accent; "Here and There," meanwhile, a central poem in the volume, takes the form of a 144-line meditation partly arranged as a dialogue in correspondence between Dunn and an English literary friend who finds the former's new dwelling place "provincial." The verse provides a kind of aesthetic justification for Dunn's return to Scotland. He is back because "literature ought to be everywhere," because his "accent feels at home / In the grocer's and in Tentsmuir Forest." Though beautifully constructed in rhyming twelve-line stanzas, the piece perhaps overstates its sense of the significance of this writerly move and can seem rather beside the point to writers who have never left Scotland. Near the poem's end the poet invites his friend to visit, to

Come by the backroads with a sense of time.
Come like Edward Thomas on a holiday
In search of passages of wild-flowered rhyme
No Scot or Irishman would dare betray.

(p. 30)

If the "backroads" have an implicit sense of time, Dunn is also advising this sense for his friend. If that "No" is hyperbolic and a touch sentimental, it also indicates something of Dunn's willful extravagance of sentiment, his thrawn romanticism against a poetic fashion for irony that also gives the poet much of his sympathy as an editor and a critic of catholic, if rigorous, taste.

He seems on stronger ground in *Northlight,* however, in a poem such as the ironically titled "The Country Kitchen," which describes the narrator's experiences preparing slaughtered rabbits and hens for the pot on a holiday in France, this largely in a diction as blunt as the experience. Peeling rabbit skin "felt like peeling plasters off your leg— / The pain and noise of skin and hair." Near the end of the poem, the narrator looks "with envy at the walnut trees / Flourishing in botanical liberty." The van of the visiting fishmonger, in a vivid description

was maritime,
Cold, dripping with melting ice,
An edible museum of the sea.

(p. 77)

Against these, Dunn imagines, with his characteristic sensitivity to the weak, the rabbits in their hutches, "When ringed fingers dropped in / On a carnivorous visit." This modest and anecdotal poem, vividly and sparsely written, is a world away from the Horatian gravitas on display elsewhere in *Northlight.* It was a clarity that Dunn's next book, among his most substantial, would benefit from.

DANTE'S DRUM-KIT *(1993)*

This collection took its title from the 387-line central poem, "Disenchantments," written in terza rima, Dante's stanza in *The Divine Comedy.* "Disenchantments" is described as "[a nine-part] meditation on the afterlife," which Dunn concludes is literary posterity or "in the mind / Of anyone who thinks about the dead / With what respect or disrespect's examined / by knowledge." Dunn's complaint that MacDiarmid after his epic poem "A Drunk Man Looks at the Thistle" lacked a "fiction-making"—presumably narrative-based—element can also to some extent be made of this poem. The difficulty with meditative verse is that, lacking real narrative progression, it may lose itself in inconsequentiality. The sheer quality of writing has to sustain the reader's interest. One of the main achievements of "Disenchantments" is in fact a dramatic range of registers, from a slangy conversational vernacular to a stately lyricism, all bonded by the requirements of this strict form. Prefaced by a quote from Edwin Muir—"It is a world, perhaps; but there's another"—it begins impressively:

Microbiologizing love, despair,
Delight, bountiful dregs, the pulse can stick
On its heirloom heartbeat. The wear-and-tear

Inherited by who-we-are, echoic
Molecular chronology, begins
At birth. Congenital, genetic,

Against know-nothing, careless inclinations,
Death starts with prophecies half-heard in dreams'
Instinctive narratives. A life's toxins—

Psycho-pollution, maverick spiremes—
Gather like gut-data in the underjoyed
Body's puddles, sponges, muscles, pumps and streams.

(p. 31)

The poem offers no real illuminations on the afterlife, concluding, understandably enough, with "Look to the living, love them, and hold on." Rather, the main pleasures of "Disenchantments" are in its linguistic hijinks, such as the sudden switch in the lines quoted above from those "maverick spiremes"—a "spireme" is the mix of DNA and RNA that forms the nucleus of a cell—to the yoking together of the brute and technical in "gut-data" and the wonderfully muscular and relishingly rhythmical bodily catalog in the final line.

Dante's Drum-kit shows a continuing development in Dunn's style. The first of its five sections contain some sprightly and—for Dunn—uncharacteristic light verse, often written in a long Kiplingesque line. "Kabla-Khun" is an engaging fictive narrative, if somewhat mannered in tone, on the spiritual cost of making art. It imagines Samuel Taylor Coleridge visiting his Person from Porlock—whose visit, he claimed, prevented him from completing "Kubla-Khan." The "person," it turns out, is his pharmacist and drug supplier. Dunn's "Henry Petroski, The Pencil. A History. Faber and Faber, £14.95" is a verse review of this apparently engaging volume. The opening stanza gives something of the swing of the metric:

As something to write with a pencil is cute
  engineering.
For how did they manage to squeeze that cylindrical
  lead
Into the timber to make what we all find endearing
Even when marking exams in satirical red?

(p. 9)

Another fine poem, "Libraries. A Celebration," amply confirms the statement of its title. Here, in an anecdotal verse, unrhymed but with lively conversational rhythms, Dunn praises libraries much in the manner of Frank O'Hara praising film stars in his "To the Film Industry in Crisis." Like O'Hara's, Dunn's poem has a winning hyperbole and anecdotal vividness, recalling:

The middle-aged black in Akron at his favourite table
Reading *The Journal of Negro History* end-to-end
Behind a Kilimanjaro of books on Africa
And every book written by blacks in America,
When asked what he was doing, smiled at me, and
  said,

"Invisible examinations on the subject of skin
Hey, boy! You, go get me this, if you have it."
Or the young man in Port Glasgow, studying madly
For raggedy credentials, poverty's homework,
The table-slog of his instinctive scholarship.
Or my old boss, Philip Larkin, holding a book
Written in Indonesian, published in Djakarta,
As if it were a toad that spoke back to him, saying,
"Isn't it *wonderful*? That someone *understands* this?"

(p. 19)

Reading this one thinks of Robert Frost's observation that sheer subject is probably the most important element of any writing.

Section 3 of the book contains a number of poems in Dunn's romantic-pastoral mode, often historically based; central to these is "Gaberlunzie"—an old Scots word for a wandering beggar. He is the "national waif, / Earth-pirate of the thistle and the thorn" but also, it is implied, an instinctive aspect of the poet's aesthetic. The section has a worn, autumnal feel; the spirit of the gaberlunzie pervades it. In "Swigs," a dozen stark vignettes on alcoholism and vagrancy, and "Poor People's Cafés," Dunn returns to his theme of fascination with the dispossessed. "Swigs" is a powerful sequence, made all the stronger by its anecdotal bareness. Scottish poverty is bleakly delineated in a dozen poems, featuring such as

The woman at Waverley
Wearing two coats, holding
Several poly-bags,
Telling the travelling world—
"Ye think ye're miserable?
Juist listen tae this …"

(p. 69)

Waverley is Edinburgh's main railway station. The verse is perfectly unadorned: its bare technique mirrors the subject matter. There is black comedy in the Scots dialogue: here, linguistic register is synonymous with dispossession. The police lead her away, and with her, "her story / only she can tell." That "only" indicates Dunn's sensitivity to the complexity of an individual life and of that life's right to make its own sense of the world.

Section 4, by contrast, has a gentler, sometimes celebratory and often retrospective air. The poet walking past a man painting a fence in "Preserve and Renovate"—a title that refers both to the physical activity described and to a potential aesthetic strategy—is reminded of his father, though the man looks at him "with almost-cross surprise" for walking "past his house four times today, / And yesterday." Dunn courts the man's suspicion and uncomprehension for the sake of the memory of his father, admitting: "It's what I do / This risk of feeling, that the sweet and true / Might be preserved." "Middle Age" and "One Thing and Another" similarly find the poet reminiscing about childhood. In the former, he revisits the Inchinnan field where in 1951, at the age of nine, he and a friend had buried a rabbit; now he finds himself looking for the dessert spoon they used. The poem dramatizes the middle-age tendency to reflect on one's childhood—its importance and its relative insignificance to anyone but ourselves, its "demented pathos looking for a spoon / In which to objectify itself." The Heaneyesque "One Thing and Another," in blank verse, dramatically contrasts and connects an exploding can of "old tractor drip" burned in a farm bonfire, whose "gas hoof" sends the narrator flying, with his young daughter's sudden kick in his arms as he holds her. Other fine poems include the little lyric hymn to fruit "Spanish Oranges"; "To My Desk," a pleasing meditation in Dunn's comic-celebratory mode—"You know me better than anyone. / Thank God you're inanimate," he quips—and "Long Ago," a lyric about the final dissolution of the past that is also inevitably about the present, as exemplified by a memory of an old man in Dunn's childhood.

Dante's Drum-kit closes with the script for the film *Dressed to Kill,* a polemic about war screened on British television's BBC2 in 1992. The script, in prose and verse, is of considerable power, not least for what it reveals of the grievous poetry of fact. Section 9 deals with Renfrewshire's Erskine Hospital, opened in 1916, which "specialised in artificial limbs and rehabilitation." After recounting how Clydeside shipbuilders transferred their skills to making prosthetics, fitting 2,697 limbs by 1918, Dunn writes:

7,000 tons of cotton wool were used by the Royal Army Medical Corps in the Great War. Can you imagine even one ton of cotton wool?—A county covered in snow. How many times round the globe would the bandages of modern wars wind, allowing room to tie them in a big, global bow? The planet's ribbons are white, with red seeping through.

(p. 138)

Dunn's next book would continue this preoccupation with war, though in this case the narrative would stop before the real carnage.

THE DONKEY'S EARS *(2000)*

The full title of the volume is *The Donkey's Ears: Politovsky's Letters Home.* E. S. Politovsky served as flag engineer on the fifteen-thousand-ton flagship *Kniaz Suvorov.* The vessel is among a fleet headed for "the biggest naval gun battle in history," the Russian-Japanese Battle of Tsushima, in May 1905. (The "donkey's ears" of the title is a translation of "Tsushima," named for the "twin peaks of the islands near which the battle was fought.") The poem's 160-odd pages are divided into nine parts, each subdivided into numerous sections, all in quatrains, rhyming *abba.* The entire narrative, the underpinning of which is the Russian Imperial Navy's inexorable voyage to probable destruction under the command of the mercurial Admiral Rozhestvensky, takes the form of Politovsky's letters home to his wife, Sophie. He complains about the ineptitude of the commanders and records in passing the sailors visiting the local brothels en route, but the core of the narrative, and its most touching element, is the engineer's love for his wife, his hope that they will be reunited, and his fears that they will not be. This intimate emotional scenario is played out against a backdrop of life at sea and Politovsky's never-ending work—he was the only engineer on the ship. The letters are all written late at night and, in an embellishment of fact, Dunn makes Politovsky a secret poet, a self-confessed amateur at times apologizing for his ineptitude. The book ends shortly before the fleet engages with the Japanese, with Politovsky dressed in his pressed uniform, ready to meet "the horrid sea" and a battle in which he will perish.

Reviewers were divided on the book's merits. At one pole was the American poet-critic X. J. Kennedy, writing in the *Dark Horse,* who expressed admiration for its sheer technical accomplishment, calling it "one of the finest and most rewarding long poems of the Twentieth Century" (*Dark Horse* 11, p. 68.) At the other was the *Times Literary Supplement* reviewer, Roger Caldwell, who found it, finally, pedestrian and at times clichéd.

The reality for many readers will probably lie somewhere in between. A record of a long sea voyage in which little happens could have sunk like the Russian fleet, yet the reader's attention is engaged by Dunn's sympathetic central character and his pining for his enigmatically silent wife (she has one word in the entire narrative, the endlessly enigmatic "*Well,*" written in a telegram). A little flutter of excitement occurs every time mail arrives, storms provide the opportunity for some fine maritime descriptions, and occasional narrative episodes embedded in the main story add anecdotal interest. These include the famous Dogger Bank incident, in which some of the Russian warships attacked three trawlers of Hull's Gamecock fleet, mistaking them for the enemy. The fishermen held up their fish—"A man beside me saw / Two fishermen hold up four half-dead haddocks," Politovsky recounts—as proof of their harmlessness; nonetheless, two trawlermen were killed, others wounded, and the incident created a short-lived international crisis. And section 26 of part 4 has Politovsky imagining himself, having survived the battle, back home at a dinner party with Sophie. He is recounting an incident in which a sailor, who has stolen church offerings to buy drink, was sentenced to death, a judgment Politovsky disagrees with, because

> officers
> Drank like fish, and they didn't have to steal
> To do so. They just ran up a big bill
> In the wardroom, and that man called them "Sirs."
>
> (p. 85)

Politovsky and his author seem to share similar egalitarian sentiments. When the firing squad misses at its first attempt—a silent protest, though, ironically, all are drunk—the commanding officer orders that "all" rifles be loaded with live ammunition for a second attempt. The sequence finishes:

> And there was something almost like tenderness
> In how their bullets this time didn't miss
> Their handsome target. But what was his story?
>
> "It's the mops I hear, swabbing the gundeck clean,
> Washing the blood away, the human stains,
> Twelve bullets' worth, heartblood, and the spilled
> brains.
> It's the mops I hear. Do you know what I mean?"
>
> And then I'll go quiet. I'll sink in my chair.
> There are those who'll think it's all for effect
> And quite beneath their hardnosed intellect.
> Later, I'll jump up and shout, *"I've been there!"*
>
> (p. 86)

Such episodes of sheer narrative interest, bloody though they are, provide respite for the reader from Politovsky's preoccupation with his wife and duties. Dunn's decision to concentrate throughout on quatrains, which must have become second nature to him, also helped foreground the story he had to tell; he could take his manner for granted from a technical standpoint, though the verse is by no means repetitious: the poet constantly varies the rhythm of his lines.

THE YEAR'S AFTERNOON *(2000)*

Published in the same year as his long maritime narrative, *The Year's Afternoon* has a meditative and somewhat subdued air. Dunn often worked on these poems as a break from the marathon of *The Donkey's Ears,* as he indicated in a note in the Poetry Society's *Bulletin* in 2000, when *The Year's Afternoon* was a Poetry Society Book Choice. Solitude and melancholy prevail—Dunn had separated from his second wife in 1997—and the poet saw fit to include only ten of its pieces in his *New Selected Poems.* The book shows the almost sixty-year-old poet, a tenured academic at a foremost Scottish University, living predominantly in memory. In "East Riding," implicitly about his first wife, Lesley Wallace, his way of preserving the past is, ironically, to refuse to revisit a once-loved haunt lest the memory be sullied by the changed present:

Some landscapes never change, because they stay
Unvisited as too significant
For a return, and must remain the same ...

(p. 67)

His first wife's spirit recurs throughout the book. A related poem, the touching if overlong "Martagon Lilies," constructs an idealized aesthetic landscape from a painting by the Scottish colorist Samuel Peploe to "commemorate" what appears to have been Dunn's first wife's "colourist philosophy." The poem is an act of artistic defiance against duty: "I keep my liberty," the poet writes, "To dream myself into a 'piece of true'" (p. 74). The piece reveals how much his first wife's taste in art still influences him almost twenty years later. The poem concludes with a brief paean to botany and flora and states his belief "In being kind, in the holding of hands" (p. 76).

Lesley Dunn appears again in "On Whether Loneliness Ever Has a Beginning," a sort of emotional stocktaking of and meditation on the poet's relationships with women. A poem of nine sections written in short-lined quatrains at once gloomy, touching, and lyrical, it finishes with the solitary poet in his garden at 2 A.M. in January. Elsewhere, he concludes "If Only," a delicate reminiscence of waiting for his first wife after work in Giffnock on the outskirts of Glasgow in the early 1960s, "If only I knew then what I still don't know." The line has the memorable surprise of an epigram.

Some of the volume's poems are less self-preoccupied. "Teachers" is a celebratory reminiscence of an English lecturer, Margaret Espinasse, who taught Dunn at the University of Hull between 1966 and 1969; he holds up her example as a scholar and philologist, among other things, to help him "give the slip" to his "depressions." "Scott's Arks" is a socio-documentary piece in Dunn's lyric style, contrasting "a girl in service" in Broughty Ferry near Dundee, who sees through a steamy window the *Discovery,* Scott's vessel of Antarctic exploration (1901–1904) built on the Tay, sailing off down the Firth. The poem is in the same stanza form as *The Donkey's Ears* and closes:

What did *she* feel watching *Discovery*'s
Departure? Probably nothing, as steam
Re-clouded the window—she, too, a dream,
Or less than that, in the world's stories.

(p. 16)

The poem is underpinned by polarity: the privileged "vainglorious Scott's" prominence set against the serving girl's obscurity, elucidated obliquely by the space given to each. (She occupies only the first and closing stanzas of this eleven-stanza poem, and a single line in stanza eight.) The girl is part of the same imaginative cast in which Dunn features gaberlunzies and old destitute women at railway stations.

Also in this group is "A Complete Stranger," in which "the soft, faint thud" of a woman committing suicide in front of a train the poet is traveling on while he is daydreaming about fruit is registered as a "train's klaxon crying" and "a minor shock" in his arthritic knee. The grimness of the suicide is sharply delineated by the sudden silence of the halted train and the newly arrived policemen's walkie-talkies. The poem concludes:

I knew her only as an anonymous thud—
And as pears, damsons, and speculations—
As a complete stranger, and as this.

(p. 31)

The poem's obscurely touching quality comes from Dunn's understatement, the vital whimsicality of autonomous inner life as exemplified by his daydreaming, and his recognition of the way the tragedies of others can barely impinge themselves on us and that there is nothing that can be done about this. The dead woman becomes a simple occasion for a poem, an irony not lost on the poet in his closing line.

"Three Poets," by contrast, is a formal celebratory elegy for three of Scotland's finest poets, who all died in 1986—Norman MacCaig, Sorley MacLean, and George Mackay Brown, the first two in their eighties, the latter in his mid-seventies. The elegy is anecdotal, commemorative, and at times hyperbolic—Dunn's calling three fine poets "great men" seems a conflation of two different ranges of quality and brings to mind Laura Riding's notion that the truly great, being egoless, are least likely to have been heard of. The poem's affection is touching, but many readers would raise an eyebrow at some of its more extravagant assertions, as when Dunn calls the three "Our chiefs of men." The poem is strongest for its anecdotal reminiscences, especially of Norman MacCaig, whom Dunn probably knew best (Sorley MacLean is referred to as being six feet tall; he was two or three inches shorter). Here he is remembering MacCaig:

Norman, when asked, "Norman, do you smoke?"
Answered politely with his polished joke—
"Almost professionally."

...

Norman, when asked, "Norman, do you drink?"
Thought for a second, and said, "Do I *think?*"

(pp. 32, 33)

Douglas Dunn can certainly take his place in such distinctive and distinguished company. A sense of integrity, an unfashionable social conscience, an engaging, thrawn romanticism, and a generosity of feeling are all bound together in his work by scrupulous craftsmanship. In the *Verse* interview he observed:

Decency is in knowing about what's happened, and what can happen, and being aware of the possible squalor and toxicity of life, but at the same time—without evasions—of refusing to allow one's own life to become contaminated with the crimes against humanity and nature.

(p. 30)

It is a humane and responsible statement, rewardingly exemplified by one of the most substantial bodies of work by any contemporary Scottish poet. The best of it can stand comparison with the finest British poetry of the last fifty years.

Selected Bibliography

WORKS OF DOUGLAS DUNN

POETRY

Terry Street. London: Faber, 1969; New York: Chilimark, 1969.

Backwaters. Oxford: The Review, 1971.

The Happier Life. London and New York: Faber, 1972.

Love or Nothing. London: Faber, 1974.

Barbarians. London and Boston: Faber, 1979.

St. Kilda's Parliament. London and Boston: Faber, 1981.

Europa's Lover. Newcastle upon Tyne: Bloodaxe, 1982.

Elegies. London and Boston: Faber, 1985.

Selected Poems, 1964–1983. London and Boston: Faber, 1986.

Northlight. London: Faber, 1988.

The Poll Tax: The Fiscal Fake. Counterblasts series. London: Chatto & Windus, 1990.

Dante's Drum-kit. London and Boston: Faber, 1993.

Selected Poems. Edited by Alasdair D. F. Macrae. York, U.K.: Longman, 1993.

The Donkey's Ears: Politovsky's Letters Home. London: Faber, 2000.

The Year's Afternoon. London: Faber, 2000.

New Selected Poems, 1964–2000. London: Faber, 2003.

SHORT STORIES

Secret Villages. London: Faber, 1985; New York: Dodd, Mead, 1985.

Boyfriends and Girlfriends. London: Faber, 1995.

EDITED WORKS AND TRANSLATIONS

New Poems, 1972–73: A Pen Anthology of Contemporary Poetry. London: Hutchison, 1973.

A Choice of Byron's Verse. London: Faber, 1974.

Two Decades of Irish Writing: A Critical Survey. Manchester: Carcanet, 1975; Chester Springs, Penn.: Dufour, 1975.

What Is To Be Given: Selected Poems of Delmore Schwartz. Manchester: Carcanet, 1976.

Poetry Book Society Supplement. London: Poetry Book Society, 1979.

The Poetry of Scotland. London: Batsford, 1979.

A Rumoured City: New Poets from Hull. Newcastle upon Tyne: Bloodaxe, 1982.

Racine, Jean. *Andromache.* (Translation.) London: Faber, 1990.

Scotland: An Anthology. London: Fontana, 1992.

The Faber Book of Twentieth-Century Scottish Poetry. London and Boston: Faber, 1992.

The Oxford Book of Scottish Short Stories. Oxford and New York: Oxford University Press, 1995.

Entering the Kingdom. Kirkcaldy, U.K.: Fife Council Libraries, 1998.

The Essential Browning: Selected and with an Introduction by Douglas Dunn. New York: Ecco Press, 1990.

ESSAYS

"Hugh MacDiarmid: Inhuman Splendours." *New Edinburgh Review* 52:110-123 (November 1980).

Under the Influence: Douglas Dunn on Philip Larkin. Edinburgh: Edinburgh University Library, 1987.

"Importantly Live": Lyricism in Contemporary Poetry. Dundee: Dundee University, 1987.

"Scottish Cadence and Scottish Life." *Times Literary Supplement,* October 28, 1988, pp. 1202-1203.

"'As a Man Sees …': On Norman MacCaig's Poetry." *Verse* 7:55-67 (summer 1990).

"Language and Liberty." Introduction to *The Faber Book of Twentieth Century Scottish Poetry.* London and Boston: Faber, 1992.

"A Difficult, Simple Art." In *Strong Words: Modern Poets on Modern Poetry.* Edited by W. N. Herbert and Matthew Hollis. Tarset, Northumberland, U.K.: Bloodaxe, 2000. Pp. 163-166.

CRITICAL AND BIOGRAPHICAL STUDIES

Ash, John. "Pleasures of Invention, Rigours of Responsibility: Some Notes on the Poetry of Douglas Dunn." *PN Review* 34:43-46 (1983).

Crawford, Robert, and David Kinloch. *Reading Douglas Dunn.* Modern Scottish Writers Series. Edinburgh: Edinburgh University Press, 1992.

Duxbury, Robert. "The Poetry of Douglas Dunn." *Akros* 14:47-61 (August 1979). Also in *Nine Contemporary Poets: A Critical Introduction.* Edited by P. R. King. London: Methuen, 1979. Pp. 221–228.

Killick, John: "Raising the Soul Up: A Brief Guide to the Poetry of Douglas Dunn." *North* 29 (autumn 2001).

O'Brien, Sean. "Douglas Dunn, Ideology and Pastoral." In his *The Deregulated Muse: Essays in Contemporary British and Irish Poetry.* Newcastle upon Tyne: Bloodaxe, 1998. Pp. 65-80.

INTERVIEWS

Baer, Bill. "An Interview with Douglas Dunn." *Formalist* 8:19-36 (1997).

Cambridge, Gerry. "Douglas Dunn in Conversation." *Dark Horse* 8:20-31 (autumn 1999).

Crawford, Robert. "Douglas Dunn Talking with Robert Crawford." *Verse* 4:26-34 (1985).

Dunn, Douglas. "Dimensions of the Sentient." In Colin Nicholson, *Poem, Purpose and Place: Shaping Identity in Contemporary Scottish Verse.* Edinburgh: Polygon, 1992. Pp. 183-201.

Haffenden, John. "Douglas Dunn." In his *Viewpoints: Poets in Conversation.* London and Boston: Faber, 1981. Pp. 11-34.

MacNaughton, Maureen, and Ian White. "Interview with Douglas Dunn." *Fife Lines* 3:23-26 (winter 1999–2000).

PROFILES

Bruce, Keith: "Perfection Personified." *Herald Weekend Living,* January 11, 2003, p. 14.

Crawford, Robert. In *Devolving English Literature.* Oxford: Oxford University Press, 1992. Pp. 276–282.

MacIntyre, Lorn. "Poetic Justice for Dunn, the Rejected Student." *Glasgow Herald,* March 4, 1991, p. 9.

Nye, Robert. "A View beyond the Gasworks." *Scotsman Weekend,* October 30, 1993.

Taylor, Alan. "The Mellow Barbarian." *Observer Scotland,* September 24, 1989.

Wroe, Nicholas. "Speaking from Experience." *Guardian Review,* January 18, 2003, pp. 20-23.

ROMESH GUNESEKERA

(1954–)

Gautam Kundu

IN COLONIAL TIMES under British rule, creative prose in Sri Lanka was mostly in the hands of the island's elites; written primarily in English, this literature had little to say about the actual Sri Lankan realities and experiences. After Sri Lanka's independence from Britain in 1948 (and its subsequent entry in the British Commonwealth of nations shortly thereafter), the situation did not change much, due largely to the fact that the academic community in Sri Lanka tended to dismiss this body of writing as being unrepresentative, and creative work in English was actively discouraged. With the exception of the work of Punyakante Wijenaike and James Goonewardene, English fiction in Sri Lanka was mediocre at best, with virtually no other writers of national or international reputation. However, the remarkable variety and vitality of Sri Lankan writing in English over the past three decades, especially fiction, has demonstrated that it is no longer inhibited by its own linguistic or creative diffidence. The skeptics, who for years had bemoaned the lack of any significant literary activity on the island and had darkly predicted the inevitable decline of English writing in postindependence Sri Lanka, have been proved wrong. The international successes of Michael Ondaatje's *The English Patient* (1992), Yasmine Gooneratne's *Pleasures of Conquest* (1995), and Ambalavaner Sivanandan's *When Memory Dies* (1997) are testimony to the impressive achievement of literature in English from Sri Lanka. While Sri Lankan poetry in English in the hands of such writers as Gooneratne, Patrick Fernando, Ashley Halpé, Jean Arasanayagam, and Rienzi Crusz has acquired a measure of success, it is the English-language fiction from the Sri Lankan diaspora that has helped put postindependence Sri Lankan writing firmly on the map of world literatures written in English. And the writer who

has contributed most to this visibility, besides Michael Ondaatje, is Romesh Gunesekera, whose collection of short stories *Monkfish Moon,* and three novels, *Reef, The Sandglass,* and *Heaven's Edge,* have been hailed as a substantive body of work.

LIFE

Romesh Gunesekera was born in Colombo, Sri Lanka (then Ceylon), on February 26, 1954, the son of Miriam and Douglas Gunesekera. In 1961 he and his family moved to the Philippines, where his father, an economist, helped set up the Asian Development Bank in Manila. When the family relocated to England in 1972, Gunesekera, bilingual in Sinhala and English, attended the University of Liverpool, studying English and philosophy. While a student he won the Rathborn Prize in Philosophy in 1976. In 1988 he was awarded first prize in the Afro-Caribbean/Asian section of the Peterloo Open Poetry Competition. After an initial foray into writing and publishing poetry, Guneskera began to focus on fiction. Between 1988 and 1992 he published his work, both poetry and fiction, in such literary journals and magazines as *Granta, London* magazine, *Strand, London Review of Books, Poetry Durham, Poetry Now,* the *Guardian,* and *Time,* among others.

Monkfish Moon, a collection of nine short stories, was Gunesekera's first book. Published in 1992, the collection offers an intriguing blend of nostalgia, character study, and sharply observed vignettes of Sri Lankan life and its varied local charms, as well as the menacing realities of its ethnic and political tensions. *Monkfish Moon* was a *New York Times* Notable Book of the Year. In

ROMESH GUNESEKERA

1991 Gunesekera was awarded an Arts Council Writer's Award, which temporarily freed him from the constraints of having to earn a living and allowed him to concentrate on his writing instead. *Reef,* his much-acclaimed first novel, was published in 1994. An allegorical tale of Sri Lanka's gradual decline into political anarchy and social chaos, the book was short-listed for Britain's prestigious Booker Prize in 1994. The novel was praised for its finely modulated prose and deeply elegiac tone mourning the demise of the Sri Lanka of Gunesekera's childhood. Translated into languages including Dutch, French, German, Italian, Norwegian, Spanish, and Chinese, *Reef* was also nominated for the 1995 New Voices award. Gunesekera's second novel, *The Sandglass,* published in 1998, was awarded the BBC Asia Award of Achievement in Writing and Literature. His third novel, *Heaven's Edge,* came out in 2002 and has since been translated into French, Dutch, and Spanish.

POETRY

Today Gunesekera is known mostly for his fiction, but poetry was his proverbial first love, and he continues to work in this form. Although he has yet to publish a collection of poems, a study of his poetry reveals some recurring themes and concerns.

The idea of home (and the complicated notion of belonging) recur in several of Gunesekera's poems of the mid-1980s. In "Circled by Circe" (1985), the speaker mulls over the complexity of an immigrant's yearning to return "Back 'home,'" his "conversation" increasingly "spiced / with images of gold sand, tamarind trees, / the cacophony of traffic—lorries, cars, / bullock carts, bicycles—." Circe-like, the island beckons, but the truth is that for the exile a return home is every bit as tentative and uncertain as the "fragile memory" of a past that "might have been" which haunts his psyche. If exilic roots need the replenishment of "native" soil, then, by the same token, return and relocation are illusions. In "Going Home (A Letter to Colombo)," the poetic persona acknowledges the difficulty of return: the "old house is in ruins" and "every clock / in this

house has stopped": its ruinous present casts a very long shadow on the "home," which is being destroyed slowly but irreversibly from within, an allusion to Sri Lanka's ethno-political difficulties. In "House Building" (1985), Gunesekera plays with an interesting irony. Both "old houses"—Sri Lanka and Britain—are "losing." While "so much of the island"—Sri Lanka—"seems to burn," singed by the flames of its political passions, life in Britain too is being wasted by the corrosive power of the "politics and grit" of devouring Capital. As social engineering in the adopted "home" subtly but surely erodes the immigrant's own cultural consciousness, the speaker "would like to build a house, to keep something in, / something out": in other words, create a space for himself where he would preserve what was worth preserving and reject all that was not. And the "house" he builds is the house of art, of imagination, deeply infused with the memory of a "private past" and "a wealth of ancestral / anecdotes" ("An Honourable Estate," 1985) that gives such effort its energy and meaning.

Gunesekera's writing, whether poetry or prose, is particularly rich in the journey motif, with its connotations of quest and discovery. An early poem, "Captain Nemo" (1985), celebrates such journeys as "always precious" because they are usually about "something elsewhere, out of sight, something in the imagination." (in Erny, p. 5). Journeys also bridge distances and create new worlds—important to a postcolonial writer for whom the search for union, for a past that breathes life into a bare history of present global diaspora, is vital and necessary. In Gunesekera's poetry, journeys are more than physical and geographical; oftentimes they are allegories of quest: "excursions into the interior" as he calls them in "Indefinite Exposure." For the poet there is no "illusion of a captured moment," as in photography. Time is rendered concrete and real through art, but in order to do that the poet (and his poetry) must "travel / into an indefinite past" of the "beamed green" of the countryside and the "warm gold / of harvest paddy" ("Indefinite Exposure"). Landscape and space become crucial aspects of remembering and of the narrative of human relationships.

ROMESH GUNESEKERA

If there is a clash between the inherited and the acquired in the language of postcolonial writing—that is, between the mother tongue and a European language—then writing in English in Sri Lanka has only rarely been regarded as a form of cultural treason. Yasmine Gooneratne, in her "This Language, This Woman," approaches English as a lover, and Gunesekera does no less. In "Frontliners" he writes: "In a post-colonial / spice garden / I grew up out of step: / dreaming in English." Gunesekera's poems possess a framework provided by a cross-cultural mishmash: Robin Hood ("Sherwood Forest / of tropicalized longbows"), James Bond, and rock and roll. Such self-confessed drollery is matched by the poet's sly deflation of the imperial culture, which, he implies, takes its form and content from "a pile of tatty war comics / and second-hand adventure stories." And in "Pigs," the poetic persona ruminates on the universality of violence and the elegant "repackaging" of death in Europe/London: "At dinner the pig's head / with an apple in its mouth / grinned from a silver tray." The wry tone of the closing lines strips the imperial of its pretensions: "I quickly learned the art: / chucking English carcasses / off my back."

Finally, Gunesekera's poetry depicts a revelatory quality, a sudden awareness of connections—across peoples, geographies, and nature—that resist the anxieties of dispersal and fragmentation inherent in the postcolonial condition. "Indian Tree" and "Watermark" speak with quiet but gentle eloquence about human connections withstanding, indeed defying, the proverbial ravages of time and the notion that the mighty world of "eyes and ears" is but a *maya,* an illusion, a "swatch / of time bound to desire" ("Watermark"). It is the "fresh blend" of cultures, of "entangling / east to west" that makes the poet feel "a delicate / prescience" ("Indian Tree") of love and continuity, of "something of ourselves met," as he notes elsewhere ("Mountain Shadow").

SHORT FICTION: MONKFISH MOON

Monkfish Moon (1992) serves as a precursor text to the author's later works. Several themes that run through the stories are echoed and reformulated in his novels, including home, leave-takings, and exile; memory, loss of innocence, and nostalgia; the difficulties of return and reconnection in the wake of postcolonial diaspora and displacements of peoples and cultures; and Sri Lanka's political violence. In "A House in the Country," an expatriate's return and his dreams of rebuilding a life in Sri Lanka are shattered by terror attacks and death. "Stormy Petrel" narrates a similarly troubled story of a returning expatriate whose good intentions of setting up a hospitality business in Sri Lanka collapse in the face of the grim reality of ethnic strife. In "Batik," the theme of ethnic violence at home and its emotional and psychological consequences finds a poignant expression in the gradual estrangement of a London-based Sri Lankan couple of Tamil and Sinhalese origins. One of the most complex stories in the collection, "Captives," is a subtle but complicated tale of sexual desire and artistic achievements interwoven with a familiar trope of postcolonialism, the so-called politics of tourism. And the title story of the book articulates a compelling anxiety about the precolonial cultural wholeness of Sri Lanka giving way to its postindependence social, cultural, and political fragmentation, an important theme in Gunesekera's novels.

REEF

Like *Monkfish Moon,* Gunesekera's debut novel, *Reef* (1994), explores the themes of exile, wanderings and relocations in the diaspora, and the ambivalence and fragility of returns and reconnections. But the predominant theme of the novel is that of "despoiled paradise," of a postlapsarian Eden haunted by a sense of irredeemable loss and melancholy.

Structurally the book is divided into five parts. A prelude of sorts called, appropriately, "The Breach," introduces the narrator, Triton, a Sinhalese émigré in London, and his metaphoric double, a young Tamil refugee from Sri Lanka, who meet across the reinforced service windows of a dimly lit London petrol station. The chance meeting sets in motion a "long fugue of memory" that takes Triton back some thirty years, to 1962, and six thousand miles to a "bay-fronted house" (p. 13) in his native Sri Lanka. Told in a series of flashbacks, Triton's story unfolds and reaches its climax in the remaining four chapters. The first-person narrative begins with a recollection of Triton's arrival as a young domestic in the household of Mr. Ranjan Salgado, a "product of modern feudalism" (p. 16) and a largely self-educated but wealthy Sinhalese marine biologist and conservationist working to save some endangered coral reefs around Sri Lanka. The rest of the story is developed around the motif of the master-servant relationship that Gunesekera had first introduced and explored in his short story "A Home in the Country" in *Monkfish Moon.*

Moving from boyhood through adolescence and into adulthood, Triton eventually becomes Mr. Salgado's cook and caretaker. Intelligent and creative, Triton learns quickly; he soaks in as much as Mr. Salgado is able to offer. As Triton remembers, "I watched him, I watched him unendingly. All the time, and learned to become what I am" (p. 53). Soon he becomes something of a culinary expert, preparing both spicy native dishes as well as some Western cuisine. Triton, who "creates" "wondrous" meals for his patrons, appropriately stands for the fledgling artist: concentrated, dedicated, and proud of his culinary artistry. Underscoring the cook-artist's emerging voice is Triton's stream of memory, which according to the author serves a Proustian function of setting into motion the processes of remembering (in Davis, p. 50).

Triton also wants to experience, as he says, "Mister Salgado's famous ocean and the life beyond our garden gate" (p. 62). The world outside the sequestered Salgado estate is a tumultuous one, for political and social changes of cataclysmic proportions have threatened the stability of the island nation since its political independence from Britain in 1948. These historic events are presented in and through the narrative point of view of the young houseboy-cook, whose grasp of the nature and meaning of such momentous occasions in Sri Lankan national life is understandably limited. When Mr. Salgado falls in love with the fetching Miss Nili, Triton

helps the two come together. However, sooner than anyone can anticipate, the lives of the three are irrevocably changed by the far-left insurgency in Sri Lanka and the civil war between the Sinhalese and Tamils that follows. Mr. Salgado fails in his effort to save the eroding reefs from destruction, and he decides to leave troubled Sri Lanka for London; a willing Triton accompanies him there. As days slowly fade into months and then years, the two drift here and there in England before Mr. Salgado decides to buy a property in London. But soon he has to return to Sri Lanka to care for an ailing Nili, now a casualty of the civil war. As the opening chapter makes apparent, Triton decides to stay on in London, the owner, presumably, of his own restaurant, serving ethnic food to "bedraggled cosmopolitan itinerants" (p. 190) and refugees like himself. In these intervening years Triton has finally found his own voice, reflecting on his yesterdays and on his present identity as an exile in London "without a past, without a name" (p. 190).

Much postcolonial literature, fiction especially, is marked by an irreducible sense of loss, which carries with it a vast weight of hidden pain and anguish. In *Reef* what Triton remembers most, with an overwhelming sense of regret and nostalgia, is a collapse of the relationships and nurturing he associates with his homeland, its beauty and innocence threatened with destruction under the burden of its present political and civic chaos. What Triton mourns for in people is commitment to tolerance, kindliness, and personal loyalty, exemplified by Mr. Salgado and Miss Nili, both ironically members of the Sri Lankan Sinhala elite, many of whom either emigrated to the West in the early 1960s or, as in the case of Ranjan Salgado, found the communist-led insurgency and ethnic civil war a baffling and profoundly disturbing experience.

Respectful toward Mr. Salgado, Triton sees him more as a mentor than as a master. However, in the hierarchical society of Sri Lanka, mutuality between master and servant is unworkable. What emerges instead is a narrative of dependence in which Triton's existence is shaped by Mr. Salgado, largely because Triton himself has ceded his personhood to his master. So when Mr. Salgado decides to leave Sri Lanka for London, Triton has nothing to do but follow him there. Similarly, in his respectful and adoring relationship with Miss Nili, Triton is grateful for her humane treatment of him even as he, mirroring his master's growing love for her, develops platonic longings for Nili. However, Triton is careful not to transgress the codes of accepted social behavior or to undermine his role of sympathetic but nonparticipatory observer. Such dependencies are no longer tenable in times of revolutionary changes in Sri Lankan society. Hence Triton yearns after the lost norms of a relatively innocent precolonial time and in Sri Lanka's mythic past, which Mr. Salgado associates with "paradise" (p. 94) and the "Garden of Eden" (p. 95). This mythic past is reconstituted in the very act of remembering, and the "loss" that the novel mourns is recuperated in and through the processes of memory. As Ranjan Salgado wistfully tells Triton, "we are what we remember, nothing more" (p. 190).

Much as memory is instrumental in recovering the past, it is also something that Triton shores up against the ruins of time: memory provides distance, and with it, the advantage of perspective and understanding. Memory also helps Triton cope with the apparent ambivalence of his diasporic identity and the cultural and psychological implications of his displacement and relocation in postcolonial metropolitan London. The "voyage of discovery" (p. 184) he alludes to in the end is in good measure engendered and sustained by his memory—as is the elegiac tone that permeates the novel. Triton's "discovery" of who he is or wants to be is best understood in the context of reading *Reef* both as a bildungsroman ("formation novel") and a *Kunstlerroman* ("artist novel") Considered thus, the novel charts two related aspects of Triton's intellectual growth and maturity: his emerging sense of self, embedded and implicated in the intricacies of the human condition; and the genesis and evolution of his artistic destiny. Triton's encounter with Joseph, the head servant in the Salgado estate, brings him to a confrontation with deceit, disloyalty, petty tyranny and the compulsions of power, and

with the threat of sexual abuse. When Joseph loses his job because of his drunkenness, Triton assumes the responsibilities of running the household. He learns his duties quickly; he also begins to acquire formal education under Mr. Salgado's tutelage. Part of Triton's education is understanding the worth of human dignity, his subaltern status notwithstanding. In fact Triton's interactions with Lucy-*amma,* the cook-woman, and with Ranjan Salgado and Miss Nili (who gives him a cookbook as a Christmas gift) are all positive. Each in his or her own way accords Triton personhood well beyond his socially and culturally designated role as a houseboy.

If Nili is an essential part of what has been called Mr. Salgado's "sentimental education," then her presence in the Salgado home marks Triton's first exposure to woman as an object of male desire. Paralleling his master's love for Nili, Triton too has romantic fantasies about her. For all his youth and his easy impressionability, Triton realizes that Nili's decision to move in with Mr. Salgado signals the "beginning of a new era" (p. 113); he observes that "the changes in our household were momentous" (p. 118). Ironically, Triton draws a parallel between the "unorthodox changes" (p. 107) in the Salgado family with the changes in Sri Lanka: the nation, "sliding into unparalleled debt, girded itself for a change of a completely different order: a savage brutalizing whereby our *chandiyars*—our braggarts—would become thugs, our dissolutes turned into mercenaries and our leaders excel as small-time megalomaniacs" (p. 118).

As the "walls" around them "crumble" and "nothing" threatens to "remain the same" (p. 175), Mr. Salgado and Triton emigrate to London, where Triton completes the final phase of his growth as an individual. He becomes a consumer of books and words as well as a restaurateur. When Mr. Salgado decides to return to Sri Lanka to care for Miss Nili, Triton, with the "whole geography of [his] past ... reconstructed" (p. 175), also paradoxically confesses that he is "emptied of the past" (p. 61) and that he is not especially burdened with it or with a name (p. 190). Gunesekera sees this repudiation of the past as Triton's strategy of survival in the West (Davis,

p. 51). Distanced from personal, cultural, and historical ties, and finally freed from his alter ego, Ranjan Salgado, Triton learns to "live on his own" and create for himself his own space whose parameters are flexible and porous enough to accommodate his adaptive strategies in the West. Put differently, what Triton has been able to achieve in his exile is something modest and intimate but which is also, from his point of view at least, something profoundly important. Like Voltaire's Candide, he has learned to cultivate his own garden and invest in people—in "the line of bedraggled, cosmopolitan itinerants" on a "voyage of discovery" (p. 184)—and hence, in his own "future" (p. 188). More crucially, Triton's exilic status forces upon him the importance of the past and the need to remember it and turn it into narrative, for, as he muses, "without words to sustain it, the past would die" (p. 49). In the end, it is memory shaped by narrative that gives life and meaning to Triton's experiences, first as a "native" in Sri Lanka and then as a Sri Lankan "exile" in postimperial London, even though his expatriate identity still remains contingent.

Closely intertwined with Triton's narrative of growth and maturation is the gradual unfolding of his artistic destiny. In interviews with Rocio Davis and Hans-Georg Erney, Gunesekera emphasizes that Triton "functions as an artist" in *Reef* and points out the importance of culinary art as a "memory," a "trigger" in the processes of remembering (Davis, p. 50). The diligence and care that Triton lavishes on his cooking, indeed his entire approach to culinary art—most memorably seen in the chapter called "Cook's Joy," where Triton prepares an elaborate Christmas dinner for Mr. Salgado and his invited guests—is analogous to a painter working on his canvas or a writer painstakingly discovering her own niche or signature voice. Read this way, *Reef* functions as an allegory of a cook-waiter's emergence as an artist in his own right, one who is both a witness to and a native informant of his nation's (mythic) past and its reconstituted present. Like an artist committed to paint and brush or a writer wedded to words, Triton likes to "reach the mind" (p. 97) of his diners; his special work of art—a roasted turkey, "beautifully brown, ready to

burst" (p. 96)—conveys an aesthetic message that is sensuous and personal. Triton in Greek mythology is a demigod who possesses the magic powers to calm and enrage the ocean waters, much as an artist ensouls and disciplines his artistic creation with the powers of his imagination. Gunesekera's Triton is the author's archetypal artist figure: the storyteller who finds his authorial voice and is able, as Gunesekera has said, to "integrate lots of different things" (Erney, p. 6) into a narrative that can, potentially at least, make the river of time stand still.

Discussions of *Reef* invariably lead to a consideration of its compelling central symbol—the coral reefs that surround the island, the delicate organic systems that keep the ebb and flow of the ocean waters from gradually but irreversibly eroding the shores. It is parts of these reefs that Mr. Salgado is determined to survey, map, and preserve from the eroding waters of the sea (a motif that recurs through the novel) and from human destruction. As a conservationist, Ranjan Salgado has a twin objective, one immediate and the other long-term. First, he wants to save the coral reefs; second, more ambitiously, his overarching concern is with the delicate balance of the "*immediate* environment" (p. 58)—the danger of the beach yielding to the rushing sea, a fate from which he is committed to saving the island. As Triton says at one point, Mr. Salgado was "going to save the island from the sea and the mind from forlorn darkness" (p. 65), thus connecting the inevitable passage of time with the urgency to protect and conserve the natural world through environmentally responsible action. It is the ocean's "hunger for land" (p. 93)—nature's devouring urges—that Mr. Salgado sees as the principal threat to the coral reefs. As the crisis of the reefs' threatened disappearance looms ever larger, Mr. Salgado's gloom deepens: "Now as the coral disappears," he warns, "there will be nothing but sea and we will all return to it" (p. 182).

It is the reefs' inevitable destruction that portends the "death" of Sri Lanka itself: its internal dissension brings ruin to an island of near-paradisial beauty and made of the very stuff of myths and legends. In symbolic terms, the endangered reefs represent the precolonial *Ratna-dip* (island of gems), the "wife of many marriages, courted by invaders who stepped ashore and claimed everything with the power of their sword or bible or language," as Michael Ondaatje ruefully notes in his fragmentary 1982 memoir of Sri Lanka, *Running in the Family* (p. 64). For Gunesekera's Triton, it also represents a *way* of life, a stability, a certain fixity of values that is now contested by the ethno-political violence and civil war in Sri Lanka. The "encroaching sea" (p. 93), the "pressing ocean" (p. 164), the "hungry sea" (p. 187) is a recurring metaphor for the changes that are taking place as Sri Lanka decolonizes itself, changes that keep "eroding" the very fabric of the civic and political life of the nation. "Trapped inside what [he] could see, what [he] could hear ... and what [he] could remember from ... [his] mud-walled school" (p. 40), the young Triton is unable to fathom these momentous changes. It is as if they were quite beyond the pale of the "undefined boundaries" (p. 40) Triton traverses, and he seems to remain magically untouched by these events.

The references in *Reef* to contemporary political events in Sri Lanka, as Neil Gordon has provocatively argued, create a peculiar problem. While the major political events from the mid-1950s to the early 1980s are alluded to in the novel, they do not form "an organic part of Triton's story" (Gordon, p. 2). These events include the de-anglicization of Sri Lanka in 1956 that led to the ethnic disturbances of 1958; the new left and ultra-left inspired insurgency of 1971, which marked the first large-scale revolt in Sri Lankan history of the mostly urban poor Sinhalese and Buddhist youth; and finally, the armed confrontation between the Tamil "Liberation Tigers" and the Sinhalese state in 1983, civil strife that remains unresolved in the early twenty-first century. The threat of a Che Guevera–style revolution in Sri Lanka, with its potential for violent class conflict, is articulated by Wijetunga, Mr. Salgado's assistant and a would-be revolutionary. "You know, brother," he tells the young Triton, "our country needs to be cleansed radically. There's no alternative. We have to

destroy in order to create. [Maybe then] ... one day we will be able to live by ourselves" (p. 121).

Clearly Gunesekera has not avoided acknowledging the troubled march of Sri Lankan postcolonial history, and these events are framed in the larger context of the currents of violent changes in world history: "Belfast, Phnom Penh, Amman, places I had never heard of," recalls Triton, "as well as our own small provinces" (p. 175). Yet for all these references to history and politics, Neil Gordon is right to point out that the narrative of the political remains extrinsic to the story of Triton's intellectual growth. As Triton himself confesses, "In those days I had no real interest in politics of the countryside: we each have to live by our own dreams" (p. 118). Triton's dreams have to do with acquiring culinary skills: he is an artist in the making and so he remains till the end, "taking in thought after thought" (p. 62), mixing and voicing memory and desire, fusing the present with the past. The adult Triton is certainly more educated, more knowledgeable and aware than his younger self, but he is not necessarily more politically conscious. His attitude to the question of Tamil separatism in Sri Lanka is simplistic, locked within the familiar binaries of reason and passion, humanistic and revolutionary socialist values, and the Sinhala and Tamil religious and cultural divide. There is not one Tamil character in the novel, and the revolutionary aspirations of a petit bourgeois like Wijetunga are eventually marginalized. Without going into the debatable and largely fruitless question of where the author stands vis-à-vis the politics of the novel, or whether Ranjan Salgado is the authorial mouthpiece, suffice to say that while *Reef* does offer readers specific historical and political markers in the life of the Sri Lankan nation since its independence from Britain in 1948, it does not provide them with an understanding of or fresh insights into the genesis and evolution of these defining events. For instance, whereas the insurgency of 1971 involved some notions of class within Sri Lankan economic and social stratifications, the civil war of the 1980s and beyond called attention to the issues of ethnicity and identity and contested the idea of the (unitary) nation itself. *Reef* does not offer readers awareness of these issues.

THE SANDGLASS

Gunesekera's second novel, *The Sandglass* (1998) , returns to the theme of exile (and of the exilic self) with greater emphasis and complexity than in the earlier work. Here the postcolonial tropes of a ruined, feminine, and eroticized nation (p. 134) are interfused with Gunesekera's meditations on mortality and the inevitable passage of time—hence the central metaphor of the sandglass in the book's title, with its suggestion of sands running through an hourglass, and chapter references to the movements of the hours from morning to dusk to night. Like *Reef, The Sandglass* is set in post-empire London, and again like the first novel, it has a narrative frame. Chip, the book's first-person narrator and a Sri Lankan émigré, repeatedly goes over in his mind the story of his friend Prins Ducal, who has disappeared without a trace; Prins's mother, Pearl; and the complicated tale of two feuding families, the Ducals and the scheming and conniving Vatunases, "who seemed forever coiled around them" (p. 2). The nonlinear plot, composed of a series of fragmented flashbacks on the domestic and business tragedies of the Ducals, and to a lesser extent those of the Vatunases, mirror the political schisms that underlie the multiple national tragedies of Sri Lanka and its splintering along ethno-political lines (a point Jacqueline Carey makes in her review). As Jason Cowley observes, Pearl's death, with which the novel opens, prefigures the death of a nation, and the Ducals' mansion, appropriately named Arcadia, "serves as a metaphor for the former Ceylon itself: a home acquired, like the independence of the island nation, in a spirit of renewal but which, as decades pass, increasingly becomes the object of discord and ruin" (p. 49). These structural techniques give the narrative design of the novel a metafictional quality, but the tone of the work is touched by a deep sense of personal loss— of "parents, homes and homelands" (Wickramagamage, p. 112).

Exilic, deterritorialized existence, whether voluntary or "chosen," is not an enabling form of dislocation in *The Sandglass;* the Sri Lankan exiles in the novel carry the burden of their cultural baggage, often with unhappy consequences. Pearl, Prins, Ravi, and especially Chip may possess what Edward Said has called a "plurality of vision"—an awareness of more than "one culture, one setting, one love" (p. 185), but that does not necessarily mean that their lives have a stable center or coherence, either cultural or psychological. In their awareness of what has been left behind—home, history, culture, the relationships and mutual dependencies of a lifetime—and what they actually possess after their "voyage in" to the West (Edward Said's phrase), Gunesekera's characters suffer a rootlessness that saps the very cores of their being. Virtually every expatriate character in the novel, from Pearl Ducal and her sons Ravi and Prins to Chip, struggles with his or her "exilic identity" (to borrow a phrase from Walter Perera). Pearl's life, Chip says, is "sedentary" and "inert" (p. 187); but while she "knitted shawls or cardigans" (p. 10), her symbolic acts of trying to "knit" an identity for herself (and for the rest of the Ducals in England) remain at best incomplete. The case of Ravi, her second son, is even more tragic. Doubly marginalized as an exile and as the racialized Other, Ravi cuts himself off from all meaningful human contact, and on his forty-second birthday he effects a final erasure by committing suicide. Ravi's "secondary migration" to America—to "find it" and "discover it like the Inuit or Alastair Cook (p. 63)—fails, and he returns to London and to his death. Gunesekera has compared Ravi to Melville's Bartleby, whose rejection of society's material demands on him takes the form of an existential withdrawal into the silence of the self and eventually into the unquiet darkness of death. If Ravi's suicide marks an alternative voyage toward discovery in a world that has (for him, at least) lost its reasons for being, then his choice to write himself out of a specific narrative of the present suggests an impasse, a regression into self-annihilation that speaks compellingly of the unfortunate consequences of some boundary crossings.

Prins, Pearl's eldest son and the protagonist of the novel, suffers a fate that is only marginally different in its tragic implications. A restless globe-trotter, Prins lacks fixity and stability, a condition common to many postcolonial immigrants and exiles. Prins's return to "an old island" (p. 44) is also a form of reverse migration to his "dreamland" (p. 82). With its connotation of the imagined and the unreal, the island (and his return to it) is expressive of a longing, which is alive and vital—but only in the imagination. Prins's restless search for antiquity, and by implication something that is more authentic than the dubious present he faces in the West as well as in Sri Lanka, is scarred by repeated failures. He cannot marry Lola Vatunas, the love of his life, because, as he tells Chip, "Marriage is all family stuff, you know. Always a mess" (p. 232). More centrally, Prins's efforts to "combine business acumen with ethical considerations" (p. 99) and to "develop a modern cultural identity alongside the traditional tourist industry on the island" (p. 129) are undermined by its pervasive violence and corruption. In the end, inexplicably and mysteriously, he disappears, leaving unresolved and unfathomed the truth of his father's much publicized "accidental death" forty years earlier.

Prins may be obsessed with reconstructing the past as much as he is haunted by it, yet the irony of his situation is that he chooses to walk away from it, leaving unscrutinized the burden of his paternal history, with which his own is irrevocably enmeshed. Read allegorically, Prins's reluctance to confront the truth of his father's death—his father's history—speaks for Sri Lanka's refusal to face the contested nature of its own national history: Sinhalese-Buddhist instead of multiethnic and secular. Like Triton in *Reef,* whose survival in the West is predicated upon his ability to forge for himself an identity which in a sense is unstable, Prins Ducal turns away from the truth of his own discovery that Jason Ducal's death "was murder and it was fixed" (p. 267). Prins's "freedom," such as it is, is achieved at the cost of his flight from memory and history. Ironically, this freedom is a disabling one, for, among other things, Prins's "voyage in" experiences, initially to England, and his later return to Sri Lanka, leave him precariously disengaged and without a center.

As his name suggests, Chip is yet another fragmented and deracinated soul drifting across the bleached landscape of the novel. Beside his exilic present, he has little by way of his past to draw upon. Confidant to Pearl, to Prins, and to the rest of the Ducals, he is a passive witness to and a sympathetic narrator of their collective history of exile, psychological and social fragmentation, and cultural loss. As an observer and a secret sharer, Chip's "uncertain identity" (p. 10) and his "orphaned" past urge him toward greater involvement in the lives of the Ducals. He tries to fashion a narrative out of the discontinuous, misshapen, and often truncated memories of the Ducals and their fractured lives. Shadowy and ill-defined as his own past is, Chip hungers for the memories of other people, as if these stories were invested with a nourishing power of their own. Musing on Pearl's habit of recounting her past, Chip says, "She fed me stories, just as she fed me heart-stopping fried breakfasts and enormous buttery dinners" (p. 61): together, they "imagined other worlds for [themselves]" (p. 268). Ironically such "feeding" and emotional nourishments go only so far. Despite his involvement in the lives and destinies of the Ducals, Chip remains a neutral register of sorts, through whom the intertwined fates of the Ducals and the Vatunases are given form and coherence, if not an overarching meaning. Like Horatio in *Hamlet,* surveying the ruins of the past and a death-haunted present, Chip offers a requiem and brings closure to the multiple family tragedies of the novel. Standing alone amid the mutilated lives of the Ducals and their heap of broken dreams, Chip looks forward, albeit tentatively, to the day when "history would be freed from the shadows of the past" and when Dawn, Pearl's granddaughter and the "last of [her] displaced dreamline," would "spin us forward from this hurt earth to a somehow better future" (p. 278).

The idea of Sri Lanka as a fallen paradise, central to *Reef,* also forms the core of *The Sandglass.* If the civil war is one of the principal reasons for Sri Lanka's ruinous problems, then the introduction of global capital in the wake of decolonization is another. The march and spread of capital takes two forms in Gunesekera's second novel: one, the rise of indigenous capital represented by the Vatunases, whose sharp business practices and ruthless competitiveness are hugely destructive; and two, the introduction and subsequent popularity of the business of tourism, which peaks Prins's interest. In an unpublished conference paper on the topic, Helen Kapstein has suggested that for this "new" postcolonial tourism in Sri Lanka, "violence is the authenticating pull" (p. 11). Prins's potential success as an entrepreneur, packaging and selling a particular kind of "safari" to his Western clientele, depends upon its "flexibility," Kapstein posits. Such tourism accommodates two kinds of sightseers: those who want to see violence as a blood spectacle and those who prefer to be blind to it. On the one hand, Prins "finally ... seemed on the verge of turning blood into wine in the garland of stunning tourist hotels" (p. 224). On the other, he is "selling the paradise experience between death camp and suicide bombers to tourists who don't care" (p. 195). In postcolonial Sri Lanka the national (and local) economy is far from being truly national or free; it has taken on a neocolonial form. Under the guise of nationalization ("Ceylonisation"), the entrepreneurial class—the national bourgeoisie and Sri Lankan expatriates (such as Prins)—is intent on replacing the old and "ramshackle empire" of colonial Britain with a new kind of "subtle empire" (p. 103) operated by the natives, who rely on a "truly indigenous empire of growth" (p. 101). At least a part of that "empire of growth" consists of a postcolonial brand of tourism that thrives on "war-watching" (p. 229), as Prins, in a moment of black humor, claims.

What *The Sandglass* critiques is the moral and ethical bankruptcy of the new ruling classes in Sri Lanka. Jason Ducal's attempt to market a native beverage fails, undermined by the monopolistic business practices of Esra Vatunas, and Prins's entrepreneurial practice is no less rapacious and irresponsible. His "new kind of safari" would invite tourists to turn their (indifferent) gaze on human destruction and death. However, the fact that his tourist business does not even get started is a measure of the duplicitous power of the indigenous capitalists to effectively shut out expatriate competition.

As in *Reef,* in *The Sandglass* the political encircles the personal and the national in a serpentine, deadly embrace; here the family histories of the Ducals and the Vatunases are entwined with the narrative of the nation. As Robin Visel has shown in her study of the *The Sandglass,* references to historical events abound in the novel, and in virtually all cases these are tied to the lives of Gunesekera's central characters in one way or another. For instance, Pearl Ducal dates her first trip to England by recalling it was the same year of Neville Chamberlain's Appeasement Pact with Hitler back in 1938. The year 1948 brought Sri Lanka's independence, when "pundits argued about the color of a free flag" (p. 22); it is also the year when Jason Ducal buys his first home, "Arcadia," which borders Esra Vatunas's mansion, Bellevue, a fact that irreversibly circumscribes the lives and destinies of the two families. Jason dies of a mysterious gun wound in 1956, the year that Solomon Banderanaike's populist Sri Lanka Freedom Party defeated the United National Party and initiated a far-reaching nationalist agenda that led to the establishment of a majoritarian Sinhala-Buddhist identity for Ceylon/Sri Lanka. Jason Ducal's death, then, coincides with the "death" of a multiethnic, multi-religious Sri Lanka, which results in a crisis of confidence among Sri Lankan minorities. As in *Reef,* national history in *The Sandglass* is connected to the larger march of international events, notably the nationalization of the Suez Canal by Egyptian president Gamal Abdel Nasser in 1956. Thus the death of Jason Ducal is tied to an important moment in world history: decolonization. The year of Pearl's death and Prins's disappearance is 1993, a year marked in Sri Lankan history by the gory assassination of its president, Ranasinghe Premadasa. Hence the individual and family histories of the Ducals and the Vatunases, with their mutual antagonisms and feuds, are tied to the larger national history of postindependence Sri Lanka (and to that of the rest of the world), fraught with ethnic division and civil war, the consequences of short-sighted Sinhala nationalism and the politics of exclusion.

The all-too-discernible connection between the personal and family saga on the one hand, and the nation and its history on the other, might invite politically allegorical readings of *Reef* and *The Sandglass*. Such readings would seem to validate Fredric Jameson's pronouncement that in "Third world texts … *the story of the private individual destiny is always an allegory of the embattled situation of the public third world culture and society*" (p. 320; emphasis in the original). It is true that Gunesekera traces the workings of Sri Lanka's troubled postcolonial history in the lives (and fates) of his characters as well as in the narrative structures he employs—the fragmented story line in *The Sandglass,* for instance, reflects authorial anxieties about the chaos of present-day Sri Lanka. But the matter is more complicated than any generalized theory of national allegory might seem to suggest. Fragments of the national life in *Reef* and *The Sandglass* (and in some of the stories in *Monkfish Moon*) belie any desire on the author's part to use the novel form to create an overarching "national framework" for postcolonial Sri Lanka; in Timothy Brennan's words, "to assemble the fragments of a national life and give them a final shape" (Brennan, pp. 52, 61). In Gunesekera's work, these fragments of the nation's history and the (often) shredded lives of his characters resist any such neat or ordered containment. Focused as these narratives are on the private lives of individuals and their "libidinal dynamics" (Jameson, p. 330), they define themselves as "fictions" but not necessarily as "fictions of postcolonial Sri Lanka." As Robin Visel correctly points out, references to the historical and the political in Gunesekera's work are mixed with the literary and the aesthetic: his postmodern concern with language, writing, and textuality; his imagistic prose; his frequent allusions to and evocations of national myths; the symbolic geography of his settings; the delicately spun webs of cross-cultural references; and the ambiguous, open-ended plots that often resist structural closures.

In his 1996 interview with Hans-Georg Erney, Gunesekera explains his inclusion of the political in his writing by saying that "In a sense, everything we do is a political act, there is a political dimension to everything" (p. 7). The issue, however, is the nature of political discourse one finds in his short stories and novels. Some novelists tend to be radical voices while others support the dominant sociopolitical and cultural ideologies. The political in Gunesekera's fiction, too, needs to be viewed either as radical discourse or that of social hegemony. In the same interview, he also claims that he is not a polemical writer and that he writes a "different kind of work" (p. 70) that offers reassessment—"reviving values of being able to look again, look freshly at something, not to prejudice it" (p. 7). Clearly his position is that of a liberal humanist writer who offers sympathetic, compassionate, nonpartisan, nonjudgmental engagement with fictional characters and their lives. His fiction is not narcissistic, nor does it lack the consciousness of its own "concrete historical situation" (Jameson, p. 329).

On closer examination, though, Gunesekera's statements raise some uncomfortable questions: How "fresh" is the authorial look at the political situation in Sri Lanka, and how nonpartisan, as it is depicted both in *Reef* and in *The Sandglass*? True, the characters (and the implied author) are understandably repelled at the beheadings on the beach in *Reef* (p. 183) and with "war-watching" in *The Sandglass* that turns Prins's "dreamland" into a "hole" (p. 269), a wasted Arcadia of failed promises from which, in the end, the returning exile must flee. The fact remains, however, that the complex history of the civil war in Sri Lanka and its contributing causes are elided in favor of a narrative and myth of a nation that tells the story of a homogeneous and unitary past. It is also true that there is no nationalistic fervor or cultural jingoism in either *Reef* or *The Sandglass,* only a deep sadness at the passing away of a certain kind of life in Sri Lanka, premodern in its stability and contentment. However, it is the absences and silences in the two novels that speak compellingly of the lives of ordinary Sri Lankans, of the Tamils and their subaltern histories and complex destinies. This muting of marginal and minority voices complicates Gunesekera's intentions to "see freshly" or whole. His principal

ROMESH GUNESEKERA

fiction through *The Sandglass* does not articulate radical voices, politically speaking. Rather, it offers discourses in social hegemony, in which certain negative stereotypes of the East—Sri Lanka as a barbarous place, with people who have no sense or understanding of their own plural histories—are reiterated.

HEAVEN'S EDGE

Gunesekera's third novel was published in 2002, nearly four years after *The Sandglass*. Once again, memory and remembering are enmeshed as the past is visited, resurrected, and examined, and once again the first-person narrator, named Marc, is trying to disentangle events that have happened elsewhere. As in *Reef* and *The Sandglass*, then, *Heaven's Edge* is set in two locations: a "rowdy" and "congested" (p. 6) postcolonial London; and "this apparent pearl of an island," which, even though it remains unnamed, resembles the strife-torn Sri Lanka projected thirty years into a dystopian future. Where the earlier two novels were deeply felt narratives of loss, regret, and nostalgia at the death of a certain idea of home and a sense of national history and way of life, *Heaven's Edge,* science-fiction-like, is set in the bleak future, on an island once thought to be at the edge of heaven but now barely recovering from an unspecified disaster. It is ruled by a brutal military regime whose marauding, gun-wielding soldiers practice a scorched-earth violence that wreaks havoc on the land, its flora, and on its animal and human inhabitants. A secret but disparate band of rebel eco-warriors try mightily to save the island for future generations. Marc, the novel's British-born narrator of mixed racial origin, travels to this island, "infused with myth and mystery" (p. 10), in search of his ancestral roots and his "peculiar inheritance" (p. 14). Eldon, Marc's pacifist grandfather, had emigrated from the island years ago, refusing to fight for a popular cause; it is commitment to that same cause that brings Marc's pilot-father back to the island, where he eventually loses his life in the strife. Thus orphaned early, Marc decides to leave behind a "life of junk, grease, and sloth" in the "fig trees and rat ruins" of a suburban London where he lives and sets out on a journey to the island. "I was like a man in search of his father," Marc says, "or perhaps in search of himself" (p. 14), whose mission it is to "explore an older terrain and discover for myself what was best to remember and what might be best to forget" (p. 5).

The opening chapter, "Nuburn," establishes the island setting. With its plundered and abandoned farms and derelict homesteads, its empty schools and poisoned water cisterns, and its "past choked with wars, disputes, borders as pointless as chalk lines in water" (p. 102), the island resembles a place of complete natural depredation and spiritual emptiness. It is here that Marc meets the beautiful Uva, releasing a pair of "emerald doves" (p. 21) into the wild. Uva's illegal farm in the countryside, her "ashram," as she calls it (p. 21), is a kind of sanctuary for hurt and maimed birds; it is also a place where hatched birds are nurtured and set free in the hope of replenishing and renewing a devastated ecosystem. Like Ranjan Salgado in *Reef,* Uva is an arch-conservationist, but unlike her fictional predecessor she is also a committed activist, an eco-warrior of sorts, and a strong and independent presence in the book. The birds Uva nurtures back to health are more than denizens of a natural world and the agents of its renewal. In the larger design of the novel they symbolize the potential of "all god's creatures ... [bound] in one eternal space" (p. 147) to live and love, and the human and artistic freedom to dream, imagine, and create.

Predictably Marc and Uva fall in love, at the same that the world around them explodes in violence, followed by Uva's disappearance. The rest of the narrative recounts Marc's action-filled odyssey across the benighted island in search for Uva. Battling all sorts of dangers on the way, Marc and his companions, Jaz, a gay transvestite, and Kris, a metalworker, reach the "carpet green" of Samandia, the site of Marc's ancestral home. Here Marc finds Uva in a finale that is steeped in violence and resonates with irony. Confronted by a group of blood-smeared soldiers carrying the head of a freshly butchered monkey, the once-pacifist Marc, instead of "forgiving and forgetting (p. 234), shoots and kills them in a moment of supreme reckoning. Uva joins him in avenging the destruction of the environment. The very knife that she had once used to set her birds free now becomes, in her hands, an instrument of terrible but cleansing violence. This apocalyptic conclusion, in which Marc and Uva finally confront evil and destroy it, also raises, for Gunesekera and his readers, a question laced with irony. As the author says in an interview with Aamir Hussein, "I am posing the question of whether the act of being like someone else involves a certain kind of violence—to yourself and to your ideas, if nothing else."

Gunesekera has repeatedly emphasized the theme of quest and the "voyage of discovery": a consciousness of the self embedded in the *un*-rootedness of the human condition. The initial journey (the "voyage out") from London to the island that Marc undertakes to retrace his father's return generates one of the most enduring themes in Gunesekera's fiction: the drawing power of myths and memories. As Marc remembers his grandfather Eldon, his grandmother Cleo, and his father Lee, he reimagines their individual and family histories. Out of these variously sedimentary and fragmented memories of the past, Marc "writes" his own narrative, in which his patrimonial heritage, recollections of his own tenuous, marginalized life in London, and especially his pacifism, clash with a swiftly evolving if violent present. The conflict provides Marc with the impetus to confront his own bewilderment and his hunger for meaning and purpose. What he learns of the past is that it cannot be erased or written out. To be "free of the past" (p. 91), Marc realizes, is an illusion, as is the notion that history can be separated from myth (p. 154), for each of us creates his or her own or replaces one narrative of the past (and its myth) with another.

Marc's "voyage of love," like his father's journey, leads to a discovery that underscores the provisional and ambiguous nature of reality. As Lee says in a taped message to his wife (and intended for Marc), "Separating myth from history is impossible now. Everyone has a fantasy with which to stake their claim for territories in our heads … Who can tell where the truth lies?"

(p. 154). The question is not a rhetorical one. The novel suggests that truth, in all its protean possibilities, lies in the very act of remembering and writing—in other words, in memory, imagination, and art. This is an idea that is vividly evoked in a moment of epiphany Marc experiences in a temple cave reminiscent of the legendary Hindu-Buddhist caves of Ajanta and Elora in western India. Gazing at an ancient fresco on the cave, Marc muses, "These were the memories I wanted to trace: history, myth, legend all defined in one single line marrying the seen to the unseen, the spirit to the bone" (p. 93).

Gunesekera's "mythic imagery of freedom, flight, and rebirth" in the novel (in the words of Maya Jaggi) reinforce several themes, one of which is the philosophical and practical issue of whether (to quote the author) "violence is ever justified." Fear of and anxiety about violence is an important subtext in nearly all of Gunesekera's fiction. Like the rushing, destructive sea in *Reef,* it is an ever-threatening presence, eroding the very structures of life and society in postcolonial Sri Lanka. In *Heaven's Edge,* the idea of violence is inextricably tied to pacifism, however, and is embodied in the figure of Mark's grandfather Eldon. Eldon's pacifism is "awkward" (as Marc wryly observes) in that it recognizes its own limitations: appeasement invariably fails, and tyrants use violence with impunity. So how does one fight evil? Marc wonders aloud, to which Eldon replies with an unshaken faith in the moral virtue of nonviolence: "Yes, of course, but the question is how do you do it [that is, achieve nonviolence that is workable and effective]? By fighting for peace? By violent retaliation? Revenge? … We now know, don't we, that if you try to teach someone a lesson, the lesson you teach him is to hit" (p. 99). The cost of violence is a long-term one, as it "accrues over years, decades, lives" (p. 99); it destroys the present and darkens the future. The issues Eldon raises are familiar and, from a philosophical standpoint, may even be unresolvable. He, however, is optimistic that "we can learn—that the young will see more clearly" (p. 99) through the dilemma that nonviolence faces in its encounter with evil, especially in the form of wars, mass killings, or political-military tyranny.

As Gunesekera's characters, especially Marc, travel their separate paths in *Heaven's Edge,* the choices are starkly defined. On the one hand there is war, tyranny, rape, pillage, incarceration, and a systematic oppression wrought upon man and nature; on the other, there is freedom, love, companionship, and the possibility of rebirth and regeneration of the earth through a respect for and restoration of the physical and moral balance of all lives. While Eldon might continue to debate in the abstract the moral dilemma of pacifism in a world torn asunder by evil, for his grandson Marc, the choice is already made. Rejecting his earlier pacifism, Marc decides to throw in his lot with Uva, and for the first time in the novel he deals with the death and violence around him proactively. Gripping his gun "hard," he sprays a hail of bullets at a group of soldiers who had "come to take everything" (p. 234). In the carnage that follows, Uva joins him a final "dance" of death, killing the last of the soldiers with her butterfly knife and a "sun-stained machete" (p. 234). The irony of the situation and consequent moral dilemma it raises are compelling. If freedom is to be protected, if the protean possibilities of life are to be nurtured and brought to their multiple completions, and if the "ruptured" earth is to be restored to its original state of natural abundance, then it is well worth the effort to fight for these greater ideals. As Marc says at the very end, "We do it because we must. For love as we know it" (p. 233). Yet at the very moment that he commits himself irrevocably to Uva's way of confronting evil directly and forcefully, he is aware that his resolve to do the right thing has somehow altered the moral balance of an already "fragile world" (p. 34). Violence, as Marc realizes, always exacts a certain price: loss of the sense of one's essential being, even as the world is altered for good. The final lines of the book underscore this paradox: "The whole sky darkened as a legion of trident bats, disturbed from their brooding trees by the gunshots, took to the newly burnt air, drawing a broken eclipse over another fragile world for ever altered; riven" (p. 234).

In his interview with Hussein, Gunesekera talks of "identity and difference—the whole notion that no one ever really belongs in one place. Even birds migrate." A condition of homelessness is both a consequence of postcolonial scattering and a predicament of modernity; rootlessness and mobility are an increasingly common fate among cultures and peoples. The sense of a provisional identity, of belonging everywhere and nowhere, of home being here *and* there, resonates across the spectrum of Gunesekera's fiction. In *Reef,* Triton tries to forge a community for himself among the itinerant immigrants and émigrés in a postcolonial London, and in *The Sandglass,* Prins is a "permanent temporary" who in the end simply disappears, erased (like his brother Ravi) from the familial and national narratives altogether. In *Heaven's Edge,* Gunesekera's concern for "identity and difference" and with location and the meaning of "home" assume a sharper sense of urgency. Unlike Prins, Marc does not return to the island only to disappear later; indeed, like his father before him, Marc chooses to come to the island and then decides to stay. He is both an uprooted lost soul and a new hybrid person. With his mixed background, Marc cannot live without taking on, in some sense, a provisional unsettled history and a sense of home that is forever shifting and changing. In this, "our ruptured world," his home is located not in any specific location from his own past or in some symbolic geography of the present, be it London or the island, but in a place "[he] could only imagine" (p. 233). Thus "home" for Marc is not a specifically bounded place. Rather, it exists in the rich complexities of the human imagination, wherever independent and interdependent hearts are locked in one embrace, and in a love that defines, nurtures, and sustains a more hopeful future.

As he waits for Uva on the plains of Samandia, a place redolent with the magic of Eldon's memories and where growth is still possible, Marc finds a storybook house "dappled in dream light" (p. 175), a place, he says, he had "always been waiting for" (p. 176). Here, in a spirit of mourning for the island and its lost past, rich in history, legend, and myth and infused with the memories of his ancestors, Marc begins to nurture a garden. Slowly he works out a strategy for survival in a world that has come unhinged from its moorings. Under these reduced circumstances, Marc says, "Ours will be a need to forget as much as to remember" (p. 233): to forget the debilitating present and remember that which is regenerative, life-affirming, and free. For all his engagement with his ancestral history, which is intimately woven with the paradisial myth of the island, Marc clearly subordinates a concern for the past to the need to live and act in the present.

Heaven's Edge is different from Gunesekera's earlier novels in that the narrative offers an amalgam of genres and styles, from science fiction to expressive realism to fable and magic realism. A more interesting difference, however, is in the novel's depiction of Uva, an eco-warrior who is strong, determined, courageous, bold, and principled. She is the only woman character in Guneskera's fiction to be presented thus. A good part of her appeal has to do with her active pursuit of conservation and biodiversity. It is through Uva that the novel's "green" philosophy is effectively articulated. As she releases a pair of emerald doves into the open air made rancid by years of violence and wars, she performs a ritualistic enactment of "green peace" (Maya Jaggi's phrase) amid ecological ruins. In her passion for the earth, renewed and repopulated, and in her love that gives freely of itself, even as it leaves him hungry for more, Marc finds that "All [I] wanted from my life, from everything, around me and before me, coalesced into her" (p. 28). Yet ironically it is she, the "Eve" in Marc's "little Eden," who initiates a "fall": her knowledge that innocence (or moral naïveté) needs to be sacrificed in order to protect and preserve "this world" that men (and Marc) "believe in" and "care so much for" (p. 228). In *Reef,* Gunesekera's first conservationist, Ranjan Salgado, had struck a dire note about an impending ecological disaster affecting a whole culture and a way of life. In *Heaven's Edge,* that future is already a reality in the form of a devastated landscape dotted with the maimed and the dead—men and women, animals and birds, and a ravaged natural world. But whereas Mr. Salgado in *Reef* virtually writes

himself out of the narrative of conservation by choosing to emigrate to the West, Uva is an active agent of change. Her theorization of the need for biodiversity and ecological balance strengthens her moral resolve to take up arms to fight for her cause.

Along with conservation and "green peace," the book articulates other themes: home, migration and settlement, love and loss, the fragility of dreams and the innocence lost to preserve them (as Maya Jaggi has noted), pacifism and violence, and the need to voice memory and confront a more or less mythological past in search of a meaningful life lived in the present. Some of these themes surface in *Reef* and in *The Sandglass,* and in that sense, the connections between *Heaven's Edge* and the earlier novels are apparent. Structurally, however, Gunesekera's third book presents some interesting differences. *Reef* is cohesive in its plotting, and *The Sandglass* brings an innovative structural technique to its narrative design that uses flashbacks, journal entries, and temporal shifts to compress and encompass the events of two decades or so. In *Heaven's Edge,* the circuitous movement of its plotline and its "up and down" tempo effectively capture the meandering nature of Marc's dangerous journey, which follows an "escape-pursue-fight" pattern. The rush of the book's wildly violent action and feats of aerial heroics often resemble staged tableaux: Marc flying an antique glider or Uva swinging from tree limbs with her butterfly knife to kill the killers. Undoubtedly the most action-filled of all Gunesekera's novels to date, *Heaven's Edge* uses its random violence to underscore the sheer scale of the human and natural destruction that takes place on the island (and elsewhere in the world). The violence forces the readers to recognize one of the central arguments of the book—that regardless of how it is used, whether as an instrument of terror or as a necessary means to resist and combat it, violence invariably diminishes both the perpetrator and the resisting human subject. While it lacks the structural cohesiveness of *Reef* and the modernist fragmentation of *The Sandglass, Heaven's Edge* succeeds in putting a consistently sharp focus on violence and pacifism, on environmental protec-

BELMONT UNIVERSITY LIBRARY

tion and eco-diversity, and on the urgent need to give and receive love.

Where the novel falters is in its lack of political vision beyond its activist philosophy of "green peace." The island and its multiple histories are de-historicized. As an Everyman figure, Marc, like Triton and Chip before him, is apolitical. Marc does not experience (or reveal) any of the island's deep, hidden truths. And seldom, if at any time, does he probe or question the sources and character of the island's myths and legends or, more important, put the history of the violence of its most recent past or its harrowing present in context. There is no desire on his part for political or cultural knowledge of this once "emerald island" (p. 19). But then Marc is not a colonist or ethnographer. True, he comes to the island partly to retrace his father's (and grandfather's) history there and partly in "search of himself" (p. 14), but his seemingly "longer journey" (p. 14) is not directed at arriving at a specific place so much as it is a search for a certain vision, an idea, of the island. It is this vision or idea that is delocalized and drenched in the luminous abstraction of myths. De-historicized, the island resembles a "pearl," a "little Eden," with bougainvillea, "hundreds of butterflies," and "a breadfruit tree" (p. 8); it is predictably associated with "paradise" (p. 8), as Sri Lanka is in *Reef* and *The Sandglass*. The history of the island (now a fallen paradise) speaks eloquently on behalf of a traditional (if unprobed and untheorized) past, with its primal stories and exploits that must never die. Occasionally Gunesekera's version of it falls rather too easily into an elegiac lament for the vanishing—or rather, an already vanished—mythic and premodern world.

In his poetry and fiction to date, Romesh Gunesekera has thoughtfully articulated the complex ideas of home, expatriation and cultural loss, and especially Sri Lanka's mythic associations with a fallen Eden. Additionally he has time and again insisted on the related themes of quest and discovery—of memory and remembrance and their shaping influence on the human imagination and on the art of writing, as it gives voice and substance to such journeys and discoveries. From his finely crafted poetry and its multiple ironies to the thematic and structural complexities of his fiction shown in *Monkfish Moon, Reef, The Sandglass,* and *Heaven's Edge,* Gunesekera's work is marked by an intense and evocative lyricism, a sympathetic portrayal of the experience of expatriation and exile, and by his complex if arguably problematic use of Sri Lanka as a signifier of loss and nostalgia, whose long and tangled history is rooted in British colonialism. While his work has received critical accolades in the West and an international readership, cultural nationalists in Sri Lanka such as Suvani Ranasinha and Walter Perera, for instance, have faulted Gunesekera for harboring Orientalist assumptions and negative stereotypes of the Asiatic Other as exotic, mysterious, and in the end, unknowable. As an expatriate writer, these cultural nationalists argue, Gunesekera fails to offer his readers a nuanced understanding of the historical, political, and cultural significance of the civil war violence and social upheaval in Sri Lanka and instead reverts to narratives of nostalgia and loss. Such views notwithstanding, the layered richness and maturity of Romesh Gunesekera's fiction and poetry have singled him out as a major talent among contemporary writers in English.

Selected Bibliography

WORKS OF ROMESH GUNESEKERA

NOVELS AND SHORT STORIES

Monkfish Moon. London: Granta, 1992; New York: New Press, 2002. (Contains "A House in the Country," "Captives," "Batik," "Ullswater," "Storm Petrel," "Ranvali," "Carapace," "Straw Huts," and "Monkfish Moon".)

Reef. London: Granta, 1994; New York: New Press, 1994.

The Sandglass. London: Granta, 1998.

Heaven's Edge. London: Bloomsbury, 2002; New York: Grove, 2002.

STORIES IN ANTHOLOGIES AND MAGAZINES

"The Storm Petrel." *Stand* 26, no. 2 (spring 1985). Reprinted in *Different Places Different Voices,* Copenhagen: DR Multimedie, 1996.

"The Green Line." *London* 29, nos. 3–4 (July 1989). Reprinted in *Telling Stories: The Best of BBC Radio's Recent Short Fiction*. Edited by Duncan Minshull. London: Coronet, 1992.

"The Batik Cup." *Sunk Island Review* (winter 1989).

"The Golden Boat." *Sunk Island Review* (winter 1989).

"Night of the Juggernauts." *Artrage* 11 (1985).

"Dream Shop." *London* 26, nos. 9–10 (January 1987).

"Dancing in South India." *London,* winter 1990.

"Wild Duck." In *New Writing 3*. Edited by Andrew Motion and Candice Rodd. London: Minerva, 1994.

"The Hole." *Granta* 50 (1995).

"Stringhoppers." *Granta* 52 (1995). Reprinted in *Wine, Food & the Arts*. San Francisco: American Institute of Wine & Food, 1997; *Kunapipi* (1999); and in *Banquet of the Mind*. Edited by Don Anderson. New South Wales: Random House, 2000.

"The Lover." In *New Writing 5*. Edited by Christopher Hope and Peter Porter. London: Minerva, 1996.

"Lucky's Bantam." In *Shorts: New Writing from Granta*. London: Granta, 1998.

"The Emporium of Durians." *Wasafiri* 29:62 (spring 1999).

"The Photograph." *Dimsum* 1, no. 3 (2000). Reprinted in *Sightlines*. Edited by P. D. James and Harriet Harvey Wood. London: Vintage, 2001.

"Jubilee." Pulp.net. (http://www.pulp.net)

POETRY IN ANTHOLOGIES, MAGAZINES, JOURNALS

Poetry Durham 1 (1982), 5 (1983), 9 (1985), 10 (1985), 11 (winter 1985). (No. 11 is a special issue devoted to "Poems by Romesh Gunesekera and Jamie McKendrick." Includes Gunesekera's "Captain Nemo," "Circled By Circe," "Going Home [A Letter To Colombo]," "House Building," "An Honourable Estate," "Target Practice," "A Map of the World," "The Garden Storm," "Dream Killing," "Lodestar," and "Indian Tree.")

Artrage 11 (1985).

Other Poetry 16 (1985).

Ambit 103, 106 (1986).

Poetry Now 6 (1986).

Artrage 15 (1987).

"Watermark." *Poetry Durham* 18 (1988).

"Indefinite Exposure." *The Pen* 24 (1988).

"Frontliners" and "The Blade." *Poetry Matters* 6 (1988). "Frontliners" reprinted in the *Guardian,* 22 April 1988.

"Mountain Shadow." *London* 28, nos. 7, 8 (November 1988).

"Turning Point" and "Pigs." *London Review of Books,* February 1989.

Wasafiri 21 (1995)

"Turning Points" and "Wanderlust." In *The Redbeck Anthology of British South Asian Poetry*. Edited by Debjani Chatterjee. London: Redbeck, 2000.

Banquet of the Mind. London: Random House, 2000.

Identity Papers. Brussels: British Council, 2001.

POEMS IN ANTHOLOGIES FOR CHILDREN

Red Sky at Night and Other Poems. Compiled by John Foster. London: Oxford University Press, 2000.

A Trunkful of Elephants. Compiled by Judith Nicholls. London: Mammoth, 1994.

A Cup of Starshine. Selected by Jill Bennett. London: Walker, 1991. (Title poem and others.)

Early Years Poems and Rhymes. Compiled by Jill Bennett. London: Scholastic, 1993.

The Faber Book of Contemporary Stories about Childhood. Edited by Lorrie Moore. London: Faber, 1997.

OTHER WORKS

"Looking for a Genie." *Time,* February 9, 1998.

"Reading the Moon." *Far East Economic Review,* January 27, 2000.

"Who Do You Think You Are?" In *Literature Matters*. London: British Council, 2000.

"My Commonwealth." *Guardian,* July 19, 2002.

"All the Raj." *Evening Standard,* February 21, 2003.

CRITICAL AND BIOGRAPHICAL STUDIES

Aloysius, Carol. "Novels of Love, Intrigue, and Courage." *Sunday Observer,* May 31, 1998, p. 24. (Review of *The Sandglass*.)

Brennan, Timothy. "The National Longing for Form." In *Nation and Narration*. Edited by Homi Bhabha. London and New York: Routledge, 1990.

Burnett, Paula. "The Captives and the Lion's Claw: Reading Romesh Gunesekera's *Monkfish Moon*." *Journal of Commonwealth Literature* 32, no. 2:3–15 (1997).

Carey, Jacqueline. "Family Feud." *New York Times Book Review,* January 17, 1999, p. 17. (Review of *The Sandglass*.)

Chew, Shirley. Review of *The Sandglass*. *Times Literary Supplement,* February 13, 1998, p. 21.

Cowley, Jason. "It's Time to Say That We All Need Time." *New Statesman,* February 20, 1998, p. 49. (Review of *The Sandglass*.)

Davis, Rocio G. "'I Am an Explorer on a Voyage of Discovery': Myths of Childhood in Romesh Gunesekera's *Reef*." *Commonwealth* 20, no. 2:14–25 (spring 1998).

Erney, Hans-Georg. "Modes of Exile in Romesh Gunesekera's *The Sandglass*." Paper presented at the Twelfth Annual Conference of British Commonwealth and Postcolonial Studies Conference, Savannah, Ga., February 2003.

Gooneratne, Yasmine. "The English Educated in Sri Lanka: An Assessment of Their Cultural Role." *South Asian Bulletin* 12, no. 1: 24 (1992). Cited in Perera, "Images of Sri Lanka through Expatriate Eyes: Romesh Gunesekera's *Reef.*"

Gurnah, Abdulrazak. "Return to the Island." *Times Literary Supplement,* April 12, 2002, p. 10. (Review of *Heaven's Edge.*)

Hajari, Nisid. "An Ill-Fitting Tale." *Time,* April 13, 1998. Available online (http://www.time.com/time/magazine/1998/int/980413/the_arts.books.an_illfit22.html). (Review of *The Sandglass.*)

Iyer, Pico. "Elegy and Affirmation." *Time,* September 7, 1998, p. 79. (Review of *The Sandglass.*)

Jaggi, Maya. "The Eden Project." *Guardian Unlimited,* May 11, 2002. (Review of *Heaven's Edge.*)

Jameson, Fredric. "National Allegory in the Era of Multinational Capitalism." In *Jameson Reader.* Edited by Michael Hardt and Kathi Weeks. London and Malden, Mass.: Blackwell, 2000. Pp. 315–339.

Kapstein, Helen. "Serendipity: Violence and National Form in Romesh Gunesekera's Novels." Paper presented at the Twelfth Annual Conference of British Commonwealth and Postcolonial Studies Conference, Savannah, Ga., February 2003.

Kapur, Akash. "The Present Is Foreign Country." *New York Times,* February 23, 2003, Section 7:6. (Review of *Heaven's Edge.*)

Khair, Tabish. "Where Hell Begins." *Hindu,* July 7, 2002. (Review of *Heaven's Edge.*)

Mel, Neloufer de. Review of *Monkfish Moon. Wasafiri* 17:54–55 (spring 1993).

Nasta, Susheila. "Romesh Gunesekera: Critical Perspective." British Council, London. Available online (http://www.contemporarywriters.com/authors).

Packard, Wingate. "Veiled Locale Obscures Novel's Impact." *Seattle Times,* April 20, 2003.(Review of *Heaven's Edge.*)

Perera, Walter. "Images of Sri Lanka through Expatriate Eyes: Romesh Gunesekera's *Reef.*" *Journal of Commonwealth Literature* 30, no. 1:63–78 (1995).

———. "The Perils of Expatriation: Romesh Gunesekera's *The Sandglass.*" *Commonwealth* 22, no. 2:93–106 (1998).

Perry, Michele. "Moving Heaven and Earth." Available online (http://www.theblurb.com.au/Issue19/Heaven.htm). (Review of *Heaven's Edge.*)

Ranasinha, Ruvani. "Romesh Gunesekera's *Reef:* Writing Expatriation." *Phoenix: Sri Lanka Journal of English in the Commonwealth* 5 and 6:87–86 (1997).

Rubin, Merle. "Love and War in Paradise." *Times* (London), March 10, 2003. (Review of *Heaven's Edge.*)

Roussan, Rasheed al. "Romesh Gunesekera: On Writing and Identity." *Star Weekly.* Available online (http://www.arabia.com).

Said, Edward W. *Reflections on Exile and Other Essays.* Cambridge, Mass.: Harvard University Press, 2000.

Sarvan, Charles. Review of *The Sandglass. World Literature Today* 72, no. 4:903 (autumn 1998).

Singh, Ajay. "Tales Born of Anguish." *Asiaweek.* Available online (http://www.asiaweek.com/asiaweek/99/0305/feat6.html). (Review of *The Sandglass.*)

Singh, Lisa. Review of *Heaven's Edge. Star Tribune,* February 23, 2003.

Visel, Robin. "Romesh Gunesekera, Michael Ondaatje, and Sri Lankan Paradise Lost." Paper presented at the Twelfth Annual Conference of British Commonwealth and Postcolonial Studies Conference, Savannah, Ga., February 2003.

Wickramagamage, Carmen. "Many Questions, Few Answers: Romesh Gunesekera's *The Sandglass.*" *Navasilu: Journal of the English Association of Sri Lanka* 15 and 16:112–117 (1998).

INTERVIEWS

Aziz, Afdel. "Of Reefs and Men: Interview with Romesh Gunesekera." *Sunday Times* (Sri Lanka), October 2, 1994, p. 13.

Davis, Rocio G. "'We Are All Artists of Our Own Lives': A Conversation with Romesh Gunesekera." *Miscelanea: A Journal of English and American Studies* 18:43–54 (1997).

Erney, Hans-Georg. "'Culture Is Not Contained, It's All Over the Place': An Interview with Romesh Gunesekera." Erlangen Centre for Contemporary English Literature, Erlangen, April 12, 1996.

Hussein, Aamir. "After an Odyssey, Paradise Regained." *Independent* (London), April 13, 2002.

JAMES HOGG

(1770–1835)

Les Wilkinson

To most readers in the twenty-first century, James Hogg is an obscure writer from the Romantic era, best known, if known at all, for his extraordinary novel *The Private Memoirs and Confessions of a Justified Sinner* (1824). In his own time, however, writing under the soubriquet of the Ettrick Shepherd, he was primarily recognized and admired by his contemporaries as a poet of considerable distinction. He was the friend of many great literary figures, particularly Sir Walter Scott, who perhaps patronized him a little; admirers of William Wordsworth will remember that one of his finest late poems, "Extempore Effusions," was occasioned by the death of Hogg, who was his exact contemporary, both men being born in 1770. Byron, in a letter to Thomas Moore, thought him "a strange being" but recognized his "great, though uncouth, powers," adding: "I think very highly of him as a poet." Beethoven was interested in setting some of his songs to music; his work was published not only in England and Scotland but also in Philadelphia, New York, and Connecticut. The *Analectic Magazine,* published in Philadelphia, assured its readers in February 1814 that Hogg's poetry was capable of "soaring to the furthest regions of human thought," and Bostonians were assured by the *American Monthly Magazine* of October 1829 that the Ettrick Shepherd "listened with the ear of genius to all the breathings of passion."

In his own time, then, James Hogg was recognized as one of the great poetical talents of the era. He is indeed a writer of some significance, largely because of the unique blend of influences that formed his cast of mind.

LIFE

The cottage in Ettrick where Hogg was born in 1770 no longer exists, but its vicinity is marked by a brown stone obelisk; his grave is only a few miles away in Ettrick kirkyard, fittingly next to his mother's, as she was perhaps his greatest formative influence. Today the landscape of the Ettrick Valley and the neighboring Yarrow Valley, the two places where Hogg spent most of his life, is still as wild as it was two hundred years ago: the hills, or laws, are high and steep, grass-covered in the main although in places outcrops of gray rock jut out; the glens are broad but often contain treacherous bogs. Between the Ettrick and Yarrow valleys lies the expanse of water known as St. Mary's Loch, a place Hogg loved and where to this day his statue gazes out, somewhat incongruously, over its waters. Much of the best of Hogg's poetry and prose is written in the language and dialect of these valleys that were so close to his heart.

Unusually for a poet of the modern era, Hogg came to writing comparatively late in life, in the most literal sense. He learned to read to a rudimentary degree during the six months he spent at school, but he was forced to leave formal education at the age of six when his father went bankrupt and he had to begin work as a cowherd in order to contribute to the family income. For the next ten or so years Hogg worked in the most menial types of farm service, often in conditions of physical hardship, until he became a shepherd in the service of the Laidlaws of Willenslea. Here he was encouraged by his employer to read (a skill he had almost forgotten) and to learn to write. Although he then began to read voraciously and extensively, for the formative years of his life Hogg relied essentially on his memory; he belonged firmly to the oral tradition of performance, and this influenced his method of composition well into his mature years. He never drafted a poem, preferring to work from notes made on a slate with a slate pencil until he had the poem complete in his head, at which point he wrote it out as a fair copy, with few if any corrections.

But the oral tradition had deeper roots than this. Hogg is very much a writer of his own land; his writing is essentially specific and local in the same way as Wordworth's is local to the Lake District and Hardy's to Dorset. That is not to say that he did not leave his native valley: he spent ten years of his life (between the ages of thirty-nine and forty-nine) in Edinburgh with the aim of establishing himself as a professional writer, and he made visits to London, where he was treated as a literary celebrity. But whereas Scott was seen as a figure on the European stage, Hogg was always associated with the locality of his birth—he was, after all, "The Ettrick Shepherd"—and this was largely because of the way Hogg himself wished to be perceived. He spent the first thirty-six years of his life working on farms in various capacities in the Ettrick Valley, and after his abortive attempts at farming in Dumfriesshire between 1807 and 1810 and his period based in Edinburgh (1810–1820), he returned to the neighboring Yarrow Valley in 1820, where he lived his last fifteen years on the farm at Altrive, let to him for a nominal rent by the duke of Buccleuch. These last years were extremely happy for him, despite financial worries at times; in 1820, at the age of forty-nine, he had married Margaret Phillips, eighteen years his junior, and their marriage was very strong, resulting in the birth of five children. The friendship and good sense that sustained this marriage is evident from the exchange of letters quoted in the anthology *A Shepherd's Delight* (1985). Hogg, while staying in London, writes to his "Dearest Margt" to ask whether she would like to become Lady Hogg or remain the Ettrick Shepherdess, as the queen is intent on offering him a knighthood. The prospect of the honor makes him uncomfortable, and he asks his wife "to dissuade me from it"; Margaret accordingly complies, replying that "it is an honour you may be proud to refuse but not to accept[.] I think a title to a poor man is a load scarcely bearable." It is clear that she and her "ever affectionate husband James Hogg" are of one mind on this issue, and the easy tone of their correspondence suggests that this would be the case in many other areas of their life together.

Hogg became seriously ill in October 1835 and died the following month at home at Altrive. The farm has now been renamed Eldinhope, Altrive Lake having been drained and long since disappeared, and today it remains a working farm rather than a literary shrine.

"OF BROWNIES AND BOGILLS"

John Buchan, in his 1932 biography *Sir Walter Scott,* notes that Hogg "came of interesting stock, for there had been witches on his paternal side, and his maternal grandfather, Will of Phawhope, was the last man on the borders who had spoken with the fairies" (pp. 62–63). Buchan (and the modern reader) may be skeptical of talk of witches and fairies, but for Hogg they were very real and form an important and distinctive element in his work. As a writer and a man, he was very conscious that there are more things in heaven and earth than are dreamt of, or capable of being defined, in our philosophy, and he turned to fairies, brownies, and witches to explain such things. As he explained in his poem "Superstition":

If every creed has its attendant ills,
How slight were thine!—a train of airy dreams!
No holy awe the cynic's bosom thrills;
Be mine the faith diverging to extremes!

The "extremes" that Hogg writes of here show that he did not think his strong Christian belief incompatible with his belief in the world of fairies and spirits.

Hogg inherited his belief in the supernatural—both the Christian supernatural and the world of fairies—from his mother, perhaps the greatest formative influence in his life. Mrs. Hogg, known according to the contemporary custom by her maiden name, Margaret Laidlaw, was a principal source of many of the songs and ballads collected by Scott in his *Minstrelsy of the Scottish Borders* (1802–1803). She had learned these in the oral tradition. In her own words, quoted by Buchan: "My brother and me learned … many mae frae auld Andrew Moor, and he learned it frae Baby Mettlin, who was housekeeper to the first laird o' Tushielaw." She in turn passed them on to her son. From her, too, he learned by heart passages from the Bible and all the Psalms in the Scottish metrical versions. He may not have been able to read until the age of seventeen, but his memory was stored with a host of ancient ballads and with the metrical psalms.

As a young man, Hogg taught himself to play the violin and become known in the Ettrick Valley as a brilliant fiddler before he earned the title of "Jamie the Poeter." He took great pleasure in music, as he himself describes in his *Memoir of the Author's Life:*

> We had our kirns at the end of the harvest, and … in almost every farm house and cottage, which proved a weekly bout for the greater part of the winter. And then, with the exception of … a little kissing and toying in consequence, song and song alone was the sole amusement.

According to his friend William Laidlaw, Hogg was a handsome man, above middle height, "of faultless symmetry of form," broad-shouldered and with a head of auburn hair usually worn under his bonnet but which, when this was removed in kirk on Sunday, flowed down his back "and fell below his loins" (quoted by Judy Steel in her introduction to *A Shepherd's Delight*). He was clearly attractive to women and, as a result of the "kissing and toying in consequence" noted by Hogg above, he became the father of two illegitimate daughters whom he was proud to own and recognize as his responsibility.

OVERVIEW

Hogg represents a range of contradictions both as a man and as a writer. He is perhaps an example of what a later poet, Hugh MacDairmid, would call the "Caledonian Antisyzigy": that is to say, "the defiant determination not to chose the bland middle way but 'aye to be whaur extremes meet." He came to be equally at home in both the houffs, or taverns, of Ettrick and Yarrow and the drawing rooms of Edinburgh—two locations with a mere forty or so miles between them, but two

very different worlds indeed. He was a man who saw himself as a shepherd and farmer and yet relied almost exclusively on writing for an income, a man whose formal education ended at the age of six and yet who was the companion of university professors and their like. He was one of the foremost literary intellects of his day and yet allowed himself to be caricatured as an ill-mannered buffoon in the *Noctes Ambrosianae,* a series of fictional conversations on a wide range of topics which appeared in *Blackwood's Magazine.* He was a committed Christian and devoted family man who believed in fairies and who also fathered two illegitimate children. As Scott's friend, he allowed himself to be patronized by "The Lion of the North" and yet succeeded in writing a novel more ambitious and groundbreaking in its narrative technique and psychological insight than the former. Scott himself recognized that "if a vile sixpenny planet presided at Hogg's birth, then so did the dancing star under which Beatrice was born."

This study will explore some of these paradoxes by looking at James Hogg's poetry and then his prose, finishing by looking at some length at the novel the twentieth century has come to recognize as his greatest work, *The Private Memoirs and Confessions of a Justified Sinner.*

EARLY POEMS

Hogg's first published work, *The Mistakes of a Night,* appeared anonymously in the *Scots Magazine* for October 1794. In it we can see that blend of the literary and the oral traditions which are a distinctive characteristic of Hogg's work as a whole. The title is taken from the subtitle of Oliver Goldsmith's comedy *She Stoops to Conquer* (1773), and yet its action is rooted in the folk tradition of bawdy night-visiting songs: young Geordie Scott crosses the moor to court the beautiful Maggie, but in the darkness he sleeps with her widowed mother by mistake. When brought before the elders and charged with fornication he makes a stout denial, but when the widow proves to be with child he acknowledges his fault and marries her, living to regret the night "he cross'd the muir to Maggie." The theme and tone are those of the songs and ballads of the Ettrick Valley, but the language (in its use of Scots dialect), the verse form (which echoes the "standard habbie" (a verse used by several eighteenth-century Scots poets, and particularly popularized by Burns) in its use of tetrameters and the concluding two-foot "wheel" at the end of each verse), and the scene in which Geordie is confronted by the dour Presbyterian elders are all reminiscent of Burns and perhaps denote Hogg's ambition to follow in the footsteps of the "heaven taught ploughman," seeing himself one day as Burns's successor.

Hogg's first taste of popular success, however, came not as a poet but as a songwriter, with "Donald MacDonald," written around 1799, by his own account when he was "a barefoot lad herding lambs on the Blackhouse Heights." Hogg first sang it in "a celebrated chophouse in the Fleshmarket Close" in Edinburgh after he had driven his sheep to market, and soon it was sung throughout Scotland: according to the *Edinburgh Literary Journal* of May 1830 "the whole country rang with the patriotic strain." Although dealing ostensibly with the Jacobite rebellion, the song's rousing chorus and its indication of what the Scots would do to Bonaparte if he were to land at Fort William struck a chord with contemporary feelings regarding the threat of invasion at this time:

Stanes an' bullets an' a'
Stanes an' bullets an' a;
We'll finish the Corsican Callan
Wi' stanes and bullets an' a'.

Hogg published two volumes of verse in the first decade of the nineteenth century, *The Mountain Bard* (1807) and *The Forest Minstrel* (1810). They contain some of his loveliest lyrics, including "Love Is Like a Dizziness," "so long a favourite with the country lads and lasses," despite the fact that Hogg himself dismissed the song as "ridiculous":

O Love, love love!
Love is like a dizziness
It winna let a poor body
Gang about his biziness!

THE QUEEN'S WAKE

Hogg first came to real poetic acclaim, however, with the publication of *The Queen's Wake* in 1813. The poem tells the story of the arrival of Mary, Queen of Scots in Edinburgh from France on August 20, 1561, to take up her personal rule. Having been moved by the "notes of runic fire" and the poem sung by a Caledonian bard to greet her at the gates of Holyrood, she sends out the command that

Each Caledonian bard must seek
Her courtly halls in Christmas week …
He then before the court must stand
In native garb, with harp in hand.
At home no minstrel dare to tarry:
High the behest.

The bards obey; each performs his lay in succession before the court over the coming nights. The structure of the *Wake* as a whole can therefore be seen to owe a great deal to Boccaccio's *Decameron* or Chaucer's *Canterbury Tales:* it is a sequence of poems bound loosely together by the fictional narrative of a bardic competition for the queen's approval. Hogg translates this into a specifically Scottish context, however, principally by adopting for his introduction to the poem as a whole the same verse form that Scott uses for his narrative poems: couplets of iambic tetrameters. In addition, the minstrel who ravishes the queen's ear before the gates of her palace with a "simple native melody" bears more than a passing resemblance to Scott's Last Minstrel, the narrator of his first successful poem, *The Lay of the Last Minstrel.*

The first of the two poems from *The Queen's Wake* to be considered here in detail, "The Witch of Fife," shows other sources of Hogg's inspiration for this work. It opens:

Quare haif ye been, ye ill womayne
These three lang nightis fra hame?
Quhat garris the sweit drap fra yer brow
Like clotis of the saut sea faem?

It fearis me muckil ye haif seen
Quhat good man never knew;
It fearis me muckil ye haif been
Quare the grey cock never crewe.

But the spell may crack and the brydel breek
 Then sherp yer werde will be;
Ye had better sleip in yer bed at hame
 Wi' yer deire littil bairnis and me.

We notice immediately Hogg's command of the ballad form: not only is he master of the ballad stanza but also of its technique, beginning the poem with direct speech taking us to the heart of a discussion between husband and wife. The structural repetition of the first and third lines of the second stanza, together with the internal rhyme in the first line of the third, is common in the border ballads Hogg learned from his mother. The defiant use of Lowlands Scots dialect words—*garris, muckil, bairnis*—places the poem firmly in the oral tradition of border ballads. The spelling, however, hints at a different tradition of literature: *quare* and *quhat* for "where" and "what," together with plurals spelled *-is,* are deliberate archaisms that recall the work of the medieval Scots makars (poets), William Dunbar (1456?–1513?) in particular. In this way Hogg makes it clear to his reader that he is writing in the tradition of Scots rather than English verse, contributing to a national literature harking back to the sixteenth century.

The wife answers her husband's questions by describing her antics with her companions, a coven of witches, telling of how she has ridden over all Scotland on a wooden horse, sailed to Norway and Lapland in a cockleshell, and finally learned to fly, ending up in the bishop's wine vault at Carlisle Castle. The comic tone of the poem is established when she tells how a Lapland warlock washed her and her companions with "witch-water," making their beauty bloom like the Lapland rose. Her husband interrupts:

Ye lee, ye lee, ye ill womyne,
 So loud as I heir ye lee!
For the worst-faur'd wife on the shoris of Fyfe
 Is cumlye comparet wi' thee.

Interestingly, the husband's Presbyterian remonstrance to his wife to stay home "wi' yer deire littil bairnis and me" disappears when he hears of the bishop's wine, and he begs to be taken with her when they next return. She refuses, but he eavesdrops on their next meeting, learns

their flying spell, and follows them to Carlisle, where he and the witches get drunk on the bishop's wine. Whereas the others leave as soon as they scent the morning wind, however, he sleeps and snores on the floor of the cellar, to be arrested by "five rough Englishmen" and condemned to die at the stake. The original ending leaves him to burn to death, pointing out the stark moral:

Let never an auld man after this
 To lawless greide inclyne;
Let never an auld man after this
 Rin post to the deil for wyne.

Scott, however, persuaded Hogg to change the ending to one more in tune with the comic tone of the poem: his wife returns to him, flying in to give him the secret word to enable him to ascend from the flames and fly back to Fife with her. The moral with which the revised version ends is more lighthearted:

May everlike man in the land of Fife
 Read what the drinkers dree;
And nevir curse his puir auld wife
 Richt wicked though she be.

We may hear in this an echo of Burns's injunction in *Tam O' Shanter* to his hero to "heed his guid wife Jean's advises." Indeed, there are other reminiscences of Burns's poem than this: the energy of the witches in their flight and in their revel in the bishop's cellar reminds us of the dance of witches in Alloway Kirk; the downfall of the hero of both poems is as a result of an inclination to strong drink and a weakness of will; finally, in both poems the closing injunction to virtue can only be taken ironically, given the exuberance that has gone before. Hogg is writing not only in the tradition of Dunbar but of Burns too.

"KILMENY"

"Kilmeny" is the offering of the thirteenth bard of *The Queen's Wake,* and the song he sings is perhaps Hogg's most admired poem. Originally written in the archaic spelling of *The Witch of Fife,* Hogg wisely dropped this from subsequent editions of the poem, which tells how Kilmeny disappears from this earth for a period of seven years, only to return to tell of her sojourn in a land

> Where the cock never crew,
> Where the rain never fell, and the wind never blew,
> But it seemed as the harp of the sky had rung
> And the airs of heaven played round her tongue.

Kilmeny proves too good for this world, however, and after a further month and a day, she returns to "the land of thought" again.

The influence of the border ballads is immediately apparent in the theme of the poem: both *Thomas the Rhymer* and *Tam Lin* are ballads that deal with a mortal being taken away from this world to another by fairies, to return at a later date. Significantly the span of seven years is mentioned in each: "Till seven years were gone and past" Thomas was held in fairyland before he was allowed back into our world by the queen of fair Elfland; in *Tam Lin,* the fairies have to pay a *tiend,* or tithe, to hell every seven years, and Tam fears that the tithe will be himself. Other aspects of the poem recall the traditional superstitions linked with the ballads: for example, when Kilmeny returns to the earth she wears "a joup (skirt) of the lilly scheen" and a "bonny snood (ribbon worn in the hair) of the birk (birch) sae green." Men and women of the Ettrick Valley would remember that when the sons of the Wife of Usher's Well, in the ballad of that name, return to visit their mother from beyond the grave, "their hats were o' the birk"—a sacred plant associated with death and the otherworld in folk mythology.

Hogg may make use of ballad tradition here, but he takes it into a new direction. Whereas Thomas the Rhymer spends his seven years in fairyland, Kilmeny does not; it is clear that she is transported not by fairies but by angels, not the land of fairie but to heaven. That this is essentially a religious poem is evident from the nature of the bard who tells it. As with Chaucer's *Canterbury Tales,* there is in *The Queen's Wake* sometimes a strong relationship between the teller and the tale and sometimes not. In the case of

The Witch of Fife, our knowledge of the teller adds little to the poem, but here our introduction to the bard is of significance. Hogg tells us that he was a solitary hermit, "well versed in holy lore," and that

> Religion, man's first friend and best
> Was in his home a constant guest;
> There sweetly every morn and even,
> Warm orisons were poured to heaven …

The holy man sings his queen a song of religious import. Kilmeny has been chosen for her heavenly journey because of her singular purity:

> Never, since the banquet of time
> Found I a virgin in her prime
>
> …
>
> As spotless as the morning snaw …
> I have brought her away from the snares of men,
> That sin and death she may never ken.

The world she visits is "a land where sin has never been," which is contrasted sharply with our world "of sin, of sorrow and fear." When she returns to this earthly life she brings an inner peace and visible radiance with her that cheers the wild beasts of the hill and seems to return her native valley to an Edenlike state: "It was like an eve in a sinless world." When she finally leaves earth again after a month and a day, her friends and family no longer mourn her. The ending is not sad but transcendental:

> She left the world of sorrow and pain
> And returned to the land of thought again.

In his introduction to his edition of Hogg's *Selected Poems,* Douglas Mack makes a convincing case for the way the poet "articulates a deeply Christian view of the human situation" through the mythical structure of the poem: Kilmeny has seen in heaven the potential for the world without sin, and therefore she cannot remain in our world below. While she does remain, however, she can

> Tell of the joys that are waiting here
>
> …
>
> Of the times that are now and the times that shall be.

Mack goes on to find the scenes in heaven "the least successful part of the poem." These are fascinating, however, because of their echoes of Dunbar's medieval vision poetry. The colors of Kilmeny's heaven are intense, enameled, almost jewel-like. She sees heaven's blue gates with sapphires glowing; "the sky was a dome of crystal bright"; and the sun shines "wi' a borrowed gleid frae the fountain of light." She sees "clouds of amber sailing by," "emerald fields," forests green "of dazzling sheen," and lakes "like magic mirrors." All this is reminiscent of the landscape of Dunbar's dream vision in *The Goldyn Targe:*

The cristill air, the saphir firmament,
The ruby skies of the orient
Kest beriall bemes on emerant bewis grene.

The jewel imagery intensifies the natural colors to an artificial brightness that makes them otherworldly. In the same way, Hogg borrows the device of political allegory from Dunbar's *The Thrissil and the Rois* to represent Kilmeny's vision of the future: we can recognize Queen Mary in the fairest lady on whom sun ever shone and John Knox in the "gruff untoward bedeman," but just as Dunbar uses the animal and plant imagery of heraldry to symbolize the wedding of James IV to Margaret Tudor (James is not only the thistle but also the Stewart lion and the eagle), Hogg uses the same symbols in a different way to symbolize the eventual triumph of the lion of the Great Britain over the eagle of Napoleon's empire. Once again we see Hogg borrowing an idea or device from the medieval Scots makars and developing it in a new way.

The poem also shows Hogg's deft command of a range of language. It is noticeable that the opening and closing sections of the poem, where Kilmeny is on this earth, make abundant use of dialect forms and are written in the language of the Lowlands:

Lang may her minny look o'er the wa'
And lang may she seek in the green-wood shaw;
Lang the laird of Duniera blame
And lang, lang greet or Kilmeny come hame!

Some of the most effective lines in the poem owe their power to the use of dialect forms:

"Late, late in the gloamin' Kilmeny came hame!" In heaven, however, Hogg writes verse predominantly in standard English to great effect:

They seemed to split the gales of air
And yet nor gale nor breeze was there.

Hogg's ear is equally attuned both to standard English and dialect.

THE POETIC MIRROR

Hogg's fine ear for the cadences of language is clear in *The Poetic Mirror,* published in 1816. His original idea was for a series of contributions from the leading poets of the day, but when they were reluctant to contribute, Hogg decided to produce his own imitations of their work instead. It should always be remembered, however, that his imitations here are a sincere form of flattery.

His parody of the style of Robert Southey (1774–1843), the poet laureate, is masterful, but as few people read Southey nowadays, it is difficult to relate Hogg's imitation to the original. Those with an acquaintance with the blank verse of William Wordsworth, however, are more likely to recognize his skills as a parodist from this extract, taken from the beginning of *James Rigg,* subtitled *Still Further Extract from The Recluse, A Poem.* The poet describes the scene from his door of

        the sparkling lake
Just then emerging from the snow-white mist
Like angel's veil slow folded up to heaven.
And lo! a vision bright and beautiful
Sheds a refulgent glory o'er the sand
The sand and gravel of my avenue!
For standing silent by the kitchen door,
Tinged by the morning sun, and on its own
Brown natural hide most lovely
Upstretching perpendicularly, then
With the horizon levell'd—to my gaze
Superb as horn of fabled unicorn

       ...
       a beauteous ass,
With panniers hanging silent at each side!

Hogg catches exactly the rhythm and vocabulary of Wordsworth's more exalted blank verse in the opening lines here, descending to the prosaic description of his graveled drive. This is then followed by the bathos of the vision of a creature likened to the fabled unicorn but which turns out to be a lowly beast of burden.

Wordsworth was perhaps an easy target and the subject of Hogg's most successful parodies, but he also imitated Scott's verse very well in "Wat o' the Cleugh"—and his own in "The Gude Grey Katt," a self-mocking look at his own style as represented in *The Queen's Wake*.

OTHER POEMS AND SONGS

This detailed consideration of a sample of Hogg's best work cannot suggest the full extent of his achievement as a poet. In considering "Kilmeny," we noted that Hogg had a good command of standard English as well as dialect in his verse, and poems such as "Superstition" show his ability to sustain a "philosophical" poem of some length in this register. His achievement as a songwriter should not be underestimated either; he wrote songs of considerable range, from the pastoral calm of "When the Kye Comes Hame" to the rousing verses of "Lock the Door, Lariston":

Lock the door, Lariston, lion of Liddesdale
Lock the door, Lariston, Lowther comes on,
    the Armstrongs are flying,
    their widows are crying
Their castletown's burning, and Oliver's gone;
Lock the door, Lariston—high on the weather gleam
See how the Saxon plumes bob on the sky.
    Yeoman and carbineer,
    Billman and halberdier;
Fierce is the foray and far is the cry.

The shifting rhythms between lines of two and four feet, coupled with the effective use of alliteration, help to suggest the turmoil created by the approach of a feuding border family of previous centuries. The reader who wishes to learn more of Hogg as a songwriter should consult David Groves's edition of the *Selected Poems,* which prints the music (often from the original printed score) alongside Hogg's words.

PROSE

Hogg wrote a good deal of miscellaneous prose, as one would perhaps expect from someone whose principal income was derived from writing. He contributed to a whole range of magazines over many years (the *Quarterly Journal of Agriculture, Ackerman's Juvenile Forget-Me-Not, Chamber's Edinburgh Journal, Blackwood's Edinburgh Magazine,* the *Scots Magazine*), besides being the editor and principal contributor to the *Spy,* which ran for a year from September 1810. These contributions varied widely in their nature, from observations on changes in the lives of the people of the Ettrick and Yarrow Valleys over the years to descriptive pieces, philosophical speculation, and most importantly narratives that seek to capture the atmosphere and nature of the kind of oral tales Hogg listened to around the hearth as a boy in the Ettrick Valley. The most successful of these are perhaps "The Brownie of Black Haggs," "The Cameronian Preacher's Tale," "Mary Burnet," and "The Witches of Traquair": they preserve the loose narrative structure typical of a tale handed down by oral transmission rather than the tighter plot of a modern (or even later-nineteenth-century) short story. They also preserve the Scots language of the Lowlands, although unfortunately later editors often felt it their duty to remove the dialect forms that give Hogg's prose its characteristic tone and flavor with a view to "improving" his work. Douglas Mack gives the example in his introduction to Hogg's *Selected Stories and Sketches* of how a sentence from "Tibby Hyslop's Dream"—"Tibby appeared a little brawer at the meeting house"—is "improved" to the more conventional (and more bland) "Tibby displayed a little more finery at the meeting house," the sentence thereby losing its immediacy and more importantly its locality. Unfortunately Hogg's prose texts were principally known in these bowdlerized forms throughout the nineteenth century and for much of the twentieth. Fortunately the meticulous work of Douglas Mack in particular and also the other editors commissioned by the James Hogg Society has ensured that today we can read Hogg's prose as he intended we should, rich in the dialect forms of his native Lowlands.

THE BROWNIE OF BODSBECK

Hogg's first full-length novel, *The Brownie of Bodsbeck,* was published by Blackwood in 1818 in two volumes along with two other tales, "The Wool-Gatherer" and "The Hunt of Eildon." It is an important work not only in its own right but also as one of several novels—including Scott's *Old Mortality* (1816)—by roughly contemporary novelists dealing with events surrounding the Covenanter rebellion of 1679 and ensuing years, known in Scotland as the Killing Time. We can learn a great deal about both Hogg and Scott by comparing *The Brownie* with *Old Mortality.*

The dates of publication of *The Brownie of Bodsbeck* and *Old Mortality* might suggest that the former was written as Hogg's response to his friend's interpretation of the Covenanting period. In a conversation recorded by Hogg in his *Anecdotes of Sir W. Scott* he records his friend's opinion of *The Brownie* as "very ill ... because it is a false and unfair picture of the times altogether." Hogg defends his work for its historical truth—"There is not one incident in the whole tale which I cannot prove to be literally true from history"—but concedes that Scott would have had a right to be angry if he thought *The Brownie* had only been written as "a counterpoise to Auld Mortality." However, Hogg asserts, and Scott reluctantly concedes, that both knew Hogg's novel was written in manuscript long before Scott's. Although Scott claims the original draft may have been augmented since the publication of his own novel to exaggerate the two men's different views, it is far more likely that these grew naturally out of the differences in approach and outlook between them than any deliberate attempt to create controversy on Hogg's part.

Conflict over the Solemn League and Covenant was a major factor in seventeenth-century Scottish politics. This grew initially out of Charles I's desire to impose the rule of bishops and a Book of Common Prayer on the Presbyterian Church of Scotland, which provoked strong resistance among the Scots and resulted in many ministers being turned out of their parishes. Although government measures to reconcile the Covenanters to Episcopalian government met with some success after the Pentland Rising of 1666, support for the Covenanters grew and culminated in open rebellion following the assassination of Archbishop Sharp on Magus Muir near St. Andrews in May 1679. After early success in battle at Drumclog, the Covenanters were decisively beaten by the Duke of Monmouth at Bothwell Brig in June of the same year. Monmouth, however, treated the defeated Covenanters with leniency and most of their support drifted away, although a number of religious extremists, known now as Cameronians, refused to be reconciled and were hunted down mercilessly over the next eight or nine years by government forces under the command of John Graham of Claverhouse, Viscount Dundee, in a period known as the "Killing Time." The action of *The Brownie of Bodsbeck* takes place toward the end of this era.

The novel concerns the family of Walter Laidlaw, who farms the lands of Chapelhope (only four miles from Hogg's birthplace), on whose hills a group of Covenanters have taken refuge in an underground cavern. Walter decides to help them by supplying them with food, thereby putting himself outside the law; as a consequence, he is arrested by Claverhouse and his troopers and taken to Edinburgh to stand trial. In his absence, his wife, Maron, a religious fanatic, arranges for the local minister to spend the night with his daughter, Catherine, in order to exorcise her, as she is believed to be involved in witchcraft and under the influence of an evil spirit, the eponymous Brownie of Bodsbeck. The minister abuses this trust and uses the opportunity to attempt to rape Catherine, but he is thwarted by the arrival of the Brownie and a group of his followers. Meanwhile Walter is set free on bail at his trial, and the change of government attitude ends the persecution of the Covenanters. This allows Catherine to explain to her father the true identity of the Brownie, who turns out to be John Brown, the deformed leader of the Covenanting band living in a cave they have hollowed out of the hills in the vicinity of Walter's farm. In return for Catherine's help and support, they have been helping her secretly at night with tasks around the farm in her father's absence.

Besides the members of the Laidlaw family and the depiction of Claverhouse, the novel also contains some strong characters. These include the Highland soldier Roy Macpherson, Walter's guard on the journey to Edinburgh, and Catherine's nurse, Old Nanny, whom Scott declared to Hogg to be "by far the best character you ever drew."

One of the major differences between *Old Mortality* and *The Brownie of Bodsbeck* is the treatment of the character of Claverhouse. In many ways he is the hero of Scott's novel, speaking "the standard English of a romantic hero" (according to Peter Davidson and Jane Stevenson, editors of the Oxford World's Classics edition) rather than being presented by Hogg as someone "whose fame remains for the most profane curser ever heard," illustrated by such speeches as:

> May the devil confound and d–n them all to hell! May he make a brander of their ribs to roast their souls on! … G-d d–n you for an old, canting hypocritical +++++!
>
> (p. 56)

While Scott presents Claverhouse as a flawed hero, a gentleman of refinement and someone to be allowed qualified admiration, he is a very different man according to Walter Laidlaw's experience: "He always said that though he was disposed to think well of Clavers before he saw him, yet he never was so blithe in his life as when he got from under his jurisdiction: for there was an appearance of ferocity and wantonness in all his proceedings that made the heart of any man … revolt" (p. 105).

Walter witnesses a man who refuses to take the oath of allegiance ordered behind the ranks and summarily shot; we as readers hear Claverhouse's callous command as to the treatment of a prisoner whose interrogation makes up chapter 7 of the novel: "Take the old ignorant animal away—Burn him on the cheek, cut off his ears and do not part with him until he pay you a fine of two hundred merks, or value to that amount." As John Hoy, Walter's shepherd, is dragged off to his punish-

ment, his words to his judge give an indication of Hogg's attitude too: "I fear our country's a' wrang thegither. … Gude-sooth, lad, but ye'll mak mair whigs wherever ye show your face, than a' the hill-preachers o' Scotland put thegither" (p. 66).

This difference between the two novelists in the characterization of one of the protagonists is a symptom of their different aims and intentions in writing their novels. Scott is consciously writing a historical novel, aiming to put into context for a nineteenth-century audience the religious turmoil and excesses of a century and a half earlier. This is particularly apparent in the scene in the Covenanters' camp on the eve of the Battle of Bothwell Brig. Interestingly too, he also uses the device of placing a nominal hero, Henry Morton, in the midst of the action, who sees everything from the point of view of a conservative unionist from the beginning of the nineteenth century; to some extent we come to see and make sense of the past through the medium of Morton's understanding of events. Hogg's novel, however, is set in a world that has remained unchanged over the years between the Killing Time and his own. He is not interested in the forces of history that shape the past of Scotland as a nation but rather in the incursions to the continuum of life on the farm that would be just as disruptive were they to occur today as they were 150 years previously: fences still have to be mended; the old cattle need to be herded by the Quive Burn, and the Winterhopeburn sheep still need to be "turned aff." Scott's sources were exclusively literary—he made himself "complete master if the whole history of those strange times, both of the persecutors and persecuted" by reading his way through accounts of trials, sermons, historical works, and personal memoirs (see the introduction to the Oxford Classics edition, pp. xi–xii). But Hogg relied far more on stories of the period handed down to him in the oral tradition over three or four generations in his depiction of events and the character of Claverhouse. By his own testimony, "The local part (of the novel) [is taken] from the relation of my own father who had the best possible traditionary account of the incidents," although he did use

Robert Wodrow's *History of the Sufferings of the Church of Scotland* to verify historical detail, as he revealed in the introduction to a new edition of the novel which appeared after his death in 1837. As Douglas Mack points out, Walter Laidlaw's account of his trial "formed one of his winter evening tales as long as he lived"; in his youth, Hogg must have listened to many such tales himself.

In keeping with the strong oral element in its genesis, Hogg's use of Scots in this novel is uncompromising. Much of the narrative is related by Walter himself in a broad Lowlands dialect that might well leave some modern non-Scots readers fainthearted before the end of the first chapter. That Hogg delights and takes pride in the richness of his local speech as opposed to the blandness of standard English is clear from the following exchange, when Claverhouse is interrogating Old John Hoy, the shepherd of Muchrah:

> "How did it appear to you that they had been slain? Were they cut with swords or pierced with bullets?"
>
> "I canna say, but they were sair hashed."
>
> "How do you mean when you say they were hashed?"
>
> "Champit, lie—a' broozled and jerjummled, as it war."
>
> "Do you mean they were cut, cloven or minced?"
>
> "Na, na—no that ava—But they had gotten some sair doofs—they had been terribly paikit and daddit wi' something."
>
> "I do not in the least conceive of what you mean."
>
> "That's extrordinair, man—can ye no understand fock's mother-tongue?"
>
> (p. 61)

Hogg likewise refuses to make linguisitic concessions to a reader unwilling to respond to the richness of the language spoken in the Ettrick and Yarrow valleys two hundred years ago.

One final observation on the novel is upon the spirit in which it was written. Hogg's sympathies clearly lay with the Covenanters as human beings. Unlike Scott, who was at pains to reveal their religious and political extremism (one of his major characters, John Balfour, advocates assas-sination as a justifiable political tool), Hogg stresses the basic humanity of the men hiding among the moss haggs of Chapelhope; after all, outlaws who mend fences cannot be all bad. When Walter addresses his daughter at the end of the novel to praise her for the succor and support she has given the Covenanters in hiding, he speaks for the novelist himself:

> Deil care what side they were on, Kate! ... Ye hae taen the side o' human nature: the suffering and the humble side, an the side o' feeling, my woman, that bodes best in a young inexperienced thing to tak. It is better than to do like yon bits o' gillflirts about Edinburgh; poor shilly-shally milk-an'-water things! ... Ye hae done very right, my good lassie—od, I wadna gie ye for the hale o' them, an' they were a' hung in a strap like ingans.
>
> (p. 163)

The novel rejects both the narrow religious doctrine of the Covenanters and the inquisitorial approach of Claverhouse to speak for a common humanity shared by all.

THE THREE PERILS OF MAN *AND* THE THREE PERILS OF WOMAN

A similar humanity is evident in Hogg's next two novels, *The Three Perils of Man* and *The Three Perils of Woman*. The first is a strange fusion of medieval chivalry, realism, and the supernatural. Its central character, the humble Charlie Scott, is sent to the great magician Michael Scott to ascertain (by divination) which side his master, Sir Ringan Redhough, should back in the siege of Roxburgh Castle, captured by Lord Musgrave and the English. Charlie's experiences lead him to be held captive in the magician's tower, where he and his fellow captives tell stories (rather like Chaucer's pilgrims) to wile away the time— stories that reveal their interlocked fates. Finally Michael Scott turns his captives into cattle, an experience Charlie later turns to good use by disguising himself and Sir Ringan among a herd of beasts to be driven into the castle by its English captors. Once inside, they throw off their ox hides and lock the English soldiers outside the gates, thereby recapturing the castle for Scotland.

The novel has a diffuse structure and did not meet with critical success on publication, although it has aroused interest in modern readers since the appearance of Douglas Gifford's edition.

The Three Perils of Women is likewise a loosely structured work following three separate but related stories and culminating in the aftermath of the Battle of Culloden. Although its early stages incorporate many of the elements of nineteenth-century genteel fiction together with some elements of the Gothic (such as dreams used as omens), the climax of the last section is both melodramatic and tragic, with the recently married husband of the heroine, Sarah, and her former lover mortally wounding each other in a duel. Although the two men live for a few days and are reconciled to Sarah, they are arrested and executed by Whig soldiers. Sarah goes insane, finally dying of exposure. Although David Groves finds this "Hogg's most unsettling and searching work," contemporary reviewers were less kind, condemning it as "profane and revolting to good feeling" and "in the worst possible taste."

THE PRIVATE MEMOIRS AND CONFESSIONS OF A JUSTIFIED SINNER

The work for which Hogg is particularly recognized today was published in 1824. Although *The Private Memoirs and Confessions of a Justified Sinner* was badly reviewed in contemporary magazines (the *Westminster Review* found it "an experiment intended to ascertain how far the English public will allow itself to be insulted"), twentieth-century reactions have been very different. Walter Allen, in *The English Novel* (1954), described it as "a remarkable work by any standard"; in 1947 André Gide had found it an "astounding book" and could not account for its lack of fame at that time. The enthusiasm of scholars and general readers has subsequently amended this fault.

The *Confessions* is a hard book to summarize: because of its structure, it is difficult, if not impossible, to say with any certainty *exactly* what happens during the course of the events, which are described twice—first (apparently) objectively, then subjectively. Indeed neither of the two narrators can be wholly trusted, as both are limited in their understanding of events. An outline of the novel's plot and structure can however be given as follows.

The Editor begins by outlining the history of the Colwan family: the pleasure-loving Laird of Dalcastle marries a pious Glasgow girl, but irreconcilable differences lead to the marriage breaking up, the Laird taking comfort in his "housekeeper," Arabella Logan, and his wife gaining support from the Reverend Robert Wringham, her minister from Glasgow. Two children are born: the first, George, is acknowledged by the Laird and brought up by him; the second, Robert, is repudiated and brought up by his mother and Reverend Wringham, eventually taking his name. (Indeed, as the Laird and his wife spent only one night together in their married life, it seems that this repudiation is wholly justified and that the minister's readiness to adopt Robert is owing to more than merely Christian charity.) The two brothers are brought up separately and meet for the first time as young men in Edinburgh, where Robert interferes in a tennis game George is playing. As a result Robert is knocked down and his legitimacy questioned. George is then apparently haunted by his brother everywhere he goes. One morning on Arthur's Seat, a hill on the outskirts of Edinburgh, he sees an apparition of his brother, who is in fact crouching behind him and seems ready to kill him. Eventually George persuades Robert to leave him alone, but shortly afterward George is found dead, apparently murdered by a drinking companion, Mr. Drummond, in a duel outside an Edinburgh brothel. The Laird dies of a broken heart, and his mistress, Mrs. Logan, determined to find out the truth about the young master's death, discovers that a prostitute, Bell Calvert, was a witness to the murder. She identifies Robert—who has subsequently inherited Dalcastle—and a mysterious companion as the murderers. The two women go to Dalcastle, intending to confront him with his crime. There they encounter him in the company of someone who appears to be the dead George himself but turns out to be Robert's mysterious companion, who leaves him to his fate at their hands. They tie him up, but when arresting officers arrive from Edinburgh, Robert has mysteriously disappeared—and at this point, the Editor's narrative breaks off.

The novel continues with Robert's account of events, told in a journal he had intended for publication that was found in his grave along with his mysteriously preserved body. Significantly, Robert describes himself as "an outcast in this world" in the second paragraph of his narrative yet feels he is "destined to play so conspicuous a part" in it. He recounts his upbringing, including his jealousy of a fellow pupil at school and how he used cunning and trickery to defeat him and become "king of the class." He then deals with the first important event of his life, when his "reverend father" dedicates him to the Lord and recognizes Robert as one of the elect, a "justified person, adopted among the number of God's Children, ... and no bypast transgression, nor any future act of my own, or of other men, could be instrumental in altering that decree" (p. 124). As he walks from the house to thank God for his elevation, he meets a mysterious stranger whose concurrence with his own religious beliefs seems to exalt him even further. The stranger calls himself Gil-Martin, and we quickly see what Robert cannot—that he is the Devil, under whose influence Robert is first led to kill the moderate preacher Mr. Blanchard and then his own brother. However, Robert's grip on reality seems to be tenuous from now on, as he often finds himself accused of crimes, including rape, seduction, and matricide, of which he has no recollection. In vain he tries to escape Gil-Martin, whom he now fears, but supernatural events haunt him. He tries to have his memoir printed in Edinburgh, even setting the type himself, until Gil-Martin intervenes and Robert flees once more. In an attempt to escape his tormentor, who has previously told him "Never shall I depart this country until I can carry you in triumph with me" (p. 187), he turns to suicide, and his journal ends in a desperate prayer of self-doubt: "Almighty God! What is this I am about to do! the hour of repentance is past, and now my fate is inevitable.—Amen, for ever!" (p. 230).

The third section of the novel is narrated by the Editor once again, who recounts how, having read a letter in *Blackwood's Magazine* describing the discovery of a mummified corpse in a grave near Altrive, he went disguised as a wool merchant to Thirlstane sheep fair to meet the writer of the letter, a shepherd by the name of James Hogg. He does in fact meet the latter there, who repudiates him gruffly and walks away. But two other shepherds act as guides, and the Editor, in the company of his friend Mr. Lockhart, is present as the body is exhumed a second time and the manuscript discovered. The Editor, so confidently the man of reason and superior intellect in the first part of his narrative, is forced to concede of Robert's journal: "I do not understand it. ... I do not comprehend the writer's drift."

Certainly one of the main attractions the novel holds for a modern reader is its sophisticated narrative technique. Hogg took great care to establish the veracity of the tale he had to tell: the letter mentioned above in the Editor's final narrative did indeed appear in *Blackwood's* in August 1823, a year before the publication of the novel. Having established the "reality" of the novel, however, thereafter nothing seems to be objectively verifiable: even the factually-minded Editor's first paragraph, on closer reading, offers few "facts," as revealed by phrases such as "It appears from tradition ..." and "the family was supposed. ..."

Much of the novel's sophisticated ambiguity comes from the fact that we cannot trust either of its narrators absolutely. From his first paragraph, the Editor's style reveals him as a man of scholarship and research; the pedantry and the qualifying antithetical structure of the sentences establish him as a scholar of the Enlightenment. Yet the second paragraph, by revealing his prejudices, alerts us to the fact that we cannot trust him to be objective: when he comments on "the stern doctrines of the reformers" and "the severe and carping" nature of the Presbyterians, yet alludes to the "free principles cherished by the court party," we can have no doubt as to where his religious and political sympathies lie. Indeed, his Tory sympathies make him ready to overlook or to play down many of the faults of the Colwans:

the fact that both father and son drink to excess, that George has no occupation beyond tennis and sport and that he visits a brothel are glossed over and certainly not condemned. George, it seems, can be forgiven all because of his superiority over Robert "in personal prowess, form, feature and all that constitutes gentility in deportment and appearance" (p. 44). Consistently George is presented as heroic, whereas Robert is not: after his first encounter with his brother, he is "an object to all of the uttermost disgust ... a rueful looking object, covered in blood, that none of them had the heart to kick, although it appeared the only thing he wanted" (p. 48).

The Editor's eighteenth-century rationalism is confirmed to his reaction to George's experiences on Arthur's Seat. Whereas George is "struck motionless" by the beauty of a pale, rainbow-like halo that rises over his head as he climbs through the early morning cloud, the Editor comments:

That was a scene that would have entranced the man of science with delight but which the uninitiated and sordid man would have regarded less than the mole rearing up his hill in silence and in darkness.

(p. 62)

While George's reaction is in tune with Romantic sensibilities and wins our support, there is a smugness in the Editor's gloss that alienates us. Yet significantly, when George sees the giant apparition of his brother rising up before him moments later, the Editor can offer no explanation, merely reporting George's perception that it was "a blown-up, dilated frame of embodied air, exhaled from the caverns of death or the regions of devouring fire" (p. 63). Increasingly the editor is at a loss to explain the events he records and can only offer the rationalization of others.

However, as a narrator, Robert is no more reliable. His distinctive literary style is likewise established in the first paragraph of his memoir, with its paired nouns ("trouble and turmoil ... change and vicissitude ... sorrow and vengeance"), its theological references to faith and the justification by grace, and its imagery of "gods of silver and of gold" together with blood and sacrifice. There is no claim to objectivity here: the first five sentences begin with either "My" or "I." His smugness alienates us, and his treatment of his rival in school, McGill, and of John Barnet, the Reverend Wringham's servant, make us ready to see him reap his deserts as the novel progresses.

It would be wrong to see Robert simply as a villain, however: Hogg is at pains to portray him as a victim too. From his first meeting with Gil-Martin, we are aware of a dramatic irony that Robert is blind to: when he returns from his first encounter, even his adoptive father is aware of a change in him: "You are transformed since this morning, that I could not have known you for the same person. ... Satan, I fear, has been busy with you, tempting you in no ordinary degree" (p. 129).

Robert insists that he has been conversing only with one whom he took "for an angel of light." When his mother reminds him that "it is one of the devil's most profound wiles to appear as one," she is cut off by Reverend Wringham, who, after establishing that Robert's companion adheres strictly to "the religious principles in which I have educated you," confirms that Gil-Martin could not be a devil. Those who know the border ballads, however, would recognize an affinity between Gil-Martin and the False Knight on the Road, who tempts those he falls in with on his travels. (In the ballad, the young boy so tempted sees through the devil's wiles, unlike Robert.) As the novel progresses, the dramatic irony becomes more apparent: for example, when Robert later asks whether all his subjects are Christians, Gil-Martin replies; "All my European subjects are, or deem themselves so ... and they are the most faithful and true subjects I have" (p. 142).

Another source of ambiguity in the novel arises over whether the strange events surrounding the protagonist are psychological or supernatural in origin. For André Gide, Gil-Martin is "one of the most ingenious personifications of the Devil ever invented" because "the power that sets him in action is always of a psychological nature." As Elaine Petrie observes, in many ways Robert's account of his experiences is an accurate account of a mind clinically both paranoid and schizophrenic. Gide observes that Gil-Martin first appears after Robert's confirmation as one of the elect and helps to confirm him in his sense of superiority, "looking down with pity and contempt on the grovelling creatures below" (p. 125). The acts of seduction and rape of which Robert is accused but cannot recollect could conceivably result from his repressed sexuality making him blot out from his memory acts of sexual indulgence. For him, it could be as though "another person" had done these things, yet a person who is as much a part of him as Mr. Hyde is a part of Dr. Dr. Jekyll in Robert Louis Stevenson's story. His suspected matricide as also explicable in these terms: there is clearly tension between mother and son in his curt manner of addressing her after his first encounter with Gil-Martin:

> "Do you see anything the matter with me?" said I. "It appears that the ailment is with yourself, and either in your crazed head or your dim eyes, for there is nothing the matter with me."
>
> (p. 128)

Such a psychological interpretation of the novel, however, has its limitations: if Gil-Martin is no more than an emanation of Robert's mind, how can others see him? Even Gide has to concede that "the fantastic part (of this novel) is always psychologically explicable *except in the last pages*" (emphasis added). It is clear that Gil-Martin must have an objective reality, but it is one that is impossible to pin down: he can look like Robert, or his brother, or adopt the features of Dr. Blanchard, it would seem, at will. Part of the novel's power arises from the fact that the reader can never be sure exactly of the nature of the reality of this character, no more than Robert himself:

> That time will now soon arrive … and when it hath come and passed over, when my flesh and my bones are decayed, and my soul has passed to its everlasting home, then shall the sons of men ponder on the events of my life; wonder and tremble, and tremble and wonder at how such things could be.
>
> (p. 125)

As a writer, Hogg has created in previous works a strong sense of the supernatural, but in this novel (unlike, for example, in *The Brownie of Bodsbeck*) he chooses not to explain away events rationally. Rather, the power of the book comes from the fact that Robert—and we as readers—cannot ever be sure what—or whom—he is dealing with. The Editor too is at a loss to explain events, and so are Mrs. Logan and Bell Calvert: How can Drummond, George's murderer, seem to be in two places at once immediately before George is assassinated in the Edinburgh close? How can they see the murdered George apparently restored to life at Dalcastle toward the end of the Editor's narrative? As Bell Calvert exclaims; "We have nothing on earth but our senses to depend on: if these deceive us, what are we to do" (p. 95). We depend on our senses for dealing with the natural world; can we expect them also to deal with the supernatural?

One of the most striking symbols of the novel comes near its conclusion, when Robert is fleeing in disguise from both his tormentor and the law. He sleeps in the house of a weaver; on awakening, he finds the disguise he had borrowed the previous day from Gil-Martin has transformed itself into his habitual cocked hat and black coat. In his confusion and in the darkness he becomes entangled in the weaver's loom "and could not get out again … My feet slipped down through the double warpings of a web … and to extricate myself was impossible" (pp. 209–210). He calls for help and is berated by the weaver as "a servant of the de'il's" who has "fawn inna little hell, instead o' a big muckle ane." He is soundly beaten and as a result becomes increasingly entangled in the loom. Robert's hell is the tangle and confusion of threads of theological sophistry, from which there is no escape for him. The trap that ensnares him progressively during the course of the novel is the warp and weft of theological debate so carefully laid out by his antinomian father, Reverend Wringham. For Hogg, evil does not lie so much in the human heart as in the corruption of religious doctrine by hubristic men.

It would be wrong, however, to see the *Confessions* as a work attacking religion. While it is true that the particular brand of Calvinism depicted here is very much local to Scotland (where it also gave rise to Burns's great satirical poem "Holy Wullie's Prayer"), Hogg is not attacking religious belief in this novel but rather its perversion by zealots. There is clearly a degree of religious satire in the work, but the voice of true religion is also strong in the novel, for example in the character of Dr. Blanchard, or in John Barnet, the minister's servant, whose sense of fair play and integrity in his dealings with the Wringham family lead to him losing his job.

CONCLUSION

It is hoped that this summary of Hogg's life and work conveys a sense, however limited, of the range and variety of his achievement. He is a unique writer, standing as he does between the oral tradition and the literary world, and the distinctive blend of the two that he brings to his greatest poetry and prose make him a writer of outstanding note.

Selected Bibliography

WORKS OF JAMES HOGG

POETRY

The Mountain Bard. Edinburgh: Constable, 1807; London: Murray, 1807.

The Forest Minstrel. Edinburgh and London: Constable, 1810.

The Queen's Wake. Edinburgh: George Goldie, 1813; London: Longman, Hurst, Rees, Orme & Brown, 1813.

The Poetic Mirror. Edinburgh: Ballantyne, 1816; London: Longman, 1816.

The Jacobite Relics of Scotland. 2 vols. Edinburgh: Blackwood, 1819; London: Cadell, 1819, 1821.

The Poetical Works of James Hogg. 4 vols. Edinburgh: Arch, Constable, 1822; London: Hurst, Robinson, 1822.

Queen Hynde. Edinburgh: Blackwood, 1824; London: Longman, 1824.

Songs, by the Ettrick Shepherd. Edinburgh: Blackwood, 1831; London: Cadell, 1831.

NOVELS AND OTHER WORKS

The Shepherd's Guide. Edinburgh: Constable, 1807; London: Murray, 1807. (Hogg's treatise on diseases in sheep.)

The Brownie of Bodsbeck and Other Tales. Edinburgh: Blackwood, 1818; London: Murray, 1818.

The Three Perils of Man. London: Longman, 1822.

The Three Perils of Woman. London: Longman, 1823.

The Private Memoirs and Confessions of a Justified Sinner; Written by Himself. London: Longman, 1824.

MODERN EDITIONS AND COLLECTIONS

The Private Memoirs and Confessions of a Justified Sinner. Edited by John Carey. London: Oxford University Press, 1969.

The Private Memoirs and Confessions of a Justified Sinner. Introduction by André Gide. London: Cresset Press, 1947; reprinted as a London Panther paperback, 1970.

James Hogg: Selected Poems. Edited by Douglas S. Mack. Oxford: Clarendon, 1970. (References in the text are to this edition.)

Memoir of the Author's Life and Familiar Anecdotes of Sir Walter Scott, Edited by Douglas S. Mack. Edinburgh: Scottish Academic Press, 1972.

The Brownie of Bodsbeck. Edited by Douglas S. Mack. Edinburgh: Chatto & Windus, 1976.

James Hogg: Selected Stories and Sketches. Edited by Douglas S. Mack. Edinburgh: Scottish Academic Press, 1982.

Anecdotes of Sir W. Scott. Edited by Douglas S. Mack. Edinburgh: Scottish Academic Press, 1983.

The Private Memoirs and Confessions of a Justified Sinner. Edited by John Wain. Middlesex, U.K.: Penguin, 1983. (References in the text are to this edition.)

James Hogg: Selected Poems and Songs. Edited by David Groves. Edinburgh: Scottish Academic Press, 1986.

A Shepherd's Delight: A James Hogg Anthology. Edited by Judy Steel. Edinburgh: Canongate, 1985.

The Three Perils of Man. Edited by Douglas Gifford. Edinburgh: Scottish Academic Press, 1989.

CRITICAL AND BIOGRAPHICAL STUDIES

Groves, David. *James Hogg: The Growth of a Writer.* Edinburgh: Scottish Academic Press, 1988.

Hughes, Gillian, ed. *Papers Given at the Second James Hogg Society Conference (Edinburgh, 1985).* Edinburgh: Association for Scottish Literary Studies, 1988.

Petrie, Elaine. *James Hogg's "The Private Memoirs and Confessions of a Justified Sinner."* Scotnotes, no 4. Aberdeen: Association for Scottish Literary Studies, 1988.

Scottish Literary Journal 10, no. 1 (May 1983). (James Hogg issue.)

ALAN HOLLINGHURST

(1954–)

Clare Connors

ALAN HOLLINGHURST'S NAME is one that elicits lofty comparisons. On the strength of his three superbly literate novels, he has been likened to such literary giants as Vladimir Nabokov and Jane Austen. The perennial matter of literature is all there—love, death, age, mourning, ennui, manners, and memory—but the perspective is, to use one of his own favored words, queer. Hollinghurst's novels play across the many senses of this resonant adjective. These works are by turns surprising, funny, perplexing, peculiar, remarkable, unexpected, and deviant. They are also, in both their subject matter and range of literary references, "queer" in the sense of homosexual. Unlike nineteenth- and early-twentieth-century writers such as Oscar Wilde or E. M. Forster, Hollinghurst does not have to present homosexuality through innuendo, allusion, and coded references. On the other hand, unlike many more recent gay novelists, including Edmund White, he does not feel obliged to follow the naturalistic conventions of the "coming out" narrative, slowly presenting the tortured arrival in consciousness of a gay man. One of the chief pleasures in reading Hollinghurst, in fact, is seeing the rich stylistic resources that have developed in earlier "queer" literary texts as a result of centuries of homosexual repression blending with an explicit presentation of late-twentieth-century gay culture, where homosexual identity is taken for granted. Hollinghurst's touching, erotic, and erudite novels represent a new literary departure not so much because of the frankness of their subject matter as because of the way they rethink and develop the literary tradition in which they are situated.

BIOGRAPHY

Alan Hollinghurst was born on May 26,1954, in Stroud, Gloucestershire, and went to school in Canford, Dorset. Initially he did not aspire to write but wanted to follow in his father's professional footsteps and become an architect. This ambition, which soon gave way to the lure of literature, has left its mark on Hollinghurst's writing; several of his most eloquent review articles discuss architectural tomes, and in his novels buildings are described with an informed sense both of their aesthetic qualities and of the history they embody.

At the age of eighteen, Hollinghurst went up to Oxford University's Magdalen College, where he read English. He remained there after graduation, working as a lecturer between 1977 and 1978 while completing his M. Litt. thesis, which he submitted in 1979. Magdalen was a place where literary talent was intelligently encouraged. The college's flourishing literary culture, fostered in particular by one of its English fellows, the poet and scholar John Fuller, had proved to be the ideal environment for a succession of young writers. As an undergraduate Hollinghurst won the prestigious Newdigate Prize for literary verse, an award that has marked the beginning of many literary careers including those of Oscar Wilde and Matthew Arnold. John Fuller owned the private press on which Hollinghurst's first volume of poetry, *Confidential Chats with Boys* (1982) was produced, in a print run of two hundred copies. With poems already in print in a variety of journals and gathered together in a Faber *Poetry: Introduction* volume in 1978, it must have seemed likely that Hollinghurst, too, was set to become a poet and an academic. Further lectureships ensued at Somerville College in the academic year 1979–1980 and in the following year at Corpus Christi College, the alma mater of William Beckwith in *The Swimming Pool Library.*

Moving to London in 1982, Hollinghurst took up a lectureship at the University of London, a job he held for only one term before his career changed direction and he became deputy editor at the *Times Literary Supplement* (*TLS*), one of Britain's foremost literary magazines. He was to remain with the journal until 1995 in a variety of capacities, latterly as poetry editor. His work writing and commissioning reviews demanded eclectic as well as discriminating reading, a literary apprenticeship that might go some way toward explaining the erudition of his own novels. Hollinghurst also helped to set the *TLS*'s weekly competition "Author Author," which invites readers to identify the source of literary quotations, and edited *Nemo's Almanac*, an annual literary competition along the same lines. Here, too, we can see the origin of traits that recur in his fiction, where bookish puzzles, teasing citations, and even anagrams pepper the narratives. Readers who share his thrill in the covert reference may be intrigued to learn that the "winner" of one of the weekly competitions in 1984 was a certain William Beckwith: the first outing of a resonant name.

It was during his time at the *TLS* that Hollinghurst's writing career took off. On the back of his early poetic achievements, he won a contract with Faber and Faber for a volume of poetry, an achievement that seemed to stifle his muse. The volume never appeared, and Hollinghurst has barely written a poem since. Instead, in 1988 his feted first novel, *The Swimming Pool Library,* was published to panegyrics from all quarters of the literary world, earning a series of prizes including a Somerset Maugham Award and the 1989 Gay/Lesbian Book Award from the British Library Association. In 1993 he was deemed one of the twenty best young novelists in *Granta*'s decadal nominations, a judgment amply confirmed by publication the next year of *The Folding Star,* which was short-listed for the Booker Prize and won a shelf-full of other awards, including the James Tait Black Memorial Book Prize for fiction. A third novel, *The Spell* (1998), completes the list of his major fictional publications to date, although his involvement in the world of letters has extended further, including

introductions to editions of works by Ronald Firbank, Francis Wyndham, and A. E. Housman, and the translation of a seventeenth-century French play by Racine, *Bajazet.* These diverse literary interests are by no means marginal to the main business of his writing but in fact constitute the very ether of his allusive and supremely literate novels.

EARLY WORK AND LATER CRITICAL INTRODUCTIONS

Hollinghurst's early academic and poetic works are interesting both in themselves and as precursors of his mature fiction. His unpublished M. Litt. thesis on *The Creative Uses of Homosexuality in E. M. Forster, Ronald Firbank, and L. P. Hartley* is concerned with what he (and his character James Brooke in *The Swimming Pool Library*) will later call "deflected" expressions of homosexuality. Here we see limned the partial outlines of a queer canon that Hollinghurst's own novels will both join and reread. The aim of the thesis is not to decode the works of his three authors, or to point out a series of signs (like the word "earnest" in Wilde) only otherwise decipherable by an initiated cognoscenti. Rather, in a series of patient readings, Hollinghurst explores the resources and characteristics of literary style that evolved in these early-twentieth-century texts, written in a culture where homosexual love was illegal and descriptions of it taboo. Discussing the kinds of literary artifice engendered by the unavowed homosexuality of his authors, he argues that their distinctive literary worlds are produced by the tension between the aspiration to realism and the prohibition of desire. In the most successful cases, the collision within these texts between the drive to convey truths about the world and the social refusal of the legitimacy or propriety of homosexuality, which means that the "truth" can only be expressed obliquely, creates a distinctively homosexual aesthetic. Although his approach is not especially "theoretical," Hollinghurst's early academic work in many ways anticipates the insights of queer theorists of the 1980s and 1990s such as Eve Sedgwick, who are interested in "queerness" as a textual phenomenon rather than simply as a concealed or revealed identity.

Its theoretical prescience aside, Hollinghurst's graduate thesis is notable for the way it outlines a set of concerns that appear, transmuted, in his later work. Specifically, the championing of Ronald Firbank's writings as the apotheosis of the "creative use of homosexuality" strikes a keynote that will resound throughout Hollinghurst's writing, both critical and literary. Firbank (1886-1926) was a highly idiosyncratic figure, who lived the life of an aesthete, and wrote short, satirical and almost plotless novels, peopled by eccentric characters. In 1991 Hollinghurst provided an introduction to Steven Moore's edition of *The Early Firbank* and in 2000 introduced a new Penguin edition of *Ronald Firbank: Three Novels*. In both he makes bold claims for Firbank's literary status, asserting in former, for example, that *Vainglory*'s (1915) "fragmented texture, elliptical structure and suppression of plot entitle it to be considered the most advanced and concentrated modernist novel that had so far appeared in England" (p. viii). The highly aestheticized world Firbank conjures, with its antirealist representation of characters and emphasis on female sexuality is of course a far cry from the milieus Hollinghurst evokes in his novels. It would be wrong to see Firbank's "remarkable economy, brilliant humour and disconcerting pathos" (p. vii) in any literal sense as an influence on Hollinghurst's own more discursive style, funny and moving as the latter often is. What Firbank stands for, however, is the successful integration of homosexual desire into a properly literary and aesthetically convincing and distinctive form. It is this that Hollinghurst seeks to emulate in his own writing.

There were detours, however, before Hollinghurst discovered his true literary medium; his earliest excursions into print were poetic. There is perhaps too little of the poetry to identify in it a voice or definitive style, and certainly the poems collected in Faber's *Poetry: Introduction 4* (1978) might properly be classed as juvenilia. Nevertheless, they have a clarity of diction and a precision in their evocation of the English landscape that points to the maturer literary tal-

ent of the novels. There are references to Forster and Christopher Isherwood and tonal similarities to the Romantic and Georgian poets (beloved by Edward Manners in *The Folding Star*) in the combination of colloquial language with lyricism and nostalgia. In both "Christmas Day At Home" and "The Drowned Field," for example, the acts of reminiscing, repeating and shuttling back and forth between then and now are dynamically enacted. Of Christmas, Hollinghurst writes "the idea makes us children / and says something of being old." There is nostalgia here, but also a more cautious, reflective distance that wards off sentimentality. A certain nostalgia, probed rather than indulged but never simply ironized, will be one of the abiding interests of Hollinghurst's later work. It is also one of the qualities he finds interesting in Housman, another poet invoked in this volume in the poem "Nightfall (For an Athlete Dying Young)," which reprises in its subtitle and twilit pathos one of A. E. Housman's poems in "A Shropshire Lad." Much later in his literary career, Hollinghurst celebrated Housman in a special edition of his poetry selected for Faber, *Poems. Selected by Alan Hollinghurst* (2001), exploring the way in which the poet enlists the "time-honoured forms" of ballad, song, and epigram to his own "less licensed [because homosexual] sufferings" (p. ix).

Nascent homosexual identity, along with certain myths and truths about childhood, are the subject of Hollinghurst's slim, privately published volume *Confidential Chats with Boys* (1982). Containing five poems each of five quatrains, the book shares its title with one dating from 1913 written by a William Lee Howard, M.D., which offers advice to adolescent boys about various aspects of sexual development and vehemently warns of the dangers posed by homosexual men: "There are things in trousers called men, so vile that they wait in hiding for the innocent boy. These things are generally well-dressed, well mannered—too well mannered in fact—and pass as gentlemen; but they are really human skunks hatched from rattle-snakes' eggs" (p. 94). The first poem in *Confidential Chats* picks up on this surreal image and its homophobic conflation of pedophilia with homosexual desire, working it into verse; the last line ends by repeating Howard's violent imprecation "scar the skunk and coward for life."

The terrifying images with which Howard presents the growing boy are ironically juxtaposed in the rest of the collection, however, with explorations of more complex, if less melodramatic, trajectories toward maturity. Hollinghurst here evokes the atmosphere of mild repression, enclosure, and inactivity he is later to celebrate in the stories of Francis Wyndham. In his introduction to *Francis Wyndham: The Collected Fiction* (1992), he identifies "an atmosphere of misunderstanding and ennui" as characteristic of the distinctive tonality of Wyndham's stories about the Second World War, stories in which people subsist "as if in a state of suspended animation … prey to boredom, deprivation and a mood of unfocused expectancy" (p. viii).

In *Confidential Chats* this mood is embodied in the rather uncomfortable power exerted on the speaker by the reproduction of Walter Sickert's painting *Ennui*. We also see in this reference the first occurrence of the Hollinghurst motif of a painting too intolerable to look at, an idea that will crop up later in *The Swimming Pool Library* and *The Folding Star*. In the poem, the Sickert painting, in which the image of a domestic interior seems also to represent the enclosure of the self, both repels the speaker with its pinioned stillness and "the orchid silence" it evokes and mirrors his own "ennui." "Orchid" puns on "awkward," of course, but also recalls the hothouse flowers of decadent writers and thus functions as a signifier of homosexuality. Relatedly, we learn about the cultural images of masculinity and femininity the speaker mimics. "When I was very young" he begins the fourth poem, in an allusion to A. A. Milne's rather saccharine poems for children, "my thrill was travesty"—both of femininity and of the machismo of Don Giovanni, and the "wonderful soprano prince" in Johann Strauss's operetta *Die Fledermaus*. The nascent sexuality of the speaker is by no means the only preoccupation of the poems, however. He jokes at one point about his "hard-core / innocence." The relatively familiar genre of the "coming out" narrative is eschewed

in favor of a more complex depiction of cultural and intellectual influences and an atmosphere of subdued constraint.

In fact only once, and then obliquely, does Hollinghurst treat the theme of "coming out," and that is in his third early publication, the short story "A Thieving Boy," published in *Firebird 2: Writing Today*. Here the perspective is no longer that of the child, or of the adult recalling childhood, but of the (foster) parents of a child. In an unusual narrative maneuver, the story is recounted in the first-person plural, a "we" that makes it impossible to know whether it is the husband or wife who is speaking. The plot is slight. The Taylors foster Tim, the young son of friends who die in a car crash, bringing him up as their own until, at the age of eighteen, he leaves them to travel and does not return. Years later the couple, on holiday in Egypt, encounter Tim again. They visit his home and meet his "servant" Mustafa, who turns out—in a revelation the Taylors receive with "all the embarrassment, the gaucherie, of good intentions" (p. 107)—to be his lover. At the conclusion of the story, in an irony "that showed life for a while to be as structured and monumental as fiction," the Taylors read in a newspaper article that Tim has been robbed by his servant while he had been showing them around the Pyramids, edifices themselves robbed by "those most trusted to keep [their] secrets" (p. 108). They fail in their attempts to contact him to commiserate and are left wondering whether he, like them, has recognized "how much we learn from those who betray us" (p. 109). This concluding sentence makes clear that the "thieving boy" of the title is not only Tim's lover but, in his relationship to his foster parents, Tim himself.

In this first piece of published prose Hollinghurst proves himself already a master of nuanced observation and controlled phrasing, maintaining an impressive balance of sympathies between the narrators and their foster son. There is no caricatured homophobia in the presentation of the foster parents' response to the revelations of Tim's sexuality, which is nicely poised between liberal acceptance and a "sense of upset" (p. 107). One simultaneously identifies with their hurt at Tim's repudiation of their care and has an intimation that there might have been something stifling in their relationship to him. In the obliquity of the narrative approach to questions of sexuality, however, there is perhaps a certain discomfort attributable not to the story's characters but to its author. Certainly the indirect treatment of gay life—glimpsed by the narrator only in a "split second" view of Mustafa's naked back in the kitchen "shielded off" (p. 107) by Tim—makes for a strange constrast with the more frank descriptions of Hollinghurst's first novel.

THE SWIMMING POOL LIBRARY

Hollinghurst's first novel, and the work with which he came to public attention in 1988, shares with his earlier short story both its Egyptology (in the form of embedded diary entries from Khartoum) and the element of shock revelation. It is also—as all its reviewers remarked—beautifully written, and it displays a relish for the aesthetic in any form, corporeal, literary, artistic, or architectural. A story about desire, *The Swimming Pool Library* plays with the reader's desire in two ways. On the one hand, the writing renders a shiftless, promiscuous eroticism. The novel is narrated in the first person by William Beckwith, a wealthy and charming young egotist whose main aim in life is sexual pleasure. Narcissistic as he may be, we are seduced both by him and by his seductions. In the course of the novel he has two relatively long-term relationships, with Arthur and Phil, as well as numerous thrillingly described casual encounters. His prose lovingly dwells on the male body and "the difference of man and man" (p. 164), the rhythms and tempos of sex, lust, love and liking, and the etiquette of pickups. The book's reviewers all noted the frankness, precision, and savor with which sex is treated. There are romantic deflowerings, pornographic set pieces, and ritual locker-room stripteases, the swimming pool of the book's title providing the scene for many of the latter. Tugging against the repeating rhythm of desire and satisfaction, on the other hand, is a sequential "detective story" narrative that plays on a more cerebral need to know, to uncover, to find out. In one of the novel's many ironies, Will, the Oxford

history graduate, is provided with the historical vision that he lacks as he gradually learns startling facts both about his own family's past and about the recent history of homosexuality in Britain. The plot itself thus performs a slow-motion striptease, leading not only to a culmination but to an education of sorts, both for the reader and the novel's narrator.

The London Underground, which forms one of the novel's leitmotivs, might serve as a metaphor for both tendencies of the story, the rhythmically erotic and the teleological. The map of the underground has a "fastidious rectilinearity" and a "Roman straightness" that Will also admires in architecture and landscape gardening (p. 46). However, his journeys on it are less straightforwardly linear. He finds it "often sexy and strange, like a gigantic game of chance, in which one got jammed up against many queer kinds of person" (p. 47).

Will's historical education, in fact, is achieved through a chance encounter with a queer kind of person. Early on in the novel, Will, pursuing sex in Hyde Park, saves the life of Charles Nantwich, an elderly peer who has collapsed with a heart attack. On the strength of this exceptional meeting Nantwich asks Will to save his life in another sense, by writing his memoirs. Someone else's story and a different point of view are thus introduced into Will's narrative of erotic and present-oriented drifting. Charles was born in 1900, an authorial contrivance that allows Hollinghurst in effect to sketch in eight decades of homosexual life. Charles's diaries, interleaved into Will's accounts of his love affairs and pickups, give us miniatures of boarding school life during the First World War, glimpses of a Brideshead-like Oxford, and a slice of his experience in Egypt as a district commissioner in the 1920s. Later volumes allow us to see him in 1940s and 1950s London, first cruising in the way Will does, then becoming a victim of the 1950s vilification of homosexuals as he is set up by the police for cottaging (using public toilets for homosexual sex) and imprisoned. The novel's shock revelation is that Will's grandfather, the paterfamilias whose money allows Will to spend his days "prancing around making passes at anything in trousers" (p. 264) rather than earning a living, was the key figure responsible for the anti-gay prosecutions of the 1950s that put Nantwich behind bars. Will is obliged to recognize his own implication in a history of persecution, as part of the structure of class and money that upholds it.

Historical vision does not simply entail a knowledge of the past, however. Will's education about the mid-twentieth-century spate of persecutions of gay men in which his grandfather was involved goes hand in hand with his recognition that such prejudice and violence still exist. As he says to his brother-in-law Gavin: "that's really not another world ... it's going on in London now almost every day" (p. 265). He reaches this realization painfully. Returning from a failed visit to the home of his missing lover Arthur, he is set upon by skinheads and violently beaten in an attack motivated both by homophobia ("You can tell he's a fuckin' poof," p. 172) and racism ("I think his friend must be one of our little coloured brothers, don't you?," p. 173). Attacked and beaten, Will says to himself: "It was actually happening. It was actually happening to me" (p. 174). "Actually" here conveys at once the shocked realization of a hitherto blessed youth that he is not invulnerable to pain and violence, and also a more temporal sense (as in the French *actuellement*) that this is happening *now,* in the present, the late twentieth century. The final image of the attack, of "a boot drawn back, very large and hard, then slamming towards my face" (p. 174) recalls Orwell's black vision of the future in *Nineteen Eighty-Four* as "a boot stamping on a human face—for ever."

The invocation of this novel, indeed of this date in particular, is significant. Hollinghurst's novel is set in 1983, in "the last summer of its kind there was ever to be" (p. 3) just before the sinister rumors of AIDS became awful facts. The novel is aware of this—its characters are not. In this context the reference to the year 1984 calls up a specific and imminent set of horrors. Will's growing realization of the fragility of his own beauty ("At least I saw it before they spoilt it," says Nantwich of his bruised and beaten face [p. 185]) takes on a terrible pathos. More generally,

the Orwell reference invokes the world of state control over the individual and the policing of all areas of personal life, including the sexual. Such policing, clearly evident in the 1950s, is seen in the world of 1983, where there is still a gap of five years between heterosexual and homosexual ages of consent and where Will's friend James can therefore be set up by a "pretty policeman" (p. 222) and prosecuted.

The presence of the police is also implied more cryptically. This novel, indeed, relishes the cryptic and the coded even as it celebrates the fact that in the twentieth century homosexuality, while still policed, does not have to have recourse to riddles in order to signify. Hot on the heels of the revelation about his grandfather comes Will's discovery that his boyfriend Phil is sleeping with an older man, Bill. The echo chamber of names here—Will, Bill, Phil—about which Will jokes bitterly ("It's like one of those frightful seventeenth-century epitaphs: I've had my Will, I've had my Fill, and now they've sent in my Bill" [p. 278]) alerts the reader to the possibility of a more than literal interpretation. Indeed, names in Hollinghurst's novels always repay attentive scrutiny. Here, Will's disillusionment about the object of his adoration, however hypocritical it is, is most obviously just a further blow to his narcissism. His "little Philanderer" (p. 276), who has been dutifully reading his way through the adventures of Fielding's *Tom Jones,* turns out to be a philanderer in earnest. The object of his choice, the older man Bill Shillibeer, who knows Nantwich from their prison days, is also allegorically significant. Shillibeer's name (which he says he will explain to Will but never does) comes undone anagrammatically to give the graffito "Bill is here." This is true in the literal sense that Bill poaches Will's lover Phil, but it also has more sinister connotations. "The Bill" are the police in English slang, and Bill's encoded surname seems to imply that, as Will finds out, the police are often present where one least expects to find them, in the middle of one's private life. Homosexuality, the novel suggests, is still policed in a way that heterosexual desire is not.

ALAN HOLLINGHURST

It is on the novel's politics—its treatment of the relationship between sex and power, both historically and actually—that recent criticism of *The Swimming Pool Library* has centered. While all readers agree that Hollinghurst intends to criticize homophobic state intervention into men's private lives, some have argued that the novel is in fact complicit with other, equally negative, structures of power. Coming in for particular scrutiny have been the novel's treatments of race and of the pornographic. Will's first lover, Arthur, is black, and he is the prompt for many encomia to the beauty of black bodies. "Oh, the ever-open softness of black lips" (p. 2) Will eulogizes, in a way that seems to reduce his lover to his skin color and a series of body parts. Arthur is also young, poor, and working class, and thus in all respects disadvantaged vis-à-vis the affluent and slightly older Will. Both Arthur and Will's second boyfriend, the white but working-class Phil, are eroticized in part because of their lack of eloquence and education.

It is clear that we are not supposed to treat Will's relationships here any less critically than we do other aspects of his narcissistic if charming character. The moment when Will, reeling from his recent historical discoveries, is bent over a table in the kitchen of the club he has hitherto visited as a privileged guest and is unceremoniously spanked and penetrated by Abdul, symbolically suggests an inversion of the power relationships that have hitherto pertained. Perhaps more complicated is the fact that this leaves Will "gurgling with pleasure and grunting with pain" (p. 262): the relationship between power and pleasure is more complicated than left-wing critics might suggest.

But what are we to make of Charles Nantwich's relationship to his African servant Taha? Nantwich brings Taha back with him from Egypt and continues to idolize him, even after his marriage, until he is murdered in a racist attack while Nantwich is in prison. A clear link is effected here between homophobic and racist violence. The critic David Alderson has suggested, however, that such violence is only condemned because the novel surreptitiously endorses Nantwich's archaically feudal view that the present is more violent and less pure than what it replaces. He argues in an essay called "Desire as Nostalgia: The Novels of Alan Hollinghurst" that the book can be read only as a criticism of the present "because it is not an unqualified condemnation of the colonially and sexually circumscribed past" (p. 33).

Readers must decide for themselves whether they think the novel simply endorses Nantwich's views. His surname might, however, provide ammunition for a counterargument. Its first syllable reminds us of the French verb *nantir,* which means "to provide." In itself this suggests a perhaps laudable philanthropy (another one of the "phil" words the novel plays on), and indeed Charles is involved with a variety of charitable institutions and private benevolences. He is a provider in a less than disinterested sense, however, when he supplies all the boy actors for his friends' pornographic filmmaking enterprises. "They like to do what I want," he tells Will, before adding, "But then I got them all their jobs" (p. 245). This admission comes shortly after Charles's nostalgic speech—"There are times when I can't think of my country without a kind of despairing shame"—and his disavowal of any racist content to his films: "I don't think *race* comes into it, does it? I mean, Abdul is black and the others aren't … but I don't want any rot about that" (p. 245). A complex view of his character is thus presented, at once nostalgic and feudally benevolent, self-interested and potentially dangerous. It is questionable whether the novel as a whole either simply upholds or completely criticizes such an amalgam of qualities.

More pertinent perhaps might be to consider how nostalgia and the relationship to the past are themselves treated by Hollinghurst. Hollinghurst's review articles can provide us with some useful insights here. When writing for the *TLS,* the books he most often reviewed were not works of fiction but architectural studies. Hollinghurst's love of the architectural is clear—he describes the heft and mass and detail of buildings beautifully, much as he does the male body. But part of the interest in buildings lies in their relationship to time. A building registers and displays the changes it undergoes; it shows history in the present, a fragment of the past simultaneously adapted to new requirements and different urban configurations. Hollinghurst reviewed, in one form or another, most of the revised "The Buildings of England" series, those famous British architectural guides originally written by a German, Niklaus Pevsner, and updated in the second half of the twentieth century. In "Keeping Up with the Past," a pertinently titled discussion of Cherry and Pevsner's *London 2: South,* it becomes clear that Hollinghurst's interest in the Pevsner guides is twofold. First, they are attentive to the ways in which the shape of London changes, describing how the past gets updated in the city landscape of the present. Second, the Pevsner guides themselves embody this process of recording but updating: Pevsner's jerky notes, with their residues of German word order, get converted into smooth essays but with small moments of homage remaining and the inspiration of Pevsner shining clear through the modernizations. In a sense both the guides and the buildings are celebrated as palimpsests, neither fetishizing the past nor destroying it completely in attending to the demands of the present.

We might view *The Swimming Pool Library* as a similarly palimpsestic text. This strange "library" is full of books. The novel's title literally refers to a memory of Will's schooldays. He explains how, at his prep school, prefects were named "librarians" and how he himself, having been passed over for positions of responsibility for many terms, was eventually nominated the "Swimming-Pool Librarian." As with the later swimming pool at Will's club, the Corinthian, this pool, too, is presented as a place devoted to exercises other than the aquatic. Will writes:

Sometimes I think that shadowy, doorless little shelter—which is all it was really, an empty, empty place—is where at heart I want to be. ... Nipping into that library of uncatalogued pleasure was to step into the dark and halt. Then held breath was released, a cigarette glowed, its smoke was smelled, the substantial blackness moved, glimmered and touched. Friendly hands felt for the flies. There was never, or rarely, any kissing—no cloying, adult impurity in the lubricious innocence of what we did.

(p. 141)

There is a nostalgia for an innocent time before history. And yet *The Swimming Pool Library* itself re-situates these shelters and empty places in history. The school pool has both historical antecedents and literary ones. The fact that Will's club is called the Corinthian implies a Greek prehistory for the pool, while the Roman baths concealed in the basement of Nantwich's home point to its existence also in Roman Britain. "Imagine all those naked legionaries in here" (p. 80) says Nantwich salaciously. Nantwich's diaries, too, form part of this library of swimming pools: he recalls, nostalgically, the innocence of river bathing in Egypt. And Hollinghurst, former graduate researcher into the novels of E. M. Forster and L. P. Hartley, cannot but have one eye on the homoerotic bathing scenes in their novels, too. This palimpsest of pools participates in the larger literary history the book cites from and incorporates, in a deliberate remaking or refiguring—we might say "queering"—of the literary canon.

What might it mean to say that Hollinghurst's novel "queers" the canon? "Queer" is a word found often in *The Swimming Pool Library,* both in its homosexual sense and in its other meanings implying peculiarity, unexpectedness, or deviance. It can also be used as a verb, as in the phrase to "queer the pitch" (p. 97). That this is going to be a queer novel in all respects is advertised in its opening paragraph, as Will tries to imagine the back-to-front regime of the maintenance workers on the London underground:

I looked at them with a kind of swimming, drunken wonder, amazed at the thought of their inverted lives, of how their occupation depended on our travel, but could only be pursued, I saw it now, when we were not travelling.

(p. 1)

Hollinghurst's book, full of swimming wonders, reverses the stigmatizing nineteenth-century notion of homosexuality as inversion, making central "inverted lives" and avoiding the journeys of heterosexual plotting which culminate in marriage or childbirth. In doing so, however, it eschews the metaphorical and stylistic obliquities to which early twentieth-century gay writers such as Firbank and Forster had recourse—the "deflected" language of covert homosexuality—in favor of more overt description. Hollinghurst has no need to use the literary strategies his graduate thesis explored. Indeed his novel is remarkable for the frankness with which it discusses all aspects of sexuality and physicality. The challenge it faces, however, is to mark itself out as "queer" not only in terms of what it represents but also stylistically. This opening set piece gives a taste of how Hollinghurst sets about this. The language is at once realistic, describing an actual experience in immediate, sensually attentive prose, and carries a more symbolic, encrypted freight of meaning. In Hollinghurst's case, oblique, allusive, punning, or "deflected" ways of signifying are not required to point mutely to a meaning that cannot be expressed literally. However, this palimpsestic novel deploys the force of citation and covert reference both in an homage to those writers whose "queerness" could not find explicit expression and to convey to the reader a historical and a literary past that presses on the present even when it is not consciously recognized by the novel's characters.

Will's own name is a richly resonant example of this process. In literary-historical terms, William Beckford, author of the orientalist Gothic novel *Vathek* (originally published in French in 1782) is invoked. Beckford's story in fact resembles Charles's more than Will's. Like Charles, Beckford was ostracized for his sexuality, living abroad for some years before returning to England to eccentric isolation with a servant. Will Beckwith's own sexual freedom is thus placed in ironic counterpoint to the more censored pleasures of his namesake. In addition we might note that both "will" and "beck" are phallic puns (the latter from the colloquial French word *bec*) while simultaneously connoting imperious willfulness, having others at one's beck and call. In a similar vein, the name of Will's heterosexual brother-in-law Gavin conceals a near-anagram of the female genitals.

It would be neither practical nor particularly productive, however, to expound all the book's puns, allusions, and references. The invocations of Pope, Yeats, Forster, T. E. Lawrence, Wilde, Genet, Gide, Waugh, and so on have a variety of functions. Often they provide local significances and ironies as when, for example, we learn that Maurice from the Corinthian, who shares his name with Forster's only overtly gay hero, is straight. Many of the names recall a history of state repression and stigmatization of homosexuality. For example, one of Nantwich's Oxford contemporaries, mentioned frequently in the diaries, is Sandy Labouchère, a name that ironically (since Sandy is openly gay) invokes that of Henry Labouchere, the author of the "gross indecency" clause in the British 1885 Criminal Law Amendment Act, the so-called "blackmailer's charter" that made homosexual sex illegal even in private. Similarly ironic and allusive is the name of the hotel in which Phil works, the Queensberry, recalling as it does Sir John Sholto Douglas, Marquis of Queensberry, the man who was responsible for the conviction of Oscar Wilde.

Specific ironies aside, the allusions create for the book its own literary milieu, constructing the tradition in which it is to be read. The book's treatment of Ronald Firbank is exemplary in this respect. Hollinghurst accords to Will's friend James Brooke his own passion for Firbank (along, interestingly, with his vegetarianism, in what is perhaps a covert act of identification). This enables us to see Will becoming persuaded, through his friend's encouragement, of Firbank's literary genius; indeed of Hollinghurst's belief that Firbank is the greatest neglected literary modernist. Firbank becomes the literary patron saint of Hollinghurst's first novel. Firbank's novel *The Flower beneath the Foot* (1923) takes on a symbolic significance. The pristine first edition of the book that Nantwich gives to Will is crushed beneath the skinhead's boot just as Will is. The "flower beneath the foot" represents both a general idea of youth and beauty and more specifically and proleptically the homosexual lifestyle that is soon to disappear. At the book's close the odious Ronald Staines (whose name perhaps suggests a debasement of the Firbankian ideal) uncovers some film footage of an elderly Firbank, walking in his famously distinctive jerky manner along the street. Encapsulated here is a tribute to the queeny past and to a literary forebear as well as another depiction, like a memento mori, of imminent death. In all respects it seems a fitting image for the final pages of *The Swimming Pool Library*. Hollinghurst's first novel is both a lover's book and a book-lover's book, and this final summoning of the ghost of Firbank, while invoking a certain romantic pathos in its homage to the queer literary past, also serves boldly to assert Hollinghurst's own claims to literary importance and place in the canon.

The literary echoes in *The Swimming Pool Library* last right to the end. Will's closing sentence, "And going into the showers I saw a suntanned lad in pale blue trunks that I rather liked the look of" (p. 288), gently recalls the famous ending of Gide's *Les faux-monnayeurs* (*The counterfeiters*, 1926), which concludes with the narrator, Edouard, who has spent the novel cultivating the friendship of young Olivier, saying nonchalantly, "I should like to know Caloub." William Beckwith is beckoned onward, blithely disregarding the lessons of the literary and historical past even while his actions echo it.

THE FOLDING STAR

The allusive ending of *The Swimming Pool Library* also points toward the future and Hollinghurst's second novel, *The Folding Star* (1994). The narrator of *The Folding Star* happens to be called Edward, thus sharing a name with the main protagonist of Gide's novel. Edouard in *Les faux-monnayeurs* is a writer obsessed with the seventeen-year-old Olivier. Edward in *The Folding Star* is a writer (of sorts) who is teaching seventeen-year-old Luc and is similarly obsessed by him. This intertexual link is in keeping with the ghostly spirit of *The Folding Star*, which unobtrusively summons a variety of literary and historical figures into its pages and quietly invites

its reader to discover hidden connections, rather like the cloze tests Edward sets his pupils.

Obsession is the dominant mode of *The Folding Star*. If a relatively free and easy desire was both the subject and motive force of *The Swimming Pool Library*, Hollinghurst's second novel is concerned with darker and more fetishistic feelings and with death, disappearance, and mourning. Even its moments of happiness are slightly unbalanced—the words "hilarious" and "hilarity" occur at least eight times. The narrator, Edward Manners, is thirty-three years old and, as he describes himself in a moment of self-disgust, a "pudging bespectacled school teacher" (p. 16). He has come to the unnamed Belgian town in which the story is set and which is presided over by the patron saints of its churches, St. Ernest and St. Narcissus, to teach two boys, the beautiful Luc Altidore and the sickly Marcel Echevin. The novel follows the progress of the infatuation. Like Will Beckwith, Edward Manners has other relationships—with the French-Algerian Cherif and the Flemish Matt—but in his case these are peripheral distractions. The main burden of his thoughts and of his narrative is Luc, whose surname, Altidore, which Manners guilelessly likens to "the name of a knight-errant out of *The Faerie Queene*" (p. 16), is an anagram of "idolator." Manners is a Luc-idolator, and we follow his obsession as it proceeds from moony romanticism through voyeurism and seedy fetishism to melancholy despair. The consummation of the obsession, when it comes, is climactic in all senses: "I had a high starlit sense of it as the best moment of my life," says Edward (p. 337). The almost shocking intensity of this fulfillment after dry months of longing soon gives way, however, to loss. Luc vanishes, and the last image we see of him is among "the named photos of the disappeared" (p. 422). Only belatedly, after he has vanished, do we learn that he too has idolized where he was not adored. The object of his passion is his friend Patrick Dhondt, whose very surname suggests a repressive refusal of all advances: "Don't." In a final shock to our distraught narrator, Edward discovers that his lover Matt has also slept with Luc: a callous act of betrayal.

ALAN HOLLINGHURST

Two other stories of idolatry, thwarted love, and betrayal intertwine with Edward's. The first of these turns, as in *The Swimming Pool Library*, on a shocking revelation from the past. Edward learns that his older friend and employer Paul Echevin has a dark secret. Echevin, whose surname, meaning "alderman," connotes his respectability, is the curator of the Edgaard Orst museum and knew Orst as a child. Echevin confesses to Edward that during the occupation he betrayed the elderly artist, whom he was supposed to be looking after, to his lover, a member of the occupying forces. It is through Echevin's story that a third narrative reveals itself: the biography of the painter himself. Like Manners's own life, this is a tale of obsession. Orst was in love with a woman named Jane Byron, with whom he had an affair before she disappeared, presumed drowned while out swimming. Obsessively, he continued to paint her for decades, her figure haunting all his canvases, until he saw her "reincarnation" in the person of the similarly red-haired prostitute Marthe.

The novel's use of literary allusion—even more pronounced here than in *The Swimming Pool Library*—continues the theme of obsession but also renders it more than simply thematic. On the one hand, the story echoes other accounts of erotic fixation and fascination. On the other hand, Edward Manners's own propensity to quote and allude forms part of his obsessive character. Indeed, this is not only a novel about obsession but an obsessed novel, possessed by the ghosts it summons, unable to leave them alone. In addition to Gide, the two most obvious thematic sources for *The Folding Star* are Thomas Mann's novella *Death in Venice* and Vladimir Nabokov's *Lolita*. Mann's account of an elderly writer suddenly besotted with a golden youth, Tadzio, is alluded to in the very opening paragraph of *The Folding Star*. Manners says of a man seen waiting for a tram, "I decided to follow him," in a phrase that echoes Gustav von Aschenbach's final resolve in Mann's novel: "as so often, he set out to follow him." Manners's first chase fizzles out, but it prefigures the later pursuit of Luc. The relationships to Nabokov are in a sense more intimate. As Hollinghurst said in an interview

with Philip Gambone in *Something Inside: Conversations with Gay Fiction Writers,* the *Folding Star* parallels Lolita "in a sort of gender-flipped way" (p. 232). It is more than just the content of Nabokov's novel that is mimicked, however, but also its verbal texture. In its wordplay, punning, sly anagrams and palindromes, clues, and even red herrings, there is homage to Humbert Humbert's famous testimony of his erotic obsession with the twelve-year-old Dolores Hayes. In his most Nabokovian moment, Manners meditates on the name Luc "being a backward offering of cul, Luc's cul a dream palindrome—the two round cheeks of it and the lick of the s between: I was nonsensing and spoonerising it in my mouth all day long" (p. 178). Words substitute for bodies here; Edward's prose enacts a textual eroticism.

While some of the literary ironies of the book are Hollinghurst's rather than Manners's (the latter's lover Cherif, for example, is named for the hero of Firbank's novel *Santal,* a fact never remarked), Hollinghurst fends off potential criticisms of the book's literariness by making Manners a pedant whose life is books. "I'm a bit of a quoter myself," he says truly (p. 132). This is not simply an authorial convenience, however. A predilection for quotation is shown to belong to the same psychological makeup that can fetishize Luc's undergarments or spy on him voyeuristically as he sunbathes. In all these, a part of something, an appurtenance, a textual fragment, a telescopically framed image, has to stand in for the real thing in its entirety.

This is not to say that *The Folding Star* presents Edward as uniquely pathological. In some ways, in fact, the novel suggests that anyone with feeling is necessarily a fetishist. Thus Cherif, whose adoration for Edward matches Edward's for Luc, is glimpsed in a changing room poring lovingly over and sniffing a letter that his now distinctly cool lover sent him in the early days of their relationship. On the other hand, Edward's other lover, the duplicitous and unfeeling Matt, who is a "fetish merchant" selling schoolboys' underwear to desperate clients, seems himself to idolize no one, and he is presented as inhumanly callous as a consequence.

One of the things that makes such ostensible "perversions" seem natural and indeed almost universal is the way that obsession is linked to mourning. Manners eventually loses Luc, but he mourns others in the novel too, notably his "dear dead father" (p. 81) and his friend Dawn, who (in a cruel irony, since he is dying from AIDS) is killed in a car crash. But what the book shows in an unsettling way is how little there is to choose between cherishing the memory of the dead and doting on the image of the living. Thus when Manners first hears the story of Orst's posthumous devotions to Jane Byron, he imagines consecrating his life to the image of Luc in the same way, before realizing that he has "killed him off already, perhaps too high a price" to pay (p. 68). Obsession seems to kill the object it seeks to cherish. Invoked here is the terrible Romantic paradox, dwelled upon in poems such as Keats' "Ode on a Grecian Urn," that art is deathly even as it preserves the image of life. Death and duplication are repeatedly linked in *The Folding Star*. The photograph Edward has of Luc at the start of the novel, and with whose image he is in love before he even meets the real Luc, is no different from the photograph of him at the end of the novel that advertises his disappearance and speaks of his possible death. Recorded voices sound ghostly even while their speakers are alive: Edward remembers the uncanny frisson of listening to radio interviews given by his musician father, and having "the feeling that his voice was being brought to us from the beyond" (p. 198). Indeed, inasmuch as art is shown in this novel to be a part of life in a way that makes it difficult to separate one from the other, so death too becomes hard to separate from life.

In another scene that links the duplication of a person to mortality, Edward, during his last meeting with the terminally ill Dawn, recalls meeting his friend's gaze in the mirror and thinking "he is looking at his death" (p. 206). This is just one of many mirror scenes in this uncannily glittering novel. The mirror always reflects back the possibility of one's own death in that it shows an image, and an image is what can outlast life. But mirrors do other things too. The triptych Echevin is busy assembling consists of a left-hand panel of "Jane" whose face is only glimpsed in a mirror, a central panel of a city, and, on the right, a picture of the sea. When challenged by Paul to interpret the painting, Edward flounders. "'There's a sort of movement outwards,' I hazarded. 'From the interior, to the city, to the open sea. It's like a kind of ... spiritual journey?'" (p. 282). Paul is unimpressed, replying "I'm not sure that's quite how it works," and it is only when, looking at the painting again and meeting in the painted mirror "the halting gaze of chrysanthemum eyes" (p. 311) that Edward recognizes that the image is not of Jane but of her prostitute double, Marthe. The idea of a "spiritual journey" is debunked here. The painting does not show a progression but only an obsessive repetition. Jane, who was drowned, is reflected back in the mirror as her successor and surrogate, Marthe. Critics who wish to view *The Folding Star* as a bildungsroman, in which the narrator Edward journeys from his childhood haunts in Rough Common to greater spiritual enlightenment through his experiences abroad, would do well to take heed here. The spiritual journey provides neither progress nor insight, and mirrors distort rather than providing knowledge.

If mirrors do not provide illumination, however, they are often useful for the purposes of espionage. As in Charlotte Brontë's *Villette*, surveillance is everywhere. Houses are equipped with spy mirrors, hotels with two-way mirrors, and changing rooms with closed-circuit television. One begins to wonder who is watching whom. Edward loiters adoringly outside Luc's house, unaware that his pupil can see him in the spy mirror without appearing at the window. In an inversion of this power relationship, Edward recalls in one of his many flashbacks to childhood, camping on the common and watching a man observing him. What fascinated the young Edward, we learn, was the man's "thinking himself the observer" (p. 248). There is a temporal mirroring in this episode, too—the man tells the seventeen-year-old Edward that he is thirty-three. We have earlier seen the thirty-three-year-old Edward spying on the seventeen-year-old Luc, who is holidaying with friends by the seaside. "Oh, they were only kids, they were only camping out" (p. 112), exclaims the mature Edward, in a comment that could also apply to his own younger self.

The closing note of the encounter on the common adds a new dimension to the idea of watching someone. Edward speaks with the man who's been spying on him, and tells him of his father's death. Dawn, suspicious of the attention being paid to his friend by an apparently predatory older male warns the man off fiercely. But he responds by claiming that his concern is pastoral rather than sexual: "He just wants looking after," he says defensively of Edward. Looking at someone shades into looking after them here. It becomes hard to tell the difference between voyeurism and sympathetic concern. *The Folding Star* is interested in the relationship between the two things—between watching out for someone (as Edward's female friend Edie and Edward's mother do for him) and watching them: between the pastoral and the pornographic. It is this "pastoral" theme that explains the book's title. The "folding star" names the evening star: "the star that bids the shepherd's fold," as Milton's Comus calls it, or the "folding star" as it is named in William Collins's "Ode to Evening." Collins's epithet is pithier, but the Milton reference is perhaps more apt. Comus presides over similar unchaste festivals of misrule to those enjoyed by Manners on twilight commons and in hermitage gardens. As a tutor, Edward ought perhaps to be caring for his wards in a strictly nonerotic way. Questions of responsibility arise. Hollinghurst does not present us with a tract on pedophilia—the age of consent for both sexes in Belgium is sixteen, so the reader is not distracted by issues of legality, and there is none of the moral queasiness that attaches to Nabokov's Humbert Humbert. But we are invited to ask what it means "to care for someone." It is these issues that Paul's revelations focus for us. Edward points out to him, consolingly, that he does not know that he was responsible for Orst's death—that the house was already being watched, that he doesn't know how Orst died. Paul replies, "But how does

one know what one is responsible for?" (p. 414). Retrospectively here, we have the reason why Paul keeps the Orst museum. It is a way, again, of memorializing someone, keeping them alive through their belongings and artifacts. For Paul, though, this posthumous fidelity is undertaken more out of duty and conscience than passion or obsession.

Paul's confession goes further, from a confidence to an avowal. He tells Edward that he has often thought of prolonging the work on the Orst catalog, on which they are both engaged, "just to keep you busy and looking after me, to keep us looking after each other" (p. 415). This idea of a mutually caring, pastoral relationship seems not to be shared by Edward. Hugged clumsily by Paul, he looks at himself in the mirror over his shoulder. Whether this glance signifies complacent self-love, troubled distraction, or simply the fact that any image of coupledom in the novel, whether amicable or erotic, is far from serene, it is hard to say.

Whatever the reason, it is clear that, as Luc queerly misquotes, "the course of true love never did run straight" (p. 322). Lovers in this novel are more star-crossed than starlit. The relationships among Luc's trio of friends are particularly complex. Patrick and Sibylle, it transpires, have been lovers, although Sibylle is now smitten with Luc, who in turn loves Patrick in as hopeless, obsessive, and romantic a way as Edward loves *him*. Similarly Cherif loves Edward, who loves Luc.

As if to mock the possibilities of coupledom, three is this novel's dominant number. Structurally it is divided into three sections, the first and third in present-day Belgium, the middle one in England and returning in memory often to the past. Paul's quest throughout the novel is to reunite a triptych. Edward aims, conversely, to break into a threesome—Luc's liaison with Sibylle and Patrick. Luc, so bizarre family mythology has it, is related to the Holy Trinity. Paul too is part of a threesome, with Maurice and Lilli. The town has three towers. There are three "Eds" in the novel—Edgaard, Edward (who is thus Edward the second, as it were) and Edie, Edward's female friend. "Edward Manners" was also, we might note, the name of a sixteenth-century British aristocrat, the *third* Duke of Rutland, an amusing alias for our narrator.

It is perhaps no wonder that Edward suffers from vertigo—literally, when he climbs the bell-tower, and metaphorically twice: first when he confronts via the Jane Byron story the "vertigo" of the idea of a total disappearance—a phrase that is proleptically ironic—and second, looking at himself in the mirror just before he seduces Luc, experiencing "a vertigo of detachment." Hitchcock's film *Vertigo* (1958), with its themes of obsession and pursuit, as well as the giddying way in which people substitute for other people and can be remade in their image, is a resonant allusion here. Vertiginous remaking and doubling clearly happens in the case of Orst, who seeks to paint his prostitute-lover Marthe in the image of the dead Jane, but it occurs in the present-day narrative too. "I felt I was getting the benefit of some stored-up passion intended for someone else, but brimming and spilling," Edward says of Luc (p. 335). After Luc's vicarious passion is spent, Edward falls asleep and dreams of a man he calls Luc even while he is "almost certain that wasn't his name" (pp. 339–340).

The giddying and disorienting relationships of substitution and displacement charted by Hollinghurst's second novel could imply an ultimately hopeless view of human relationships. According to this reading, we are condemned forever to repeat our early loves and obsessions, watched all the while by the ironic ghosts of the past, who mock our attempts to break free from habitual patterns of feeling and reaction. The tyranny of habit is certainly another of this book's themes. On the other hand, and given that the notion of "watching" in this book has a deeply ambivalent ethical charge, we might see the presence of ghosts and repetitions as more benign. Even as we watch over other people, so our ghosts keep watch over us. The dead are kept alive in the living. Whether Edward Manners draws either of these morals from his experiences is uncertain. The novel ends without resolution, with the stark fact of Luc's disappearance. What is clear, however, is that whereas Will Beckwith in *The Swimming Pool Library* beck-

oned blithely into the future, without much sign that he had learned from his recent history lesson, Manners will continue to be possessed by his past.

BAJAZET *AND* THE SPELL

Commenting on the bewildering permutations of Luc's friendships toward the end of *The Folding Star*, Edward says "I felt I'd have had to be Racine to keep abreast of this convulsive trio" (p. 398). In 1991 Hollinghurst had translated just such an emotionally complicated Racinian tragedy, *Bajazet*, into English. Set in a harem in Constantinople, the play shows the complicated shifts of relationship among its three main protagonists. While it is not difficult to see why Hollinghurst might have been attracted to the play's content, it is formally very different from the stylistic preoccupations he demonstrates in his first two novels. As he writes in his translator's introduction, "the static, concentrated austerity of his neo-classicism is bewilderingly alien to English taste and tradition" (p. ix). His rendition of Racine's poetry is faithful to its simplicity, its clarity, and the compact and charged structure of repetitions in the original, converting its alexandrine couplets into supple but patterned blank verse.

If neoclassical austerity is hard to find in Hollinghurst's own fiction, his third novel *The Spell* (1998) certainly marks a stylistic departure for him in its shift toward greater simplicity. Lighter, brighter, and more sparkling, it does not turn on a cataclysmic moment of revelation. Neither is it particularly allusive. And what is most immediately notable is that it has, unlike the first-person narratives of *The Swimming Pool Library* and *The Folding Star*, a third-person narrative voice. The voice is far from omniscient, however: the narrative keeps shifting from one character's perspective to another's, perpetually undermining the notion of a single, transcendent viewpoint. In some ways this seems to mimic the work of time, showing how one can always be betrayed, not (as in the earlier novels) simply by a person but by the very fact of time's passing.

"Plot" is hardly the appropriate word to describe the structuring of events in this narrative. Rather there is, as in Racine's play albeit in comic mode, a sense of the characters being choreographed, as they move back and forth between town and country, and change partners and allegiances. The central characters are Robin, Justin, Alex and Danny. All are gay, and Danny is Robin's son from an early marriage. The novel begins, in fact, with Robin learning of his imminent paternity and then leaps forward in the next section some twenty years. In the interim, Robin has left his wife and lost a lover to AIDS; he is now living in the Dorset countryside with Justin, who used to be Alex's partner. Justin, motivated by ennui and an instinct for troublemaking, invites Alex to stay for the weekend in order to display his domestic happiness. While there, Alex falls in love with Danny, and once back in London they begin a relationship. Alex cannot keep hold of twenty-year-old Danny boy for long, ending up at the book's close in a mature if slightly dull relationship with Nick, who, in Alex's own terminology, is like him a "giver" in relationships rather than a "taker." Justin, emphatically a taker, leaves Robin just as a few years previously he had left Alex. On this occasion, however, he returns. To add to the novel's sense of moonstruck and chaotic sexual partnering, Danny, Robin, and Justin all sleep with the local odd-job man Terry Blodgett.

Although permutations in relationships form the main movement of the novel, they are not necessarily where its significance resides. *The Spell* derives its meaning more from its generic affiliations than from the sequential events of its narrative. This is a comedy—both a romantic comedy in the Shakespearian sense and a more Wildean social comedy of wit and mannered repartee. The party at the novel's center happens on Midsummer's night, and as in Shakespeare's play the apparently motiveless, enchanted errancy of desire is Hollinghurst's main preoccupation and explains one of the resonances of his title. Just as in *A Midsummer Night's Dream* the enchantment is literally attributed to the potion produced from the juice of a flower, so here a kind of magic is worked through drugs. Alex

(whose name ironically means "outside the law" even though he is the most law-abiding, deskbound, and conscientious of middle-age men) is inducted into the delights of the dance-scene drug ecstasy by young Danny. One of his ecstatic revelations is that "It seemed that happening and happiness were the same" (p. 84), though the novel proves this precisely not to be the case. Changes happen in time, but ecstasy is outside of temporality.

Change is explored in two modes, in fact. On the one hand the novel looks at the circumscribed but still significant capacity of the individual to change. Alex undergoes "a general rejuvenation" and acquires a "hip new taste for life" (p. 152), stops lamenting the past, and has two lovers in the course of the novel. Robin and Justin's relationship undergoes a power shift. Danny, as he tries to break off the relationship with Alex, says in the itself time-worn language of such scenes, "I've changed, darling. People change" (p. 238). On the other hand, the inevitability of aging, change, and decay is also mourned. The Puckish Justin, for example, seems at the start of the novel to resemble Shakespeare's mischievous sprite, relishing human folly while not participating in it himself. His brief sojourn away from Robin, however, seems to precipitate a panicky crisis of confidence. The glimpse in a barroom mirror of the "alien stiffness and slackness" (p. 201) of his own face functions as a memento mori and propels him back into Robin's arms. Death haunts the novel, even if the mood is less mournful than in *The Folding Star.* Robin's earlier lover Simon has died of AIDS, Jason's father has died, and Robin's client Toby Bowerchalke dies before his "rogue Gothic" mansion can be renovated. The novel ends with Robin, Justin, Alex, and Nick looking out to sea in the autumnal early evening: "then as the sun dropped westward, the surface of the sea turned quickly grey, and they saw the curling silver roads of the current over it" (p. 257).

Death, mortality and mutability are all hinted at here, as the sun sets and the gray sea continues its incessant motion. But in the group of men facing it, and gathered in an awkward group embrace, there is also the sense of the compromised but still necessary partial triumph of human feeling and community. Love might well turn out to be time's fool, but—if only for a spell—it is also the sole magic that will arrest time, or at least (to use Robin's high-scoring Scrabble word) to "temporise" a little. *The Spell* eschews transcendentals. Frequently adjectives are qualified with "half-": Justin is "half-grieved, half-gratified" by the intensity of Alex's kiss (p. 27); Robin has a "fixated half-smile" as Alex talks to him (p. 59); Danny sees his times with Robin as "half-vacations" (p. 60); Alex finds himself "half-forgetting" that Danny is younger than he is (p. 72) and "half-expecting" to be jumped by the drug squad (p. 81); Danny gives the banker in his office an "unallowed half-smile" (p. 145); Justin thinks fondly of "half-conscious" morning bouts of sex (p. 89). These qualified expressions traverse all the narrative voices, suggesting a general quality of inadequacy or incompletion rather than the thought patterns of timorous characters. In fact the expressions are all in keeping with what is perhaps the motto of the book as a whole—the fragmented word "Sempe" printed on the piece of porcelain that Robin finds in the desert in the first chapter. As he explains much later to Lars, a guest at his party, "it's trying to say SEMPER, which is Latin for always." Lars responds, "So it's almost always" (p. 132). "Almost always" could mean "nearly all the time," but it could also mean "never quite always": something approximating, but never reaching, the absolute or the eternal. Such a flawed and compromised "forever" is the nearest we come, this novel suggests, to flouting time's ravages with our defiant human impositions.

If *The Spell* does not, then, have the historical vision of *The Swimming Pool Library* or the psychological intensity of *The Folding Star*'s obsessions, it does strike a new note in Hollinghurst's work. Ostensibly less weighty, its philosophical aspirations are at least as profound. The first two novels were careful to situate themselves in a variety of literary traditions, but this most recent work wears its learning more lightly. There is less need to hark back now to literary forebears,

for Hollinghurst has triumphantly established himself as an important literary voice in his own right.

Selected Bibliography

WORKS OF ALAN HOLLINGHURST

NOVELS AND SHORT STORIES

"A Thieving Boy." In *Firebird 2: Writing Today.* Edited by T. J. Binding. Middlesex, U.K.: Penguin, 1983. Pp. 95–109. (The volume also contains stories by Kazuo Ishiguro, Fay Weldon, and Angus Wilson.)

The Swimming Pool Library. London: Chatto & Windus, 1988; New York: Random House, 1988. (In this essay the 1989 Penguin edition is cited.)

The Folding Star. London: Chatto & Windus, 1994; New York: Pantheon, 1994. (Vintage's 1998 edition has been cited in this essay.)

The Spell. London: Chatto & Windus, 1998; New York: Viking, 1999. (Vintage's 1999 paperback edition has been cited in this essay.)

POETRY

"Over the Wall," "Nightfall," "Survey," "Christmas Day at Home," "The Drowned Field," "Alonso," "Isherwood Is at Santa Monica," "Ben Dancing at Wayland's Smithy," "Convalescence at Lower Largo," and "The Well." In *Poetry: Introduction 4.* London and Boston: Faber and Faber, 1978.

Confidential Chats with Boys. Oxford: Sycamore Press, 1982. (Printed by hand in a limited edition of 200 copies.)

"Sugar Mill." *Times Literary Supplement,* May 7–June 2, 1988, p. 579.

"Brain Garden." In *Magdalen Poets: Five Centuries of Poetry from Magdalen College.* Edited by Robert Macfarlane. Oxford: Magdalen College, 2000. (This volume also reprints sections from *Confidential Chats with Boys.*)

CRITICAL INTRODUCTIONS AND EDITIONS

Introduction to *The Early Firbank.* Edited by Steven Moore. London and New York: Quartet Books, 1991.

Introduction to *Francis Wyndham: The Collected Fiction.* London: Vintage, 1992.

Introduction to *Ronald Firbank: Three Novels.* London: Penguin, 2000.

ALAN HOLLINGHURST

Introduction to A. E. Housman, *Poems. Selected by Alan Hollinghurst.* London: Faber and Faber, 2001.

REVIEW ARTICLES

Listed below is a selection of those articles most relevant to the preoccupations of Hollinghurst's fiction.

"Keeping Up with the Past." *Times Literary Supplement,* January 6, 1984, p. 8. (Review article discussing architectural books by Cherry and Pevsner, Stephen Croad, Edward Jones, and Christopher Woodward and Hugh Casson.)

"The Dwelling Places of Obsession." *Times Literary Supplement,* April 26, 1985. (Review of Francis Wyndham's *Mrs. Henderson and Other Stories.*)

Review of J. Mordaunt Crook's *The Dilemma of Style: Architectural Ideas from the Picturesque to the Postmodern. Times Literary Supplement,* March 18–24, 1988, pp. 295–296.

Review of Bridget Cherry and Nikolas Pevsner's *London 3: North West. Times Literary Supplement,* December 13, 1991, p. 229.

OTHER WORKS

The Creative Uses of Homosexuality in the Novels of E. M. Forster, Ronald Firbank, and L. P. Hartley. M. Litt. thesis, Magdalen College, 1979. (Unpublished. A copy of the manuscript can be consulted in the Bodleian Library, Oxford.)

Jean Racine, *Bajazet.* (Translation.) London: Chatto & Windus, 1991.

New Writing 4. (Editor with A. S. Byatt.) London: Vintage, 1995.

CRITICAL AND BIOGRAPHICAL STUDIES

Alderson, David. "Desire as Nostalgia: The Novels of Alan Hollinghurst." In *Territories of Desire in Queer Culture: Refiguring Contemporary Boundaries.* Edited by David Alderson and Linda Anderson. Manchester and New York: Manchester University Press, 2000.

Annan, Gabriel. "Love's Old Sweet Song." *New York Review of Books,* November 3, 1994, p. 23. (Review of *The Folding Star.*)

Baker, Nicholson. "Lost Youth." *London Review of Books,* June 9, 1994. (This essay is also collected in Nicholson Baker, *The Size of Thoughts: Essays and Other Lumber.* London: Vintage, 1997.)

Bradley, John. "Disciples of St. Narcissus." *Oxford Quarterly* 1–2:8–24 (spring-summer 1997).

Bristow, Joseph. *Effeminate England: Homoerotic Writing after 1885.* Buckingham, U.K.: Open University Press, 1995.

Brown, James. "Race, Class, and the Homoerotics of *The Swimming Pool Library.*" In *Postcolonial and Queer Theories: Intersections and Essays.* Edited by John C. Hawley. London and Westport, Conn.: Greenwood Press, 2001.

Chambers, Ross. "Messing Around: Gayness and Literature in Alan Hollinghurst's *The Swimming Pool Library.*" In *Textuality and Sexuality: Reading Theories and Practices.* Edited by Judith Still and Michael Worton. Manchester: Manchester University Press, 1993.

Corber, R. J. "Sentimentalizing Gay History: Mark Merlis, Alan Hollinghurst, and the Cold War Persecution of Homosexuals." *Arizona Quarterly* 55:115–141 (winter 1999).

Davies, Alistair, and Alan Sinfield. *British Culture of the Postwar: An Introduction to Literature and Society, 1945–1999.* London and New York: Routledge, 2000.

Hopes, David. "Alan Hollinghurst." In *The Dictionary of Literary Biography.* Vol. 207, *British Novelists since 1960.* Third series. Edited by Merritt Moseley. Detroit: Gale Group, 1999.

Kemp, Peter. "Aesthetic Obsessions." *Times Literary Supplement,* May 27, 1994, p. 19. (Review of *The Folding Star.*)

Jensen, Hal. "Pastoral in Passing." *Times Literary Supplement,* June 26, 1998, p. 25. (Review of *The Spell.*)

Rees, David. "Beckwith, Beckford, Boy and O." In his *Words and Music.* Brighton: Millivres, 1993.

Simpson, Catherine. "Not Every Age Has Its Pleasures." *New York Times Book Review,* October 9, 1988, p. 9.

Wood, Michael. "A Bathing Beauty's Belle Èpoque." *Times Literary Supplement,* February 19–25, 1988, p. 85. (Review of *The Swimming Pool Library.*)

———. "Tight Little Island." *New York Review of Books,* June 24, 1999, pp. 56–59. (Review of *The Spell* alongside Julian Barnes's *England, England.*)

INTERVIEWS

Burton, Peter. "Alan Hollinghurst." In *Talking To . ...* Exeter, U.K.: Third House, 1991. Pp. 47–50.

Canning, Richard. "Alan Hollinghurst." In his *Conversations with Gay Novelists: Gay Fiction Speaks.* New York: Columbia University Press, 2000. Pp. 331–365.

Gambone, Philip. "Alan Hollinghurst." In his *Something Inside: Conversations with Gay Fiction Writers.* Madison: University of Wisconsin Press, 1999.

135

ROHINTON MISTRY

(1952–)

Yumna Siddiqi

OF THE GROWING cadre of Anglophone writers from India who have acquired an international reputation, Rohinton Mistry stands out for his rich and sympathetic portraits of the lives of the people of Bombay, or Mumbai as the city is now called. He tells the stories of ordinary people, sketching in fine detail the relationships among families and neighbors in the setting of an apartment block or a neighborhood. The nation-state forms the backdrop to his stories. Though the state is remote, the common man or woman, who is the focal point of Mistry's fiction, feels its pressures and violent tactics. He also deftly sketches the economic strains that middle- and working-class Indians face every day. Mistry's style has often been compared to that of the great realist writers of the nineteenth century, particularly Charles Dickens. He entirely eschews postmodern techniques and the assumptions associated with these techniques, such as the fragmentation of subjectivity and the discontinuous nature of history. Rather, Mistry advances an old-fashioned humanism, emphasizing the interconnection between characters and their similar struggles and triumphs.

Rohinton Mistry was born in Bombay, where he received his primary and secondary education, and then a degree in mathematics at St. Xavier's College of Bombay University. As he explains in an interview, the natural step for middle-class Parsis was to look for a future abroad. Mistry emigrated to Toronto in 1975, where he met and married Freny Elavia. He worked as a clerk at a bank for ten years and during this period obtained a second degree in English and philosophy at the University of Toronto. While working, he began to write. At the urging of his wife, Mistry entered a literary competition at the University of Toronto, which he won two years in a row. He has been a full-time writer ever since. While some of his stories are about the experience of immigrants in Canada, the greater part of his writing is set in India, the wellspring of his creative talent.

Mistry's fiction centers on the tiny community of Parsis who live in Bombay. As the name suggests, the Parsis originated in Persia, where the prophet Zarathustra is believed to have lived in the sixth century B.C. They were forced to flee Persia when the Persian empire fell to the Arabs in 651, and they arrived in India in the tenth century. Now nearly a third of the world's 125,000 Parsis live in Bombay, many in housing colonies set up specifically for Parsis. During the period of British rule in India, the Parsis were a colonial elite. They had a privileged status in Anglo-Indian society because they spoke English, were able traders, and had a global outlook. They were an especially Westernized group within India, emulating the tastes of the British in literature, dress, music, and food. One can see the marks of such anglicization in the milieu of which Mistry writes. One might argue that the Parsis to a great extent fulfilled the British will to, as Thomas Babington Macaulay put it in 1835, "form a class who may be interpreters between us and the millions whom we govern; a class of persons, Indian in blood and colour, but English in taste, in opinions, in morals, and in intellect." At the same time, one finds in Mistry's novels many references to Parsi religious rituals and other cultural practices. For example, Mistry refers to the *kusti,* a muslin shirt with a sacred cord tied around the waist, worn by all Parsis; to the death rituals and the *dokhma,* or tower of silence, where the dead are left for vultures or other birds of prey; and to the ceremonies in the fire temple where the *afarghan,* or holy fire, is kept burning. In making reference to these and other Parsi customs, Mistry alerts us to the continued existence of a specifically Parsi way of

ROHINTON MISTRY

life alongside the adoption of European habits. Today, while the Parsis continue to be relatively well-off, their numbers have dwindled sharply because of intermarriage and emigration. Mistry's fiction commemorates the life of the Parsi community in Bombay in the face of its possible extinction.

SWIMMING LESSONS

In 1987 Mistry published a collection entitled *Swimming Lessons and Other Stories from Ferozsha Baag.* Each of the stories is about a different set of residents of a Parsi housing estate (apartment block) in Bombay. The stories are loosely linked by the associations between the different families and with the people who live in the vicinity of the estate. The similarity of each story's milieu contrasts with the variety of the characters and indeed of the narrative voices, which include those of a servant, children and teenagers, and the middle-class men and women who live in Ferozsha Baag. Mistry renders with artistry and sympathy the lives of the inhabitants, giving equal attention to mundane and momentous events. In the first story, "Auspicious Occasion," Mistry takes us into the apartment of Rustomji and his wife Mehroo on Behram Roje, a holy day of the Parsi calendar. He deftly contrasts the characters of husband and wife. Mehroo, a devout Parsi, prepares to leave for the fire temple, looking forward with pleasure to the coming ceremonies. Her husband is in a foul temper, having been soiled by a leaking water closet. He sits drinking his tea and reading the newspaper, grumbling and secretly ogling the maid. By the end of the day when the couple meets again for tea at home, Mehroo has been shaken by the murder of the elderly priest at the temple, while Rustomji has had a close escape from an irate and xenophobic crowd. Yet it is not these dramatic events that make up the story but the quotidian affairs of this middle-age Parsi couple, which Mistry sketches with affectionate detail— their struggle to pay the bills and to stem the decay of their apartment.

In "One Sunday," Mistry takes us out of the home of a solitary family to the larger world of the neighborhood and the people who work for the middle-class inhabitants of Ferozsha Baag. Francis, one such young man, who sleeps under the awning of the furniture store across the road where he used to work, is asked by Najamai, proud owner of a refrigerator that the neighbors use, to help with a chore. When she accuses Francis of stealing some money from her home, the neighbors join in to chase him down, and Francis is eventually hauled away by the police. The story shows the vulnerability of a character like Francis and his dependence upon his more prosperous neighbors for his livelihood and indeed his freedom. It also underscores the paranoia with which the middle classes maintain a grip on their possessions and their status. Francis is one of many indigent and marginal characters who populate Mistry's fiction.

Another such character is Jaakaylee, an ayah—a combination child-minder and maid— who works for yet another family in Ferozsha Baag. In "The Ghost of Ferozsha Baag," Jaaykalee tells the story of how she was first visited by a ghost and was then herself mistaken for a ghost. She begins her first-person narrative with her early experience of ghosts. In three sentences, Mistry sets the scene for the most poignant story in the collection. We learn that Jaqueline (for that is her name, only no one can be bothered to pronounce it correctly) is a domestic worker who migrated from Goa at the age of fourteen and has worked for the same family in Ferozsha Baag for the forty-nine years since. She speaks English, a mark of middle-class status, but her family lost its toehold in the middle class, and she was forced to seek a job in the city. In this her situation is like that of the thousands who come to Bombay every day—only she has the minimal comfort and security of a lifelong job. Jaakaylee describes how she encountered a ghost one night on the landing in front of the flat in which she works and lives. When she tells her employers of this encounter, they ridicule her, and she becomes the laughingstock of the colony. A few months later, the ghost begins to pay her nightly visits, lying with her in her bed, only she tells no one about this. Then one day, when she is standing out on the balcony with a white sheet wrapped

ROHINTON MISTRY

around her for warmth, her mistress sees what she believes is a ghost as she enters the compound in her car. At this point, instead of acknowledging her presence on the balcony, Jaakaylee remains quiet. She is enthusiastically taken into the confidence of her mistress, who now believes her maid's account of the earlier ghost.

The story explores the experience of what one might call the subaltern, following the work of Indian subaltern studies and the cultural critic Gayatri Spivak. By "subaltern," postcolonial scholars mean the hyper-exploited, often Third World subjects who are so marginalized from social and economic power that they have no voice in public discourse. Jaakaylee is not necessarily a subaltern by Spivak's reckoning: as an ayah in a middle-class household, she is relatively comfortable and secure, and Mistry, in making her the narrator, gives her voice and agency in the story. However, her circumstances make her largely invisible to the other residents of Ferozsha Baag. The story underscores this subaltern status by framing her as the "ghost" of the community. At the same time, Mistry elevates her shadowy status such that by the end of the story, everyone believes in the existence of the ghost of Ferozsha Baag. Her marginal status is articulated specifically in relation to her repressed sexuality, the necessary condition of being a female live-in domestic worker. Jaakaylee recounts her teenage escapades in Goa with Cajetan, a neighbor, who, she states, "made all funny eyes at me, like Hindi film hero, and put his hand on my thigh." He refuses to stop, though she tells him to and threatens to tell her father. Years later, when the ghost begins to visit Jaakaylee, it reminds her of Cajetan and his illicit touch. The "ghost" that visits her nightly is a phantasmic projection of the sexual desire she has had to excise from her life.

Several of Mistry's stories center on the children of Ferozsha Baag and their relationships with friends and neighbors. These children are beguilingly precocious yet innocent, conveying the flavor of adolescence in the large, colorful, and often harsh city that is Bombay. In "The Collectors," Jehangir, an introvert and reader who avoids the games of his rowdy fellows, is befriended by Dr. Mody, disappointed father of the leader of the rowdies. To make up for his son's bullying, Dr. Mody shows Jehangir his stamp collection. Dr. Mody and Jehangir soon become fast friends and meet every Sunday morning to swap philatelic notes. Jehangir goes so far as to enter into an exchange of stamps for sexual fondles with one of his classmates in order to augment his collection. Then one day Dr. Modi discovers that his precious Spanish dancing lady stamp is missing. He believes that Jehangir has stolen his prized stamp, and their friendship cools. Two years later Dr. Mody dies suddenly. His wife, who has always resented her husband's interest in Jehangir rather than their own boisterous son, invites Jehangir to her house and presents him with Dr. Mody's entire collection. She explains tearfully that it was she who destroyed Dr. Mody's treasured stamp. The story ends on a bittersweet note: Dr. Mody's stamps, which Jehangir has stored under his bed, are eaten by cockroaches. The story uses symbolic objects and events to fashion the birth and death of an unlikely friendship between a man who is disappointed in his own son and a boy who has few friends.

Some of the children of Ferozsha Baag grow up in the course of the series of stories. Jehangir, the pretty young boy of "The Collectors," is, in "Exercisers," a nineteen-year-old who is caught between his desire for his girlfriend and his mother's disapproval. The family consults a holy man about the young man's future. Mistry deftly renders the guru's pronouncement as the obliquely reported comment that "all life is a trap, full of webs." These words perfectly capture the substance of Jehangir's world: his struggle with family expectations, the pull of his girlfriend, the physical constraints of space in Bombay, and his own wish to be independent. He finally gets to spend an amorous evening with his girlfriend, but he cannot rebel entirely and goes home abruptly, afraid of being locked out of his home. As he explains bitterly to his incredulous girlfriend, he cannot bear to make his mother more unhappy than she already is. Mistry captures perfectly the denials and compromises that people are forced to make when they live in tight-knit families and in close quarters. In the final scene we leave Jehangir waiting on the floor outside the flat, dozing until the unlatching of the lock wakes him.

"Of White Hairs and Cricket" also takes us into the world of a young boy and his family in Ferozsha Baag. Kersi, whom we have met before in "One Sunday," shares with us in his own voice his thoughts about his middle-age father, whose white hairs Kersi plucks in anticipation of a job interview that never arrives. Kersi performs his task with a mixture of resentment and love. He recalls the games of cricket chaperoned by his father at a nearby field adjoining the sea and notes sadly that his father no longer organizes these communal matches. Kersi's thoughts turn to his grandmother Mamaji, who sneaks him spicy snacks that wreak havoc with his bowels. She sits spinning thread for the sacred *kustis,* of which the family has a plentiful supply. His mother, meanwhile, makes toast on an old Primus that imparts the smell of kerosene to her creations. He encounters his friend Viraf, whose own father is very ill, but rather than consoling him Kersi runs away. The story, entirely a fabric of mood and setting rather than of events, builds to a melancholy crescendo, in which he expresses grief for the sadness of the lives of those he has known, as well as his own. Kersi's lament bespeaks a young adult's awareness of the pathos of the everyday, a gloomy knowledge of the constraints on experience and on expression that any adult will remember as "the blues." Mistry gives these adolescent "blues" the shades and textures of middle-class life in Bombay.

Mistry portrays the hardships of life in Ferozsha Baag from the perspective of adults as well. In "Condolence Visit," a grieving widow, Daulat, must contend with the prospect of unwelcome calls by her family and neighbors: "They would come to offer their condolence, share her grief, poke and pry into her life and Minocher's with a thousand questions. And to gratify them with answers she would have to relive the anguish of the most trying days of her life" (p. 59). Mistry makes us aware of the intrusiveness of the neighbors and, by implication, our own role as readers who are secret shar-

ers in the widow's pain. At the same time, we honour Daulat's strength and dignity when she gives her dead husband's pugree (turban) to a young man who is soon to be married, despite the aghast interjections of her neighbors, and keeps her husband's sacral lamp burning beyond the religiously prescribed period because it gives her comfort. In "The Paying Guests," what starts out as a mutually satisfactory arrangement between two couples deteriorates into a vicious battle waged with ordure. Mistry conveys with sympathy and an appreciation for the absurd the efforts of Boman and Kashmira to evict their tenants, elderly Khorshedbai and her meek husband, Ardesar. Khorshedbai empties out the foulest rubbish she can find on her landlords' veranda; she does this with impunity until she teeters over the edge of sanity and puts the couple's newborn in the cage of her no-longer-living-but-still beloved parrot. Mistry succeeds in making us feel for both couples, one tormented by their elderly "paying guests," the other pitiable in their old age and near-destitution.

In three of the stories, Mistry takes us beyond the world of Ferozsha Baag to the realm of immigrants to North America. The postcolonial critic Homi Bhabha, in his essay "The Commitment to Theory," privileges the interstitial realm of diasporic and migrant life as a "Third Space" of cultural hybridity that is new, "neither the one nor the other" (*The Location of Culture,* p. 36). While Bhabha by and large celebrates the destabilizing dynamics of this "Third Space" of hybridity, Rohinton Mistry's stories suggest that this space can also be problematically unsettling and ridden with pitfalls.

"Squatter," the most complex and memorable story in the collection, is about a young man, Sarosh, who travels to Canada. The title "squatter" refers to the man's need to squat in order to relieve his bowels. Driven to distraction, Sarosh finally seeks advice from the Immigrant Aid Society, which sends him to a doctor, but he is loath to take the drastic measure of having a device—a CNI, or Crappus Non Interruptus—implanted in his bowels. His inability to use a Western-style toilet signifies his failure to assimilate to his new surroundings. The title is at the same time a tongue-in-cheek reference to the unwanted presence of immigrants in the West. The story is a cautionary tale: the young man eventually returns to India, where he exists in a sort of hapless limbo. Sarosh's words of advice to those who might want to travel abroad are that "the world can be a bewildering place, and dreams and ambitions are often paths to the most pernicious of traps." In "Squatter," this space proves to be treacherous, not offering the migrant a foothold, a place to "squat."

In a second story about migrant experience, "Lend Me Your Light," Mistry explores another pitfall of migration from India to North America: an alienation from and extreme denigration of India and an excessive valorization of the West. The first-person narrator, Kersi, of the earlier story "Of White Hairs and Cricket," travels to Toronto at about the same time that his brother's friend Jamshed moves to New York. When Jamshed returns to Bombay for a visit, he disparages every aspect of life there—from the presence of street vendors to "the dust and heat and crowds" (p. 191). Jamshed's attitude has antecedents in his childhood snobbery toward "ghatis" (which literally means hill folk), who are supposedly flooding the schools of Bombay and lowering their caliber. This snobbery, a hangover of colonial rule and a common attitude of the Westernized elite of Bombay, is rendered by Mistry with unerring skill. It is exaggerated in the person of the NRI, or nonresident Indian, exemplified by Jamshed, who perceives only the worst of India. With his characteristic humanity, Mistry explains this attitude as a defensive reaction:

> I thought of Jamshed and his adamant refusal to enjoy his trips to India.... Perhaps the contempt and disdain which he shed was only his way of lightening his load.
>
> (p. 192)

While Kersi acknowledges that cultural strains have exacerbated Jamshed's disdain for his native country, he unequivocally rejects this attitude and literally tosses Jamshed's next letter unread into an incinerator.

If the Scylla that threatens the migrant's integrity in the course of a passage to the West is a defensive disdain for and rejection of his or her "home," and the Charybdis that menaces from the other side is an inability to adjust to and embrace the new, then the third story about migration, "Swimming Lessons," envisions the possibility of a successful passage—successful in the sense that the protagonist maintains his appreciation of and attachment to his home in Bombay and at the same time learns to "swim" in North America. The narrative of "Swimming Lessons" moves back and forth between Mother and Father, at home in Bombay, and their son, who has emigrated to Toronto. The parents are perplexed and frustrated by the fact that the narrator tells them little of his new life in his prosaic letters. The narrator, in the meantime, tells us about his aborted attempt to learn how to swim, as well as his fleeting acquaintance with an aging neighbor who often sits in his wheelchair in the lobby of their apartment block. Then Mother and Father receive a gift: a collection of stories that the narrator has written unbeknownst to them, the very collection that we have just read. Not only has the narrator negotiated the passage to the West with integrity, humor, and a continued attachment to his "home"; he has made his passage the subject of a story. Indeed, one might argue that he has been able to bridge the cultural distance between his old and new home precisely because he takes his inspiration for his writing from his life in Bombay and makes a gift of his labor to his parents. "Swimming Lessons" is clearly a reflection on Mistry's own migration to Toronto, his foray into unknown territory, his relationships with his neighbors—and his efforts to please his readers.

Indeed, two of the stories about migration are also about storytelling. Mistry frames "Squatter" as a tale told by one of the residents, Nariman Hansotia, to a group of boys in the compound. Nariman first tells another story, about a young sportsman's prowess at cricket at the Marlybone Cricket Club, to whet his audience's palates. In Nariman's fashioning of his story, in his masterful manipulation of his listeners' curiosity, we can see Mistry reflect on his own art as a storyteller.

Mistry's tales from Ferozsha Baag are not without their share of pain and hardship, and yet there is a quality of innocence in them. Though the lives of the residents of the Baag may be troubled, they are protected and secure. This is not to say that the stories idealize middle-class life in Bombay. On the contrary, the power of Mistry's fiction lies in his ability to convey both the petty struggles and larger travails of the middle classes and also to animate the small people of his world: the pavement dwellers, the servants, the children, the elderly. Yet the stories have a buoyant quality that derives perhaps from Mistry's tone, from the brevity of the tales, or from a relative absence of the oppressive political forces that are much more clearly delineated in his novels. *Such a Long Journey, A Fine Balance,* and *Family Matters* take us away from the coziness of Ferozsha Baag to a more politically unstable, precarious, and even violent milieu.

SUCH A LONG JOURNEY

Mistry established his reputation as one of the foremost Indian novelists writing in English with *Such a Long Journey* (1991), for which he won a Books in Canada First Novel Award, a Governor-General's Prize, and a Commonwealth Writers Prize; the novel was also was short-listed for the Booker Prize. Like *Tales from Ferozsha Baag, Such a Long Journey* is set in an apartment block, but it focuses more fully on the life of a single character and his family, and the presence of the outside world is felt much more strongly than in *Tales.* The novel's protagonist, Gustad Noble, a middle-age Parsi, lives with his wife and three children in Khodadad building in Bombay. As in *Tales,* Mistry writes in a realist vein, but the more extended and rounded novel form gives Mistry the chance to convey a complex and dynamic social totality. The various dimensions of this social totality include the texture of Parsi life, the struggles of a middle-class family, the urban landscape and the nature of urban pressures, the tensions of a multireligious society, the circum-

stances of the poor of Bombay, and the activities of a corrupt and coercive state.

We are introduced to Gustad as he says his morning *kusti* prayers. Khodadad Building, like Ferozsha Baag, is a middle-class community of Parsis, and we are given a sense of its close, intimate nature. Parsi ritual and faith are part of the fabric of Gustad's everyday life. At the end of the novel, at the funeral rites for Gustad's friend Dinshawji, Gustad expresses a deep connection with the religion that he has for the most part practiced in a rather automatic fashion. Running through the novel is a sense of the cultural and spiritual elements of Parsi life, a religion that is shown to be in decline yet is rich with significance.

At the heart of the novel, however, are Gustad Noble's relationships with his family and neighbors. His son Sohrab has just been admitted to the prestigious and exclusive Indian Institute of Technology, and Gustad is keen to celebrate. However, Sohrab insists that he will remain at the local college, much to his father's chagrin. Gustad's anxiety for his son's future is expressed as anger, and the ensuing quarrel between father and son results in Sohrab's departure from his home. Mistry brilliantly conveys the worries and ambitions of a lower-middle-class father who has seen his own father experience economic bankruptcy and social decline and wants his son to have a better life. These hopes are offset against a gifted young man's desire to fashion his own life and to study the humanities rather than a scientific or technical field that is likely to assure a prosperous future. Gustad's second son, Darius, and his daughter, Roshan, are younger and do not oppose their father's will, but Darius' flirtation with a neighbor's daughter and Roshan's illness are a cause of further irritation and anxiety. We see the misguided attempts of Dilnavaz, Gustad's wife, to restore harmony to her family and health to her daughter in the face of forces that seem mysterious and insurmountable. Discouraged by the travails of her family, she turns to an elderly neighbor, Mrs. Kutpitia, who promises to rid the Nobles of bad luck using sorcery. Dilnavaz anxiously awaits the results as Mrs. Kutpitia hatches her spells with lemons and lizards' tails and attempts to transfer the Nobles' bad luck to a hapless neighbor, Tehmul.

Tehmul, a young man who is crippled and mentally impaired because of a childhood fall from a tree, is the most striking character in the novel. By and large Tehmul hangs around with the children of the compound, though he is exceedingly fond of Gustad. Tehmul's singular way of running his words together—"ListeninglisteningGustadlisteningveryvery-verycarefull"(p. 90)—makes him incomprehensible to most of the residents of the building, but Gustad, through long practice, has learned to make sense of the man-boy's speech. Tehmul is a misfit and an innocent in ways that are sometimes disturbing. His strangeness is manifest in his torturing and killing of rats, whose pain he seems not to recognize. It also takes the form of a sexual attachment to Roshan's gorgeous, near-life-size doll, which Tehmul steals. Yet Tehmul's guilelessness makes him one of the most sympathetic characters in the novel, and his death at the end from a blow by a flying brick is the novel's greatest moment of tragedy.

While Mistry homes in on one family in a single building, he also conveys the full variety of life in Bombay. He describes Gustad's office at a bank, with its contingent of lecherous middle-age men who lust for the smart young secretary; its regimen of lunch breaks, when the bankers and clerks are brought home-cooked meals by the famous *dubbawallas,* or box-runners, of the city; and the bank's location in the bustle and noise of Flora Fountain in the southern part of Bombay. Mistry also brings to life other locales in the city: the noisome and crowded Crawford market, where Gustad buys a live chicken to slaughter for a family celebration; the House of Cages, a brothel in the red-light district; and life on the street itself. Thus the novel—in the person of the protagonist—traverses different social and economic milieus, and we become aware both of the level of deprivation of the poor of Bombay as well as their resourcefulness and buoyancy. In one striking episode, Gustad comes upon four children, all bone-thin and dressed in tatters, trying to drink the dregs of flavored milk that a man at a stall sells to customers. When the seller chases away three of the children and whacks the fourth, Gustad grabs him by the collar. The man complains that he loses customers when they see beggars, whereupon Gustad buys milk for the little girl. She tries to share her bottle with her brothers—for whom Gustad proceeds to buy bottles of chocolate milk. The scene is poignant and unsettling, underscoring the painful inadequacy of Gustad's compensatory gesture and the violence and precariousness of the lives of children on the streets of Bombay.

Mistry, far from representing the poor of Bombay as pathetic and miserable, accords these characters considerable verve and strength. For instance, the narrator refers periodically to a street artist who draws murals on the pavement. Gustad employs him to paint the wall of Khodadad building with images of gods to deter people from urinating against it. When Gustad questions him about his evident knowledge of different religions, the artist explains, "I have a BA in World Religions. My specialty was Comparative Studies. Of course, that was before I transferred to the School of Arts." The artist voices the predicament of many of the slum-dwellers of Bombay, who are educated professionals who can make a living in the big city but have no permanent housing. The artist takes up a spot in the compound of Khodadad building and paints a pantheon of gods there (p. 184). Far from characterizing the artist as a hapless mendicant, the narrator attributes to him an independence of spirit and freedom that is a secular version of the ideal of the *sanyasi,* or ascetic, who frees himself of worldly attachments and desires. The artist's lack of a home and routine denote not the precariousness of his life but rather an experience of ever-spontaneous journeying that has its own logic and value.

In the figure of the mural artist, Mistry expresses not only the dignity of the person who lives on the street but also a commitment to secularism and interreligious amity that runs through the entire novel. When Gustad had asked the artist whether he could cover a three-hundred-foot wall with pictures of gods, the artist had answered, "I can cover three hundred miles if necessary. Using assorted religions and their gods, saints and prophets. ..." (p. 182). Here Mistry is referring to an actual strategy that was followed in Bombay in the 1970s, when a team of artists painted the wall around the Prince of Wales Museum. This vision of religious syncretism is of course a humorous one: the divine figures of different faiths are meant to discourage people of a variety of religions from using the walls to relieve themselves. The crossing of religious boundaries is also suggested by Gustad's visit to his friend Malcolm Saldana's church, where he offers votary candles. In counterpoint to this vision are references to the activities of the Shiv Sena, which has historically been a pro-Maharashtrian organization, with a regional identity, but which has in recent years taken on a religious identification and aligned itself with the family of Hindu organizations: "And today we have that bloody Shiv Sena, wanting to make the rest of us into second-class citizens" (p. 39). In Mistry's later novel *Family Matters,* the betrayal of secularism is a central theme; in *Such a Long Journey* it is hinted at and criticized obliquely.

Mistry's fullest portrait of the working people of Bombay is his depiction of the neighborhood around the House of Cages, the brothel in the red-light district. Gustad is familiar with this part of the city from visits to his family physician, Dr. Paymaster. Mistry's description (p. 155) of this locale highlights the haphazard mix of old and new that is the mark of postcolonial modernity. His facetious account of the so-called modernization of India contravenes the country's nationalist discourse on the blessings of industrial development and progress. Mistry continues in the same vein in his descriptions of the movie houses in the same area (p. 156)

Mistry alludes to the enormously popular musicals of "Bollywood," or Bombay's film industry, the most prolific cinema industry in the world with an output of more than one thousand films a year. Bollywood cinema has become iconic of a kitschy Bombay cultural aesthetic and is the subject of pastiche and parody in diasporic Indian fiction such as Salman Rushdie's *The Satanic Verses* and films such as *Bhaji on the*

Beach and *Masala.* Here Mistry parallels the overblown, melodramatic idiom of Bollywood with the specious rhetoric of national progress. The third establishment that weathers the changes of a modernizing India is the House of Cages. Its residents are at once purveyors of fantasy, hard-working women, and practitioners of the oldest profession amid the glitz and grit of the new industrial and business city. Once again Mistry accords these social outcastes dignity and vitality, describing them with a bawdy humor that is nonetheless tinged with sympathy.

While *Such A Long Journey* is chiefly about social relationships, it brings political events much more clearly into the reader's vision than do the tales of Ferozsha Baag. Domestic life is intertwined with public affairs from the outset, when the novel harkens back to the Indo-China war of 1965, of which traces linger in the Noble household in the form of permanently blackened windows. The novel begins against the backdrop of the looming 1971 war with Pakistan and describes the continuing hegemony of the Congress Party after independence from Britain in 1947. An important subplot of the novel is an intrigue that involves Gustad's vanished friend Jimmy Billimoria—who, it turns out, is recruited by a corrupt Prime Minister Indira Gandhi to pursue her own political agenda, though he believes he is helping the freedom fighters of Bangladesh or Mukti Bahini. Gustad becomes involved in this intrigue when Jimmy asks him at a distance to bank some money supposedly earmarked for this. Jimmy later recounts his discovery of the prime minister's fraudulence and his own imprisonment—before he is murdered. Pakistan's leaders are characterized as equally scurrilous. Peerbhoy Paanwaala, who plies his famous *paan,* or flavored areca leaf (eaten after meals), recounts in a salacious allegory shenanigans of Pakistan's generals, entertaining a crowd of customers. At the local level, meanwhile, people have organized a march to the municipal ward office to protest "overflowing sewers, broken water-pipes, pot-holed pavements, rodent invasions, bribe-extracting public servants, uncollected hills of garbage, open manholes, shattered street lights—in short, against the general decay and corruption of cogs that turned the wheels of city life" (p. 312). The novel depicts the political and physical decay of the country at every level. *Such a Fine Balance* conveys in a nuanced way a social totality that is shaped by this institutional and infrastructural decay and chronicles a variety of human responses to it.

A FINE BALANCE

With its complexity, richness, and expansive humanity, *A Fine Balance* (1995) is Mistry's most ambitious novel. It chronicles the attempts of a young Parsi widow, Dina Dalal, to eek out an independent existence as a lone manufacturer of garments for export by employing two tailors, Ishvar Darji (*darji* means "tailor" in Hindi) and his uncle Omprakash. The two men have traveled to Bombay from their village in the North of India to seek work. The fourth principal character in the novel is Maneck Kohlah, the son of family friends of Dina's, who comes to live as a paying guest in her small flat while he attends college. Set during the mid-1970s, *A Fine Balance* is a far more politically charged piece of fiction than Mistry's other stories. At the national level, it describes the period of Indira Gandhi's conviction for electoral fraud in 1975 and her declaration of emergency soon after. During the emergency—which involved the suspension of the constitution and direct rule by the center until Mrs. Gandhi was ousted from power in 1977—thousands of her political opponents were imprisoned, press censorship was imposed, and thousands were victims of compulsory sterilization programs. Again using the literary form of the realist novel, Mistry attempts to convey a totality of social experience in India and weaves together personal stories that are shaped by public events.

Mistry's account of Dina Dalal's life conveys the enormous strains upon and limited possibilities for single lower-middle-class women in Bombay and in India in general. As a widow, Dina is dependent on her bullying and stingy brother to pay her rent and support her. Her one domain of independence is the low-rent flat she lived in with her husband and which now has

passed to her. Using her skill as a seamstress and her more prosperous contacts from school, she obtains orders from a garment export outfit to sew dresses. She employs Ishvar and Darji in the hopes of filling the company's orders. We see her struggle to make ends meet, to preserve her independence and dignity, and to manage her two tailors, one of whom is deeply resentful. The three, along with her lodger, Maneck, make up a makeshift but nonetheless interconnected family.

Through the characters of Om and Ishvar, Mistry introduces his readers to a very different milieu, that of a rural village where the bonds of caste are inexorable and violently policed. Born into a caste of *chamars,* or tanners, traditionally considered untouchables and denied schooling by the Brahmins, Ishvar and his brother Narayan are sent by their father to a nearby town to apprentice as tailors. For the "uppity" attempt of Narayan to vote in the local elections when they return, the Thakurs, or landlords of the village, torture and kill Narayan and two other untouchables who attempt to follow suit, then round up the family and torch them as well. Only Ishvar and his nephew Om, Narayan's son, escape. The account of this horrific incident is straight from the annals of the caste violence that thousands in India continue to experience today. In a parallel account of the village where Ishvar and Narayan apprentice, Mistry tackles another important historical problem, that of communal violence. The two brothers are taken in by a Muslim tailor, who is later threatened by an aggressive Hindu mob; the two young men save their teacher by deflecting the anger of the crowd. In this episode, Mistry sketches the virulent communal hatred that has increasingly marred social relations in India but also depicts a relationship of solidarity and affection across religious lines.

The tailors inhabit yet another milieu that Rohinton Mistry renders with verisimilitude and sympathy: the slums of Bombay. During the period of which Mistry writes, of the eight million inhabitants of Bombay, roughly five million lived in slums and on the street. Bombay had the dubious distinction of hosting the largest slum in Asia, Dharavi. Om and Ishvar buy squatting rights in such a slum, where they become part of a community. Befriended by their talkative neighbor Rajaram, they learn the ins and outs of life in a shantytown: how to line up for water, where to relieve themselves, whom to trust. As in *Such a Long Journey,* Mistry brings to life the lives of the urban poor and infuses them with dignity and whimsy:

> Mirror, razor, shaving brush, plastic cup, loata, copper water pot—Ishvar arranged them on an upturned cardboard carton in one corner of the shack. He hung there clothes from rusted nails protruding through the plywood walls. "So everything fits nicely. We have jobs, we have a house, and soon we'll find a place for you."
>
> Om did not smile. "I hate this place," he said.
>
> (p. 167)

The description of the tailors' shack is so matter-of-fact that it leaves no room for condescending horror or cloying sympathy, as one sometimes finds in the writings of, for instance, Charles Dickens. Instead, Mistry introduces a note of self-conscious humor in Ishvar's invocation of an ideal domestic scene. At the same time, it hints at how soul-sapping existence in slum conditions might be with Om's unequivocal words "I hate this place."

The college student Maneck introduces a different set of circumstances to the novel, those of the middle classes who live in the smaller towns and send their children to cities to be educated. Maneck grew up in an idyllic landscape on the border with Pakistan; his father's considerable property vanished on the wrong side of the border during the partition of India in 1947, and they were left with a small shop. In his description of Maneck's home, Mistry sketches a way of life that is relatively tranquil, far from the strains and noise of the city. Here is an India that might be unspoiled but for the ravages of development: "The destitute encampments scratched away at the hillsides, the people drawn from every direction by stories of construction and wealth and employment. But the ranks of the jobless always exponentially outnumbered the jobs, and a hungry army sheltered permanently on the slopes. The forests were being devoured for firewood; bald patches materialized upon the body of the hills"

(p. 215). Here, as in the city, the forces of modernization are ruining the environment, and the pressures of population growth and poverty threaten to destroy the countryside. When Maneck's parents decide to send him to Bombay for college, he is reluctant to go but gives in. In the college hostel, he is subjected to the humiliations of ritual hazing and becomes desperate to return home. Guessing that there is something wrong, his mother arranges for him to rent a room in Dina's apartment. There he finds some peace from the callow depredations of his classmates.

The relationships among the odd ménage in Dina's house, combining different religions and social classes, are symbolic of how difference may be negotiated in a nation that is so diverse. For the four to live together, huge barriers must be overcome—on the one hand, Omprakash's resentment of Dina and his belief that she is exploiting them, and on the other, Dina's sense of middle-class superiority, which keeps her from taking them in when their hut is violently torn down and they are left homeless. However, a camaraderie and love grows between Om, Ishvar, Maneck, and Dina, so much so that they are able to build a fragile sense of home and belonging together. In this vision, the novel holds out the possibility of a humanity that transcends economic pressures and social differences. However, the relentless political forces that swirl around them wreck any possibility of a stable and secure home.

The most overtly political of any of Mistry's fiction, the novel depicts the full range of these forces, particularly in the context of the state of emergency. Mistry describes the rounding up of ordinary people for political rallies; the destruction of shantytowns in the name of progress; the murder of Indira Gandhi's political opponents, such as Maneck's erstwhile college roommate Avinash; the abduction and coerced labor of supposed "beggars"; and the forced sterilization of scores of people in makeshift camps. At the same time, he infuses even the more predictable political episodes in the novel with complexities and contradictions. For instance, one of the more outlandish characters in the novel is Beggarmaster, who makes his living off the takings of his beggars, whom he protects from harassment and violence. When he is stabbed at the end of the novel, Dina wonders whether he in fact served a desirable social purpose in looking after his mendicants. A second complex character is Ibrahim the rent collector, who is Dina's adversary for circumstantial reasons but who warns Dina when she is about to be evicted from her flat—and whose eyes become tearful when she addresses him as a father. Once again, Mistry offsets the grim ways of the world with the compassion of individuals. *A Fine Balance* is ultimately the most tragic of Mistry's novels and stories: three of the four characters are crushed by social and economic forces and by state violence, and the fourth is only able to make a living by leaving India for the Persian Gulf. Forced out of her apartment, Dina becomes a virtual servant in her hated brother's home. After Ishvar loses his legs in an accident and Om is forcibly sterilized, the two become beggars. In the closing pages of the novel Dina feeds them surreptitiously, then returns to her household chores. In painting their lives in such bleak hues, Mistry mounts a thoroughgoing critique of modern India and its pledges of development.

FAMILY MATTERS

In his third novel, Mistry returns to the intimate space of a single family, as its name suggests. *Family Matters* (2002) is set once again in Bombay but this time in the 1990s, against the backdrop of rising communal tension, the destruction of the Babri Masjid historic mosque, and the mobilization of the Shiv Sena. At the center of the novel is a frail, elderly Parsi man, Nariman Vakeel, who is suffering from Parkinson's disease. The different parts of the family have severe quarrels and show a meanness of spirit that is exacerbated by the strains of limited space and means. After Nariman breaks his ankle, he is shunted from one part of the family to another and suffers from physical neglect and, consequently, pain and humiliation. Mistry develops the characters of Nariman's two stepchildren—the domineering and conniving Coomy and her weak, mild-mannered brother, Jal—and their

stepsister, Roxana, in relation to Nariman. As a family drama unfolds, Roxana's husband, Yezad, becomes embroiled in an intrigue that involves the Shiv Sena and results in the death of his employer, Mr. Kapur. The novel indirectly portrays the rising power of the Hindu Right in Bombay.

On first reading, *Family Matters* appears to be a much simpler and less ambitious novel than *A Fine Balance,* but as a narrative it is in fact the more intricate of the two. As Mistry has put it, the novel "has an internal canvas which is as complex as the external canvas of *A Fine Balance* (in Shaikh). Its complexity lies in the subtlety with which it explores the different characters and moves in and out of their perspectives—perspectives that are often at odds with each other. The most poignant of these is that of Jehangir, Nariman's grandson:

> Up on one elbow, Jehangir listened to Grandpa having that same dream about Lucy singing their favourite song. Now he was asking her to step down, it was dangerous to stand up there. But he could only catch bits of Grandpa's dream. Like Daddy's badly working radio, where the sound came and went.
>
> He turned the phrases over in his mind, storing them away with the other fragments he was saving. Some day, it would all fit together, and he would make sense of Grandpa's words, he was certain.
>
> (p. 325)

Jehangir tries to piece together Grandpa's most intimate dream thoughts. From the perspective of a child, he attempts to make sense of fragments of phrases to better understand his grandfather's tragic past. We sense his deep love for his ailing grandfather, as well as his curiosity about events that have clearly shaped the lives of his family but about which he is kept in the dark. We learn later that Nariman's former mistress Lucy has jumped off a terrace along with his wife. Here the tragedy is only hinted at, in a subtle and oblique way that is quintessential Mistry.

To put into relief the contours of Mistry's fiction, and of *Family Matters* in particular, it is helpful to compare his writing with that of the other best-known writer of postcolonial fiction about Bombay, Salman Rushdie. Indeed, critics have implicitly held Mistry to the postmodern literary standard set by writers such as Rushdie. When asked in an interview about why he used modes of representation associated with nineteenth-century fiction—social realism, linear narrative, elegantly plain prose—rather than self-consciously playful postmodern narrative techniques, Mistry commented, "I don't like clever books, I like honest books. For me telling the story and being true to your characters is more important than demonstrating your skill with words, all your juggling acts, the high-wire acts, the flying trapeze acts" (interview with Oprah Winfrey, January 2002). Rohinton Mistry clearly views his realist literary style as a less showy and more honest means of representing people's lives.

His use of a realist mode of narrative has more profound implications, however. These implications might best be viewed in terms of a debate about the politics of modernism that took place in the 1930s in a group of essays published as *Aesthetics and Politics*. In his essay "Realism in the Balance," the Czech philosopher Georg Lukacs argued that whereas realist fiction was able to portray the historical forces at work, abstract expressionists, in favoring fragmentary and disjunctive modes of representation, obfuscated the totality of social relationships. In response Ernst Bloch argued, in "Debating Expressionism," that discontinuity and fragmentation were crucial aspects of the present historical moment, and that the modernists were able to express this formally in their work. Of course, one would have to characterize Rushdie as a postmodern writer rather than a modern one, but his emphasis on fragmentation and discontinuity, conjoined with the more postmodern elements of pastiche, irony, self-conscious narration, and the like, are similarly at odds with Mistry's realist mode of representing Bombay. Rushdie, in *The Moor's Last Sigh,* uses postmodern narrative to underscore the plural, discontinuous nature of Bombay, to which a more unitary and totalitarian vision put forward by the Shiv Sena is contrasted. Mistry, rather than privileging difference, uses a realist mode of writing to represent a complex, dynamic social totality that is shot through with tensions and contradictions but nonetheless holds

together. He thereby explores the possibility and difficulty of coexistence in a city under the enormous pressures of social and economic deprivation, sharp divisions of wealth, potentially murderous religious politics, and a crumbling infrastructure. Addressing these differing approaches, Laura Moss, in her essay "Can Rohinton Mistry's Realism Rescue the Novel?," makes the important point that although there has been a recent tendency to read realism as inherently conservative not only in literary but also in political terms and to see postmodern writing as necessarily liberational, Mistry's realism affords a critique of forces of social oppression that is no less trenchant than that of postmodern writers who are celebrated for articulating a resistance to postcolonial modes of domination.

CONCLUSION

In January 2002, the talk-show host Oprah Winfrey chose *A Fine Balance* as the featured title for her book club. This is not an honor that every accomplished writer of literary fiction would court, and certainly not a writer known as Mistry is for his extreme privateness. Welcome or not, Winfrey's accolade brought Mistry considerable literary fame and a wide readership. It brought to that readership an intimate imaginary encounter with the lives of the people of Bombay and of India and, one hopes, an appreciation of the variety of challenges that they face and surmount everyday. Rohinton Mistry's work is akin to that of the great nineteenth-century realists in that he portrays a rich individual as well as social landscape, conveying a complex totality of relationships and events in a richly detailed setting. As such, it is a grave mistake to read "India as a metaphor" in his fiction and to place more emphasis on the supposedly universal themes of the novel than on the cultural and historical specificity of the novel, as do some readers and critics (see, for example, Robert L. Ross's essay "Seeking and Maintaining Balance"). Rather, the novel affords an imaginative journey through the fertile yet bleak social landscape of India, with its vibrant, cosmopolitan cities; its skyscrapers and shantytowns and close rural communities; its web of class, caste, and gender politics; its crushingly powerful state apparatuses; and its brutal economy. This journey is not illuminated by the verbal pyrotechnics and self-conscious irony that we have come to expect of contemporary writers; nor does it take into account poststructuralist critiques of representations of subjectivity, of history, and of the social. Yet it is precisely in its gracious, perhaps old-fashioned yet politically trenchant humanism that the power of Rohinton Mistry's fiction lies.

Selected Bibliography

WORKS OF ROHINTON MISTRY

NOVELS AND SHORT STORIES

Swimming Lessons and Other Tales from Ferozsha Baag. New York: Vintage, 1987.

Such a Long Journey. London: Faber, 1991; New York: Vintage, 1991.

A Fine Balance. New York: Vintage, 1995; London: Faber, 1996.

Family Matters. London: Faber, 2002; New York: Knopf, 2002.

CRITICAL AND BIOGRAPHICAL STUDIES

Bhabha, Homi K. *The Location of Culture.* London and New York: Routledge, 1994.

Bloch, Ernst. "Debating Expressionism." *Aesthetics and Politics.* Edited by Ernst Bloch et al. London: NLB, 1977.

Lukacs, Georg. "Realism in the Balance." *Aesthetics and Politics.* Edited by Ernst Bloch et al. London: NLB, 1977.

Macaulay, Thomas Babington. "Minute on Indian Education." 1835. In *Imperialism & Orientalism: A Documentary Sourcebook.* Edited and introduced by Barbara Harlow and Mia Carter. Malden, Mass.: Blackwell, 1999.

Nanavutty, Piloo. *The Parsis.* New Delhi: National Book Trust, India, 1977.

Moss, Laura. "Can Rohinton Mistry's Realism Rescue the Novel?" In *Postcolonizing the Commonwealth.* Edited by Rowland Smith. Waterloo, Ontario: Wilfred Laurier University Press, 2000.

Ross, Robert L. "Seeking and Maintaining Balance: Rohinton Mistry's Fiction." *World Literature Today* 73: 239-244 (spring 1999).

Spivak, Gayatri. *Critique of Postcolonial Reason: Toward a History of the Vanishing Present.* Cambridge, Mass.: Harvard University Press, 1999.

INTERVIEWS AND PROFILES

Bogaev, Barbara. *Fresh Air.* National Public Radio, September 26, 2002.

Lambert, Angela. *Guardian,* April 27, 2002, Saturday Pages, p. 6. (Profile.)

Shaikh, Nermeen. "Family Matters: An Interview with Rohinton Mistry." *AsiaSource: A Resource of the Asia Society* (http://www.asiasource.org/news/special_reports/mistry.com), November 1, 2002.

NANCY MITFORD

(1904–1973)

Patrick Denman Flanery

NANCY MITFORD, BEST known for her two semi-autobiographical postwar novels *The Pursuit of Love* and *Love in a Cold Climate,* was born into a family with a talent for popular literature. Her paternal grandfather, Bertram Mitford, was the author of the hugely successful *Tales of Old Japan* (1871), while her maternal grandfather, Thomas Gibson Bowles, had founded the magazines *Vanity Fair* and *The Lady.* The more immediate influences on Mitford's work—both fiction and nonfiction—came from her now-fabled family. Mitford strained family relations when she began to mine her childhood—and the characters of her siblings and parents—for the benefit of fiction. Her works are peppered with autobiographical detail, family jokes, and unfailingly sharp, merciless portraits, barely disguised by the veil of fiction. The six Mitford daughters, whose talent for scandal cemented their celebrity status as an increasingly anachronistic curiosity, alternately adored and reviled, have evolved in the public consciousness into a beguiling and indomitable hydra known collectively as the Mitford Girls. The steamroller force of their celebrity has perhaps undermined the longevity of Mitford's own literary reputation, which has often been regarded as the featherweight hobby of an overprivileged and undereducated woman. Not long after her death, the critic John Atkins accused her of descending into base snobbery, assuming that her fictions were essentially statements of personal philosophy and allowing neither for Mitford's creativity nor her ironic, often self-mocking distance from her characters. Allan Hepburn has speculated that her low critical profile may be due to sexism and xenophobia on the part of critics and academics who take umbrage at her disregard for marriage, tolerance of adultery, Gallic sensibility, and (apart from her nonfiction) entirely comedic oeuvre.

EARLY LIFE

The Honourable Nancy Freeman Mitford was born in London on November 28, 1904, the first of David and Sydney Bowles Mitford's seven children, followed by Pamela in 1907, Thomas in 1909, Diana in 1910, Unity in 1914, Jessica in 1917, and Deborah in 1920. As the eldest (and the only child lacking the Mitford Teutonic blondness), Nancy tormented her siblings with endless teases, not limited to childhood pranks, though these were the least malign.

The Mitford children were mostly raised by nannies, particularly Laura Dicks, known within the family as Nanny Blor, a model for Nanny in Mitford's seventh novel, *The Blessing,* and subjected to benign nonfictional treatment in Mitford's collection of essays and journalism *The Water Beetle.* At the age of five Nancy was enrolled in the Francis Holland School in London, which she continued to attend until 1914. David Mitford was then working for his father-in-law's magazine, *The Lady.* He left this position in 1914 to serve in World War I but had to be discharged by 1917 because of severe exhaustion. He had lost a lung in the Boer War and was never again in perfect health. David's elder brother, Clem, was killed in France in 1915, and his father, Bertram, by then Lord Redesdale, died in 1916, so David succeeded to the title as the second Baron Redesdale, allowing the family to move into the Redesdale estate, Batsford Park, with its extensive library. Nancy had three years in which to scour the library, reading widely in French and English before her father decided to sell the house in 1918. He bought Asthall Manor, where the family lived during the construction of the hideous family home, Swinbrook House, which Nancy dubbed Swine Brook.

Nancy was particularly close to her wildly eccentric and unpredictable father, whom she would immortalize as Uncle Matthew in *The Pursuit of Love, Love in a Cold Climate,* and *Don't Tell Alfred.* While her brother, Tom, was allowed to go to Eton, David did not believe that girls should be sent to boarding school, and Nancy resented her lack of formal education for the rest of her life. The biographical consensus seems to be that David believed school would make the girls vulgar, not that he believed they should be unlettered, though he was himself no great reader; some biographers have speculated that he may have suffered from undiagnosed dyslexia.

At sixteen, Nancy attended a finishing school at Hatherop Castle, which led to a chaperoned tour of the Continent in 1922, introducing her to Paris for the first time; she instantly fell in love with the city that would be her future home. She was presented to court in 1923, and allowed greater social liberties, such as a season in London (with its attendant balls) and the freedom to entertain both male and female friends at home. Nancy was largely on the fringes of the Bright Young People scene, as evoked in Evelyn Waugh's *Vile Bodies* and painted to similar though less cynical effect in Nancy's first novel, *Highland Fling.* Nancy developed a lifelong friendship with Mark Ogilvie-Grant, who introduced her to the aesthetic Oxford set, much to her father's despair; David strongly disliked the effete (and often homosexual) young men in whose company Nancy revelled.

In 1926, David sold Asthall, and the family moved to Paris for three months while Swinbrook House was completed. Nancy was enrolled in art lessons but failed to excel; she had a vibrant social life largely centered around the British embassy, whose world she would farcically evoke in her last novel, *Don't Tell Alfred.* This brief residence in Paris confirmed Nancy's love for the city. Returning to England for Christmas 1926, the family moved to a house near Hyde Park. Nancy enrolled in a course at the Slade School of Fine Art, but she had no native talent for the visual arts and soon turned to writing to supplement her meager allowance.

In 1928, Nancy fell in love with one of the circle of Oxford aesthetes, Hamish St. Clair-Erskine, with whom her brother, Tom, had had an affair at Eton. To everyone apart from Nancy, Hamish (euphemistically described by Harold Acton as a "narcissist") was a thoroughly inappropriate choice. Neither David nor Hamish's father approved of the relationship.

Nancy's sister Diana married Bryan Guinness in 1929, providing Nancy with new bases (and new freedom) to meet Hamish via the Guinnesses' houses in London and Wiltshire. Through Diana's mixing with the artistic intelligentsia, Nancy became friendly with Evelyn Waugh and lived in his London flat for a period, just as his marriage to his first wife, Evelyn Gardner, was disintegrating. When Gardner confessed to Nancy that she was having an affair, Nancy sided with Waugh, bolstering what would become a lifelong friendship.

Jonathan Guinness dates the end of Nancy and Hamish's romance to the summer of 1933. Charlotte Mosley contends that they were never formally engaged, though the relationship was sufficiently serious and fraught enough that Nancy once tried to commit suicide by putting her head in a gas oven. A month after Hamish contrived what Mosley considers to have been a false engagement to another woman, Nancy became engaged to Peter Rodd, second son of Lord Rennell of Rodd. Peter, partial model for Evelyn Waugh's archetypal ne'er-do-well Basil Seal in *Black Mischief* and *Put Out More Flags,* had been sent down from Balliol College, Oxford, for having women in his rooms; he subsequently worked for a bank in Brazil and as a journalist in Berlin before accompanying his elder brother on a two-year expedition to the Sahara. At the time of his engagement to Nancy, Peter was working for a London bank. They were married on December 4, 1933, and honeymooned in Rome; Nancy seems quickly to have recognized him for the bore that he was. Returning to London, they had very little money and lived in a small cottage near Kew Bridge. Peter failed to keep his bank job, and the young couple were forced to rely on the rather mean generosity of both sets of parents. Economies were nearly impossible, as Peter was a lavish spender, heavy drinker, and frequent visitor to costly nightclubs. Nancy's writing, far from being a mere hobby, was a very necessary means of increasing the household income.

In 1930, Nancy had been hired to write a weekly column for her grandfather Bowles's magazine, *The Lady,* and began work on her first novel, *Highland Fling,* published in 1931 by Thornton Butterworth. In her memoir *Hons and Rebels,* Jessica Mitford recounts Lady Redesdale's horror that Nancy should publish the novel under her own name, given its barely disguised portrait not just of Lord Redesdale but of various other friends and members of the extended family. Ultimately, Jessica concludes, David Mitford relished his multiple fictionalizations and was perhaps mellowed by them, while the larger Mitford clan seemed generally proud of Nancy's achievement.

HIGHLAND FLING

In biographer Laura Thompson's view, Mitford's first novel was lucky to be published. It is a slight work, borrowing from Evelyn Waugh, P. G. Wodehouse, and Aldous Huxley's *Crome Yellow.* Though it is generally unsure of its aims and intended tone, it was well received in the press and not just by Nancy's friends, who might have felt some obligation to soften their criticism. At the core, it is a mildly cynical comedy exploring the conflict between the aesthetic Bright Young People and the athletic country set, who collide at a shooting party in Scotland.

The punningly named artist Albert Memorial Gates—partially based on Hamish St. Clair-Erskine—is an Oxford graduate who returns to London from his beloved Paris after a two-year stint of the artistic life. He has missed his perpetually broke friends Walter and Sally Monteath and has been offered an exhibition of his paintings by a London gallery. Echoing a note from Waugh's *Vile Bodies,* Albert's copy of James Joyce's *Ulysses* is seized by customs officials in London. Jonathan Guinness identifies Albert as an early, and poorer, prototype for Waugh's Ambrose Silk in *Put Out More Flags*

and Anthony Blanche in *Brideshead Revisited,* but denies that Hamish bore much resemblance to Nancy's creation, suggesting that inspiration perhaps came in part from the writers Brian Howard and Harold Acton, both models for Waugh's characters.

When Walter and Sally are invited by her aunt and uncle to host a shooting party at their Scottish home, Dalloch Castle, they convince Albert and Sally's friend Jane Dacre (the first of many Mitford self-portraits) to accompany them. The shooting party is rounded out by a group of hearty athletes: Captain and Lady Brenda Chadlington, General Murgatroyd (the first fictional rendering of David Mitford), Admiral Wenceslaus, Mr. Buggins, and Lord and Lady Prague.

Thompson contends that Albert would have been a more successful character if Mitford had written him as unswervingly homosexual and suspects that Mitford's inability to acknowledge Hamish's homosexuality affected her rendering of his fictional counterpart. This seems unlikely, however, given Albert's high-camp behavior and overt though short-lived affections for the ruggedly masculine General Murgatroyd. Albert might rather be seen as the first example of a string of male characters with ambiguous rather than rigid sexual orientations who occur throughout Mitford's fiction. Some are plainly homosexual; others are bisexual or simply effetely unconventional heterosexuals.

Jane finds herself romantically inclined towards Albert, whose extravagantly flamboyant clothes set him apart from the others. Albert is initially more interested in Dalloch's collection of Victorian objets d'art, which he and Jane sort, catalog, and photograph—a mania borrowed, in Harold Acton's opinion, from the habits of Mitford's friend Robert Byron, author of the now classic travel narrative *The Road to Oxiana* (1937). While Jane's feelings cool, Albert's become inflamed, and on an evening stroll he tells her that he has fallen in love with her and kisses her. She initially resists his advances but ultimately agrees to marry him.

Mitford's plotting is inexpert; she contrives a fire that burns Dalloch Castle to the ground and forces her characters back to London, where Albert's exhibition of his terrifying mixed-media surrealist paintings bemuses the hearties from Dalloch. The exhibit opening gives Mitford an opportunity to represent the madcap surrealist quality of the Bright Young People who so dominated London society at the time and anticipates a not wholly dissimilar scene in Evelyn Waugh's *Brideshead Revisited,* in which Charles Ryder's aesthete friend Anthony Blanche interrupts the opening of Ryder's art exhibit. In spite of its insignificance in Mitford's oeuvre, *Highland Fling* is worth revisiting, if only as a companion to Waugh's *Vile Bodies,* which Mitford herself acknowledged was unusually like her own book, though its similarities remain primarily tonal rather than narrative in nature.

CHRISTMAS PUDDING

Under pressure from her publisher for another comic novel, Mitford began work on her second book, *Christmas Pudding,* which Butterworth published in 1932 with illustrations by Mark Ogilvie-Grant. As light as *Highland Fling,* it paints London and the countryside in equally world-weary winter grays, and by 1951, when Hamish Hamilton asked to republish it, Mitford felt it was too facetious and poorly written. Evelyn Waugh classed it, hardly more generously, as mere juvenilia.

The protagonist, earnest young writer Paul Fotheringay (modeled on the poet John Betjeman), has published his first novel, *Crazy Capers.* Intended as a serious romantic tragedy about two lovers who make a suicide pact but fail to kill themselves, Paul is distressed to find that everyone is reading the book as farce—and thoroughly enjoying it. Even Paul's pseudo-fiancée, the social climber Marcella Bracket, fails to see its intended seriousness. The only person who seems to guess that Paul's novel is not meant to be funny is the reformed, stylish prostitute-turned-hostess Amabelle Fortescue, whom Laura Thompson describes in her biography as the first "properly Mitfordian character" (p. 92). Amabelle warns Paul that "it's no good writing about the upper classes if you hope to be taken

seriously. ... Station masters, my dear, station masters." Paul, perhaps speaking for Mitford, objects, "But you see my trouble is that I loathe station masters, like hell I do, and lighthouse keepers, too, and women with hare-lips and miners and men on barges and people in circuses; I hate them all equally. And I can't write dialect" (p. 38). When Amabelle suggests Paul try biography instead of fiction he consults the *Dictionary of National Biography* and decides to write the life story of Victorian poet Lady Maria Almanack. Her unpublished personal papers are still held by her descendants at the family home, Compton Bobbin, current residence of Lady Gloria Bobbin and her son, Sir Roderick, or Bobby (modeled on Hamish), who is currently at Eton. Failing to gain Lady Gloria's permission to consult the papers, Paul turns to Amabelle (one of Bobby's dearest friends), who arranges for Paul to be engaged as Bobby's holiday tutor under the false identity "Paul Fisher."

Predictably, Paul falls in love with Bobby's sheltered but beautiful sister, Philadelphia, who is the only person who properly understands—and even cries while reading—his novel. Philadelphia is also pursued by her cousin and Amabelle's former admirer, Lord Michael Lewes, recently returned from a diplomatic posting in Cairo. Bobby and Amabelle do not see Paul as a proper match for Philadelphia, who must marry well in spite of loving Paul more than Michael. Paul and Philadelphia become secretly engaged, but after returning to London, Paul begins seeing Marcella Bracket, and Philadelphia maintains a correspondence with Michael, who, under Amabelle's influence, presents her with a dazzling Cartier diamond bracelet. Paul undermines his own desires when Philadelphia comes to London, distraught, and finds him in a stupor. He drunkenly tells her to go away and later reads of her marriage to Michael. The book ends with Paul setting to work on his biography of Philadelphia's ancestress Lady Maria Almanack.

Mitford's characterization of Amabelle is the novel's greatest and perhaps sole strength, and Thompson considers it early evidence of Mitford's inherent (though possibly then unconscious) sympathy for older sophisticates rather than the brash Bright Young People. Selena Hastings records that though Mitford was concerned Hamish would be offended by his unveiled portrait as Bobby, he embraced the new name and went so far as to sign himself "Bobby" in his letters to her.

WIGS ON THE GREEN

In 1934, Mitford began work on *Wigs on the Green,* a partial satire of British fascism and a barely concealed critique of two Mitford converts, sisters Diana and Unity. In 1932 Diana had left her husband Bryan Guinness for the British fascist leader Sir Oswald Mosley, founder of the British Union of Fascists, dubbed the "Blackshirts." In 1933, Diana and Unity visited Germany and became close friends of Adolf Hitler. Mitford and Peter Rodd had a brief flirtation with fascism but quickly saw it for what it was and condemned it. (See Wodehouse's, *The Code of the Woosters.* [London, H. Jenkins, 1938] for a fictionalized portrait of Oswald Mosley as Sir Roderick Spode, leader of the "Blackshorts.") Though difficult for today's readers to fathom, given the result of German fascism, for many conservative and center-right British writers and intellectuals in the 1930s, Fascism seemed an appealing, intriguing, and preferable ideological movement compared to Soviet-styled communism. Laura Thompson speculates that Mitford's brief involvement with British fascism may largely have been rooted in natural curiosity, and affected by her siblings' fervent Germanophilia. Whatever the cause, it was not long before she was vehemently opposed to it.

Fascism is but one of a number of causes, ideologies, and human foibles that Mitford parodies in a novel that Thompson regards as the first to show signs of her growing literary maturity and hints of what might be described as the Mitford style. The protagonist, Noel Foster, inherits £3,314 from a dead aunt, immediately quits his job, and calls to brag to the Peter Rodd–inspired perennial mooch Jasper Aspect. Aspect convinces Noel to pursue the mysterious and extremely wealthy heiress Eugenia Malmains, a blue-eyed, blonde follower of the fascist

Union Jack Movement. Malmains, who is directly modeled on Unity Mitford, gives speeches from an overturned washtub in the Chalford village green: "Soon your streets will echo 'neath the tread of the Union Jack Battalions, soon the day of jelly-breasted politicians shall be no more, soon we shall all be living in a glorious Britain under the wise, stern, and beneficent rule of Our Captain" (p. 20).

Noel and Jasper join the Jackshirt movement to gain Eugenia's favor, but they are equally intrigued by two mysterious ladies, the Misses Smith and Jones, staying at the Jolly Roger Inn in Chalford. Jasper sees Miss Jones picking ducal coronets out of her underwear, and when he investigates her rooms he finds masses of jewels and steals two pounds in cash. The newspapers soon explain the mystery: Miss Jones fled from her wedding and is actually Lady Marjorie Merrith, the wealthiest heiress in England, second only to Eugenia Malmains. Miss Smith, her friend, is actually Eugenia's cousin, Mrs. Poppy St. Julien, whose husband wants to divorce her in order to marry a younger woman.

Noel falls under the influence of the local culture vulture, Mrs. Anne-Marie Lace, who, after six months of singing lessons in Paris as a girl, returned to Britain having lost her birth name— Bella Drudge—and gained an affected French accent. Mrs. Lace is a slightly more mature version of Philadelphia from *Christmas Pudding*—a woman longing for the excitement she associates with bohemian intelligentsia. She relies on the advice of Mr. Leslie Leader, an ascetic, aesthete pacifist who lives in nearby Rackenbridge and leads a group of effete artistic male hangers-on. Noel begins an affair with Anne-Marie, who, thanks to Jasper, believes that Noel is minor middle-European royalty in disguise, while Jasper embarks on an affair with Poppy.

Poppy is recruited by Eugenia's grandmother and guardian, Lady Chalford, to help plan a pageant garden party for Eugenia. Predictably, Eugenia sees this as an ideal opportunity to hold a Jackshirt rally and intends to invite Jackshirts from all over the country. She opens a Jackshirt headquarters in the village and decorates it with life-size photo portraits of Hitler, Mussolini, Roosevelt (then regarded as a model socialist leader because of his New Deal reforms, but no doubt included with the others for comic effect), and the Jackshirt captain. The climactic pageant descends into ironic chaos as Mr. Leader's pacifists sabotage the event, overturning a coach carrying Mrs. Lace and attacking the Jackshirts with "life preservers, knuckle-dusters, potatoes stuffed with razor blades, bicycle bells filled with shot, and other primitive, but effective, weapons" (p. 235). Eugenia rallies the Jackshirts, who turn on the pacifists and defeat them, forcing them to flee.

Under pressure from Unity, Diana, and Oswald Mosley, Mitford made substantial changes to *Wigs on the Green* before it was published, cutting, she claimed, almost three chapters, which effectively limited her parody of Mosley to one of reference rather than direct representation. The sisters, and Diana in particular, were still deeply irritated. Laura Thompson attributes this to the conflict between their wholehearted belief in the seriousness of purpose behind the British fascist movement and the flippancy with which Mitford treated the subject, regarding it as both fundamentally ridiculous and dangerously xenophobic. The relationship between Mitford and her sisters came under serious and enduring strain. Prior to the book's publication, Mitford tried to calm Diana, insisting in a letter that the book was actually pro-Fascist and that her light treatment of the movement was defensible on the grounds that "Fascism is now such a notable feature of modern life all over the world that it must be possible to consider it in any context, when attempting to give a picture of life as it is lived today" (*Letters of Nancy Mitford,* p. 100). When Hamish Hamilton asked to reprint *Wigs on the Green* in 1951, Mitford refused, recognizing that her prewar jokes on Fascism and its association with Nazism were in terrifically bad taste given the atrocities of the Holocaust.

PREPARING FOR WAR

In 1936, Diana Guinness married Sir Oswald Mosley in the presence of Hitler; still angered by *Wigs on the Green,* the Mosleys forbade Nancy to stay in their home. In the same year, Peter and Nancy moved to the Maida Vale district of London. The marriage was in a poor state, weakened by Peter's alcoholism and infidelities. In 1938 and 1939, Nancy edited and published the correspondence of her Victorian ancestors under the titles *The Ladies of Alderley* and *The Stanleys of Alderley.* She also became pregnant in 1938 but suffered the first of several miscarriages.

Early in 1939 Peter went to Perpignan, France, to help Spanish Republican refugees, and Nancy soon joined him, working as a driver. James Lees-Milne credits the experience with concretizing Nancy's unbending hatred of fascism and eventual self-identification as a socialist. Nancy later incorporated her experiences in Perpignan in her fourth novel, *The Pursuit of Love.*

On the day war was declared in September 1939, Unity was in Germany and unsuccessfully attempted suicide by shooting herself in the head. Hitler arranged for her to be moved to Switzerland for treatment, and Nancy's sister, Deborah (later Duchess of Devonshire), and her mother, Lady Redesdale, were dispatched to bring Unity home to England in January 1940.

The war years were a particularly fraught time for the Mitford family. Unity, Tom (who served in the Rifle Brigade but at his request was sent to Asia so he would not have to kill Germans), Pamela, and the Mosleys were all in favor of appeasement, while Jessica was staunchly pro-war. Even the Mitford parents had been introduced to Hitler and were immediately charmed by him. When war was declared, however, David reverted to supporting the British, though Sydney remained ambivalent. Nancy was fervently pro-war and worked at a London hospital while Peter took up a commission in the Welsh Guards. Money was extremely tight for them, as Nancy's allowance from her father had been cut. She began to take in paying guests and stretched the household budget by raising hens, growing vegetables, and writing a comic spy novel, published by Hamish Hamilton in 1940 as *Pigeon Pie: A Wartime Receipt.*

NANCY MITFORD

PIGEON PIE

The timing of Mitford's fourth novel was unfortunate, as the "phony-war" quickly turned into an active war. The book achieved little success at the time of first publication, only to find renewed life when reissued in 1951. Though dismissed by Jonathan and Catherine Guinness as her weakest novel, Mitford's evocation of the phony-war period was astute and colloquial. It captures the feverish absurdity of a London still untouched by the Blitz but buzzing with stories of spies and assesses in inimitable Mitford style the international situation:

> By about a month after the war had been declared, it became obvious that nobody intended it to begin. The belligerent countries were behaving like children in a round game. … England picked up France, Germany picked up Italy. … Then Italy's Nanny said she had fallen down and grazed her knee, running, and mustn't play. England picked up Turkey, Germany picked up Spain, but Spain's Nanny said she had internal troubles, and must sit this one out. … America, of course, was too much of a baby for such a grown-up game, but she was just longing to see it played. … They were longing for the show, and with savage taunts, like boys at a bull-baiting from behind safe bars, they urged that it should begin at once.
>
> (pp. 36–37)

The exasperatingly dotty Lady Sophia Garfield has fallen out of love with her appeasement-minded businessman husband, Luke, who has recently joined an American-based religious cult called the Boston Brotherhood and invites its members to congregate in their hundreds at the Garfields' London house. While Luke is having an affair with Florence—a fervent follower of the Brotherhood who moves into the Garfields' house and keeps a pet pigeon in her room—Sophia turns to the former journalist and troublemaker Rudolph Jocelyn for romance. Jocelyn insists that she must do something to help the war effort, so he arranges for Sophia to volunteer at a first aid post at St. Anne's Hospital while he is sent with his battalion to a training camp on the coast.

Sophia's godfather, the beloved Sir Ivor King—the "King of Song," who can sing higher and lower than any human ever has before and has a particular penchant for blond wigs—is found brutally murdered in the pagoda at Kew Gardens. When news leaks that he was about to begin a propaganda campaign with the Ministry of Information, everyone suspects sabotage, leakage of information, and possibly German spies. But Sir Ivor soon appears to turn up in Germany, not dead at all; the body found at Kew was merely a disfigured pig. Sir Ivor announces his apparently enthusiastic involvement in a world-wide anti-British propaganda campaign in nightly radio broadcasts, which seems to be transmitted from Germany.

Sophia eventually discovers that Florence and two other members of the Boston Brotherhood, Heatherley and Winthrop, are all German spies. Ivor, it turns out, is loyal to Britain. He never left the country and is working with the spies as a double agent, sending broadcasts from the drains under the first-aid post. He warns Sophia that the Germans are planning a major operation. Though under constant surveillance by the spies, Sophia manages to slip a message to Jocelyn. Scotland Yard arrives in time to thwart the spies' plan to blow up London's drains, and Sir Ivor is the hero of the hour.

Based in part on Mitford's experiences as a volunteer at St. Mary's Hospital, *Pigeon Pie* exhibits her growing maturity as a writer, bridging the light early fiction with her three strongest novels. Written in only three months, the plot is absurdly tortuous, and the protagonist's naïveté strains credibility. But a new, more worldly tone befits the developing conflict at the time of its composition, and sustained passages of prose do not merely seek to entertain but seem to indicate Mitford's greater confidence in her metier. Ever autobiographical, she modeled Lady Sophia Garfield on herself, Sir Luke Garfield on her brother-in-law Francis, Rudolph Jocelyn on Peter Rodd, and the bewigged Sir Ivor King on Mark Ogilvie-Grant.

THE WAR AND PALEWSKI

Peter Rodd was sent to France in late spring 1940, and Sir Oswald Mosley was arrested and incarcerated in Brixton Prison for his fascist activities. Nancy warned the Home Office that her sister Diana was equally dangerous and should also be arrested; Diana was subsequently incarcerated in Holloway Prison for two years, after which time Mosley was allowed to join her. Nancy did not reveal her actions to Diana but maintained a steady correspondence and sent care packages to prison. Nancy's parents, Lord and Lady Redesdale, separated at this time, perhaps under the strain of Unity's illness following her suicide attempt, Diana's incarceration, and worries over Tom's mobilization. David retreated to his Scottish island, Inch Kenneth, while Sydney looked after Unity in a cottage in Swinbrook. Unity eventually died at Swinbrook in May 1948 after contracting meningitis.

In 1940, Nancy became pregnant and again miscarried. She worked at a London canteen, and when the Blitz began she moved from the heavily targeted Maida Vale district to the family house in Rutland Gate, living in a small flat while the main house was occupied by evacuees from the badly bombed East End. Peter and Nancy's marriage was by this time almost nonexistent. When he was in London on leave he would stay at the Savile Club, begging friends like Harold Acton not to tell Nancy he was in town. After his father died in July 1940, Peter stopped receiving an allowance, and as a result Nancy herself had very little on which to live. Selina Hastings records that in 1941 Nancy began to frequent the Free French Officers Club, where she was a great success, and had an affair with Roy André Desplats-Pilter. She became pregnant by Desplats-Pilter but suffered an ectopic pregnancy, and in November of that year she lost both the fetus and any hope of ever having a child.

In spring 1942, Nancy began working in Heywood Hill's bookshop in Curzon Street, attracting the intelligent and fashionable literati. Later in the year Nancy met the great love of her life, the Free French colonel Gaston Palewski, the model for Fabrice de Sauveterre in *The Pursuit of Love* and Charles-Edouard de Valhubert in *The Blessing* and *Don't Tell Alfred*. Palewski had been commander of the Free French in East Africa and in September 1942 came to London to be General

Charles de Gaulle's *directeur du cabinet*. Nancy was overwhelmed by Palewski and enjoyed an extended period of great happiness until he left with De Gaulle to fight in Algeria. He returned to London for a brief period in summer 1944 before going to France for the invasion and permanently resettling in Paris.

With Evelyn Waugh's encouragement, Nancy began work in 1945 on her fifth novel, *The Pursuit of Love*. During its composition she received word that her brother, Tom, had been killed in combat in Burma. At the end of the war David Mitford gave Nancy a large sum of money, and she used a portion of it to buy a partnership in Heywood Hill's bookshop with the intention of increasing its stock of French literature. With this legitimizing cover she obtained permission from the government to visit Paris on a book-buying trip. The real impetus for the trip was, of course, Gaston Palewski. Though lodged in a dreadful hotel, Nancy again fell in love with Paris and made plans to move there.

THE PURSUIT OF LOVE

Published in December 1945, *The Pursuit of Love* achieved a huge and lasting success, selling over a million copies. It is Mitford's chef d'oeuvre, arguably her best novel and the one for which she is most remembered. Harold Acton argued that its success was largely attributable to timing, as it hit the right moment in the psychology of the British nation; Waugh's equally nostalgic *Brideshead Revisited* was published earlier in 1945, laying the groundwork for the success of Mitford's book. Acton believed that *The Pursuit of Love*'s greatest contribution to literature was as a pseudo-historical documentary record of country-house life among the upper classes in the interwar years. The novel is of course considerably more than that. Among other things, it is largely responsible for the mythologizing of the Mitford family: through *The Pursuit of Love*, together with Jessica Mitford's *Hons and Rebels*, fact and fiction have become almost inextricably entangled. By no means a direct portrait of the actual Mitford family, it borrows liberally from certain aspects of Nancy's family members' lives and idiosyncrasies.

Narrated by the Honourable Frances "Fanny" Logan, the story centers around her cousin, Linda Radlett, one of Aunt Sadie and Uncle Matthew's seven children. Fanny is the daughter of "wicked" parents: her mother, "the Bolter" (a type identified by the Guinnesses as a "female rake" [p. 473]), has fled from one husband to another. As a result, Fanny has been raised by her Aunt Emily but usually spends her holidays at the Radlett home, Alconleigh, where Uncle Matthew's unpredictable temper keeps the children and the house permanently off balance. Uncle Matthew is an undisguised portrait of David Mitford, who, like his fictional persona, was fond of cracking a whip on the front lawn early in the morning, playing opera records on the gramophone, dismissing unfavorable people as "sewers," hating Germans ("the Hun") and foreigners in general, and regularly holding a "child hunt," in which he chased the children across fields with a pack of bloodhounds.

The children take regular happy refuge in the "Hons Cupboard," an overheated linen cupboard high in the otherwise freezing house where meetings of the "Hons" are held: "The Hons was the Radlett secret society, anybody who was not a friend to the Hons was a Counter-Hon, and their battle-cry was 'Death to the horrible Counter-Hons.' I was a Hon, since my father, like theirs, was a lord" (p. 14). Membership of the Hons (short for "honourable," but pronounced with an aspirated "h") was not limited to the children of aristocracy but extended to sympathetic people like the Alconleigh groom, Josh.

On Boxing Day, Aunt Emily arrives with her fiancé, the hypochondriac aesthete Captain Davey Warbeck. Contrary to expectation, Uncle Matthew instantly likes him, as does everyone else. Davey is another of Mitford's ambiguous men; he has identifiably effeminate characteristics, but his marriage to Aunt Emily, the reader is guaranteed, is happily (and unusually in Mitford's fiction) unmarked by adultery or jealousy. This may, however, be Mitford's code for a marriage of convenience that is at root platonic.

As Linda and Fanny grow older, they become obsessed with romance: "What we never would admit was the possibility of lovers after marriage. We were looking for real love, and that could only come once in a lifetime; it hurried to consecration, and thereafter never wavered" (p. 37). When Sadie and Matthew give their eldest daughter, Louisa, a coming-out ball, they are at pains to provide enough men—let alone young eligible men—to balance the numbers and are forced to call upon their flamboyantly aesthetic neighbor, Lord Merlin. Based on the real-life Lord Berners, Merlin has his whippets wear stunning diamond necklaces, and his house is a center of art and youth: "Modern music streamed perpetually from Merlinford, and he had built a small but exquisite playhouse in the garden, where his astonished neighbours were sometimes invited to attend such puzzlers as Cocteau plays, the opera 'Mahagonny,' or the latest Dada extravagances from Paris" (p. 40).

Depressed in the wake of the ball, Linda is taken under Lord Merlin's wing; he provides the education in art and literature she had previously lacked. Like earlier Mitford heroines, Linda desires the witty, bohemian intellectual world but, unlike Philadelphia, Bobbin or Anne Marie Lau, understands that education is required if she can ever hope to find her place among the glittering literati.

Two years later, Linda meets and becomes engaged to the small-minded bourgeois Tony Kroesig, whose family collects houses all over the world and, though English (too recently English for Uncle Matthew's tastes), shows no particular allegiance to Britain. Mirroring Mitford's experience with Hamish Erskine, both fathers are furious about the engagement, and Tony is sent to New York to work in a bank. He soon returns and convinces his father to allow the marriage. No one wants Linda to marry Tony, but Lord Merlin is the only one to speak plainly, arguably echoing Mitford's own philosophy: "You will discover that [love] has nothing to do with marriage" (p. 75). The couple is married nonetheless; Tony soon secures a Conservative seat in the House of Commons and reveals his truly pompous, miserly personality. As Linda is a child of the landed gentry and Tony of the nouveaux riches, class becomes a growing obstacle in the marriage, manifesting itself as much in vocabulary (a theme Mitford enlarges upon in her contribution to *Noblesse Oblige*) as anything else:

> the Kroesigs said notepaper, perfume, mirror and mantelpiece [instead of the upper class equivalents: writing-paper, scent, looking-glass, and chimney-piece], they even invited [Linda] to call them Father and Mother, which, in the first flush of love, she did, only to spend the rest of her married life trying to get out of it by addressing them to their faces as "you," and communicating with them by postcard or telegram. Inwardly their spirit was utterly commercial, everything was seen by them in terms of money.
>
> (p. 78)

Like E. M. Forster's Wilcox family in *Howards End,* the Kroesigs exist solely for the twin causes of capital acquisition and social advancement and find fault with Linda for failing to be an asset and credit to Tony. Linda gives birth to a daughter, Moira, in whom she takes no interest; the child is clearly a Kroesig and a "Counter-Hon" to the marrow. It is a difficult pregnancy, and Linda is warned that she should never again become pregnant. Fanny, meanwhile, marries Alfred Wincham, a young theology don at St. Peter's College, Oxford. She also has a child, though in much happier circumstances, and moves to Oxford with her husband.

Tony and Linda settle into a marriage of mutual convenience. Lord Merlin introduces Linda to London's chattering classes, while Tony busies himself with social and political advancement. Moira, fat and ugly (and all but ignored by Linda), is raised by nannies at her paternal grandparents' house in Surrey. Circumstances change quickly when Linda meets Christian Talbot, a communist journalist modeled in part on Peter Rodd. Linda leaves Tony, who starts divorce proceedings so that he can marry his mistress, Pixie Townsend. Linda and Christian have nothing on which to live, and though Lord Merlin also disapproves of Christian, fearing, as others do, that she is chasing another mirage, he gives Linda the freehold of a house in Cheyne Walk. Linda and Christian have a dreary wedding, with only Fanny and Davey Warbeck representing her side of the family. To make ends meet, Linda starts working in a communist bookshop, attracting her fashionable bohemian set and managing to make it the first profitable English communist bookshop as she stocks it with books people actually want to read.

Christian Talbot travels to Perpignan to help the Spanish Republican refugees, and Linda soon follows, making her first trip abroad, and echoing Mitford's experience with Peter Rodd. Tony was never interested in travel, and Uncle Matthew believed that "abroad is unutterably bloody and foreigners are fiends" (p. 114). While Linda helps by driving a van and visiting the refugee camp, Christian falls in love with Lavender Davis, one of Linda's girlhood friends who, coincidentally, has also come to assist the relief effort. Seeing the inevitability of the situation, Linda quietly departs for Paris, leaving Christian a note suggesting he marry Lavender. Retrospectively she fears she may be turning into another Bolter, just like Fanny's mother, running from one man to the next.

Arriving in Paris, Linda bursts into tears in the Gare du Nord when she discovers that her ticket has expired and she hasn't enough money to return home. She is rescued by a mysterious Frenchman whom she soon discovers is a duke, Fabrice de Sauveterre. He puts her up in a hotel, pays for everything, and in a few days' time has installed her in a flat, taking her as a lover. Like Gaston Palewski (to whom the book was dedicated), Fabrice is not conventionally attractive, but Linda knows that she has truly fallen in love for the first time. She settles into a routine, shopping and sunbathing naked in her flat during the day, entertaining Fabrice at night. When she discovers that he has another mistress, she realizes the futility of making a scene; she knows that, having accepted the terms of the relationship, she can make no claim on him without jeopardizing her happiness and newfound security.

War is looming, and in April 1940 Fabrice urgently sends Linda home to England and her family. Sadie and Matthew still believe she is with Christian, who conveniently does not want a divorce. Linda sits out the first months of the war in her Cheyne Walk house, waiting for news from Fabrice. Finally, in August, Fabrice manages to visit and tells her for the first time that he is truly in love with her. Leaving quickly, he warns her that he may not return until after the war. It is the last time they see each other.

Linda soon finds herself pregnant, and when her Cheyne Walk house is bombed she finally consents to retrench to Alconleigh with the rest of the family. Uncle Matthew prepares to fight the Germans when they come, hoping to hold them off for a few hours at least. The Bolter arrives, with her Spanish lover, Juan, who turns out to be an excellent chef and expert black marketeer, vastly improving everyone's diet, health, and spirits. In May 1941, Linda and Fanny both give birth on the same day. Linda has been looking forward to the birth of her second child, a boy, named Fabrice, but she tragically dies in childbirth. At the same time, the baby's father, Fabrice, is captured and killed by the Gestapo. With the consent of Christian, the legal father, Fanny adopts the baby.

Owing to its aesthetic superiority and lasting popularity, *The Pursuit of Love* has attracted the most critical attention, though even that is scant. Mitford's biographers deal with the novels to a varying degree, focusing most often on the (auto)biographical elements of the fiction rather than assessing them in literary critical terms. The Guinnesses make some efforts in this direction, concluding that Linda is incapable of change, remaining fairly static from her teens to her death. Attempting to distinguish her from any real-life model, they contend that she lacks the trademark Mitford family willpower and native intelligence that might have led to comparisons with Mitford or with any of her sisters. Oddly, this seems to ignore Mitford's professed self-identification with Linda.

In his article "The Fate of the Modern Mistress," Allan Hepburn argues that in *The Pursuit of Love* and its sequel, *Love in a Cold Climate,* marriage and love are portrayed as two independent states that are not necessarily unified or codependent. He contends that Mitford borrowed a model from eighteenth-century French literature, portraying marriage as a business transaction in which love is almost wholly separate. Further, he asserts that Mitford always looks benignly on adultery and treats it as a fact of life rather than as a phenomenon. This is not entirely true, however; in *The Blessing,* the very crux of the novel concerns Grace's despair over Charles-Edouard's penchant for younger women. Hepburn does not consider Linda's death as punishment for her adultery; he argues rather that death is the natural result of motherhood triumphing over—or replacing—the idealized state of love with Fabrice. The reverse occurs in *Love in a Cold Climate,* in which Polly's child dies so that she can find happiness in an adulterous relationship. Mitford was reading Marcel Proust's *À la recherche du temps perdu* throughout the 1940s, and Hepburn conjectures that her satire of the socially aspirant Kroesigs and the snobbish Lord Merlin and other aesthetes might be traceable to Proust.

LOVE IN A COLD CLIMATE

Mitford's sixth novel was published in July 1949; like its predecessor, it achieved great critical and commercial success. *Love in a Cold Climate* takes place roughly in the same period as *The Pursuit of Love,* and Fanny again narrates a lighthearted story of adultery and love gone awry. Backtracking to her late adolescence, Fanny forges a friendship with the Montdore family, lately returned from India where Lord Montdore was viceroy. Lady Montdore takes an immediate liking to and interest in Fanny, who is the same age as the Montdores' only child, Polly. Though the Montdores' fortune will go to Polly, their beloved home, Hampton, must pass to a mysterious male heir, cousin Cedric from Nova Scotia, whom everyone fears is sure to be a typically uncultured North American.

Polly and her mother don't get on with each other, and the stresses grow as other young women, like Fanny, begin to get engaged. Lady Montdore makes clear her disapproval of Alfred Wincham as a husband for Fanny; he has no social standing and is merely a university don at

NANCY MITFORD

a minor Oxford college. Lady Montdore tries to cancel the announcement of their engagement in the papers until Fanny protests that she is genuinely in love. Lady Montdore scoffs: "I should have thought the example of your mother would have taught you something—where has love landed her? Some ghastly white hunter. Love indeed—whoever invented love ought to be shot" (p. 110).

Shortly after Fanny and Alfred's wedding, Polly's aunt, Lady Patricia Dougdale, unexpectedly dies. A few weeks later Polly announces that she and her uncle by marriage, the "Lecherous Lecturer" Boy Dougdale, are going to marry. Boy, unbeknownst to Polly, had once been Lady Montdore's lover and shares her passion for amateur painting and embroidery. The Montdores are furious (Lady Montdore particularly) and disinherit Polly. Both the estate and fortune will now pass to Cedric Hampton. Having only £800 annually, Polly and Boy are forced by finances to live abroad.

Fanny, meanwhile, settles into Oxford's grim social life:

Oxford is a place … designed exclusively for celibate men, all the good talk, good food and good wine being reserved for those gatherings where there are no women; the tradition is in its essence monastic, and as far as society goes wives are quite superfluous.

(pp. 183–184)

Fanny distinguishes herself in Oxford social circles by revealing that she was present for Polly's scandalous wedding. Lady Montdore is a frequent visitor, insulting Fanny's housekeeping and her husband and running up Fanny's phone bill. Lady Montdore soon decides to invite Cedric Hampton to come stay with her in order to get to know the man who will one day bear the Montdore title. Surprisingly, Cedric is currently living in France, where, it transpires, he has been the kept lover of a wealthy baron. He is hardly the backward colonial they had all expected:

He was a tall, thin young man, supple as a girl, dressed in rather a bright blue suit; his hair was the gold of a brass bed-knob, and his insect appearance came from the fact that the upper part of the face

was concealed by blue goggles set in gold rims quite an inch thick.

(p. 210)

Cedric is flamboyantly camp and immediately charms the Montdores, who seem oblivious to his sexual orientation. He convinces his aunt to unearth all her jewels on the night of his arrival, and the two of them spend hours dressing up and applying makeup. Over the course of several months Cedric takes Lady Montdore under his wing, transforming her into a preening peacock, teaching her how to use beauty creams and hair dyes, showing her the benefits of fasting cures and cosmetic surgery. He is not all superficialities, either: he can intelligently discuss Hampton's art and book collections with Lord Montdore. He also becomes a close friend of Fanny's, who takes pains to prevent him meeting any of her young undergraduate friends, worrying that he might be a bad influence. This is virtually the only note of moral concern in what constitutes a revolutionary portrait of homosexuality. Harold Acton regarded Cedric as Mitford's great stroke of originality; to create a happy homosexual was almost unknown in literature, and Cedric stands in stark contrast—perhaps even in rebuttal to—Evelyn Waugh's alcoholically self-destructive Sebastian Flyte in *Brideshead Revisited*. Acton went so far as to suggest that Cedric may have played a role in the growing public tolerance for homosexuality, at least in Britain. American reviews at the time were censorious, seeking in vain for a note of moral indignation in Mitford's characterization of Cedric.

Perhaps even more revolutionary, however, is the novel's conclusion. Boy and Polly, now pregnant, return to Britain, facilitated by the death of an aunt who left Polly everything. Polly has quite plainly fallen out of love with her husband. Supporting Hepburn's argument about the incompatibility of love and motherhood, Polly's baby dies shortly after birth, and she soon takes a lover, while Boy, whose embroidery hobby seems to have been more than idiosyncrasy but an early clue to the true nature of his romantic inclinations, embarks on an affair with Cedric. The fluidity of Boy's sexuality and Cedric's unashamed, even celebratory (albeit stereotypical) homosexuality is a landmark in English literature, not least for the matter-of-factness with which Mitford describes queer relationships.

The Pursuit of Love and *Love in a Cold Climate* have twice been combined under the title of the second novel and adapted for British television: in 1980 by Thames Television and in 2001 by the BBC.

POSTWAR PARIS

Flush with cash from the success of *The Pursuit of Love*, Mitford moved to Paris in spring 1946, living in various borrowed flats before settling in 1947 into her beloved ground-floor rooms at 7, rue Monsieur ("Mister Street") in the seventh arrondissement. Gaston Palewski remained quite formal in their relationship and took care to prevent them from being publicly identified as a couple. To Mitford, he was the love of her life. Beevor and Cooper contend that Palewski discouraged her move to Paris and made clear to her that marriage was impossible, as he would never marry a divorced woman—though Mitford and Rodd would not divorce until 1957. Perhaps more importantly, Mitford could no longer conceive the children Palewski desired.

In 1949, Mitford began contributing a weekly column to the *Sunday Times,* selected installments of which are reprinted in *A Talent to Annoy.* With her indisputable success as a novelist, the 1950s ushered in a period of stability for Mitford, providing her with ample money to indulge her passions for fashion and antiques and eventually allowing her to secure a long-term lease on her rue Monsieur flat. In 1950, Mitford translated two works from French: Madame de Lafayette's novel *La Princesse de Clèves* and André Roussin's play, *La Petite Hutte,* which was produced in the West End and filmed by MGM in 1957 as *The Little Hut,* starring David Niven, Ava Gardner, and Stewart Granger.

In 1951, Mitford published her penultimate novel, *The Blessing,* followed in 1954 by the first of four biographies, *Madame de Pompadour.* Almost certainly enriched by an element of autobiographical passion—many critics have

been tempted to view the choice of subject as elaborate self-portraiture—the book was arguably in the vanguard of the popular biography genre. Greeted with mixed critical response, it was nonetheless a great commercial success and was followed in 1957 by *Voltaire in Love,* which recounts the writer's affair with the Marquise du Châtelet.

Nancy edited and contributed to the 1956 collection *Noblesse Oblige,* a pseudo-serious examination of the (mostly verbal) habits of the English upper-classes that attempted to distinguish between "U" (that is, upper class) and "Non-U" speech.

THE BLESSING

Regarded by Harold Acton as Mitford's finest novel, *The Blessing* reincarnates Linda and Fabrice (again quite transparent portraits of Mitford and Palewski) from *The Pursuit of Love* as the Honourable Grace Allingham and Charles-Edouard de Valhubert. Dedicated to Evelyn Waugh, who at the time also thought it Mitford's finest work—an opinion he would later revise—the book was poorly reviewed and considered to be a step backward in quality from the previous two novels. Nonetheless, it was yet another commercial success. Laura Thompson regards the novel not just as an explanation of French sensibility to an Anglophone audience but, more personally, Mitford's explanation to herself of Gaston Palewski's frenetic philandering. Thompson believes the novel's great strength is its frankly realistic, rather than romantic, representation of the nature of relations between the sexes. As with the two previous novels, there is no authorial moralizing over adultery and fidelity, even if Grace's ultimate self-sacrifice for the sake of love effectively relegates the novel to the prefeminist past. Thompson argues, somewhat unconvincingly, that the novel is *not* prefeminist, simply because Mitford concedes that women may have affairs as readily as men.

Based on a plot developed by the film producer Alexander Korda and subsequently passed to Mitford, *The Blessing* traces the marriage, divorce, and remarriage of Grace and Charles-Edouard, separated for the first seven years of their marriage by World War II. Returning from the war, Charles-Edouard unceremoniously moves Grace, the nanny, and their six-year-old son Sigismond to France, stopping first in Provence, at the family estate of Bellandargues, where he introduces them to his mother, La Marquise, and aunt, Madame Régine Rochard des Innouïs. Charles-Edouard's family privately believes the marriage won't last, not least because it was only a civil and not a Catholic wedding. In the eyes of the church, Charles-Edouard and Grace are not even married, and she has yet to discover his fondness for other women—and most importantly for his "foster sister" and longtime mistress, Albertine Marel-Desboulles. Grace is stunned when La Marquise warns her that the only way for the marriage to survive is if she allows Charles-Edouard everything—and everyone—he desires.

Charles-Edouard and Grace move to his house in Paris, followed some weeks later by Nanny and Sigi. Grace loves Paris, and after Charles-Edouard has outfitted her with better clothes, he begins to introduce her to his extensive extended family, consisting largely of aged ladies: members of the Légion d'Honneur and guardians of the French literary establishment. Grace is awed by their intellectual conversation and is gradually accepted by them and Parisian society. Charles-Edouard recommences his old habit of seeing Albertine every day for tea and discovers that she is having a romance with Grace's ex-fiancé, Hughie Palgrave. Charles-Edouard begins a new affair himself, with the dazzlingly silly (and married) coquette Juliette Novembre de la Ferté. Grace is not oblivious to her husband's interest in Juliette, whom he persistently corners at dinner parties.

In contrast to the witty and glamorous French society in which Grace is increasingly moving, Mitford describes a dinner held by Grace's friend, Carolyn Dexter, and her boorish American husband, Hector Dexter. In Hector, Mitford brilliantly eviscerates the boasting, all-knowing character of postwar Americans abroad. In jargon-larded language, Hector pontificates on every possible subject. Reflecting the early years of the Cold War, Mitford satirizes American attitudes to the arms race by having Dexter implore his fellow Americans to discuss the A-bomb:

> the authorities have issued a very comprehensive little pamphlet entitled "The Bomb and You" designed to bring the bomb into every home and invest it with a certain degree of cosiness. This should calm and reassure the population in case of attack. There are plenty of guidance reunions, fork lunches, and so on where the subject is treated frankly, to familiarize it, as it were, and rob it of all unpleasantness.
>
> (p. 105)

Mitford's famous "anti-American" streak is most obvious in *The Blessing* and in her final novel, *Don't Tell Alfred*, in which Dexter returns. Doubtless tinged by real concern for the assault on European values by the economic and military force of postwar America, Mitford's characterization of Dexter and his fellow Americans is astute and finely wrought satire, though it sits incongruously in the midst of the narrative as an amusement and political aside rather than an integrated element of the plot, which is primarily concerned with Sigi's increasingly calculating efforts to keep his parents apart once they begin to drift.

When Charles-Edouard's mother dies, the family goes into deep traditional mourning, and as a result Sigi spends more time with his father and meets Albertine by chance. Grace becomes aware of her husband's regular tea-time rendezvous and begins to grow jealous, though he assures her it is merely lifelong habit. Grace is increasingly suspicious of her husband, and the suspicions are finally justified when Grace discovers Charles-Edouard and Juliette together in bed. The next day Grace returns to England, taking Sigi and Nanny with her. Sigi, for the first time since his parents were reunited after the war, is the center of attention. He relishes his new status and hopes that his parents will divorce and remarry, providing him with two sets of parents and even more gifts and more attention. Grace's father, Sir Conrad, notably fails to sympathize with Grace's decision, but Charles-Edouard and Grace nonetheless arrange to be divorced; Sigi will spend six months of the year with each parent. When Charles-Edouard comes to fetch his son in

England, Sigi connives to prevent his parents from meeting, though both, feeling ambivalent about the divorce, want to see each other.

Shortly after the separation, Hughie asks Grace to marry him, as he has finished his affair with Albertine, whom he caught in bed with Charles-Edouard. Grace finds that she is not bothered by the news and wonders if she is adopting a more European attitude towards marriage. Sigi, meanwhile, is having a wonderful time with his father, learning about art and antiques and being thoroughly spoiled; in his continuing effort to keep his parents apart he tells his father that Hughie is the love of Grace's life.

The divorce is finalized, and Sigi keeps up a campaign of misinformation and lying obstructionism. Juliette and Albertine, both determined to win Charles-Edouard, recognize that Sigi is the route to his father's heart. Juliette lets Sigi drive her car in the country but makes a misstep when she suggests that if she were his mother, he might have some little siblings. Sigi doesn't want any competition and tells his father that he certainly doesn't want Juliette as a mother, and Charles-Edouard consequently puts Juliette out of his mind.

Grace, meanwhile, has been courted by Ed Spain, owner and manager of a small experimental theater staffed by the "Crew," a group of Marxist young ladies who do all the work and look after Ed, a pompous, self-indulgent hedonist. Spain is an unflinching caricature of Cyril Connolly and his then recently disbanded group of female assistants and secretaries at the magazine *Horizon*. Connolly was a favorite butt of Mitford's barbed private jokes, particularly in her correspondence with Evelyn Waugh.

Sigi returns to England, where Hughie, also recognizing the boy's importance in his mission to win Grace's heart, tries to woo him with outdoor sport but makes a fatal mistake when he takes Sigi to visit Eton, assuring Grace that he can pull the necessary strings to get him enrolled. Sigi is horrified by Eton's penal atmosphere and stories of beatings and warns his mother that she must never marry Hughie.

Grace takes Sigi to see a play at Ed Spain's theater, and Spain, also recognizing Sigi's importance, decides to cast him as the lead in a new play, an obvious Marxist takeoff of *Little Lord Fauntleroy,* which Spain has decided should be transposed from Communist Bratislava to Victorian England. When the Crew hear of his brazenly commercial plans, this is the last straw. Spain's association with the rich bourgeois world was bad enough, but an assault on the Crew's sacrosanct Marxist aesthetic is insupportable. Spain goes to Grace's house to ask her to marry him and asks Sigi to fetch his mother, giving him a miserly small tip. Sigi, used to much bigger payoffs, tells his mother that Spain is a "bloody bastard" and she mustn't marry him.

As is often the case, Mitford relied on a deus ex machina to resolve her plot: Madame Rocher des Innouïs—concerned that Sigi is running amok and that Charles-Edouard is unbalancing Parisian society by having affairs with countless married women—decides that Grace and her nephew must remarry, but in a Catholic ceremony. Visiting London, Madame Rocher suggests to Grace that she must take the first step and allow Charles-Edouard his philandering, which will almost certainly subside as he gets older. Grace agrees, and Sigi is unable to meddle in his parents' relationship when he is suddenly taken to the hospital with appendicitis. Charles-Edouard flies to London. He and Grace finally have the opportunity to see each other alone and manage to piece together Sigi's long string of deceptions. They agree to remarry and, as soon as Sigi is well, make plans to return to Paris. They return in *Don't Tell Alfred,* apparently happy and proving the fruitfulness of Grace's sacrifice.

Notably, Allan Hepburn does not address *The Blessing* in his assessment of the role of adultery in Mitford's oeuvre. This would have effectively undermined the basis of his argument as Grace is deeply pained by Charles-Edouard's affairs, and ultimately, after her reconciliation with her husband, she is able to be both mother and lover simultaneously.

The Blessing was adapted for feature film by MGM in 1959 as *Count Your Blessings,* starring Deborah Kerr, Rossano Brazzi, and Maurice Chevalier, whose casting in an invented role as Sigi's aristocratic French uncle horrified Mitford.

DON'T TELL ALFRED

In 1960, Mitford published her final novel, *Don't Tell Alfred*. An uneven return to the narrative voice of Fanny Logan, the novel sold well but was critically very poorly received. The 1960s saw the deaths of many of Mitford's closest friends and the forward march of an increasingly mechanized modern world from which she felt distinctly estranged, as evidenced at least in part by the despair with which the older characters in *Don't Tell Alfred* face the unrepentant and unapologetic iconoclasm of their children. Consisting largely of farcical episodes and lacking a discernible plot, *Don't Tell Alfred* is arguably the weakest of Mitford's novels in terms of narrative coherence. Even she disliked it and found the process of writing it arduous.

Set in the world of the British Embassy in Paris, Fanny's husband, Alfred Wincham, is appointed Ambassador to France when the former ambassador, Lord Leone, retires. His wife, Lady Leone, refuses to vacate the entresol flat of the Embassy even after Fanny and Alfred arrive. Aided by her former protégé Philip Cliffe-Musgrave, Fanny desperately tries to get rid of Lady Leone, who upstages the Winchams with an endless parade of society visitors. Fanny calls on her Uncle Davey Warbeck, who bribes a man well-known in Parisian society to take the names of all who visit Lady Leone, and who puts out the word to the most fervent gossips that her visitors will be denied invitation to all official Embassy functions. The scheme works, and Lady Leone is spurred to decamp from the Embassy, though not without upstaging Fanny in the process.

The balance of the novel is largely concerned with Fanny's niece, Northey, who arrives to act as social secretary. Northey is beautiful and charming and soon has a flock of the most important men in France pursuing her, while she pines unrequitedly after Philip (who is himself unrequitedly in love with Grace de Valhubert). Northey delegates all of her responsibilities to Fanny, Alfred, and other embassy staff members, allowing her time to practice her French, shop, and look after wayward animals. Even worse, Northey becomes friendly with Amyas Mockbar,

savage columnist for the *Daily Post*, who has a grudge against Alfred and repeatedly publishes libellously false reports about the Winchams. Northey also catches the attention of Charles-Edouard de Valhubert. Horrified that he might be taking advantage of her niece, Fanny confronts him, but he assures her that, if anything, he is doing all he can to encourage the relationship between Northey and Philip, to distract the man from Grace.

Adding to Fanny's problems, she receives a phone call about her youngest sons—Charlie and Fabrice—from their master at Eton, saying that they and Sigi de Valhubert have left the school in a Rolls-Royce, complaining of the appalling food. Fanny goes to London to bring them home, but they now have jobs packing shavers for the astonishing sum of £9 a week and refuse to return to Paris with her.

The novel reaches its climax as a diplomatic dispute erupts between France and Britain over a small cluster of Channel islands, and the Embassy is surrounded by crowds of apparently protesting youths. In fact, they have come to see Yanky Fonzy, the "jazz pop star" for whom Charles and Fabrice are now acting as publicity agents. They arrive on the roof of a black London cab, along with Fanny's aged Uncle Matthew. Alfred and all of the nonmusic press continue to believe the crowds of youths are protestors, and the demonstration effects a resolution of the diplomatic storm. Charles and Fabrice tell Fanny that they are going on a grand tour to Moscow with Yanky Fonzy, but when the pop star reads the next day's papers and sees nothing about his appearance, he fires the boys and leaves without them. The boys, thankfully, seem only too happy to return to normal life.

Harold Acton credited Mitford with a good grasp of the popular youth idiom of the late 1950s but believed the plot was weakened by the weight of Fanny's rather improbably behaved children, whose unpredictable actions force the plot into a farce more characteristic of Mitford's earliest work. Laura Thompson, more correctly, judges Mitford's attempt at capturing the essence of youth culture painfully wide of the mark, failing to evoke accurately the slang of the time (for example, "jazz pop star") while undeniably recognizing the inevitable triumph of youth culture over the establishment. In a review for *London Magazine,* by contrast, Evelyn Waugh claimed that Mitford's skill had reached full maturity in *Don't Tell Alfred.* He regarded the book as an openly socialist novel and considered its narrative incompleteness its greatest feature. One wonders to what extent this judgement, given Waugh's conservative politics and own narrative formality, was a subtle attack on his old friend's work.

LATER YEARS

In 1961, much to Mitford's distress, another of Gaston Palewski's lovers (and a married one, to make things worse) gave birth to his son. Mitford was sure this augured the end of their relationship, but Gaston assured her it did not. He returned to Paris in 1962, after an extended posting as French Ambassador to Rome, to become a minister in Pompidou's government. In the same year, Mitford published a collection of her journalism and essays, *The Water Beetle.*

In 1966, Nancy published her biography of Louis XIV, *The Sun King,* in a lavish illustrated edition that was a phenomenal success and an archetypal "coffee table" book. The following year she left Paris and settled in Versailles, at 4, rue d'Artois. Peter Rodd died in Malta in 1968, and in the same year Mitford began to feel the first symptoms of the illness that eventually killed her. In 1969, Palewski married his son's mother, the recently divorced Violette de Talleyrand-Perigord, duchesse de Sagan. It was a doubly bitter blow, and not long after, Mitford had a large, malignant tumor removed from her liver. Though the doctor told her sisters that Nancy had only four months to live, they kept the diagnosis secret from her and she lived a further four years, suffering from almost constant and debilitating pain, which was somewhat mediated by morphine. She consulted numerous doctors and only in 1972 was properly diagnosed as suffering from Hodgkin's disease.

After a physically taxing research tour of East Germany as a guest of the government, she published her last book, the biography *Frederick the Great,* in 1970. In 1972, she was awarded the French Légion d'Honneur and appointed CBE in Britain.

She died on 30 June 1973, at home in Versailles, with Gaston Palewski beside her. By sheer coincidence, he had been passing and claimed to have had a presentiment of her death. Her ashes were buried at Swinbrook, alongside her sister, Unity, and her parents.

Selected Bibliography

WORKS OF NANCY MITFORD

NOVELS
Highland Fling. London: Butterworth, 1931.
Christmas Pudding. London: Butterworth, 1932.
Wigs on the Green. London: Butterworth, 1935.
Pigeon Pie. London: Hamilton, 1940.
The Pursuit of Love. London: Hamilton, 1945; Garden City, N.Y.: Sun Dial Press, 1947.
Love in a Cold Climate. London: Hamilton, 1949.
The Blessing. London: Hamilton, 1951; New York: Random House, 1951.
Don't Tell Alfred. London: Hamilton, 1960.

ESSAYS AND JOURNALISM
The Water Beetle. London: Hamilton, 1962; New York: Harper & Row, 1962.
A Talent to Annoy: Essays, Articles, and Reviews, 1929–1968. Edited by Charlotte Mosley. London: Hamilton, 1986.

BIOGRAPHIES
Madame de Pompadour. London: Hamilton, 1954: New York: Random House, 1954.
Voltaire in Love, London: Hamilton, 1957.
The Sun King. London: Hamilton, 1966; New York: Harper & Row, 1966.
Frederick the Great. London: Hamilton, 1970.

TRANSLATIONS
La Fayette, Madame de (Marie-Madeleine Pioche de la Vergne). *The Princess of Cleves.* London: Euphorion, 1950.
Roussin, André. *The Little Hut.* London: Hamilton, 1951.

EDITED WORKS
The Ladies of Alderley: Being the Letters between Maria Josepha, Lady Stanley of Alderley, and Her Daughter-in-

Law Henrietta Maria Stanley during the Years 1841–1850. London: Chapman & Hall, 1938.

The Stanleys of Alderley: Their Letters between the Years 1851–1865. London: Chapman & Hall, 1939.

Noblesse Oblige: An Enquiry into the Identifiable Characteristics of the English Aristocracy. London: Hamilton, 1956; New York: Harper & Row, 1956.

CORRESPONDENCE

The Letters of Nancy Mitford: Love from Nancy. Edited by Charlotte Mosley. London: Hodder & Stoughton, 1993. As *Love from Nancy: The Letters,* Boston: Houghton Mifflin, 1993.

The Letters of Nancy Mitford and Evelyn Waugh. Edited by Charlotte Mosley. London: Hodder & Stoughton, 1996.

ADAPTATIONS

Count Your Blessings. Screenplay by Karl Tunburg. Directed by Jean Negulesco. Metro-Goldwyn-Mayer, 1959.

The Little Hut. Screenplay by André Roussin. Directed by Mark Robson. Metro-Goldwyn-Mayer, 1957.

Love in a Cold Climate. Screenplay by Simon Raven. Directed by Donald McWhinnie. Thames Television, 1980.

Love in a Cold Climate. Screenplay by Deborah Moggach. Directed by Tom Hooper. BBC, 2001.

CRITICAL AND BIOGRAPHICAL STUDIES

Acton, Harold. *Memoirs of an Aesthete.* London: Methuen, 1948.

———. *More Memoirs of an Aesthete.* London: Methuen, 1970.

———. *Nancy Mitford, A Memoir.* London: Hamilton, 1975.

Allen, Brooke. "A Talent to Delight: Nancy Mitford in Her Letters." *The New Criterion* 12:58-62 (1994).

The Letters of Evelyn Waugh. Edited by Mark Amory. London: Weidenfeld & Nicolson, 1980; New York: Ticknor & Fields, 1980.

Atkins, John Alfred. "Nancy Mitford: The Uncrossable Bridge." In his *Six Novelists Look at Society: An Enquiry into the Social Views of Elizabeth Bowen, L. P. Hartley, Rosamund Lehman, Christopher Isherwood, Nancy Mitford, C. P. Snow.* London: Calder, 1977. Pp. 166–199.

Amory, Mark, ed. *The Letters of Evelyn Waugh.* London: Weidenfeld & Nicolson, 1980; New York: Ticknor & Fields, 1980.

Balfour, Patrick. *Society Racket: A Critical Survey of Modern Social Life.* London: John Long, 1932.

Beevor, Antony, and Artemis Cooper. *Paris after the Liberation, 1944–1949.* London: Hamilton, 1994.

Byron, Robert. *Letters Home.* Edited by Lucy Butler. London: Murray, 1991.

———. *The Road to Oxiana.* London: Macmillan, 1937.

Carpenter, Humphrey. *The Brideshead Generation.* London: Weidenfeld & Nicolson, 1989.

Dalley, Jan. *Diana Mosley.* London: Faber & Faber Ltd., 1999; New York: Alfred A. Knopf, 1999.

Davie, Michael, ed. *The Diaries of Evelyn Waugh.* London: Weidenfeld & Nicolson, 1976; New York: Little Brown, 1976.

De Courcy, Anne. *Diana Mosley.* London: Chatto & Windus, 2003.

Devonshire, Deborah Vivien Freeman-Mitford Cavendish, Duchess of. *Counting My Chickens: And Other Home Thoughts.* Introduction by Tom Stoppard. Illustrated by Will Topley. Edited by Sophia Topley and Susan Hill. Ebrington, U.K.: Long Barn Books, 2001; New York: Farrar, Straus, and Giroux, 2002.

Fussell, Paul. *Wartime: Understanding and Behaviour in the Second World War.* New York and Oxford: Oxford University Press, 1989.

Forbes, Alastair. "The Mitford Style." *Times Literary Supplement,* September 12, 1975, pp. 1020-21.

The Essays, Articles and Reviews of Evelyn Waugh. Edited by Donat Gallagher. London: Methuen, 1983.

Greenidge, Terrence. *Degenerate Oxford?* London: Chapman & Hall, 1930.

Griffin, Roger. *The Nature of Fascism.* London: Pinter Publishers, 1991.

Griffiths, Richard. *Fellow Travellers of the Right: British Enthusiasts for Nazi Germany, 1933–39.* London: Constable, 1980.

Guinness, Jonathan, and Catherine Guinness. *The House of Mitford.* London: Hutchinson, 1984.

Hastings, Selina. *Evelyn Waugh.* London: Sinclair-Stevenson, 1994.

———. *Nancy Mitford.* London: Hamilton, 1985.

Hepburn, Allan. "The Fate of the Modern Mistress: Nancy Mitford and the Comedy of Marriage." *Modern Fiction Studies.* vol. 45, no. 2. Baltimore: Johns Hopkins University Press, 1999.

Brian Howard: Portrait of a Failure. Edited by Marie-Jacqueline Lancaster. London: Anthony Blond, 1968.

Lees-Milne, James. *Another Self.* London: Hamish Hamilton, 1970.

Lovell, Mary S. *The Mitford Girls: The Biography of an Extraordinary Family.* London: Little, Brown, 2001.

McDonough, Donald. "Off With Their Heads: The British Novel and the Rise of Fascism." *Tennessee Philological Bulletin: Proceedings of the Annual Meeting of the Tennessee Philological Association* 33:34-42 (1996).

Mitford, Jessica. *A Fine Old Conflict.* London: Michael Joseph, 1977.

———. *The Making of a Muckraker.* London: Michael Joseph, 1979.

———. *Hons and Rebels.* London: Gollancz, 1960.

Mosley, Diana. *A European Diary: Notes from the 1950s and 1960s.* Francestown, N.H: Typographeum, 1990.

———. *The Duchess of Windsor.* London: Sidgwick & Jackson, 1980.

———. *A Life of Contrasts.* London: Hamish Hamilton, 1977.

———. *Loved Ones.* London: Sidgwick & Jackson, 1985.

Mosley, Nicholas. *Rules of the Game.* London: Secker & Warburg, 1992.

———. *Beyond the Pale.* London: Secker & Warburg, 1993.

Mosley, Oswald. *The Greater Britain.* London: BUF Publications, 1932.

———. *Tomorrow We Live.* London: Greater Britain Publications, 1938.

———. *My Answer.* London: Mosley Publications, 1946.

———. *The Alternative.* London: Mosley Publications, 1947.

———. *Europe, Faith and Plan.* Dublin: Euphorion Books, 1958.

———. *My Life.* London: Thomas Nelson & Sons, 1968.

Murphy, Sophia. *The Mitford Family Album.* London: Sidgwick & Jackson, 1985.

Palewski, Gaston. *Hier et Aujourd'hui.* Paris: Plon, 1975.

———. *Mémoires d'action, 1924–1974.* Edited by Eric Roussel. Paris: Plon, 1988.

Parise, Marina Patta. "Nancy Mitford: A Bibliography." *Bulletin of Bibliography* 46:3–9 (1989).

Payne, Stanley. *A History of Fascism, 1914–45.* Wisconsin: University of Wisconsin Press, 1995; London: UCL Press, 1995.

Pryce-Jones, David. *Unity Mitford: A Quest.* London: Weidenfeld & Nicolson, 1976.

Skidelsky, Robert. *Oswald Mosley.* London: Macmillan, 1975.

Stannard, Martin. *Evelyn Waugh: The Early Years, 1903–1939.* London: Dent, 1986.

———. *Evelyn Waugh: No Abiding City, 1939–1966.* London: Dent, 1992.

Thompson, Laura. *Life in a Cold Climate: Nancy Mitford, a Portrait of a Contradictory Woman.* London: Review, 2003.

Thurlow, Richard. *Fascism in Britain, 1918–1985.* New York and Oxford: Basil Blackwell, 1987.

Waugh, Evelyn. *Brideshead Revisited: The Sacred and Profane Memories of Captain Charles Ryder.* London: Chapman & Hall, 1945; Boston: Little, Brown, 1945.

———. *Put Out More Flags.* Chapman & Hall, 1942; New York: Little, Brown, 1942.

———. *Vile Bodies.* London: Chapman & Hall, 1930; New York: Cape, Smith, 1930.

Wodehouse, P. G. *Code of the Woosters.* London: H. Jenkins, 1938.

JAN MORRIS

(1926–)

Michele Gemelos

JAN MORRIS IS an extraordinarily prolific and celebrated Anglo-Welsh writer who has sustained commercial and critical success through her versatility in form and subject, engaging descriptions of people and places, and zest for life. Her curiosity and enthusiasm for exploration has fueled her career as a journalist, historian, reviewer, essayist, editor, and novelist for over fifty years. Morris' works display her carefree approach to travel and a romantic sympathy for arcane figures and ideas, which are often illuminated by her evocative and insightful commentaries. Between 1956 and 2002 Morris produced more than forty publications, all of which underscore her allied interests in literature, history, biography, art, and politics. They include eight volumes of essays, more than two dozen travel books, and three novels, the first of which—*Last Letters from Hav*—was short-listed for the Booker Prize in 1985. Morris decided to formally end her book-writing career at age seventy-five, using the publication of *Trieste and the Meaning of Nowhere* in 2001 as an autobiographical adieu. She continues to contribute reviews, articles, and letters to many literary, specialist, and popular periodicals and newspapers both in North America and Europe. Additionally she has written introductions for essay collections, some of which she has also edited.

The British journalist Alistair Cooke once called Morris "the Flaubert of the jet age," and the *Times Literary Supplement* described her as a "motorized scholar gypsy" in a review of her book *Oxford* (1965). These compliments verge on caricature, and they gloss over Morris' complexity as a writer and as a personality while encouraging the interchangeability of the "public" and "private" Jan. Morris is, however, as challenging to pigeonhole as her work is to categorize: formerly James, Jan underwent a sex change, which she cataloged in a revealing 1974 autobiography entitled *Conundrum*. Well-publicized and a best-seller, the text has been praised for its candid but sensitive reflections on being transgendered and on society in general in the 1970s.

Whether writing as James or as Jan, Morris has been called both capricious and predictable. Morris' style and oeuvre have been mostly admired, occasionally mimicked, and very rarely completely dismissed by other writers and reviewers. Critical reception of her work has fluctuated over time, but her contribution to twentieth-century travel writing is indisputable. The allure of her writing goes beyond the enticing exoticism or cozy familiarity of her chosen subject, whether geographical or philosophical. Her trademarks include paradoxical tendencies toward dreamy subjectivity and wry observation, hyperbole and nuance, reflection and prognostication. These cross-impulses propel, rather than hinder, her work, which is full of anecdotes and character sketches, wordplay and narrative meandering. Morris' lyrical prose also showcases her masterful eavesdropping skills and her eye for patterns, rhythm, and neologism.

The journalist Paul Clements, who has written the only manuscript-length study of Morris' life and work to date as part of the Writers of Wales series, adds the following elements to her stylistic repertoire: paradigms, eponyms, linguistic compression, acronyms, initialisms, ciphers, abbreviations, reduplication, and a "distinctive Morrisian battery of much-favoured words" (Clements, pp. 39, 5). Readers can quickly discover these after scanning her essays—the form that provides the most succinct introduction to her diction and method. Many of these have been collected (and some are reduplicated) in volumes simply entitled

Cities (1963), *Places* (1972), *Travels* (1976), *Destinations* (1980), *Journeys* (1984), and *Locations* (1992).

Although Morris has undeniably influenced the contemporary genre of travel writing, she has often done so while producing texts that celebrate old-fashioned virtues, as her writings on the British Empire, the Commonwealth, and Wales reveal. Furthermore, she is not fond of her labeling and marketing as a "travel writer," preferring, if pushed, to call herself, a "traveling writer." She has pleaded passionately that her publications should belong to categories of their own. Morris used her contribution to a 1992 collection of women's writing entitled *The Writer on Her Work* to underscore this opinion:

> I am a travelling writer—not a travel writer, a category I reject, but a writer who travels. That I write about place is almost incidental to my vocation. I am really an essayist, often of an all too protracted kind, but it so happens that the Second World War, by making me a traveler whether I wanted it or not, provided me with a particular range of subject matter—the matter of place, which I have manipulated ever since in works of memoir, description, history, and fiction.
>
> (Steinberg ed., p. 95)

As evident in that manifesto, self-representation and transition are dominant themes of Morris' work. The figurative language she uses encourages readers to see her writing as a process akin to trying to mold a form out of ethereal substances—manipulating the raw material only to find that the shape can shift endlessly. Regardless of her desire to make her writing the most central concern of her readership, her public transformation during the 1960s and 1970s from James to Jan has been the most compelling of her shape shifts. *Conundrum* is a retrospective study of "incessant wandering as an outer expression of my inner journey" as a transsexual (p. 88). In a new introduction to the 2001 edition, Morris emphasizes that her gender conundrum was more than just a social or biological riddle:

> I thought it was a matter of spirit, a kind of divine allegory, and that explanations of it were not very important anyway. What was important was the liberty of us all to live as we wished to live, to love however we wanted to love, and to know ourselves, however peculiar, disconcerting or unclassifiable, at one with the gods and angels.
>
> (p. x)

The metamorphosis from James to Jan is only one of many gradual changes that provide an organizational frame for her oeuvre. Morris' professional development from journalist into essayist and novelist has paralleled very orthodox stages of a privileged mid-twentieth-century life, which included attending Oxford both as a boy chorister and as a mature student of English literature, military service in World War II, marriage, and fatherhood. Within each of her works, readers can sense her acute awareness of natural cycles and learning processes. Morris presents investigative and preliminary hypotheses rather than authoritative declarations, calling her life "a quest for unity," noting that "Every aspect of my life is relevant to that quest—not only the sexual impulses, but all the sights, sounds and smells of memory, the influences of buildings, landscapes, comradeships, the power of love and of sorrow, the satisfactions of the senses as of the body (p. 6).

Current book-length scholarship about Morris' writing is limited to Clements' 1998 Writers of Wales monograph, but reviews of her books abound, and within them critics have focused on her evolving style and political views, which are shaped by her cautious Europhilia and lifelong republicanism. Although she does not actively subscribe to "traveling theory" or employ jargon from literary criticism or political science, Morris does obliquely discuss the dynamics of exchange between disparate cultures and the manipulation or interference involved in observing and penetrating spaces, histories, cultures, and personalities. One subject that benefits from her multidisciplinary approach to travel is the history and significance of Wales, not only to her own worldview but to Western civilization. Her championing of Wales stems from a deep admiration for the land and the Welsh language, and this has earned her membership into the Gorsedd of Bards, an association of individuals who have made significant contributions to Welsh culture.

Nevertheless, her timely commentaries on Eurofederalism and Welsh devolution have drawn more interest from her British and Continental readers than from readers in North America, where Morris has enjoyed a greater reputation for her travel impressionism and autobiographical revelations. There have been notable exchanges in various literary journals and newspapers about Morris' sex change and its possible effects on her writing—the contentious issue being whether her writing has suffered as a result of becoming a woman. For Morris and for her audience, the biographical sometimes competes with the bibliographical for attention. Her opinion of public interest in her gender fluctuates between gracious understanding of what is mainly natural curiosity and sheer outrage at invasive questions.

In the past, Morris also wrote several letters to editors in response to imbalanced reviews about her work. Some of these letters chastise critics for lapses in their research, but they all indicate her disdain for negative comments and the needless backbiting within the literary establishment. A positive result of her feedback to the press is the additional insight it provides into her writing process and self-image. One such response appeared in a January 11, 1974, letter to the editor of the *Times Literary Supplement,* in which Morris rejected a reviewer's categorization of her and her work, proclaiming that *Heaven's Command* (1973), part of her Pax Britannica trilogy, belongs

> immodestly perhaps, in a literary category of its own, being an amalgam of travel writing, reconstruction, retrospect and imagination. ... If there is one status in my life to which I vehemently do not aspire, it is that of "academic commentator." I write simply to give pleasure to myself and others of similar taste.
>
> (p. 32)

Immensely quotable, Morris often portrays herself as a literary free agent by rejecting institutional affiliations and labeling. She can be critical of academic writing and the formal study of literature; moreover, she does not find the application of the term "journalistic" to her work dismissive, contrary to certain trends in literary criticism and history.

Morris tended to agree, however, with the scholarly backlash against *Lincoln: A Foreigner's Quest* (1999), which was seen as a "fantastically self-indulgent concoction of suppositions" by the conservative British historian Andrew Roberts. Nonetheless, other critics ignored the historical inaccuracies of the work and celebrated Morris' frank exploration of the mythology surrounding the sixteenth American president. Although she has always defended her personal and imaginative approach to history, Morris decided that her impressionistic book *Trieste and the Meaning of Nowhere* (2001) would be the last she would publish.

The pursuit of pleasure through travel and writing has taken Morris around the world, and her popularity has been bolstered by her sustained appeal to individualism as well as collective human experience. Fans of her brand of "historical romanticism," Welsh patriots, Europhiles, transgender activists, and armchair travelers make up her motley readership. At age seventy-five, however, Morris has settled into the corner of the world she finds most habitable and hospitable— Wales, in close proximity to her birthplace in western England.

EARLY LIFE: FROM COLLEGE CHORISTER TO QUEEN'S SOLDIER

Catherine Jan Morris was born James Humphry Morris in Somerset, England, on October 2, 1926, to a Welsh father, Walter Henry, and an English mother, Enid. The Morrises had two older sons, Gareth and Christopher. Young James's love of this western county of Britain and, more importantly, of Wales, was solidified as a child while exploring the surrounding landscape with a telescope that gave him "a private insight into distant worlds" (*Conundrum,* p. 3). Jan Morris has discussed her "double possession" of England and of Wales afforded by a childhood on the border of the two nations and by mixed parentage. Precocious thoughts about the land were coupled with James's preternatural awareness of having been born into the wrong body, thinking as a child that "Perhaps one day, when I grew up, I would be as solid as other people appeared to be: but perhaps I was meant always to be a creature of wisp or spindrift, loitering in this inconsequential way almost as thought I were intangible" (*Conundrum*, p. 5).

In 1936 James was sent to the choir school of Christ Church, Oxford University. This early identification with a select group, specifically trained for service, continued later in life in the army and as a newspaper correspondent. Morris has proclaimed that "Oxford made me," as the contemplative and mystical environment of the cathedral nurtured the longing to be female. Here the young James "moulded my conundrum into an intent" and literally prayed for divine intervention (p. 14). After six years as a chorister, James began boarding at Lancing College, a private boy's school that was forced to move its campus from Sussex to the Welsh-English border county of Shropshire at the outbreak of World War II. The atmosphere at Lancing, dominated by the activities of the Lancing College Officers Training Corps and corporal punishment, left him perpetually scared save for two pleasures: cycling in the countryside and the admiration received from older boys. He left Lancing at age seventeen to pursue journalism, covering war news in Britain before volunteering for the army and training at the Royal Military Academy, Sandhurst. Morris served as an intelligence officer in the Ninth Queen's Royal Lancers in Italy, Egypt, and Palestine at the end of the British mandate of the area. While serving in this regiment Morris felt "more proudly feminine at heart" and was able to acquire the analytical and observational skills crucial for a career as a writer, developing "an almost anthropological interest in the forms and attitudes of its society. ... It was like eavesdropping by license" (*Conundrum*, pp. 23, 27). In her writings about these years, Morris relays her sense of alienation despite the camaraderie of the regiment: "It is a fine thing to be independent in life, and a proud sensation to know yourself to be unique: but a person who stands all on his own, utterly detached from his fellows, may come to feel that reality itself is an illusion" (p. 33).

To overcome this distance, Morris embraced the familial aspects of regimental life and was treated by fellow soldiers as a confidant. As a lancer, Morris was also able to travel extensively throughout the Mediterranean, which provided the rich first impressions that would inform her later travel writings.

LIFE AFTER DEMOB: JOURNALISM

After demobilization, James Morris moved to London, where he took a short course in Arabic. He also met and fell in love with Elizabeth Tuckniss, who had been working in the Women's Royal Naval Service. Morris hid nothing about his sexual predicament from Elizabeth, who married him in 1949 and ardently supported Morris' career as well as his decision to change sex. First as James then as Jan, Morris has dedicated many books to Elizabeth, and together they had five children between the early 1950s and early 1960s: Mark, Henry, Twm, Susan, and Virginia, who died in infancy. Although they divorced later on, Jan and Elizabeth still live together today in the small north Wales village of Llanystumdwy. In *Conundrum*, Morris reflected: "It was a marriage that had no right to work, yet it worked like a dream, living testimony, one might say, to the power of mind over matter—or of love in its purest sense over everything else" (p. 51).

James Morris worked in Egypt for a short time as a journalist with the Arab News Agency but returned to Oxford to study English as a mature undergraduate at Christ Church, where he also edited the university's student publication *Cherwell* and worked as a trainee subeditor on the *Times* foreign desk in 1951. While he was working with the *Times*, his big journalistic break came when, in 1953, the twenty-six-year-old Morris was selected by Sir John Hunt to accompany the British Mount Everest expedition and to detail the challenges and progress of the Himalayan journey. Morris' exclusive reports were sent back to the *Times* in clandestine code in order to prevent interception and disappointment. A leak justified this plan: Morris was scooped, but the report led newspapers to believe that Sir Edmund Hillary and the Nepalese sherpa Tenzing Norgay ascended on 29 May. Hunt's crew reached the peak one day before Queen Elizabeth's coronation, which took place on June 2, 1953. The story of the ascent seized the British public's interest, providing an extra reason for celebrating imperial virtues on Coronation Day. Morris' retrospective book *Coronation Everest* (1958) is enlivened by his race against other reporters as well as the crew profiles interspersed through the narrative. As a *Times Literary Supplement* reviewer recognized, "Mr. James Morris's story is really of newsgathering, not climbing" (E. Coxhead, "News from the Mountain Top," *Times Literary Supplement,* March 14, 1958, p. 136).

Two years before *Coronation Everest* appeared, Morris published his first book of travel writing entitled *As I Saw the USA* or *Coast to Coast* in the United Kingdom. As a Harkness Commonwealth Fund fellow, Morris studied international relations at the University of Chicago and toured the States with his family in tow. He wrote a series of articles for the *Times* and conducted a lecture tour much in the spirit of earlier British literary travelers to America, such as Charles Dickens or Oscar Wilde. Morris articulated the book's aim in a revised introduction: "to demonstrate that behind the lacquered façade of the affluent society many an old cranny, alley-way and courtyard unexpectedly survives" (*Coast to Coast,* p. 12). Yet Morris' infatuation with New York as a capital of culture and commerce gave the city a privileged place in his survey; he calls it "the gateway of America, and the most dazzling expression of its lingering diversity"(p. 12). This introduction to the United States planted impressions and ideas that Morris would follow up with subsequent essays and books on American places and civilization in the 1970s and 1980s.

Morris returned to the Middle East as a *Times* correspondent to report on the British withdrawal from the region and its fallout—most notably the Suez crisis. Building on his interest in the changing Middle East, developed while serving with the Ninth Royal Lancers, he gathered materials for two books on aspects of modern Arab life: *Sultan in Oman* and *Market of Seleukia* (both

1957), but he resigned from the *Times* because the newspaper had a policy preventing its writers from publishing books. He then joined the editorial staff of the *Guardian* in 1957, moved his family to the French Alps, and pursued book writing full-time. While living there Morris published *South African Winter* (1958) and *The Hashemite Kings* (1959); the former is a study of the social and political impact of the apartheid regime and the latter is a dynastic history.

Morris expanded the scope of his writing to include a political review of Britain in the early 1960s. *The Outriders: A Liberal View of Britain* (1963) presents Morris' fervent belief that Britain had a moral and social responsibility to engage with Europe: "our role should be that of Outriders to the main army—out in front, independent-minded and resourceful." That same year, Morris was commissioned to write *The World Bank: A Prospect,* which was published as *The Road to Huddersfield: A Journey to Five Continents* in the United States, where it was a Book-of-the-Month Club selection. Rather than presenting a technical analysis of the World Bank's projects and structures, Morris examined the organization's effectiveness as an agent for sustained development, tracing the impact of its policies on a range of newly industrialized regions.

By 1960 Morris' restlessness within the confines of journalism increased, and he rejected a move to the *Observer,* citing philosophical differences with the paper. Morris negotiated a part-time reporting schedule with the *Guardian* from 1957 to 1962 that allowed him to write with more freedom. Despite having won the George Polk Award for Journalism in 1961, Morris eventually ended his full-time newspaper work after establishing his name as a traveling writer with a seventh book, *Venice* (1960), published to critical acclaim.

(E)VOCATIONAL WRITING: MORRIS' TRAVEL LITERATURE AND HISTORIES

Jan Morris has written that the decade spent as a foreign correspondent instilled in her "a cynical disregard for fame, power, and consequence: but it also disqualified me once and for all for the routines and preoccupations of life at home" (in Steinburg, p. 96). Her travel literature exhibits belletristic elements of late nineteenth- and early-twentieth-century writing; it is elegant and modulated, dealing with social issues coolly and stylishly rather than crudely remonstrating. Critics have seen thematic and stylistic similarities between Morris' work and the writings of Joseph Conrad, Rudyard Kipling, Osbert Sitwell, Ford Madox Ford, and James Pope-Hennessey, among others. To call Morris' writing "belles lettres" may seem like disapprobation, but many of her essays and books unfold in an anachronistically charming manner—conducting a traditional type of *flânerie* as she observes the "oriental" features of her subjects with an awareness of the "occidental" orientation of her audience. This is particularly evident in her writings about the declining British empire. Morris' ability to launch discussions on the formation of national character based on quotidian observations shows her aptitude for balancing the lightweight and the serious as well as the particular and the universal. As she vacillates between them, Morris searches for connections between places across time, all while summarizing the epistemological process that goes beyond the simple viewing of a landscape. At its best, her portraiture invites her readers to join her, promoting her belief that her evocations can bridge gaps in time and distance. In some reviewers' estimations, Morris' sentimentality and gentility toward her subjects has increased since the 1970s.

Her most celebrated travel "portraits" are of *Venice* (1960), *Oxford* (1965), and *Spain* (first published as *The Presence of Spain* in 1964). Along with her Pax Britannica trilogy about the peak and decline of the British empire, the 1960s travel texts have received the most substantive praise from critics. Both cities of the mind and modern metropolises have a venerated place in her corpus, with Venice, New York, Oxford, and Trieste ranking high in her considerations. Her rapture with these places is evolutionary: she has modified her opinions in revised editions and in new introductions, prefaces, envois, and afterwords. Although her love of fabulous and famous cities has not waned, Morris used her last book to challenge her readers to see the exceptional in a seemingly unremarkable, passed-over place like Trieste. More straightforward if only by comparison to *Trieste,* Morris' earlier city portraits often reaffirm the reputations of these centers of civilization.

James Morris first visited Venice as an army officer, but in 1959 he returned to live there with his family. *Venice* (1960) presented his not "merely sensual, but actually sexual" experience of the city (Clements, p. 22). The Royal Society of Literature acknowledged Morris' achievement in 1961 with an award intended, paradoxically, to promote the work of lesser-known writers whose work might not succeed commercially. It quickly became a classic of twentieth-century travel writing and Morris' most successful book, selling over two hundred thousand copies and still in print in a third paperback edition. As a report on the contemporary state of the city at the end of 1950s, *Venice* eschews a linear presentation of the city's history; instead, factual fragments are enmeshed in scenic descriptions. In later years Jan Morris identified the opening passage of *Venice* as her favorite extract:

> At 45° 14'N., 12° 18'E., the navigator, sailing up the Adriatic coast of Italy, discovers an opening in the long low line of the shore: and turning westward, with the race of the tide, he enters a lagoon. Instantly, the boisterous sting of the sea is lost. The water around him is shallow but opaque, the atmosphere curiously translucent, the colours pallid, and over the whole wide bowl of mudbank and water there hangs a suggestion of melancholy. It is like an albino lagoon.

For Morris, labyrinthine Venice is a conundrum with no clear solution: caught between tradition and modernity, the city faces destruction either from external developers or from nature: If left alone, Morris couches the city's fate in bleak terms: "She potters down the years as a honeymoon city, part art gallery, part burlesque, her mighty monuments mere spectacles, her wide suzerainties reduced for ever to the cheap banalities of the guides" (p. 247).

This use of obsolete words or jargon such as "suzerainties" (meaning "spheres of influence" or "positions of authority") has elicited mixed reviews. On the one hand, the retrograde tone of the term taps into Venice's past grandeur and emphasizes Morris' consumption of the complex history of the place. On the other, the strangeness of it distances the reader. Bridging the gap between the city and the reader is made more difficult by the layout of Venice itself, floating tentatively in the present on dissolving foundations, and Morris attempts to preserve in print the potency of the eroding landscape. In a review entitled "Venice Preserved" in the *Times Literary Supplement* (August 12, 1960), John Russell noted that, among the many volumes about the city, Morris admired the American writer Mary McCarthy's *Venice Observed* and also drew inspiration from older accounts such as John Ruskin's *The Stones of Venice*. Russell nevertheless compliments Morris' ambitious project, analyzing the process behind it:

> To attempt a new kind of book about Venice is almost as daring, in its field, as to climb nearly to the top of Mount Everest with no experience of mountaineering, and Mr. Morris does the one as he did the other, with every appearance of aplomb. "Overconfidence" in descriptions moves from strained description to "an unfeigned easiness." He makes no attempt, moreover, to hide his weaknesses—good on history, not great on painting, sculpture or architecture.

(p. 515)

As Morris was a former reporter for the *Times*, it seems appropriate, if only coincidental, that the *Times Literary Supplement* has been a lively forum for Morris' debates about literary categories and style. Russell's contribution is characteristic of the balanced reception Morris has received on the pages of the *TLS*.

Morris prefers not to view her movement away from factual reportage as a digression from her craft, as other journalists might. She constantly reevaluates, amends, and combines her interpretations of places in new editions or collections that benefit from the sum total of her writing experiences. Whether by simply updating information or by retracing her steps, Morris seems to enjoy the "revision" of her visions, and this is apparent after reading her many updated introductions and epilogues.

She has unabashedly expressed her admiration for certain writers while paving her way apart from earlier practitioners of her craft. Morris' influences abound, drawn from journalism, visual art, music, and literature. Among the artists, thinkers, and adventurers she most admires or feels akin to she lists Jane Austen, Robert Browning, Benjamin Disraeli, Harold Nicholson and Vita Sackville-West, John Ruskin and J. M. Turner, T. E. Lawrence, and the poet and British consul J. E. Flecker, with whom Morris shares a more ambassadorial experience of the Mediterranean and the Middle East (*Conundrum*, p. 82). Morris' enthusiasm for illustrations led to her collaborations with the photographer Paul Wakefield on *Wales, the First Place* (1982), *Scotland, the Place of Visions* (1986), and *Ireland, Your Only Place* (1990). The photographs serve as touchstones and enhancements of Morris' rich descriptions, and in the relationship between the photos and her texts one is reminded of the symbiosis between art and literature exemplified by Turner's painting *Ruskin's View*, so named after Turner heard of Ruskin's enthusiasm for the work.

In writing about her literary influences, Morris reserves a special recognition for Alexander Kinglake, the Somerset-born author of *Eothen* (1844) and avid supporter of women's rights. A starkly personal collection of impressions from Eastern Europe and the Near and Middle East, *Eothen* was instrumental in expanding the reach and deepening the tone of travel literature. Morris has discussed the similarities between her style and Kinglake's, such as the presence of the writer's personality in every aspect of the prose (Clements, p. 96). In the introduction to the Oxford University Press 1982 edition of *Eothen*, Morris writes:

> Such was the journey this book describes—or rather, does not describe, for there was never a travel book more intensely subjective and selective, more immune to the orthodox demands of descriptive reportage[...] *Eothen* is sub-titled Traces of Travel, but it is not the travel that is important in

this work, only the traces it left upon its author's very particular sensibility.

(pp. ix, x)

The term or name "Eothen" means "from the early dawn" or "from the east," and the book's full subtitle is "Traces of Travel Brought Home from the East." As with Kinglake, many of Morris' writings have sprung from her Eastern travels and from similar self-revelation and illumination. In her travel essays, as in *Trieste and the Meaning of Nowhere,* the juxtaposition of east and west as well as light and dark is extensive. Some of the traces left on Morris' sensibility are easily perceptible while others require a gradual piecing together of impressions from her evolving and tangential narratives. Kinglake's effect on Morris' writings about empire extend beyond the paradigm of slightly condescending colonial observer to include humor and self-awareness. Kinglake's legacy is one that allows Morris to continue to transform her subjective impressions into art while making her writings the focus of new critical attention about imperialism, colonialism, and nationalism in travel literature.

As a companion piece to Venice, *Oxford* (1965) is more of a social and intellectual history, though Morris draws heavily on experiences there as a young chorister, an undergraduate, and a longtime resident. Morris addresses the reader in the second person—a favored technique—and adopts an ambassadorial pose in encouraging the reader to visit. The opening of *Oxford* utilizes a mise-en-scene approach, as the sweeping bucolic landscape of the first chapter gives way to hurried snapshots in the second. Given the diminutive size and provincial location of the city, Morris finds a morning scene in the bustling Covered Market jumbled and stimulating and fears that one might possibly find it "a little too rich" in its diversity (p. 15). Rather than dismantling the dreaminess of the spires or indulging in sycophantic admiration of Oxford traditions, Morris combats the university's obscurantism by revealing some facts about its operations and the governing academic culture. Quick glances at the natural environment, the university, and civic history in early sections resurface to allow for lengthier meditations on climate, town-and-gown conflicts, horticulture, the automobile industry,

architecture, and the effects of world wars and imperial decline.

With the publication of *Oxford,* Morris earned the label of "motorized scholar-gypsy" by describing the experience of camping out in a Volkswagen bus in Oxford's Radcliffe Square, home of the Bodleian Library: "I dream of it still: it is like sleeping in some private inner chamber of the city, where old letters are bundled, locks of hair are kept in envelopes, and the air is thick with memories" (p. 264). Like earlier writers, Morris surveys the metaphors used to summarize Oxford: it has been called an ark, an argosy, the navel of the empire, an island city, a microcosm, and a compact version of England. Oxford has produced politicians, scientists, musicians, artists, fine essayists, and champions of quick wit, but Morris humorously concludes that it has truly excelled in hymns and official notices that admonish students and tourists alike. The city is reminiscent of only one foreign place Morris has visited: Kyoto, in Japan, a comparison that is explained in philosophical terms: "In both cities you feel that a manner of thought is stubbornly defying all that the world can do to humiliate it. … [T]hey are both cities that reached their heydays in the era of the nation-States, and that era is now passing" (p. 270).

In the 1968 edition of *Oxford,* Morris included a list of corrections after many Oxford devotees and historians pointed out small misprints and factual inaccuracies. The author's note self-effacingly admits the dangers of writing about a much loved and examined place. Morris has also edited *The Oxford Book of Oxford* (1978), a colorful anthology of quotations tracing the history of the university from its monastic beginnings to the present-day confederation of modern colleges.

The Presence of Spain, later published as *Spain,* is also deeply influenced by Morris' interest in fallen empires and the impact of industrialization. The theme of decline extends beyond the book's treatment of the palatial Escorial and other royal sites. Early on in the text, which is accompanied in the 1964 Faber edition by atmospheric photographs and ghostly portraits by Evelyn Hofer, Morris discusses the formalities of the evening stroll—the paseo—in the main squares of the cities. The movement of the people becomes a metaphor for Spain's passage from antiquated empire to modern European nation. The scene belongs to

> Some long-dead Europe, the England of Barchester and the Proudies, perhaps, or Gogol's vanished Russia. [...]It is very charming to see, but sometimes the nostalgia of Spain has a more elemental quality[...].
>
> (p. 16)

Morris' elemental view of modern Spain is often enhanced by the ability to match it to British (or more familiar) scenes from classic works of art and literature. The result is that readers are transported to a contemporary Spain that is timely via cultural references and through allusion. To remark on the unappealing side of Spain's archaism, Morris lingers

> In some hangdog mining town, Dickensian in filth and gloom, where the old women grub for waste coal among the railway sidings, and make you think of Poor Susan;[...] or in the Hogarthian slums of Barcelona, where the sailors' brothels are, where the prostitutes are busted like pouter pigeons, and at the end of every dingy alley you may see the trams go by.
>
> (p. 28)

PAX BRITANNICA *TRILOGY: A DECADE OF EMPIRE WRITING*

Although the effects of her self-discovery and transformation are often the subject of Morris' writings of the last fifty years, her history writing of the 1960s and 1970s does not reveal the anguish she felt in those decades, as revealed in *Conundrum*. It was within those decades that she completed her gradual change of sexual role; in 1972, Morris underwent sex reassignment surgery in Casablanca, Morocco, because the health authorities in Britain insisted she would have to divorce Elizabeth before the procedure. During these tumultuous years Morris also undertook the immense research for the three volumes that would become known as the Pax Britannica trilogy: *Heaven's Command* (1973), *Pax Britannica* (1968), and *Farewell the Trumpets* (1978). (Though *Pax Britannica* was the first to be written and published, it is actually the second volume of the completed trilogy.) The ruling narrative of these historical books is "the rise, climax and fall of the Victorian Empire," and Morris surveys the pervasive influence of the queen's ethics and tastes on the formation of modern Britain's individuals and institutions (*Heaven's Command*, p. 9). Critics enthusiastically reviewed the trilogy, likening Morris' style and format to that of Edward Gibbon's *History of the Decline and Fall of the Roman Empire* and noting Morris' debt to Kipling. Morris' optimistic twinning of events in *Coronation Everest* reveals hopes for a similar relationship between the current monarch and her dominion. However, unlike Victoria's supremacy, the reign of Elizabeth II has paralleled a steady decline in the eminence of the monarchy.

All three volumes of *Pax Britannica* begin with an epigraph by Oscar Wilde. These lines of Wilde's 1881 poem "Ave Imperatrix" emphasizes Morris' concerns about the formation of the empire's reputation:

> *Set in this stormy Northern sea,*
>   *Queen of these restless fields of tide,*
> *England! what shall men say of thee,*
>   *Before whose fee the worlds divide?*

Underlying Wilde's triumphant lines are the provocative questions about heritage and historiography that Morris uses to propel her investigation. Her methodology combines reportage, journalism, archaeology, and impressionism, looking to extract collectible minutiae with which dioramic scenes of the empire can be constructed. The trilogy challenges traditional historical modes and argues in its methods for an ontological view of the empire's existence. Although Morris' attitudes toward the empire are somewhat outmoded, her approach in these books reflects elements of debates about the study of contemporary social, intellectual, and cultural history.

The green and pleasant view of the nation is replaced with a commanding vision of an industrial and expansionist empire. Interviews and epistolary evidence gathered by Morris' visits to former colonial locales are balanced to create portraits of Britain's power brokers and eccentrics that frame the narrative of each volume. Some excerpts appeared in the transatlantic literary and political journals *Horizon* and *Encounter,* but all three volumes were reissued in paperback in the late 1970s as well as in 1998 by Faber, complete with new introductions by Morris, in which she explains the impulses behind the writing of the books and offers her thoughts on the notion of empire at the end of the twentieth century. The trilogy's long publication history is a testament to Morris' popularity as a historiographer and to the books' significant contributions to this controversial subject, which is central to her oeuvre.

Heaven's Command: An Imperial Progress traces the development of the British empire from Victoria's 1837 accession until 1897—the year of her Diamond Jubilee and the empire's halcyon days. In *Heaven's Command,* Morris underscores the pivotal force driving the participants in British empire-building, which was an escapist desire akin to the impulse behind much travel writing: that is, a desire to "break out of their sad or prosaic realities and live more brilliant lives in Xanadu." She presents intriguing snapshots of reformers and rebels alike, most of whom show the abandonment of an initial idealism and the subsequent violence and fragmentation characteristic of the last decades of the empire.

Searching for a figure on which to model herself as arranger and narrator, Morris seizes on the image of a Roman centurion reflecting on the fall of Rome and vividly recalling both the facts and deeply personal impressions. Morris' reporter-like command of current events and ability to be in the "right place at the right time" extended to this project:

I was in time to witness the immense imperial organism uniting for the last time to fight the greatest war in history; and I was in time, in 1947, to spend my 21st birthday on a British troop train travelling from Egypt (where the Empire was noticeably not wanted) to Palestine (which the Empire emphatically did not want). For the next fifteen years or so I found myself vocationally

engaged in the dissolution of the British Empire, and I watched with mixed feelings the changes that were occurring in Britain itself—its loss of power, its shifts of purpose, its adaptations, sometimes skilful, sometimes clumsy and reluctant, to the new balances of the world.

(*Heaven's Command,* pp. 10–11)

Morris was interested in the ways that the creation of empire inspired individuals to chase their own political and commercial ambitions. This relationship between a national vision and individual dreams fostered impulses that in Morris' eyes were both brutal and benevolent. She admits that her treatment of those employed by the empire "display[s] a certain sympathy for them," "Just as the centurion of mine, I do not doubt, however tender the circumstances of his retirement, would have looked back upon the arrogant march of the legions with comradely understanding" (p. 10).

Heaven's Command concludes with the Diamond Jubilee of Victoria in 1897. This key event also inaugurates the second volume of the series, *Pax Britannica: The Climax of an Empire.* However jarring, it is significant that the second volume was written and published before the first volume. Morris has called *Pax Britannica* a "self-contained" work that addresses the impact of "a spectacularly theatrical event." The Jubilee is a bookend to a period of British history that had entered the realm of myth by the time the volume appeared in the 1960s. The citizens whose responses she tallied share Morris' astonishment at the empire's magnitude and achievements. As primary sources, their recollections illustrate how "institutions, customs and traditions" supported the "immense muddle of motives good and bad" (p. 11) cultivated by the empire. The celebratory tone turns elegiac as Morris acknowledges in the preface to the 1998 edition that the jubilee could not shield the empire from the realities of military conflicts and uprisings:

I have not tried to conceal, either, a sensual sympathy for the period, haunted as it is in retrospect by our knowledge of tragedies to come—for soon after the Diamond Jubilee the miseries of the Boer War cracked the imperial spirit, and still more terrible events would presently destroy it.

(1998 edition, p. 11)

The last book in the series, *Farewell the Trumpets: An Imperial Retreat,* surveys the aftermath of the "frisson of imperial achievement" (p. 12), ending with the death of Winston Churchill in 1965. Morris sees the finale as tattered, with the empire "reduced to a ragbag of islands and an amorphous society of independent States called simply The Commonwealth" (p. 9). Yet Morris resuscitates the grandeur, while providing streaming commentary on the political realities. Her trilogy owes much to Lytton Strachey, the author of a celebrated study of Victoria and artful, psychological biographies of Florence Nightingale, Charles Gordon, Cardinal Manning, and Dr. Arnold collected in *Eminent Victorians* (1918). Strachey's essay, which he called "Victorian Visions," can be read as a reaction to the panegyrics of nineteenth-century scholarship." Morris enhances her psychological profiles and sensory reactions to the empire with details from both visual and aural culture:

I have fondly imagined the work orchestrated by the young Elgar, and illustrated by Frith; its pages are perfumed for me with saddle-oil, joss-stick and railway steam; I hope my readers will feel, as they close its pages, that they have spent a few hours looking through a big sash window at a scene of immense variety and some splendour, across whose landscapes there swarms a remarkable people at the height of its vigour, in an outburst of creativity, pride, greed and command that has affected all our lives ever since.

(*Farewell the Trumpets,* p. 12)

Although Morris did not intend the work to be used as a register of modern British political history, the Pax Britannica trilogy is encyclopedic and useful, as it transcends its own chronological accounts and creates a sentient past. Each of the volumes is used by Morris as a "flare" or "window" or envisioned as part of a "triptych"— all of which emphasizes her reliance on frames and metaphorical devices, perhaps to combat the meandering that takes place within these structures. In *Pax Britannica* she attempts to categorize the work, calling it "a kind of historical travel book or reportage"—a description that seems quite haphazard compared with her carefully articulated views about form in other pieces. But as both a witness and agent of change in the empire, Morris confidently dons the role of the imaginative historian who is both credible and "immediately less reliable" (*Farewell the Trumpets,* p. 10). She makes the case for her suitability to her subject, underscoring both the personal and the universal impact of imperialism:

I do not come from an imperial family, and could write about the nineteenth-century Empire with absolute detachment, but in the first half of the twentieth century few of us were immune to the imperial effects. Even my poor father was gassed for his Empire. ... Even I found myself, for a decade of my life, embroiled in the imperial mesh, as I followed the retreating armies of Empire from one after another of their far-flung strongholds.

(p. 10)

Morris' desire for travel during her military service and afterward can be seen as her small-scale imperialism. The traveler searches for new experiences to tag with his or her characteristic vocabulary. Morris' expeditions constitute an intellectual, rather than political, type of conquest, and her "empire" writing asserts this impulse best. The "events, loyalties and excitements" (*Heaven's Command,* p. 9) chronicled in the trilogy resonate and gain significance in her later reactions to the Commonwealth, specifically in her investigations of architecture in *The Stones of Empire: The Buildings of the Raj* (1983) and her studies of *Hong Kong: Xianggang* (1988) and *Sydney* (1992). Additionally, a long fascination with the Admiral of the Fleet Lord "Jacky" Fisher resulted in Morris' book *Fisher's Face,* started in the 1950s but eventually published in 1995. This biography is a celebration of Fisher's bravery and innovation in military leadership and as a naval reformer.

MORRIS' AMERICANA: DEEPER INTO THE AMERICAN SCENE

The publication of *Coast to Coast* in 1956 and Morris' trip to the United States inaugurated two relationships that have shaped the author's writing life. The first was with Faber and Faber, who published Morris' first book and have supported subsequent works. The second was with the United States of America. Morris' views of the country in which she has spent the most time outside of Britain are shaped by a curiosity about its cultural and political imperialism.

Morris' initial infatuation with New York City developed into a questioning of the city, one that mirrors other literary travelers' attitudes but which also reveals much about her interests as a writer. She has visited Manhattan almost every year of her adult life and was eager to accept a commission by the Port Authority of New York and New Jersey in the 1960s to write a study of the metropolis's infrastructure. But *The Great Port: A Passage through New York* (1969) is also a biography of the city that details its impact on the exchange of both capital and ideas. Like *The Stones of Empire,* the book is organized allegorically, allowing Morris to reflect on the relationship between space, structures, movement, and the spirit of place. By contrast, *Manhattan '45* (1987) is a departure from her contemporary analyses of the city. The book reconstructs New York City circa 1945 as the self-congratulatory nation welcomed back its soldiers from World War II service. Morris displays her affection for both "high society" and "low life" as she tries to capture the infective spirit of this "golden age" of American youthful optimism and possibility. The book's section titles reflect her ambitious project: she moves skillfully from issues of style and entertainment to more sober but equally intriguing matters of infrastructure, race, class, industry, and commerce. In the epilogue, Morris admits that she chose her title "Because it sounded partly like a gun, and partly like champagne, and thus matched the victorious and celebratory theme of my book. But like bubbles and victories, that moment of release, pride and happiness was not to last" (p. 269).

In a later attempt to understand that optimistic ambition permeating American popular history and mythology, Morris embarked on a pilgrimage of sorts to trace the transformation and legacy of one of America's most revered leaders. In *Lincoln: A Foreigner's Quest* (1999), Morris struggles to understand the nation's fascination with and worship of its sixteenth president. Skepticism controls her view of Lincoln; this was planted during her first visit to the States when she became frustrated with the saccharin renditions of Lincoln's life and achievements. Memorably she admits that she was tempted to call the book *Grape Jelly,* as the foodstuff was the only other thing that irritated her more than Lincoln's legacy when she visited the country in the 1950s.

Morris' opinions of Lincoln permeate her portraits of other "supermen": in a review of Sir Edmund Hillary's 1997 autobiography, Morris likens the champion of Everest at his less appealing moments to "that other archetypal hero, Abraham Lincoln, who spent so many of his middle years as a not very admirable party politician" (*Literary Review,* July 1997). Although her Lincoln project begins as a revisionist biography, the result is a personal and impressionistic collage of presidential "lore" that illustrates Morris' growing sympathy toward her subject. The work concludes, however, with the suggestion that Lincoln's domestic imperialism and iron-fisted treatment of the South's secession during the Civil War set precedents for the nation's strong-willed future foreign policy and global image.

Some critics regaled in the mistakes that went unnoticed by the editors of *Lincoln.* For some readers, numerous geographical and historical errors seemed only to distance Morris further from her subject and audience. Her interests in Lincoln's class-based conflicts as a young man were dismissed by some reviewers as part of the anglicized approach to history. Angrier responses were elicited from historians who felt that Morris was out of her league and that her informal style did not suit the gravity of her subject. Her interrogation of Lincoln's mental state and sexual orientation did little to endear her to those readers already outraged by her project. On the other hand, the book was hailed by U.K. and U.S. newspapers and journals as both absorbing and persuasive in its honest presentation of humanizing idiosyncrasies about the subject and the author. Morris confessed later that she, too, believed the book was riddled with mistakes, and the negative responses (notably the hurtful review of the book by the conservative historian Andrew Roberts) made Morris reflect on the future of her writing.

ESSAYS AND AUTOBIOGRAPHICAL WRITINGS

Although Morris transgresses the rules of the forms in which she writes, her interest in motifs such as the quest show her desire to both belong to and move away from literary traditions. In an article for the *Times Literary Supplement* she describes how she looks to nineteenth-century guidebooks for solace when the desolation of modern life sets in. In her use of the quest motif, Morris can be compared to another eccentric former student of Christ Church and literary exile of sorts, W. H. Auden, whose verse has provided epigraphs and touchstones in Morris' prose. Moreover, as with Auden's oeuvre, stark contrasts can be made between Morris' early and later writing, if only because she is keenly aware of the changes that have taken place in the usage of English and in literary production over the past century. As she encourages in *Conundrum,* her life and writing process can be read as a quest for unity and clarity.

Finding pleasure is paramount to Morris. In her eight volumes of travel essays and in *Pleasures of a Tangled Life* (1989) she discusses ways in which she has achieved this through her work and relationships. The essays in *Pleasures* read like extemporaneous pieces, improvised as she muses on how the pursuit of pleasure has informed her literary choices. Contrary to the impression gleaned from these entries and other pieces, Morris shows us in *Pleasures* how meticulous she is with drafting, thus countering the argument that her breezy style is a disguise for makeshift research or composition. Her eight volumes of travel essays serve as useful introductions to the methods she expands on in her longer city portraits and in her historical writings. They are well-informed, humorous, and timely sketches of places she has lived (such as Oxford, London, and Venice) or studied (such as Hong Kong and

Delhi). Many of the essays are reprinted or reworked throughout the volumes. For example, in *Among the Cities* (1985), Morris designs an exhibition of profiles selected from travel essays that first appeared in *Cities* (1963). *Places* (1972) includes reflections on the profession of travel writing and the genre of the travel essay interspersed in pieces about former imperial locales; it shares some themes in common with the *Travels* (1976) collection, which also discusses classic guidebooks. *Destinations* (1980) is a collection of essays commissioned by *Rolling Stone* magazine, while *Journeys* (1984) and *Locations* (1992) represent final attempts to fulfill her ambition to visit and write about the entire urban world.

Morris' enthusiasm and flights of fancy are often channeled and refined by her rigorous attention to detail and tireless observation—an example of Morris applying her journalistic skills to temper unruly bursts of creativity. The years between 1962 and 1972 were a period of discovery, transformation, and greater clarity for Morris: in this decade she found a trademark style and voice, along with completing her change of sexual role. Some critics argue that this "epiphany" merely uncovered elements of her style during her shift from journalism to book writing. One element that became incontrovertible was her attraction to revision: although she had a policy with her travel essays of not revisiting places, she often readdresses ideas that were initially introduced in earlier writings. This allows for a refreshing transparency, as the reader can follow the flow of ideas from the mind to the page to her mind, but this has also elicited the response that she is an unreliable guide. Her organization of texts, as well as her choice to embellish some of them with footnotes and leave them out altogether of others, can be read as her dismissal of literary or publishing conventions. As can be observed in the *Pax Britannica* trilogy and her city portraits, reliability is often shelved in favor of subjectivity. What Morris' readers can rely on her to provide is visceral, sensory description that has one goal: transporting the reader to the moment in time. For example, the two different introductions to editions of *Coast to Coast* are not wildly incongruous, but they exhibit her commitment to clarity in conveying her mood and the mood of the United States as a complex tangle of evolving cultures.

CONUNDRUM

In 2001 Morris provided an introduction for a new edition of *Conundrum* in which she asserts that she has not amended anything but a few facts and that the "fundamental attitudes" remain intact. Yet Cyril Connolly, reviewing the first edition for the *Sunday Times,* felt that *Conundrum* did not hold together as a book. His review did not disparage the work: the collection of "snapshots," as he called them, showed how "the suggestible, Romantic James is now the enlightened, Classical Jan, and no writer of such intelligence, humour and sensitivity has ever undergone a complete sex-change and written about it so well" (in Clements, p. 47). By contrast, the *Times Literary Supplement* thought that *Conundrum* "represented only the chin-up half of a far more stressful inner dialectic; the forces of darkness, on the whole, are inadequately represented" (in Clements, p. 47). The *New York Review of Books* went further and proclaimed that, in Morris' postoperative writing, "purple passages and flights of Celtic fancy proliferated as the author's male hormones lost out to female ones" (in Clements, p. 48).

Morris' autobiographical writing seductively emphasizes her ability to control the conundrum over gender—but on a practical level, her femininity did have an impact on the execution of her research. Critics such as Patrick Holland have looked at her specific treatment of cities like Cairo and her metaphorical use of veiled figures as ways of suggesting a relationship between gender and travel in her work, in which being female has afforded her, ironically, greater ease of movement in male-dominated societies that might question the motives of an inquisitive Western male. Her Middle Eastern travel essays do reveal her comfort in moving through such societies clothed or cloaked as a woman. But tensions can be sensed as Morris relinquishes some of the male traveler's general freedoms—of access, of expression, or from certain threats.

Any sense of Morris' belonging to a male, female, English, or other narrative tradition seems somewhat paradoxical when contrasted with her suspicions of nationalism, her literary rebelliousness, and her disregard of generic conventions. As with the quest motif, the theme of exile finds a range of outlets in Morris' work. She has asserted that "all of my own excursions into the expatriate condition have been temporary but that has not made them any the less exciting." In a November 2002 *Atlantic Monthly* piece, Morris described herself as "a traveler by profession but not by instinct," citing the fact that her English and Welsh ancestors never lived outside the British Isles and that "the Welsh have never been easy migrants" (pp. 136, 137).

THE MATTER OF WALES *(1984)*

Morris' admiration for and fascination with Wales and Welsh culture, personally and professionally, have heightened her profile as a Welsh patriot and devoted republican. As M. Wynn Thomas has noted, Morris' work is to be considered alongside the best writing about and from Wales in the twentieth century; the works "come from the peregrine imaginations of migrants—individuals who sought out or stumbled upon, who 'discovered' and/or constructed, a culture more spiritually congenial than the one to which they were actually native" (p. 157). Paul Clements' 1998 critical and biographical study of Morris devotes two sections to the charting of Morris' writing on Wales, although he cites the influence of Wales on her other writing. Thomas' comments of the congeniality of Welsh identity find resonance in Morris' evolving love of Wales—which began with skepticism but has become a source of deep pride.

Anglo-Welsh by birth, Morris' literary involvement with Wales can be traced to a 1958 article in *Wales,* a national monthly magazine. In "Welshness in Wales," Morris discusses the principality's insular, romantic, and anachronistic attitudes, which she dubs "Welshry." The general secretary of Plaid Cymru (the party of Wales) contacted Morris in the 1960s to express his concern with her views. Clements quotes Morris' reaction to the secretary's suggestion that she embrace Wales as an insider: "I was flattered that such an ultra-Welshman should consider me fit for inclusion. … I took his advice, and if I have fulfilled myself anywhere, I have fulfilled myself in Welshness" (p. 50).

Her association with the Gorsedd of Bards is a testament to her support for the preservation of the nation. Druidic in origin, the Gorsedd inducts its members at the Crowning of the Bards, which takes place at the weeklong national Eistedfodd folk festival, held annually since the late twelfth century. Morris describes the festival as having a powerful influence on Welsh life as it celebrates language as the basis for the cultural separateness of Wales from the rest of Britain—a distinction about which Morris has written extensively and thoughtfully. Morris also reflects on Welsh connections and contributions to a wider definition of what constitutes British history; discussions of Welsh exclusivity and the culture's harmony with the rest of the world are equally present in Morris' writing. Yet, the dilemmas of a culture that is resistant to progress, undergoing rapid modernization, and also receiving only limited sovereignty from Britain find their way into her writing about Wales, evident in her outline of fairy-tale-like Celtic curses that she names the "torments of Wales." They are the Torment of the Confused Identity, the Torment of the Torn Tongue, the Torment of the Two Peoples, and a "more elemental *Angst*" that she describes in the epilogue of *The Matter of Wales* as "the yearning, profound and ineradicable, for their own inviolable place in the world" (p. 423). She elaborates on this last torment in her album of a half-century of travels in Europe entitled *Fifty Years of Europe* (1997), in which her homeland of Wales figures quite prominently. In those decades of rapid globalization, Morris calls this lasting angst the Torment of Dispossession.

The Matter of Wales: Epic Views of a Small Country (later published as *Wales: Epic Views of a Small Country*) stands out from Morris' other treatments of Wales, such as her photographic study *Wales, the First Place* (1982) and the collection of excerpts she edited as *The Small Oxford Book of Wales* (1982). *The Matter of Wales* is a heroic exploration of the nation's history and future goals, shaped by her intense love of it. Morris uses the story of Owain Glyndwr, a hero of the ill-fated fifteenth-century Welsh resistance movement, as "a symbolic index" for her study. She credits Glyndwr with defining Welsh identity in triumphant and positive terms. Using "artistic hindsight," Morris sees Glyndwr's vision of Wales as "a vision of the place as a human entity, not just a country but a nation, not just a State but a fellowship, and a culture, and a heritage, and a sense of home, and a reconciliation of time, in which the affairs of the remotest past might overlap the present and embrace the future" (*Wales*, p. 6).

The book became one of her best-sellers, and it reinforced her authority as a member of the Welsh intelligentsia. With loving detail, Morris evokes the nation for her readership and cements the landscape and the language as continual inspiration for her work. Comparisons to Wales abound in her writings about other places; Morris' forays into fiction also extend her discussions of the numinous quality of the nation.

MORRIS AND THE NOVEL: A MACHYNLLETH TRIAD, LAST LETTERS FROM HAV, *AND* OUR FIRST LEADER

Owain Glyndwr's legacy and the Welsh town of Machynlleth provided the inspiration and setting for Morris' next significant book on Wales. *A Machynlleth Triad* (1994) was written nearly a decade after Morris' Booker Prize–nominated novel, *Last Letters from Hav* (1985), and is also a continuation of her experiments with fiction. Although *A Machynlleth Triad* is difficult to categorize, the narrative encompasses the past, present, and future, illustrating the historical underpinnings of the hopes and fears of a future independent republic. Morris reflects on Machynlleth as the temporary seat of Glyndwr's parliament in the early fifteenth century and charts its transformation into the hybrid Anglo-Welsh market town of 1991. In the last section, she envisages the twenty-first-century establishment of Machynlleth as a vibrant and savvy capital of the Welsh Republic but with potential internal conflicts brewing. Interestingly her later novel of Wales, *Our First Leader* (2000), coauthored with her son Twm Morys, is a satirical fantasy of an independent Welsh nation-state established by Adolf Hitler as the victor of World War II.

Last Letters from Hav blends Morris' early interests in fantasy with her interests in ethnicity, imperialism, and colonialism. The first-person epistolary narrative follows a writer who has been sent to a fictional independent city-state. Writing about a nonexistent place, Morris created an appropriate setting for the investigation of the themes that resonate throughout her earlier works and those that would ultimately impact on her later writings. Hav is an amalgam: it is described in the book as an eastern Levantine city, a crossroads for explorers, tycoons, and artists. Morris was disappointed by the shaky results of her fictional experiment, and also by the confusion that beset reviewers of the work, some of whom assumed that Hav was a real place. Moreover, she was surprised that the book made the prestigious Booker Prize shortlist. The novel explores the pitfalls of a metaphor often used by travel writers: "map-making," or prescribing ways of seeing and, therefore, of controlling a space. It is in the tentative sketching of Hav that Morris acknowledges the problems and opportunities endemic in real sites throughout the postimperial and postcolonial world.

FIFTY YEARS OF EUROPE *AND* TRIESTE AND THE MEANING OF NOWHERE

Morris' memorable treatment of postimperial Hav laid some of the thematic groundwork for her investigation of a former site of imperial power and cultural exchange: the city of Trieste, which occupied the center of *Fifty Years of Europe,* a memoir of travel and a striking collection of meditations on modern European civilization and culture. With its history as the capital of the Austro-Hungarian Empire and potential as an allegory of transience and limbo (*Trieste,* p. 7), Trieste demanded its own forum. *Trieste and the Meaning of Nowhere* (2001) is a characteristic example of Morris' anthropomorphic treatment of place: a complex but graceful interweaving of personalities and impressions rules the narrative. She presents the city as a faded contact zone, to borrow the term from Mary Louise Pratt, who uses the phrase in her 1992 interdisciplinary study of travel writing entitled *Imperial Eyes* to refer to the space of colonial encounters in which peoples geographically and historically separated come into contact with each other and establish ongoing relations. In an article entitled "Doing the Continental" for the *Spectator* (December 14, 2002) Morris confesses the joy she found in viewing "from a safely vicarious distance" Trieste's "relics of that bewitching earlier version of a half-united Europe, the Austro-Hungarian Empire." The elements that grab her attention are "the yellow of its barrack walls, the pomp of its railway stations, the sickly thump of its waltzes," as well as the lives of exiled Napoleonic nobles and questing writers like Italo Svevo and James Joyce. Constructed specifically to serve as a commercial port, Trieste is now an abandoned, hallucinatory model of compromise and collaboration that—unlike its eulogizer, who insists on the parallel—has been relegated to the position of a retired and fidgety specialist. The once cosmopolitan town, now Adriatic backwater, serves as a metaphor for Morris' life—one that she first embraced as a young soldier, enchanted by its multiculturalism and melancholy. Morris' subject in *Trieste* encompasses more than just a geographical place: she presents her views on origins, purpose, and community—and draws a number of conclusions that can be seen to be drawn from her entire writing life.

The epigraph to *Trieste* consists of two lines by the poet Wallace Stevens: "I was the world in which I walked, and what I saw / Or heard or felt came not but from myself." In this book, as in most of her later writings, Morris becomes a more assertive medium of her experiences, ducking in and out of the limelight of her scenes, gesticulating to the others on the sidelines, and pairing her swashbuckling through time and facts with the gentleness of a goodly spirit. On the final page of the book, a quartet of lines by Rudyard Kipling appears:

Something I owe to the soil that grew—
More to the life that fed—
But most to Allah Who gave me two
Separate sides to my head.

The tension between the separate "sides" eventually led to Morris' twinning of physical and material satisfaction with spiritual fulfillment. Of her writing, Morris says in *Trieste* that "the books I have written are no more than smudged graffiti on a wall, and I shall write no more of them. Money? Enough to live on. Critics? To hell with 'em. Kindness is what matters, all along at any age—kindness, the ruling principle of nowhere" (p. 186).

CONCLUSION

Compared to the critical and commercial success of works by James Morris, Jan Morris' writing since 1972 has not been as wholeheartedly praised as the early books, but her whole oeuvre both anticipates and celebrates trends and styles of later twentieth-century travel writing, such as the work of Paul Theroux, Jonathan Raban, and Pico Iyer (who has been called her "heir"). Morris has also engaged with contemporaries such as the late Bruce Chatwin and the popular philosopher Alain de Botton, finding elements in their styles of writing to both kindly praise and shrewdly criticize.

Critics have argued that were it not for her gender reassignment, Morris fits the archetype of the genial British literary traveler of the early twentieth century. Her groundbreaking explorer narratives and intimate views of personalities and moods faithfully represent the spectrum of travel-writing styles in the twentieth century. But Morris further complicates, and prevents her easy categorization. She blurs generic boundaries as well as elements of patriotism, style, irony—the

skewing of which remind the reader that her writings go beyond journalists' exposés or the satirical speculations of a litterateur. Morris' fellow Trieste exile James Joyce once claimed that "a writer should never write about the extraordinary. That is for the journalist." As a journalist, Morris unveiled the extraordinary even in the most quotidian of subjects—a duty she upheld as a freelance writer. Through her lifelong love, like Joyce's, of the infinite play encouraged by the English language, Morris has gone about redefining her terms and her profession to fit her special brand of commentary. Like Lawrence Sterne's "sentimental traveller," Morris has defended the maxim that witnessing and recording incidental occurrences is the reason for exploration and writing.

Of the many themes and tropes that inhabit Morris' writing, there are a handful that not only link the life and the work but that link the diverse publications together. Among these are a sense of voice, an extreme interest in sensory experience, and a desire to transport the reader to extraordinary moments and places. Another is the notion of home and belonging: the impact of homesickness and nostalgia is summarized, however abstractly, for Morris by a Welsh word she summons for her longing for Wales: *hiraeth*. For her the term's literal meaning (nostalgia, longing and grief) is abstracted by the indeterminacy of that for which one yearns. Virginia Woolf, another of Morris' beloved subjects, provides a representative motto for women writers who, like Morris, have been both insiders and outsiders: "as a woman, I have no country. As a woman, I want no country. As a woman my country is the whole world" (*Three Guineas*, p. 99). Morris' *hiraeth* for a welcoming Wales competes with the hold that the entire world has on her imagination. Unlike a writer who buries the false starts, the fears, wrong turns, prevarications, and the like in letters and diaries to be uncovered by devoted scholars in time, Morris has offered up much of herself, some of it cloaked in a charming persona but much of it honest and frank, allowing her audience to fully inhabit her incredibly wide world.

Selected Bibliography

WORKS (WRITTEN AS JAMES OR JAN MORRIS)

NONFICTION

Coast to Coast: An Account of a Visit to the United States. London: Faber, 1956. Rev. ed., 1962. (Published under the title *As I Saw the USA* in the United States.)

Sultan in Oman. London: Faber, 1957; New York: Pantheon, 1957. Rev. ed., 1983.

The Market of Seleukia. London: Faber, 1957.

Coronation Everest. London: Faber, 1958; New York: Dutton, 1958.

South African Winter. London: Faber, 1958; New York: Pantheon, 1958.

The Hashemite Kings. London: Faber, 1959; New York: Pantheon, 1959.

Venice. London: Faber, 1960. 3d rev. ed., 1993.

The Outriders: A Liberal View of Britain. London: Faber, 1963.

The World Bank: A Prospect. London: Faber, 1963. Published in the United States as *The Road to Huddersfield: A Journey to Five Continents.* New York: Pantheon, 1963.

The Presence of Spain. Photographs by Evelyn Hofer. London: Faber, 1964; New York: Harcourt, Brace & World, 1964. Rev. eds. as *Spain,* 1979, 1982, 1988.

Oxford. London: Faber, 1965; New York: Harcourt, Brace & World, 1965. 2d ed., 1986.

Pax Britannica: The Climax of an Empire. London: Faber, 1968; New York: Harcourt, Brace & World, 1968. (First published but second part of the *Pax Britannica* trilogy.)

The Great Port: A Passage through New York. London: Faber, 1969; New York: Harcourt, Brace & World, 1969. Rev. ed., 1985.

Heaven's Command: An Imperial Progress. London: Faber, 1973; New York: Harcourt Brace Jovanovich, 1974. (First part of the *Pax Britannica* trilogy.)

Conundrum. London: Faber, 1974; New York: Harcourt Brace Jovanovich, 1974. Rev. with a new introduction, 2001. (Autobiography.)

Farewell the Trumpets: An Imperial Retreat. London: Faber, 1978; New York: Harcourt Brace Jovanovich, 1978. (Third part of the *Pax Britannica* trilogy.)

The Venetian Empire: A Sea Voyage. London: Faber, 1980; Harcourt Brace Jovanovich, 1980.

A Venetian Bestiary. London and New York: Thames and Hudson, 1982.

The Spectacle of Empire: Style, Effect, and the Pax Britannica. London: Faber, 1982; Garden City, N.Y.: Doubleday, 1982.

Wales, the First Place. With Paul Wakefield. London: Aurum, 1982; New York: C. N. Potter, 1982.

Stones of Empire: The Buildings of the Raj. With Simon Winchester. Oxford and New York: Oxford University Press, 1983.

The Matter of Wales: Epic Views of a Small Country. Oxford: Oxford University Press, 1984. Rev. ed. as *Wales: Epic Views of a Small Country,* 1998.

Scotland, the Place of Visions. With Paul Wakefield. London: Aurum, 1986; New York: C. N. Potter, 1986.

Manhattan '45. London and Boston: Faber, 1987.

Hong Kong: Xianggang. London: Viking, 1988; New York: Random House, 1988. 3d rev. ed., 1996. ("The final edition.")

Pleasures of a Tangled Life. London: Barrie & Jenkins, 1989; New York: Random House, 1988. (Autobiographical essays.)

Ireland, Your Only Place. With Paul Wakefield. London: Aurum, 1990; New York: C. N. Potter, 1990.

Sydney. London: Viking, 1992.

Fisher's Face; or, Getting to Know the Admiral. London: Viking, 1995; New York: Random House, 1995.

Fifty Years of Europe: An Album. London: Viking, 1997; New York: Villard, 1997.

Lincoln: A Foreigner's Quest. London: Viking, 1999; New York: Simon & Schuster, 2000.

Trieste and the Meaning of Nowhere. London: Faber, 2001; New York: Simon & Schuster, 2001.

A Writer's House in Wales. Washington, D.C.: National Geographic Books, 2002. (Part of the National Geographic Directions series.)

ESSAYS

Cities. London: Faber, 1963; New York: Harcourt, Brace & World, 1964.

Places. London: Faber, 1972; New York: Harcourt Brace Jovanovich, 1973.

Travels. London: Faber, 1976; New York: Harcourt Brace Jovanovich, 1976.

Destinations. Oxford and New York: Oxford University Press, 1980.

Journeys. Oxford and New York: Oxford University Press, 1984.

Among the Cities. London: Viking, 1985.

O Canada! London: Hale, 1992.

Locations. Oxford and New York: Oxford University Press, 1992.

"Travelling Writer." In *The Writer on Her Work.* Edited by Janet Steinburg. London: Virago, 1992.

"Home Thoughts from Abroad." *The Atlantic Monthly* 290: 136–138 (November 2002). Reprinted in *A House Somewhere.* Edited by Donald W. George and Anthony Sattin. Pp. 1–7. London and Melbourne: Lonely Planet, 2002.

The World: Travels 1950–2000. New York: W. W. Norton, 2003. Originally published as *A Writer's World: Travels 1950–2000.* London: Faber, 2003.

FICTION

Last Letters from Hav. London: Viking, 1985. (Short-listed for the Booker Prize.)

A Machynlleth Triad. With Twm Morys. London and New York: Viking, 1994. (Welsh fantasy.)

Our First Leader. With Twm Morys. Llandysul, Wales: Gomer, 2000. (Welsh fantasy.)

EDITED WORKS

The Oxford Book of Oxford. Oxford and New York: Oxford University Press, 1978.

John Ruskin: The Stones of Venice. London: Faber, 1981.

The Small Oxford Book of Wales. Oxford: Oxford University Press, 1982.

Travels with Virginia Woolf. London: Hogarth Press, 1993.

CRITICAL AND BIOGRAPHICAL STUDIES

Clements, Paul. *Jan Morris.* In Writers of Wales series. Edited by Meic Stephens and R. Brinley Jones. Cardiff: University of Wales Press, 1998.

Holland, Patrick, and Graham Huggan. *Tourists with Typewriters: Critical Reflections on Contemporary Travel Writing.* Ann Arbor: University of Michigan Press, 1998.

Phillips, Richard. "Decolonizing Geographies of Travel: Reading James/Jan Morris." *Social & Cultural Geography* 2:5–24 (March 2001).

Thomas, M. Wynn. *Corresponding Cultures: The Two Literatures of Wales.* Cardiff: University of Wales Press, 1999.

Woolf, Virginia. *Three Guineas.* Edited by Naomi Black. Oxford: Blackwell, 2001.

Wroe, Nicholas. "The Long Voyage Home." *Guardian,* October 6, 2001. (Detailed profile of the writer.)

The *Times Literary Supplement*'s Centenary Archive contains many articles and reviews by Morris and of her work. Highly recommended; searchable by author, reviewer, titles, and dates. Subscription required (http://www.tls.psmedia.com).

ROBERT NYE

(1939–)

Helena Nelson

THE BIOGRAPHICAL DETAILS of a poet are, in one sense, irrelevant. As Nye himself might say, his true life lies elsewhere—in the poems and stories he has made from his experience. And yet Robert Nye, reluctant as he has been to divulge more than the bare details of his personal life, has always been fascinated by intrigue and anecdote, the riddle of an individual writer behind the mask.

Who but Nye would begin a literary analysis of John Donne's poetry with "Donne hated milk"? Or recall what Coleridge was wearing in April 1804 as he set sail for the Mediterranean— "four waistcoats and two pairs of flannel drawers under cloth pantaloons"? Nye loves literary anecdote, gossip and tall stories—what one of his own characters, Pickleherring, would call "country history." Yet Nye, like the Shakespeare of his 1998 novel, is also "a man obsessed—obsessed by the pen, obsessed by private terrors." The immediate source of some of these obsessions—and perhaps the key to much more—may be found in the events of his first two decades.

EARLY YEARS

Robert Nye was born in London on March 15, 1939, roughly six months before the outbreak of World War II. His mother was the youngest of twenty-one children, a farmer's daughter who left school at age twelve. According to Nye, she "never learned to read or write properly," but she could—and did—tell wonderful stories. His father worked for the Post Office, selling telephones, and enjoyed dog racing. Nye describes him as "a gentle, shy and lovely man" who "just didn't know what to do with his impossible son" (correspondence with the author, November 2002). But that came later.

As soon as bombs started dropping on London, the Nye baby was whisked off to the country with his mother and paternal grandmother while his father went off to fight. The next few years were spent in Dormans Land, on the borders of Surrey and Sussex. The connection that drew them there—Nye's maternal grandmother—was also a connection that the young poet was encouraged to avoid. His mother's mother, so Nye was assured in no uncertain terms, was a witch, and despite familial ties and proximity he was not allowed to talk to her.

Witchcraft is a pagan art. On the other side of the same family, however, Nye's grandfather (the witch's husband) had been the son of an Anglican priest. These two strands, celebrated in Nye's poem "Birthright," are seminal in the poet's life. A practicing Christian, his poetry and novels are interwoven with devils and darkness, myth and mandragora.

A late autobiographical poem, "An English Education," records the way the approved grandmother taught Nye to read "by reading verse" aloud. Although no witch, she chanted nursery rhymes "like a magic spell." Subsequently the boy devoured all the reading he could get his hands on. Some must have come his way through school: much more was from Boots Lending Library. He recalls a riot of fiction: Mother Goose, comics, Robert Louis Stevenson, Enid Blyton, anything involving Robin Hood, Scottish outlaws or Arthurian legend, Black Beauty, Dracula, the Leslie Charteris books, Bulldog Drummond, Edgar Allen Poe, Richmal Crompton, and so on. Among the most significant influences was Walter de la Mare's 1923 anthology *Come Hither*. It is hard to imagine a richer introduction to poetry, with such an emphasis on magic, music, and mystery, and such haunting inclusion of the most ancient bard of all—"anon."

At around the age of nine Nye began scribbling his own verse. He recalls Wordsworth at this time as "the first individual poet who spoke to me" (Correspondence, May 2002). A hunt for more reading matter to match his insatiable appetite led him, at age eleven, to Southend Public Library where—wonder of wonders—he discovered that families were entitled to up to three tickets for each member. Since nobody else in the family was much of a reader, he was able to use all the tickets himself.

In 1952, aged about thirteen, Nye recalls writing his first "inspired" poem. The poem was "Listeners" and came to him, as Coleridge said of "Kubla Khan," in a dream. The two brief stanzas feature a house at night with rain drumming against the glass: the words and rhythms beat like raindrops. Sound, silence, and wakefulness create a mystery: the source of sound is also the focus of silent listening, as though the rain itself were alive. After writing this poem, Nye says he "knew what [he] had to do for the rest of [his] life."

In his preface to *A Selection of the Poems of Laura Riding,* Nye recalled how, as a teenager, he read his way "through all the volumes of English poetry that I could lay my hands on, as well as several kinds of more eccentric and occult writing." Then he discovered Riding's 1938 *Collected Poems,* "the culmination of all the volumes which I had been searching through." Riding's influence would prove far-reaching; a few years later it developed into personal correspondence.

But Nye's first real literary relationship of letters was with John Cowper Powys. At the age of thirteen Nye discovered *A Glastonbury Romance* and was bowled over by it. He wrote a fan letter to its author, scarcely expecting a reply. However, an eight-year-long correspondence ensued. Powys was a generous mentor: poet as well as novelist, he read the boy's earliest poems and offered encouragement.

By the age of fourteen Nye was well into adult fiction. When his father discovered a copy of James Joyce's *Ulysses* among his son's library books, he was appalled—and confronted the head librarian. Who, he demanded, had allowed a boy of fourteen to borrow such an unsuitable book? It was pointed out to him that the volume had been purloined from the "reference only" section. There were more "stolen" books at home. Nye's father had to use a suitcase in order to return them all.

However, this minor setback did not stop the reading—far from it. Nye was already deep into Shakespeare, Arthur Rimbaud, and Sir Walter Ralegh. When the news of Dylan Thomas' death was reported in his father's newspaper, Nye shed tears. And he was not only writing seriously but also submitting poetry to leading literary magazines. In 1955, when he was only sixteen, his poem "Kingfisher" was published in *London* magazine. That same year he left school with never a qualm. Most of the poets he admired had felt no need of higher education—he would make his own way. Which he did.

THE YOUNG ADULT

From here the personal details of Nye's life remain mostly private. In early 1959, aged only nineteen, Nye was married to Judith Pratt, to whom his first two books were dedicated. The couple were hard-pressed to make ends meet—Powys paid for the wedding license. At first Nye took on whatever work was necessary to survive. By 1961, however, following the publication of his first poetry collection, *Juvenilia 1,* he was determined to support his growing family as a freelance writer. By this time Nye and his wife were living in a remote cottage in North Wales with no electricity and water only from a well. Here their first son was born; two others would follow.

Meanwhile Nye took up serious reviewing by the simple expedient of approaching editors and offering his services. Fueled by dogged determination, he forged ahead. Poems published in *Juvenilia 2* (1963) reflect some of the difficulties of this period: stories at bedtime on Christmas Eve, candles, firelight and shadows, washing in rainwater.

There may have been difficulties but there were also compensations. A correspondence with Laura Riding was thriving—it lasted four years. Friendships also flourished with established poets like Martin Seymour-Smith and James Reeves. *Juvenilia 2* won an Eric Gregory Award, designed to encourage young writers. Poems continued to be published in prestigious magazines.

Meanwhile, Nye had begun writing children's books, exploiting his love of myth and folktale. In 1966 Faber published *Taliesin,* a retelling of the ancient Welsh story found in the *Mabinogion* (and a key tale in Nye's personal mythology). In the same year, correspondence with Laura Riding suddenly ended—a break that may have been connected with changed domestic circumstances. Nye was working on his troubled and troubling first adult novel, *Doubtfire*—and his marriage was on the rocks.

ESTABLISHING A LITERARY CAREER

In 1967 *Doubtfire* was published, Nye was appointed poetry editor for the *Scotsman,* and he and Judith were divorced. He continued writing both poetry and children's fiction. In 1968 his children's book *Bee Hunter: Adventures of Beowulf* was illustrated by Aileen Campbell, who that same year became his second wife. The couple moved to Edinburgh, where they stayed for the next decade.

In 1969 *Darker Ends,* Nye's third book of poems, was published. It is, as the title suggests, a book full of foreboding. About three-fifths of the poems were new; the rest had appeared in earlier volumes. Some were reprinted unchanged. Others had been altered—sometimes radically, sometimes in title alone. It was the first indication of that continuous self-editing which is a feature of Nye's work.

Nye, prolific in prose, if not in verse, now expanded his interests into radio plays, screenwriting, and editorial work. He was also publishing adult short stories. By 1971, in addition to writing for the *Scotsman,* he was poetry critic of the *Times* as well as contributing reviews of new fiction to the *Guardian.* He wrote articles and essays on Thomas Chatterton and planned an edition of his poems. He published a remarkable essay on the poetry of John Donne in the *Critical Quarterly* and edited a book of Sir Walter Ra-

legh's verse; later there were also selections from Barnes and Swinburne.

In 1976 a literary breakthrough came with the publication of *Falstaff,* Nye's second adult novel, which won both the Hawthornden and Guardian prizes for fiction. The book was justly praised: a vein of high spirits and sheer delight in language runs through it, as well as extraordinarily bawdy sexual exploits. Translated into several languages, it proved a best-seller in Poland as well as Britain. That same year Nye completed his fourth collection of poetry (*Divisions on a Ground*), edited the *Faber Book of Sonnets,* published (in one volume) two radio plays and a surrealistic film script, edited a selection of English sermons, and finally, took up the post of writer in residence at the University of Edinburgh. On the one hand he was writing about Sir John Fastolf's noble penis: "It was her joy to tie ribbons about it, taking them from her hair, and then to dance her fingers round and round his towering pillar of flesh like maids about the maypole." On the other hand, he was exploring, with equal attention, two centuries of sermons, while writing poetry that evoked "an orthodox theology of tears." Such apparent contradictions, though, are part of what makes Nye what he is.

RETREAT TO IRELAND

After the Edinburgh residency, Nye and his family moved to southern Ireland (where the poet still lives). Although mostly withdrawn from public life, he continued to flourish as a novelist. Between 1979 and 1998 he produced a further seven adult novels, his reputation growing. However, a gap of thirteen years stretched between *Divisions on a Ground* in 1976 and *A Collection of Poems 1955–1988.* The back cover of the latter asserts that Nye's "principal calling is poetry, and he has never followed any occupation which interfered with that vocation." It is true that Nye's dedication to poetry has never been less than absolute; whether it is true that nothing interfered with that vocation is open to question. This volume reprints (or reworks) many previously published poems, adding only about twenty completely new ones. It is hard to see why this poet, whose early inspiration was so highly charged, should have produced so little during his main period of success as a novelist unless the novel writing in itself was using up more of the poet in him than he admitted.

The publication of *A Collection of Poems, 1955–1988* took place in the same year, 1989, that correspondence with Laura Riding was finally renewed. In 1995 Nye was summoned to come and see her in Wabasso, Florida. She was in her nineties, frail but fierce as ever—and delighted to see him. Perhaps this experience was, to some extent, the completion of a circle in Nye's life. He spent three days with her, three days in which they talked and talked. Riding presented Nye with the unpublished manuscript of her early poems—surely no gift could have moved him more deeply.

In 1995 Nye brought out his *Collected Poems*. The volume encompassed his whole writing career and was divided chronologically. Once again, however, there were few completely new poems, and some of those were closely connected by theme, tone, and language with the poems of *Juvenilia 2*. But it was an important watershed and an opportunity for Nye, by this time known much better as novelist than poet, to reach new readers.

In 1998 Nye published what he claimed was his last novel. *The Late Mr. Shakespeare,* according to the author, took only five months to write. It is a masterpiece. The process of penning may have taken five months, but the execution of thought represents a lifetime's work, bringing together all that is elemental and diverse in Nye's interests. It is the novel of a poet.

Since the publication of *Mr. Shakespeare,* new poems by Nye have appeared in a range of literary publications. There is palpable excitement in them, as well as a sharp sweetness (absent from his midlife satires) and a lyric quality older than the poet himself. Before closely examining his poetic development (which is how he would most want to be discussed) it is necessary to consider his work as a novelist. Some connections between the poems and the novels are too significant to overlook.

THE NOVELS: DOUBTFIRE

Robert Graves, in the first chapter of *The White Goddess,* uses words that might describe Nye himself: "Prose has been my livelihood, but I have used it as a means of sharpening my sense of the altogether different nature of poetry." Nye, though a very different novelist from Graves, shares the older poet's unwavering belief that prose, as a medium, is inferior to poetry. Instructed (as Graves himself was) by Laura Riding, Nye holds that poetry is a matter of truth-telling, with plainness and simplicity at its core. But it isn't easy to live from day to day with an art that requires absolute adherence to truth. In the introductory note to the second edition of *Tales I Told My Mother* (an early collection of short stories), Nye remarks that his "stories are intended as a relief from the truth-telling which poetry requires of its adherents" as well as to "amuse both poets and children."

Putting aside, for a moment, the veiled "muse" reference in that last remark, the literal desire to amuse is important. It highlights a feature of this writer that is easily forgotten: in prose he is witty, clever, and funny (also in satirical verse), and though darkness and nightmare run insistently through his work, so does delight. Rabelais and Sterne make him laugh, and their influence echoes through his fiction.

However, his first novel is not at all amusing. *Doubtfire* (1967) spills anguish onto the page in a fractured outpouring that has palpable designs on the reader. It mixes stream-of-consciousness reflection, prose narrative, screenplay, theatrical sequences, literary quotation and allusion, repeated and edited versions of itself—and poetry. One particular sentence extends over more than ten pages, tempting the reader to wish that the young Nye had never "borrowed" *Ulysses* from Southend Library.

Much of *Doubtfire* is interesting—especially to a student of Nye's work—but as a narrative it fails to make the reader care what happens next. Having said this, *Doubtfire,* like the first two collections of poetry, *Juvenilia 1* and *2,* is the molten lava from which all Nye's later work emerges. It focuses obsessions which do not leave him and which will reemerge. No doubt similar observations could be made of the early work of other writers. But in Nye's case, it is different. His obsessions repeat themselves literally. For example, the description of a well-spring in *Doubtfire* recurs in *The Life and Death of My Lord Gilles de Rais,* published twenty-three years later. The well-spring also pops up in verse form in the Irish magazine *The SHOp* in spring 2001. The descriptions are not identical, but the detail is. In *Doubtfire,* the water is "cold and good," pouring from a "place he has scooped clean and keeps filled with plausible white pebbles." In *Gilles de Rais,* "it comes out in the hillside, in this place I have scooped clean and keep filled with white pebbles … cold and good." In the poem "The Well-Spring," "the spirit flows / Bloody and hot, but comes out cold and good / In this place I've scooped clean and filled with pebbles." In this way, images, characters, and precise singing phrases haunt this writer's work. The reader starts to be haunted by them too, meeting half-echoes and reminiscences in different novels, stories, and poems.

The feature of conscious repetition is significant in many senses. In the prefatory note to his children's version of *Beowulf,* Nye says, "To me it is an essential story, and therefore never to be fixed." Essential tales, so far as Nye is concerned, can—and should—be told and retold. They possess the quality of living material: he picks them up and handles them and the substance quickens. Renewing what is old—and even what is ancient—is part of Nye's calling. *Doubtfire* seethes with lines from poems already written and poems not written yet.

FROM FALSTAFF TO BYRON

Two years after *Doubtfire,* the collection of short stories *Tales I Told My Mother* (1969) replayed more poetic extravagances. Again the tales are often hard work for the reader. However, although there is "the terror of transsexual nightmare" to contend with, "comic liveliness" starts to get a look-in in the shape of Mr. Benjamin, who escapes from a snowdrift by melting the snow with his "swelling cockerel of a cock." Then in 1976, *Falstaff* appeared, the novel which, according to its author, allowed him to find "my own voice and pitch."

Certainly, there is a huge difference between *Falstaff* and what has gone before, not only in terms of assurance, control, and readability, but more importantly in a sense of sheer delight in language. William Saroyan, on the Penguin back cover, describes it as "a riproaring, rollicking romp and riot of scholarship and neat, horny writing." For once the blurb is an understatement: the book is all these things and more. It is also sad at heart. Falstaff's purported memoirs are fabrications of a fat old man who fantasizes about his niece, a man who in real life "found lust easy and love difficult," who saw his true love three times and doesn't even know her name.

The next two novels, *Merlin* (1979) and *Faust* (1981), pursue familiar obsessions, though less successfully. Perhaps the financial success of *Falstaff* led Nye to write too much, too quickly. Merlin is the son of devil and virgin; Faust makes a pact with the devil. Thus the play between good and evil, dark and brightness continues. However, the "root at the dark root of all—an erotic nerve below everything, a source of all manner of imaginations and enchantments" (elsewhere an important idea) is diluted into erotic fantasy. Favorable criticism credits the novelist at this point with success as an erotic writer, but the reader looking for Nye the poet and thinker will be disappointed by long pornographic sequences that advance little. The style is thin in both *Merlin* and *Faust*—short chapters, speedy easy-read dialogue, a great deal of white space on the page.

There is a change again, however, with the next two novels, both of which are biographies. *The Voyage of the Destiny* (1982) tells the story of Sir Walter Ralegh's last voyage and death. *The Memoirs of Lord Byron* (1989) rewrites Byron's famously lost papers. Both novels convey a sense of genuine (and carefully researched) engagement with the real poets who are their subjects, and both books take the reader back to the poems. For that alone, they are valuable. But Nye the poet-novelist is back too: Ralegh, anchoring off the Leeward Islands, finds "a medicinal spring." The description is oddly

ROBERT NYE

familiar: "It must start hot down there, sown hot and sulphurous down there under the black, but by the time it comes out in the bank here, in this place I have scooped clean and keep filled with white pebbles like pearls, it is cold and good." Issues of sex and sexuality are not far away, but in these two novels they are integral to the thinking—and love is important too.

THE LIFE AND DEATH OF MY LORD GILLES DE RAIS

All Robert Nye's main characters are tempted by evil—or at the very least crookedness. But Gilles de Rais was around from the start and was the most terrifying embodiment. He featured in *Juvenilia 1*; he was—at least in one sense—the central character of *Doubtfire*. He is the "Lord Fox" who appears in both adult and children's stories, the uneasy heart of sadistic eroticism, sexual ambiguity, magical dabbling, and base matter—and yet he is indivisibly connected with the pure woman, the virgin Joan of Arc.

Gilles de Rais, the wealthy marshal of France who fought beside Joan of Arc at Orléans (and the probable origin of the Bluebeard folktale) was also a serial killer who confessed to the sadistic murder and sexual abuse of over 140 children in 1440. How could this epitome of evil have been associated with the young woman later accorded sainthood? That question is at the heart of Nye's thinking, perhaps because of his own attraction toward both innocence and carnal knowledge, goodness and cruelty. "I did what others dream," says de Rais in his confession. "I am your nightmare." The novel is a remarkable and authentic piece of writing, characterized by a sort of poetic plainness. There is no eroticism in it, no whimsy. It flinches neither from fact nor mystery. Just as, for Nye, poems should only appear when they "have to be written," so this novel was the product of a compelling necessity.

MR. AND MRS. SHAKESPEARE

Two more novels appeared in the 1990s: *Mrs. Shakespeare: The Complete Works* and *The Late*

Mr. Shakespeare. The first of these had its origin in a short story written a decade earlier. The novel is lightly, jokily written, the style thin, though not unattractive. It pales into insignificance though, beside *The Late Mr. Shakespeare,* which of all Nye's novels is the richest and the most beautifully developed. Here the mature novelist and poet is immediately evident, effortlessly drawing on a lifetime study of poetry and story. He plays his reader like a fish, with confidence, craft, and half-flirtatious charm. Among its many ideas, the novel pursues the theme of erotic love in a newly poignant way: "It is through suffering in love, erotic suffering, that we grow." The narrative is full of jokes and irony, both public and personal. Pickleherring, narrator and onetime actor in Shakespeare's company, quotes Nye's own words while purporting to recall Mr. Shakespeare's remarks. The novel has much to say about Shakespeare. However, at heart it is about Robert Nye. Readers who want to find Nye, the poet as well as novelist, could do worse than start here. Or they could start with the poems, which is where the author himself started and where—perhaps—he would most want to be found.

THE WHITE GODDESS

Before looking at the poetry, it is necessary to address this whole business of white goddesses. Nye himself does not use the term, but it is a handy coinage to describe the muse who flits through his work severally as Hecate, Habundia, Eurynome, Caridwen, the Queen of Elphame, Nimue, Erato, Diana, Helen, Sappho, Luna—all names for a feminine inspiration who is essentially nameless. Robert Graves thought every poet worth his salt had drawn on this source and wrote *The White Goddess* to prove it. Nye, in a review of Graves's *Some Speculations on Literature, History, and Religion,* called Graves a "master poet" but also remarked that "outside his poetry, he could be quite barmy." So is a belief in muse-inspired poetry also barmy? Perhaps. Nye himself, the tersely clear-thinking poet-critic, is the last person to attract such a description. And yet he believes in some form of mystical inspiration, just as he believes in God. "All I

196

ROBERT NYE

know about poems," he said in *Book and Magazine Collector* (1999) "is that the true ones are not the product of the will." If he chooses, as critic, to praise a poet, he will remark on their poems in terms of inspiration. Of Chatterton's "Rowley" poems, he says they "were written because they had to be written." Of Ralegh, he "wrote poems only when he had to." Of Graves, "Page after page bears the unmistakable impress of necessity." What kind of poet thinks like that? What does it mean when Nye says on the flyleaf of *A Collection of Poems, 1955–1988,* "As for poems, I hope never to write more of them than I have to"? For Robert Nye, the muse calls the tune. Without her intervention, poetry will simply not happen.

Is Graves to blame for this curious approach? Not at all. That sense of poetry's magical source was with Nye from the start, and he has never lost it. He talks of it in terms of magical personae, but also as that strange well-spring, which recurs in his writing and comes from the darkness within himself. Besides, Nye is not uncritical of Graves's thinking. "*The White Goddess,*" he says, "is dangerous stuff, especially for young poets." Dangerous in what sense? Perhaps the whole idea can sound too attractive, leading to Shelleyan flights of fancy. But not in any poet who has also been strongly influenced by that indomitable twentieth-century presence Laura (Riding) Jackson.

Riding's uncompromising beliefs about poetry dominated the theory and practice of Robert Graves: for a time she *was* his "muse." Other poets, too, spoke of her in terms of power and witchcraft. Nye himself fell under the spell of her poems at the age of thirteen, corresponded with her during four key formative years, and was different as a result. He was subsequently drawn to poets equally affected by Riding's thinking: Norman Cameron, James Reeves, Martin Seymour-Smith, Terence Hards, and those whose approach to the art is not dissimilar—C. H. Sisson, Malcolm Lowry, Warren Hope. Such poets do not form a school. Neither do they, despite the attempts of some critics to credit both Nye and Cameron with "Gravesian lyrics," share

a style. What binds them is a belief in poetry as something rich, rare, strange—and involuntarily chosen.

So exactly what did Laura Riding say to exert such power? In the preface to the 1938 edition of her poems (the one Nye found in Southend Public Library), she describes a poem as "an uncovering of truth of so fundamental and general a kind that no other name besides poetry is adequate except truth." Of all statements about poetry over the centuries, this must be among the most potent. No wonder those who share her beliefs write sparingly. The complexity of Riding's message is as enduring as Keats' "Beauty is truth, truth beauty." It takes an instant to understand intuitively, a lifetime to comprehend. And the reasons for writing poetry? According to Riding, "a tremendous compulsion that overcomes a tremendous inertia." Poems that *have* to be written.

THE FIRST TWO COLLECTIONS: JUVENILIA 1 *AND* JUVENILIA 2

Robert Nye's first collection was published in 1961, only six years after Philip Larkin's *The Less Deceived* had asserted a presence strong enough to be described by Michael Schmidt in *Lives of the Poets* as "the characteristic voice of the 1950s and 1960s." Nye, on the other hand, was always *un*characteristic. His work did not spawn a generation of imitators and stamp its indelible impress on the school curriculum. Neither did he go through pardonable phases, as many young writers do, of sounding "like" other poets. Nye sounds like himself in these early volumes—and often something much older than himself. If there is a voice that is not his own, it belongs to anonymous ballads and folk rhyme. At the same time—and running counter to this—there is a highly allusive (and elusive) complexity, a heady intoxication with language and verbal fencing.

But what about the titles of the first two books—*Juvenilia 1* and *2*? Such titles are usually used of posthumous collections, or sections thereof—the young work of a great writer collected for posterity. The term is at once dismissive (juvenilia are of literary interest only because of what came next) and highly ambitious (it implies that the magnum opus is on its way.) Nye's sense of his vocation as poet is in these titles: he knew he would go on to work on poetry all this life. His conviction was never less than absolute.

Juvenilia 1 is a puzzling little volume. Its contents were written between 1952 and 1957—that is to say between the ages of roughly thirteen and eighteen, forty-five poems by a very young writer. Yet the very first poem, "Preamble," has an ancient feeling about it. It is odd but not mannered: it reads like a medieval riddle:

Here comes I, as ain't been yet,
    A stem of that pluperfect
    I, who passed and came not,
Child among children I was not

Enigmatic phrasing introduces a dominant concern: the issue of identity. Who is "I"? The poem answers its own question—or appears to:

    At last I am intransitive:
A boy who cannot tell the time—
And you late coming home.

The simple complexity of the piece is astonishing. An intricate play of verb tenses—combined with literal and aural ambiguity of word and phrase—leads the reader into a spiral of thought that riddles itself perpetually. The last line ("And you late coming home") is all about time but has no finite verb at all, a timeless line. And the whole small poem evokes a huge sense of vulnerability and lostness.

However, if "Preamble" serves to entice the reader into *Juvenilia 1,* subsequent poems perplex in a different way, perhaps even alienate. While Nye's simplest poems are essentially (and beautifully) mysterious, some of the complex pieces are completely mystifying. From the depths of Southend Library, he returns with a theatrical company, the cast of which includes Joan of Arc, the Devil, God, King Pellam, Gareth, Byron, Iseult, Amfortas, the Virgin Mary, Pan, Robin Hood, Queen Habundia, Arthur, Parsifal, Hebenon, Adam, Othello, Christ, the Moon, George Fox. The collection reflects a troubled psyche: a deep absorption with death, blood,

alchemy, God, spiders, ghosts, spells. The world is gothic and shadowy, attractive but terrifying. Whirling words and medievalisms (lethlen, manchyn, chrissom, thistle-warp, dream-elsing, thraslark, lovendrinc) attest to an intoxication with language that attracts and also, in some poems, shuts the reader firmly out.

At the same time, there is no doubt of the deep personal meaning. In "Murder," for example, which is impenetrable to a casual reader, we find "God was my foster: Jarmara difference." Jarmara? A beautiful name, but meaning—what? In fact, Jarmara is a cat's name, the name of a witch's familiar. There is meaning if you know where to look: Nye is speaking of the same birthright he will later describe as "half Hecate and half Christ."

Stylistically the young Nye employs syntactical and typographical complexity that later he will take pains to avoid: ellipsis, inverted commas, frequent parentheses, polyhyphenated words, odd capitalization, e. e. cummings-type compressions, frequent use of ampersand. Such features reflect typical experimentation of that period, as does the occasional Eliot-like tendency to switch rapidly from discursive to lyrical tone.

But Nye's underlying voice is distinctive, as is the compelling movement toward form and music. Even in the middle of a whirlwind of obscurity, there are some wonderful lines: "As I have felt the soft fists of the rain / Tack on my shoulders, and a window pour / With the powers of darkness."

And of course there are whole poems that work completely. Of these, "Preamble," "Huntsmen," "That Raven," "Belladonna," "Undressing," "The Listeners," and "Kitchen Window" are particularly haunting. "Other Times" is a poem that would be noticed in any collection. The expression is wholly authentic. It is not necessary to know what the poem is "about" to feel that on an intuitive level it can be understood:

And you have gone, but still your foolishness
Imprisoned in the semblance of midsummer
Disturbs the rumor of oncoming snow.
'Do not remember me for I am here
At other times' you said. At other times
I can remember but have loved enough.

The early poems, in fact, can be divided into those that are often mysterious but intuitively understandable and those that are too obscure for most readers to bother with. The elliptical nature of Nye's early prose writing, compared with the purity and accessibility of *Gilles de Rais,* makes an interesting parallel.

There is a strong difference between the first *Juvenilia* volume and the second, even though the flyleaf instructs the reader that the two "should be considered as a whole." The second set of poems spans 1958 and 1962—the first four years of Nye's life as a young adult, the first two years of his marriage. The language is less difficult, though there is still plenty of playful coinage and syntactical complexity. There are more short, pleasurable lyrics, often with an incantatory quality. At the same time, the world of the poems is even more gothic, with a disturbing emphasis on damage and dysfunction. The preoccupation with dreams, sleep, identity, God, evil, death, spiders, blood, cobweb, snow—all of which are present in the first volume—continues. Repeated words and phrases are worth noticing because they will not go away: for the rest of Nye's career certain allusions will recur, certain words will acquire greater and greater significance. For example, we find recurring mention of lies (for Nye, as for Shakespeare, the word "lie" can never have only one meaning). Even those poems that look, at first sight, like simple lyrics are characterized by doubt and ambiguity. The first two metrically regular, perfectly rhyming stanzas of "True Love," for instance, have a lyrical purity and sharp spareness that is deceptive in its simplicity:

You say I love you for your lies?
  But that's not true.
I love your absent-hearted eyes—
  And so do you.

You say you love me for my truth?
  But that's a lie.
You love my tongue because it's smooth—
  And so do I.

The long pauses created by alternate short lines—and the dash at the end of the third line of each stanza—emphasize both parallels and contradictions. The poem sings, but it also thinks, and the thought stretches the ambiguity of words like "lie" and "truth" to the utmost. "You" and "I" exist in dramatic and syntactical tension. The form and style are more characteristic of an Elizabethan songbook than a twentieth-century poem—and yet the poem is also completely accessible—timeless, in fact. It is one of the poems that Nye does not change in any way—apart from the title, which in later books (including the *New and Selected*) becomes "Familiar Terms." Interestingly Nye avoids Latinate words almost entirely in this early poem and moves, with three notable exceptions, in monosyllables (as George Gascoigne, in his *Certayne Notes of Instruction concerning the making of verse or ryme in English,* 1575, would have approved). The longest (and most obviously Latinate) word is "absent-hearted"—and it is also the most complicated word in the poem. Not the "mind" (as might have been expected), but the "heart" is elsewhere, and this complex adjective describes "you," not "I." "True Love" sings sweetly and at the same time communicates a terrible bitterness. The final stanza drives this home:

You say they love who lie this way?
  I don't agree.
They lie in love and waste away—
  And so do we.

"Waste" is one of the significant repeating words in *Juvenilia 2.* Mirrors are also sinisterly important, as well as the general idea of "likeness." The word "crooked" recurs ominously, as does "break," "broken," and "shroud." "Shadow" is pregnant with meaning. There are references to exorcism, faithlessness, and raising the dead. Behind all the poems an intricate network of story is establishing itself.

"THE ONLY GHOST I KNOW"

All human beings have stories that are important to them. Some of these are part of personal experience. Some are stories they have read or heard. The old tales that still live, commonly known as myth and folk narrative, have survived because they are important to all of us. The story of Gilles de Rais has fascinated Nye all his life. Either we find our own stories, or they find us. Something in our consciousness seems to recognize a personal relevance that feels larger than we are. However, it is a rare writer who also creates his own myths, and this is an added source of interest in Nye's work. His repeated reference to specific images based on personal experience evokes a cumulative feeling of recognition. Often it is hard to tell whether he is drawing on a real incident in his life or an imaginary detail. In the end, it may not matter: once the story acquires mythic resonance, the original incident is unimportant.

Still, some haunting images do make the reader want to pursue their origins—for example, the shoes at the side of the bed that sit "heels under, to ride away nightmare" in "Undressing" (*Junvenilia 1*) and in at least two later poems. Equally, the story in "The Eaves" (*Juvenilia 2*) of the woman found hanging "Half-strangled in her sluttish hair" exerts considerable fascination (it recurs in *The Late Mr. Shakespeare* as Pickleherring's recollection of his wife's death and—by remote allusion—in a different but closely connected poem, "The Rain in the Eaves" [*Collected Poems*, 1995]). Such images feel like moments out of time, and when they recur, they actualize as timeless allusions, not imprisoned in one poem but escaping in several directions.

DARKER ENDS *AND* DIVISIONS ON A GROUND

So much then, for juvenilia. Except that Nye's first two books cannot be so easily dismissed. He is not a writer who moves on to the "real, mature work." Maturity of thought and expression, in verse form, was there from the start and persists. And the poems that preserve his early inspiration stay with him—quite literally.

The two *Juvenilia* volumes contain between them ninety-seven poems. *Darker Ends* (1969) and *Divisions on a Ground* (1976) jointly comprise only sixty-nine. But of that sixty-nine, twenty-four poems are either reworked or reprinted poems from the *Juvenilia* volumes. That leaves only forty-five completely new poems produced over a period of about thirteen years—

just over three poems per year. Obviously it is inappropriate to measure poems by numbers: quantity is insignificant compared to quality. But clearly something was going on here. Robert Graves said that he wrote poems at the fairly constant rate of four or five a year. Both Graves and Nye subscribe to the idea that poetry should be inspired or should not happen at all. Yet Nye's output, unlike Graves's, has not been steady. And it has been characterized by an unparalleled need to go back and rework previously published poems.

An editorial note in *Darker Ends* reads, "Drafts of some of these poems first appeared in *Juvenilia 1* (1961) and *Juvenilia 2* (1963)." A similar note in *Divisions on a Ground* suggests that "the sequence entitled *Expurgations* consists of final versions of poems which appeared in earlier drafts in *Juvenilia 1* (1961) and *Juvenilia 2* (1963)." Drafts? Final versions? Several poems reproduced in *Darker Ends* are unchanged from their first versions ("True Love," for example, is simply retitled); others change radically—generally by becoming shorter and simpler, with eccentricities of typography and line layout removed.

In *Divisions on a Ground,* the poems that form the sequence "Expurgations" are mostly fragments of longer early poems. One combines parts of two poems. Another, "The Furies," rephrases "The furious blow / Half their brains out" in favor of "Some poets blow / Half their brains out"—a neatly ironic twist in meaning. It then goes on to comment on how poets "fool with their verses / To please the Furies." "Fool," of course, is another Nye word; it connects with the term "joculator" defined in *The Late Mr. Shakespeare* as "A fool who knows the wisdom of foolishness," or with the "comedian" Pickleherring, whose desire is "to come at the truth by telling lies." At the same time, there is a feeling that "Expurgations" purged little. These poems come back to haunt him in terms of both form and thought.

But what about the new poems in these two later volumes? *Darker Ends* is in many ways the more satisfying of the two collections. The title poem opens the volume in a strongly personal, intimate tone. The poet is at the bedside of his young son, both entertaining and scaring the child:

Here's my hand turned to shadows on the wall—
Black horse, black talking fox, black crocodile—
Quick fingers beckoning darkness from white flame,
Until my son screams, "No! chase them away!"

The father's hand (it is worth noting that Mr. Shakespeare in Nye's novel also makes shadow pictures) creates familiar creatures. But the images increase in menace—first a horse, then a fox (with more sinister connotations) and finally a crocodile (the most threatening of all—even in a Punch and Judy show). The "quick fingers beckoning darkness" evoke black magic. This poem is not lyrical. It treads a careful pace, varying the meter in tune with the thought, employing sound echoes but no regular rhyme scheme:

Why do I scare him? Fearful of my love
I'm cruelly comforted by his warm fear,
Seeing the night made perfect on the wall
In my handwriting, if illegible,
Still full of personal beasts, and terrible.

The question "Why do I scare him?" leads to a truthful attempt to resolve the answer—and more. It opens the poet's mind, "full of personal beasts." A desire to protect his child is stronger than the impulse to frighten him, but Nye fully acknowledges that impulse, though it clearly scares him, too.

There is much unease in *Darker Ends*. "Anniversary" has a resonant and powerful bitterness, while "A Trout," "A Leaf Blown Upstream," and "Not Looking" suggest a new love—difficult too, but potent. "Crowson" represents a change in style. It is a narrative poem, based on explicit personal experience, the first (but not the last) of its kind. "Fishing," with which the book ends, has autobiographical significance—and it is about poetry. "At thirteen he went fishing for stars," but later the fisher-poet learned "how not to fish too much / Or, rather, how to fish for more than stars / With less than mussels or a singing line." It spells out a credo: a belief in truth rather than glitter, meaning rather than decorative sound.

Lastly, "The Boys" cannot pass without mention. It is a horrible (and excellent) poem that connects with a central concern: violence and darkness. The boys in the woods are out hunting: "obeying its curse, / they kill what the dark loves." The short poem ends with violence: an image of what the boys do *not* do, and yet even that act is imaginatively realized:

Poet, be grateful they do not run
nor hammer yet at your door,
to drive your pen through your open eye
and follow the night to its source.

The word "curse" finds an assonantal echo in the "source" of this last line, and the half-rhyme is sharp—sharp as the pen, bringing a shock—like static charge. The "open eye" aurally introduces "I," the source of the night, the source of darkness. We are reminded of the last lines of the volume's title poem:

To tell the truth, when he is safe asleep,
I shut my eyes and let the darkness in.

As for what it may mean, to be the source of darkness, like Joan of Arc who says "I am the dark" but who exudes a light like glory—that is a big question, and not answered yet.

Divisions on a Ground introduces another type of poem new to Nye's repertoire: the playful satire. "Henry James," "To a Dictionary Maker," "Interview," and "Reading Robert Southey to My Daughter" fall into this category. The first sentence of "Henry James" unfolds with a grave formality worthy of its subject:

Henry James, top hat in hand, important, boring,
Walks beautifully down the long corridor
Of the drowned house just off Dungeness
At the turn of the century.

Like all Nye's poems, the opening is characterized by immediacy, but here darkness has given way to merciless satire. The poet goes on to describe James's face with a gleeful sideways swipe at his novel *The Golden Bowl:*

It is a face which looks like the face of a goldfish
Fed full of breadcrumbs and philosophy, superbly
Reconciled to its bowl.

Other poems, such as "Hong Kong Story," may or may not be satirical—it is hard to tell. The last

ROBERT NYE

mentioned is as surreal and as baffling as some of the early poems in *Juvenilia 1,* but without the linguistic richness. "Agnus Dei," on the other hand, is an interesting piece, again untypical of what has gone before and based on a precise series of visual images, like snapshots. Nothing happens; there are no finite verbs; but the image is sharp and clear. A few poems ("Traveling to My Second Marriage on the Day of the First Moonshot," "In More's Hotel," "My Uncle") evoke that lyric grace of thought and expression which sounds so resonantly through Nye's oeuvre. "The Seven Deadly Sins: A Mask," which concludes the volume, is a verse play based on "The Lord's Prayer"—something completely different again, serving as a reminder, if one were needed, that Nye is not only a Christian, but also a Christian poet. His allusion to "the seven sins of contradiction to eternal grace" connects with the seven chambers in Lucy Negro's house in *The Late Mr. Shakespeare,* as well as (more obviously) to the central idea of grace important both in earlier and later poems. The "specific antidote / Which is called Christ" is the only answer to sin—and sin, in Nye's world, is serious. At the same time, the deadliness of sin does not obliterate a wry humor:

You may suppose your own death to be a mistake
At least until you have been mistaken by it

As a whole, *Divisions on a Ground* is a motley: hard for a reader beginning here to get a sense of where Nye stands or where he is headed. It may be no accident that one poem, "The Long-Ago Boy," suggests lost direction, a predominant sadness, only dispelled by evoking the past:

The boy's ribs are bruised
By the bullying northpaw wind.
When he weeps, it's hailstones.
When he laughs, the lake gets gooseflesh.
The sun is bleeding to death in a puddle of slush.
O long-ago boy, let's spit at it. Tonight
We'll claw all the stars down
That dangle from Orion's stupid belt.

TWO SETS OF COLLECTED POEMS

A Collection of Poems, 1955–1988 (1989) brings together poems (or versions) from all previous volumes; in all it includes eighty-nine poems. They are not consistently chronologically presented, though thematic links are preserved. So far as revisions are concerned, this volume includes a few that are markedly unsuccessful (in several cases, Nye will return to the earlier version in his next book). The very beautiful early poem "Christmas Eve," for example, becomes "Song of the Fourth Magus," with a new final stanza immeasurably inferior to the original. (Mercifully, it is restored in the 1995 *Collected Poems.*) Approximately twenty-four poems are new, though it is easy to get confused since some of these preserve whole lines from earlier poems. Above all, it is clear to see that the production rate has not increased: perhaps a couple of new poems each year. "A Charm against Amnesia" may well record a sense of lost direction connected with this sparse output. It immediately recalls the early lyric purity of "True Love," "The Listeners," and "That Raven" in *Juvenilia 1:*

No name you know reminds you now
Of who you are or why you go
Alone about your trouble in the snow.
Forgetting whom you would forget
You have forgotten more than that
And lost your mind's distinctive alphabet.

The poem reads simply and timelessly, its tercets like a magical incantation. Nye is never afraid of formal patterns, and here the singing structure works, quite deliberately, like a spell. It is a poem in which he is talking to himself—in fact giving himself "a bit of a talking to." He reassures himself at the end (as Nimue reassures Merlin, "But it is not too late yet"):

That half-loved other is your fate—
Her name can turn you from hell's gate
And bring you home again before too late.

Such lyrical beauty also characterizes "A Bit of Honesty," "The Rain upon the Roof," "Round

Table Manners," and "A Leaf Used as a Bookmark." Others take biographical narrative one stage further: "Childhood Incident," for example, describes how the poet's mother once appropriated a volume of Elizabeth Barrett Browning's poems, bought at "junk-stall" by her young son, and heated it in the oven "to kill all known germs." The truth of the experience is palpable in both tone and detail:

I can still see those pages that curled and cracked,
And the limp green leather cover that peeled away
  like lichen
From the body of the book, and the edges turning
  gold,
And the hot glue's hiss and bubble down the spine.

But most clearly I recall as if this was just yesterday
An odd but quite distinct and—yes—*poetic* scent
Which arose from the remains of Mrs. Browning's
Poems. ...

The later volume, *Collected Poems* (1995), is divided chronologically into five sections. The sections span, respectively, four years, four years, six years, six years, and—finally—eighteen years. A few uncollected early poems are included, too. There is a handful of notable new poems, in particular "Admonition on a Rainy Afternoon," "Eurynome," "The Sewage Pipe Pool" and "The Frogs." The last of these is fascinating—it stands out because it is *not* sweet: it rhymes but it does not sing. It connects with themes of sexuality and voyeurism obvious in the novels but rarely appearing explicitly in the poems. Its positioning in the book is also significant—it follows a prayer-poem in the words of Joan of Arc ("If I am not in the grace of God / May God place me there") and precedes the elegantly literary "Sappho." "The Frogs" is not like either of its companion poems and resembles little else in Nye's work except possibly "The Holy Experiment" in *Juvenilia 1,* which recalls Byron's sexual interest in his half-sister Augusta's "shrewd behind." But that poem works by mischievous allusion. "The Frogs" is completely direct. It recalls a paragraph in *Doubtfire,* where Retz sees "two frogs, like frogs, upon the porch, inadequately copulating. I shook with fury not a

little less than their infuriation, losing reason, stamping on them until their antique emerald no more amused the moon, and they were dead as stone." There was significance in that incident for Nye, and so he returns to it in verse. In rhyming couplets he describes the frogs' sexual congress. The narrator's role is that of fascinated (and excited) observer (the same role occupied by Pickleherring in *The Late Mr. Shakespeare,* watching his young neighbor through a hole in the floor—his "secret erotic theatre"):

The female frog was small and plump.
She shook with lust and took him up her rump.

Their eyes were bright, their mouths agape;
It was a sweet unconscionable rape.

This is a risky poem. It summons erotic danger; "forbidden" pleasures. It is about sex, not love. It drops in the dark phrase "unconscionable rape" without shame or embarrassment. And this time, unlike the narrator in *Doubtfire,* the voyeur does not stamp on the frogs. Quite the reverse:

An age I watched them in their slime
Doing what I do now in my black rhyme.

Their frogging done, they had a piss.
Christ send me, quick, another night like this.

What is going on in this poem? The title reminds us of Aristophanes' comedy by the same name (which features Dionysus in a central role). So there is a sense of the comic there, the sense perhaps of coming at the truth by telling lies. There is something absurd, after all, about being "turned on" by observing frogs copulating. Besides, the frogs' pleasure is an anthropomorphic fantasy. But the poet says the frogs are "Doing what I do now in my black rhyme." Doing what? Perhaps coupling, as the poet makes couplets. Or perhaps the poet is deliberately "playing" his readers: attracting them into a "foul pool," a "black rhyme," a forbidden territory for poetry—because he knows the attraction is real, and therefore part of life, and therefore part of poetry, too. But there is another consideration yet: Nye is a Christian poet, so the invocation of Christ in the last line cannot be taken lightly. But

how should a poet appeal to Christ for "another night like this"? Possibly "The Rotter," a poem published only once in book form
A Collection of Poems, 1955–1988) offers a partial explanation. The first line of "The Rotter" features in two other early poems: "He wished his bones might dream without his flesh." The line implies an instinctive unease about sexual pleasure. However, the poem also recognizes that the flesh itself, if obeyed in terms of simple need, may have its own kind of purity:

He wished his flesh might act without his mind—
A lovely need. But then he was dismayed
By love, and never much cared for touching.

"The Rotter" is a sad poem; "The Frogs" is much more carefree, and it may, perhaps, finally satisfy that "lovely need"—simple sexuality with no intellectual complications. And the voyeur may take delight in that, because "touching," in every sense, is much more difficult. There is a kind of complicit innocence in "The Frogs."

In the last section of the *Collected Poems,* apparently covering the years 1977–1995, the poet does something quite idiosyncratic. Certain poems are presented as having been written during this period, when in fact they stem from much earlier. "Poppies," for example, is almost completely faithful to the first stanza of "A Necessary Blindness" in *Juvenilia 2.* Similarly "The Devil's Jig" is drawn from the second part of "Boyhood" in *Juvenilia 2,* though the lines are rearranged to make a much more fully effective poem. Several things seem to be happening here—it is much more complicated than a simple preoccupation with revision.

FOOLING WITH HIS VERSES

In a review of the *Complete Poems of Robert Graves: Volume 1,* Nye draws attention to Graves's "obsession with getting a poem right." He notes five textual emendations to "The Cool Web" between 1927 and 1975 and wholeheartedly approves the changes: each is not only "an improvement both in sound and in sense" but also "evidence of a moral struggle to make words enact what they are saying, make the poem truthful as well as true."

Such a moral struggle, then, partly explains what underpins Nye's revisions: the truth of the matter is so important that he will not let it be until he thinks it is achieved. Such an attitude must be respected. At the same time, a reader tracing the changes through cannot help feeling that a poem originally written in the early 1960s, if represented as belonging to that period, might be allowed its original expression. For example, "At Last," which was printed originally as "The Empty Heart" and later as "An End," has traveled through four variations on the fifth line. It isn't immediately obvious why the last version is the best.

But some late poems have connections with earlier versions that are striking in their oddness. For example, the poem "Storm," which had its genesis in "Any Other Enemy" in *Juvenilia 2,* was originally a single five-line stanza:

Bemused by nightmare, unable to dream,
Half sleepily awake in the crook of my arm,
You change your mind back to sleep, complaining 'I love you'
Who might as well love any other enemy
And would, no doubt, in wartime.

It is a poem that focuses key aspects of Nye's world: nightmare, a slant reference to the muse in "bemused," the crookedness of the arm, the love that is also a complaint, an ironic uneasiness about sexual fidelity—and finally an essential opposition between lover and enemy. The poem reappears in *Darker Ends,* but the "you" of the first version shifts significantly to become a "friend of mine," perhaps to emphasize the friend/enemy opposition but in fact distancing the narrative voice from the intimacy of "you." When the poem resurfaces in *A Collection of Poems, 1955–1988,* "you" is back, bringing with it an intimate danger. The poem has now doubled in length, formalized its versification, changed its title, and accommodated a storm—perceived both as outside the window and inside the relationship. Once again the loved one is "complaining," but this time the complaint is much more serious— "that I wish you harm." The last two lines resume familiar bitterness, the rhyme and the bleak foreshortening of the last line evoking an Othello-like obstinacy:

Who might as well love any other foe—
And do, for all I know.

Both versions of this poem carry real authenticity, but only "Storm" makes it to the 1995 *Collected Poems,* where it is included in the 1977–1995 group, along with "Poppies," "The Devil's Jig," "Enough," and "Lullaby," all of which have ur-texts in the *Juvenilia* volumes.

Why, then, does Nye keep resurrecting or reworking old poems? An unkind critic might suggest it is a way of masking lack of inspiration—padding out a new book. In Nye's case, this explanation won't wash. Quite apart from the fact that his aim was always quality, not quantity, if he had needed to swell the pages of his slender poetic volumes, whole paragraphs of some of the novels could easily have been construed as half-decent verse. There are poems inside the novels, too, which have not been included in verse collections. Most poets have to write numerous forgettable poems in order to win their way to the handful of lyrics that may ensure their immortal memory. In Nye's case, he began with certain remarkable poems that need, in more than one sense, to be contemporaries of his later work.

In Nye's work, old poems resurface for several reasons. One certainly has to do with his belief that it sometimes takes decades to "finish" a poem. Another is the need to rework an image that never leaves him. And finally, something that should not be forgotten is personal context: "Any Other Enemy" was written when Nye was married to Judith Pratt. "Storm" dates from the period of his second marriage to Aileen Campbell. Both poems summon that crippling fear which may threaten the heart of a loving relationship. The poem has acquired new resonance in different circumstances. The repetition is chilling.

Other texts, by the time they reach the 1995 *Collected Poems,* are allowed to appear in two versions—the original and a related (but different) poem. For example, "A Former House," which originally derives from "The Looking Glass" in *Juvenilia 2,* has traveled through part 7 of

"Expurgations" to appear separately (and under both titles) here. Similarly "Moon Fever," which began as "The Heron" in *Juvenilia 2,* appears in both versions in the 1995 collection. In some cases Nye, having taken a poem through a second version, restores it to its original. This is true of "Kingfisher," for example, as well as "Five Dreams" and "Christmas Eve." Sometimes the restoration comes as a relief; at other times less so.

This is a poet grappling with a tortuous thinking process. His poems are an attempt to think something enormously difficult right through to its logical conclusion. There is also, perhaps, a fundamental refusal in Nye to consign poems to the past. Their meaning and their lyric beauty is still as alive to him as though he had written them yesterday. He comes to them in a different period of time, and they are at once familiar and completely new. In *The English Sermon, 1750–1850* he remarks, as editor: "John Keble was one to whom the new is but the old understood more clearly." Robert Nye is another.

NEW POEMS

At the time of this writing, a new volume of verse is in preparation. Judging by poems published over the last few years in the small press, it will be a compelling read—and the volume contains more than thirty new pieces. To anyone who has followed not only Nye's lyrical gift—the feeling that his voice belongs to a tradition far older than itself—there are poems that revive a kind of grace he has always been able to summon. "The Task" renews his sense of spiritual vocation as poet; "The Well-Spring" confirms its inexhaustible source; "Down Darkening" and "The Spider" retread the floorboards of fear and nightmare; "Birthright" and "The Prize" suggest that somehow both darkness and light have been accommodated and that redemption is possible. Many of Nye's poems are about love, but just as many are about poetry itself. One new poem, "Song Talk," seems to comment, in beautiful and lyrical terms, on the whole process of writing (and revision) in Nye's life, as well as his belief that truth is more important than understanding.

"Song Talk" reads simply, but what it says has taken a lifetime to learn:

Some say the nightingale improves his song
By adding new notes to it, year by year,
Correcting any bits he first gets wrong
Until the whole is simple and sincere.

But others say that bird sings from the heart
And does not need to add or change a thing
Because he is inspired from the start
To know what song a nightingale should sing.

I say it does not matter which is right
So long as the bird truly tells his tale;
Nor do you need to understand the night
To sing your heart out like a nightingale.

MAKING AN ENDING

"In my beginning is my end," says Eliot memorably in "East Coker." Nye makes such lines come true. In his early novel *Doubtfire,* the narrator in the first paragraph evokes "the void, the good void, the aching void of the good, which is his source and port and target." Near the end of *The Late Mr. Shakespeare,* "the void, the good void, the aching void of the good" is Shakespeare's "source and port and target." What can this possibly be—the "aching void of the good"? And how could such a destination be at all desirable? How can Joan of Arc be the dark itself and at the same time a source of light? How can a Christian believer be so drawn to witchcraft? How can the web of pure thought kill? Nye, who writes both prose and poetry with his "pen dipped in darkness," is trying to understand this himself; he invites us to share that process.

In one of Nye's children's tales, the eponymous poet Taliesin meets a man who asks him, "Will you make me a poet like yourself?" Taliesin replies, "Only the Muse makes poets." His companion points out that there are plenty of poets in the court who write about "important matters" with no reference to muses or witches. "Tell me this," counters Taliesin, "listening to the songs of these bards did you ever feel … that you remembered all this from somewhere else? And yet, when you searched your memory, you knew

that it was not just an old song, nor just a new song, but a song both old and new, original and remembered?" The man admits that he has never felt this before. "Well then," says Taliesin, "they are no true poets."

If Taliesin's test is applied to most twentieth-century poetry (and nearly all of what has so far appeared in the twenty-first), little of it will pass as "true." In an interview in the e-zine *Tryst* in 2002, John Sweet expressed a view shared by many: "In a good month, I'll write 40 or so poems. When I get jammed up, only 10 or 20. … I'm not a big believer in 'the muse.' If you want a poem, you have to work for it." Sweet is a typical twenty-first-century writer—perhaps typical of most poets at any period of writing. Robert Nye belongs to a rarer breed: he holds back until necessity dictates; his sparse production results in short, intense, oddly familiar poems. Life is not long enough to read thousands of poets all writing forty poems a month. It is, however, not too late to be enriched by a few darkly rich poems, which linger in the heart and mind long after the reading. When a man writes only what he sees as fundamental truth—sometimes no more than two poems in a year—it is time to listen to what he has to say.

Selected Bibliography

WORKS OF ROBERT NYE

POETRY
Juvenilia 1. Suffolk: Scorpion Press, 1961.
Juvenilia 2. Suffolk: Scorpion Press, 1963.
Darker Ends. London: Calder & Boyars, 1969; New York: Hill & Wang, 1969.
Divisions on a Ground. Manchester: Carcanet, 1976.
A Collection of Poems, 1955–1988. London: Hamish Hamilton, 1989.
Collected Poems. London: Sinclair-Stevenson, 1995. Reissued by Carcanet, 1998.
Henry James and Other Poems. Edgewood, Kentucky: R. L. Barth, 1995.

The Rain and the Glass: New and Selected Poems. London: Cecil Woolf; New York: Arcade. Forthcoming.

NOVELS

Doubtfire. London: Calder & Boyars, 1967; New York: Hill & Wang, 1968.

Falstaff. London: Hamish Hamilton, 1976; Boston: Little, Brown, 1976.

Merlin. London: Hamish Hamilton, 1978; New York: Putnam, 1979.

Faust. London: Hamish Hamilton, 1980; New York: Putnam, 1981.

The Voyage of the Destiny. London: Hamish Hamilton, 1982; New York: Putnam, 1982.

The Memoirs of Lord Byron. London: Hamish Hamilton, 1989.

The Life and Death of My Lord Gilles de Rais. London: Hamish Hamilton, 1990.

Mrs. Shakespeare: The Complete Works. London: Sinclair-Stevenson, 1993; New York: Arcade, 2000.

The Late Mr. Shakespeare. London: Chatto & Windus, 1998; New York: Arcade, 1999.

SHORT STORIES

Tales I Told My Mother. London: Calder & Boyars, 1969; New York: Hill & Wang, 1969.

The Facts of Life and Other Fictions. London: Hamish Hamilton, 1983.

PLAYS

Sawney Bean. With Bill Watson. London: Calder & Boyars, 1970.

The Seven Deadly Sins: A Mask. London: Omphalos, 1974. (Also included in *Divisions on a Ground,* 1976.)

Penthesilea, Fugue and Sisters. London: Calder & Boyars, 1975.

CHILDREN'S FICTION

Taliesin. London: Faber, 1966; New York: Hill & Wang, 1967.

Bee Hunter: Adventures of Beowulf. London: Faber, 1968. Published as *Beowulf: A New Telling,* New York: Hill & Wang, 1968.

Wishing Gold. London: MacMillan, 1970; New York: Hill & Wang, 1971.

Lord Fox and Other Spine-Chilling Tales. London: Orion, 1997.

NONFICTION

"The Sleepless Soul That Perished in his Pride." *Times Saturday Review,* March 18, 1970. (Article written on the bicentenary of Chatterton's death.)

"The Body Is His Book: The Poetry of John Donne." *Critical Quarterly* 14:345-360 (winter 1972).

"Robert Nye." In *The Tiger Garden: A Book of Writers' Dreams.* Edited by Nicholas Royle. London: Serpent's Tail, 1996. (In this short autobiographical piece, Nye records his experience of writing the poem "Listeners.")

"The Point of Poetry." *The Tablet,* April 1, 2000. (Nye comments here on the nature of poetry and the role of inspiration.)

REVIEWS

"Vision and Revision." *Scotsman,* January 1, 1996. (Review of Robert Graves's *Complete Poems: Volume 1.*)

"Here Is the Muse." *Scotsman,* December 13, 1997. (Review of Robert Graves's *The White Goddess* and *Complete Poems: Volume 2.*)

"Exploits of a Holy Opium Addict." *Scotsman,* October 17, 1998. (Review of Richard Holmes's biography *Coleridge: Darker Reflections.*)

"Here Is the Muse." *Scotsman,* December 16, 2000. (Review of Robert Graves's *Some Speculations on Literature, History, and Religion.*)

"Do Universities Kill Off Poetry?" *Scotsman,* November 17, 2001. (Review of Robert Crawford's *The Modern Poet: Poetry, Academia, and Knowledge since the 1750s.*)

EDITED WORKS

A Choice of Sir Walter Ralegh's Verse. London: Faber 1972.

William Barnes: Selected Poems. Manchester: Carcanet, 1973.

A Choice of Swinburne's Verse. London: Faber, 1973.

The English Sermon: An Anthology. Vol. 3, *1750–1850.* Manchester: Carcanet, 1976.

The Faber Book of Sonnets. London: Faber, 1976. Published as *A Book of Sonnets,* New York: Oxford University Press, 1976.

First Awakenings: The Early Poems of Laura Riding. Manchester: Carcanet, 1992; New York: Persea, 1992.

A Selection of the Poems of Laura Riding. Manchester: Carcanet, 1994; New York: Persea, 1996.

CRITICAL AND BIOGRAPHICAL STUDIES

Hobsbaum, Philip. "Robert Nye." In *Contemporary Poets.* 5th ed. London and Chicago: St. James Press, 1991. Pp. 708-709.

Matcham, Clive. "Robert Nye." *Book and Magazine Collector* 180:74-86 (March 1999).

"Robert Nye." In *World Authors, 1970-1975.* Edited by John Wakeman. New York: Wilson, 1980. Pp. 589–592.

MARGARET OLIPHANT

(1828–1897)

Antonia Losano

ONE OF THE most prolific, versatile, and popular of Victorian writers, Margaret Oliphant produced over ninety novels, more than twenty-five histories and biographies, at least fifty short stories, and over three hundred literary or cultural essays published in periodicals of the time. She was reported to have been Queen Victoria's favorite novelist and was for many years a major and regular contributor of reviews, editorials, and other nonfiction pieces to the prestigious journal *Blackwood's Magazine.* Oliphant's seemingly endless stream of popular novels quickly made her a well-known and well-loved literary figure in England. Her equally steady production of literary and cultural criticism meant that she knew and was known to most of the writers, thinkers, and politicians of her time and was one of the most influential critical voices in London literary circles.

During her lifetime Oliphant was considered one of the country's foremost writers—if not on a par with the extremely highbrow George Eliot, then certainly similar in reputation to Wilkie Collins or Anthony Trollope. When Oliphant died her publisher William Blackwood wrote that she had been as important for England's literary world as Queen Victoria was to the larger society. After her death, however, her reputation quickly diminished, and she became known as merely a popular novelist rather than a producer of literature. Late Victorian and particularly modernist critics considered that Oliphant's productivity was in fact overproductivity; they felt that she might have laid claim to a more solid place in the literary canon if she had concentrated her efforts in fewer novels. Even the writer Virginia Woolf, who admired Oliphant's intellectual powers, bemoaned the fact that because of her family's poverty Oliphant was forced to publish enormous quantities of work without having the leisure time to focus her energies. During much of the twentieth century and now into the twenty-first, Oliphant's literary reputation continued to suffer because of her status as the Queen of Popular Fiction. Critics often assumed that anyone who could write so much simply could not be producing quality work. Such an assumption depends much upon a conception of artistic genius as consisting of irregular bouts of wild inspiration rather than upon a steady industriousness. This ideology of genius as explosive rather than sedate became current only in the Romantic era (roughly 1790 to 1830) and has only rarely been supported by actual facts: many accepted, canonical "geniuses" like Wordsworth, Austen, Dickens, Eliot, and others never fit the pattern of unpredictable Romantic genius.

The value of Oliphant's productivity, like that of her contemporary Trollope, is at last being reconsidered. In the 1990s Oliphant's literary output began slowly to undergo serious reevaluation. This resurgence of interest has brought many of her works, long unknown, back into print. A nuanced understanding of the quality and historical importance of her work—both fiction and nonfiction—is gradually evolving. But Oliphant's writing offers scholars numerous difficulties. Within the academy, most recovery work of little-known women writers like Oliphant has been carried out by feminist scholars who are eager to redress the wrongs done to past women writers simply because of their gender. Undeniably many women writers were neglected, rejected, or misinterpreted by their contemporaries and by subsequent readers and critics solely because they were women writers. But the case of Oliphant's erasure from the literary canon is proving to be an interesting phenomenon, raising dilemmas both for traditional and feminist scholars. For the more traditional critic, Oliphant's fiction is of questionable quality, often primarily because of its subject matter (domestic, feminine, and religious rather than political or historical). For the feminist scholar, Oliphant's work is marred by her conservatism on women's issues. One of the main goals of late-twentieth-century feminist scholarship was the recovery and reevaluation of lost women writers, particularly those whose work (like the Brontë sisters or the New Woman novelists of the 1890s) clearly argues for at least some kind of women's emancipation. Oliphant's work, however, is not so easily subsumed under a feminist agenda and often specifically argues against feminist causes. Nor do her novels offer readers explicit critiques against the Victorian patriarchal system. Oliphant certainly does criticize the way women of energy and intellect were curtailed by their social environment, but this criticism is oblique rather than strident, and Oliphant's heroines, though lively and socially powerful, generally remain within the strict bounds of social convention. As a result Oliphant has remained outside both the male and the female literary traditions—too interested in women's issues to be considered among the "great" realist writers of the Victorian age, but at the same time too ambiguous in her treatment of women's issues to be embraced by contemporary feminist scholarship. It is to be hoped, however, that as scholars continue to reexamine her fiction and her impressive body of essays and other nonfiction works, a more comprehensive and balanced picture of Oliphant's contributions to literature should emerge. The question of what to make of Margaret Oliphant is very much still under debate.

BIOGRAPHY

Oliphant was born Margaret Wilson in Wallyford, a town just outside Edinburgh in Scotland, on April 4, 1828. Although she lived most of her life in England or Europe, Oliphant maintained close emotional ties to her Scottish homeland and proudly retained a certain Scottishness in manner throughout her life. Although formally part of Great Britain in the nineteenth century,

Scotland had a long previous history of failed struggles for greater independence, and the Scots jealously maintained autonomy in various aspects of life. For example, Scots were subject to different laws than the English (most famously, Scottish marriage laws were considerably more lax than English marriage laws; hence the Scottish town of Gretna, just across the border from England, was a popular elopement destination in the early nineteenth century). The British government attempted many times (through legal, military, or other routes) to stamp out the more rebellious aspects of Scottish culture, particularly in the remoter Highland regions. The public conception of the Scots as daring, warlike, and boldly independent was reinforced by Scottish literature, which was in vogue throughout the British Isles during the late eighteenth and early nineteenth centuries, in large part because of the influence of Sir Walter Scott, whose historical novels sparked a fad for all things Scottish. Oliphant, particularly in her early novels, drew heavily on her Scottish heritage and contributed to the reading public's concept of the brave and bold Scot.

Oliphant's father, Francis Wilson, had a minor job with the customs service and had little impact upon the young Margaret. He was by all accounts a weak and ineffectual figure, and his lack of character is echoed in many of the men in Oliphant's fiction. Her mother, on the other hand, was more powerful, and her intelligence and energy had a great impact upon Oliphant's life. Although both parents were Presbyterian (as were many Scots), Oliphant chose to become Anglican (a member of the established Church of England). She had two elder brothers (Frank and William, known as Willie), but there had been a girl and two boys who had died before Margaret was born.

Oliphant was educated at home, largely by her mother. Oliphant wrote her first novel at age seventeen, but her first published work, *Passages in the Life of Mrs. Margaret Maitland of Sunnyside,* appeared in 1849 when Oliphant was twenty-one years old. She was not certain she wanted to send the work out for consideration, but her brother Willie stole the manuscript and sent it without her knowledge to the publisher Henry Colburn, who published it to reasonable success. (The book went into three editions and was praised by such contemporary writers as Charlotte Brontë and Charles Dickens.) Oliphant published a few other novels through Colburn, but in 1853 she became permanently attached to the well-known Blackwood publishing firm, which was to be her most important professional relationship. For the first few years of her publishing career, Willie continued to negotiate with publishers, as was common in the period. Women were rarely permitted access to the business world; any financial or professional interactions were carried out by male relatives. Women writers also regularly published novels under masculine pseudonyms (for example, George Eliot and the Brontë sisters) or simply anonymously, "by a Lady" (as did Jane Austen). Willie, because he carried out all the dealings with publishers in Oliphant's early career, managed to have four of Oliphant's novels attributed to himself when published.

In 1852, with three novels under her belt, Margaret married her cousin (a common occurrence in the nineteenth century) Francis Oliphant; she published under the name "Mrs. Oliphant" for the rest of her life. He was ten years her senior. Francis was a painter who specialized in designing stained glass, but he was financially irresponsible; for most of their married life Oliphant wrote consistently to earn money to support her husband and their growing family of children. The marriage appears to have been relatively happy but marred by financial woes and the fact that Oliphant's much-beloved mother intensely disliked her daughter's new husband. Relations between husband and mother were so strained that Oliphant was forced to visit her mother in secret.

From this point Oliphant's biography reads like an extended tragedy. Her marriage to Francis Oliphant was to last only seven years. He contracted tuberculosis (also called consumption) and took the family to Italy in hopes that the warmer climate would improve matters. It did not, and he died in 1859, leaving Oliphant penni-

less, pregnant, and with two small children, Maggie and Cyril. A son Francis (called Cecco) was born two months after her husband's death. From then on, writing became not just a vocation but a practical necessity for Oliphant. She needed money to support herself, her three children, and eventually other family members who came to rely on her for emotional and financial support. Her brother Willie had trained as a clergyman and had held a post as minister for a short time, but his alcoholism quickly became apparent to his parishioners and he was forced out. He became Oliphant's dependent for the duration of his surprisingly long life as a permanent wastrel and alcoholic. Her brother Frank, devastated by the death of his wife and unable to work, turned over the care of his children to Oliphant; one of her nieces even changed her last name to Oliphant in honor of the woman she called "mother" for most of her life.

In 1864 Oliphant suffered the greatest tragedy thus far in her life: her daughter Maggie, age ten, died after a short gastric illness in Italy. Oliphant had lost three children previously—a daughter who died at eight months, a day-old boy, and a nine-week-old boy (the death of young children was, in the days before antibiotics and antiseptic medical practices, all too common)—but the death of Maggie, her firstborn, was crushing. After Maggie's death Oliphant returned with her two sons to England, settling at Windsor, which was to be her home base for the next thirty years. Both her remaining children predeceased her as well, dying in their thirties of lung disorders after unfortunately dissolute and unproductive lives. Cyril died in 1890, and Cecco, her last surviving child, died in 1894.

Throughout all these tragedies and hardships, Oliphant wrote and wrote and wrote. She wrote for money, certainly, but she also seems to have written for emotional solace—her work provided an imaginative realm far away from the depressing reality of her daily life. After experiencing the deaths of her parents, her husband, two brothers, one sister-in-law, her six children, and numerous friends, Oliphant ended her autobiography with two stark lines set in almost poetic isolation:

And now here I am all alone.
I cannot write any more.

(Autobiography and Letters, p. 150)

She did continue to write, however, even after writing these fatalistic words; she continued to produce essays and fiction up until the week of her death. As she lay dying, too weak to hold the pen herself, she even dictated a poem that she asked to be published as a kind of epitaph.

After her death the literary world took stock of her accomplishments. The writer Henry James wrote one of her many obituaries, her publisher Blackwood another. Queen Victoria, whom Oliphant had met personally and whose two published memoirs Oliphant had reviewed for *Blackwood's* (a difficult task), made formal declarations of her sadness. From her rather humble origins as the daughter of a Scottish clerk, Oliphant had raised herself purely by hard work to a prestigious social (if not economic) position, one that resulted in friendships with world-renowned writers and invitations to tea with the queen. Oliphant stands as a success story for the middle-class working woman, whose professional skill allows her to move steadily up the social ladder.

Her unfinished *Autobiography* was posthumously published in 1899 along with a selection of her letters. The *Autobiography* is a powerfully moving account of her struggles, her friendships, and her literary interests. Unusually, Oliphant chose to write her autobiography not in the standard linear sequence but rather in a fragmented, almost thematic way. Instead of tracing her life from birth through childhood to marriage, motherhood, widowhood, and a busy career, Oliphant attempts to explain the complexities of her life and work in a series of only roughly chronological vignettes, touching sometimes on family, sometimes on current events, sometimes on her works-in-progress. She never attempts, as did many writers of the time, to offer a coherent narrative of artistic development (a narrative of "progress" toward ever-increasing artistic confidence).

In fact Oliphant's self-representation in her *Autobiography* questions the whole notion of the writer as an "artist" at all. She consistently portrays herself as professional workman (or workwoman), someone who plies her craft with time, patience, and sweat rather than some kind of semidivine inspiration. What often emerges from reading Oliphant's *Autobiography* and her letters is the startling intensity of her self-awareness and her frequent bouts of self-pity. Oliphant herself rarely commented on her own fiction; she refused to write about her work as "art" or to consider herself a serious artist. At the start of her *Autobiography,* she writes:

> I have been tempted to begin writing by George Eliot's [the pen name of the contemporary highly respected novelist Mary Ann Evans] life—with that curious kind of self-compassion which one cannot get clear of. I wonder if I am a little envious of her? I always avoid considering formally what my own mind is worth. I have never had any theory on the subject. I have written because it gave me pleasure, because it came natural to me, because it was like talking or breathing, besides the big fact that it was necessary for me to work for my children. … I feel that my carelessness of asserting my claim [to being a great novelist] is very much against me with everybody. It is so natural to think that if the workman himself is indifferent about his work, there can't be much in it that is worth thinking about.

(pp. 4–5)

Oliphant refers to George Eliot frequently throughout the opening of her *Autobiography;* Eliot, who was lucky enough to have the time, money, and support to give her work careful attention, represented the kind of writer Oliphant herself could not be due to circumstances. At one point she writes in despair, "No one even will mention me in the same breath with George Eliot" (p. 7).

The modernist novelist and critic Virginia Woolf, in her extended essay *Three Guineas,* writes that Oliphant "sold her brain, her very admirable brain, prostituted her culture and enslaved her intellectual liberty in order that she might earn her living and educate her children" (p. 166). Woolf seems to believe that Oliphant *could* have written better novels (more erudite, more polished) but for her dismal personal situation, which Woolf argues stemmed directly from gender concerns. Oliphant's husband's inability to support her, the fact that having children was not really a choice for married women at the time, the various failings of her brothers and sons, and so on—all these contributed to locking Oliphant into a role that did not allow her the leisure to refine her undeniable literary talent. Woolf saw Oliphant as a victim of Victorian patriarchal culture, too worried about making a living to have time to worry about making art. Oliphant herself sets out a similar argument when she writes in her *Autobiography:*

> I don't quite know why I should put this all down. I suppose because George Eliot's life has, as I said above, stirred me up to an involuntary confession. How I have been handicapped in life! Should I have done better if I had been kept, like her, in a mental greenhouse and taken care of? ... It is a little hard sometimes not to feel ... that the men who have no wives, who have given themselves up to their art, have had an almost unfair advantage over us who have been given perhaps more than one [dependent] take care of. Curious freedom! I have never known what it was. I have always had to think of other people, and to plan everything. ... I have not been able to rest, to please myself, to take the pleasures that have come in my way, but have always been forced to go on without a pause.
>
> (pp. 5–6)

As these quotes suggest, Oliphant persistently refused to elevate her profession into a romanticized calling, but she was extremely aware how much her personal circumstances influenced her abilities.

OLIPHANT AND THE VICTORIAN REALIST NOVEL

Oliphant's writing varies wildly; she produced works in almost every category, from sensation fiction to provincial religious fiction to domestic tales, romances, and supernatural thrillers, along with innumerable book reviews, cultural and literary essays, historical scholarship, short stories, travel books, and biographies. Perhaps her greatest skill was the ease with which she shifted genres. Any discussion of Oliphant's career must consider the diversity of her writings; we will start here with her novels.

The novel is generally considered the central literary form of the Victorian era (much as poetry is associated with the Romantic period). Understanding the enormous popularity and centrality of the novel throughout the nineteenth century is a necessary background to understanding Oliphant's life, work, and literary reputation. Novels were most frequently offered to the public first in serialized form, published in literary magazines in numerous small segments (often the longer novels of Dickens or Trollope would run to sixty or more installments). Readers would purchase each issue of the magazine as it came out, and when the novel had run its course a publisher might then (if the novel had been popular enough in serial format) publish the novel in three volumes, each volume again appearing individually. Eventually the three-volume format gave way to the single editions with which we are familiar today. The serial format meant that readers were constantly attuned to the world of fiction, as they waited impatiently for the next installment of their favorite novel-in-progress. It also meant that novels were constantly evolving as the serialization went on; writers often didn't have the entire plot mapped out in their heads beforehand. Oliphant, for example, wasn't certain whether her novel *The Perpetual Curate* would be a novel at all when she began it; she thought it might turn out to be a novella, or even shorter. Under the serial system, publishers and even readers had a great deal of influence upon what might happen next in a novel. Writers also couldn't go back and revise earlier chapters, which made the entire process of writing fiction very different from that of today.

It is also crucial to understand that the modern distinction between popular "fiction" (which was read for entertainment) and erudite "literature" (which was read for education or moral improvement) was not a distinction yet recognized by the Victorian public. The novels of the most famous writers of the period—George Eliot, Charles Dickens, Charlotte Brontë, William Thackeray—were read by the intellectual elite and the middle classes (and often working classes) alike. Oliphant's work was read by a similarly wide range of people.

The dominance of the novel coincided with the dominance of a particular literary style: realism. Realism attempted to represent the actual daily emotional, religious, domestic, and political experiences of ordinary individuals rather than the fantastic adventures of heroes or kings. The Victorian reading public expected that the novel would show them themselves—their interests, their activities, their culture. Although the Gothic or sensation novel was also popular, realist fiction dominated for most of the century, and most of Oliphant's more than ninety novels are in the realist mode. Oliphant also produced numerous historical novels, curiously one of the least respected of the novelistic genres of the nineteenth century. George Eliot encountered this problem when her novel *Romola,* which traced the romantic and political intrigue surrounding a young woman in fifteenth-century Florence, received significantly less acclaim than any of her domestic tales set in contemporary nineteenth-century England. Historical fiction had reached its apex with Sir Walter Scott's Waverly novels at the end of the eighteenth century, and none of the Victorian novelists seemed able to repeat his success in the genre, although all of the major novelists tried (perhaps the one judged most successful was Dickens' *A Tale of Two Cities,* set during the French Revolution). The adult Victorian reading public by and large seemed to prefer tales set in their own time, in their own land.

Her first novel, *Passages in the Life of Mrs. Margaret Maitland of Sunnyside* (1849), is told in the first person and traces the life of a religious Scottish spinster, Margaret Maitland, who becomes the guardian of a young relation, Grace Maitland. The novel is quiet and largely descriptive, with greatly detailed renderings of the Scottish landscape and the Scottish character; the only real dramatic element in the plot comes from the budding romance between Grace and the minister Claud, Margaret Maitland's nephew. Oliphant later wrote a sequel to *Margaret Maitland* titled *Lilliesleaf,* published in 1859.

For the fifteen or so years after the publication of *Margaret Maitland,* Oliphant continued to produce novels with a Scottish setting: many of these early works are subtitled "A Story of Scottish Life." Then in 1861 Oliphant published the novella "The Rector," the first work in the *Chronicles of Carlingford* series which was to make her truly famous and which went on to include the novella "The Doctor's Family" (1861–1862) and the novels *Salem Chapel* (1862–1863), *The Perpetual Curate* (1863–1864), *Miss Marjoribanks* (1865–1866), and *Phoebe Junior* (1876). The series, set in an imaginary country town (Carlingford) not far from London, explores the lives of the middle-class inhabitants (doctors and other professionals, clergy, and tradesmen and their families) during the mid-nineteenth century. Carlingford is represented as a quiet, prosperous, sheltered (socially as well as geographically) community:

> It is a considerable town, it is true, nowadays, but then there are no alien activities to disturb the place—no manufactures, and not much trade. And there is a very respectable amount of very good society at Carlingford. To begin with, it is a pretty place—mild, sheltered, not far from town; and naturally its very reputation for good society increases the amount of that much-prized article.
>
> (*The Rector and The Doctor's Family,* p. 1)

Carlingford itself is much like Elizabeth Gaskell's Cranford in its atmosphere, while the series bears a resemblance to Anthony Trollope's popular Barsetshire series, which also features novels linked by a place and (loosely) by a common cast of characters. Many of the works in the series focus on religious issues and provide an interesting introduction to the intricacies of Victorian Christianity.

"The Rector" details the spiritual and social crises of a new reverend, who has embarked upon a religious life purely to sustain his elderly mother. "The Doctor's Family" shows us another side of Carlingford by introducing us to Edward Rider, the local surgeon (at this point in history an inferior position, below official doctors), a weak young man with social pretensions. His alcoholic elder brother Frank returns from Australia with his children, his wife, and her sister Nettie, a strong-willed young woman who becomes the novella's heroine and eventually agrees to marry Rider. Richard Chatham, an Englishman who lives in the wilds of Australia, appears suddenly in town to startle the hidebound inhabitants and to hint at the world events occurring beyond the safe bounds of Carlingford. Oliphant calls him "The Bushman" and writes:

> A very small stretch of imagination was necessary to thrust pistols into his belt and a cutlass into his hand, and reveal him as the settler-adventurer of a half-savage disturbed country, equally ready to work or to fight, and more at home in the shifts and expedients of the wilderness than among the bonds of civilization; yet always retaining, as English adventurers will, certain dainty personal particulars—such, for instance, as that prejudice in favour of clean linen, which only the highest civilization can cultivate into perfection.
>
> (*The Rector and The Doctor's Family,* p. 143)

Chatham offers to squire Nellie and her now-widowed sister back to Australia; Nettie refuses, but she is torn between her desire to return to "the colony" and to remain in England. In her fiction Oliphant only rarely engages with the complex issues surrounding British imperialism; "The Doctor's Family" provides but a brief glimpse into her ideas on the subject.

The first full novel in the series, *Salem Chapel,* was serialized (as were the first two novellas) in *Blackwood's Magazine* from 1862 to 1863. The novel focuses on Arthur Vincent, the nonconformist minister of Salem Chapel, which is the only dissenting religious institution in the town of Carlingford. Nonconformity is the name given throughout the nineteenth century to the group of English Christians, also called Dissenters, who do not belong to the established national Church of England (Anglicans); although technically this applied to Roman Catholics as well, the name in practice was used only for Protestant groups. The nineteenth century saw an enormous increase in the numbers and influence of Nonconformist churchgoers; by the end of the century the number of nonconformists exceeded the number of practicing Anglicans. Scottish Presbyterians (to which group belonged Oliphant's parents) were the dominant Scottish Nonconformist group.

Oliphant herself became an Anglican when she moved to London. It is possible that Arthur Vincent reflects Oliphant's own transition away from nonconformity. Vincent begins his ministry with high ideals but is gradually disillusioned by the reality of life as experienced by his lower-middle-class parishioners. During the course of the novel Vincent loses his sense of vocation and falls in love with a society woman. He leaves the church and takes up journalism as his new calling; he founds a journal called the *Philosophical Review* to espouse his new beliefs. Alongside this study of religious politics Oliphant sets a subplot of the sensation variety in which one of the members of the Nonconformist church, Mrs. Hilyard, has a secret past. She has fled from an evil husband, Colonel Mildmay, who continues to stalk her and her abused daughter. Mildmay, in disguise, is also courting Vincent's sister Susan; when she discovers his villainy she shoots him. She is arrested for the crime but Mildmay, having a slight change of heart, refuses to testify against her, and she is released. The unusual double plot of *Salem Chapel,* blending as it does the quiet comic realism of a religious story with the heightened melodrama of a sensation plot, has caused some critics to consider the novel unbalanced. However, critics also have compellingly suggested that the double plot was intended by Oliphant as a commentary on both literary genres: religious or "clerical" fiction, as it was often called, and sensation fiction.

The Perpetual Curate, the fourth work in the Carlingford series, again focuses (as the title suggests) upon religious issues. Curates are low-ranking clergymen in the Church of England hierarchy; in Victorian fiction they were often poorly paid, overworked, and frequently figures of pathos. Oliphant's novel explores the experiences of a young curate, Frank Wentworth, who, although an Anglican clergyman, has leanings toward Catholicism. The Church of England was often divided into High and Low Church sides: the High Church was the closest to Catholicism and emphasized tradition, sacraments, ritual, and the authority of clergymen. The Low Church was nearer to the Nonconformists in ideology. Many Church of England members who became attracted to High Church ideals eventually officially converted to Catholicism (as did the theologian John Henry Newman), often with radical personal consequences. In Oliphant's novel Frank's half-brother George, who has a wife and five children, is tempted to resign his well-paid position as rector and become a Catholic priest, which would leave his family fatherless and penniless. Frank's own leanings toward Catholicism lead him in more positive directions; he helps organize a sisterhood and preaches to the poor in the slum districts. In the end, however, both men compromise: George does convert to Catholicism but does not become a priest, and Frank becomes rector at Carlingford but does not wholly renounce his High Church leanings.

Miss Marjoribanks (pronounced "Marchbanks") is often considered Oliphant's best novel and has garnered the most scholarly interest in modern times. Published in book form in 1866, this fifth volume in the Carlingford series is the least interested in religious matters. The novel displays Oliphant at her most sophisticated; the narrative is tightly controlled and almost sardonic in its mock-heroic tone. This is not her most common literary technique, however; the current critical centrality of *Miss Marjoribanks* can give readers new to Oliphant a skewed idea of her style. Rather, Oliphant's fiction is generally characterized by a light tone and focuses upon daily activities and domestic objects that are invested with simple psychological meaning. Oliphant's characters are rarely larger than life, rarely cast in the heroic mode. But in *Miss Marjoribanks* Oliphant offers a witty and strident critique of a social order that prevents women from becoming the larger-than-life heroines they want to be; the novel makes fun both of the society that confines women and the pathetic attempts of women to gain power in their narrow world.

The novel begins with the death of the mother of the young heroine, Lucilla Marjoribanks. Lucilla is seventeen, still at school, and filled with romantic ideas about how one should act upon the death of one's parent. Oliphant's sarcasm is biting here; she portrays the young heroine consciously acting the part of the grieved child with evident enthusiasm and remarkable calculation. Everything Lucilla does, in fact, is done with calculation. She is obviously too intelligent for her environment but too ignorant (because of her education and upbringing) to escape into something more challenging. Instead she focuses her enormous energies upon reorganizing polite society in Carlingford. She begins by instituting genteel social gatherings, upon which inordinate time, money, and thought are expended. Lucilla is absurdly pleased with the success of her parties, and considers herself the "Queen of Carlingford," a majestic leader of the community. She busies herself by planning dinners and marriages and becomes the arbiter of fashion and morality.

Yet for all the sarcasm Oliphant uses to describe Lucilla's activities, the narrative is still in sympathy with her; she is not portrayed as a mean or bad character. Oliphant's point seems to be that Lucilla is confined to such a narrow, inane, ludicrously unimportant sphere of activities because of her gender. Oliphant is extremely concerned in this novel, as in a great many of her novels, with the idea of women's work. Lucilla's desire to become the monarch of her small world stems not from vanity but from a desperate desire to do something, to be active and engaged in the world. But the real world of midcentury England, Oliphant tells us, offers very little for the middle-class woman to do. For an intelligent woman this limitation can pose serious problems. Early in the novel Lucilla's father bemoans the fact that Lucilla is a girl; he recognizes that she is more intelligent than her male relatives and would have benefited more from the professional education and training that tradition dictated be given to her male cousins. Instead of becoming a doctor or lawyer, Lucilla is forced to work out her enormous energies in the narrow confines of "woman's sphere." The wonderful irony of the novel is that Lucilla embraces precisely the kind of female power that conservative Victorian conduct books said women should have: absolute power in the home, power over fashion, morals, food, and polite society. But Oliphant's language and symbolism consistently represent this power as analogous to larger-scale political power; she regularly refers to Lucilla as "the young sovereign" or "this distinguished revolutionary." The novel also makes it quite clear that this kind of female domestic power has an unavoidable tendency to bleed over into other aspects of the world; the second half of the novel focuses a good deal on Lucilla's involvement in a local parliamentary election. As a woman she has no vote, but her private influence in the town is enormous and can sway the electorate.

At the end of the novel Lucilla finally agrees to marry her cousin Tom Marjoribanks, thus assuring that her married name will, significantly, remain the same as her maiden name. Oliphant makes it quite clear that their future will include no wifely passivity on Lucilla's part. When they become engaged, their discussions as to how their married life will proceed are unusual for Victorian fiction and display Oliphant's persistent belief in women's superiority to men (in terms of intellect, energy, and organization). Lucilla announces that she must have "something to do" after she is married; Tom replies with the standard middle-class Victorian male ideal: "That is what *I* want … but as for you, Lucilla, you shall do nothing but enjoy yourself and take care of yourself. The idea of *you* wanting something to do!" (p. 481). She insists that she must be occupied, and he cries out, "But now you are in my hands I mean to take care of you, Lucilla; you shall have no more anxiety or trouble. What is the good of a man if he can't save the woman he is fond of from all that?" (pp. 481–482). To this Lucilla says nothing, but she thinks to herself, "What was to be done with a man who had so little understanding of her, and of himself, and of the eternal fitness of things?" (p. 482). Her belief is that the "eternal fitness of things" requires a powerful woman in control of men and society in general; Oliphant's narrative seems to agree with her in many regards. Lucilla succeeds in convincing Tom to purchase the estate of Marchbanks and has dreams of influencing behavior in the small village near the estate, just as she had tried to reign in Carlingford. Oliphant writes, "Lucilla's eyes went over the moral wilderness [of the village] with the practical glance of a statesman, and, at the same time, the sanguine enthusiasm of a philanthropist" (p. 494). Marriage for Lucilla will increase rather than decrease her scope for activity.

The final novel in the Carlingford series, *Phoebe Junior,* was published in 1876. Its heroine, Phoebe, similar in liveliness and intelligence to Lucilla, comes to Carlingford from London and eventually marries the son of an extremely wealthy contractor. The son is too ignorant and ineffectual to take up his father's business, but Oliphant makes it clear that Phoebe is more than equal to the task. In marrying Clarence (whom she does not love), Phoebe will gain not just a husband but a career as well.

Many of Oliphant's subsequent novels also focus heavily on the theme of women's work. Oliphant herself was, after all, a working woman who struggled to balance the demands of career and family in a way almost unprecedented for her era. Novels like *The Three Brothers* (1870), *Kirsteen* (1890), and *Diana Trelawny* (1892) explore the lives of working women, showing the effects of work upon their personal lives or vice versa. Oliphant also engages with various strains of public opinion on the subject of women in general. The Victorian era is well known for its enormous concern for "The Woman Question"; women's domestic, moral, physical, and political character was fiercely debated during the century. The question of the fitness of women for work was particularly pertinent because the reigning monarch of the period was Queen Victoria, herself a hardworking woman and mother of nine children. Oliphant's female characters (particularly Lucilla Marjoribanks) engage with issues along the same spectrum, if not of the same magnitude, as those that occupied the queen in her professional and personal life.

In *Hester* (1883), Oliphant introduces us to a woman banker, Catherine Vernon. She is the despotic head of the Vernon family, having sacrificed her private hopes to provide for her family. Her financial acuity and the power her profession gives her is what turns the male heir against her (a circumstance familiar to Oliphant, who was a similar figure in her family and was greatly resented, as well as loved, by her grown-up sons, who themselves failed to make anything of their lives). Although treated sympathetically, Catherine isn't represented as a positive model for women; her niece Hester wishes to follow her lead and take up a career, but Catherine won't hear of it, feeling that Hester ought to follow the traditional female path of marriage and motherhood instead. The novel leaves Hester on the brink of marriage to one of two honorable suitors, but she loves neither passionately. Hester has longed to do something unusual, even dangerous, but it is uncertain whether she will ever truly be permitted to break out of the mold in which society has placed her.

Oliphant's novel *Joyce,* published in 1888, traces the life of a heroine who is raised by rustic foster parents; she becomes a schoolteacher and gets engaged to a local schoolmaster who wishes her to stop working when they marry. She resists this, and he considers her ambition overly masculine. Joyce is removed from her dilemma by the discovery of her true parentage; she joins her middle-class father and is raised into a new social class. Joyce falls in love with a well-to-do young man whose family does not want him to marry a girl with a lower-class past. Joyce is convinced to sacrifice her desires for happiness, and she returns to her foster parents and a life as a spinster schoolteacher. The novel offers no way out for an intelligent, independent woman—she can neither marry "beneath her" (the schoolmaster) nor marry above her station; she must resort to solitude.

In *Kirsteen: The Story of a Scotch Family Seventy Years Ago* (1890), Oliphant returns to her Scottish roots and continues to explore the problems faced by intelligent professional women. The novel focuses on the aristocratic but impoverished family of Douglas, headed by a destructive and vicious father with four daughters. Kirsteen is the rebellious daughter who rejects her father's demand that she marry a wealthy suitor; she runs off to London and becomes a successful businesswoman. The plight of women in a stultifying, materialist society is given voice in the novel by the Douglases' outspoken servant, Marg'ret, who appreciates the lively and intelligent Kirsteen and provides money and advice for her escape from home. Kirsteen travels first to her sister Anne's home in Glasgow; Anne has married a doctor (against the wishes of her family, who feel that any contact with a working

man is dishonorable) and is happy with her husband and children. Kirsteen then moves to London, where she stays with Marg'ret's sister Jean, who runs a mantua-making business (mantua-maker is the older term for a dressmaker). Kirsteen goes to work for Miss Jean; Kirsteen's aristocratic manner makes her an extraordinary asset in the business, and she is quickly promoted to serving the wealthiest customers. Eventually Miss Jean offers Kirsteen a partnership, and the business quickly becomes the most exclusive and profitable in the city.

Kirsteen is then recalled to her family home by the news that her mother is dying. There she reconciles with her father, who is willing to use the money she has made (although he despises her for working at all) to repurchase some of the family's estates. The sum he wants is beyond even her means, but she determines to work herself to the bone if necessary to gain the money, and does. She also uses her worldly knowledge to save her youngest sister, Jeanie, from the dishonorable advances of a local aristocrat. Kirsteen's father, living as he is in a fantasy of his family's importance, envisions that the man means to marry his daughter: only Kirsteen can understand that he simply means to seduce the penniless young girl.

Kirsteen is an unusual heroine in many ways. Although she is shrewd, lively, and powerful, she is not without serious flaws. She is consistently snobbish, believing with her father that her sister Anne, by marrying a working man, had hopelessly de-classed herself—even though Kirsteen herself works for a living. She steadfastly refuses to trade under her family name, Douglas, since that would bring dishonor upon the family; instead she simply uses her Christian name in her business. In her business dealings she refuses to make dresses for any but the upper crust, refusing even to make a dress for her younger sister Mary, who has married a man whom Kirsteen believes has insufficient social rank. Her emotional life, too, is unusual and ambiguous. Her refusal to marry, for example, is complex: her solitude is both empowering and emotionally debilitating, as scenes of late-night tears show.

Yet at the end of the novel, Kirsteen is living as a wealthy single woman, active in trade and appreciated by her remaining family. Oliphant's last word seems to be that a working woman can achieve *some* measure of contentment.

In addition to her interest in the lives of working women, several other themes appear with surprising regularity in Oliphant's enormous oeuvre of realist fiction. Although Oliphant was conservative in her political writings on the subject of women's legal rights (she wrote against women's suffrage, for example, a fact that has greatly contributed to contemporary feminist disinterest in Oliphant's work), she consistently portrays women in her novels as stronger, cleverer, and more active than men, who are represented as weak, self-indulgent, and ineffectual in both public and private life. Men are never evil, never villainous, just simply trivial and incompetent. Perhaps because of this lack of masculine power in Oliphant's fictional world, women in the novels are also—unusually for Victorian fiction—almost wholly uninterested in romantic love. Few if any of her novels end with the traditional "happy ending" in which a man and a woman in love head off together into the proverbial sunset. Intense romantic happiness is virtually unknown in Oliphant's novels, although mild married contentment is occasionally achieved. Certainly her heroines marry, but they are not portrayed as indulging in any kind of real or deep passion for the men they eventually choose. Oliphant's view of marriage (possibly because of her personal experiences with it) is consistently unsentimental, practical, and businesslike. In her *Autobiography,* Oliphant writes, "the love between men and women, the marrying and giving in marriage, occupy in fact so small a portion of either existence or thought" (p. 10). The powerfully romantic scenes of novels like *Wuthering Heights* and *Jane Eyre* find absolutely no echoes in any of Oliphant's fiction.

Oliphant consistently shows in her novels that marriages based on convenience, common sense, and nothing stronger than mild affection (if even so much) are in fact more successful than those entered into because of a mistaken (for Oliphant) belief in romantic passion. Eddy and May in *The*

Railway Man and His Children (1891), for example, enter into matrimony for completely unsentimental reasons and prove to be well suited and quite content. Couples in *The Sorceress (1893), Phoebe Junior,* and *Sir Tom* (1884) marry under similar circumstances (for money, or out of boredom, or simply because it is what people thought they should do), and Oliphant deems the matches successful. Even the heroine of *Miss Marjoribanks* announces her decision to marry her cousin whom she does love by the bland pronouncement that "after all it was Tom" (p. 497).

Oliphant's depiction of women who do love powerfully is, on the contrary, generally negative. Such women are punished for what Oliphant represents as unrealistic expectations or self-indulgence. Her novels undermine or make ridiculous the Romantic urge toward heroism, passion, or extreme states of any kind. Her fiction consistently exposes the blandness of women's daily existence, making a mockery of those women (and novels) that strive toward the melodramatic or tragic. Oliphant's novel *Janet,* for example, published in 1891, offers a parodic twist on Brontë's Gothic romance *Jane Eyre.* The heroine of *Janet* sets off to become a governess like Jane Eyre; Janet is ready and willing to become a victim and subsequently a heroine but is disappointed at the warm and cozy welcome she receives from the Harwood family. But the Harwoods have their own dark secret; instead of a madwoman in the attic as in *Jane Eyre,* Janet discovers that Mr. Harwood is mad. His wife has spent her life protecting him from harm and protecting their children from discovering the sad truth about their father. But no danger besets Janet; the novel treats madness as a horrible and depressing part of life rather than a Gothic excitement.

Other main themes in Oliphant's fiction include religion, politics, and the problems of social class. As we have seen, religion and religious debates are a primary focus of several works in the *Chronicles of Carlingford* series; to these one can add *Caleb Field: A Tale of the Puritans* (1851), *A Son of the Soil* (1866), and *The Curate in Charge* (1876). Political elections and radical political ideology can be seen in *Miss Marjoribanks* and *He That Will Not When He May* (1880). In *Squire Arden* (1871), its sequel *For Love and Life* (1874), *It Was a Lover and His Lass* (1883), and *The Cuckoo in the Nest* (1892), as well as in many other novels, Oliphant tackles the complex problems of the class hierarchy in Great Britain. She covered a wide range of topics, themes, and issues in her fiction, which is not surprising given her enormous productivity.

SUPERNATURAL TALES

Even though much of her fiction went out of print in the years after her death, Oliphant's supernatural fiction has remained consistently popular. She published numerous short stories and novellas with supernatural themes, some of which were eventually collected into *Stories of the Seen and Unseen*. Two of her best stories, "The Open Door" and "The Portrait," are in this collection. She also published the novella "A Beleaguered City" (1879), which is often considered her best work.

The extraordinary story "The Open Door" traces the gradual awakening of a brusque and rational military man, Mr. Mortimer, who must learn to believe in the supernatural and in the power of human love in order to save his dying son. The son is haunted by a spirit crying for help in the garden of their home. The spirit is the ghost of a boy who is crying for his dead mother, and Mortimer must confront the ghost and try to aid it. Eventually a local minister releases the spirit out of the purgatory-like state by telling the ghost:

> Your mother's gone with your name on her lips. Do you think she would ever close her door on her own lad? Do ye think the Lord will close the door, ye faint-hearted creature? You'll find her with the Lord. Go there and seek her.
>
> (*Stories of the Seen and Unseen*, p. 74)

The novella contains a clearly symbolic encounter between rationalism (the father), science (in the figure of Simpson the doctor) and faith (the minister); only the latter can release both the ghost boy and the living boy from their turmoil. "A Beleaguered City" focuses on similar issues of faith. In the novella, a small French cathedral town is taken over by a "presence" that forces the inhabitants out of the town. The townspeople are represented as being devoted to the rational, skeptical of anything religious or supernatural. At last the mayor's wife, who has just lost her daughter, realizes that the presence is in fact the ghosts of the dead, trying to bring the living a message about faith (the story was originally conceived as a Christmas tale). The living people of the town must reassert their faith to be allowed back into their homes. They do, but the tale ends ironically, as the townspeople quickly revert to their irreligious ways.

Oliphant offers a metaphoric account of the woman writer in her short story "The Library Window," published in *Blackwood's* in 1896 (the year before her death). The story is told in the first person by a young woman who spends her time looking out her window into one particular window in the university library across the street. The act of looking becomes for the developing young woman a refuge from the boredom of her own banal feminine life, which offers only sewing, tea parties, and an elderly aunt for interest. Gradually the narrator begins to discern the outline of a figure, which turns out to be a young man sitting in the room beyond the library window; he is sitting at a writing desk, utterly absorbed in his work. Only the narrator can see into the window at all; other viewers think it is merely a painted window, or a fake window with nothing beyond it, or an old window that has been filled in with boards. Yet the narrator continues to see the young man writing in the room; the vision becomes a symbol for a world outside the narrator's grasp, a fantasy of a world that would include education (it is a university library window) and imaginative work (writing) but that is wholly a male domain. At the climax of the story, the young man turns and nods to her; after this she never sees into the window again. The window of imagination has disappeared.

NONFICTION: ESSAYS, REVIEWS, HISTORY AND BIOGRAPHY

For thirty-plus years Oliphant was a regular contributor to *Blackwood's,* the enormously popular and prestigious literary magazine that published poetry, fiction, book reviews, political and cultural essays, and translations of foreign literature. The magazine, which ran from 1817 until 1980 (one of the longest-circulating literary magazines in history), was published by the firm Blackwood and Sons, the preeminent Scottish publishing house for the nineteenth century. It set up London offices in 1840 and consistently attracted writers of a high caliber, both for its magazine and its three-volume publications. The magazine was published monthly, which made it an ideal vehicle for fiction (as opposed to the more infrequent quarterly publications of the time, which made readers wait many months for the next installment of a story). *Blackwood's* serialized major novels of the period by prominent writers such as George Eliot (who published most of her major novels through Blackwood and Sons), Anthony Trollope, and Joseph Conrad, in addition to Oliphant. Much of Oliphant's early fiction appeared in *Blackwood's,* as did almost all of her literary criticism. One of her last works was a history of Blackwood and Sons titled *Annals of a Publishing House,* published in 1897, the year she died.

Oliphant's influence as a literary critic cannot be overrated. As a frequent reviewer for one of the most prestigious literary journals in the country, she had the chance consistently to mold public opinion in a profound way. She reviewed works by some of the best-known writers of her day (some of whom are now considered the great writers of the nineteenth century): Thomas Hardy, Jane Austen, Henry James, Honoré de Balzac, William Wordsworth, Charles Dickens, and others. She also reviewed the two published works (both personal memoirs) of Queen Victoria—a job that required considerable tact on Oliphant's part, since the queen was very eager to be considered a real literary talent.

One of her most widely quoted reviews helped to establish, define, and popularize an entire literary subgenre. In a *Blackwood's* essay on Wilkie Collins' novel *The Woman in White,* Oliphant helped to define the character of sensation fiction in terms we still use today. Sensation fiction, considered to have officially come into being in 1862, was one of the more popular nonrealist genres in the Victorian era. It arose out of the Gothic fiction of the late eighteenth century and gave way to detective fiction by the end of the century. In her essay titled "Sensation Novels," published in 1862, Oliphant claimed that Collins' novels marked a new beginning in novel writing. Although numerous authors (Dickens, Oliphant herself, Nathaniel Hawthorne) had previously published novels that partook of sensational elements, it was Collins, Oliphant argued, who combined the elements to produce a truly new genre. Sensation fiction is characterized by psychological suspense, an interest in lunacy and madness, family scandals (divorce, bigamy, illegitimacy) and their legal repercussions, personal secrets, sexual passion, and a focus on criminal characters, particularly criminal women. While sensation fiction rarely crosses the line to represent supernatural events, the atmosphere in sensation novels is such that the possibility of paranormal events is always right around the corner. The genre has been extensively studied by contemporary scholars, particularly those interested in gender issues in the Victorian era. Oliphant flirted with the sensation fiction genre in a subplot of her novel *Salem Chapel.*

In her reviews Oliphant typically took a conservative, pragmatic approach. She approved of fiction and poetry that represented the ups and downs of daily life rather than writing that displayed heightened, lurid, melodramatic, or exalted emotions. She believed too that fiction should avoid any mention of sexuality, a belief that became increasingly old-fashioned as the century wore on. One of her best-known late reviews, "The Anti-Marriage League" (1896), took Thomas Hardy and other fin de siècle writers to task for what Oliphant perceived as their immoral obsession with the details of sex. Her critique of Hardy's *Jude the Obscure* in this review was scathing; her misunderstanding of his literary aims has unfortunately colored scholars' opinion of Oliphant's literary taste. As a whole her reviews are balanced, tolerant, nuanced, and intelligent. They offer us an interesting example of Victorian middle-class taste.

Oliphant's non-review essays in *Blackwood's* ran the gamut from an article on the painter J. M. W. Turner (1861) to "Historical Sketches of the Reign of George Second" (1868–1869) to a discussion of the current status of women ("The Condition of Women," 1858). Her research skills were extraordinary, as was her ability to quickly translate large amounts of historical data into easy, readable prose. Her essays in history or travel often expanded to become full-scale books. Her nonfiction works include a series of what we might call today coffee-table books: large, copiously illustrated, simple cultural histories: *The Makers of Florence* (1876), *The Makers of Venice* (1887), *Royal Edinburgh* (1890), *Jerusalem: Its History and Hope* (1891), and *The Makers of Modern Rome* (1895). She also produced *Literary History of England in the End of the Eighteenth and Beginning of the Nineteenth Century* (1882) and *The Victorian Age of English Literature* (1892), two works of literary history in which she assesses the accomplishments of writers in her own time. She wrote biographies of Edward Irving (an early-nineteenth-century Scottish preacher), Laurence Oliphant (an eccentric novelist, lawyer, traveler, and utopianist who, though bearing the same last name, was no relation to Margaret), the Count de Montalembert (a politician and historian influential in religious debates in nineteenth-century France), Molière (the seventeenth-century French comic dramatist), Richard Sheridan (the English Restoration dramatist) and Thomas Chalmers (another Scottish preacher and theologian; Irving had been his assistant at one time).

CRITICAL ASSESSMENT OF OLIPHANT'S WORK

Oliphant's popularity as a novelist and essayist was perhaps highest during the 1860s and 1870s. As she grew older her work, though still popular, was often considered old-fashioned, and her reputation began to decline. In the decades after her death, her books gradually fell out of print (except for her supernatural tales, which remained popular) and scholarly consideration of her work ceased almost entirely. Robert and Vineta Colby's book *The Equivocal Virtue: Mrs. Oliphant and the Victorian Literary Marketplace,* published in 1966, was the first serious critical reassessment of Oliphant's work. While still voicing disapproval for Oliphant's enormous output, the Colbys attempted to position her work within the larger context of canonical Victorian literature rather than to view it as merely popular or inadequate. Since then more and more of Oliphant's works (both fiction and nonfiction) have been reprinted; concomitantly there has been a steady increase in the number of scholarly books and articles devoted to Oliphant.

Much of the recent scholarship on Oliphant has focused on gender issues. Part of the reason for the tentativeness with which twentieth- and twenty-first-century scholars have approached the critical reassessment of Oliphant's work is largely due to her aforementioned article "The Anti-Marriage League," in which she blasted Thomas Hardy's novel *Jude the Obscure* (along with a number of other novels) as sex-crazed and immoral. Oliphant had previously reviewed Hardy's novel *Tess of the D'Ubervilles,* giving it solid if qualified praise. But in *Jude the Obscure,* Hardy had gone too far, Oliphant felt. Subsequent critics (and Hardy himself, who was outraged by the review) painted Oliphant as an ignorant prude, unable to see beyond her Victorian moralities to the greatness of Hardy's technique. But more recently critics have reconsidered Oliphant's opinion of Hardy and the other novels she discussed in the famous review. Read carefully, the review does not claim that sex per se is indecent or repellent; rather, Oliphant seemed to be objecting to what she saw as Hardy's insistence upon sex as the central facet of human life, almost the sole motivating force in (particularly) women's existence. Oliphant saw Hardy's female characters—the seductress Arabella and the ascetic Sue—as unnatural not in their approach to sex but in their one-sided characterization. They were simply not represented as anything like the women Oliphant knew in her daily life.

Yet Hardy was not attempting to produce the kind of realism that Oliphant evidently valued; he cannot really be faulted in creating such female characters. In a sense, then, Oliphant's distaste for the works of Hardy and those other authors she associated with his brand of sexual frankness arose not from repression but from her belief that realist fiction should represent a more balanced picture of the individual's daily domestic existence—an existence into which sexuality and passion figured only peripherally, in Oliphant's personal experience.

Oliphant has also been labeled an antifeminist by contemporary critics because of her steadfast refusal to support women's suffrage. Other critics, however, have taken a more extensive look at Oliphant's writings and argued that she was, in fact, quite feminist in her own way—a way profoundly influenced by her personal circumstances. The title of a 1995 book of critical essays on Oliphant, *Margaret Oliphant: Critical Essays on a Gentle Subversive*, shows the transformation of critical opinion. Oliphant's "gentle subversion" of Victorian gender norms is one of the focuses of the book. Another title shows a similar take: *The Novels of Mrs. Oliphant: A Subversive View of Traditional Themes* (1994). Oliphant's work has been reevaluated from other angles as well, including articles on Oliphant's relationship to British imperialism, her influence on Victorian literature, her theory of tragedy, her place in the Scottish literary tradition, her correspondence with Queen Victoria, the religious debates represented in her fiction, the unusual form of her *Autobiography,* and on numerous aspects of her literary style. Readers interested in learning more about Margaret Oliphant might well begin with Elisabeth Jay's outstanding critical biography titled *Mrs. Oliphant: "A Fiction to Herself"* (1995). In addition to providing a balanced and thorough biography of Oliphant, Jay gives excellent summaries and analyses of most of her works. As the scholarly interest in Oliphant grows, publishers have begun to reprint her work, both fiction and nonfiction; most of the titles in the Carlingford series are now available and make an excellent introduction to Oliphant's extraordinary talents.

Selected Bibliography

WORKS OF MARGARET OLIPHANT

FICTION

Passages in the Life of Mrs. Margaret Maitland of Sunnyside, Written by Herself. London, 1849.

Caleb Field: A Tale of the Puritans. London, 1851.

Harry Muir: A Story of Scottish Life. London, 1853.

Katie Stewart. Edinburgh and London: Blackwood, 1853.

Magdalene Hepburn: A Story of Scottish Reformation. 1854.

Lucy Crofton. London, 1859.

The Last of the Mortimers: A Story in Two Voices. London, 1862.

The Rector and The Doctor's Family. 1863. Reprint, London and New York: Virago, 1986. (First two works in the Carlingford series.)

Salem Chapel. 1863. Reprint, London and New York: Virago, 1986. (Third in the Carlingford series.)

The Perpetual Curate. 1864. Reprint, London and New York: Virago, 1987. (Fourth in the Carlingford series.)

Agnes. London, 1865.

Miss Marjoribanks. 1866. New edition, edited and with an introduction by Elisabeth Jay, London: Penguin, 1998. (Fifth in the Carlingford series.)

A Son of the Soil. London, 1866.

The Minister's Wife. London, 1869.

The Three Brothers. London, 1870.

Squire Arden. London, 1871.

At His Gates. London: Tinsley Brothers, 1872.

May. London: Hurst & Blackett, 1873.

For Love and Life. London: Hurst & Blackett, 1874.

The Curate in Charge. London, 1876.

Phoebe Junior. London, 1876. Reprints, London and New York: Virago, 1988; Peterborough, Ontario: Broadview, 2002. (Sixth and final work in the Carlingford series.)

The Primrose Path. London: Beccles, 1876.

He That Will Not When He May. London: Macmillan, 1880.

A Little Pilgrim in the Unseen. Edinburgh and London: Macmillan, 1882.

Hester. London: Macmillan, 1883. Reprint, Oxford: Oxford University Press, 2003.

It Was a Lover and His Lass. London: Hurst & Blackett, 1883.

The Ladies Lindores. Edinburgh: Blackwood, 1883.

Sir Tom. Edinburgh and London, 1884.

The Wizard's Son. London: Macmillan, 1884.

Effie Ogilvie. Glasgow: J. Maclehose, 1886.

Joyce. London: Macmillan, 1888.

8000# MARGARET OLIPHANT

The Land of Darkness. Edinburgh and London: Macmillan, 1888.

Kirsteen. London: Macmillan, 1890. Reprint, London: Everyman, 1984.

The Railway Man and His Children. London: Macmillan, 1891.

Janet. London: Hurst & Blackett, 1891.

The Cuckoo in the Nest. London: Hutchinson, 1892.

Diana Trelawny. London: Blackwood, 1892.

The Sorceress. London: F. V. White, 1893.

Two Strangers. London: T. Fisher Unwin, 1894.

Old Mr. Tredgold. New York: Longmans & Green, 1895.

STORY COLLECTIONS

The Doctor's Family and Other Stories. Oxford: Oxford University Press, 1986.

A Beleaguered City and Other Stories. Edited by Merryn Williams. Oxford: Oxford University Press, 1988.

"A Beleaguered City" and Other Tales of the Seen and Unseen. Edinburgh: Canongate Classics, 2000.

Stories of the Seen and Unseen. 1889. Reprint, Freeport, N.Y.: Books for Libraries Press, 1970.

NONFICTION

Memoir of the Life of Laurence Oliphant and of Alice Oliphant His Wife. Edinburgh and London: 1891. Reprint, New York: Arno Press, 1976.

Life of Edward Irving, Minister of the National Scotch Church, London. London, 1862.

Francis of Assisi. 1868.

Historical Sketches of the Reign of George Second. Edinburgh and London, 1869.

Memoirs of the Count de Montalembert: A Chapter of Recent French History. 1872.

The Makers of Florence: Dante, Giotto, Savanarola, and Their City. London, 1876.

Literary History of England in the End of the Eighteenth and Beginning of the Nineteenth Century. London: Macmillan, 1882.

The Makers of Venice: Doges, Conquerors, Painters, and Men of Letters. London: Macmillan, 1887.

Royal Edinburgh: Her Saints, Kings, Prophets, and Poets. London: Macmillan, 1890.

Jerusalem: Its History and Hope. London: Macmillan, 1891.

Victorian Age of English Literature. London: Percival, 1892.

The Makers of Modern Rome. London: Macmillan, 1895.

Annals of a Publishing House. Edinburgh and London: Blackwood, 1897.

ESSAYS

"Sensation Fiction." *Blackwood's Magazine,* May 1862, pp. 564–584.

"The Anti-Marriage League." *Blackwood's Magazine,* January 1896, pp. 135–149.

AUTOBIOGRAPHY

Autobiography and Letters of Mrs. M. O. W. Oliphant. Arranged and edited by Mrs. Harry Coghill. New York: Dodd, Mead and Company, 1899.

The Autobiography of Margaret Oliphant: The Complete Text. Edited by Elisabeth Jay. Oxford: Oxford University Press, 1990.

CRITICAL AND BIOGRAPHICAL STUDIES

Barros, Caroline. "A Fuller Conception of Life: The Transformation of Margaret Oliphant." In her *Autobiography: Narrative of Transformation.* Ann Arbor: University of Michigan Press, 1998. Pp. 143–195.

Colby, Robert A., and Vineta Colby. *The Equivocal Virtue: Mrs. Oliphant and the Victorian Literary Marketplace.* Hamden, Conn.: Archon, 1966.

Corbett, Mary Jean. *Representing Femininity: Middle-Class Subjectivity in Victorian and Edwardian Autobiographies.* Oxford and New York: Oxford University Press, 1992.

d'Albertis, Deirdre. "The Domestic Drone: Margaret Oliphant and a Political History of the Novel." *Studies in English Literature, 1500–1900* 37, no. 4:805–831 (1997).

Heilmann, Ann. "Mrs. Grundy's Rebellion: Margaret Oliphant between Orthodoxy and the New Woman." *Woman's Writing* 6, no. 2:215–233 (1999).

Heller, Tamar. "'No Longer Innocent': Sensationalism, Sexuality, and the Allegory of the Woman Writer in Margaret Oliphant's *Salem Chapel.*" *Nineteenth Century Studies* 11:95–108 (1997).

Houston, Gail Turley. *Royalties: The Queen and Victorian Writers.* Charlottesville and London: University Press of Virginia, 1999. Pp. 139–163.

Jay, Elisabeth. *Mrs. Oliphant: "A Fiction to Herself."* New York: Oxford University Press, 1995.

Jones, Shirley. "Motherhood and Melodrama: Salem Chapel and Sensation Fiction." *Women's Writing* 6, no. 2:239–250 (1999).

Langland, Elizabeth. *Nobody's Angels: Middle-Class Women and Domestic Ideology in Victorian Culture.* Ithaca, N.Y., and London: Cornell University Press, 1995.

Michie, Elsie. "Buying Brains: Trollope, Oliphant, and Vulgar Victorian Commerce." *Victorian Studies* 44, no. 1:77–97 (2001).

O'Mealy, Joseph H. "Mrs. Oliphant, *Miss Marjoribanks* (1866), and the Victorian Canon." In *The New Nineteenth Century: Feminist Readings of Underread Victorian Fiction.* Edited by Barbara Leah Harman and Susan Meyer. New York and London: Garland, 1996.

Rubik, Magarete. *The Novels of Mrs. Oliphant: A Subversive View of Traditional Themes.* New York: Peter Lang, 1994.

Sanders, Valerie. *Eve's Renegades: Victorian Anti-Feminist Women Novelists.* Basingstoke, U.K.: Macmillan, 1996.

———. "Mrs. Oliphant and Emotion." *Women's Writing* 6, no. 2:181–189 (1999).

Schaub, Melissa. "Queen of the Air or Constitutional Monarch?: Idealism, Irony, and Narrative Power in *Miss Marjoribanks.*" *Nineteenth Century Literature* 55, no. 2:195–225 (2000).

Terry, R. C. *Victorian Popular Fiction, 1860–80.* Atlantic Highlands, N.J.: Humanities Press, 1983.

Trela, D. J., ed. *Margaret Oliphant: Critical Essays on a Gentle Subversive.* Selinsgrove, Penn.: Susquehanna University Press, 1995.

Williams, Merryn. *Margaret Oliphant: A Critical Biography.* New York: St. Martin's Press, 1986.

Woolf, Virginia. *Three Guineas.* London: Hogarth Press, 1938.

BIBLIOGRAPHY AND OTHER RESOURCES

For a complete list of Oliphant's fiction, consult John Stock Clarke, *Margaret Oliphant (1828–1897): A Bibliography.* Victorian Fiction Research Guides 11. St. Lucia, Australia: Dept. of English, University of Queensland, 1986. Many of Oliphant's short stories are now available online.

DENNIS POTTER

(1935–1994)

Fred Bilson

POTTER, ONE OF the most celebrated of British television dramatists, was born Dennis Christopher George Potter on 17 May 1935 at Brick House, Berry Hill, in the Forest of Dean, Gloucestershire, England. His father, Walter Edward Potter, was a coal miner and his mother, Margaret Constance Wale Potter, had been a worker in a bakery before her marriage.

The Forest of Dean, on the English side of the border with Wales, was at this time an isolated area. Unusually for England, it was extensively forested and picturesque; there was no agriculture. The coal miners were "free miners"; they had acquired by squatters' rights the concession to mine for coal in shallow drifts. In competition with the deep mines of Wales or Yorkshire, their production was marginal, and they lived in poverty. Potter says that his father never worked a full week until 1940, when World War II led to a desperate need for coal. The Forest was an inward-looking area with close solidarity; people rarely moved away, and new people rarely moved in. They spoke a marked local dialect. The people were almost universally Methodist and Labour Party voters. Potter attended Sunday school at chapel and was steeped in the King James Bible and Methodist hymns. He felt a deep nostalgia for this area all his life and settled within eight miles of it when he was able to buy his own home.

When the war ended in May 1945, Mrs. Potter and the children went to London looking for a better life. Here they lodged with her father in Hammersmith in overcrowded conditions. Mr. Potter remained behind in the Forest of Dean. Strict government policies continued to regulate the employment of miners; he had been exempt from conscription into the army during the war, but now he could not be released from his job because of the continued coal shortage.

During that summer in London, when he was ten years old, Dennis Potter was sexually abused a number of times by his mother's brother. He did not reveal this fact publicly until 1984 and claimed that the incidents were trivial. The effects, however, were profound. The boy had been taken away from his father to a new location, where he had his mother's company without his father's presence. He had been taken from the forest he loved to a depressing, shabby London. On top of this was piled the guilt he felt about the sexual abuse, and he would become aware in time that the family realized the uncle in question was deviant. All this, of course, happened in the fashion of the time, without a word of discussion or explanation. Potter was always to feel a deep guilt, which he projected onto later relationships and which informs much of his work.

He won a place at New College, Oxford, where he studied PPE (politics, philosophy, and economics). PPE was the royal road to a career in politics, and what Potter wanted was to be a Labour member of Parliament. Before starting at Oxford, however, Potter had to do two years' military service, and like many other writers of his generation, he spent it learning Russian. Though he succeeded in mastering the language, he did not pass with sufficient marks to transfer to the officers' course for further study at Cambridge. Almost certainly his social class and accent additionally disqualified him. He remained an enlisted man and worked in Whitehall, London, in MI3 (Military Intelligence section 3), which monitored the Russian press and news broadcasts to pick up clues about the location of Russian troops in the Soviet Union. Here he came up against the English class system at its worst, suffering the snubs of the commissioned officers in whose office he worked. He then had to take a year out to pass Oxford's qualifying examination in Latin, without which no student, however talented, could be admitted.

At Oxford he was a charismatic figure, active in politics and the Oxford Union, the prestigious student debating society. But Oxford is a society where women are disprized and held to be of little account. For all his radicalism, Potter adopted this attitude as his own; it went with the working-class separation out of women into subservient roles. At the same time, while on holiday at home he met Margaret Morgan, a girl from exactly the same background as he, and they married on January 10, 1959, before he graduated. She was totally devoted to him throughout her life until she died only a short time before he did. His view of women would always be paradoxical, complicated by the guilt of that summer in London as a boy.

After Oxford he joined the BBC (British Broadcasting Corporation) as a trainee, that is, a member of a scheme designed to train an elite of producers, journalists, and other specialists. He participated in a documentary program, *Between Two Rivers* (1960), in which he reflected on the distance he felt both from the world of Oxford and from his original home in the Forest of Dean. The program included shots of his father with a voice-over commentary that, because of its patronizing comments on working-class life, must surely have caused his father offense. He was selected to be the Labour candidate for East Hertfordshire, a dreary agricultural constituency with a solid Conservative majority. He ran in the election of 1964, but, though it was a good year for Labour, he was not elected. Other constituencies were offered him, and he would almost certainly have been elected in 1966, but he had realized he had no taste for organized politics.

In 1965 three television plays were produced that placed Potter in the forefront of dramatists for that medium; these were *Alice; Stand Up, Nigel Barton;* and *Vote, Vote, Vote for Nigel Barton.* He would spend the rest of his life as a television dramatist, working at different times for the BBC and for ITV (Independent Television—the commercial sector), and as a journalist.

On May 24, 1962 he was diagnosed with the psoriatic arthropathy that was to continue throughout his life. It produced two serious effects. Arthropathy caused stiffness in the joints, so walking was difficult and he could not type or hold a glass easily; he wrote his scripts by hand because he found it impossible to dictate. Psoriasis led to a painful blistering of the skin all over his body, so that he was covered in sores, like a biblical leper in the Sunday school stories that carried the message that leprosy was a punishment for sin. Psoriasis ran in the family (though his was by far the worst case), and he was convinced that its severity in his case was a product of his guilt. Drugs gave only intermittent relief.

Potter and his wife were both to suffer from cancer. Margaret Morgan Potter was first diagnosed in 1992 and Potter himself in February 1994. She died on May 27, 1994, and he died just eleven days later, on June 7. In an interview given after the diagnosis, Potter mentioned his determination to live at least till his fifty-ninth birthday on May 17, 1994 and to complete two final sets of plays, the four-part series *Karaoke* and *Cold Lazarus.* He was determined that BBC and ITV should cooperate in the showing of these plays. He wanted *Karaoke* shown on BBC and repeated on ITV on consecutive nights and *Cold Lazarus* shown on ITV and repeated on BBC, so that there would once again be a television event that could attract a universal viewing audience. In effect he used his imminent death as a lever to persuade the two channels, and after his death his request was accepted. On this topic, and a wide variety of other questions in the reception of Potter's work, there are useful articles in *The Passion of Dennis Potter,* edited by Vernon Gras and John R. Cook.

PARADOXES IN THE WORK OF DENNIS POTTER

Clearly there are a number of paradoxes in the experience described above, and these are creatively productive in the work. First there is the paradox of the Forest of Dean. As a children's environment it is a paradise of great natural beauty; as an adult environment it offers only poverty and narrow, constricted lives. Contained within this double environment is the dysfunctional family, where children not only witness terrible events but also experience them, as in *Blue Remembered Hills* (1979).

Second, there is the paradox of a religion that is rich and sustaining in its words and imagery but also black in the way it brands us all as sinners, on whom the punishment of leprosy can be visited. Potter's experience of religion began with absolute belief; for a child of his generation in his place there was no other existing world picture. It ended with absolute rejection. David Lodge, the critic and novelist and a contemporary of Potter, describes this process, which he also experienced, as the failure of an existential bargain with God. We agree to limit our behavior in certain ways and He agrees to exist. But He fails to keep his bargain. Two of Potter's greatest plays, *Son of Man* (1969) and *Joe's Ark* (1974), address this theme.

Third, there is the sexual paradox. It seems clear that Potter was totally devoted to his wife; whether he was totally faithful to her cannot now be determined. But his initiation into sexual activity brought with it guilt, reinforcing dichotomous feelings about his mother. In his work Potter writes out of the values of a working-class upbringing of the 1930s, in which women are madonnas (wives, mothers) or whores. Sometimes even the mothers are whores, as in *The Singing Detective* (1986), where Philip Marlow as a boy witnesses his mother's adultery in the Forest of Dean. Clearly Potter is displacing onto women the guilt of the experience of abuse as a child, and he does not censor his feelings. Germaine Greer, the feminist author and critic, compares him to the Italian film director Federico Fellini, who, she points out, is also criticized for "giv[ing] shape to male fantasies of women. They are not saying this is how it is, they are saying this is how we see you" (in Carpenter, p. 505).

Carpenter records (though his family deny the suggestion) that Potter had a number of sentimental relationships with younger women; one element of these relationships is that he sought out situations in which he encountered women who could not contemplate a sexual relationship with a man disabled by arthritis and psoriasis. Regularly in Potter's work sexual encounter ends only

in disgust. In contrast to this is the world of sexual warmth and fulfillment suggested by the popular music of the 1930s that surrounded Potter as a boy, which figures a magical, dreamlike world very different from that of our real lives but imaginatively potent. *Pennies from Heaven* (1978), a six-part television series later to be rewritten as a film, and *Blackeyes* (1987) are typical documents here. Potter also directed *Blackeyes,* which he came to see as an artistic failure, partly because his camera work handles Blackeyes, the beautiful young heroine, in a voyeuristic way.

Such a view of sexuality is evident in Potter's work, but one should avoid seeing it as a reflex of his life or put too much reliance on his own report of himself. He was a consummate self-publicist, and much of what he said was intended for effect. Glen Creeber's *Dennis Potter: Between Two Worlds* (1998) is to be recommended for attempting to break out of the standard approach to Potter's work, which describes it sequentially in time, as though one play evolved out of the previous play. Instead Creeber adopts a thematic approach, and it will be obvious that Potter's talents were fully developed from the first; there is no apprenticeship work in his drama. Humphrey Carpenter, in *Dennis Potter: A Biography* (1998), chronicles Potter's life together with full coverage of the creation, production, and critical reception of his works.

THE GOLDEN AGE OF TELEVISION

The context within which Potter's work must be judged is the debate on whether the 1960s marked a "golden age" of British television. During this period the BBC, using a public services model, enjoyed domination in laying down the parameters, and commercial television followed them. Under its charter, the corporation was given an obligation to educate and entertain, and it set out to diffuse an overtly high culture in programs aimed to increase public awareness of art, literature, and science. The two series of "one-off" dramas (individual, self-contained plays) called "The Wednesday Play" and the later "Play for Today" represented part of the best of the achievement—the best, that is, if this diffusion model, in which knowledge passes down from an educated (and privileged) elite to the public, is considered to be the ideal one for television.

Those modern critics who reject the theory of the golden age suggest that the work produced then was elitist and condemn such diffusion praxes, substituting an appreciation of schedules that are constructed around the soap, the chat show, and reality television. These programs attempt to represent the language and mores of the majority of viewers and to give expression to them. Viewers read for meaning "across" from screen to personal experience, not "up" or "down." Television drama of this sort, it may be said, whether for soap or series, is almost inescapably realistic and representative of general experience. Soaps are written by a series of writers who follow a treatment, a scenario that dictates locale, characterization, and so on. Access to the treatment is the beginning of access to the writing team. Though the writing may be excellent and is almost universally highly competent, it rarely bears the marks of one individual writer. It can powerfully summate experience, but it offers little surprise.

POTTER'S EARLY TELEVISION DRAMAS

When he started writing drama, Potter, like most of his generation, produced one-off plays on the single commission basis, with half the fee up front and the other half on delivery. The total fee for each play would be about half the annual salary of a high school teacher or better. Thus, especially if writers did some journalism as well, they could live on two plays a year, and Potter worked much harder than that. At least in Potter's case, on the rare occasions the expected play did not materialize, the BBC did not reclaim the up-front half fee.

Production was in monochrome recorded onto a tape, which was difficult to edit. Motion picture film could be prerecorded and included in the master recording, but its use was discouraged on grounds of cost. Cameras (usually two were available per production) were fairly static, and maximum use was made of studio sets. The cast

rehearsed as for a stage production and then attempted a single-take performance. There was an edge to these productions as a result. To modern eyes they are very static and seem locked in the studio. Sets and props are often ludicrous, but the acting is of the very highest caliber. Creeber argues that these circumstances meant that early production teams tended to handle plays as though they were being produced in the theater, and this explains why the writer is seen as the major creative agent in television rather than the director, as in cinema.

From the very first, Potter's work was marked by innovation in technical terms and a willingness to explore the rawest of emotions. He pursued a totally non-naturalistic, non-representational approach to drama. He is with Brecht here; the audience must constantly be challenged to "reread" what it is watching, never forgetting that drama is a reordering of life, not a depiction of it. Potter had no interest in the work of, for example, Ken Loach, whose enormously successful and influential production of Jeremy Sandford's *Cathy Come Home* (1966) was realistic and documentary in its approach to the problem of homelessness (Carpenter, pp. 178–179).

MASTERY OF THE GRAMMAR OF TELEVISION

To begin with the most basic requirement, Potter had an acute ear for the varieties of English speech, conditioned as it is by location and social class. To cite an example where the ability is of dramatic importance, Nigel Barton's speech to the Oxford Union in *Stand Up, Nigel Barton* (1965) is a perfect reproduction of the combination of lightness of tone and vapidity of content that characterizes such speeches, which can be done easily by those who can learn the trick.

Television plays aim to have a large variety of rapidly changing scenes within which it is important to be able to catch an image that sets the circumstances of the play in visual form. Two openings from Potter's early plays will illustrate this.

Alice opens in a railway compartment in the 1860s; on the seats to the left is a middle-age man, Charles Dodgson (Lewis Carroll); on the right a young couple clearly recently married. The compartment has a door on each side to reach the platform, but there is no way through to the rest of the train; it looks like an old-fashioned stagecoach. Once the train has started, you cannot leave the compartment, nor can anyone join you. Your situation is privileged (it is a first-class compartment), but claustrophobic. In this it exactly represents the Oxford world in which Dodgson lives.

In *Stand Up, Nigel Barton,* Nigel, home on holiday from Oxford, is walking with his father to the club. His father, like Potter's own father in the Forest, walks straight down the middle of the road. Nigel follows a pace or two behind, unable to make up his mind whether to walk with his father or at the side of the road, which is the "proper" thing to do. This catches Nigel's feeling that he has lost the sense of how to relate to his father.

Potter also had the confidence to break the grammatical rules of television drama for effect. It is a convention of the genre that actors do not look out of the frame and straight at the viewer; that would suggest the news bulletin or the political broadcast. In *Vote, Vote, Vote for Nigel Barton,* Nigel is making a speech that fails to move his audience. Suddenly he makes the right move and mentions the old-age pensioners. His worldly-wise agent (campaign manager) turns full face to the camera and reverently makes the sign of the cross. Nigel has just said the magic word.

Potter is responsible for two innovations that have not been much imitated but remain very much part of his own individual language for television. The first is the adult actor in a child role. In *Stand Up, Nigel Barton* he wanted at one point to switch the action back to Nigel's school days. He did not want to use flashback, which he never found natural on television; it would also entail using a second actor to play the young Nigel, which he felt would dislocate the viewer. So he had Keith Barron, the adult Nigel, play the boy Nigel as well; his costume represented the dress of a 1940s schoolboy, and all the other children in the school were played by adult ac-

tors using the mannerisms of children. Potter later used the convention again for the whole of *Blue Remembered Hills.*

Potter's other innovation is his particular use of lip sync, a technique in which actors move their lips in synchronization with a live or recorded voice from another source. Usually the suggestion is that the voice represents what the character is saying or singing. In Potter's work, however, the use of lip sync depends on the fact that the voice is clearly not the actor's. First used in *Moonlight on the Highway* (1969), this technique is central in much of Potter's later work and first features prominently in *Pennies from Heaven.* Here no one would mistake Bob Hoskins, whom we see as Arthur Parker, for Al Bowlly, whom we hear singing. Instead, when Arthur mimes to Al Bowlly's song, it represents a desire that the promise of the song might be fulfilled in his own life.

RECEPTION AND CRITICAL REPUTATION

Potter was a hardheaded businessman and a skilled manipulator of the levers in television companies and the film world. He was enormously prolific and is often accused of recycling his work. This is a misjudgment. In fact his style is personal, and he regularly returns to the same themes. For example, *Lay Down Your Arms* (1970) and *Lipstick on Your Collar* (1993) both deal with the experience of working in MI3 but are quite different in tone and structure.

Potter was from the first critically acclaimed; his best work attracted major viewing figures throughout his career, and some of his work has cult status. But there has always been dissension, originally political in nature and dating back to *Vote, Vote, Vote for Nigel Barton* (1965), in which Potter describes the experiences of Nigel Barton as Labour candidate in a safe Conservative district. The reception of this play, which was disliked by many both on the right and left, provided a paradigm for the future.

For right-wingers the play was an attack on British values. Particular offense was caused by one incident during a speech at a formal dinner by Sir Hugh Archibald-Lake, the Conservative candidate. Claiming the hegemony of British ideas within the world, and the hegemony of Conservative ideas in Britain, he refers to the fact that many of the greatest modern inventions are British (and, by implication, stolen by the Americans):

ARCHIBALD-LAKE: "Who invented penicillin? A Briton … jet propulsion? A Briton … and television? hellip;

NIGEL: (quietly) And the water closet.

ARCHIBALD-LAKE: Personally, I always think of my country when I use these things.

(*Nigel suddenly hoots with laughter. He cannot avoid it.* Anne [Nigel's wife] is horrified.)
(*The Nigel Barton Plays,* p. 118)

Reduced to incoherence during his own speech as he tries to talk about his father's life as a miner while the audience jeers, Nigel ends by making a rude gesture at Archibald-Lake.

For many left-wingers, Potter was a privileged dilettante who failed to engage in true political debate, and the play was marked by a deep cynicism. It suggested that the Labour party at this time was disguising its opposition to racism to avoid alienating prejudiced voters. And Anne, Nigel's wife, who has been lukewarm throughout the campaign, ("I thought you were just a party hack," p. 123) now reacts to his speech at the dinner by saying "You're not meant for the sidelines, Nigel; you should be in the middle of the field … you will have to compromise, smile, concern yourself with your public image, measure your words as carefully as possible. …" The stage direction that follows reads: "*While she is talking—with Nigel staring at her in horror—her face slowly, slowly dissolves into the grinning, winking face of Jack Hay*" (p. 124).

Jack Hay, the Labour organizer, is not a cynic. He is a dedicated politician who will do anything to keep the party vote up, and his surface cynical attitude, the result of years of hopeless contests, conceals a genuine commitment. Nigel sees the paradox of Jack Hay's position clearly, but if

politics is what Anne and Jack understand, it is not for him. And it was not, in the end, for Potter either.

Later work was criticized on the grounds of Potter's approach to women, which is generally both aggressive and voyeuristic. The critical incident here was the refusal of the BBC in 1976 to air his play *Brimstone and Treacle*. This deals with how a girl left in a vegetable state after an accident is restored to consciousness when she is raped by a visitor to her house, who may or may not be the devil. For Potter it was an illustration of the fact that good can come of evil; for the BBC's television program director, Alasdair Milne, it was "repugnant" and "an outrage." The play was not shown until 1987, though a film version was released in 1982.

As a result, by the 1980s Potter had become a regular target of the prurient right-wing press, especially the *Sun*. The agenda was political; Rupert Murdoch, the owner of the paper, who also had a television empire, sought an end to what he called the BBC's privileged status. And any attack on Potter was an attack on the BBC. Other papers (the *Mirror, Mail,* and *Express*) joined in, so that by the end of his career Potter was "Dirty Den," writer of filth. Less and less serious criticism was published. Potter was now a personality, covered less on the review pages and more on what were still, for historical reasons, called the news pages.

CHILDREN AS INNOCENTS AND AS VICTIMS

The deepest buried of Potter's themes is the question of how far children connive in their own victimization and how this relates to the nature of childhood innocence. Potter is one of the most interesting writers on childhood and makes two central points. First, children cannot always distinguish truth from the well-told tale, even when they themselves tell the tale, as we see in *Stand Up Nigel Barton* and *Blue Remembered Hills*. Second, they take adult behavior as their model, so whatever adults do is normative, even if different adults provide contradictory models, as we see in *Alice* and *Where Adam Stood*.

DENNIS POTTER

ALICE

As described earlier, *Alice* (1965) opens with Dodgson encountering a young married couple on the train. The wife recognizes Dodgson as a man with whom she had played as a young girl. She is keen to introduce herself and her young husband, but Dodgson is cold, even rude. The girl is hurt, her husband baffled. ("Oh, I say," he remarks, as people do when they cannot find words.)

Dodgson is a student of Christ Church (in other words, a fellow of the college) and a mathematics lecturer; the play traces his relationship with Alice Liddell, the daughter of the dean, and their increasing estrangement as she grows up. Feelings are ambivalent and unspoken; Mrs. Liddell both burns Dodgson's letters to her daughter and allows him to photograph the girl. In the famous scene on the river where he tells her the first *Alice's Adventures in Wonderland* story, Alice humiliates him and splashes him with water, then at her mother's insistence apologizes and kisses him on the cheek, offering him "my prettiest handkerchief" to dry himself with. Carpenter says this is done "flirtatiously" (p. 176), but that might be a misreading. She teases him, but she teases him as she might her doll or her cat. Her behavior is not innocent, but it is naive. It is a reflex of the confusion her mother exhibits.

Carroll's deviant sexuality and the nature of the childhood innocence of the girls he associated with are of course central, and the dynamics are repellent. But the play does not stop there. Carroll's incoherence (he stammers except when he talks to the girls) is mirrored in the inability of Alice's mother and the young wife on the train to comprehend the situation and in the husband's strangled "Oh, I say." All this raises for most readers the question of how far we can suppress our knowledge of Dodgson'psychopathology and still read *Alice's Adventures in Wonderland* innocently. Potter himself regarded it as an example of the "considerable art [that] can come from repression" (Carpenter, p. 177). Possibly, he saw his own work in that light, too. Oxford, it has been suggested above, confirmed in Potter a confusion about the status of women. It is incoherent in its attitudes toward women and sex,

and continues to revere authors like Carroll. can *Alice's Adventures in Wonderland* really be described as "consdierable art"? Carroll/Dodgson is an image of such peculiar confusions at the heart of Oxford, and Potter shares many of them.

STAND UP, NIGEL BARTON

This is a very comic play ("I lay claim to be, at times … an extremely amusing writer," says Potter in his introduction to *Blue Remembered Hills and Other Plays,* p. 21). It intercuts scenes from Nigel Barton's life at Oxford, from his holidays back in the mining village where he grew up, and from his childhood.

The moral crisis in the childhood scenes comes when Nigel steals the class daffodil. The teacher says she has her methods of finding the thief. "Stand up, Nigel Barton," she says. He rises shamefaced. "Do you know anything about this? I cannot believe it was you!" Nigel looks up, "a faint hope glimmering." He confesses he may have had it, "the stem was all broke—somebody gave it to me." He incriminates his enemy, Georgie Pringle, and the class goes "Aaah." The children then join in the persecution of Georgie. "I saw him," says one girl. "By the bread shop. And him had the daffodil, Miss. The stem was all broke, like Nigel said." "Thank you for being so truthful, Nigel," concludes the teacher.

The ability of Nigel to seduce the other children in the class is significant. For these children truth is the well-told tale. The little girl is convinced she saw Georgie at the bread shop—how else could she tell the story? "I used to tell lies at school and get away with it," the adult Nigel remembers; "it gave me a sort of power" (*Nigel Barton Plays,* pp. 63–65).

WHERE ADAM STOOD

In his memoir *Father and Son* (1907) the writer Sir Edmund Gosse (1849–1928) describes his relationship with his father Philip Henry Gosse (1810–1888). Philip Gosse was a distinguished marine biologist who kept up a correspondence with the leading scientists of the day. He was at the same time a fundamentalist Christian and creationist; he went to the same seaside town each summer, and here he was a lay preacher for a meeting of the Plymouth Brethren. His faith was totally unshaken by the death of his wife from cancer, and he treated his son as an intellectual equal. One year, while they were holidaying at their usual resort, Edmund wanted his father to buy him a model yacht that was for sale. His father suggested that he ask God whether God wanted him to have the yacht. A few days later his father asked if he had prayed. Edmund answered that he had and that God wanted to him to have the yacht. So his father bought it.

This typifies much of the Protestant approach. Nothing is too trivial to be taken to the Lord in prayer, and prayers are answered, sometimes positively, sometimes negatively. Philip Gosse is not hiding behind God; if he had thought Edmund should not have the yacht, he would have said no on his own account. He cannot predict God's answer—yes is as likely as no. At the start of the book Edmund says the relationship with his father in later years became "a struggle between two temperaments, two consciences and almost two epochs" (his father Christian, creationist, convinced; Edmund agnostic, Darwinian, doubting), but he is making the point that at this particular time in his life, he and his father accepted the same values. Philip above all is granting Edmund autonomy, responsibility for his own moral decisions, and the incident has the shape it does because Philip believes Edmund to be truthful. At the same time, Philip's calm acceptance of his wife's death and his son's chronic illness may look like apathy rather than acceptance.

Certainly Potter thought so when he came to take *Father and Son* as the basis for his play *Where Adam Stood* (1976), which cannot be described as an adaptation. He made two substantial changes. One was to introduce into the life of the seaside town a madwoman, Mary Teague, who performs an act of sexual liberation for Edmund, which Potter called "just one of those things that would happen in a village at that time" (in Carpenter, pp. 326–327). The other was to

change the course of events to make the yacht incident the moral crisis and climax of the play. Sexually initiated, Edmund now realizes he too can play God as his father does, and Edmund faces his father down as he responds with rage to the reply "The Good Lord God says I am to have the ship, father." The play ends here.

Edmund has learned that the world is a more violent and sex-obsessed place than conventional Christianity allows, and it is only through the experience of liberating sex that we can break out of the "mind-forged manacles." Yet his experience with Mary Teague was closely akin to rape, and as we have seen, the notion of rape as a liberating experience was also present in *Brimstone and Treacle*, written about the same time. Liberating for Edward, that is, in Potter's view, and this raises two problems. First, the woman is objectified as a kind of mad spirit of the woods, deriving nothing from the experience herself. Secondly, Edward has been sexually abused, and that is not a liberating experience.

BLUE REMEMBERED HILLS

This 1979 play has remained popular, available in an acting edition and regularly performed. *Blue Remembered Hills* is unusual among his work, as Potter points out in his introductory note, in that it takes place in real time, on a single afternoon, with events following one another sequentially (*Blue Remembered Hills and Other Plays,* p. 21). The cast is made up of seven year-old children played by adults, whose depiction of child behavior Potter found more controlled than that of child actors. They are out in the Forest of Dean during the long summer holiday of 1943, a magic time when it was at long last clear that Germany and Japan were going to be defeated in World War II and before the terrible knowledge of Auschwitz and Hiroshima. The play has several touches that place it in that time—references to comic books, to collecting jam jars for the war effort, and to parents fighting in the war. One of the girls has brought a pram; one of the boys has a box of matches—England's Glory matches. On the front of the matchbox is a depiction of a battleship of about 1910, and on the back is a joke—a nice image of the combination of aggression and comedy that marked the English approach to the war.

These children have complete freedom to wander the countryside in a day that will go on forever; because of double daylight saving time, the sun will not set till nearly 11 P.M. They play the usual games of children (families, fights for domination) as well as games conditioned by the war (the play opens with one of the boys pretending to be an airplane, running with both arms extended full out, like the wings.) Often their language and mannerisms are imitative of the adults among whom they live; they are learning codes for the expression of meaning.

The sound of a siren from the local prisoner of war camp that signals a prisoner has escaped sends them into a panic, and they hide in a hollow. Eventually they begin to recover their courage. The boy who is the leader of the group picks the boy he has just replaced as leader to go with him to recover the pram one of the girls has left in the open. As the rest continue to cower in the hollow, the pram suddenly hurtles down on them. The terror of this breaks the tension and they recover their nerve.

One of the group, called Donald Duck, is in a barn. The other children decide they will frighten him by pretending to be Italians (using the mock Italian English drawn from comic strips). They shut him in the barn by moving a stone that holds the door open. Unknown to them, Donald Duck is trying to start a fire, which takes as they shut him in. He panics, traps himself deeper in the barn as it blazes, and is burned to death. The play ends with the children sobbing over their friend but inventing the lies they will tell to absolve themselves of blame. In voice-over we hear the A. E. Housman lines (from *A Shropshire Lad*) that give the play its title: "Into my heart an air that kills / From yon far country blows / What are those blue remembered hills? ... That is the land of lost content ... The happy highways where I went / And cannot come again."

It is a morally complex play. In his introductory note, Potter writes: "childhood is not transparent with innocence. ... [I]ts apparent simplicities ... are the very anxieties and aggressions which we ... seek to evade by a misplaced nostalgia for those 'blue remembered hills.' ... [W]e also experience a countervailing grace when we actually look at children at play" (p. 40).

It is interesting that these children are seven, not eight as Potter himself was in summer 1943. Under English law, seven is the age of criminal responsibility, when a child is considered capable of forming a criminal intention and committing a crime. But these children are not likely to face much investigation—Donald Duck is an abused boy whose family does not care for him and is already known as a firebug. The event will quickly be forgotten, but in the minds of the surviving children there will be a growing guilt, aided by the fact that there will be little talk of it in the children's families. They did not intend Donald Duck's death and could not have foreseen the result of their closing the barn door, but what they did led to his death. The real reason for wanting to come again to the land of lost content is not nostalgia, which is an infantile regression, but a desire to do things differently, to go back to when the barn door was open and never shut it.

A critical commonplace is to compare the play to William Golding's *Lord of the Flies* (1954). Both are set in a world where only children are found; in both, some echo of war in the adult world leads to a game that ends in death. In Golding, it is the body of an airman trapped by his parachute harness in a tree; in Potter, the sound of the siren that tells that an Italian prisoner of war has escaped. Golding's story illustrates by analogy the notion of original sin. Sin is alienation from God, resulting in actions that are chaotic and self-centered. Original sin, which comes from Adam's decision to take the apple and the consequent loss of Eden, is in all of us, including children. For Potter, however, the death is the result of the nature of child play. The bully of the group, Peter, does not know his own strength and exerts it to its maximum without considering the consequences. So too when the game of being menacing Italians begins, the children do not stop to think what might happen in the barn. The responsibility lies in the terror that the adult world brings into these children's lives; the menacing Italian game is an attempt to naturalize and neutralize that terror.

However, Potter appears to play with the notion of original sin. *Blue Remembered Hills* opens with Willie, who is imitating the airplane, deciding he has been shot down. He reflects, "Them be all dead. Dead, dead. Burnt to nothing" (p. 41), clearly foreshadowing the end of the play. But he is also eating an apple. The Forest is not Eden. Adam has already eaten the apple and fallen. "Them be all dead."

Such a reading as this does not distract from a richness of interpretation, and of course for a writer of Potter's generation such references to biblical imagery are always close to the surface. But it is possible he is attempting a comic approach to satirize the seriousness of such neo-Christian writers as Golding. For what follows is a beautifully observed power struggle between Willie and the more robust and aggressive bully Peter. The apple is the object of this struggle. Peter wants part of Willie's apple, but Willie wants to keep it all and points out that it is a bitter cooking apple, not a dessert apple, neatly inverting Eve's desire to share the fruit with Adam.

Children then are single-hearted, living within the moment in a state of innocence like William Blake's—intelligent and creative in play. It is the adult world that brings terror, confusion, and violation. But children can assimilate and naturalize this, as Edmund Gosse does. In the film *Dreamchild* (1984), which looks at Alice Liddell as an old woman, Potter gives her the interesting and significant line "I was too young to see the gift whole … and to acknowledge the love that had given it birth. Thank you, Mr Dodgson." He has made her what she is.

THE DEATH OF GOD

Aberfan is a community in South Wales which in the 1960s had been a coal-mining town for a hundred years. The waste from the mines (small rocks and mud) had simply been piled on the hillside above the town. In October 1966 the waste heap slipped down into the town, engulfing the local school and killing 144 people, of whom

116 were children. Potter, who came from a mining community himself, was one of the reporters who filed copy on this incident. The effect of the deaths of so many innocent children was devastating, especially in religious terms; among other effects, membership of chapels in Wales declined even more sharply than previously.

Television writers at the time (especially Welsh writers like Elwyn Jones and Ray Jenkins) felt that they had to tackle this incident in their work. The results would be harrowing, but it was important to show that television as a medium had the maturity to depict the reality of suffering. Potter too wanted to tackle head-on the questions of pain and death. He had no Christian belief, but because of his upbringing he did have Christian impulses; he was conditioned to see pain and death as religious problems and to experience natural beauty (what he called "seeing the blossom") as evidence of a benevolence in the universe, and he would revisit these themes several times.

SON OF MAN

For post-Christians of Potter's sort, the personality of the historical Jesus is often a preoccupation. He explored this preoccupation in *Son of Man* (1969). Although many Christians found the play stimulating and moving, some right-wingers objected to this filthy writer handling the theme, and there was a great furor about it. But, above all, it was puzzling at the time because it was a presentation of Jesus as simply a man, avoiding any suggestion of his divinity. Potter had been thinking for some time of writing a play about a preacher obsessed with Jesus and then decided to cut through and write a play about Jesus himself. He handles it as an adaptation, selecting from the Gospel narratives to produce a limited but coherent portrait of Jesus as reluctant prophet. He begins with the temptation in the wilderness, takes the story through the ministry in Galilee and up to the fatal decision to go to Jerusalem. (There is no reference to miracles—Jesus is the preacher, repeating the message "Love your enemies.") There Jesus runs athwart the ruthless political power of Rome and the colluding Temple authorities. Ruthless political powers use their power ruthlessly, and Jesus is crucified.

Potter stresses the full humanity of Jesus. At first he is uncertain of his calling. "Is it me?" he asks. But then he comes to accept it, along with the death that goes with the acceptance. At one point he addresses a cross that has been left standing by the wayside. "You should have stayed a tree," he says, "and I should have stayed a carpenter." It is because of this acceptance that he is unwilling to answer his accusers and remains silent at his trial. Potter insists in the stage directions that the full cruelty of the crucifixion should be emphasized to point up the cost.

It is a bleak message. To accept one's humanity is to accept the pain that goes with it. There is no consoling resurrection at the end—this is Good Friday. Potter ended the television play with the line "Father, why have you forsaken me?" But the stage play adds the line "It is accomplished": it is all over. Possibly Potter did not wish to leave open the hope offered by the line "Why have you forsaken me?" He would have known it as the opening of Psalm 22, which is traditionally read by Christians as prophetic of both the crucifixion and the resurrection. Both versions end in darkness and silence, challenging the God who is dead.

JOE'S ARK

The work that most overtly responds to Aberfan is *Joe's Ark* (1974). Potter set it in South Wales, though he found the Welsh unsympathetic—a hereditary prejudice among the border people—and this gives his portrayal of the character of Joe Jones an interesting complexity; Joe is both moving and slightly contemptible.

The play opens in Joe's pet shop ("Joe's Ark"). Animals of all sorts are clearly visible. Outside it rains. We hear the voice of a preacher, remembered from Joe's attendance at morning chapel, on the theme of Noah's flood ("It repented God that he had made man"). Joe makes his first prayer, "Please God … let it go on raining for ever and ever." The cockatoo lets out a loud

shriek. "Shut up … you'll wake Lucy, you feathery idiot!" But Lucy, in the bedroom upstairs, is already awake. She is about eighteen years old and very ill—she cannot even reach a glass of fruit juice. "Sunday," she mutters. "Sod it! Sod it!" Downstairs, Joe addresses the cockatoo, "comically, yet disturbingly": "'You just wake her up, boyo … and I'll wring your scrawny neck. … Keep quiet all of you. … Don't like the rain, do you?' (*Grim chuckle*) … 'Perhaps this time it won't stop.'"(*Blue Remembered Hills and Other Plays,* p. 92).

Potter is attempting a delicate balance here. Lucy has terminal cancer—she will die in the course of the play. Yet he wants the tone of the play to be comic as well as solemn because, according to his introductory note, "there is something jauntily comic about our mortality. … I think we are all far less frightened of death than custom and language delude us into thinking we are" (p. 89). The original cast could not bring this off (except perhaps Angharad Rees, who played Lucy)—perhaps it is impossible.

John Brady arrives, hoping to see Lucy. He believes himself to be in love with her—they had met at Oxford where they were both students. Joe receives him brusquely, unwillingly. He is reluctant to let him see Lucy, who "is not going to die." (John had originally been misled into thinking he was too late by the fact that the curtains were drawn.) Joe tells John he no longer believes in the Bible; he had attended the service where the preacher told the story of Noah and had walked out in the middle. "The one just man in those bad times. So God let him live and killed all the rest, men, women, kids, the lot …" (p. 97).

The exchange that follows is significant. John is an agnostic—the Bible is a set of myths; "It's a legend. A sort of fable." For Joe, who has been a believer, the price is higher: "It's in the Bible, ennit? … Either it is or it is not so." The price of this experience will be his faith. But Joe lets John go up to Lucy. John has brought her a present, a book. "A book," repeats Joe bitterly.

The next scene is a flashback to morning in the chapel. The preacher, Dan Watkins, is giving a sermon (a masterpiece of satirical writing that

catches the tone of such occasions) that concludes, "We are none of us good enough for this
earth. We all of us lack the holy imagination that
could see life as the thrilling wondrous gift that
it really is." But Joe rises in his place. "No, no,
that's not true. ... You've had your life, Daniel.
You've lived it. You've got no right..." (p. 99).
The definition of the "holy imagination" will be
a theme of the play.

An "over-careful" John goes into Lucy's
bedroom. The room is darkened, and she is
propped up. It has been about two months since
he last saw her at Oxford. She takes him for her
brother Bobby and cannot hide her
disappointment. John asks, "Is it bad? Do you
feel ..." "Tired, mostly tired," she replies. (There
is an *awkward, sick-room pause.*) But she is
comic above her pain:

> LUCY: If I was you I wouldn't visit you if you were
> me.

> JOHN: That sounds more Irish than Welsh.

> LUCY: Celtic, anyway.

He offers the book—*Wordsworth's Hawkshead,*
by T. W. Thompson, a masterly wrong choice. It
reflects the interests she had had at Oxford, which
are now irrelevant to her in her illness.

> LUCY: But, John—it's—look at it—as fat as an old
> Bible.

> JOHN: You can dip into it. It's full of stuff. ... It even
> finds out what sort of cakes Wordsworth had for
> tea. ... I've written inside it.

> LUCY: What, the recipe I suppose ... for the tea-cakes.

(*He is hurt, the wet lad.*)

Apart from the fact it took sixty years to write,
she no longer "cares about that sort of detail":

> JOHN: ... What do you care about?

> LUCY: The way carrots taste different from cabbage.

...

> JOHN: I've missed you a lot. I keep thinking about
> you.

> LUCY: So do I.

> JOHN: (*Brightening*) Really?—Oh, Lucy, you.

> LUCY: Keep thinking about me I mean.

He tells her he has come down to "spill it all
out":

> LUCY: Spill out what? *Blood*?

> JOHN: No, what I feel about y— [you].

> LUCY: Oh words ... Piss off, John.

But she relents a little and asks after her father.
"His Christianity survived the death of my
mother and the defection of my brother, but not
this, I think." She makes him promise to get Joe
to write to her brother: if he will not, John must
do it. She tires.

> LCUY: ... I'm—tired. Go downstairs.

> JOHN: Can't I just sit here?

> LUCY: No, I want to break wind.

(*His face a comic mixture of embarrassment, and
even disillusion, he gets up quickly.*)

This masterly scene (pp. 100–105) works on
many levels. First there is exposure of the one-
sided love affair, as John builds up the relationship into something it wasn't, then lets it go
again. Then there is the mismatch between the
interests of the dying (Lucy now) and those of
the living (John and, subtly, Lucy then). Finally
there is the complete self-centeredness of the dying; for Lucy things that matter have shrunk to
the immediate and the there, the carrots and the
cabbages. She has the holy imagination to see
life as it is, as the pure now.

The preacher, Dan Watkins, calls, but he cannot reach Joe, who talks about killing the animals.

PREACHER: No, no. You are not a cruel man.

JOE: No! and if I was God, see, I wouldn't do what *He's* doing to our Lucy.

...

PREACHER: We shall all die, Joe. ... We have our cycle. Our time.

JOE: Not a young girl! ... That can never be right!

...

PREACHER: Even Our Lord ... thought God the Father had forsaken him.

...

JOE: Perhaps Our Lord was forsaken! ... have you thought of that?

(p. 112)

Disturbed by what he has just said (a line, it should be noted, that echoes *Son of Man*), Joe sinks to his knees and prays in Welsh, "that strange, moving, beleaguered tongue of his childhood," as Potter calls it. What he says (slightly mistranslated in the footnote of the published play) is, in part, "Don't let her die, I cannot bear the pain. Take me and all I own in her place, yes take me and let the dear girl find life." It is moving, yet somehow staged. It is not natural for Joe to speak Welsh; this is a regression to childhood, when all was simpler. The scene makes the case against God, the case of Aberfan. The death of the innocent Lucy is forcing Joe away from his faith almost against his will. And Potter forces us to watch.

John writes to Bobby, who is working as a stand-up comic, disgusted at his own material and disgusting his girlfriend Sally. Then Joe tells John he must go but asks if Lucy was happy at Oxford.

JOE: Was she happy there? Was it like all she hoped it was?

...

... Lucy couldn't help standing by the signpost ... and look[ing] at it. The one to [route] A40. Second name from the bottom was Oxford, see.

JOHN: ... yes, I think so ... She seemed to glow—there.

...

... words ideas all that you know

JOE: (*Flat*) Words.

...

JOE: You didn't mess her about or anything like that?

JOHN: Pardon?

JOE: Spoil her!

JOHN: N-No.

JOE: She was a good girl, see ...

JOHN: Was? I didn't say was! She isn't going to—...

...

(*[John] cries hard, but perhaps with an enjoyable self-pity.*)

(pp. 117–119)

Lucy had foreseen this, that they would "grieve ... without having the responsibilities of a *real*— a *real*— commitment" (p. 113). She had also foreseen the incident that follows, which is typical of her brother's behavior and which she had seen as parallel to Joe's behavior in chapel. On his way down to see her, Bobby makes a scene in a diner, upbraiding the waiter for sweeping up while he is eating. He ends up shouting, "I'm a shareholder in this company! And I shall do something about it!" Joe, Lucy felt, when he made his scene in chapel, could hardly claim to be a shareholder in God.

Lucy is sinking fast. She can no longer eat. The doctor calls and Potter again forces us to watch as she asks him about death. When her father's animals die, "they sort of hood their eyes and— (*pleased*) relax." "Yes." "Don't lie to me." "I have never known a person die who … did not accept in peace." "And serenity?" The doctor repeats the different word, "In peace."

But the pain-killing injection has not worked this time and he gives her the final stronger injection from which she will not awake. "It'll go," he whispers, "Good girl, good girl" (pp. 123–126).

When Joe sees her dead, he cannot accept it, repeating his prayer in Welsh. But by the time Bobby arrives, Joe is ready. "She's with your Mam," he announces. "I was with her. … She sent her love and said she was going home." We know this is not true, but like the little girl in Nigel Barton's class, Joe is able to believe what he knows not to be true. And that is one kind of religion. "Is it raining out?" Joe asks. "I didn't want it to be raining. Not for our Lucy …" He breaks off. He cannot say "our Lucy's funeral" (pp. 130–131).

FACING DEATH: KARAOKE *AND* COLD LAZARUS

All these themes culminate in Potter's last works, and he probably writes better for writing in a compressed but oddly unhurried way. On March 15, 1994, in his last interview (aired April 5), Potter talked to Melvyn Bragg about his coming death and his desire to have his two last series, *Karaoke* and *Cold Lazarus,* shown both on the BBC and ITV. Potter stresses the immediacy of his experience, his discovery that he is not a coward, his seeing the blossom under his window in Ross as the "whitest, frothiest blossom that there could ever be." He reports "the nowness of everything is absolutely wondrous … if you see the present tense, boy do you see it and boy do you celebrate it" (*An Interview with Dennis Potter,* pp. 5–6). We might say he has arrived where he placed Lucy in *Joe's Ark,* as one in a state of "holy imagination."

The central character of both series is Daniel Feeld, like Potter a successful author of television plays facing death from an incurable disease. His name is modeled on Dennis Potter's by a series of verbal connections like those used by James Joyce. Daniel abbreviates to "Dan," about as close as possible to the way Dennis had been abbreviated to "Den" (or even "Dirty Den") by the right-wing press. Potter connects to Feeld; in the New Testament when Judas hanged himself, the bribe he had been offered to betray Jesus remained uncollected, so the Sanhedrin used it to buy the potter's field to use as a cemetery "to bury strangers in." The story is about the disposal of money after death, a preoccupation of both Potter and his creation Feeld. Symbolically death claimed Judas twice, once when he killed himself and once when his inheritance became a cemetery. Death also claims Daniel Feeld twice.

Elsewhere in the plays Potter metathesizes the Forest of Dean to the Forest of Nead, which echoes the "need" he feels for his childhood home. Similarly "field" is metathesized to "Feeld." In the language of Potter's youth, "feeled" was the past tense of "feel" when it was used in the sense of attempting to fumble a girl. Daniel is "feeled" by the intrusive procedures of the hospital in *Karaoke* and the laboratory in *Cold Lazarus,* all of which he must suffer passively.

Karaoke arose from Potter's realization that a writer providing a script for his cast to follow is like a karaoke system in which people who want to sing are prompted by being fed the words by a machine. Feeld, already terminally ill and possibly delusional, becomes convinced that people in real life are using the words of his latest script, especially a man and a young woman whom he sees in a restaurant. He follows the woman, Sandra, to the karaoke bar where she works and discovers that she is planning to murder the owner of the bar, Pig Mailion, who has scarred her mother for life. Feeld, infatuated with Sandra, writes a will that leaves her sufficient money to live on and then murders Mailion himself. At the same time, his producer, Peter Beasley, is distorting Feeld's script in the editing process by cutting to reaction shots by the actress Linda, with whom he is infatuated. She is simply not a good enough actress to carry them off. Also under the influence of Mailion, Linda becomes involved in a plot to blackmail Peter. As a result his infatuation ends, but he is beaten up by two of the villain's thugs. When Feeld murders Mailion, he frees Peter too. Pig Mailion is, of course, Pygmalion, who in Greek mythology created the perfect woman; Pig Mailion is thus a mirror image of Feeld.

Feeld's agent, Ben Baglin, who is very supportive of him, is troubled by a trick of speech in which his words come out as spoonerisms: "he who fays the piddler" is his version of "pays the fiddler." This is not so much comic in itself but marks a difficulty of communication galling in someone who works with creative people. Ben's difficulty communicating is seen in a dysfunctional relationship with his senile mother, and a displacement of the creative urge makes him spend most of his spare time building a model of Notre Dame from matchsticks.

So despite his illness, Feeld is above his production team and his agent. The writer as maker of scripts and modeler of life has almost godlike power. When Feeld steals Sandra's gun to prevent her murdering Mailion, he thinks of this as "changing the script." Once completed, the script is permanent, though the editing may change the emphasis; we realize this as we listen over and over again to the same scrap of dialog in the cutting room. Or, musically, where others simply sing along to the karaoke words, Feeld is able to allow himself the voice of Bing Crosby as he sings "Pennies from Heaven."

If *Karaoke* shows the writer as all-powerful, *Cold Lazarus* shows him as powerless.

It is the year 2368. England as such no longer exists; it is only a province of Westeuropa (German for Western Europe). It is a place of scientific advance (cars are voice-controlled) but social breakdown (urban guerrillas battle the militia with no regard for civilian casualties).

In a laboratory, a despised operation of a powerful worldwide medical cartel, a team is experimenting with a head that has been in cryogenic storage for four hundred years. They are trying to stimulate the cells that contain memory. So once again Daniel Feeld's memories are being shown on a television screen. To save the laboratory from closure, the scientists are turning Feeld into a source of round-the-clock entertainment. He will be traded among organizations, as professional writers must trade themselves among organizations today. His work becomes a commodity.

We also deepen our picture of Feeld himself, seeing the incident that marked him as a child, when a tramp killed his dog and violated the young Feeld. We see his first death, when he cries, "No biography." He touches the people in the laboratory by remembering a soccer game in front of a crowd of 75,000. So many, they ask, how could they trust one another?

But the act of remembering brings too much pain. In life he had had to ask himself on what terms he would buy a longer life, and he had chosen to be cryogenically preserved. But it was the wrong answer. Better to let go. So he dies a second time, released by a laboratory worker who is a member of the rebel guerrillas. As he goes, he remembers a chapel hymn—"Will there be any stars, any stars in my crown / When at evening the sun goes down?"—and greets it with "a triumphant cry, repeated in increasing joy." It is Molly Bloom's last life-affirming word, with which James Joyce closed *Ulysses:* "Yes."

Selected Bibliography

WORKS OF DENNIS POTTER

PUBLISHED EDITIONS OF WORKS FOR TELEVISION

The Nigel Barton Plays. Harmondsworth, U.K.: Penguin, 1967. (*Stand Up, Nigel Barton* and *Vote, Vote, Vote for Nigel Barton.*)

Son of Man. London: Deutsch, 1970.

Pennies from Heaven. New York: Quartet Books, 1981. (Edition cited in this essay is London and Boston: Faber, 1996.)

The Singing Detective. London and Boston: Faber, 1986.

Blackeyes. London and Boston: Faber, 1987.

Christabel. London and Boston: Faber, 1988.

Lipstick on Your Collar. London and Boston: Faber, 1993.

Blue Remembered Hills and Other Plays. London and Boston: Faber, 1996. Previously published as *Waiting for the Boat,* London and Boston: Faber, 1984. (Includes *Joe's Ark* and *Cream in My Coffee.*)

Karaoke and Cold Lazarus. London and Boston: Faber, 1996.

STAGE PLAYS AND NOVELS

Brimstone and Treacle. London and New York: Samuel French, 1978. (Stage play.)

Sufficient Carbohydrate. London and Boston: Faber, 1983. (Stage play.)

Ticket to Ride. London and Boston: Faber, 1986. (Novel.)

NONFICTION

The Glittering Coffin. London: Gollancz, 1960.

The Changing Forest: Life in the Forest of Dean Today. London: Secker & Warburg, 1962.

CRITICAL AND BIOGRAPHICAL STUDIES

Carpenter, Humphrey. *Dennis Potter: A Biography.* London: Faber, 1998.

Creeber, Glen. *Dennis Potter: Between Two Worlds.* Basingstoke, U.K.: Macmillan, 1998.

Gilbert, W. Stephen. *Fight & Kick & Bite: The Life and Work of Dennis Potter.* London: Hodder & Stoughton, 1995.

Gras, Vernon W. and John R. Cook, edd. *The Passion of Dennis Potter: International Collected Essays.* London: Macmillan, 2000.

INTERVIEWS

Fuller, Graham, ed. *Potter on Potter.* London and Boston: Faber, 1993.

An Interview with Dennis Potter. London: Channel 4 Television, 1996 (Transcript of the Melvyn Bragg interview of April 5, 1994.)

Seeing the Blossom: Two Interviews and a Lecture. London: Faber, 1994. (The Melvyn Bragg interview, an interview with Alan Yentob, and the McTaggart Memorial Lecture of 1993.)

IAN RANKIN

(1960–)

John Lennard

I want to explain Scotland to myself, to fellow Scots and to the outside world.

Ian Rankin, 2000

SCOTTISH LITERATURE IS complex. There are works in Gaelic, the tongue of the highlands and islands; works in what used to be called "Braid Scots" or "Anglic" but is now usually called "Lallans," the lowland speech of Robert Burns (1759–96) and Hugh MacDiarmid (1892–1978), which can be regarded as a dialect of English or a language in its own right; and works in standard English (sometimes enlivened with dialect) by writers born or resident in Scotland. Gaelic literature, whether Scottish or Irish, is generally freestanding, protected by its incomprehensibility to most Britons, but the major Lallans writers often have been annexed by "English literature," and those primarily using standard English, from David Hume (1711–1776) to James Hogg (1770–1835), Sir Walter Scott (1771–1832), Robert Louis Stevenson (1850–1894) and beyond, struggle to retain a Scottish literary identity even when their works are distinctly Scottish in content.

The erosion of Scottish identity began with the yoking of the English and Scottish thrones in 1603 and accelerated with formal political union in 1707 and the Jacobite defeats of 1715 and 1745. In the eighteenth- and nineteenth-century heyday of British empire, intranational concerns were suppressed, and with the Victorian emergence of the English canon as a preeminent world literature there was little incentive for British writers to claim or struggle to defend an un-English identity. But with the passing of empire, and the rise of devolutionary movements claiming Scotland as a victim of English colonialism, matters have changed. The later twentieth century saw a revival of Gaelic, notably in the poet Sorley Maclean (Somhairle MacGill-Eain, 1911–

1996), and the aggressive promotion of Lallans as a mother-tongue in re-spelled editions of Burns and MacDiarmid. Scottish nationalism was also boosted from the 1970s by the North Sea oil and gas booms. With the reestablishment of a Scottish parliament and executive in 1999, Scotland began the twenty-first century with greater autonomy than at any time since 1707. Yet the diaspora of the imperial years followed by the internationalism of modernity—especially the pervasive influence of American technoculture and the global reach of the oil industry—has made it less clear than ever what a Scottish literary identity might be.

Ian Rankin, creator of Edinburgh policeman John Rebus, is the youngest writer of international standing to be commonly identified as specifically Scottish. He writes in English, but dialect figures in his dialogue and narrative prose; and though Rebus has had outings south of the border, usually to London, most of Rankin's work describes, analyzes, celebrates, and curses a Scotland centered on the urban belt of Edinburgh and Glasgow and extending north through Fife to Aberdeen, the Highlands, the Orkneys, and Shetland. In one view he clearly belongs to a cohort of Edinburgh novelists and should be considered alongside Iain (M.) Banks and Irvine Welsh, but all three writers have obvious debts to English as well as Scottish predecessors within the British canon and to twentieth-century American literature—in Rankin's case, the California tradition stretching from Raymond Chandler to James Ellroy. No account of Rankin's work can ignore the specifics of modern Scotland, and his acknowledged masterpiece, *Black and Blue* (1997), is a state-of-the-nation novel. Yet it was written in France and is among other things a frontier tale drawing on American westerns, signaling the complexity of modern Scotland and of Rankin's approach to his homeland.

Ian James Rankin was born on April 28, 1960, in Cardenden, a mining town of seven thousand souls in the Kingdom of Fife, about forty miles north of Edinburgh. His father, James, was a grocer's assistant, and his mother, Isobel (née Vickers), was a canteen worker. Neither were great readers, but Rankin was allowed a generous supply of comics and at an early age began to write and draw his own. Mining was in decline, and though the nearby Rosyth Naval Dockyard continued to provide employment, Cardenden (nicknamed "Car-dead-end") otherwise offered very little: from Beath Senior High, the comprehensive school Rankin attended, the only escape routes were university or the army. Alternative visions were, however, constantly advertised at the local cinema, and an astonished Rankin discovered at about thirteen that while he was too young to be admitted to *Shaft, The Godfather,* or *One Flew Over the Cuckoo's Nest,* no one stopped him from reading the books on which they were based. Schoolwork added some classics, notably by Stevenson, and Rankin's life took a literary turn.

His other great interest was music, and his first publication was a lyric for a fantasy band that won him the second prize of five pounds in a school poetry competition. Playing music was another matter, and when he left school Rankin had secured a place at Edinburgh University to read English. Living in Edinburgh, seeing tourists and façades but sensing darknesses and discovering grim history, was a revelation Rankin continues to explore. Despite the death of his mother during his first year and the impossibility of financial support beyond the state grant and odd-jobbing, he completed his degree, taking a special paper in American literature, and immediately began a Ph.D. on the Edinburgh novelist Muriel Spark.

Rankin's own writing was then in the form of short stories for competitions: one, winning second prize, was published in the *Scotsman;* a second, winning outright, was broadcast on local radio. About a year into the Ph.D. he found himself increasingly repelled by the academic industry he was discovering and began to write more for himself than for his supervisor; one short story soon ran out of control and became a novel, *The Flood* (1986). It was accepted by Polygon in Edinburgh, and both *Knots and Crosses* (1987), the first Rebus novel, and *Watchman* (1988), a spy novel, were published by the Bodley Head in London. In 1986, with grants exhausted and no thesis in sight, Rankin married Miranda Harvey, his girlfriend since undergraduate days, and moved to London, where she was working as a civil servant.

Like many in British academia, Rankin seems passively to have absorbed the critical snobbery that sees crime writing and other "genre fiction" as déclassé and intrinsically unliterary. He knew, however, that continental European and American critics took popular culture seriously, and as a graduate student he began more systematically to read avowed crime fiction, particularly American noir writers, and was surprised by the formal capacity and moral engagement he found. At the same time, financial need drove him to a succession of odd jobs, from secretarial work to editing a hi-fi magazine, and he produced a fourth novel, *Westwind* (1990), partly set in an America he had never visited. But Muriel Spark remained on the back burner, and Rankin began to realize both that he wanted to write full-time for himself, and that Rebus could become an adequate mouthpiece for what he wanted to say.

In 1990, after four struggling years in Tottenham, the Rankins made a complete break and moved to France to practice subsistence farming in the Dordogne. The idea was that enforced tranquillity and simple physical labor would allow Rankin to write, and despite what sounds in many ways like a predictable nightmare, and the birth in 1992 of his first son, Jack, write he did. Six Rebus novels and a collection of stories appeared in the next six years—*Hide and Seek* (1990), *Wolfman* (1992; later *Tooth and Nail*), *A Good Hanging and Other Stories* (1992), *Strip Jack* (1992), *The Black Book* (1993), *Mortal Causes* (1994), and *Let it Bleed* (1995). Sales

IAN RANKIN

stayed low, but in 1992 a $20,000 Chandler-Fulbright fellowship enabled him to travel with his family for six months in the United States. Rankin also regularly produced short stories (including two Crime Writers' Association dagger winners), and wrote three thrillers as "Jack Harvey": *Witch Hunt* (1993), *Bleeding Hearts* (1994), and *Blood Hunt* (1995). The demands of Rebus were taking Rankin back to Edinburgh several times a year, and finances became still more pressing with the birth of his second son, Kit, in 1994. But money soon became in a horrible way at once the least and worst of his worries, for in 1995 it became clear that Kit had been born with Angelman syndrome, a genetic disorder affecting vision, speech, and motion.

During the terrible year of hospital visits and twisting hopes that followed, struggling with medical French and Kit's need for constant care, Rankin wrote *Black and Blue* (1997). It was twice as long as and infinitely more powerful than any previous Rebus novel, and after a slow start it won the Crime Writers' Association Gold Dagger for best novel and exploded onto the best-seller lists. Even before its successor, *The Hanging Garden* (1998), confirmed Rankin's new maturity and mass popularity, the Rebus backlist, rapidly issued in a smart uniform edition that made them a recognizable brand, had begun to sell, especially in Scotland. Since then Rankin has regularly occupied multiple places in the annual best-seller lists there and in the U.K. as a whole. Subsequent Rebus novels—*Dead Souls* (1999), *Set in Darkness* (2000), *The Falls* (2001), and *Resurrection Men* (2001)—have each sold in hardback by the tens and paperback by the hundreds of thousands, as has a collection of stories, *Beggars Banquet* (2002); *A Question of Blood* will presumably follow suit. A walking tour of Rebus's Edinburgh is now a popular tourist attraction. Rankin's present contract, for two Rebus novels, specified an advance of 1.3 million pounds; he has received honorary degrees from the universities of Abertay Dundee (1999) and St. Andrews (2000), and in 2002 was awarded the OBE for services to literature.

Money is thus no longer a problem, but one-third of Rankin's income goes to a trust for his children, and Kit will require complete medical care throughout his life. The first real effect of wealth was the purchase in 1997 of property in Edinburgh, where he and his family now live (though he retains the French farmhouse). The move was partly prompted by Jack's arrival at school age and Kit's needs but also responded to urgent pleas from Rankin's publishers, Orion, to arrange promotional tours and events. Though he confesses in interview to finding the discipline of writing harder when there is no financial need, Rankin is not yet bored with Rebus, but as the two-book contract implies, he has no wish to be bound to his creation, who is in any case aging toward retirement. Late in 2002 Channel 4 TV in the U.K. broadcast a three-part series written and presented by Rankin on the understanding, genesis, and punishment of evil: though unsurprisingly inconclusive, the programs, which included interviews with criminals and the criminally bereaved, showed him as an understated interviewer, kindly and thoughtful but steely in confronting guilts, vengefulness, and (strikingly) forgiveness. Other televisual or cinematic opportunities are likely to arise, and it is a shock to remember that Rankin is, at this writing, only forty-two years old: his forties and fifties, commonly a novelist's most richly productive decades, are still to come.

THE "ACCIDENTAL CRIME WRITER," 1986–1990

Right from the very beginning I knew I wanted to write palpably Scottish fiction.

Ian Rankin, 2001

Rankin has called himself "the accidental crime writer," comically protesting that he was "appalled" (when his second novel, *Knots and Crosses,* was marketed as a crime novel) to find he had "*written a whodunit*" and confessing that he "used to go into bookstores and ... take [copies of] my book off the Crime Fiction shelves and put them in with Scottish Fiction" (in Pierce, "Ian Rankin"). It's a good story at his own expense, wryly suggesting the absurdity of academic disdain for "genre" fiction, but it begs the question of how a highly literate twenty-six-year-old could be genuinely surprised by the marketing as crime fiction of his novel about a policeman investigating multiple murders. On reflection one wonders just how tongue-in-cheek Rankin's self-mockery is and whether he was really as unaware of crime writing as he claims.

Nor is that the only oddity. Rankin has also said, for example, that he "started off life as a short story writer" (*Beggars Banquet*, p. 1), commenting that he finds writing short stories "good ways of experimenting with narrative voice, structure and methods of economy" and enjoys "reading other people's" aesthetically for their minimalism (p. 3). Yet despite this credo, and despite the profitable respect Rankin's name would guarantee now, his early stories remain uncollected and in interview are skimmed over. Presumably, as with his early poetry published in student magazines, he doesn't "want any of that stuff coming out" (in Pierce, "Ian Rankin"). In consequence the earliest stories available are the Rebus ones collected in *A Good Hanging* (1992), all deliberate crime writing in which the isolated protagonist of *Knots and Crosses* develops into the proto-serial character of *Hide and Seek* (1990) and *Wolfman* (1992).

Moreover, though Rankin's first novel, *Summer Rites* (written 1984–1985), was apparently "a black comedy, set in a Highlands hotel," it was "Never published, though my wife says it's my best book." What part, if any, crime plays in its "black comedy" is therefore uncertain. The question matters, because while Rankin describes his first published novel, *The Flood* (1986), as "a bildungsroman [literally, a "formation novel"] about a young man growing up in Fife and dreaming about moving to Edinburgh," it is also an investigation that contextualizes the self in the world by burrowing inward and outward to reveal past crimes and present betrayals. As such it joins a literary criminal tradition stretching back to Oedipus. It begins with a young girl, Mary Miller, who is so rashly teased and tormented by two slightly older boys that she falls into the hot, polluted stream running from the local mine. Rescued without obvious injury, she is so traumatized that the next morning her hair has turned white—famously the fate of the narrator

in Poe's "A Descent into the Maelström" (1841). Her freakish appearance blights her life and contributes to a second criminal victimization, her rape at sixteen by a drunken neighbor—and perhaps also by her father; certainly in his sodden presence—leaving her pregnant with a son, Sandy, the "young man growing up in Fife."

Much of *The Flood* is, as Rankin suggests, about Sandy's maturation, and the central action is his first love for Rian, a traveler or gypsy girl with whom he is desperate to lose his virginity, and his eventual discovery of her prostituting herself with a fat school bully whom he loathes. The Madonna/whore portrait is a malevolent cliché, and the lesson of the bildungsroman is the general one of recognizing the construction, projection, and danger of clichéd sexual roles and appearances. But Rian is also recognizably a femme fatale, suggesting some years before Rankin says he read them a debt to Chandler's and Dashiell Hammett's Los Angeles noir (perhaps via the films of *The Maltese Falcon* and *The Big Sleep*), while other plot strands persistently turn on the consequences of crime. Mary Miller, unable to articulate her rape, is socially stigmatized and suffers a traumatic frigidity that keeps her celibate, despite an increasingly desperate desire (half-wittingly shared with Sandy) to become for the first time a sexually active adult. The drunken rapist, unable for fifteen years to commit suicide (as Mary's father did within months), becomes a roly-poly sweet-shop owner tormentedly slipping free sweets to the teenager he believes to be his son, before finding whisky and pills preferable to public responsibility—a suicide that triggers a third criminal assault on Mary by a man utterly ignorant of the truth. All in all, it would be poetic justice if *The Flood* were to be moved on republication from the Scottish fiction shelves where it sat in 1986 to crime fiction, beside the Rebuses.

Turning around Rankin's joke like this suggests that the problem is not only his failing to understand *Knots and Crosses* as crime writing but also his not having recognized *The Flood* as a very good criminal beginning. If, as seems to have been the case, he then thought of "crime writing" as comprising only the English variant exemplified by Agatha Christie—unreal amateurs in a closed setting—the narrow misconception would explain both his early disdain for the genre and his apparent belief (in McCrum, "Gothic Scot") that it has no history in Scottish literature:

> in Scotland there was [when I started writing] no tradition of the crime novel. The English crime novel was perceived as being an entertainment, a puzzle. In Scotland, the tradition I was coming from was much more the Gothic novel.

Though a critically sexy idea, this is misleading, for while Christie-type murder mysteries never flourished in Scotland, the Scottish contribution to crime writing at large is considerable. Sherlock Holmes himself was created by a Scotsman (Conan Doyle) and partly modeled on an Edinburgh physician (Joseph Bell); the fictional Scots of Scotland Yard are beyond counting; and American and Commonwealth crime-writing shelves are bulked by a host of authors whose names begin "Mc" or "Mac." Nor can Rankin's opposition of crime writing to the Scottish Gothic tradition pass unchallenged, for it depends on the same narrow definition of crime writing that wrongly excludes it from Scottish literature in the first place. The Scottish Gothic tale Rankin most often and explicitly invokes is Stevenson's *The Strange Case of Dr. Jekyll and Mr. Hyde,* published, like the first Holmes novel, in 1886, equally centered on murder, and (though full of expatriate Scotsmen) set in the same dangerous and fogbound London.

Taken all in all, the key to Rankin's odd self-understanding as an "accidental crime writer" would seem to be that his initially narrow notion of crime writing and exclusion of it from Scottish Gothic blinded him to a wider understanding of what he was writing until the commercial sense of his London publishers forced him to rethink. His degree work in Edinburgh would have reinforced received prejudices about "genre" writing, both by excluding anything so labeled and by denying the label to authors who were taught. The books Rankin most passionately responded to were *Dr. Jekyll and Mr. Hyde* and James Hogg's great novel of Calvinist psychosis *The Private Memoirs and Confessions of a Justi-*

fied Sinner (1824): both are de facto mainstream Scottish crime writing but also prime examples of Scottish Gothic, and in academic approaches their narrations of criminal activity have usually been seen only as a handy springboard for the metaphysical and theological discussion of evil.

Knots and Crosses was written exactly one hundred years after *Dr. Jekyll and Mr. Hyde* and explicitly recasts Stevenson's novella for 1980s Edinburgh as a battle between policeman Rebus and a serial child-murderer. Like tormented Jekyll, crying denials of the brute within and the evidence of its escapes, Rebus is repressing a traumatic episode in his military past that explains the violence erupting in the present—a structure that allows Rankin to consider how social façades conceal violence and the damage done, and how self-perceiving minds at once confess and deny the mental cancers that gnaw at them. But his adaptation abandons the fundamental tenet of Stevenson's classic and its *doppelgänger* (literally, "double-goer") tradition—that Jekyll and Hyde are one—and his "policeman versus murderer" plot is progressively skewed by attempts to bring Rebus and the murderer into an identity they do not really share.

Apart from anything else, Rebus, though a far more objective creation than Sandy in *The Flood,* remains a direct imagination of a man Rankin (or his father) might have become, escaping working-class Fife via the army but crashing traumatically out of Special Air Service training and into the Lothian and Borders police. If Rebus is a morally gray and deeply troubled Jekyll, he is no more a Hyde than Rankin himself, and the book's real Hyde, an ex-army colleague of Rebus's who spells out his revenge with the initials of his victims, is nothing like either Rebus or his creator. This weakness is damaging, for as Scottish Gothic the plot must allow narrative illustration and analysis of Fife and Edinburgh society, not simply catch a criminal. But its increasing and necessary domination by Rebus's personal history means that in the end Rankin uses Edinburgh only to stage a private drama. It could be argued that the book fails either to reinvent Stevenson or to be satisfactory crime writing, but it remains a fascinating (and gripping) read, and even if Rankin didn't really understand what he was doing, the link it forged between Stevenson's Gothic representation of hypocrisy and modern Scottish policing has been at the heart of his success.

The difficulties with *Knots and Crosses* help to explain why Rankin did not at first see the value of Rebus and why the novel initially sank without trace. But his imagination knew what it was about, and his third published novel, *Watchman* (1988), though abandoning Rebus, developed the approach he represents with greatly increased control and range. The protagonist is Miles Flint, a Scotsman working as a surveillance officer for the security services in London, who finds that he must watch his back as closely as his targets. At first Flint's professionally low profile and personal mildness keep the action low-key, but it rapidly escalates when he is sent to Belfast supposedly to observe an arrest, narrowly escapes execution, and finds himself on the run with an Irish Republican Army man. The title derives, via the seminal graphic novel *Watchmen* (1986–1987) by Alan Moore and Dave Gibbons, from Juvenal's famous question, *Quis custodiet ipsos custodies? (Satires* VI, 347)—Who watches the watchmen? Within the narrative conventions of the action thriller, Rankin reapplies the Jekyll-and-Hyde, smiling faces/black hearts formula to superb effect.

Rankin describes *Watchman* as "a LeCarré-ish spy novel" (in Pierce, "Ian Rankin"), but his narrative reveals far more about Flint's inner life than LeCarré reveals about Smiley's, partly via a brilliantly exploited obsession with beetles:

> *Platyrhopalopsis melyi* was a small beetle, not much more than a centimetre long, which lived in ants' nests, and was sustained by the ants, who in turn licked a sweet secretion from the beetle's body. Miles had never been able to find out as much as he would have liked about this faintly arousing symbiosis. The first time Partridge and he had met, Partridge had reminded him of the tiny beetle, something in the man's attitude prompting the comparison.
>
> Perhaps, though, this had been a rash decision, for the more Miles saw of Partridge, the more there

was in him of the tiger beetle, *Cicindelidae,* a ferocious and powerful predator.

(p. 19)

From a dense base of narrated details about Miles's daily life as a watchman, through the slow arousal of his suspicions about his colleagues, to the thrilling chase sequences, the novel's real target is the Irish "Troubles" as an arena enabling governmental and private criminality, an inviting slippery slope from half-official expediency to customized murder. The eventual exposure of a corrupt villain in authority is structured much as LeCarré might the hunt for a mole. But the deeper resonance with Stevenson (even the beetles are two-faced and Jekyll-ish, with *Platyrhopalopsis* concealing Hyde-like *Cicindelidae*) is enough to take the novel to Edinburgh for climactic scenes in Princes Street Gardens and Waverley Station, while Flint's final exit to the French countryside is simply what Rankin himself was about to do.

In the late 1990s Rankin openly regretted that *Watchman* "is almost impossible to get now," commenting that "recently re-reading [it] I thought the writing had a lot of maturity to it" and was "some of my best" (in Pierce, "Ian Rankin"); it was republished in 2003. He has no such feelings about the unavailable *Westwind* (1990), an exciting but slight tale crossing a Bond film with superhero comics: mild-mannered astronomer Martin Hepton and over-the-hill astronaut Michael Dreyfuss save the West from a cabal of NATO generals who have decided a military dictatorship is the only way to deal with those wishy-washy politicians. There was apparently substantial editorial interference with the plot, doubtless doing more harm than good, and its imaginations of near-future politics have not stood up to European history since 1989. Well-written as hack work goes, it seems disconnected from the far more substantial work Rankin was doing at the same time on what became his first avowed crime novels, *Hide and Seek* and *Wolfman.*

A fuller understanding of Rankin's genesis as a crime writer must wait on a proper literary biography, but one interim conclusion is that he was not so much an "accidental" crime writer as an unwitting and misinformed one. The Scottish works to which he was most attracted and found most apt to his concern with the Scotland he knew were centered on crime but labeled as Gothic, and it was as Gothic that he conceived his work—which did not stop publishers from realizing that his product was clearly most marketable within the massively larger, international, and increasingly lucrative field of crime writing. When the surprised Rankin stopped moving *Knots and Crosses* out of crime fiction and began instead to read the contemporary British and American novels it had been placed beside, he found it easy to forget indignation. The volume of international crime writing sold in London's bookshops must also have given him canny pause for thought, while the specialist crime bookshops and cosmopolitan intellectualism of the British capital would have provided the means to reassess a genre his school and university teaching had sold short. Whatever the immediate spur, Rankin soon realized that to write serious Scottish fiction selling sufficiently well to provide an income, all he needed to do was to embrace his ready-made series protagonist.

REBUS IN HARNESS, 1990–1995

The real mystery in these books isn't the crime … underneath, the real mystery is Rebus coming to terms with Edinburgh.

Ian Rankin, 2001

The legacy of *Knots and Crosses* saddled Rankin with some features he might not consciously have chosen for a serial detective. Rebus was forty-one years old, divorced for five years, and in only occasional touch with his ex, Rhona, and near-teenage daughter Samantha (Sammy). He had a brother, Michael, once (like their father) a stage hypnotist but now in jail for drug offenses. Even before that embarrassment, Rebus had found his CID career stalled at Detective Sergeant (DS), implicitly because the Lothian and Borders police had not much cared to have a broken-down army dropout foisted upon them. His police partner and narrative foil was DS Jack Morton,

even closer to alcoholism than he, and his lover was a superior, Detective Inspector Gill Templer, whose greater respect for the rules and vulnerability as a woman in a male-dominated world were at odds with Rebus's trust in his instincts and burnt-out drinker's indifference to risk. But he had also just solved a child-killer case attracting national media attention, and Rankin neatly used the horrors within that success to separate Rebus from Morton and Templer (both posted away) and its prestige to promote him to inspector, while filling the gaps with a consistent subordinate, Detective Constable (later DS) Brian Holmes; an immediate superior, Detective Chief Inspector Frank Lauderdale; and a boss, Detective Chief Superintendent "Farmer" Watson.

Hide and Seek (1990), true to its punning title, again sticks close to *Dr. Jekyll and Mr. Hyde,* from which it takes striking epigraphs; Rebus even reads the novella in the course of investigating the death of a young homeless heroin addict—a death generically "unimportant" but somehow niggling in Rebus's mind. The vectors that limited *Knots and Crosses* by making the violence and hypocrisies of Edinburgh life a reflection of Rebus's inward troubles are reversed, and he becomes the weary-eyed, enduring sleuth whose moral ambivalence and attraction to violence are both the history of the city whose meanest streets he must walk and the pragmatic shell necessary for hard men to survive hard lives. The dead man's life points to rent-boys (young male prostitutes) used in high places. But half-healed bruising on the corpse remain a puzzle, and the grimmer truth proves to be not the predictable scandal of politicians, celebrities, and prostitutes but a real horror: the use of rent-boys for bare-knuckle, no-rules fights on which the jaded rulers and glitterati of the city love to bet; an occasional corpse is a piquant inconvenience, necessitating disposal in a handy building site. Yet for all the studied amorality of both punters (those spending money) and providers (those making money), the true lure of the fight club is its evil. Its corruption extends into boardrooms and council chambers because without contacts turning blind eyes as the money slips from hand to hand the evil could not thrive, and in the nature

IAN RANKIN

of the beast those it is consuming know their condition as they do its will. As Rebus probes the decay, the use of blackmail and murder to keep him off the scent inevitably backfires and arrests are made. But in a sharp lesson for readers and Rebus alike, some all-too-convenient suicides and accidental deaths curtail the scandal, and an Establishment lid comes firmly down. It is the British way, trading some sacrificial pawns and at least the appearance of a private house-cleaning for the quashing of public scandal and the preservation of careers amid the social status quo.

Wolfman (1992; now *Tooth and Nail*) is by contrast something of an oddity, taking Rebus to London to help chase another serial killer, frightening enough for the poor victims but a pale imitation of a far more complicated and fully-realized killer in James Ellroy's stunning novel of McCarthyism, *The Big Nowhere* (1988). Rankin has indicated that these early Rebus novels took him about three months each to write, and by his later standards the haste shows. It all ends implausibly quickly in an absurd but enjoyable high-speed chase through the central London rush-hour traffic. It is the least morally engaged of the Rebus novels, but it does accomplish some important things. Rhona and Sammy Rebus are living in London, and Rebus is able, in his traumatized way, to reestablish some kind of proper contact with them. He also makes some friends in the Metropolitan Police who facilitate later plots, while Rankin intermittently begins to size up the view of Edinburgh from London.

Most interestingly, the necessity of imagining Rebus in conversation with a London copper made Rankin think about his creation as a specifically Scottish voice:

"So," said Chief Inspector Laine, "you're here to help us with our little problem?"

"Well," said Rebus, "I'm not sure what I can do, sir, but rest assured I'll do what I can."

There was a pause, then Laine smiled but said nothing. The truth hit Rebus like lightning splitting a tree: *they couldn't understand him!* They were standing there smiling at him, but they couldn't understand his accent. Rebus cleared his throat and tried again.

"Whatever I can do to help, sir."

(pp. 19–20)

So a linguistic joust begins between Rebus and his de facto partner, Detective Inspector George Flight, whose cheerful use of cockney rhyming-slang goads Rebus at a difficult moment into using (for the first time in Rankin's writing, barring a single word in *The Flood*) the Fife and Edinburgh dialect such a man would speak:

Flight stared at [Rebus]. The fun was over. "There are some rules, John. We can get away with breaking a few, but some are sacrosanct, carved into stone by God Almighty. And one of them states that you don't muck around with someone like Laine just to satisfy your own personal curiosity." Flight was angry, and trying to make a point, but he was also whispering, not wanting anyone to hear.

Rebus, not really caring any more, was half-smiling as he whispered back, "So what do I do? Tell him the truth? Oh hello there, Chief Inspector, my daughter's winching with someone I don't like. Can I have the young man's address, please, so I can go and belt him? Is that how I do it?"

Flight paused, then frowned. "Winching?"

Now he too was smiling, though trying hard not to show it. Rebus laughed aloud.

"It means dating," he said. "Next you'll be telling me you don't know what hoolit means."

(p. 195)

From this point on Rankin has skillfully worked Scots words into his writing, using them in contexts where the meaning is either obvious—the Glaswegian "polis" for "police," "skiting" on an icy pavement, getting "hoolit" on a pub-crawl, seeing "haar" drifting in over sea cliffs—or can be explained (to a non-Scots listener, for example). Though never overwhelming, such words add considerably to the texture and specificity of the world Rebus inhabits.

Just as each of the dozen Rebus stories in *A Good Hanging* (1992) adds a facet to him or his daily working life—court appearances, Sundays off, the advantages and disadvantages of his army experience—so each subsequent Rebus novel has added a substantive new element to Rankin's Edinburgh and Scotland. *Strip Jack* (1992) revolves around a well-liked local Member of Parliament, Gregor Jack, dismayingly apprehended in a raid

IAN RANKIN

on a brothel. The press vultures gather, and Jack's wife goes missing from a holiday cottage in the Aberdeenshire Highlands, drawing Rebus for the first time into the farther North. *The Black Book* (1993) deals with an old unsolved murder and arson affecting one of Edinburgh's brewing dynasties and takes Rebus back to the town he (and Rankin) grew up in, Cardenden in Fife. *Mortal Causes* (1994), set against the colorful backdrop of the Edinburgh Festival, turns grim attention to what Rankin calls "the umbilical cord between Northern Ireland and Scotland" (*Rebus: The St. Leonard's Years,* p. viii), a cord that carries both orange Protestant and green Catholic bile as well as guns, explosives, fugitives, favors, and other corruptions of justice. "Getting mortal" means getting drunk, and Rankin's analysis includes the effects on Rebus of his increasingly dedicated drinking, not least by looking at one of its causes—his memories of serving in Ulster in 1969, when the Troubles were well underway (and Rankin's future wife was growing up in Belfast). *Let it Bleed* (1995) no less explosively delves into the opportunities for massive fraud made possible by European Union startup grants to Scotland's "Silicon Glen," pitting Rebus against the righteous hypocrisy of Establishment figures beyond his powers of retribution.

Novel by novel, Edinburgh itself assembles like a jigsaw, from the tourist center of Princes Street, the Castle, and Arthur's Seat to the Old and New Towns, the upmarket districts of Duddingstone Village, Morningside, and Canongate, and the more numerous downmarket suburbs and estates of Corstorphine, Gorgie, Colinton, Oxgangs, Niddrie, and Craigmillar. Similarly the Leith waterfront and the coastal towns to east and west—South Queensferry, Cramond, Newhaven, Joppa, Musselburgh, Prestonpans, Cockenzie and Port Seaton—slot in as Rebus journeys to and fro, with the surrounding dormitory towns (bedroom communities), hulking Glasgow further to the west, and industrial Fife (as well as the distant highlands) to the north over the Forth Bridge. The cast also grows to include pathologist Dr. Curt, rival Detective Inspector Alister Flowers, Detective Constable Siobhan Clark (English despite her name, and doubly valuable

to Rankin as a woman and an outsider), Detective Sergeant Holmes and his girlfriend Nell Stapleton, journalists Jim Stevens and Mairie Henderson, returning Detective Chief Inspector Gill Templer, Rebus's brother Michael (released from prison), Patience Aitken (his on and off lover), Sammy Rebus (returning to Edinburgh as an adult), a range of superiors (the "high-heidyins"), and above all the arch-villain Morris Gerald ("Big Ger") Cafferty, who jeeringly calls Rebus "the Strawman" even after Rebus forces him to control his criminal empire from a cell in Barlinnie prison. Each place and person, like each individual case, could be analyzed in detail, but over all of them arch four major themes, the hammer-beams of Rankin's Scotland: Calvinist guilt; profit and hypocrisy; sectarianism; and drugs, most commonly alcohol and street heroin.

Rankin's representations of Edinburgh and Scotland substantially depend on intertwinings of these themes that Rebus both uncovers and himself embodies. The alcohol to which he is dangerously addicted functions (much like the illegal drugs he seeks to interdict) both to sustain and to help him deny the monkeys on his back, haunted and self-loathing memories driven by the pervasive personal guilt Calvinism taught him is the proper lot of the Fallen. Such gloomy and pathologically extreme Protestantism in turn sustains and is used to justify the vicious sectarianism that is notoriously expressed in the soccer rivalries of Glasgow (Celtic/Rangers) and Edinburgh (Hibs/Hearts) and which is deeply entrenched in many areas of Scottish life. As in Ulster, Freemasonry flourishes, particularly within the police, and the whole Northern Irish situation feeds and is fed by its elder Scottish twin:

As Rebus drove to St Leonard's, he rubbed at his jaw and chin, enjoying the feel of the bristles under his fingertips. He was remembering the very different feel of the AK47, and thinking of sectarianism. Scotland had enough problems without getting involved in Ireland's. They were like Siamese twins who'd refused the operation to separate them. Only one twin had been forced into marriage with England, and the other was hooked on self-mutilation. They didn't need politicians to sort things out; they needed a psychiatrist.

(*Mortal Causes,* pp. 113–114)

What is at stake is not only terrorist and political connections but also the whole panoply of crime that surrounds terrorism—protection rackets, punishment beatings and killings, fiscal and ideological corruptions of everyday life—and the inevitable involvement of organized crime in money-laundering and smuggling operations. In the end, even with the supposedly absolute but in fact pragmatic and hypocritical opposition of the police (and behind them the Establishment) factored in, it is usually impossible to tell whether the flow of profits masks and lubricates ideological commitments to violence and hatred or vice versa.

As naturally happens in series novels, particular themes or members of Rebus's supporting cast wax and wane in importance, sometimes all but disappearing only to reappear from another angle later on. The skill with which Rankin orchestrates these movements has led to a specific comparison with the twelve-volume sequence *A Dance to the Music of Time* (1951–1975), a *roman-fleuve* (flowing novel) of mid-twentieth-century English bohemian and patrician life by Anthony Powell (1905–2000). Rankin sometimes mentions him in interview as a favorite author, and Gill Plain in *Ian Rankin's* Black and Blue, the most substantial critical monograph on Rankin yet to appear, considers Powell a primary model for the "interconnectivity" of Rankin's characters and themes over time and at different scales (p. 14). In a general sense the comparison has virtue, but neither the steady iteration of Powell's structural method (each chapter recounts a social occasion where assorted cast-members meet; each novel has four to six chapters), nor the invariably detached amusement of Nick Jenkins, Powell's self-effacing narrator, have any resonance with Rankin's work. The more obvious comparison with Powell would be James Tucker (b. 1929), author of *The Novels of Anthony Powell* (1976) and since 1985, as Bill James, of twenty very evenly paced and savagely ironic crime comedies featuring the policemen Colin Harpur and Desmond Iles. Where James's debt to Powell remains tonally clear however dark the world of Harpur

and Iles becomes, the idea that Rankin owes Powell anything substantive is as faint as Rebus's hopes of happiness. At the heart of Powell's sequence, for better or worse, is a persistent narrative refusal—blithe, blind, and just occasionally stoic—to abandon a moneyed and usually snobbish comedy of manners. Rebus, however, whatever else he may be, is a proletarian who has become a petit bourgeois and who, like all good Calvinists, abandons manners for tragedy whenever the chance comes his way.

What is very clear, reading Rankin in chronological order, is how the Rebus novels have grown in length and complexity. From the early games-playing titles (the atmosphere in which the name "Rebus" was chosen) to the far more basso rumble of *Mortal Causes,* things get steadily less satisfying for Rebus and more so for the reader. One index is Rebus's transfer in *The Black Book* from the fictional and nonspecific Great London Road station to the real St. Leonard's Station (Great London Road being conveniently burned down to remove it from the map). Another is Rankin's inspired development of an idiosyncratic CID and wider police slang for his fictional force, peppering Rebus's dialogue with "the biscuit-tin" (interrogation-room), "woolly suits" (uniformed officers), and "furry boot town" (Aberdeen).

Rankin's commitment to quality is also illustrated by the fate of "Jack Harvey," the pseudonym under which he had (mostly for the money) written those thrillers. In his own summary:

Witch Hunt [1993] was about a female assassin who goes after a Member of Parliament in the U.K. *Bleeding Hearts* [1994] was about a male assassin, who's being tracked by a really dodgy private eye. And the last one was called *Blood Hunt* [1995]. What was that one about? I think it was about the beef scare in Britain and a government cover-up, with people dying under mysterious circumstances.

And that was all I wrote of those. Thrillers take a lot of time and research, because thriller readers demand lots of detail.

(Pierce, "Ian Rankin")

With the Rebus novels taking longer and longer to write, Rankin could no longer maintain additional research. As well as regretting the loss of much-needed income, Rankin had relished the way that "Jack Harvey" "let me go off the leash a little bit and let me do things that I couldn't do in the Rebus books." Those creative ambitions would now have to be curbed—or somehow channelled within the Rebus series. And at the same time Rankin's life was turned upside-down, and his financial situation made potentially desperate, by Kit's diagnosis with Angelman Syndrome.

REBUS ON SONG, 1997

Rankin attributes the relative lightness of *Strip Jack* to his "surroundings … [the] rolling hills, time and space" of the Dordogne (*Rebus: The St. Leonard's Years,* p. vii). His need while in France for frequent visits to Edinburgh, "spent mostly in the Oxford Bar" (p. viii), also suggests the importance to him of atmosphere and ambience, soaked up at ease. Probably, therefore, the jagged, hurtling movements of *Black and Blue,* criss-crossing Scotland from Glasgow to Sullom Voe, and its constant soundtrack of 1960s and 1970s rock, should be related to the circumstances of its prolonged composition: Kit's referral to a regional pediatric hospital, with all the attendant displacements of home and routine: overnight stays and living out of suitcases; rollercoaster hopes and fears; disrupted sleep, endless waits, and late-night vigils with all words spent and only a Walkman for refuge.

Rebus has always listened to music at home, usually on vinyl, initially jazz but expanding to blues and rock, and he sometimes drops by secondhand shops to buy rare pressings. His favorite listening is the Rolling Stones, and rock became Rankin's usual source of titles: *Let it Bleed* and *Black and Blue,* like the recent *Beggars Banquet,* borrow titles from Stones albums. But the new density of musical reference in *Black and Blue,* linked to multiple song titles used as a narrative index of Rebus's passing thoughts and emotions, is tied to a new fragmentation of prose and the word "segue":

He tried not to think about what he'd done, about what Brian Holmes had done. The Pet Shop Boys inside his head: "It's a Sin." Segue to Miles Davis: "So What?"

(p. 13)

The media started sniffing their story, Spaven's life and death big news. And now … three things.

One: the incomplete third volume of autobiography had been published. …

Two: a prisoner was released, and told reporters he was the last person to see or speak to Spaven alive. …

Three: a new TV series was launched, *The Justice Programme,* a hard-hitting look at crime, the system, and miscarriages of justice. High ratings for its first series … so now a second series was on the blocks, and the Spaven case—severed head, accusations, and suicide of a media darling—was to be the showcase opener.

With Lawson Geddes out of the country, address unknown, leaving John Rebus to carry the film-can.

Alex Harvey: "Framed." Segue to Jethro Tull: "Living in the Past."

(pp. 40–41)

Derived from eighteenth-century music (*seguire* means "to follow"), "segue" became widely used in 1940s and 1950s American jazz and bebop parlance to describe medleys and movements from one passage or solo to another. Its figurative use to indicate thought processes was popularized in the 1980s by James Ellroy's novels of midcentury Californian corruption— "Mal segued, new colleagues to old business, thinking that …" (*The Big Nowhere,* p. 70)—and like other innovations by Ellroy it allows rapid sequences of disparate or conflicting data and emotions, juxtaposed by association in the protagonist's mind, which may be wildly paranoid or hideous glimpses of a big picture. It functions similarly in *Black and Blue,* threading patterns through the unceasing movement necessary as Rebus tracks one murderer to Aberdeen and another into the past, spanning the gaps produced by geographical and historical expansion.

As some reviewers realized, there are nods to Chandler in Rankin's use of the names "Moose Molloy" and "Eddie Segal," and the whole

Californian tradition of crime writing presses on the book—but it is longer and much wider-ranging than anything in that tradition before Ellroy, and Rankin's real breakthrough is structural. Earlier Rebus novels had been fattened by side plots and denser description, but *Black and Blue* is built on a bigger scale, combining three major plotlines which slowly collide. The first is the reopened Spaven case, in which the young Rebus half-wittingly supported evidence assembled by his police mentor, Lawson Geddes, that now looks like a frame-up. The second is the brutal murder in Niddrie of an oil-rig maintenance worker, which leads Rebus to Aberdeen, the oil-frontier installations of the far North, and a drug supply route to the rigs run by a Glasgow gangster, "Uncle" Joe Toal. The third, itself doubled, is Rebus's obsession with the real-life 1960s serial killer "Bible John," never caught, and a fictional new copycat case, "Johnny Bible"—a murderous act of homage that brings Bible John angrily out of retirement. The sheer scale of Rankin's design, enabled by the expansion of his prose technique, forces on readers a wide-angle consciousness, even when the narrative is in tight local focus. It is that as much as anything that makes *Black and Blue* not just a very good crime novel but a devastating report on the state of Scotland.

Reunited with Jack Morton, now a member of Alcoholics Anonymous (the "Juice Church") and back in control of his life, Rebus is forced to confront his own alcoholism and self-destructiveness, and the novel is for him a long black-and-blue night of the soul. But beyond his private struggle, and the mellow riffs of the 1976 Rolling Stones album invoking black American experience and lament, *Black and Blue* names the colors of bruising and the beaten; of depression, Scots moodiness, and shadow; of Thatcherite conservatism, ink, and pornography; of oil and the sea from which it must be pollutingly claimed, and of the police and the criminals they battle. The memory of Bible John, like the touch of oil wealth, opens strange doors and makes for odd allies, criminals and police alike haunted by the unsolved murders of the past and enraged by their modern duplication. Traveling from the black granite façades of Aberdeen to the blue reaches of Shetland, turning in his mind the black hearts of killers and the blue appeal of women, Rebus's investigations of resilient evil and his own razor-wire emotions scour out a portrait of a nation in cultural crisis and a people in thrall to their own history and diet. No one can escape the bruises, and all need the blues: *Black and Blue* isn't a relaxing read, but the narrative packs a formidable punch, and the analysis of Scotland, once absorbed, is not easily forgotten.

As well as being the book that secured mass-market success, *Black and Blue* is the first of Rankin's novels to receive extended critical treatment, in Gill Plain's 2002 reader's guide in the Continuum Contemporaries series). Plain's section headings usefully adumbrate her analysis: "Genre and Contemporary Fiction" and "The City, the Frontier and the Law" (pp. 31–47) deal with literary contexts and Rankin's fusion of police procedural, Californian PI, and western "frontier-novel" frames; "The Problem with Women" and "Big Men in Crisis" (pp. 47–62) turn to gender in his representations of victims, criminals, and police; and "Guilt, Self-Destruction, Pain and the Truth" (pp. 62–67) considers Rebus's Calvinist alcoholism. Plain also deals usefully with the novel's reception in 1997 and disappointing television adaptation in 2000 and suggests further reading and discussion. The commissioning of her book reflects the rapidly growing use of *Black and Blue* as a school text, especially in Scotland, and it seems likely that similar guides to other Rebus novels and more general work on Rankin will appear before long.

REBUS AT LARGE, 1998–2003

Given the pressured sorrow of his private life, Rankin might have taken a deserved break after *Black and Blue*, but (perhaps driven by medical bills) he remained in overdrive until 2003, producing six more long Rebus novels, a pendant novella, and a volume's worth of short stories. None are as geographically extended as *Black and Blue*, and their prose style retreats from Ellroy's fragmentation and frenzy. But song titles, wide-angle history, and multiple plots have remained as structural features, while Rebus, running on whisky fumes and overextended professional credit, has struggled in a neverending and violent purgatory.

The Hanging Garden (1998)—the title of a song by The Cure—initially concerns a war-crimes case, one of the many fruitless investigations into elderly suspects that mark the last effort to prosecute perpetrators of the Sho'ah (Holocaust). Ordered to establish whether old Joseph Lintz was once barbaric Josef Linzstek, because only an investigator both maverick and dogged is thought to have any chance of a result, Rebus soon finds himself warned off by the security services and overwhelmed on two fronts: an escalating gang war as predators close in on Big Ger Cafferty's territory; and the severe injury of his daughter Sammy in a hit-and-run accident. All strands end in tragedy: Lintz is found hanged; a police operation smashes one gang but at the cost of Jack Morton's life, without whom Rebus's drinking returns; and a Faustian bargain with Cafferty to find the driver who hit Sammy turns out as all such bargains must, a peril to the soul. Sammy lives but is crippled, and though her mobility has slowly improved in subsequent books, she continues to have to use double-crutches and sometimes a wheelchair.

Rankin's canvas is again broad—the gang war demands scenes as far apart as Paisley and Newcastle-upon-Tyne, while memories of Sammy's childhood open (like the Lintz case) a variety of historical perspectives—and his command is assured. For Rebus, however, agonies pile up, and nothing is eased in *Dead Souls* (1999), an ominous title less concerned with the comic but ill-fated novel by Gogol than with the gloomy 1979 song by Joy Division. Ian Curtis, who wrote it, committed suicide, and Rankin's novel begins with the suicide of a CID officer. Like Jack Morton, he is one of the dead souls haunting Rebus as he tries to drink them away, but some dead souls still breathe—abusive pedophiles, a Scottish murderer released in the United States and deported back to Edinburgh, the tabloid reporter who cossets the murderer for his story while caring nothing for his evil, and

perhaps Rebus himself, increasingly subject to alcoholic stupor and blackouts.

Besides the antics of Cary Oakes, the released murderer, the primary concern of *Dead Souls* is with pedophilia. As anyone who keeps up with the news will know, cases stretching back decades and systematically covered up by civil and ecclesiastical authorities have occurred with hideous regularity since the mid-1980s, and the stories that have emerged beggar belief. Mainstream "literature" has been slow to respond, but crime writing has not: impressive as it is, *Dead Souls* should be considered alongside Reginald Hill's outstanding *On Beulah Height* (1998) and, in a wider view, Hill's *Singing the Sadness* (1999), Andrew Taylor's *The Four Last Things* (1997), Anna Salter's *Shiny Water* (1997), and Toni Cade Bambara's *Those Bones Are Not My Child* (1999). As well as with the abuse and custody of living children and the lives of survivors, these novels share a concern with the missing and the ways in which the trauma for families of disappearance can be worse than the trauma of known death:

> The world is full of missing persons, and their numbers increase all the time. The space they occupy lies somewhere between what we know about the ways of being alive and what we hear about the ways of being dead. They wander there, unaccompanied and unknowable, like shadows of people.

This, from Andrew O'Hagan's *The Missing* (1995), is one of the epigraphs to *Dead Souls* and links the pedophile plot to the third major strand of investigation, the disappearance of a young man from Cardenden whose mother dated Rebus at school and turns to him in her desperation. These plots resonate rather than collide, and though one terrible explanation is achieved and one arrest made, the body count is high, and the mordant ending is uncertain and in some ways surprisingly ragged.

Set in Darkness (2000) is, by comparison, much tighter, focused on the devolution debate (and reality) that engulfed Scotland after Tony Blair's election as Prime Minister in 1997. Eagle-eyed for the bottom line, Rankin's primary theme is the mass program of building work triggered by the reestablishment of a parliament and executive in Edinburgh. The corpse of a prospective Member of the Scottish Parliament at the construction site of the building in which he would have worked triggers one investigation; a second is driven by a desiccated body exposed by demolition work, which dates back to the failed devolution referendum that brought down the government of James Callaghan in 1979 and leads to the dirty world of real-estate speculation as developers anticipated the multimillion-pound contracts that never came—until now. Across this dual plot, extraordinarily, drifts a narrative about two rapists, linked to Siobhan Clark (liaising with one of the victims), but this plot-strand is never fully engaged with and terminates itself when the partners fall murderously out. And toward the end, in an explosive shock, comes the reentry of Big Ger Cafferty, conning his way out of prison by faking terminal cancer with substituted X-rays and again seizing personal control of his empire, while Rebus can do nothing to stop him and nearly loses his life in the process. It is a bleak greeting by Rankin of Scotland's new autonomy, insisting that the new homes of power, as so often in the past, are slaked and mortared with blood; that the building sites literally double as cemeteries.

Wide-angle narration remains, especially in the historical perspectives of 1979 to 1999, but *Set in Darkness* also develops to a new level a technique of multiple-angle narration. Rebus himself retreats slightly, more or less managing his alcoholism but aging, fattening, and in some ways diminished; Detective Chief Superintendent (DCS) "Farmer" Watson is heading for retirement; and younger players step forward, especially Siobhan Clark, less maverick than Rebus but willing to step over the line when it seems right to do so. Rankin has discussed Clark in interview, explaining that he finds her mixtures of wariness and loyalty, canny obedience and spirited individuality, a spur to composition, and in *The Falls* (2001) she occupies center stage as much as Rebus. The central case is another disappearance, a female student whose parents are wealthy and powerful: Clark pursues the missing girl's interest in online gaming, developing

Rankin's always-accurate portrayals of the progressive computerization of policing (and crime). Rebus meanwhile is sent by the newly promoted DCS Gill Templer to investigate a disturbing oddity, the discovery near the girl's parents' home of a miniature coffin containing a crude wooden doll.

Seventeen such coffins were found in a cave on Arthur's Seat in 1836 and are often associated with the notorious string of murders by Burke and Hare in 1827 and 1828, whose motive was sale for dissection: it was believed that the soul of a dissected body, not having received Christian burial, was excluded from heaven, and the miniature coffins are supposed to have been an attempt by a friend of Hare's, a shoemaker, to provide symbolic burial for the victims. Like Deacon Brodie (1741–1788), the town councillor executed for theft who reputedly inspired Stevenson's Jekyll/Hyde, Burke and Hare flicker throughout Rankin's work but here receive substantial attention, superbly counterpointed with the computer-gaming that eventually reveals the missing girl's fate. In parallel, tensions between Clark, Rebus, and Templer become acute, and triangulations of gender, rank, and respect for procedure richly orchestrate another novel of real power and reach.

One hopeful note is provided by Jean Burchill, widowed curator at the Museum of Scotland (where the Arthur's Seat coffins are held), with whom Rebus establishes his most sustained and loving relationship in years. Despite difficulties, the affair survives in *Resurrection Men* (2002), which sees Rebus apparently in the police last-chance saloon after hurling a mug at DCS Templer but in fact secretly investigating three other reprobates on the retraining course, suspected of stealing a drug haul and arranging the dealer's murder. Back in Edinburgh, Clark has to cope on her own with two murders that repeatedly throw up the name of Morris Gerald Cafferty. She also has to cope with the knowledge that crossing the line brings her—that Rebus and Cafferty, if similar only "like Cain and Abel were" (p. 407), are brothers of a kind, and that her own attraction to the dark side is a form of sisterhood with both. The narrative split (until their cases collide) between Rebus and Clark increases the supporting cast, bringing in Clark's contacts to overlap and contrast with Rebus's, and the outcome has repercussions throughout the Edinburgh force and beyond. The climax of the action, however, depends on a too-convenient and implausible piece of psychology, suggesting for the first time a degree of impatience and weariness in Rankin's handling of Rebus.

A Question of Blood (2003) again places Rebus under internal investigation when a severe (and unexplained) scalding of his hands coincides with the fiery death of a petty criminal who had been harassing Siobhan Clark. In parallel, both Rebus and Clark are involved in the messy and traumatic aftermath of a school-shooting, which also draws in two army investigators concerned with the motives of the apparent shooter, an ex-SAS man. This connection elicits further details of Rebus's own very damaging army experiences, and some additional light is also shed on Rebus's family and childhood. Tautly constructed in seven days of investigation, which span a tellingly blank and unreported weekend, *A Question of Blood* is in many ways a return to form for Rankin, but the denouement is again somewhat contrived, flirting with the implausible and felicitous. Though an emotional relief for readers, such felicity seems at odds with Rebus's nature—but not with Siobhan Clark's, and she again takes center stage at least as often as Rebus.

One further Rebus novel is contracted, but he is already in his mid-fifties, worn to the nub by the strains of policing Scotland, and it seems unlikely that Rankin will extend Rebus's career once his thirty-year police pension becomes available in about 2004. How peacefully he gets there, and whether he is succeeded by Siobhan Clark as the serial protagonist, remain to be seen, but for Rankin, Rebus's will be a most honorable retirement.

THE MAINSTREAM FUTURE

Life is ... full of open endings. Maybe the way forward is for the detectives not to solve the crimes, and for there to be mess and ambiguity.

Ian Rankin, 2000

Though all the stories in *Beggars Banquet* (2002) concern crime, only seven feature Rebus—a timely reminder of Rankin's range. In 1999 he became chairman of the Crime Writers' Association and has energetically promoted his constituency, repeatedly arguing in interview and in an introduction to *Criminal Minded* (2000), a crime sampler, that crime writing is enjoying a second golden (or platinum) age and should be integrated into mainstream fiction. He has also pointedly remarked that "the big breakthrough would be to see a crime novel make the Booker shortlist. A couple of years ago I would have said hell would be more likely to freeze over, but ... I think it will happen soon" (in Baxter, "Accidental Crime Novelist").

Welcome as these sallies are, Rankin apparently continues to accept (at least for polemical purposes) the erroneous historical separation of crime from mainstream writing. He also seems never explicitly to have addressed the effects on Scottish literary history and identity of demonstrating that error. Yet his own creative work has unquestionably placed crime writing at the center of modern Scottish literature, recalling the shades of Sherlock Holmes and Dr. Jekyll from their long London exile to the Edinburgh where both were conceived. The Scotland he has built in his books is a dark place soiled by its past, unhealthy in its present, and despairing of change. But the nation itself now has a power of autonomy and opportunity for self-improvement, and in Rankin it has a homegrown novelist of the first water, who has begun to refashion its literary self-understanding.

Selected Bibliography

WORKS OF IAN RANKIN

NONSERIES NOVELS
Summer Rites. (Written 1984–1985, unpublished).
The Flood. Edinburgh: Polygon, 1986.

IAN RANKIN

Watchman. London: Bodley Head, 1988; New York: Doubleday Crime Club, 1991; with a new introduction by the author, London: Orion, 2003.

Westwind. London: Barrie & Jenkins, 1990.

REBUS NOVELS

Knots And Crosses. London: Bodley Head, 1987; Garden City, N.Y.: Doubleday, 1987; New York: St. Martin's Paperbacks, 1995.

Hide and Seek. London: Barrie & Jenkins, 1990; New York: Penzler, 1994; New York: St. Martin's Paperbacks, 1997.

Wolfman. London: Century, 1992. As *Tooth and Nail,* New York: St. Martin's Dead Letter Mysteries, 1996; London: Orion, 1998.

Strip Jack. London: Orion, 1992; New York: St. Martin's Press, 1994; New York: St. Martin's Paperbacks, 1998.

The Black Book. London: Orion, 1993; New York: Penzler, 1994; New York: St. Martin's Paperbacks, 2000.

Mortal Causes. London: Orion, 1994; New York: Simon & Schuster, 1994; New York: St. Martin's Paperbacks, 1997.

Let It Bleed. London: Orion, 1995; New York: Simon & Schuster, 1996; New York: St. Martin's Paperbacks, 1998.

Black and Blue. London: Orion, 1997; New York: St. Martin's Paperbacks, 1997. (CWA Macallan Gold Dagger for best novel, 1997.)

The Hanging Garden. London: Orion, 1998; New York: St. Martin's Press, 1998; New York: St. Martin's Paperbacks, 1999.

Death Is Not the End: An Inspector Rebus Novella. London: Orion, 1998; New York: St. Martin's Minotaur, 2000. (A precursor to *Dead Souls,* using a plotline later cannibalized for that novel but with a variant outcome.)

Dead Souls. London: Orion, 1999; New York: St. Martin's Minotaur, 1999.

Set in Darkness. London: Orion, 2000; New York: St. Martin's Minotaur, 2000.

The Falls. London: Orion; 2001; New York: St. Martin's Minotaur, 2001.

Resurrection Men. London: Orion, 2001; New York: Little, Brown, 2002.

A Question of Blood. London: Orion, 2003; Boston: Little, Brown, 2003; New York: St. Martin's Minotaur, 2004.

OMNIBUS AND OTHER REBUS VOLUMES

Rebus: The Early Years. London: Orion, 1999. (Includes *Knots and Crosses, Hide and Seek,* and *Tooth and Nail* with a brief introduction, "Exile on Princes Street," by Rankin.)

Rebus: The St. Leonard's Years. London: Orion, 2001. (Includes *Strip Jack, The Black Book,* and *Mortal Causes,* with a brief introduction by Rankin.)

Rebus: The Lost Years. London: Orion, 2003. (Includes *Let It Bleed, Black and Blue,* and *The Hanging Garden.*)

Rebus's Scotland. Forthcoming, London: Orion, 2004. (Photographs of Scotland by the team that does the covers for U.K. editions of Rebus, to be published with accompanying text by Rankin.)

NOVELS AS JACK HARVEY

Witch Hunt. London: Headline, 1993.

Bleeding Hearts. London: Headline, 1994.

Blood Hunt. London: Headline, 1995. (All three have been reissued under Rankin's name, individually and, with an introduction by him, as *The Jack Harvey Novels,* London: Orion, 2000.)

SHORT STORIES

A Good Hanging and Other Stories. London: Century, 1992; New York: St. Martin's Minotaur, 2002. (Includes twelve Rebus stories: "Payback," "The Dean Curse," "Being Frank," "Concrete Evidence," "Seeing Things," "A Good Hanging," "Tit for Tat," "Not Provan," "Sunday," "Auld Lang Syne," "The Gentlemen's Club," and "Monstrous Trumpet.")

Herbert in Motion and Other Stories. London: Revolver, 1997. (Includes "Herbert in Motion," winner of the CWA Short Story Dagger in 1996; "The Serpent's Back"; the Rebus story "My Shopping Day"; and "No. 79." A stapled pamphlet of sixty-four pages, limited to two hundred copies.)

Beggars Banquet. London: Orion, 2002. (Includes seven Rebus stories: "Trip Trap," Facing the Music," "Talk Show," "Castle Dangerous," "In the Frame," "Window of Opportunity," and "The Serpent's Back." Also: "No Sanity Clause," "Someone Got to Eddie"; "A Deep Hole," awarded the CWA Short Story Dagger, 1994; "Natural Selection"; "Principles of Accounts"; "The Only True Comedian"; "Herbert in Motion," awarded the CWA Short Story Dagger, 1996; "Glimmer"; "Unlucky in Love, Unlucky at Cards"; "Video, Nasty"; "The Wider Scheme"; "Unknown Pleasures"; "The Confession"; and "The Hanged Man.")

"Get Shortie." In *Crimewave 2: Deepest Red.* Edited by Mat Coward and Andy Cox. Ely: TTA Press, 1999. Pp. 34–39. (Rebus story.)

"The Slab Boys." In *Scenes of Crime: A Crime Writers' Association Annual Anthology.* Edited by Martin Edwards. London: Constable, 2000. Pp. 187–196.

"Saint Nicked." *Radio Times* (London), December 21, 2002, pp. 25–28, and January 4, 2003, pp. 28–30. (Rebus story.)

PLAYS

The Serpent's Back. Unpublished radio play, first broadcast on BBC Radio 4's *Saturday Night Theatre,* September 30, 1995.

The Third Gentleman. Unpublished radio play, first broadcast on BBC Radio 4's *Saturday Night Theatre,* October 25, 1997.

ESSAYS AND ARTICLES

"Surface and Structure: Reading Muriel Spark's *The Driver's Seat.*" *Journal of Narrative Theory* 15, no. 2 (spring 1985).

"A Historicist Approach to Pynchon." *Pynchon Notes* 16:110–111 (1985).

Foreword to *Missing Persons: A Crime Writers' Association Anthology.* Edited by Martin Edwards. London: Constable, 1999. Pp. 7–9.

Introduction to *Criminal Minded: A Collection of Short Fiction from Canongate Crime.* Edinburgh: Canongate, 2000. Pp. 1–8. Partly reprinted in the *Guardian,* March 9, 2000, G2, pp. 10–11. Also available online (http://www.books.guardian.co.uk/departments/crime/story/0,6000,144849,00.html).

Introduction to *A Journey through America with the Rolling Stones,* by Robert Greenfield. London: Joseph, 1974; Helter Skelter, 2001. Pp. 4–5.

"Ian Rankin." *Crime Time* 28:14–15 (2002).

INTERVIEWS

Baxter, Ralph. "The Accidental Crime Novelist." *Publishing News* (London), January 14, 2000, p. 6.

"Criminal Masterminds." *Guardian,* October 15, 2002. Also available online (http://www.books.guardian.co.uk/departments/crime/story/0,6000,811925,00.html). (A conversation between Rankin and Anthony Bourdain; the online version includes four audio clips.)

Ginn, Kate. "The Devil Inside." *Daily Mail.* November 23, 2002, p. 34.

Jordan, Jon. "Interview with Ian Rankin." Available online (http://www.mysteryone.com/IanRankin.htm).

Laing, Allan. "The Suspense Is Killing Us." *Herald* (Glasgow), September 5, 2001, p. 12. (An interview with Stuart Hepburn, who adapted *Black and Blue* and *The Hanging Garden* for television.)

McCrum, Robert. "Gothic Scot." *Observer.* March 18, 2001. Available online (http://www.books.guardian.co.uk/departments/crime/story/0,6000,458332,00.html).

Pierce, J. Kingston. "Ian Rankin: The Accidental Crime Writer." Available online (http://www.januarymagazine.com/profiles/ianrankin.html).

Robinson, Peter. "At Home Online." Available online (http://www.mysteryreaders.org/athomeian.html).

Sykes, Jerry. "Ian Rankin: Puzzle Writer." *Crime Time* 7:22–24 (1997).

CRITICAL AND BIOGRAPHICAL STUDIES

Ashley, Mike, ed., *The Mammoth Encyclopedia of Modern Crime Fiction* (London: Robinson, 2002). (Restricted to work after 1950, but very full within that limit; there is a substantial section dealing with films and television, and useful appendices, including the most comprehensive listing of award-winners available.)

Binyon, T. J. *"Murder Will Out": The Detective in Fiction.* Oxford and New York: Oxford University Press, 1989.

Blincoe, Nicholas. "The Other Edinburgh Fringe." *Observer,* July 26, 1998. Also available online (http://www.books.guardian.co.uk/reviews/crime/0,6121,98978,00.html).

Chernaik, Warren, Martin Swales, and Robert Vilain, eds. *The Art of Detective Fiction.* London: Macmillan, 2000.

Earwaker, Julian, and Kathleen Becker, *Scene of the Crime: A Guide to the Landscapes of British Detective Fiction* (London: Aurum, 2002).

Friedland, Martin L., ed. *Rough Justice: Essays on Crime in Literature.* Toronto, Buffalo, and London: University of Toronto Press, 1991.

Harvey, Christopher, "Devolution Doom." *London Review of Books* 24 (17): 19–20 (September 5, 2002), pp. (An article summarizing recent Scottish devolutionary history and suggesting that "superhood Cafferty, Mephisto to Inspector Rebus, isn't just someone Ian Rankin dreamed up.")

Herbert, Rosemary, ed., *The Oxford Companion to Crime and Mystery Writing* (Oxford and New York: Oxford University Press, 1999.) (A mildly idiosyncratic A to Z by many contributors; some topic essays are provocative, and coverage of older authors is good, but treatment of living ones is scattered and often thin.)

Horsley, Lee. *The Noir Thriller.* Houndmills, U.K., and New York: Palgrave, 2001.

Klein, Kathleen Gregory, Jay P. Pederson, and Taryn Benbow-Pfalzgraf, eds, *St. James Guide to Crime & Mystery Writers* (1st ed., 1978; 4th ed., Farmington Hills, Mich.: Gale Group, 1996). (A detailed guide, with full bibliographies and in many cases brief comments by the subject as well as a short critical essay.)

Lanchester, John. "Rebusworld." *London Review of Books,* April 27, 2000, pp. 18–20.

Mandel, Ernest. *Delightful Murder: A Social History of the Crime Story.* Leichhardt, New South Wales, and London: Pluto Press, 1984.

Murphy, Bruce F. *The Encyclopedia of Murder and Mystery* (New York: Palgrave, 1999). (A monographic A to Z, well-presented and crisply written; Murphy's views are often helpfully challenging, and coverage of living authors is generally excellent.)

Ogle, Tina. "Crime on Screen." *Observer,* April 16, 2000, p. 8.

Plain, Gill. *Ian Rankin's* Black and Blue. London and New York: Continuum, 2002.

———. "Ian Rankin: A Bibliography." *Crime Time* 28:16–20 (2002).

Ousby, Ian, *The Crime and Mystery Book: A Reader's Companion* (London: Thames and Hudson, 1997). (A browsable introduction, generously illustrated with lively layout.)

IAN RANKIN

Robinson, David. "Mystery Man: In Search of the Real Ian Rankin." *Scotsman,* March 10, 2001, Weekend Section, pp. 1–4.

Rowland, Susan. "Gothic Crimes: A Literature of Terror and Horror." In her *From Agatha Christie to Ruth Rendell.* Houndmills, U.K., and New York: Palgrave, 2001. Pp. 110–134.

Symons, Julian. *Bloody Murder: From the Detective Story to the Crime Novel: A History.* London: Faber & Faber, 1972. As *Mortal Consequences,* New York: Harper, 1972; with revisions, Harmondsworth, U.K.: Penguin, 1974; 4th ed., London: Pan, 1994. (Hugely influential and pioneering history, in many ways invaluable but often tendentious and felt to embody a misguided approach.)

TELEVISION WORK AND REBUS ADAPTATIONS

Black and Blue. First broadcast on ITV (U.K.), 2000. (This and the other Rebus adaptations listed here star John Hannah as Rebus; many fans think him much too young for the role, and it has been rumored that the casting will change in future films. The series has in general been found disappointing and has not been issued on video or DVD.)

The Hanging Garden. First broadcast on ITV (U.K.), 2001.

Dead Souls. First broadcast on ITV (U.K.), 2001.

Mortal Causes. Made by ITV (U.K.), 2001. (This adaptation was pulled after the World Trade Center attack in September 2001 and has not yet been broadcast.)

Ian Rankin's Evil Thoughts. First broadcast in three parts by Channel 4 TV (U.K.), November–December 2002.

The Rebus novels have been variously adapted for radio, most frequently by BBC Radio 4 and BBC Radio Scotland. There was also an arts documentary devoted to Rankin in *The South Bank Show* series, first broadcast on ITV (U.K.) on June 18, 2001.

Rankin has an official website (http://www.ianrankin.net).

KEITH ROBERTS

(1935–2000)

Fred Bilson

KEITH JOHN KINGSTON ROBERTS was born September 20, 1935, in Kettering, Northamptonshire, in the English Midlands. His father, Lance John Kingston Roberts, was a cinema projectionist, and his mother, Laura Ellen Wells Roberts, was a nurse. His background was totally within the skilled working class, and he retained all his life an appreciation of those who belong to this class and an understanding of what it is like to acquire and practice a craft.

He qualified in 1956 as a graphic designer at the Northampton School of Art and did further study at the Leicester College of Art. At the start of his career, he was primarily an illustrator and animator. From 1966 to 1967 he edited *SF Impulse,* a science fiction magazine, and at this period he wrote his early novel *The Furies* (1966) and his best-known work, *Pavane* (1968). He continued to write prolifically throughout his life, leaving behind novels, short stories, poetry, and a collection of essays on his life and opinions, *Lemady* (1997).

Those who knew him report a personality that could be warm and friendly on first encounter. But eventually he quarreled bitterly with almost everyone he knew and sustained illogical grievances against many of the people with whom he worked, leading them to break with him. Because of his personality, Roberts never managed that rapport with readers and critics that would have established the reputation he deserved. However, he generally had some sort of coterie, and much of his later work was published partly at the instigation of others in rather overpriced limited editions by small presses, almost as though he shrank from full exposure to professional criticism. This is particularly true of publications by the Kerosina collective, named after a favorite character in *Kiteworld* (1985).

In later life his health suffered, partly as the result of drink, and in his last years he was almost unknown. An occupational therapist suggested to him during one period of hospitalization that he might like to try creative writing as a therapy, an ironic encounter given that Anthony Burgess, one of the leading English writers of the postwar period, had included *Pavane* on his list of the ninety-nine best novels in English since 1939. Roberts died on October 5, 2000.

Because Roberts loved Wessex, it is usual to suggest that Thomas Hardy was a major influence. In fact, apart from certain of his poems, Roberts disliked Hardy, finding him "an infuriating writer. Much of his output I find frankly turgid" (*Lemady,* p. 23). Roberts' depiction of the world of work, like Hardy's, is marked by a great deal of hard toil and a constant imposition of moral choice on those who toil, but there is little sense of men's achievement being wiped out by cosmic whim. More relevant as a model is Rudyard Kipling, to Roberts a poet of a "vivid, restless imagination." (p. 91). Like Kipling, Roberts represents the world of men who work with machines (the craftsmen, including writers and journalists, among whom they both lived). Like Kipling, Roberts observes the way in which the beliefs and moral systems of earlier stages of English history lie just beneath the surface of modern English life. In Roberts' Kiplingesque tale "The Grain Kings," from a collection of the same name, one of his characters (a Russian), voices the shared preoccupations of the two writers:

In Kipling's work, the machines are made to speak. They cannot; but the poet is skilful and so we believe. Soon too England speaks, as an old grey Mother. The sea speaks to the Danish women ... the

KEITH ROBERTS

little banjo speaks ... So the world, which is as it is, becomes re-peopled with mirages and Gods. ... We do not worship stones and trees, yet we listen to our poets.

(p. 169)

EARLY WORK: "SYNTH"

Roberts's reputation as a skilled practitioner was established early, largely in the field of science fiction. As an example, in 1966 John Carnell published his eighth annual *New Writings in SF* and included Roberts' "Synth" as "the major story in the collection." He describes Roberts as "one of Britain's most promising new writers" (p. 7).

The story gives a flavor of Roberts' style. The opening sets the scene in our future: "The apartment was small, as all twenty-second-century apartments had perforce to be, and looked out from its fifty-storey height over the panorama of roofs and canyons that was the latter-day London" (p. 135). The narrative technique is familiar to any reader of H. G. Wells, in such works as *When the Sleeper Wakes* (1899); it is at once authoritative in tone and alienating in its detail. Like Wells, Roberts looks back at our future, placing the twenty-second century in the narrative past. This future is both familiar ("sparrows ... most unattractive of birds, had managed to survive") and unfamiliar (the time of day is "the lull between dawn and First Shift").

A young woman moves about the flat, showering, dressing, and watching the news on television, but "the flat was unusual in ... its lack of furnishing ... and there was no calorie box ... through which ... packaged meals [were delivered]" (p. 136). By foregrounding the technology—at the risk of making a pastiche of Wells's style—Roberts persuades the reader to accept the young woman at face value; she is the one object we are sure we understand. After spending some time reading, she takes a taxi to the New Bailey, where the Supreme Court of Judicature is guarded by state troopers (the names are indicators that the legal system of England has changed, moving

it closer to the U.S. system). Here she is recognized and mobbed by reporters. Arriving at reception, she is instantly stripped of her humanity:

"Name?"

"Megan Wingrove."

...

"Identification, please."

"I'm sorry. M.E.G. one nine stroke zero two."

...

"Tag. ... Put it on, please. You know the rules. ... Your place of manufacture? ... Year?"

(p. 138)

Megan Wingrove is a synth, a synthetic human being; she is woman as absolute object onto whom any fantasy can be projected. Like a Hollywood starlet, she carries a name chosen for her by others at random. She is the property of Henry Davenport, "a famous painter ... a master of egg tempera and chocolate boxes" (p. 139)—Roberts's contempt for the untalented artist is absolute. Ira Davenport, Henry's wife, has found her husband in a compromising situation with Megan and is suing for divorce, citing Megan as corespondent.

As the case progresses, Henry's lawyer, Richard Blakeney, develops a close relationship with Pieter van Melcheren, head of the firm that made Megan, and both spend a good deal of time with her. Richard learns that if Ira wins the case she can seek an injunction requiring Megan to be destroyed. To save her he interrogates her in court, not as a witness but as a mechanical recording device on the level of a television camera security system. She tells of her manufacture as an object designed to please Davenport. Her education was an indoctrination, entirely passive. She learns to walk, to dress, to speak. Her first spontaneous action is a crime. Wishing to see if she can pass for human, she leaves the institute where she is being trained and goes out shopping; she buys some clothes and high-heeled shoes (which Davenport insists she wear).

"And where did you—ah—come by the money for this spree?"

"I stole it. ... I calculated with the profit they were making on me they could afford that at least. ... But

262

they let me keep [the clothes]. I think they were pleased too."

Van Melcheren ... grinned to himself.

(p. 166)

At the Davenport home, she is caught up in a feud between Henry and Ira Davenport. Ira mistreats Megan, and Henry comes to prefer Megan's company to his wife's. Sentimentally, he takes her out for meals and reads poetry with her. "She got vindictive," reports Megan. "She used to keep me up working till all hours. ... Once she made me use a cleaning fluid that burned my hands" (p. 168). Eventually Henry makes a drunken approach to Megan, which Ira Davenport interrupts. Richard asks Megan, "Were you conscious of doing wrong?" She replies, "I was conscious ... of an unhappy situation. But I was not a free agent. ... I was programmed to obey Mr Davenport. He was my master" (p. 171).

To save the case, Richard in effect turns on Henry. Throughout history men have sought the perfect woman; Megan is the perfect woman. Take her, he tells Henry. Repelled, Henry turns on Richard and on Megan, rejecting the synth. Triumphantly Ira withdraws the suit, seeing her rival dethroned. The story ends with van Melcheren reprogramming Megan. She tells him, "I was in love with him." Take it easy, he advises her. The story ends: "She 'felt' his hand upon her shoulder" (p. 188), where the quotation marks around "felt" remind us that the emotions of this woman, whom we were so sure we knew at the opening, in fact make her a complete stranger.

GENDER IN THE WORK OF KEITH ROBERTS

Some of the details of Megan's treatment are reminiscent of stories of life in the slave-owning South found in Mary Chesnut or Frederick Douglass, and "Synth" is an early document recording the changing position of women in the 1960s. Throughout his career, Roberts wrote fictions in which women hold the narrative center and in which he attempted to let them speak for themselves. This in itself did not make him a feminist, of course, but it did require him to consider the orientation men have toward women.

In "Synth" he does this by considering myths—a characteristic approach because Roberts' work is rich in references to several mythologies, especially Celtic and Norse. Here, in an early attempt to look at the empowerment of women, he reinterprets two Greek legends that consider the position of women in a hegemonic patriarchal society. In "Synth," Richard refers explicitly to the story of Phryne, whose death sentence was reversed when her counsel ripped off her cloak and asked the jury whether they could destroy such beauty. This legend paradoxically suggests that women may be safest when they are most exposed.

The second, more crucial, myth is that of Pygmalion, the sculptor who made a statue of a woman so beautiful that he prayed to Aphrodite to bring her to life. Richard, Henry, and van Melcheren all play out the role of Pygmalion, attempting to bring Megan to life by having her conform to their fantasies. The myth still has resonance in the modern world because even though we do not make synths, we do make frameworks that define beauty in women, so that if a woman finds herself accidentally conforming to one of such stereotypes, the result can be a loss of self-definition. Roberts will return regularly to this theme, and, like Megan, his heroines will sometimes find their independence partly through acts of petty crime.

THE FURIES (1966)

Roberts' first novel is generally considered a failure. It is a comfortable catastrophe modeled on John Wyndham's *The Day of the Triffids* (1951). In a comfortable catastrophe, humanity is overwhelmed by some disaster that wipes out civilization, and the label suggests two features of such a disaster: first, that it saves the world from some worse calamity, usually nuclear war; and second, that the central narrator can, like Robinson Crusoe, loot the wreckage and survive. The Furies are giant wasps that attack a world weakened by a geological calamity brought on by the intransigence of the United States and Soviet Union in conducting simultaneous atomic tests. The population of England is reduced from forty million to two million before the wasps degenerate and die out.

The story is told with vigor, and a varied narrative line is sustained, but the artistic failure can be seen in the conclusion:

> I don't think the wasps will ever be totally forgotten. … They're the things that rattle doors on nights of wind, the faces that watch half-seen from the deepest woods. … Our towns are small and the roads between them bad, we barricade our houses after dark. We don't know what form our New World is going to take; but … in some way it's got to be better.
>
> (p. 220)

It's hard to see how it's got to be better. After his description of the terror of survival, the optimism seems tacked on. All too often, comfortable catastrophes suggest that the world would be a better place if a few billion people were wiped out, taking the world we know with them. Roberts does not manage, as George Stewart does in the more lyrical *Earth Abides* (1949), either to convey a sense of regret for the world that is lost or to bring a creative imagination to depicting the new world that emerges. The failure is artistic: the immediate catastrophe, from the geological upheaval to the death of the wasps, occupies virtually the entire length of *The Furies*. George Stewart in his novel quickly disposes of the impact of the virus that destroys most of humanity and then follows his survivors through two or three succeeding generations, charting their evolution from urban Americans to nomadic hunter-gatherers, with both new strengths and new weaknesses.

PAVANE *(1968)*

Pavane was Roberts' greatest success, brought to the attention of a wider public in 1984 by Anthony Burgess in his *99 Novels: The Best in English since 1939*. In selecting these novels Burgess notices them very briefly; he writes in general less than a page on each. Of *Pavane* he says simply that it is a "novel of hypothesis" (a novel based on the hypothesis that history might

have been different) and that it inspired Kingsley Amis' *The Alteration* (1976).

Roberts described the book as "an albatross around my neck." He resented being asked to repeat the effect, though when he did in *Kiteworld* (1985), he produced another success. Each of these books is closer to a set of linked short stories than to a conventional novel, and Roberts' technique is to switch the center of attention so that each chapter concentrates on a different character, enabling him to build up a varied picture of the fictive world of each book. The technique will be familiar from Rudyard Kipling in such collections as *Rewards and Fairies* (1910).

Roberts suggested that the labeling of *Pavane* as science fiction was due to laziness by early readers and publishers, because his previous work had been in that genre. He preferred to think of it as a historical novel, and the central image of a pavane explicates Roberts' sense of history. A pavane is a stately dance popular at the court of Elizabeth I; the use of the term suggests that history is a dance in which we are all bound to take part. The steps we do are prescribed for us, but we might not follow the rules. A pavane traditionally leads up to a climax. One of his characters, Eleanor, describes life this way:

> It's like a dance, a minuet or a pavane. Something stately and pointless, with all its steps set out. With a beginning and an end. … Life's … all sorts of strands and threads woven like a tapestry. … So if you pulled one out or broke it the pattern would alter right back through the cloth.
>
> (p. 249)

This is the paradox. The steps are all set out—history is an inevitable single flow of events. What did happen was bound to happen. At the same time, individual events as we experience them are not inevitable, and the pattern in the tapestry can be changed.

Pavane then is an alternate world, a work that depicts what might have arisen as a result of one single change in the history of our world. Roberts handles that change in a prologue, an achieved piece of mock historical explanation that begins in July 1588: Queen Elizabeth I is on the English throne and the Spanish Armada is sailing up the English Channel to join the Spanish army in the Netherlands. In our world the Armada was destroyed, the queen lived until 1603, and England remained independent, eventually founding the American colonies, which became the United States. But suppose there had been one small initial change, given in the opening paragraph:

> On a warm July evening of the year 1588, in the royal palace at Greenwich, London, a woman lay dying, an assassin's bullets lodged in abdomen and chest. Her face was lined, her teeth blackened, and death lent her no dignity; but her last breath started echoes that ran out to shake a hemisphere. For the Faery Queen, Elizabeth the First, paramount ruler of England, was no more.
>
> (p. vii)

It is not Elizabeth's death in itself that changes history but rather the thousands of individual acts and decisions that follow. It is this complex that makes or unmakes our world. So the Protestants of England turn on the Catholics, and the Catholics in self-defense rise in rebellion and appeal to Spain for help. A joint invasion by Spanish and French troops puts Philip II of Spain back on the throne of England. Protestantism is destroyed throughout Europe, and the unchecked power of Catholic kings and the Church dominates everything. It disapproves of modern technology. Electricity, radio, petrol engines exist but are all rigorously controlled or suppressed; the rebellion is in part a call for the forbidden technology.

England returns to the medieval world of forests and castles:

> a land half ancient and half modern, split by barriers of language class and race ... mile on mile of unfelled woodland harboured creatures of another age. To some the years that passed were years of fulfilment ... to others they were a new Dark Age, haunted by things dead and others best forgotten. ... But by the middle of the twentieth century ... rebellion was once more in the air.
>
> (p. viii)

Here Roberts signals two features of *Pavane*. First, the reader may well find this alternate world both more attractive and more repellent than our own. Second, this world has parallels with our own—the description of England given above (apart from the unfelled woodland) is very much true of England as it was in the 1960s (and still is, in many ways).

In its mood, a pavane is sad, suggesting mourning and loss. What is the loss here? At first, of course, it is mourning for the loss of Elizabeth and the Britain and America that grew up under her and her successors, but the ending, as we shall see, may suggest a different reading. Roberts calls the chapters "measures," like the movements of a dance suite, and he adds a section called "Coda" as an ending. The tone of the measures may be melancholy—life does not always give us what we want. But it always gives us a chance to make a moral choice and stand by it; the sum of those moral choices makes history. The first measure and the last two tell the story of the Strange family and their part in the rebellion; the middle three tell the tales of others caught up in this world.

In the first measure, Jesse Strange, a haulier, is driving a steam locomotive named "The Lady Margaret" (the title of the measure) along the roads of Dorset, towing a train of wagons. He is making the last trip to the coast before the onset of winter 1968, when wolves and routiers (bushwhackers) will make the trip impossible. On the way he calls in at a pub kept by Margaret, the woman he loves; as a boy he had persuaded his father, Eli Strange, to name the best and newest of the locomotives after her. Eli has just died, leaving Jesse the haulage firm and making him rich. Jesse proposes to Margaret, but she refuses him. He falls in with Col, a friend from schooldays, and they have a drunken night together. The following day, as Jesse is on the next leg of the journey, Col jumps into the cab, and Jesse realizes he is a routier; Col later leads the routiers in an attack, using fire arrows. Jesse detaches the last wagon, which he has filled with gunpowder and shot. It explodes, and Col and the routiers are all killed.

Jesse is a strongly drawn portrayal of a man who lives only through and for his work with the machines he drives; his relationships with his

KEITH ROBERTS

father and his employees are based on this preoccupation. At first Col seems the exception; there is genuine warmth in their meeting and their memories of their time at college together, when Jesse was away from home. It is a more naive time than we would expect; one of their fondest memories is of a raid on a walnut tree orchard. But Jesse had left college to return to his machines, and when Col gets in the way of Jesse's ownership of them and their cargoes, he has to die. Further, naming the greatest of the machines after Margaret in effect transfers Jesse's feelings for the woman to the machine, and there is little human warmth in his proposal to her.

There are masterly descriptions of the work on the machine and of the Dorset countryside through which the journey proceeds, with its tight little fortified towns and its wild, wintry open country. But above all, what the measure stresses is Jesse's moral determination that nothing will prevent him from continuing to succeed as a haulier.

In "The Signaller," Rafe Bigland lies dying in the snow, mauled by a wild cat. He makes his way back to the hut where he works as a signaller and collapses. A flashback tells how, as a boy at his home in Avebury, Rafe becomes fascinated by the signalling system whose semaphore stations cover the land; they pass messages by a mechanical wigwag (in other words, a machine that waves flags according to a code). He attracts the attention of the local chief of signallers, Serjeant Grey, who eventually arranges for him to train as a signaller even though he is not a member of one of the hereditary signaller families. After training, he takes over a one-man station, where the wild cat attacks him.

As he lies delirious, he is visited by a young woman who tends him and cures his wounds. She tells him legends of the history of England that the Church suppresses—of the emergence of England in geological time, but above all of the pre-Christian myths of Balder, the beautiful young god who dies and whose rebirth brings the spring, and of Yggdrasil, the tree of life. Suppressed by the Church, the fairy people to whom the young woman belongs have retreated into hiding. Rafe leaves the hut, following the young

woman. Two officers come to the station, which is covered by the cabalistic sign used by the fairy people, and find Rafe's body there.

The measure considers how knowledge spreads through society. As a boy Rafe had watched the signals, realizing they must be telling some story. Only members of the secretive Guild of Signallers know the meaning of the messages; eventually Rafe joins the guild and learns the code. But the system does not carry the real knowledge that would enable Rafe to understand the world, only the information about markets and politics needed by the rich and powerful; many maintain private stations and have their own signallers.

Knowledge is hidden. In a powerful image, Roberts describes the way the people of Avebury treat the standing stone circles that are found throughout the area. Where in our world we hold them in awe because we are aware of the prehistory they represent, in the *Pavane* world they are simply the work of devils and are broken up to make walls between the fields. An absolute system must destroy history, but for Rafe history remains present in the countryside of England, recoverable at need. As a boy he had heard stories of fairy gold, and had thought he might learn the truth of them when he became a signaller. But there is no fairy gold; however, more importantly, there is the presence in England of the power of fairy magic.

In "The White Boat," Becky is the daughter of a fisherman's family in Lyme Regis; she collects the lobsters caught in the family's lobster pots. The local priest already disapproves of her because she is interested in things of which the Church does not approve—the shapes within the rocks and the fossils on the beach. She is one of Roberts' independent, self-assertive girls of whom he always wrote fondly. Lyme is a notorious place for heresy; it is the port from which the visionary priest John had sailed on his mission to see the Pope some years before, after stirring the country up to rebellion against the Church. One day Becky sees what she calls the White Boat, a trim racing vessel (a Bermudan, her father says). The crew of the White Boat buys her whole catch, but her father is far from pleased; she is to keep clear of the boat.

Taken onboard the White Boat, she realizes it is a smuggler manned by a Welsh crew; they bring in wine and cloth from France. She goes with them on a run to the French coast, and the trip on the White Boat is like a time in a different England: she is dressed in jeans and an old sweater and goes ashore to sit in a bar in France, like a tourist. She finds everything around her strange—she cannot even help in the galley because the cooking is so unusual. The White Boat also carries radio sets; we learn later that these are for the Guild of Signallers. Becky takes one of these and hides it, not knowing what it is, seeing it as the heart of the boat.

Back home, she feels betrayed; the crew of the White Boat has abandoned her and failed to fulfill the promise that England longs for:

> Where, she asked herself, was the Change once promised, the great things the priest John had seen? The Golden Age that would bring other White Boats, other days and hope: the wild waves of the very air made to talk and sing.
>
> (p. 118)

Broken by her family's disapproval and her own disappointment, she hands the radio to the village priest and tells him of the White Boat. He promptly calls the authorities.

The military arrives and occupies the village, laying a trap for the White Boat. They lay in cannon to blast it out of the water. Becky manages to evade the guard as the White Boat arrives and pull the lanyard on the first cannon. The White Boat is warned and escapes.

Like Rafe the signaller, Becky has a secret knowledge of the shape of an old, buried England, the England of sea and rocks. She also has seen some vision of the technological, liberated England that is to come.

The next measure tells the story of the priest that Becky had heard about. The rebellion at the end of the novel is backed by the ordinary people who have been inspired by John, and led by a girl with the spirit and independence of Becky. The title character of the measure "Brother John" breaks free from a hereditary calling (he comes from a family of shoemakers): he becomes a monk, working as a lithographic printer in an ab-

bey on the borders of Dorset, and he has a reputation as an artist. He is sent on a mission at the direct request of Rome to make a pictorial record of a witch-hunt in Dubris (Dover) that is being carried out by the Inquisition. His mind is destroyed by the experience and by the guilt he feels at the pleasure he took in the work. He deserts the abbey and tramps through Wessex, preaching a simplified Protestantism. His followers rise in open revolt and are suppressed by the military.

His journey ends in a village where a woman asks him to perform a miracle and cure her husband, who is a quarryman. John cannot heal his blindness and watches as the man goes to his workplace and quarries stone by touch without stopping day or night until he dies—an image of the people of England who work till death for the rich and powerful. It is here that John preaches the sermon in which he promises the Change: "He saw … the buildings of that new time, the factories and hospitals, power stations and laboratories … lightning chained, the wild waves of the very air made to talk and sing" (p. 161). This is of course the Change that Becky had heard of, and her radio foreshadows the talking and singing in the air.

John believes it is his mission to go to Rome and plead with the pope, for he has had a vision, based on what he knows of the practices of the Church, that the pope will at last release the technology he has suppressed. This decision to go to Rome is not a gesture; it is the only way out. Otherwise the human cost, in victims of the Inquisition and in lives like that of the blind quarryman, will continue.

He ends his sermon and borrows a boat to cross the channel. His followers melt away; the military, out to arrest him, finds only an empty beach and an upturned boat. It is not an escape for Brother John, however: He never makes it to Rome; he is lost at sea. The deliverance will not come yet, nor will it come this way.

At this point the action returns to the Strange family about twenty years after the first measure. Margaret Strange is the daughter of the Margaret that Jesse had loved years earlier but who had married his younger brother, Tim. After the elder

Margaret deserted Tim, however, their daughter became part of Jesse's household and his favorite. Jesse has become rich by ruining all his competitors.

Convinced that the house is haunted, the family has summoned the priest to exorcise the spirit. He is convinced that Jesse is possessed by the devil. The family has already been marked out as unsympathetic toward the Church by keeping the old Protestant custom of not naming their children after saints; the men have biblical names—Eli, Jesse, Timothy—and the women have the names of strong warlike queens from English history—Margaret (the warrior wife of Henry VI) and Eleanor (wife and bitter enemy of Henry II). The Church also disapproves of Jesse's business methods. Young Margaret is convinced that it is she who is possessed.

Margaret's childhood and schooling have made her familiar with the English people and countryside yet also capable of associating with the French-descended aristocracy. She meets and is courted by Robert, son of the Lord of Purbeck; a regular visitor to his home, she eventually consents to be his lover. The following morning she is sent out in disgrace from his castle. He will not, she believes, cross the social divide to marry her.

She calls in anguish on the old gods, Balder and Wotan. A vision is granted her; she is told, "Do not despise your Church. … Do not despise her mummeries; they have a purpose that will be fulfilled. … The Dream is ending. … The great Dance finishes, another will begin" (p. 200). But of her own individual future the Vision will say nothing. Desolate, she watches Jesse die.

In the measure called "Corfe Gate," Henry, Lord of Rye and Deal and the pope's lieutenant in England, is riding west with a military detachment to put down a revolt. On the way he attacks and kills the signallers at a station, though they have always enjoyed immunity. Things are changing violently in England.

The object of the expedition is Corfe Castle, where Eleanor is castle-holder. She is the daughter of Robert, Lord of Purbeck, and Margaret Strange. Having refused to send tribute to the pope because her people are starving, she has closed the castle, ready for a siege. She claims in response to the demands from the pope's officers that she hold the castle only from the king, not from the pope, and for that reason she resists the soldiers of the Church. When Henry arrives, she fires on him and kills him.

Other castles join in the revolt, but it is crushed by mercenaries brought from France and Spain; only Corfe holds out. All this happens in the absence of King Charles, who is visiting his American possessions. On his return, Eleanor yields the castle to him because she holds it as his vassal. To placate the pope, the king has her imprisoned for treason in the Tower of London. Later she is allowed to escape and lives in obscurity for some years until she is eventually murdered by agents of King Charles. He had never really trusted her, because those who make a rebellion against a pope can make one against a king.

She dies on the heath in the arms of John Falconer, who has been her faithful seneschal (steward). When the soldiers come for them, they find her body, but he is gone.

In the "Coda" to *Pavane,* John Falconer's son, also called John, who has been taken to America and brought up there, is sent by his father to visit Corfe Castle, where the revolt began that convulsed the world. As he reads a letter his father had given him to open on his arrival, the young man learns not to despise the Church and its oppression completely, because it had "giv[en] man time to reach … toward truer reason. Did [the Church] hang and burn? A little, yes. But there was no Belsen, no Buchenwald, no Paschendaele" (p. 275). He meets a local girl, who offers to put him up in her father's pub. She goes ahead to make sure. When he meets up with her, "he saw her cupped palm gleam. She had collected glowworms on the walk back down the path, carried them 'along of her' as the locals would say" (p. 279). The story ends here with this new friendship.

There are problems with the resolution, and not just at the level of seeing how King Charles broke with the Church, which is how the Change came about. L. J. Hurst suggests that this is a novel set in future time, not alternate time. He bases this view, in part, on the section in the letter that reads, "The Popes knew … that given electricity, men would be drawn to the atom. Given fusion, they would come to fission. Because once beyond our time, there was … a Reformation, an Armada. And a burning, an Armageddon" (p. 275). For Hurst, *Pavane* is about how the Church is able to reconstruct time, to save men from themselves, as though the Church could foresee and change the future. Though the world depicted in *Pavane* is a hard world, it is also a world that has avoided the worst horrors we have seen in our lifetimes.

THE ACHIEVEMENT OF PAVANE

The summary does not do justice to the close texture of the book, with its descriptions of England at different seasons (*Pavane* begins in winter and ends in summer) and of the heath, the towns, and the coast. Above all are the descriptions of work—with machines like steam engines and boats, with the signalling system and the stone blocks used in lithography. These are in our terms old technologies, but an alternate present is always a possible future. Ecological deterioration may force us to return to older technologies such as those Roberts presents. Further, by not using modern technologies, Roberts avoids the clichés familiar from a thousand documentary films.

The work they do defines the men and women of *Pavane*. They make their moral decisions in silence, without words, but the decisions they make shape the future. In the end, their choices matter.

THE ALTERNATE WORLD AS A GENRE

As an alternate world, *Pavane* shares some features with two American novels in the same genre. In Ward Moore's *Bring the Jubilee* (1953), Robert E. Lee's victory at Gettysburg launches a successful campaign that ends with the defeat of the Union and Southern independence; in Philip K. Dick's *The Man in the High Castle* (1962),

the Axis powers have won World War II; Japan occupies California and the western seaboard states while Germany occupies the eastern seaboard. All three novels have common preoccupations and techniques that are designed to undermine readers' expectations and alienate them from any sense of the comfortably familiar.

The first feature of these works that causes such alienation is that they represent a United States or an England that is a colonized dependency rather than a colonizing power. *Pavane* depicts the absolute poverty of a colonized England, not just in Eleanor's rhetoric but in such details as the economic status of Rafe Bigland's family. Though he is an estate manager, Rafe's father can hardly feed his family; they must grow most of their own food. Further, *Pavane* notices cultural features of colonialism, such as the use of local people as the military arm of the colonizing power, control of language and communication, and the denial of technology. The colonized lack autonomy; when they reach out for knowledge, the very diversity of the available knowledge is itself bewildering. The experience is brutalizing. Again and again in *Pavane* there are incidents where children are savagely beaten. The fighting and even the sports (cudgeling in "The Signaller") are medieval and brutal. Unlike Moore and Dick, however, Roberts is clear that the only way out of a colonial situation is through a political act that has popular support, like King Charles's decision to break with Rome as a consequence of his people's rebellion.

Alienation arises on the micro level too, and Roberts has a rich array of devices here. Names of towns are Latinized (Londinium for London) or spelled annoyingly differently (Bourne Mouth for Bournemouth). Shakespeare is there (Margaret quotes from *Richard III*), but he isn't famous. "One of those minor Elizabethans," she says. "I forget his name: I thought he was rather good" (p. 195). Then, suddenly, we are doubly alienated when something familiar from our world appears—Zeiss make binoculars and Burrell and Sons of Norwich make steam engines.

A device Roberts takes from Moore is introducing the name of an organization or person from our world but altering its significance. To us, Les Routiers is an organization of French truck drivers that approves pubs and restaurants and awards decals; these appear all over Dorset. In *Pavane* routiers are French highwaymen. Most readers on first encountering King Charles in *Pavane* probably think of Charles Stuart or Charles Windsor, but this King Charles is a Hapsburg with five hundred years of absolutism behind him.

Finally, each of these novels brings us back to our world. For Dick, who is always preoccupied by illusion and reality, the sight of a bridge that exists in our world but not in the alternate world begins a process in which the world of the Japanese occupation dissolves. The reader comes back out of the text.

Moore handles the return through the narrative. In the alternative world where Hodge Backmaker was born in a defeated New York, Lee's victory at Gettysburg had been the beginning of the Confederate victory in the Civil War. As a historian, Backmaker wanted to be absolutely sure that he was describing the battle correctly, so he traveled back to 1863 in a time machine (the pride of Southron technology) to witness the battle and placed himself at the point of the key Confederate advance. But his very presence panics the Southerners. Lee loses the battle; the time machine is never invented and Backmaker now must live out his life in the world that followed a Union victory.

Bring the Jubilee and *Pavane* both ask the reader two questions. What would be the price of the victorious South or the Catholic England that so many people seem to desire? And how might the essential U.S.A. or the essential England show through if they were deprived of all their power and wealth?

Roberts is perhaps the most subtle, because he considers the changes necessary to bring the two worlds together and how a million individual acts of will can build up to a single historic event. Further, the change is qualified. There is no sense that, as the result of the end of the pope's hegemony, England has become a democratic society. It remains one in which power is focused at the center rather than diffused.

THE GRAIN KINGS *(1976)*

This collection of short stories begins with "Weihnachtsabend" (German for "Christmas Eve"), set in a party at a great English house over the holiday in an England occupied by Germany as a result of World War II. Roberts' interests here are the nature of collaboration and the moral problems it poses; many of the Englishmen who work with the Germans have even abandoned their own language and speak only German. His hero, Mainwaring, an Englishman, must break free of the effects of his years of collaboration when faced with the demand to lie about the disappearance of an Englishwoman he brought to the house with him. In the end he shoots the German minister for whom he has worked and is hunted down as a result. His decision is brought on in part by the savagery with which the German children of the guests are treated; as part of a toughening-up process, the adults deliberately terrify them when they come down in the evening. It is an uncomfortable tale, suggesting that the English might well have compromised in building what the story calls the Two Empires, the linked British empire (ruled, of course, by Edward VIII) and the Third Reich. The ending is bleak. "We made a mistake," Mainwaring tells himself. The story is in the tradition of *When William Came* (1913) by Saki (H. H. Munro), which describes how England falls to Wilhelm II without a struggle because of the moral decadence of the English. There is one difference: Saki looks forward to what might happen; Roberts looks back over what did not happen. England was not on the losing side in World War II. Why then this preoccupation? For Roberts it is still terribly possible for the English to make a mistake, to collaborate with processes that are in themselves neo-Nazi.

The influence of Kipling shows clearly in this collection, first of all in a group of three stories— "The Passing of the Dragons," "The Trustie Tree," and "The Lake of Tuonela"—set on other worlds. Roberts here is writing about the exotic along the lines of Kipling's tales of India. For Kipling, India would never be free; it faced a future of permanent British occupation. Almost to compensate, he writes about the magic of the

Indian empire. For Roberts, that route is closed. There is no empire for him. But he realizes a disturbing fact about the effect of Kipling's imperialism: that it destroyed the people of India by removing their autonomy, their freedom to act. In "The Passing of the Dragons," a field worker watches in despair as an exotic people, the Dragons, close themselves off from communication with humans and then simply commit suicide. In the other two stories, the Kalti of Xerxes are also in decline. They are canal people. Years ago they built a mighty system of canals on their planet which now faces competition from the Earthmen's road transport. Now that the canals have lost their purpose, the Kalti have no purpose either. To justify themselves, the Earthmen create a myth that the canals are now unusable, and when Mathis attempts in "The Lake of Tuonela" to navigate the canals to their end, the trip costs the life of the Kalti who accompanies him. Such pessimism and fatalism are also found in Kipling as a reflex of triumphalist imperialism.

The title story, "The Grain Kings," is set in the future aboard a huge combine harvester built to harvest the new artificially heated wheat prairies of America. "It's like a ship or a plane" is the impression of the passengers, a group of journalists and photographers, who see little of the crew apart from the barman. The grain king must harvest near a rival Soviet machine, and an incident occurs that looks like interference by the Soviet vessel. However, it turns out to be a chart error, and the standoff between the United States and Soviet Union is resolved.

What is noticeable about Roberts' depiction of the world of work, especially here but also in *Pavane,* is the way in which men's work isolates them. Either they are craftsmen on their own or they are in a rigid hierarchic structure—of a ship, an army, a monastery—that assigns them a role within which they may find themselves isolated. There is no sense in Roberts of the way in which working in cooperation creates a community of interest. Kipling, too, characteristically focuses on the men who work alone, on the engineers aboard ship, for example, who live in the secretive world of their own competence. It is no coincidence that Kipling was a passionate

Freemason; for him, a constructed socialization of the isolated replaces the solidarity of those who work in cooperation.

KITEWORLD *(1985)*

Just before World War I, Samuel Cody designed and flew a kite capable of lifting a man in a gondola several hundred feet above the ground. He also devised the air show, designed to introduce the public to the possibilities of flying machines. In *Kiteworld* (1985), Cody's inventions are developed; his kites are the principal technology in that world.

Kiteworld starts with the men who fly the kites that line the frontier and are found all over the interior of the country as well. There is a public network of kites, and the rich and powerful have their own kites to protect their homes. The writing is full of a sense of the joy to be found in membership of a disciplined corps; from Kitecadet to Kitemaster, both fliers and ground crew take pride in their work. The chapters of *Kiteworld,* which are devoted to different characters as in *Pavane,* have titles like "Kitecadet," but there is also a "Kitewaif"—even a girl without home and family is defined by the kites.

The kites fly to protect Kiteworld from demons that fly through the air and have to be shot by the observers in the kites before they can harm the people of Kiteworld. The demons actually exist; Roberts is clear about phobia. Having an illogical phobia about spiders, for example, does not imply that spiders don't exist, only that the phobia is excessive. On the fear of these demons, an elaborate religious system has been built. The Variants, the main church, are oppressive and hierarchic, but a moderate religion, the Middlers, is tolerated. The technology of the kites and the church in this world are mutually supportive. Few are allowed outside; there are few places to visit. But there is a Kitemariner who has journeyed to the tropical islands to the south of Kiteworld.

It becomes clear that this is several hundred years in the future and that the motivation behind the fear of the invading demons is a confused memory of the nuclear weapons that flew through the air and destroyed all but such small communities as this. Outside Kiteworld, the land and sea are full of strange mutations—priests swoop down on the fishermen to condemn their catch if it is radioactive. Sometimes, even in the safe world under the kites, people are born who lack normal human characteristics—one girl has no power of speech or memory. The demons, too, are some sort of mutation of human beings.

But what *Kiteworld* centers on is the ability of those who live in this world to make something of their lives. There are long summers on country estates and trips to the capital for festivals built around the air shows. Even those at the bottom of the social structure, like the abused ragamuffin Kitewaif, learn to manage.

The characterization is stronger than in most of Roberts' work, particularly where he revisits themes he had already handled in *Pavane*—the apprentice or the older man who loses faith in what he is doing. He said that he was particularly pleased with the drawing of the relationship between the Kitemariner and his wife, based on friends of his (*Lemady,* pp. 87–88). But he was probably most pleased with his femme fatale, Madame Kerosina. She is the wife of the richest tradesman in Kiteworld, who has made his money from fuel—hence his nickname, Kerosin. She is in fact neither vulgar nor pathetic; though she takes lovers, she retains her dignity.

How would such a society break down? First, there is knowledge that comes from outside. The Kitemariner has found the life of the tropical islanders gentler and less repressive. A kiteman who has encountered the demons in the flesh has found it hard to kill them because they seemed human. Another kiteman who is grounded in their territory is helped by the demons and finds them friendly, not hostile. Each of these encounters offers a challenge to the prevailing orthodoxy.

But the collapse of Kiteworld, when it does come, is sudden and violent. Two sects form among the Variants, and a state of civil war breaks out and is barely contained. Then comes a day when there is no wind, and throughout Kiteworld not a kite flies. There is no invasion of demons—the whole belief system is invalidated, and the fighting between the warring factions

intensifies and destroys everything. Only a few of the young people escape, taken off in flying machines by the islanders.

If *Pavane* attracted readers because, among other reasons, it used a picture of an alternate England to look at what England is like, Kiteworld has a similar attraction. Roberts gives one clue in *Lemady:* "[Madame Kerosina's] name was formed in the Russian way from that of her husband who cornered the [kerosene] market" (p. 134). Why Russian? There are other clues in the text of *Kiteworld:* a signpost that says Eastern Fort, which is the meaning of Vladivostok; the stained-glass window in the cathedral that shows a line of kitemen guarding a forgotten city whose churches have onion-shaped domes; the fact that the Kitemariner sails south and reaches a tropical island; all these suggest that the location of the Kiteworld is in eastern Siberia. It is a society, despite the English names of the characters, that derives from the Soviet system.

Hence the combination of a rigid and oppressive ruling class with a marked gaiety in personal relationships, reminiscent of, for example, Vladimir Nabokov's *Ada* (1969), another picture of a displaced Russia. The Soviet system ended partly because of contact with those living abroad, especially perhaps the Czechs, with their different kind of communism. The demons from abroad that were most feared—consumerism, libertarianism—turned out to be attractive and friendly. The collapse when it came brought civil disorder, because the old belief system seemed invalidated. If this analysis is correct, then it is noteworthy that *Kiteworld* preceded these events by some years.

OTHER PROSE

Among Roberts' other work, two books deserve attention. *The Boat of Fate* (1971) is a depiction of the end of the Roman occupation of Britain; it is Roberts' attempt at a purely historical novel. *The Chalk Giants* (1974) is a particularly effective collection of short stories in which a man expecting to die in an imminent nuclear attack has a series of visions of future societies that will arise in Britain.

Some of the rest is disappointing. *Winterwood and Other Hauntings* (published 1989, but actually collecting earlier short stories) has one strong item, "Mrs. Cibber," which describes a young man's obsession with a portrait of an eighteenth-century actress that he sees in a pub. It is an interesting depiction of the development of his work as an artist in the advertising world in Covent Garden in London in the 1950s, as life became easier and more prosperous and at the same time more violent. In this it parallels Roberts' own experience.

Roberts was particularly happy with his stories about Kaeti, a young actress who is an East-End Londoner; the attempt to use her language and way of thinking gives the stories an energy and drive. *Kaeti and Company* (1986) and *Kaeti on Tour* (1991) are lively and humorous but suffer like most dialect stories from relying rather on the writer's view of how such a girl might behave than on firsthand experience. They are popular, though, with most readers of Roberts.

A HERON CAUGHT IN WEEDS *(1987)*

A number of Roberts's poems, selected by James Goddard, appeared in a limited edition of 650 copies entitled *A Heron Caught in Weeds,* published by Kerosina in 1987. About half the printing was reserved for distribution with special editions of Roberts' novel *Gráinne.* Publication of this sort within a coterie is close to vanity publishing, as though the poet wished to avoid notice and criticism, and some of the poems (pen-portraits of friends of Roberts, for example) have little general interest. But it may be that a proper edition of the poems would reveal to the public a minor poet but one capable of close observation and original expression.

The title, reflected in a graphic motif in the Celtic tradition printed on the cover, equates the heron unable to rise and fly because of the impeding weeds with the attempts at composition of the "unversed poet," as Roberts describes himself in the introduction. The reading implied by the references in these poems—Yeats, Browning, Marvell, the Protestant Episcopalian hymn-book—is old-fashioned, as the taste for Kipling evidenced in his prose is old-fashioned. In his introduction Roberts cites as a major influence the work of the Georgian poet Edward Thomas (1878–1917), best known for the poem "Adlestrop" (1915). Adlestrop is a remote station where one hot summer's day Thomas' train stopped unusually. Nothing happens—"No-one left and no-one came"—but the poet hears the singing first of one blackbird then of "all the birds of Oxfordshire and Gloucestershire." In other words, it is an occasional poem, one that depends on the close observation of some particular occasion, and similarly it is as an occasional poet that Roberts is most interesting.

The other influence he cites is the painter Paul Nash (1899–1946); as an artist recording the battlefields of World War I, Nash had depicted a world of ruined landscape, with the wreckage of war appearing almost like the skeletons of animals. His work, Roberts says, had long been a "fetish with me."

There are three sections to the collection. First comes the poem "Gráinne," which is more typical of the Welsh or Irish poetic tradition than the English, since it depends on knowledge of an accepted, mythical tale and reinterprets the experience of the hero or heroine in an allusive and sometimes teasing way. Gráinne was the daughter of Cormac, and she married Finn. She ran away with her lover Dermuid, and they were pursued throughout Ireland, hiding where they could. Dermuid was eventually killed by a boar. It is at this point of isolation that the poem begins. She is alone in a cave. Outside is a summer's day

Heat-bowl of sky, her Mother, blue,
And sunlight shafting in
Through cavemouth, never touching her
And fern leaves hanging, rich with that same light,
Unviewable, and sweetened with the wind
That comes up from the white plains, from the sea;
Nearer, his bed, the bracken pressed by limbs,
His hunting horn forsaken.

(p. 9)

A modern avatar of Gráinne is seen in a hotel room, in denim and "tart's shoes": "All is transformed now ... and Him, the lover / Stepping through Light and Time to leave her be, / Free to paint nails and wail," before we return to Gráinne in her cave:

Nothing will come; this too is afternoon

    ...

Space is made visible, while her hand
Stays firm to rock, freezing the moment there

    ...

The lorries move, along their necklace road;
A horn sounds, distant as a dream.

                        (p. 10)

Spanbroekmolen contains perhaps the most achieved writing in the collection. It is a group of thirteen poems based upon a trip to Belgium and northern France to visit the battlefields of World War I. Central to the poems is Roberts' feeling for his grandfather, who had been a soldier at the front and had survived. Roberts recreates the world of that war and the landscape of the ordinary Flanders towns with their memorials and graveyards. He is particularly effective at catching the actual feel of being one of the young men caught up in the war. For many, the arrival in France had the air of holiday, and *Spanbroekmolen* begins with an apparently simple poem, "Calais Encounter," that catches the surprise of finding oneself abroad and the need to come to terms with a new language.

"Madame," I say; you bob your head and grin
So small and square, so blonde, so very *French,*
Surprising to an Islander; that liquid chat
Can't be your native tongue ...
You've been to school too much, you'll soon slip back.

And she responds

"M'sieur—" and so the oracle is worked afresh.
I've spoken, you've responded, think of that!
Madame, there's wonder in you!

But being abroad in wartime as a young soldier is also being in a new moral climate. In "Home Thoughts from a Coach" (a coach here is a tour bus), Roberts sees in a bar a woman old enough to have been a girl when his grandfather was there and draws a shocking picture of these men, marked by the war, groping the girl:

The old men, gas capes stinking,
Roughness of drab, my Grandad, the white eyes

Haunting in haunted faces, they'd have handled
You; and you them, little one.

    ...

Blue girl in bar, *French* girl
Madame; so many memories,
Vanished, already past, yet still so fresh.

The tension of attitudes is caught in the girl being both "little one"—young, innocent—and also to the soldiers a French girl and therefore a fit target.

Then he drives on, like his grandfather had before, to a battlefield, Ypres, whose name the soldiers could not pronounce so they gave it an English shape and called it Wipers. The windshield wipers of the coach as they move back and forth recall the earlier journey his grandfather made.

Forward and back. My Grandad, bloody Wipers
Acceleration ...
... the landscape swinging round,
The first headstones in sight, blue skies.
We drive toward a terror indefinable.

                        (p. 14)

The title of the poem echoes Browning's "Home-Thoughts, from Abroad" (1845), which is about the flowers and birds of the poet's native England remembered from abroad and making England a land of peace and beauty; in 1914–1918, it was the land to be kept inviolate, whatever happened at the front. This was the root of the attitude that English girls were pure but French girls were fair game.

But at the battlefields themselves, Roberts finds only silence. "At Hellfire Corner" is set at Ypres itself. Battlefields in England from the Wars of the Roses and the Civil War still resonate for him, alive as he is to the continuing presence of history beneath the present:

Edge Hill still cries aloud, the mists collect
On Bosworth, Naseby, Marston. Great Corfe Gate
Throbs with a shattered anger, London's walls urge
  blood.

At Ypres he hears not even an echo of war, not even of the whining shells that were so terrifying they had to be given a childish nickname, the whizzbangs.

No ghosts of whizzbangs, in the glowing blue?
Least jangle of a harness, clank of tracks?
These guns, these tanks mere fossils, exoskeletal
Rusted to silence?

So the remains at Ypres (seen as Paul Nash
depicted them, like the skeletons of once-living
things) have slipped into prehistory; the once
bronze voices of the guns are silent; they are part
now of the vastness of antiquity.

Bronze voices, gods of chalk, disdain to speak.
Nothing speaks here; but this is Antic too,
Antiquity is vastness, vastness the only Age.

(p. 22)

This is not as paradoxical as it seems. The men
who came home did not speak of the war; a great
silence covered it, except for the work of very
few poets. This is the silence that Roberts finds
at Ypres. It is a part of what Wilfred Owen had
forecast for those who had lost friends or family
in the war, a future summed up as "a drawing-
down of blinds" ("Anthem for Doomed Youth,"
1917).

The strength of these poems, then, is that
Roberts does not attempt to re-create his grandfather's experience but reports a set of parallel and
illuminating incidents.

Among the rest, "Verulam" is based on a visit
to the Roman amphitheater at Verulam, near St.
Alban's in Hertfordshire; Roberts begins with the
observation that, though the Roman crowd may
have been very like us, we have no idea of the
sort of show that was put on here, as the Roman
empire came to its end. "What did they watch? ...
/ I see the gigs, carrucas all the rest / The cream
of Roman Hertford come to view." He homes in
on one imagined girl in the crowd, a servant on a
night out: "And you in your long togs, hair
garlanded / Perhaps. / Perhaps so much; your one
night off a week." But as the girl dreams, "... the
wolves close, circling through the woods / Eyes
gleaming like the yellow carriage lamps"—the
wolves and the woods long gone in our Britain
but there in Roman times, like the enemies that
circled the empire. But for her tonight, there is
promise: "Somewhere the Venus, coltish, just
like you / Holds unknown flowers." It is an
interesting meditation on the way in which,

though we live within history, we don't live
bound by the doom of history, and on the way in
which we know both more and less than those
living in our past.

RECEPTION

Roberts, partly for personal reasons of the sort
hinted at above, is not a popular writer, though
he is an achieved writer. In the end his work is
conservative and backward looking, but his view
is totally without sentimentality. History for him
is red in tooth and claw. However, he is above all
a rewarding writer, and he must surely find more
readers in an England desperately seeking to
redefine itself. In that sense, too, he is like his
beloved Kipling.

In his novel *The Alteration* (1976), Kingsley
Amis paid Roberts the compliment of taking the
world of *Pavane* as his setting, extending and
developing it. In Amis' novel Roberts himself
appears as the author of *Galliard*, a novel about
how Princess Elizabeth succeeded in seizing the
throne and establishing a Protestant Reformation.
It's a neat tribute.

Selected Bibliography

WORKS OF KEITH ROBERTS

Novels

The Furies. London: Hart-Davis, 1966.

Pavane. London: Hart-Davis, 1968; Garden City, N.Y.: Doubleday, 1968.

The Inner Wheel. London: Hart-Davis, 1970; Garden City, N.Y.: Doubleday, 1970.

The Boat of Fate. London: Hutchinson, 1971. Englewood Cliffs, N.J.: Prentice-Hall, 1974.

The Chalk Giants. London: Hutchinson, 1974; New York: Putnam, 1975.

Molly Zero. London: Gollancz, 1980.

Kiteworld. London: Gollancz, 1985; New York: Arbor House, 1986.

Gráinne. Salisbury, U.K.: Kerosina: 1987.

The Road to Paradise. Worcester Park, Surrey: Kerosina Press, 1988.

SHORT STORY COLLECTIONS

Anita. New York: Ace Books, 1970; London: Millington, 1976.

Machines and Men. London: Hutchinson, 1973.

The Grain Kings. London: Hutchinson, 1976.

The Passing of the Dragons. New York: Berkley Medallion, 1977.

Ladies from Hell. London: Gollancz, 1979.

Kaeti and Company. Salisbury: Kerosina Press, 1986.

The Lordly Ones. London: Gollancz, 1986.

Winterwood and Other Hauntings. Scotforth, U.K.: Morrigan, 1989.

Kaeti on Tour. Feltham, U.K.: Sirius Book Company, 1992.

OTHER WORKS

A Heron Caught in Weeds. Salisbury, U.K.: Kerosina, 1987. (Poetry.)

Lemady: Episodes of a Writer's Life. San Bernardino, Calif.: Borgo Press, 1997. (Autobiography.)

CRITICAL AND BIOGRAPHICAL STUDIES

Barbour, Douglas. "Keith Roberts." In *Twentieth Century Science Fiction Writers.* Edited by Curtis C. Smith. London: Macmillan, 1981.

Burgess, Anthony. *99 Novels: The Best in English since 1939: A Personal Choice.* London: Allison & Busby, 1984.

Hurst, L. J. Hurst. "*Pavane* by Keith Roberts." Available online (http://dspace.dial.pipex.com/l.j.hurst/pavane.htm).

VIKRAM SETH

(1952–)

Thomas Wright

VIKRAM SETH (pronounced "sate") is one of the most accomplished and exciting of contemporary writers. His oeuvre is characterized by its variety and its stylistic range: among other things, he has written volumes of poetry, a travel book, a verse novel, a libretto, the longest single-volume prose novel in the English language, and a collection of verse fables for children. Great stylistic variety is also displayed within his books: the travel book *From Heaven Lake* (1983) is comprised of poetry and prose.

Seth's books are heterogeneous, too, in terms of their subject and setting. As a writer he draws upon his academic training as an economist and as a student of politics as well as his gifts as a poet. His first three non-poetry titles were set in China, San Francisco, and northern India; the novel *An Equal Music* (1999) takes us on a tour of Europe. Seth's writing has a distinctly international and cosmopolitan feel; many of his poetry collections thus include translations from a number of languages, *Three Chinese Poets* (1992) being the most notable example.

For all its cosmopolitanism, many critics have suggested that Seth's work is steeped in his own Indian culture. He has been labeled a "postcolonial Indian writer" and identified as a member of an "Empire-writes-back" generation that includes other British-educated Indians such as Salman Rushdie. The issue of Seth's "Indianness" is a sensitive and rather controversial one; some commentators have even gone so far as to criticize Seth for not being "Indian" (whatever that may mean) enough.

Whether or not Seth's books are typically "Indian," it is possible to make other generalizations about them. Seth is in no sense a "conceptual" or "metaphysical" writer: he is not interested in the ideas behind a person or an object but rather in people and things in themselves. His focus is usually on surfaces, textures, and quotidian details: it is the visible world of phenomena rather than the invisible world of ideas and beliefs that exists for him.

Seth is also obsessed with matters of form and style. He is a dazzlingly gifted stylist whose love of language and literary form are infectious. The style of *The Golden Gate* (1986), a novel comprised of almost six hundred sonnets, is exhilarating and intoxicating: it offers the reader an almost Mozartean aesthetic pleasure. Seth's writing is invariably sharp, rich, and sophisticated; it brilliantly evokes the colors and surfaces of the various societies he describes. And it is the visible and social world of appearances, manners, and conversations that fascinates him. Some of his best fictional writing occurs in set-piece scenes where his characters come together to exchange gossip. In his poetry, too, he rarely retreats from the world into a private language of introspection: his muse is invariably a public one.

The characteristic themes of Seth's writing also concern the social world. His books always acknowledge the presence and the power of society; we are continually made aware of its inviolable laws and traditions. In *A Suitable Boy* (1993) characters who attempt to go beyond society's limits, or who challenge its rules, invariably come to sticky ends; those who accept those rules and limits tend to live happily, or at least comfortably, ever after. The moral (and Seth's work is unashamedly moral) is that you can never escape the world or suddenly change the way things have been for centuries.

This moral reminds us of Greek tragedy: what Seth suggests is that to overstep society's bounds is to condemn oneself to madness and exile. Throughout his books we discover the Greek idea of the "golden mean": moderation is to be preferred to excess, friendship to wild passion, and the gradual amelioration of social ills to revolutionary change. It is hardly surprisingly then that Seth has annoyed the more "radical" literary critics, because his work is essentially a celebration of bourgeois values and the bourgeois way of life.

Sensual, worldly, urbane, and flamboyant, Vikram Seth can be likened to eighteenth- and early-nineteenth-century writers such as Alexander Pope, Lord Byron, and Jane Austen. In his books he bears witness to the power of society and comments wittily on the foibles of its members. Above all else, pleasure is perhaps most important to him, and there is certainly a great deal of pleasure to be derived from his super-civilized and incorrigibly stylish writing.

EARLY LIFE AND EARLY POETRY

Vikram Seth was born in Calcutta on June 20, 1952, into a middle-class Hindu family. His father, Prem Seth, is a consultant to the leather industry and his mother, Laila Seth, is a High Court judge. In his youth he attended an English-style public school called the Doon School, then he read politics, philosophy and economics at Corpus Christi College, Oxford.

In 1975 he moved to Stanford University in California, where he studied for a Ph.D. in economics. His thesis, on the demography of certain Chinese villages, was never completed, although he has expressed an intention to return to it and rewrite it in sestinas. At Stanford he took a course in creative writing under the supervision of the poet Donald Davie. The experience, which Seth has described in his article "Forms and Inspirations," was to be a formative one: it taught him the virtues of lucidity and readability.

At Stanford, Seth also encountered the poet Timothy Steele, who was equally influential on his poetry. (In acknowledgment of this Seth was to dedicate *The Golden Gate* to him). Among other things Steele taught Seth the importance of form and demonstrated that contemporary episodes and issues could be described and addressed in traditional rhyme and meter. Prior to his arrival at Stanford, Seth had regarded tradi-

tional form as artificial and constricting; his youthful poetry, which he later destroyed, had been written in free verse. Under the tutelage of Davie and Steele, Seth discovered "the way poetic form and poetic inspiration work to search each other out" ("Forms and Inspirations," p. 18).

The debate about traditional poetic form is one of the few theoretical issues Seth has commented on (it is telling, perhaps, that it should be a purely technical one). He argues that the use of traditional form leads to greater pith, pleasure, memorability, and readability and suggests that it intensifies the emotional power of verse. On a personal level Seth found that the restrictions of rhyme and meter forced him to think harder about his own writing; he also discovered that there was something miraculous about the range of emotions and ideas that one could convey in two poems of the same tight verse form. Traditional form curbed what he saw as his worst poetical excesses and ensured that he was not continually forced to come up with something striking and original. He was no longer, to use Oscar Wilde's brilliant phrase, at the mercy of genius, and thankfully, neither was the reader.

Seth's fondness for traditional poetic form is of a piece with his awareness of the weight of history and tradition. In one of his poems he describes tradition as "the soul of art," and he has remarked that because particular rhyme schemes carried resonances of particular poets ... pouring my spirit into a cup into which some poet I admired had poured his, I found I was seized with an energy that came from outside myself" ("Forms," p. 18). It is, of course, also consistent with the public nature of Seth's writing: rhyme and meter create a sort of familiar social poetic space in which both author and reader feel comfortable.

Seth's careful observation of technical rules and limits can in turn be related to his awareness of the rules and limits of society. His comment that the constriction of traditional form is both psychologically satisfying and curiously liberating is interesting in this context. Without the safety net of a traditional form one is forced to fall back on a unique and private language; this is the fevered and incomprehensible language spoken by the characters in Seth's books that become social outcasts.

Seth's fascination with form is worth remarking upon at length because it remains constant throughout his oeuvre. Many of his books are breathtaking technical performances, and they often have their origin in some formal challenge. In *The Golden Gate,* Seth set out to evoke the world of California yuppies in Pushkinian sonnets; *An Equal Music* is perhaps his attempt to write a novel in the sonata form of classical music.

In *Mappings* (1981), his first collection of verse, Seth characteristically justifies his "unreasonable" use of rhyme by arguing that it is "fun"; he also demonstrates his masterful handling of rhyme and a variety of other traditional poetic devices and forms. The volume, which is comprised of poems Seth wrote in his twenties and dedicated to his Stanford mentors Donald Davie and Timothy Steele, was originally published (and sold) by Seth himself in 1980. A year later it was republished in Calcutta with a beautiful multicolored cover.

The poems exhibit Seth's love of the commonplace. The French symbolist poet Stéphane Mallarmé once dismissed daily life as unsuitable material for poetry. "The everyday world," he loftily remarked, "smells of cooking." To Seth, however, the everyday world positively reeks of poetry. His poems are invariably occasioned by some commonplace incident: in one he describes a moth dancing around a lightbulb, another begins with the poet dipping a cookie into a glass of tea. It is a poetry that celebrates the life of the body and the social world and seeks to find a rich and subtle language for little curiosities and everyday things.

Seth's early poems are crammed full of references to food, news, and domestic objects; they frequently describe everyday episodes, such as waking up, sex, and shopping. He juxtaposes commonplace incidents with allusions to more "elevated" and "poetical" subjects, such as metaphysics and love. In a poetical parody of Hamlet's "To be or not to be" soliloquy, he refers to a presidential election and the Olympic Games;

a sonnet beginning "O my generous and exuberant love" contains the line "You are forgiven … for beating me at scrabble" (*Collected Poems,* p. 15). The effect is often humorous and bathetic; Seth's wordplay is equally funny. In "Dubious" he undermines the seriousness of the subject—his sexuality—with a clever and epigrammatic ending:

In the strict ranks
of Gay and Straight
what is my status?
Stray or Great?

(*Collected Poems,* p. 46)

This kind of linguistic trickery may strike some as facile and inappropriate; others will discover seriousness in Seth's verse precisely because he refuses to take himself too seriously. It is perhaps his lack of self-consciousness and self-indulgence that allows him to evoke landscapes and cities in short photographic poems such as "Point Reyes"; it also lends to his verse variety and a pleasing air of sociability. Seth is always kind and considerate toward his gentle reader: on no occasion does he make us feel that we have to suffer for the sake of his art.

Seth's language is invariably as direct, colloquial, and simple as the transparent prose of *A Suitable Boy.* He attempts to introduce subtlety to the public language of everyday conversation and cliché. This does not, however, preclude powerful emotion, and often a poem that begins with small talk opens out into a moving lyrical language: "I've spoiled your mood. I'm sorry. Yes, I will / Keep clear of you … / you who infuse / My music now, my sunsets" (*Collected Poems,* p. 57). Here, as elsewhere in his work, Seth produces surprising and unexpected effects through the mixture of tones and colors.

Several of the pieces in *Mappings* concern Seth's native India; the poem "Divali" is his most personal and impassioned discussion of his Indian identity. He tells us that at school he gained "the conqueror's / Authoritarian Seal: / English!," which has left him and his fellow countrymen with the sensation of being "not home at home" (*Collected Poems,* pp. 65–66, 68). Condemned to the live the life of an exile within his own country, he chooses to travel, and yet he also feels "abroad" when he is "abroad." A sense of the restlessness of the exile informs many of the other poems in the collection, which are typically set either in transit or in a variety of exotic locations. The few people who read *Mappings* would not have been particularly surprised to discover that Seth's next publication would be a travel book.

FROM HEAVEN LAKE *(1983)*

In 1980 Seth went to China to carry out the research for his Ph.D. thesis. He stayed there, as a student of Nanjing University, for the following two years. Wishing to visit his family in Delhi in the summer of 1981, he mapped out an adventurous route back to India through the Himalayas via Tibet and Nepal. His plan was to hitchhike for most of the journey; in the end, because of terrible floods and the appalling condition of the roads, he was forced to walk some of the way. *From Heaven Lake* is the engaging account of his odyssey.

Seth's journey, and the various obstacles he is confronted with along the way, provides the narrative outline of the book. Within that narrative structure there are a poems, quotations from guidebooks, pages of dialogue, and countless digressions on a wide variety of economic, cultural, and political issues. In form the book is not unlike *A Suitable Boy:* it seems to grow organically and to have its own rather gentle momentum. It is possible that the travel genre appealed to Seth precisely because it is undefined and capacious enough to accommodate his diverse interests; it may also have provided some relief from the formal restrictions he imposed upon himself when writing poetry.

Given the desultory nature of the book, it is absolutely necessary that Seth maintains our interest by being a fascinating companion for us along the long and winding way. And this is exactly what happens: Seth is such an amiable, informed, and charming narrator that we gladly accept him as our guide. He is witty, self-deprecating, endlessly curious, and familiar, offering us the sort of unpretentious, almost throwaway, gems of wisdom that we expect from the best travel writing. "I have often thought," he comments in one of his many asides, "that those who don't know a language properly are often most expressive in it" (p. 169).

Seth is also a keen observer. As in his poetry, he occasionally presents himself as a Romantic figure (there are several occasions when he wanders off by himself to write lyrical apostrophes to the landscape), yet he never allows the concerns of his ego to get in the way of the world around him. Rather like Bruce Chatwin, he replaces the insistent "I" of the navel-gazing travel writer with the "eye" of the detached photographer, and he evokes land and cityscapes in an economical, pared down prose: "There is a pomegranate tree, a small pavilion, a few stone tablets. ... on the platform where the main hall stands are ceramic basins filled with mossy stones" (p. 30).

In *From Heaven Lake* and throughout his writing, Seth tends to be more interested in others than in himself; this in turn makes him interesting to us. He is fascinated by everything from the economic importance of yaks to children's games; he is also a good listener with a fine gift for conjuring up a character. Of all these characters (to whom the book is dedicated) the driver who takes Seth to Lhasa is perhaps the most interesting. Sui is a tough and laconic chain-smoker who spends most of his life on the road. Through his actions, mannerisms, and occasional remarks, we come to understand a great deal about contemporary China.

Seth's dealings with the Chinese authorities are equally revealing in this regard. From the moment the book opens he comes up against a wall of bureaucratic rules and regulations. In a sense he is not unlike Lata, the young female protagonist of *A Suitable Boy,* who continually finds herself at odds with Indian society. On a guided tour Seth is forbidden to walk outside the limits set down by his Chinese guide, and throughout the book he experiences great difficulty in visiting temples, buying goods, and obtaining visas.

At every point in his journey he is confronted by a representative of the state: thus at Germu he is awakened at 3:15 A.M. by the police and interrogated. The police appreciate that the hour is unreasonable but, they explain, Seth did not report to them on arrival and "regulations are regulations." This last phrase is repeated like a mantra throughout the book, curiously enough by people who, outside the context of their official duties, are often very kind and easygoing. Despite these problems, our hero proves to be extremely resourceful, and through a mixture of charm, pleading, and aggression, he manages to talk and then walk his way out of Chinese Tibet and into Nepal.

The picture Seth paints of Communist China is a rather depressing one. While he admits that some of its social and economic policies have been far more effective with regard to poverty and population growth than those of his native India, the effects of the Cultural Revolution on most peoples' lives (and particularly those of Tibetans he encounters) is shown to have been catastrophic. Seth's anger at the Chinese authorities was intensified by the events in Tiananmen Square in 1989, and in a later edition of the book he wrote a foreword in which he expressed his anger and disgust about the massacre there.

Seth's book is also a poignant lament for the history, tradition, and culture that Mao's Red Army destroyed. On entering one ruined Buddhist temple he comes across a Chinese poem, which he translates thus:

This day Zhi Xiong came to the old temple. ...
And he saw it and wept.

(p. 61)

This might have served as an epigraph for the book because Seth (who later translated works by three Chinese poets of the eighth century) evidently came to China with the idea of discovering something of its ancient spirit of serenity. When the book was published in 1983 it won the Thomas Cook Travel Book Award.

THE HUMBLE ADMINISTRATOR'S GARDEN
(1985)

One section in this volume of poetry contains poems concerning Seth's experiences in China.

Here he continues to bemoan the destruction, or as the Chinese state euphemistically puts it, the "renovation" of ancient temples. He also tries to capture the rare and fleeting moments of grace and tranquillity that the country afforded him. He does so in short poems such as "A Hangzhou Garden," which begins: "Wistaria twigs, wistaria leaves, mauve petals / Drift past a goldfish ripple" (*Collected Poems,* p. 100). These exquisite photographs, or postcards, which are infused with the spirit of Buddhism, prefigure Seth's translations of the ancient Chinese poets. The other two sections in the book concern California and India. In setting, style, and theme, they often look forward to Seth's novels *The Golden Gate* and *A Suitable Boy.*

Once again Seth demonstrates his fascination with the surfaces and the trivialities of life: one piece begins with the poet clipping his nails in a yard, another ends with an old woman contemplating how she will darn her grandson's sweater. Like *Mappings,* the collection is a feast for the senses. Allusions to Bach, hands trailing in water, and California poppies excite his readers' sense of sound, touch, and smell, and our visual sense is delighted by descriptions such as "beautiful light, / Heavy as honey" (*Complete Poems,* p. 131). There are the usual references to food: "I remember you in tastes," Seth writes of a friend, "ice-cream, garlic soup, / Cinnamon rolls, pâté" (p. 96).

In this collection we also find gentle humor, Seth's characteristically sunny philosophy, and delicate formal exercises in a wide variety of rhythms and rhymes. Sometimes Seth dazzles us with his wordplay; on other occasions, as in the two California songs in the collection, he achieves the simplicity of a ballad or pop song: "Some days I am so lonely, so content / The dust lifts up. The trees are weatherbent" (p. 124). *The Humble Administrator's Garden* was awarded the Commonwealth Poetry Prize for the Asian region in 1986.

THE GOLDEN GATE *(1986)*

In his early poetry Seth tried to invest everyday speech with resonance and subtlety rather than to

VIKRAM SETH

startle the reader with bold linguistic trickery and formal experimentation. In *The Golden Gate,* a verse-novel written in 590 Pushkin sonnets, he achieved both.

Seth imitates the stanza form of Pushkin's *Eugene Onegin* (1833): iambic tetrameter with a rhyme scheme of *AbAbCCddEffEgg* (capitalized letters indicate feminine rhymes—disyllabic rhymes, with the stress on the first syllable). The advantage of the Pushkin sonnet over other varieties of the form is that there is no abrupt transition in the stanza from the first half (usually an octave) to the second (usually a sestet). In fact, in its quick tempo and flexibility, the form is not unlike the ottava rima stanza used by Byron in *Don Juan,* a poem that influenced Pushkin.

Before embarking on the book, Seth had intended to write a series of short stories set in the Bay Area of San Francisco, but he did not have a clear plot in his mind. What he began with was the Pushkin sonnet itself, the energy and the delights of which had been revealed to him when, by chance, he happened upon a copy of *Eugene Onegin,* "In Johnstone's luminous translation": "like champagne / Its effervescence stirs my brain" (*The Golden Gate,* p. 102).

The Pushkin sonnet appealed to Seth, as he explains at the start of section 5 of the novel, because it was "fun" to work with and because he regretted the decay of the "once noble" tetrameter. He later added that he was excited by the tetrameter's narrative "propulsiveness" and by the fact that the alternation of feminine and masculine rhymes gives an easy colloquial feel to the verse.

Seth was also impressed by the extraordinary variety of subjects, moods, tones, and emotions encompassed by the Pushkin sonnet in *Onegin.* Variety is certainly one of the distinguishing characteristics of *The Golden Gate,* which includes, among other things, a paean to Mozart and Tin-tin (a famous Belgian comic book character), a prayer to Saint Francis, ad copy, highway graffiti, an antinuclear speech, an art review, personal ads, witty recitative sections of colloquial dialogue, aria-like apostrophes to San Francisco, internal monologues, and intellectual disputations. The shift between themes and emo-

tions across the book, and within individual sonnets, is breathtaking. The very first stanza begins with an abrupt invocation of the muse ("To make a start more swift than weighty, / Hail Muse"), moves to an incident in Golden Gate Park where "the ill-judged toss / Of a red Frisbee" (p. 3) nearly kills John, the poem's hero, and ends with John's rather self-pitying ruminations about his life. The next stanza starts with a number of references to electronic engineering.

It is the rather lugubrious John who sets the plot in motion by deciding, on the advice of his ex-girlfriend Janet, a Japanese-American sculptor, to advertise in the personal columns of a newspaper. This results in a date, and a love affair, with the lawyer Liz Dorati; subsequently there is a housewarming party in which we are introduced to the novel's two other main characters: Phil, a political activist who has resigned from his high-powered computer job, and Ed, the guilt-ridden Catholic who falls for the "warm, Socratic" Phil. Seth, a master of dialogue, shines at social gatherings.

Yet, rather like *A Suitable Boy,* the novel is not driven by the plot. The narrative pace is often slow, and its structure is cyclical rather than linear. The events take place in roughly the space of one year, and Seth brilliantly dresses San Francisco in the clothes of the four seasons: "the February weather / Lures the quince blossoms to a peak / Of pinkness on the leafless hedges." Then, after a time, "Mimosas bloom, and springtime edges / Into the city fragrantly" (p. 126). And so Seth's great hymn of praise to "the loveliest city in the world" goes on intermittently throughout the novel.

The themes of the novel can be briefly described. There is an ongoing dispute between the liberal, bisexual, antinuclear protestor Phil and the homophobic and politically right-wing John, whose work is somehow connected to the nuclear industry. Their argument epitomizes the larger debate that is conducted in the pages of the book. This is between those who choose "life" (by which Seth means friendship, tolerance, and a love of the earth and its fruits) and those who choose "death" (by which Seth means a life devoted to money, work, war, and the destruction of the environment). This may seem a simplistic configuration, but there is something simplistic, and almost Aesopian, about a book that sometimes reminds us of *Beastly Tales,* Seth's collection of moral fables. As an author Seth is never afraid to wear his heart on his sleeve or to take up a definite moral position: in *The Golden Gate* it is obvious where his sympathies lie.

The book is in many respects a celebration of California and its way of life, yet it is also a sharp critique of Silicon Valley's culture of money and work. John is rich, healthy, and attractive, yet he is also empty and lonely: "a linkless node" without family or real friends. Greed and worldly wisdom have lead him to Silicon Valley, which

Lures to ambition's ulcer alley
Young graduates with siren screams
Of power and wealth beyond their dreams

    ...

files take precedence over friends,
Labor is lauded, leisure riven.
John kneels bareheaded and unshod
Before the Chip, a jealous God.

                       (p. 7)

Other themes, such as attitudes toward homosexuality and the choice between platonic companionship and passionate romantic love (one of Seth's favorite topics), are addressed and commented on, either directly or implicitly. Obviously a book that reveals its author's sympathies so transparently is going to annoy critics and readers who do not share them, and this indeed proved to be the case. Few commentators, however, were able to fault Seth's magisterial handling of the Pushkin sonnet.

The Golden Gate is a dazzling poetic performance that fully merited critics' comparison of Seth to authors such as Pushkin and Pope. His delight in the form and his sheer love of language are contagious and inspiring. In the poem he combines cheeky brilliance ("Thus the young yahoos coexist / With whoso list to list to Liszt," p. 297), funny plays on clichés ("like my dad, for heaven's sakes! / Still, that's the way the biscuit breaks," p. 75), and moving lyrical passages.

Twice in the poem, in the guise of the economics student Kim Tarvesh (an anagram for Vikram Seth), the author steps in among his characters. His presence, however, is felt throughout the book as he keeps up a playful conversation with the reader and a ceaseless stream of wise and witty asides.

Seth's authorial manner recalls Byron in its swagger and self-conscious virtuosity. The contents, acknowledgments, and the "about the author" sections of the book are all written in Pushkin sonnets, and on the cover the title rhymes with the author's name: *The Golden Gate* / Vikram Seth. As is the case with Byron's writings, part of the delight of reading the poem is watching Seth work and play with the form and in particular the rhymes. Byronic, too, is the emphasis on pleasure. There are several epiphanic paeans to California wine, delicious breakfasts, sex, Scrabble, and Mozart.

Seth had great difficulty in finding a publisher for his verse novel, perhaps because it was a generically unclassifiable book that might in consequence be hard to sell. Eventually it was taken up by Faber & Faber in England and by Random House in the United States. It was a great success both with the public—its first American print run was 25,000 copies—and the critics. Gore Vidal called it "The Great Californian novel," and Seth was hailed as the boy wonder of literature in English.

ALL YOU WHO SLEEP TONIGHT (1990)

After the publication of *The Golden Gate,* Seth once again decided to combine a modern subject with a traditional form. He wrote a verse drama entitled *Lynch & Boyle,* which concerns the internal politics at an English publishing house. Although apparently completed, the play has never been produced or published, and one can only hope that Seth returns to it at some point. After writing the play he decided to embark upon a completely new writing project: a long prose novel set in postindependence India, which would become *A Suitable Boy.*

During the seven years it took to write the novel, Seth continued to compose and publish books of verse, the first of which was *All You Who Sleep Tonight*. At first glance this collection appears to bear many similarities to Seth's earlier volumes of poetry. In the sections "Romantic Residues" and "Meditations of the Heart" Seth is characteristically inspired by an everyday incident (in this case an experience at baggage claim in an airport) to ruminate about sex and love. The easy, colloquial, Larkinesque style is also familiar. One poem begins: "How rarely these few years, as work keeps us aloof ... / Have we had days to spend under our parents' roof" (*Collected Poems*, p. 207).

Elsewhere, however, new forces are at work: in particular one can discern the influence of Seth's experiences as a novelist in the section "In Other Voices." Here we find a number of internal monologues in the manner of Browning, by various narrators from different periods and cultures. These include "A Doctor's Journal Entry for August 6, 1945" (the day of the Hiroshima bombing); a verse letter written after the Indian mutiny; and a deeply moving deathbed meditation by a modern-day AIDS sufferer.

Generally the poems do not set out to dazzle the reader in the manner of *The Golden Gate*. The section "Quatrains," however, is not dissimilar to Seth's great verse novel. Here he plays with another tight and traditional verse form, using it to express a wide variety of emotions and ideas. Some of the quatrains are lyrical, others are evocative or thought-provoking, and several are comic. "Telephone" combines a variety of these moods:

I see you smile across the phone
And feel the moisture of your hair
And smell the musk of your cologne ...
Hello? Is anybody there?

(*Collected Poems*, p. 193)

THREE CHINESE POETS (1992)

Seth had translated German and Indian poets in his early poetry collections, but *Three Chinese Poets* is his most substantial work of translation. In his introduction he discusses his fascination with the art of translation and sets out his own intentions for the book. Rather than freely attempting to distill the spirit of the original in the manner of Ezra Pound, Seth admits its primacy and endeavors to stay as close to it as is linguistically possible.

In the introduction Seth includes brief biographical sketches of the three poets: Wang Wei (701–762), Li Bai (701–761), and Du Fu (712–770). He also places their poetry in its historical context and takes us through a literal translation of one of the poems. His essay and the poems constitute an excellent introduction to ancient Chinese verse.

Wang Wei's poetry is serene and rather Zenlike. The first Wei poem included in the collection begins "Empty hills, no man in sight" (p. 223), and there are several cold but exquisitely beautiful evocations of natural scenes. The more exuberant Li Bai brings us back to the world of men. Titles such as "Parting at a Wine Shop in Nanjing" and "Bring in the Wine" give a taste of his quality, as does "Drinking Alone with the Moon."

While the Confucian sage Du Fu is less energetic and raucous, his attention is similarly fixed on the social world. Seth translates a letter in rhymed couplets written from the court as well as the "Ballad of the Army Carts," which begins with sharp, realistic detail: "Carts rattle and squeak, / Horses snort and neigh" (p. 270). Seth includes a number of notes at the back of the volume that are particularly helpful with regard to Du Fu, who makes numerous references to the Chinese court and its affairs. *Three Chinese Poets* added to Seth's reputation as an international writer of considerable range and originality.

A SUITABLE BOY (1993)

Seth originally planned to write five novels set in India in the second half of the twentieth century. When he began writing the first he discovered that it would by itself cover the length of five books. At 1,349 pages, *A Suitable Boy* is in fact the longest single-volume novel in the English language; without question, it is also the heaviest. Other interesting statistics can be mentioned: it had an initial print run of 100,000 copies, and

Seth received the highest advance ever paid to a first-time novelist (the journalists didn't regard *The Golden Gate* as a real novel). With all the hype that surrounded its publication, Seth became one of the highest-profile authors in the world.

The central narrative concerns Rupa Mehra's search for "a suitable boy" for her youngest daughter, Lata. Lata is in love with a dashing Muslim cricketer named Kabir; she is also courted by Haresh, a foreman at a shoe factory, and the poet Amit Chatterji, who is Seth's alter-ego and the marvelous boy of modern Indian literature. The other main narrative strand focuses on Lata's brother-in-law, Maan Kapoor, who is looking for something to do with his indolent and rather charming life. These two narratives involve, and frequently bring together, characters from four families: the Mehras, the Kapoors, the Khans, and the Chatterjis. Most of the novel is set in the imaginary town of Brahmpur, where the first three of these families live, but Seth often takes his characters, and the reader, to the Chatterji house in Calcutta and to the country residence of the Khans.

The domestic action unfolds against a background of momentous political and social events. The year is 1950, and the newly partitioned and independent India prepares for its first general election and for a land act that symbolizes the passing of power from the old feudal class. The novel is a day-by-day account of the ensuing eighteen months: there are riots, political debates, cricket test matches, and religious festivals as well as private episodes such as marriages, births, and deaths. As with *The Golden Gate*, the structure is cyclical rather than linear; once again the rhythm of the plot is regulated by the changing seasons.

Within this cyclical structure, stories accumulate around the characters: there is little overall narrative development but instead a sort of organic growth and proliferation of subplots. In several metafictional passages, the novel is variously compared (usually by Amit Chatterji) to a *raag* (a traditional form of Indian music), a banyan tree, and to the Ganges, with its numberless tributaries. Critics have also compared the novel to a tapestry and a Victorian painting because it is at once extraordinarily detailed and vast in scale.

One other helpful comparison, erroneously attributed to Salman Rushdie, is with a television soap opera. What engages the reader's attention is the characters and their little trials and tribulations. We want to hear all the gossip about this or that person or family, and as in a Dickens novel, we need to know, every thirty or so pages, how our particular favorite character is getting on. The experience of reading the book is in fact very similar to the experience of reading nineteenth-century novels by authors such as Dickens. We derive great pleasure from empathizing and identifying with Seth's characters and from being a "fly on the wall" in their homes.

Generally speaking Seth's characters are not in-depth psychological portraits. In a society such as 1950s India, where social etiquette and appearances were everything, it would have been incongruous of him to have focused on their inner lives. Some of the characters are closer to caricatures: Rupa Mehra, for instance, is a rather absurd Lady Bracknell type, and her son, Arun, is a representative of the upper class of Indians who are still more than half in love with the culture of their former colonial rulers. What Seth gives us, in other words, is a collection of archetypal and exemplary figures who have little inner depth and who do not really develop in the course of the book. This is both appropriate for the social world he describes and congenial to his particular genius: as we have seen, his focus tends to be on the details and surfaces of everyday life.

Seth uses his archetypal characters to introduce his themes: thus Arun is a symbol of the continuing and pervasive influence of English culture in India. Lata's various attempts to thwart her mother's search for "a suitable boy" brings into focus the strict laws of Indian society and makes us realize that she is a point in a vast network of duties and affiliations rather than a free agent.

Lata's gradual understanding and acceptance of her position provides the emotional focus of the book. She comes to see that only those who recognize limitations have a chance of contentment: for her this means bending her will to that of her family. It is in this context that we must understand her decision to marry the most dependable and "suitable" yet least emotionally or intellectually exciting of her suitors. At the end of the novel she quotes the Victorian poet A. H. Clough to the effect that there are two kinds of human passion: the romantic one that excites but is usually violent and temporary, and the calmer passion that endures. It is entirely fitting that Seth should draw upon Clough here, because Seth drives his moral home with all the force and certainty of a Victorian writer.

In a broader sense, too, *A Suitable Boy* is about the power and presence of society. At every turn the characters come up against rules and laws of a legal, bureaucratic, religious, or social nature. The novel examines these laws and shows us what they are like in action. Seth spends a great deal of time explaining the intricacies of the political, economic, religious, academic, class, and linguistic situation of postindependence India. The book can indeed be read as an encyclopedia of that society or as a sort of "travel book" that explains India to Western readers.

Seth makes one thing resoundingly clear: there is nothing outside this social, political, and economic world. While religious beliefs are presented favorably insofar as they provide the glue that holds society and the family together, vague aspirations of transcendence are gently but consistently mocked in the book. Likewise the Marxist Rasheed, who in intellectual terms tries to transcend his society, is driven to madness and suicide.

The novel is also encyclopedic in its attention to detail. Among other things, it includes a list of prison rules, quotations from tourist guides and scientific manuals, instructions for feeding mynah birds, guidelines for how to play polo, and a list of Indian judges before and after 1947. Sometimes the detail is overwhelming: one might echo the charge made against Joyce's *Ulysses* (a book referred to and playfully mocked in the novel) and say that Seth has made a novel out of the Brahmpur telephone directory. Seth is all too aware of this: the two epigraphs to the novel, both of which are from Voltaire, read: "The

superfluous, that very necessary thing …" and "The secret of being a bore is to say everything."

At times, particularly in the middle sections of the book, Seth is indeed uncharacteristically dull. One of the difficulties is that the style is not interesting enough to keep hold of the reader's attention in the same way that it did in *The Golden Gate*. While Seth's prose is extremely flexible and varied—the book includes letters, telegrams, diary entries, cricket reports, religious and political speeches—it fails to create its own distinctive universe.

Throughout the novel Seth generally adopts an unadorned and transparent style and thus aligns himself with the realistic tradition of Indian writing that includes authors such as R. K. Narayan and Rohinton Mistry rather than the more experimental tradition exemplified by Salman Rushdie. In this context, but not specifically with regard to Rushdie, Seth has commented that he admires Victorian writers "who portray the lives of other people rather than those who try to emphasize technique and their own particular finesse in the use of language. That seems to me to be like using a stained glass window to look out to see a particular view. I'd much rather have a clear window" (in Pandurang, p. 112).

This may seem a little rich coming from the author of *The Golden Gate,* a novel in which style, rather than sincerity and content, is everything, but it successfully describes the style, or lack of style, of *A Suitable Boy.* There are few dazzling poetic riffs or witty authorial asides, and Seth keeps a tight leash on his love of form and language. The most entertaining parts of the book are perhaps those set in the Chatterji house in Calcutta, which are written in a sharp, slightly camp style that is closer to Oscar Wilde and Noël Coward than Narayan. At one point the poet Amit, who is writing a long and weighty novel about the Bengal famine, reflects that he might be better off turning his hand to a social comedy based on the lives of his family; some readers might apply the remark to Seth and his weighty book.

One feels a little guilty criticizing Seth, however, because there are so many wonderful things in the novel. The scenes in which his characters come together (and the essential purpose of the plot is to engineer such occasions) are excellently evoked whether they are funerals, weddings, theatrical productions, religious festivals, cricket matches, academic committees, or bridge parties. Seth has a brilliant line in bitchy gossip, and he is excellent at observing the interaction and power struggles between characters. He also has an ability to enter into the mind of his female characters in a way that is rare for a male novelist. Indeed, in its attention to details and in its gentle irony, there are times that this novel recalls Jane Austen, another author mentioned throughout the book.

In any case Seth appears to be fairly thick-skinned when it comes to criticism. Throughout his books in fact he brilliantly parodies the world of academics and journalists, and in interviews one sometimes gets the impression that he is enjoying an elaborate game of hide-and-seek. On occasion he has been openly hostile and contemptuous. In one interview, apropos of the reviews of *A Suitable Boy,* he bluntly remarked: "It doesn't matter what professors ... or critics ... think about the current state of the novel. What will last as literature and what gives pleasure is clear, affecting, straightforward writing which appeals to the general intelligent reader" (in Pandurang, pp. 111–112).

BEASTLY TALES FROM HERE AND THERE
(1992)

According to his foreword, Seth began work on his ten "beastly tales" to amuse himself during the composition of *A Suitable Boy.* The tales, which are written in the rhymed tetrameter couplets he had used for the contents page of his gargantuan Indian novel, belong to the genre of the "beast epic"—an allegorical story involving animal characters. Aesop and Chaucer contributed to this genre, as have George Orwell *(Animal Farm)* and Richard Adams *(Watership Down).* In selecting the tales, Seth characteristically cast his net very wide: they are drawn from the folklores of India, China, Greece, and Ukraine; the final two tales came directly to him from the imaginary "Land of Gup."

It is hardly surprising that Seth was attracted to the genre, because in his previous books he had displayed both a love of animals (Charlemagne the cat in *The Golden Gate,* Cuddles the dog in *A Suitable Boy)* and a fondness for sweeping moral statements. Like many authors before him, Seth uses the form to explore moral issues. In "The Frog and the Nightingale" he rides one of his favorite hobby horses when he criticizes the critics. The frog of the tale, who is a critic for the *Bog Trumpet,* becomes the agent and mentor of the gifted nightingale. Under the frog's influence, the nightingale looses its genius, pines away, and dies. This leaves the field open for the frog who, at the end of the tale, blares his dreary song unrivaled through the bog.

In "The Elephant and the Tragopan," political and environmental issues are addressed when the animals of Bingle Valley lobby the authorities about the projected building of a dam in their land. This tale is the most Orwellian in the collection and bears a striking resemblance to the antinuclear march described in *The Golden Gate* and to a number of scenes of student protest in *A Suitable Boy.* Although it is clear where Seth's sympathies lie, he declares at the conclusion that his is a "tale without a moral." Likewise, in the other tales, the expected Aesopian moral is often inverted. In the "The Hare and the Tortoise," even though the hardworking Hare wins the race, it is the more glamorous Tortoise who claims all of the media attention. Here too there are several echoes of *A Suitable Boy:* Haresh (the Hare of the novel) wins the race to marry Lata, but most readers wish that the prize had fallen to Amit Chatterji.

Beastly Tales could have been written by Amit, with a little help from his sisters Kakoli and Meenakshi, both of whom converse in funny couplets. Some of the authorial asides are written in a humorous spirit: one reads: "(Why he wept was never clear / So it can't be stated here)" (p. 29), and throughout it is clear that Seth is having a great deal of fun finding words and rhymes for his strict formal scheme. At one point Seth alludes to Scrabble, a game that requires great linguistic inventiveness and agility. It is Seth's success at a similar game—the game of writing

VIKRAM SETH

rhymed couplets—that makes *Beastly Tales* such a wonderful read.

ARION AND THE DOLPHIN *(1994)*

This verse libretto, commissioned by the English National Opera in 1992, was written for an opera by Alec Roth. The story is a retelling of the legend of Arion, a brilliant musician from Corinth who was thrown overboard while returning from a musical contest in Sicily and saved by a group of dolphins who had gathered round the ship to hear him sing.

At various points Seth's libretto recalls Shakespeare's *The Tempest.* The text alternates between Arion's beautiful arias and the colloquial recitative sections of the sailors onboard the ship. Arion is in fact the reincarnation of the tricky spirit Ariel: he serves Periander, a tyrannous master, and his songs are light, lovely, and energetic:

Bright stars, bring comfort
To those who dream.
Bright stars, guide me to fame
By land, by sea

(p. 14)

We can also detect the influence of Lewis Carroll, who probably inspired the song of the dolphins:

Our skins are smooth and rubbery,
Our bulky bodies blubbery.
    We harry herring happily
    And swallow salmon snappily.

(p. 43)

Seth had not written playful, tongue-twisting verse such as this since *The Golden Gate,* and indeed, Arion recalls Seth's great verse novel in its exuberant style and the pleasure he takes in its form.

In his poetry, Seth had often tried to find words for music and, as it were, to marry the two artistic forms. *All You Who Sleep Tonight* included an evocation of a movement of Mozart's Clarinet Quintet; *The Golden Gate* similarly includes an account of a Mozart string quartet. Seth would

try the trick again, on a much grander scale, when he came to write *An Equal Music,* and yet *Arion and the Dolphin* is possibly his most successful work in this context. One can only hope that Seth returns to the verse libretto form in the future because it is particularly suited to his genius. Seth also recast *Arion and the Dolphin* as a prose and verse tale for children and published it in an illustrated edition in 1994.

AN EQUAL MUSIC *(1999)*

Here Seth returns to a subject that appears throughout his oeuvre: music and its relationship to the world of words and men. Whole sections in *A Suitable Boy* were dedicated to discussions of the history and technicalities of traditional Indian music, and in his poetry Seth has frequently tried to translate the effect of music into verse. Here we are offered a guided tour of the world of Western classical music by Michael Holme, second violinist in the London-based Maggiore string quartet.

Michael's first-person narrative follows the Maggiore's tour from London to Vienna and then Venice; it also relates the sad and tortuous history of his relationship to Julia McNicholl, a deaf pianist. Once again, however, the plot proves to be one of the least important things in a Seth novel, and its development is cyclical rather than linear. On occasion the lack of action and dramatic tension in the book (reminiscent of the middle sections of *A Suitable Boy*) make you wonder whether you are reading a novel at all. It is indeed possible that Seth has tried to structure his story along the lines of a musical composition.

Michael is a learned and comprehensive guide (comprehensiveness is, according to one's viewpoint, one of Seth's great virtues or vices as a writer). He shows us rehearsals, backstage scenes at performances, and the power struggles between quartet members. He also introduces us to instrument makers and auctioneers, agents, critics, annoying fans, and record dealers. As ever, Seth has put an enormous amount of research into a novel, which might be described as an intelligent person's introduction to classical music.

For all his firsthand experience and comprehensiveness, Michael is a rather glum guide, and this makes us tire quickly of his company. A working-class boy from Rochdale, a town in the North of England, he has escaped his lowly origins through his musical gifts and entered a world dominated by middle- and upper-class "southerners." In this world, he feels disgruntled and uncomfortable; the price he has paid for entering it is the loss of his original identity (he soon discards his northern accent, for instance), and there is no chance of his ever returning "home." The English class system and the government's neglect of the working class and the North are two of the book's themes.

Michael is also reduced to misery by London, a city so vast and anonymous that sensitive souls such as himself have little chance of survival. Michael in fact resembles many melancholy characters from fiction set in London such as Arthur Clennam in Dickens' *Little Dorrit* and Edwin Reardon, the hero of George Gissing's *New Grub Street.* These figures are crushed under the weight and immensity of a city that adheres solely to the imperatives of money and power. Like these characters, Michael is worn down and debilitated by the ferocious energy of a place that in his eyes assumes the attributes of the inferno. "I do feel uneasy," he confesses at one point, "oppressed, dizzy: the bright lights, the large number of people all round, the heat, the colours, the sense of being underground …" (p. 229). This is strongly reminiscent of much London literature, from the novels just mentioned to Wordsworth's account, in *The Prelude,* of his visit to St. Bartholomew's Fair.

Rather like John in *The Golden Gate,* Michael is a symbol of the alienation and loneliness of modern urban life: he hardly speaks to his neighbors and recognizes that he is "one of the lonely majority" (p. 451). It is hardly surprising that Seth's latest "linkless node" seeks relief and salvation in romantic love with Julia. Unfortunately for Michael she is married with a child, and she is also a Catholic; when it comes to it, readers of Seth's earlier work know which form of love she will choose. She sacrifices her sexual passion for Michael to her family and her sense of morality, just as Lata sacrificed Kabir for Haresh. Michael, who feels an instinctive hatred for her religion, is unable to understand the reasons for her choice.

His one solace in life is music, and this novel is, among other things, an impassioned testament to the healing and consolatory properties of art. At the end of the novel Michael sits listening to Julia's piano recital, and he is blessed with a moment of tranquillity and grace. Throughout the book Michael describes music as a faithful friend: it visits him when he is in need of help and takes him out of himself into an impersonal world of perfect form.

Michael also tries to weave music into the texture of his prose, to translate it directly into language. This has been the Holy Grail of many twentieth-century writers such as James Joyce, who used a polyphonic and contrapuntal technique in *Finnegans Wake,* and Anthony Burgess, who based the structure of a novel called *Napoleon Symphony* on Beethoven's Third Symphony. As has been suggested, Seth may have attempted something similar here, because the architecture of *An Equal Music* is utterly unlike that of a conventional novel.

Michael's attempt to translate music into language inspires him to write several prose poems, or epiphanies, such as the following: "Dying, undying, a dying fall, a rise: the waves of sound well around us as we generate them" (pp. 109–110). These purple patches, which recall Joyce and certain writers of the 1890s (a decade in which literature aspired to the condition of music), become more frequent as the book goes on. By the end, the use of impressionistic descriptions, associative images, and internal rhymes becomes commonplace. "I wrote to you; I know the fax went through" (p. 388).

Michael's (and Seth's) stylistic quest is of course doomed to failure: the closest a writer has come to translating music into words is *Finnegans Wake,* a novel that is, in consequence, utterly unreadable. Throughout the novel Seth admits the difficulty of his endeavor when he suggests that the power and the secret of music are ultimately ineffable. Perhaps in unconscious acknowledgement of this, he also compiled an

Equal Music CD, comprised of music mentioned in the novel and sold along with the book.

An Equal Music is the least entertaining of all Seth's novels. His use of first-person narration denies us the multiple voices of *A Suitable Boy* and the multiple perspectives of *The Golden Gate.* Likewise, Michael cannot compete with Seth as a narrator: he lacks humor, intellectual curiosity, and emotional empathy; he has little range either as a human being or as a stylist. Most importantly, perhaps, he does not occupy a social space (Seth's favored territory) but rather a sterile and claustrophobic world of introspection, anxiety, and nostalgia. It is as if Seth had rewritten *The Golden Gate* from John's point of view or produced a revised edition of *From Heaven Lake* containing endless authorial meditations instead of his sharp observations of place and character.

CONCLUSION

Seth's next book, which will be published in 2005, will be a memoir entitled *Two Lives.* The book, which the English publisher Little, Brown has recently purchased for the enormous sum of £1.4 million, will be an account of the lives of Seth's great uncle Shanti, an Indian, and his aunt Henny, a German Jew. The couple met in Nazi Berlin and then escaped to England where they settled in North London. As a teenager Seth lived with them.

Given Seth's eclectic backlist, it should not surprise us that *Two Lives* is a work in a genre that he has never previously attempted. This habit of continually producing striking and original books may be due to Seth's temperament, but it may also be an aspect of his game with critics: he once remarked that one of its advantages was that commentators were unable to pin him down.

After *Two Lives,* perhaps he will return to his verse drama *Lynch & Boyle,* and create something that will be a landmark in the literature of the modern stage. That he is capable of achieving something of this order cannot seriously be doubted because he has already proved himself to be one of the most gifted and ambitious authors alive.

Selected Bibliography

WORKS OF VIKRAM SETH

NOVELS
The Golden Gate. London and Boston: Faber, 1986.

A Suitable Boy. London: Phoenix House, 1993; New York: HarperCollins, 1993.

An Equal Music. London: Phoenix House, 1999; New York: Broadway Books, 1999.

POETRY COLLECTIONS AND SHORT POETICAL WORKS
Mappings. Calcutta: Writer's Workshop, 1982.

The Humble Administrator's Garden. Manchester: Carcanet, 1985.

All You Who Sleep Tonight. London: Faber, 1990; New York: Knopf, 1990.

Three Chinese Poets: Translations of Poems by Wang Wei, Li Bai, and Du Fu. London and Boston: Faber, 1992. (Translations by Seth of eighth-century Chinese poetry.)

Beastly Tales from Here and There. New Delhi and New York: Viking, 1992; London: Phoenix House, 1993.

Arion and the Dolphin. London: Phoenix House, 1994. (Libretto.)

Arion and the Dolphin. London: Orion, 1994. (Children's book.)

The Collected Poems. New Delhi, 1995. (Contains all of Seth's poetry to date and includes *Three Chinese Poets, Beastly Tales from Here and There,* and the libretto *Arion and the Dolphin.*)

NONFICTION
From Heaven Lake: Travels through Sinkiang and Tibet. London: Chatto & Windus, 1983. (Travel memoir.)

"Forms and Inspirations." *London Review of Books,* September 29, 1988.

CRITICAL AND BIOGRAPHICAL STUDIES
Contemporary Literary Criticism, Vol. 43 and Vol. 90. Detroit: Gale Research: 1987, 1996. (These contain a wide selection of interviews and critical articles on Seth.)

Dictionary of Literary Biography, Vol. 120. 3d ser.,: *American Poets since World War II.* Third Series. Detroit: Gale Research, 1992. Pp. 281–285.

Pandurang, Mala. *Vikram Seth: Multiple Locations, Multiple Affiliations.* Jaipur and New Delhi: Rawat, 2002. (Includes extensive bibliography.)

JON STALLWORTHY

(1935–)

Sandie Byrne

THE POET JON Howie Stallworthy was born in London on January 18, 1935 to Dr. John Stallworthy and his wife, Peggie Howie, young New Zealanders who had come to England on a traveling medical scholarship won by Dr. Stallworthy the year before. When Jon Howie was three the family moved to Oxford, where his father took up a post as an obstetric surgeon in the Oxford University Department of Obstetrics and Gynaecology. It was in a suburb of North Oxford, "on the outer edge of the city's intellighetto," that Stallworthy's love of the music of language was born from the nursery rhymes and songs taught to him by his mother, and from the verse and prose he was encouraged to read at the local nursery and later at the Dragon School (*Singing School: The Making of a Poet,* p. 15). He wrote his first poem at the age of seven, "an execrable ballad about a fighter-pilot" (p. 46). He records that oblivion has closed over the poem "and no doubt I would have forgotten the occasion altogether but for the instant knowledge it brought that what I most wanted to do in the world was to write poems." By then he had graduated from the "Baby School" to the "Big School" at the Dragon, School where he remained until 1948. At Rugby (a public school in the Midlands of England), his twin talents for poetry and rugby were encouraged, and at fifteen he won the school poetry prize with a poem on a set subject, "The Golden Years."

In August 1952 the family left for a five-month stay in Australia and New Zealand following Dr. Stallworthy's appointment to a visiting professorship at Sydney's Royal Prince Albert Hospital. Returning to school briefly, Stallworthy gained a place at Magdalen College, Oxford, but deferred his matriculation until after his two years' National Service. These were spent as a lieutenant of the Oxfordshire and Buckinghamshire Light Infantry seconded to the Royal West African Frontier Force in Nigeria. After National Service he returned to England and matriculated into Magdalen College, where he became president of the JCR (Junior Common Room, the undergraduate body) played rugby for the Greyhounds (the university second team), and in his final year won the Newdigate Prize for Poetry for his long poem *Earthly Paradise.* After graduation he remained at Oxford, ostensibly to take a B. Litt. degree but primarily to try for a rugby Blue (a place on the Oxford University first team). However, a visit to Dublin, where he met Georgie Yeats, widow of W. B. Yeats, kindled his interest in the poet, and he wrote a thesis on Yeats's successive recensions of the drafts of his poems. This formed the basis for Stallworthy's first major scholarly work, *Between the Lines: Yeats's Poetry in the Making* (1963).

After leaving Oxford, Stallworthy went to work in the editorial department of Oxford University Press, where in 1959 he founded the Oxford Poets list, which was to become one of the most important publishers of new poetry in the country and which he was to defend vociferously when it was threatened with closure nearly forty years later. He was deputy academic publisher of Oxford University Press from 1975 to 1977 (he concurrently held a visiting fellowship at All Soul's College) and then "exchanged a publisher's office for a professor's" (*Louis MacNeice,* p. xv) to become John Wendell Anderson Professor at Cornell University. In 1986 he became a fellow of Wolfson College, Oxford, and was initially reader, later professor, in English literature at the University of Oxford. After his retirement from teaching he served as vicegerent of Wolfson College and was appointed a research fellow of the college. He married Jill Waldock in 1960; they had two sons and a daughter.

Stallworthy's 1974 biography of the World War I poet Wilfred Owen won the Duff Cooper Memorial Prize, the W. H. Smith Award, and the E. M. Forster Award of the American Academy of Arts and Letters, and his 1995 biography of the Ulster poet Louis MacNeice won the Southern Arts Literary Prize. Among his many publications are editions of Wilfred Owen's *Complete Poems and Fragments* (1983) and Henry Reed's *Collected Poems* (1991); translations, with Peter France, of *The Twelve, and Other Poems by Aleksandr Blok* (1970) and the *Selected Poems of Boris Pasternak* (1983); and a number of anthologies he has edited, such as *The Oxford Book of War Poetry* (1984) and *The Penguin Book of Love Poetry* (1973), or coedited, such as the third and fourth editions of *The Norton Anthology of Poetry* and fifth, sixth, and seventh editions of *The Norton Anthology of English Literature*. He is also the author of an invaluable and accessible essay on versification, which is included in the Norton anthologies listed above. He is a fellow of the Royal Academy and of the Royal Society of Literature.

Although he is internationally renowned as an interpreter of and apologist for literature, a biographer, scholar, and teacher, Stallworthy speaks of himself as first and foremost a poet. The account of his early life in *Singing School* ends as he is about to return from Dublin, where he has been reading the notebooks and manuscripts of W. B. Yeats. Georgie Yeats, the poet's widow, bids Stallworthy farewell and advises him not to spend all of his life on Yeats.

"I won't," I said and, even as I said it, I knew that the poem in my pocket was more important to me than all the transcriptions in my suitcase—and tomorrow's poem was more important still.

(p. 229)

POETRY

In *Singing School: The Making of a Poet,* Stallworthy tells the story of his parents' crossing from New Zealand to England aboard a dilapidated freighter. Though the crew asserted that urgent repairs were required before the ship could embark, the owner insisted that the work be carried out on the Clyde, in northern Britain, where a refit would be less expensive. As the ship rounded the Horn in the high seas of midwinter, the rudder chain snapped. Dr. John Stallworthy worked with the crew to repair the damage, and the ship won through to quieter waters, but Peggy Stallworthy, in spite of having been strapped into a bunk, was severely bruised. This hazardous passage was shared by their son, who rounded the Horn in his mother's womb, and provides the title for his *Rounding the Horn: Collected Poems* (1998), published at the same time as *Singing School.* Many of the poems collected in *Rounding the Horn* reach back and forward through time to continue the theme of the journey launched in Stallworthy's first book-length collections, *The Astronomy of Love* (1961) and *Out of Bounds* (1963). These poems, mostly written before his twenty-fifth birthday, are presciently described by the dust-jacket copy as "a fragmentary record of the first phase of a journey"; a journey "of self-discovery between innocence and experience … as old as the Book of Genesis" which "every man travels by a different route."

Several of the poems in the first collection are about the beginning of journeys. Reading them, it is possible to follow the young Stallworthy from Magdalen College to Spain, Greece, Ireland, and back to England, and to feel the influence of W. B. Yeats, Dylan Thomas, and Robert Graves in the forms and phrases of poems such as "The Common Breath," "My Man of Flesh and Straw," and "Consolation." There are also ghostly echoes of D. H. Lawrence, John Betjeman, and Andrew Marvell, but the collection is neither derivative nor self-indulgent; the voice is new and distinct, and Stallworthy seems already to have left behind the common flaw of the apprentice poet: not knowing when to stop. Stallworthy's poetry belongs to none of the schools or movements of his near contemporaries; his voices employ neither the clipped impersonality of the Movement nor the demotic idiom of the Mersey and Barrow poets. Perhaps the most distinctive feature of the collections is the assured handling of form. Stallworthy shows himself equally at home with the stricter rules of traditional verse forms and the flexibilities of free verse. Many of the lines are so neatly and perfectly formed that they strike with the force and inevitability of epigram, but never the pat slickness of easy aphorism.

"Sindhi Woman" (from *Out of Bounds*), by which Stallworthy is represented in a number of anthologies for schools, opens with a characteristically harmonious interplay of consonant and vowel, iambic and trochaic feet—an unstressed *(u)* followed by a stressed *(x)* syllable or a stressed syllable followed by an unstressed syllable—and trimeter and tetrameter (three metrical feet to a line and four metrical feet to a line) perfectly fitted to its subject. (Quotations are taken from *Rounding the Horn* except where stated):

```
x  u /  x      u / u x /
Barefoot through the bazaar,
u    x / u   x  / x u / u   x /
and with the same undulant grace
x  u / x    u  /  x    u / u   x /
as the cloth blown back from her face
```

The poem is not permitted the luxury of an unreflecting lyricism, however; the perspective is acknowledged: this is a colonized subject observed and represented by the colonizer:

```
x    u /  u   x / u x /
Watching her cross erect
u      x / u   x / u x /  u   x /
Stones, garbage, excrement, and crumbs
u   x / u x / u x / u   x /
of glass in the Karachi slums,
x  u / u   x /  x  u /
I, with my stoop, reflect
x   u / x   x /
they stand most straight
u    xm / u   x / u x / u   x/
who learn to walk beneath a weight.
```

(p. 43)

The final couplet contains a neatly encapsulated double allusion (both thematic and aural) to the final line of John Milton's sonnet "When I Consider How My Light Is Spent" (composed c. 1652): "They also serve who only stand and wait." This line has been much quoted in the context of service to empire, which makes the appropriation of it by a young man in service to country and empire gazing upon a subject of empire particularly ironic. The "weight" under which the woman walks is of course metaphorical as well as literal. As a New Zealander ("colonial"), Stallworthy was a subject of empire; as a product of the English public-school system and British army, he was an agent of empire. His autobiography records the journey from unthinking acceptance of the rhetoric of glory and duty, with its concomitant right to rule, to realization of the effects of imperialism.

Between the publication of *Out of Bounds* in 1963 and his next collection, *Root and Branch,* in 1969, Stallworthy brought out a pamphlet-size publication with a small publisher, the Turret Press, in 1967. The title poem of *The Almond Tree* was to become his best known and most frequently anthologized poem.

Section I of "The Almond Tree" begins in Oxford, as the poet drives to his wife's childbed past Magdalen College, with its happy memories, beautiful medieval tower, and graceful bridge. The city is described in terms suggesting fairy tales ("lights green as peppermints," "Trees of black iron broke into leaf") and which cast the poet as prince both rushing to the rescue of a princess under enchantment, and himself enchanted; young, fearless an indestructible.

II

Crossing (at sixty) Magdalen Bridge
Let it be a son, a son, said
the man in the driving mirror,
Let it be a son. The tower
held up its hand: the college
bells shook their blessing on his head.

III

I parked in an almond's
Shadow blossom, for the tree
Was waving, waving me
Upstairs with a child's hands.

IV

...
New-
minted, my bright farthing!

Coined by our love, stamped with
our images, how you
enrich us! Both
you make one. Welcome
to your white sheet,
my best poem!

But the joy is cut short by a brutal announcement
from the obstetrician:

> V
>
> ...
>
> *—I have to tell*
> you—set another bell
> beating in my head:
> *your son is a Mongol*
> the doctor said.

> VI
>
> How easily the word went in—
> clean as a bullet
> leaving no mark on the skin
> stopping the heart within it.

Stallworthy confronts his feelings courageously,
acknowledging that his son will never:

> VII
>
> ...
>
> come
> ashore into my kingdom
> speaking my language.

He returns to the almond tree:

> In labour the tree was becoming
> itself. I, too, rooted in earth
> and ringed by darkness, from the death
> of myself saw myself blossoming,
>
> Wrenched from the caul of my thirty
> years' growing, fathered by my son,
> unkindly in a kind season
> by love shattered and set free.

(pp. 158–161)

Denis Donoghue, writing much later in Stallworthy's career, identifies precisely the problem for any critic wanting to write about "The Almond Tree" or any other of the poems about Jon and Jill Stallworthy's firstborn child, born with Down syndrome:

> Several poems in *Rounding the Horn* ponder the tragedy, including "The Almond Tree Revisited" and "The Fall of a Sparrow." It is painful to see Stallworthy trying to maintain his refinement of tone in face of such heartbreak, but I suppose that is one of the graces a poem may strive for. It is a desperate measure to take comfort from the budding of an almond tree.
>
> I don't think I could rise to that flowering, if the tragedy were mine.
>
> (*London Review of Books,* p. 24)

What Donoghue calls the "refinement of tone" and the control of form may make reading about these poems possible, just as they made writing them barely possible, but they cannot make reading them, and less still writing about them, easy. Both the depth of pain and the painful honesty of the response make "The Almond Tree," "At Bedtime" (in *Hand in Hand,* 1974) and "Fall of a Sparrow" (in *Root and Branch*) highly emotive and viscerally affective.

As a biographer and editor of Wilfred Owen, the editor of an anthology of war poetry, and author of the companion to the (London) Imperial War Museum's exhibition on the poets of the Great War, *Anthem for Doomed Youth* (2000; the quotation is from Wilfred Owen's poem of that name), Stallworthy is well acquainted with both clarion calls to and protests against war. He has written poems about the effects of war, in particular on those bereaved by war, in *The Anzac Sonata* (1986), for example, and has included verse letters from the front in *A Familiar Tree* (1978), but he has not published poems about contemporary warfare as though from personal experience. "A Poem about Poems About Vietnam" in *Root and Branch,* his third collection, is a scathing indictment of poets who become pundits of war, famous for condemnations and evocations that are parasitic on real suffering. The biting irony of the poem comes from Stallworthy's use of the register of one semantic field, warfare ("had you covered," "combat zones," "muzzles," "opened fire," "phalanx") to write about another, those poets' performance in London's Albert Hall.

JON STALLWORTHY

The spotlights had you covered [thunder
in the wings]. In the combat zones
and in the Circle, darkness. Under
the muzzles of the microphones
you opened fire, and a phalanx
of loudspeakers shook on the wall;
but all your cartridges were blanks
when you were at the Albert Hall.

Lord George Byron cared for Greece,
Auden and Cornford cared for Spain,
confronted bullets and disease
to make their poems' meaning plain;
but you—by what right did you wear
suffering like a service medal,
numbing the nerve that they laid bare,
when you were at the Albert Hall?

(p. 78)

Though so bitter a tone is rare in Stallworthy's work, and much of his writing is autobiographical, he is not a purely lyric or personal poet. He makes a stand on content in an early poem, characteristically blending modesty with quiet certainty. Having derided non-combatant war poets in the earlier poem, he turns to the question of writing war poetry and poems of violence in "Letter to a Friend," which echoes poems of W. B. Yeats such as "On Being Asked for a War Poem."

You blame me that I do not write
with the accent of the age:
the eunuch voice of scholarship,
or the reformer's rage
(blurred by fag-end in the twisted lip).
You blame me that I do not call
truculent nations to unite.
I answer that my poems all
are woven out of love's loose ends;
for myself and for my friends.

(pp. 18–19)

Stallworthy insists that his poems are a "window," not a "looking-glass"; they show people what lies beyond, not simply what is. His are not poems of social realism, depicting "rape and death in bungalows," "the crazy gunman, or/the man who drops the bomb," but visionary art.

The entry for Stallworthy in the reference work *Contemporary Poets* contains a comment by the poet:

When a poet is asked to "make a statement" he should respond with a poem, but I am tongue-tied in police stations, so will echo Keats: "I am certain of nothing but the holiness of the heart's affection." The changing seasons of "the heart's affection" have prompted the best of the poems I have written since, at the age of seven, I set myself to learn how to make poems as a carpenter makes tables and chairs. I count myself a maker, and such other things as I have made with words—studies of Yeats "at work," translations of poems by Blok and Pasternak—have been made with one purpose in view; to learn how to make better poems.

(p. 954)

The theme of journey and continuity is also taken up in *Root and Branch*. In "Epilogue to an Empire," the statue of Admiral Lord Nelson in London's Trafalgar Square upbraids the bookish liberal poet, and by extension the modern nation, for the loss of empire. The admiral's imperialism is unpalatable to a postcolonial age, but Stallworthy allows him a voice and a point; rather than the loss of riches and of power, Nelson deplores the loss of the adventuring spirit, of the daring, energy, and above all confidence of his day.

Acknowledge
their energy. If you condemn
their violence in a violent age
speak of their courage. Mock their pride
when, having built as well, in as wide
a compass, you have none.

The poems ends wryly, perhaps ambiguously, in the twentieth century, with one of the hundreds of birds that flock the square: "And a pigeon sealed the page" (p. 73).

Similarly, in "The Peshawar Vale Hunt," the narrator raises his drink "in mock salute" to a hunt breakfast photograph from 1910, and reflects:

If they could see
themselves now, grouped on the grass
in their insolent poses! History
has put down the mighty

from their family seats; tumbled them arse
over crop, out of the saddle.

The poor inherit the earth; the middle class
Took care of the brass.

(p. 49)

But he grants the fallen huntsmen the right of reply:

Empire Builder, with your back to the wall,
Have you any last word to say?

And we sense his approval of the proud response:

"It is better to ride fierce, and fall,
than never to ride at all."

These are characteristic of the tenor of Stallworthy's poems on the dignitaries and institutions of Great Britain and its empire, which is simultaneously regretfully elegiac and critical; the nostalgic tempered by a sense of justice and the criticism by the humane.

"Sword Music" similarly reaches out to the seemingly uncongenial (Old English) in an effort to understand and appreciate:

All that Anglo-Saxon jazz
of *brond on byrnie* [brand on mail shirt] stuns the ear
attuned to higher frequencies.

But as you wield the words they welded
The great worm bleeds; nor can its venom
scald that sprung edge as it scalded

The smith and the giver of rings.
The consonants keep their balance,
dark shine of the raven's wings.

The poet forges a sympathetic identification that extends to the use of a register of battle (mailshirt, sword, smith, tempering, ore, weapons) and to reproduction of the form of Old English poetry with its four-stressed lines and alliteration, concluding:

Words so tempered, forged on the tongue
from loyalty, tenacity,
and pride, time can but sharpen. Wrung

from such obsolescent ores,
their words outlast their weapons
and may outlast ours.

(p. 76)

In "A Bottle of Ink" *(Hand in Hand)* the black thread that loops across the page in letters and poems becomes a continuous line:

a black thread
reaching from here
to God knows where

(p. 91)

Similarly, in "So Much in Common," the line of time loops so that occasions become synchronic and places can be entered one from the other:

Under the sheet you take me by the hand
to meet a boy among the dunes
who calls you beautiful. I stand
in his footprints to kiss you, brushing the down

along your cheekbones with a salty tongue.
Help me to push the dinghy out.
She gybes again! You seize my coat
with my mother's hand when it was young.

...

Our fingers meet on your father's landing,
tighten at the treacherous stair,
and we ride on a banister
into an orchard with its branches bending.

(pp. 99–100)

This theme of time as linear but looping back on itself is continued in the poignant "The Blackthorn Spray." A journey to a funeral evokes memories as real as the present moment:

As the wheels of the hearse
unreeled the road
downhill, they slowed
to let the milkman pass.
His white van showed
in the black-framed glass
and the reel went into reverse.

The first stanza's juxtaposition of lines of four syllables with lines of five, six, and eight syllables impedes the poem's progression, making this journey slow and painful.

Here the road rears
and father, setting spur
to twenty horse-power,
takes them up and over
thirty-five years,
off the edge of the map
crackling in mother's lap.

"Blue gates, the agent said—"
"We must have come too far."

JON STALLWORTHY

"No. There they are."
And here is the house of the dead.
I want to stay in the car,
but not by myself under these
fluttering, muttering trees.

(pp. 169–170)

The metaphor of journey and line surfaces again in *A Familiar Tree* (1978). Reading the poems is like turning the tuning knob on an old-fashioned radio across the thin line that marks wavelengths, but instead of a frequency line we follow a bloodline, a lifeline, a line of linked lives, seven generations of a family; and instead of snatches of broadcasts we encounter voices from the past. This journey begins in 1974, in a small Parish church in the Buckinghamshire village of Preston Bissett, where the poet, knowing that "among those lifelines [is] my own," comes to find

                    the names that are
all that remain of them, brown ink
in a parish register,
a shadow on lichened stone:

(p. 123)

The first voice we hear is a mother crooning to her child, the first John in the sequence "1738" ("Mother and Son"), and as we move through time the line intersects the voices of other Stallworthys, some also John, heard in petitions, testaments, letters, and journals, or through imaginative re-creation. The line continues through time and place, from Preston Bissett to the Marquesas, fifteen-hundred miles northeast of Tahiti; to New Zealand, to London, to West Africa, to Oxford; and finally, to the contemplation of another departure from England, for America, by the present Jon Stallworthy and his son. In "Patchwork," the line becomes a thread stretching out from home to a son bound for overseas, stitching together the pieces of a quilt which will unite the places and memories of a life, and of lives past, and under which the next lives will be conceived and born.

A house without a man
A pod without a pea
William gone under the ground

George going over the sea
Come little needle you
and I have work to do

                    ...

For Claydon Brook a ribbon
Lenborough Wood sateen
remnants of chintz and twill
the crowded fields between
and from this pair of sleeves
a border of oak leaves

Though seas be heaped between us
My son shall sleep at home
and when he takes a bride
may she find here with him
on this familiar ground
what William and I found.

(pp. 133–134)

The phrase is taken up again in the last poem, "Envoi," dated June 1977, in which the narrator sits by his sleeping son's bedside on the eve of their departure, and wishes:

may the swift bring
you and your children's children home
to this familiar, well-planted ground.

(p. 163)

While history and voices from the past haunt and inform much of the poetry, Stallworthy is also capable of living in the moment, as in the wonderfully erotic "Pour Commencer," which takes the form of a salad recipe that calls for a pair of lovers at the seaside to use their "two bellies" as plates.

Take 1 green pepper and 2 tomatoes
and cut them into rings and hearts. Mix those
with olives, black olives, and go for a swim
in a green sea with her (or him).
Then serve your salad on two bellies. Pour
a little sun-warmed olive oil in your
salt navel, some vinegar in hers
(or his), and eat slowly with your fingers.
Empty the bottle. Open a second. Then
lick your plates. You will need them again.

(p. 99)

A few pages later in the same collection comes "A Question of Form and Content," a wry, half-joking apology to one of the protagonists of Stallworthy love poems, its humor underlined by the audacious rhyme of apology/anthology, the pun on "crisp sheets" (bed and book) and the use of the technical term "enjambement" for lines in poetry that are run on rather than end-stopped (that is, the grammatic sentence does not coincide with the poetic line and so does not end with a full stop at the end of the line), as in the second and subsequent lines of this poem:

I owe you an apology.
love my love, for here you are
in a school anthology
without so much as a bra
between your satin self and those
who come between us in crisp sheets.
   The narrator concludes:

                       Let
them observe, love, our enjambement.
They shall be guests at the secret
wedding of form and content.

                           (p. 101)

The *Anzac Sonata* (1986) contains a number of poems dedicated to friends and family members, including a number on the death of Stallworthy's much-beloved mother. These are poignant and affecting poems in their own right, but they are made all the more painful by the reader's own sense of having lost sight of someone glimpsed only briefly but unforgettably on occasions across a lifetime. The poems give vivid cameos of Mrs. Peggy Stallworthy carrying her son round the Horn in her womb ("The Return," pp. 152–153), teaching and inspiring him ("Credits," in *The Astronomy of Love,* p. v; "Mother Tongue," in *Rounding the Horn,* p. 172), determined to maintain her standards of housekeeping even in old age ("Counter Attack," p. 167), and, finally, gone ("One Day," "The Rooms"). These records of endings mark the beginning of a new journey, of grief. As in many of Stallworthy's poems, the present brings the past into sudden sharp focus and connection in "One Day":

The last morning as an immortal
passed into the last afternoon

and when the bedside lamp was lit
you told me: Grandmother has died.
Died?
      She has gone to Heaven.
                        When
will she be back?
              We don't come back.
We?
      Everyone goes to Heaven.
Will you go?
        One day.
                 Black lightning
scissored the wall, and the floor
fell away in a down-draught
of terror—
          I had forgotten
that sheer shaft, the vertigo,
until the day your grandson fell
to your death and, standing astride
his darkness, I threw him
the line you lowered.

               (pp. 167–168)

Appropriately for a collection in which continuities of people and their feelings escape the linearity of time, *Rounding the Horn* ends with poems from the volume *The Guest from the Future* (1989). The collection focuses on four strong women: the poet Anna Akhmatova; the painter Françoise Gilot, one of Picasso's lovers; a survivor of the siege of Stalingrad; and "the girl from Zlot," Jade Drysz. Stallworthy's foreword explains that the "Guest from the Future" of the title poem was the name given to Isaiah Berlin by Anna Akhmatova in her "Poem without a Hero." The poem records Sir Isaiah's visit to Akhmatova's Moscow apartment in 1945, and the consequences when the visit came to the attention of Stalin. Akhmatova, already under suspicion as an intellectual and following the execution of her second husband for counter-revolutionary activities, was suspected of consorting with spies. Soon after the visit, Akhmatova's apartment was bugged, she was denounced by the Central Committee of the Communist Party and expelled from the Writer's Union. "She became convinced that, fuelling Stalin's paranoia, they had caused the first move in the Cold War" (foreword, p. 219). After her son Lev was ar-

JON STALLWORTHY

rested for the third time, Akhmatova committed her poems to memory and burned the manuscripts (p. 219).

In spite of all this, Akhmatova does not complain or deplore Berlin's arrival; rather she celebrates her guest as a harbinger of the future and hope. Akhmatova's poetry is of the "acmeist" school which, in reaction against the prevailing symbolist movement, sought lucidity and simplicity, but her poetry contains sudden shifts in perspective and chronology as well as minute detail of the seemingly insignificant. Stallworthy's poem adopts a similar style to give a sense, sometimes wistfully elusive, sometimes powerful and clarion, of Anna Akhmatova's voice.

The doorbell   a tocsin   tolling
as if the Huns were at the gate
told nothing that was not foretold
in this room   and on this date

when the stranger turned left from the bridge
along the Fontanka   and knew
the gates by the iron lions
that growled and let him through

        ...

He brought me no lilac   no ring
But something more precious than love
As the terrible downpour ceased
He brought me   like Noah's dove

a green word out of the blue
A Russian word rinsing the air
of its thunder and ash   and if
he flew off he returned later

                (p. 220)

Stallworthy's unsurpassed knowledge of the genres and forms of English poetry enable him deftly to catch the rhythms, nuances, and inflections of earlier masters. In his introduction to the poem "The Girl from Zlot" for the literary magazine *Ploughshares* (spring 1991), Stallworthy explains that the genesis of his poem was the story told to him by an old friend of a winter flight from war-torn Poland (another desperate journey), which seemed to him to have an inverted relationship with the story of Tennyson's *The Lady of Shalott* (1831–1832), the first stanza of which is given below:

On either side the river lie
Long fields of barley and of rye,
That clothe the wold and meet the sky;
And through the field the road runs by
     To many towered Camelot;
And up and down the people go,
Gazing where the lilies blow
Round an island there below,
The island of Shalott.

Just as Tennyson's Lady embroidered a tapestry, so the girl from Zlot embroiders a counterpane, but whereas the Lady of Shalott stitches images taken from the mirror and dies from her contact with reality, the girl sews love and life into her embroidery and is kept warm and alive by her art. Both poems end with the end of a journey: the Lady of Shalott drifts into Camelot and is found dead by the man she desires; the Girl from Zlot is found on a train by her lover, having survived her ordeal. Stallworthy writes: "I tried to embroider the modern story over the ghostly outline of the ancient, to point a parable about one function of art—what Heaney has called its power of 'redress'—in our, or indeed any, time."

Mile after dark Silesian mile
the river wears the forest's frown,
only venturing a smile
to greet a village or a town:
one on an island, where
four grey walls and four grey towers
see the patients come and go,
and sufferers in the small hours,
hearing a voice beside them, know
the girl from Zlot is there.

Midnight: an emergency:
at the operating table,
opposite the surgeon
she draws as deft a needle,
ties as neat a knot.
When screens are drawn about a bed,
voices lowered and feet swift,
a sick child or a wounded
miner on his final shift
asks for the girl from Zlot.

Off duty, climbing a grey tower
and in her attic opening
a window on the lights below her,
she stands a moment listening

listening for what?
Water talking to the wharves,
wind to rushes; rowlocks—a late
fisherman—where the river curves
carrying its nightly freight
of longing down to Zlot.

(pp. 210–211)

Stallworthy's form follows that of the source poem in that it is in four parts and the lines are octosyllabic apart from the shorter fifth line, but Stallworthy's stanzas have ten lines where Tennyson's have nine. Like Tennyson, Stallworthy varies the meter of the lines to achieve different effects. "The Lady of Shalott" opens with a very regular iambic tetrameter (four metrical feet, each consisting of an unstressed followed by a stressed syllable), which changes to trochaic tetrameter (four metrical feet consisting of a stressed followed by an unstressed syllable):

```
u  /  u  /  u  /  u  /
On either side the river lie
  u   /   u  /  u  /  u  /
Long fields of barley and of rye,
  u   /   u  /  u   /  u   /
That clothe the wold and meet the sky;
u   /    u  /  u  /   u   /
And through the field the road runs by
          u / u / u   / u/
          To many towered Camelot;
  u  / u   /   u  /  u  /
And up and down the people go,
 /  u  /   u  / u  /
Gazing where the lilies blow
  /    u / u   /   u /
Round an island there below,
u   /  u  u  / u
The island of Shalott.
```

Compare this with the opening of "The Girl from Zlot":

```
 /   uu  /  u/u   /
Mile after dark Silesian mile
  u / u /   u / u   /
the river wears the forest's frown,
 / u  /  u / u  /
only venturing a smile
u   /  u  /  u  / u   /
to greet a village or a town:
```

In "The Girl from Zlot" the first and last words of the first line, "mile," are balanced, and the

stresses of the line fall on "mile," "dark," and the medial syllable of "Silesian" to emphasize the long, monotonous course of the river, here darkened by forest rather than irrigating fertile arable land. The missing final syllable of the third line prevents the rhythm from becoming too predictable, as does the interlaced rhyme scheme: *ababcdedec,* which Stallworthy uses in preference to Tennyson's more repetitive *aaaabcccb.* "Silesian" has a sinuous quality fitting for a river, as well as the suggestion of "silt" and "sinister." "The Girl from Zlot" uses the reader's memory of "The Lady of Shallot" and its familiar English pastoral of gently rolling wolds, which we probably envisage in tones of green, sky blue, and gold, to set up an opposition; a foreign landscape whose river is personified to evoke a storybook-gloomy pinewood.

"My Last Mistress," a poem in the "From the Life" section of *The Guest from the Future,* has as an intertext Robert Browning's "My Last Duchess" (1842), lines of which are given below:

That's my last Duchess painted on the wall,
Looking as if she were alive. I call
That piece a wonder, now: Frà Pandolf's hands
Worked busily a day, and there she stands.
Will't please you sit and look at her?

...

          She had
A heart—how shall I say?—too soon made glad,
Too easily impressed; she liked whate'er
She looked on, and her looks went everywhere

...

          Oh sir, she smiled, no doubt,
Whene'er I passed her; but who passed without
Much the same smile? This grew; I gave commands;
Then all smiles stopped together. There she stands
As if alive.

"My Last Mistress" transfers the narrator from Renaissance archduke to modern painter, and his duchess's transformation is from figurative art's simulacrum of life to surreal art's imagined monstrosity. Stallworthy uses images of bulls, real and mythological, throughout this section of the collection, borrowing the motif from the art of Pablo Picasso, for whom minotaurs were a potent symbol in the late 1920s and 1930s. A commission from the Parisian art dealer Am-

JON STALLWORTHY

broise Vollard led Picasso to create a series of etchings known as the "Vollard Suite," many of which depict a minotaur in different poses. In Picasso's "The Sculptor's Studio" series, he depicts a sculptured bull in an artist's studio, and his "Minotauromachy" contains images of the minotaur speared by a bare-breasted woman on horseback and of a bullfight in which a horse has been disembowelled. Picasso was to use these images again in his famous mural *Guernica.*

That's my last mistress on the easel. I
call her "The Fallen Picador"—and why?
She lived ten years with the minotaur
and deserved to leave with the honours of war,
so when Vallauris last July declared
me president of the *corrida,* I shared
the honours with her. Seeing that the bull
was *my* symbol, the horse *her* symbol,
what end could be more fitting than that they
should face each other in a ritual way—
life imitating art, a masterpiece
of living theatre?

(p. 232)

The *corrida* is a bullfight. The mistress could be François Gilot but may be Marie-Thérèse Walter, whom Picasso met when she was a teenager in the 1920s. They had an intense but secret affair, and she bore him a daughter, Maïa, in 1935, before, having lived ten years with the minotaur, she took her own life.

The Uffington Horse, a Bronze Age monument cut into the side of a chalk hill, is the center of the ten-poem sequence *Skyhorse* (2002). The monument was a favorite spot for Stallworthy when he was a young boy, and he records memories of a family picnic near the Roman fort in *Singing School* (p. 68). The horse became for him the mythological flying horse Pegasus, a symbol of the wild ride of poetry, and *Skyhorse* depicts its many incarnations, from flesh-and-blood mount to rocking horse, described by voices from c. 1000 B.C. to the present day. Combined, they comprise a polyphonic celebration of the English people and their poetry over three thousand years. The scene is set by epigrams whose sources similarly range over miles and millennia: *Revelations;* Tacitus, *Germania;* G. K. Chesterton; "The Ballad of the White Horse"; an anonymous ballad, "The Ballad of the Scouring of the White Horse"; and W. B. Yeats, "Coole Park and Ballylee, 1931." The first voice is that of a priest and poet c. 1000 B.C., the earliest called to worship of the Skyhorse. The last is a "wandering scholar" on the last night of 1999, who in the bonfire and firework conflagration of the millennium celebrations is also called by the horse. He straddles the "marvellous beast," who carries him into the clouds, the wind "stitched" with the voices of poets:

one that said:
"Look at the stars! Look, look up at the skies!
Oh look at all the fire-folk in the air" ...
[Gerard Manley Hopkins]

One whispering: "Cast a cold eye
On life, on death. Horseman, pass by!" ...
[W. B. Yeats]

One a woman's,
On the obsidian disc of space:
"I, like the Earth this season, mourn in black,
My Sun is gone so far in's zodiac" ...
[Anne Bradstreet]

a distant, whispered,
"Seek out—less often sought than found—
a soldier's grave." ...
[Lord Byron]

"We didn't have to seek,"
said someone from a killing-ground
closer to home. "I am the enemy
you killed, my friend." ...

[Wilfred Owen]

The flight through the night takes the poet through England, across the Irish Sea, over the Atlantic, through the Arctic and Asia, Gallipoli and Greece, France, and across the Channel to England again. Its end, the poet's awakening alone on the grass, marks it as in the great line of dream-vision poems that stretches back to *The Dream of the Rood* and before, through *Piers Plowman* and *The Divine Comedy,* in which tradition Stallworthy wrote the prize-winning *Earthly Paradise,* his first printed pamphlet, over forty years before. The poet wakes

Surrounded
by voices interwoven with the wind:
that of a horseman who founded

a tribe singing a lay that extolled
the horse, as I walked down to Uffington
and into a future not foretold.

RECEPTION

Stallworthy's earliest collection, *The Astronomy of Love,* was well received by critics. Robin Skelton, writing in *Critical Quarterly* (summer 1961), found that Stallworthy

> has a gift which few poets possess, and which all poets wish for—the ability to strike out a memorable and epigrammatic line which is at once simple and deeply disturbing. ... There is wit and passion in Jon Stallworthy's poems, and there is also discernible a directness and honesty of attack which make him another man we must watch and pray for. This book looks like an augury of great things.
>
> (pp. 186–187)

Other critics, however, even several decades after publication of Stallworthy's statement of his poetic principles in "Letter to a Friend," were still urging him to produce more politically engaged or enraged poetry. Jeremy Noel-Tod, reviewing *Rounding the Horn* for *Oxford Poetry* (winter 1998), writes that the poetry is "well-mannered and gentle, it lilts along lyrically enough, rhyming regularly but unostentatiously" but complains that though it employs Yeatsian stanza forms, it "misses the essential Yeatsian thunder" (p. 51). Stallworthy is of course an eminent Yeats scholar, and he sometimes writes on Yeatsian themes and in Yeatsian forms, but we should remember that he is a firsthand Jon Stallworthy, not a secondhand Yeats. Why Yeatsian thunder is essential to another poet is unclear. Noel-Tod did admire Stallworthy's adaptation of Zbigniew Herbert's "The Stone," observing that it is "more than a translation, it is a very fine poem on its own terms." He also praises *A Familiar Tree* but seems mistakenly to suggest that *Rounding the Horn* "rides its momentum of inspiration into the present to produce one of Stallworthy's most arresting and personal poems, 'The Almond Tree'" (p. 53). ("The Almond Tree" was published in 1967.)

Denis Donoghue has criticisms to make, but he notes the pleasure he gains from going through *Rounding the Horn,* "quoting especially poems in which Stallworthy makes much—but never too much—of a word or a phrase that continues to disturb after it has appeared to settle for placating" (*London Review of Books,* March 4, 1999, p. 24).

A double review of *Rounding the Horn* and Stallworthy's autobiography *Singing School* provided the basis for one of the best summations of his career as a poet. The poet and scholar Peter McDonald asserts that *Rounding the Horn* makes it possible "to take stock of a complex and fascinating body of poetry which has been persistently underrated, and in which even the earliest poems have a sense of form and descriptive precision that makes them seem, by comparison with much contemporary verse, compellingly fresh" (*Times Literary Supplement,* January 8, 1999, p. 23). His assessment of Stallworthy's volumes is that they "have been both deeply traditional in their forms and concerns, and incisively original in their achievement." Discussing "Poem about Poems about Vietnam," McDonald writes that Stallworthy knows that sincerity in poetry is not in itself a virtue, since one can be sincerely wrong, wicked, or foolish, and

> poetry gains authority only from an authenticity in which voice and experience maintain mutual fidelity. The "Poem about Poems About Vietnam," in which the modish politics of 1960s literary fashion are forthrightly shamed, retains its currency thirty years later. ... The ballade says what has to be said, just as good manners demand sometimes the direct expression of a sharp rebuke; but Stallworthy's "dispatches from the front" generally know the risks they are running, in the short term at least, by insisting on the truth's relation to literary style. The wariness of the fake, which is part of Stallworthy's sense of poetic shaping, becomes more complex in his later work, and helps to give resonance to the narratives of *The Anzac Sonata* (1986) and the more recent *The Guest from the Future,* where lives and their meanings are searchingly and delicately examined.

Stallworthy is also capable of "searchingly and delicately" examining his own life, as his autobiography *Singing School* attests. In this book, which forthrightly contains much of what might in other quarters be dismissed as juvenilia, he addresses the question of why a poet should publicly display his early, unpublished, perhaps rejected work. The answer, he says, is because "to the best of my knowledge, no one else has done so" (p. 230) and because the schooling of poets seems a "potentially rewarding subject. Stallworthy explains that while he was trying to develop MacNeice's impressionistic sketches of his early reading and writing into an account of that poet's poetic apprenticeship, "I began to reflect on this curious omission in the autobiographies of poets; an omission no biographer can properly rectify." He determined to conduct an experiment with his own autobiography, in which he would trace the influences (literary and other) on his own development as a poet. He goes on to say that he will count it at least a partial success "if it encourages better poets to write better accounts of their apprenticeship."

Stallworthy's infallible courtesy and mildness of manner have sometimes misled critics; he has been accused of having had a gilded youth followed by a comfortable maturity; of having a manner unruffled by passion. Yet he was roused to passionate anger by the threat from Oxford University Press to close the poetry list he had founded in 1959, as articles in the *Oxford* magazine and letters to the press have shown. Sadly, the fight was only partially won. Critics notwithstanding, Stallworthy clearly has the respect of other poets; he has frequently been a champion of published poets as well as of those who have yet to achieve their full potential.

In the introduction to his collection of Wilfred Owen's poetry, Stallworthy quotes from a letter of Owen's to his mother: "I am held peer ... I am a poet's poet." This is equally true of Stallworthy.

Selected Bibliography

WORKS OF JON STALLWORTHY

POETRY
The Earthly Paradise. The Newdigate Prize Poem. Oxford: Privately printed, 1958.

The Astronomy of Love. Oxford and New York: Oxford University Press, 1961.
Out of Bounds. Oxford and New York: Oxford University Press, 1963.
The Almond Tree. London: Turret Books, 1967.
Root and Branch. London: Chatto & Windus/ Hogarth Press, 1969.
Positives. Dublin: Dolmen Press, 1969.
A Dinner of Herbs. Exeter, U.K.: Rougement Press, 1971.
Hand in Hand. London: Chatto & Windus/ Hogarth Press and New York: Oxford University Press, 1974.
The Apple Barrel: Selected Poems, 1955–1963. London: Oxford University Press, 1974.
For Margaret Keynes, 1890–1974. Burford, Oxfordshire, U.K.: Cygnet Press, 1975.
A Familiar Tree. London: Chatto & Windus/Oxford University Press; New York: Oxford University Press, 1978.
In Memory of Geoffrey Keynes, Kt., Late of Lammas House, 1887–1982. Oxford: Privately printed, 1984. (Printed as a keepsake for the biennial meeting of the Zamorano-Roxburghe Clubs in 1984.)
The Anzac Sonata: New and Selected Poems. London: Chatto & Windus, 1986; New York: Norton, 1987.
The Guest from the Future. Manchester: Carcanet, 1995; Oxford: Perpetua, 1989.
From the Life. New York: Norton, 1995.
Rounding the Horn: Collected Poems. Manchester: Carcanet, 1998.
Skyhorse. Oxford: Thumbscrew Press, 2002.

AUTOBIOGRAPHY
Singing School: The Making of a Poet. London: John Murray, 1998.

CRITICISM
Between the Lines: W. B. Yeats's Poetry in the Making. Oxford: Clarendon Press, 1963.
Vision and Revision in Yeats's "Last Poems." Oxford: Clarendon Press, 1969.
Poets of the First World War. London: Oxford University Press, in association with the Imperial War Museum, 1974.
The Poet as Archaeologist: W. B. Yeats and Seamus Heaney. Oxford: Clarendon Press, 1982. (Reprinted from *Review of English Studies,* n.s. 33:130, May 1982.)
Anthem for Doomed Youth: Twelve Soldier Poets of the First World War. London: Constable, 2002.

BIOGRAPHY
Wilfred Owen. London: Chatto & Windus/Oxford University Press, 1974; New York: Oxford University Press, 1975.
Louis MacNeice. New York: Norton, 1995.

EDITIONS
Yeats, Last Poems: A Casebook. London: Macmillan, 1968; Nashville, Tenn.: Aurora, 1970.

Wilfred Owen: The Complete Poems and Fragments. London: Chatto & Windus/Oxford University Press, 1983; New York: Norton, 2 vols., 1984.

The Poems of Wilfred Owen. London: Chatto & Windus/Hogarth Press, 1985; New York: Norton, 1986.

The War Poems of Wilfred Owen. London: Chatto & Windus, 1994.

Henry Reed: Collected Poems. Oxford: Oxford University Press, 1991.

TRANSLATIONS

Five Centuries of Polish Poetry 1450–1970. With Jerzy Peterkiewicz and Burns Singer. London: Secker and Warburg, 1960.

The Twelve and Other Poems by Aleksandr Blok. With Peter France. London: Eyre & Spottiswode; New York: Oxford University Press, 1970. As *Aleksandr Blok, Selected Poems,* Harmondsworth: Penguin, 1974.

Boris Pasternak: Selected Poems. With Peter France. London: Allen Lane; New York: Norton, 1983.

EDITED ANTHOLOGIES

New Poems, 1970–71. With Seamus Heaney and Alan Brownjohn. London: Hutchinson, 1971.

The Penguin Book of Love Poetry. London: Allen Lane, 1973. As *A Book of Love Poetry,* New York: Oxford University Press, 1974.

The Oxford Book of War Poetry. Oxford and New York: Oxford University Press, 1984.

First Lines: Poems Written in Youth from Herbert to Heaney. Manchester and New York: Carcanet, 1987.

The Norton Anthology of Poetry. 4th ed. With Margaret Ferguson and Mary Jo Salter. New York: Norton, 1979.

The Norton Anthology of English Literature. 5th ed. M. L. Abrams, general editor. New York: Norton, 1986.

The Norton Anthology of English Literature. 6th ed. M. L. Abrams, general editor. New York: Norton, 1993.

The Norton Anthology of English Literature. 7th ed. M. L. Abrams, general editor; Stephen Greenblatt, associate general editor. New York: Norton, 2000.

The New Penguin Book of Love Poetry. 2d ed. Harmondsworth, U.K.: Penguin, 2003.

INTERVIEWS

Ahmeen, S. "Jon Stallworthy: An Interview." *Plum Review* 4:47–54 (fall–winter 1992).

Haberstroh, P. B. "An Interview with Jon Stallworthy." *Contemporary Poetry: A Journal of Criticism* 3: 1–20 (1978).

McDonald, Peter. "An Interview with Jon Stallworthy." *Oxford Poetry* IV (spring 1988)

CRITICAL AND BIOGRAPHICAL STUDIES

Donoghue, Denis. "Untouched by Eliot: Jon Stallworthy." *The London Review of Books,* March 5, 1999, pp. 24–25.

McDonald, Peter. "Dispatches from the Front." *Times Literary Supplement,* January 8, 1999, p. 23

Noel-Tod, Jeremy. "Quiet Amid the Thunderers." *Oxford Poetry* 10 (winter 1998).

Skelton, Robin. Review of *The Astronomy of Love. Critical Quarterly* 3:186–187 (winter 1961).

MASTER INDEX

The following index covers the entire British Writers series through Supplement X. All references include volume numbers in boldface Roman numerals followed by page numbers within that volume. Subjects of articles are indicated by boldface type.

"Cap and Bells, The" (Keats), **IV:** 217

Cape of Storms: The First Life of Adamastor (Brink), **Supp. VI: 54–55,** 57

Capell, Edward, **I:** 326

Caprice (Firbank), **Supp. II:** 201, 204, 205, **211–213**

Captain, The (Beaumont and Fletcher), **II:** 65

Captain Brassbound's Conversion (Shaw), **VI:** 110; **Retro. Supp. II:** 317

Captain Fantom (Hill, R.), **Supp. IX:** 117

"Captain Henry Hastings" (Brontë), **V:** 122, 123–124, 135, 138, 151

Captain Lavender (McGuckian), **Supp. V:** 280, 287–289

"Captain Lavender" (McGuckian), **Supp. V:** 289

"Captain Nemo" (Gunesekera), **Supp. X:** 86

"Captain Parry" (Hood), **IV:** 267

Captain Patch (Powys), **VIII:** 258

"Captain Rook and Mr. Pigeon" (Thackeray), **V:** 21, 37

Captain Singleton (Defoe), **III:** 8, 13; **Retro. Supp. I:** 72

Captains Courageous (Kipling), **VI:** 204

"Captain's Doll, The" (Lawrence), **VII:** 90

Captives, The (Gay), **III:** 60–61, 67

Car, Thomas, **II:** 181

Caravaggio, Michelangelo Merisi da, **Supp. IV:** 95, 262

"Carboniferous" (Morgan, E.), **Supp. IX:** 167

Carceri d'invenzione (Piranesi), **III:** 325

Card, The (Bennett), **VI:** 250, 258–259, 266; **Supp. III:** 324, 325

Card, The (film, Ambler), **Supp. IV:** 3

Card Castle (Waugh), **Supp. VI:** 270

Cardenio (Fletcher and Shakespeare), **II:** 43, 66, 87

Cards on the Table (Christie), **Supp. II:** 131, 135

"Care" (Murphy), **Supp. V:** 327

"Careless Lover, The" (Suckling), **II:** 227

"Careless Talk" (Bowen), **Supp. II:** 93

Careless Widow and Other Stories, A (Pritchett), **Supp. III:** 328, 329

Caretaker, The (Pinter), **Supp. I:** 367, 368, 369, **372–374,** 379, 380, 381; **Retro. Supp. I:** 224–225

Carew, Thomas, **I:** 354; **II: 222–225,** 237

Carey, John, **V:** ix, xxvii, 39, 62, 73

Carlingford, Lord, *see* Fortescue, Chichester

"Carlow Village Schoolhouse" (Murphy), **Supp. V:** 328

Carlyle, A. J., **III:** 272*n*

Carlyle, Jane, **IV:** 239, 240

Carlyle, R. M., **III:** 272*n*

Carlyle, Thomas, **IV:** xii, 38, 41–42, 70, 231, **238–250,** 266*n*, 273, 289, 295, 301–302, 311, 324, 341–342; **V:** vii, ix, xii, 3, 5, 165, 182, 213*n*, 285, 319

"Carlyon Bay Hotel" (Murphy), **Supp. V:** 328

"Carmen Becceriense, Cum Prolegomenis et Commentario Critico, Edidit H. M. B."(Beerbohm), **Supp. II: 44**

Carmen Deo Nostro, Te Decet Hymnus, Sacred Poems, Collected (Crashaw), **II:** 180, 181, 184, 201

Carmen Triumphale, for the Commencement of the Year 1814 (Southey), **IV:** 71

"Carmilla" (Le Fanu), **III:** 340, 345; **Supp. III:** 385–836

Carmina V (Herrick), **II:** 108

Carn (McCabe), **Supp. IX:** 127, 128–129, 137, 138

Carnal Island, The (Fuller), **Supp. VII:** 77–78, 81

"Carnal Knowledge" (Gunn), **Supp. IV:** 258

Carnall, Geoffrey Douglas, **IV:** xxiv, 72, 156

Carnival Trilogy, The (Harris), **Supp. V:** 135, 136, 138, 140–141

"Carol" (Nicholson), **Supp. VI:** 214–215

"Carol on Corfu" (Durrell), **Supp. I:** 123–124, 126

Caroline (Maugham), **VI:** 369

"Caroline Vernon" (Brontë), **V:** 112, 122, 123, 124, 125, 138, 151

Carpenter, Edward, **VI:** 407, 408

Carr, John Dickson, **Supp. IV:** 285

"Carrickfergus" (MacNeice), **VI:** 401

Carrington, Charles, **VI:** 166

"Carrion Comfort" (Hopkins), **V:** 374

Carroll, Lewis, **V:** xi, xix, xxii, xxvi, 86, 87, 74, **261–275;** **Supp. IV:** 199, 201

Carry On, Jeeves (Wodehouse), **Supp. III:** 455, 461, 462

Carter, Angela, **III:** 341, 345; **Supp. III: 79–93; Supp. IV:** 46, 303, 459, 549, 558

Carter, Frederick, **VII:** 114

Cartoons: The Second Childhood of John Bull (Beerbohm), **Supp. II:** 51

Cartwright, John, **IV:** 103

Cartwright, William, **II:** 134, 185, 222, 237, 238

Cary, Joyce, **VII:** xvii, **185–196**

Caryl Churchill, A Casebook (King), **Supp. IV:** 194–195

"Casa d'Amunt" (Reid), **Supp. VII:** 329

Casa Guidi Windows (Browning), **IV:** 311, 314, 318, 321

"Casadh Súgaín Eile" (Behan), **Supp. II:** 68

Casanova's Chinese Restaurant (Powell), **VII:** 348–349

Cascando (play, Beckett), **Supp. I:** 60

"Cascando" (poem, Beckett), **Supp. I: 44**

Case, A. E., **III:** 25, 36

Case for African Freedom, The (Cary), **VII:** 186

"Case for Equality, The" (Drabble), **Supp. IV:** 31, 233

Case is Alter'd, The (Jonson), **Retro. Supp. I:** 156–157

"Case of Bill Williams, The" (Kavan), **Supp. VII:** 210

Case of Conscience Resolved, A (Bunyan), **II:** 253

Case of Elijah, The (Sterne), **III:** 135

Case of General Ople and Lady Camper, The (Meredith), **V:** 230–231, 234

"Case of Identity, A" (Doyle), **Supp. II:** 171

Case of Ireland . . . Stated, The (Molyneux), **III:** 27

Case of the Abominable Snowman, The (Day Lewis), **Supp. III:** 130

Case of the Midwife Toad, The (Koestler), **Supp. I:** 38

Cashel Byron's Profession (Shaw), **VI:** 102, 103, 105–106, 109–110, 113, 129

"Cask of Amontillado, The" (Poe), **III:** 339

Cassinus and Peter (Swift), **Retro. Supp. I:** 284

"Castalian Spring" (Heaney), **Retro. Supp. I:** 134

"Castaway, The" (Cowper), **III:** 218–219

Castle, The (Kafka), **III:** 340, 345; **Supp. IV:** 439

Castle Corner (Cary), **VII:** 186

Castle Dangerous (Scott), **IV:** 39

Castle of Indolence, The (Thomson), **III:** 162, 163, 171, 172; **Supp. III:** 412, **425–428**

Castle of Otranto, The (Walpole), **III:** 324, **325–327,** 336, 345; **IV:** 30; **Supp. III:** 383–384

Castle of the Demon, The (Hill, R.), **Supp. IX:** 116

Castle Rackrent (Edgeworth), **Supp. III:** 154–155; **Supp. IV:** 502

Castle Richmond (Trollope), **V:** 101

Castle–Croquet (Carroll), **V:** 274

Castles of Athlin and Dunbayne, The (Radcliffe), **IV:** 35

Casualties of Peace (O'Brien), **Supp. V:** 339

"Casualty" (Heaney), **Retro. Supp. I:** 130

Casuarina Tree, The (Maugham), **VI:** 370, 371

"Cat–Faith" (Reid), **Supp. VII:** 328

Cat Nappers, The (Wodehouse), *see Aunts Aren't Gentlemen*

Cat on a Houseboat (Desai), **Supp. V:** 55, 62

"Catarina to Camoens" (Browning), **IV:** 314

Catcher in the Rye, The (Salinger), **Supp. IV:** 28

Catepillar Stew (Ewart), **Supp. VII:** 47

Catharine and Petruchio, **I:** 327; *see also Taming of the Shrew, The*

Cather, Willa, **Supp. IV:** 151

Catherine (Thackeray), **V:** 22, 24, 28, 37

Cathleen ni Houlihan (Yeats and Gregory), **VI:** 218, 222, 309; **VII:** 4

Catholic Church, The (Newman), **Supp. VII:** 292

"Catholic Church and Cultural Life, The" (Lodge), **Supp. IV:** 376

"Catholic Homilies" (&Aelig;lfric of Eynsham), **Retro. Supp. II:** 297–298

"Catholic Novel in England from the Oxford Movement to the Present Day, The" (Lodge), **Supp. IV:** 364

Catholics (Moore, B.), **Supp. IX:** 143, 151, 152

Cathures (Morgan, E.), **Supp. IX:** 160, 164, 170

"Characters of the First Fifteen" (Ewart), **Supp. VII:** 36

Charge Delivered to the Grand Jury, A (Fielding), **III:** 105

"Charge of the Light Brigade, The" (Tennyson), **IV:** xxi, 325

Charioteer, The (Renault), **Supp. IX:** 172, 176–178, 187

"Charity" (Cowper), **III:** 212

Charles, Amy, **Retro. Supp. II:** 174

"Charles Augustus Milverton" (Ewart), **Supp. VII:** 42

Charles Dickens (Swinburne), **V:** 333

Charles Dickens: A Critical Study (Gissing), **V:** 424, 435, 437

Charles I (Shelley), **IV:** 206

"Charles Lamb" (De Quincey), **IV:** 148

Charles Lamb and His Contemporaries (Blunden), **IV:** 86

"Charles Lamb, to those who know thee justly dear" (Southey), **IV:** 85

Charley Is My Darling (Cary), **VII:** 186, 188, 189, 190–191

Charlie and the Chocolate Factory (Dahl), **Supp. IV:** 202–203, 207, 222–223

Charlie and the Great Glass Elevator (Dahl), **Supp. IV:** 207

"Charlotte Brontë as a Critic of *Wuthering Heights*" (Drew), **V:** 153

Charlotte Brontë, 1816–1916: A Centenary Memorial (ed. Wood), **V:** 152

"Charlotte Brontë in Brussels" (Spielman), **V:** 137n

Charlotte Brontë: The Evolution of Genius (Gérin), **V:** 111, 152

Charlotte Mew and Her Friends (Fitzgerald), **Supp. V:** 98–99

"Charm Against Amnesia, A" (Nye), **Supp. X:** 202

Charmed Circle, A (Kavan), **Supp. VII:** 203, 205, 206–207

Chartism (Carlyle), **IV:** xix, 240, 244–245, 249, 250; **V:** viii

Chase, The, and William and Helen (Scott), **IV:** 29, 38

Chaste Maid in Cheapside, A (Middleton), **II:** 1, 3, **6–8,** 10, 21

Chaste Wanton, The (Williams, C. W. S.), **Supp. IX:** 276–277

Chastelard (Swinburne), **V:** 313, 330, 331, 332

Chatterton (Ackroyd), **Supp. VI: 7–8**

Chatterton, Thomas, **IV:** iv, 228; **V:** 405; **Supp. IV:** 344

Chatwin, Bruce, **Supp. IV: 157–177, Supp. IX: 49–63**

Chaucer, Geoffrey, **I:** 2, 15, 16, **19–47,** 49, 60, 67, 126; **II:** 70, 292, 302, 304; **IV:** 189; **V:** 298, 303; **Supp. IV:** 190; **Retro. Supp. II: 33–50,** 125

Châtiments, Les (Hugo), **V:** 324

"Cheap in August" (Greene), **Supp. I:** 16

"Chearfulness" (Vaughan), **II:** 186

"Cheek, The" (Hope), **Supp. VII:** 157–158

Cheery Soul, A (White), **Supp. I:** 131, 150

"Cheery Soul, A" (White), **Supp. I:** 143

Chekhov, Anton, **VI:** 372

"Chekhov and Zulu" (Rushdie), **Supp. IV:** 445

Cherry Orchard, The (tr. Frayn), **Supp. VII:** 61

"Cherry-ripe" (Herrick), **II:** 115

"Cherry Stones" (Milne), **Supp. V:** 302–303

"Cherry Tree, The" (Coppard), **VIII:** 94

"Cherry Tree, The" (Gunn), **Supp. IV:** 271

"Chest" (Self), **Supp. V:** 403

Chester Nimmo trilogy (Cary), **VII:** 186, 191, 194–195; *see also Prisoner of Grace, Except the Lord, Not Honour More*

Chester, Robert, **I:** 313

Chesterton, G. K., **IV:** 107; **V:** xxiv, 60, 262, 296, 383, 391, 393, 397; **VI:** 200, 241, 248, **335–345; VII:** xiii

Chettle, Henry, **I:** 276, 296; **II:** 47, 68

Chief of Staff (Keneally), **Supp. IV:** 347

"Chief Petty Officer" (Causley), **VII:** 434

"Child, The" (Friel), **Supp. V:** 113

"Child and the Shadow, The" (Jennings), **Supp. V:** 210

Child Christopher and Goldilind the Fair (Morris), **V:** 306

"Child Dying, The" (Muir), **Supp. VI:** 207

"Child in the House, The" (Pater), **V:** 337, 357

Child in Time, The (McEwan), **Supp. IV:** 389, 390, 400–402, 404, 406, 407

Child of Misfortune (Day Lewis), **Supp. III:** 118, 130–131

Child of Storm (Haggard), **Supp. III:** 214

Child of the Jago, The (Morrison), **VI:** 365–366

Childe Harold's Pilgrimage (Byron), **III:** 337, 338; **IV:** x, xvii, 172, **175–178,** 180, 181, 188, 192; **V:** 329

"Childe Roland to the Dark Tower Came" (Browning), **IV:** 357; **VI:** 16

"Childe-hood" (Vaughan), **II:** 188, 189, 190

Childermass (Lewis), **VII:** 71, 79, 80–81

"Childhood" (Cornford), **VIII:** 112

"Childhood" (Muir), **Supp. VI:** 204–205

"Childhood Incident" (Nye), **Supp. X:** 203

Childhood of Edward Thomas, The (Thomas), **Supp. III:** 393

"Childish Prank, A" (Hughes), **Supp. I:** 353

"Children, Follow the Dwarfs" (Smith, I. C.), **Supp. IX:** 214

Children of Dynmouth, The (Trevor), **Supp. IV:** 501, 510–511

Children of Men, The (James), **Supp. IV:** 320, 338–339, 340

Children of the Chapel (Gordon), **V:** 313

"Children of the Zodiac, The" (Kipling), **VI:** 169, 189, 191–193

Children of Violence (Lessing), **Supp. I:** 238, **243–246**

Children's Encyclopedia (Mee), **Supp. IV:** 256

"Child's Christmas in Wales, A" (Thomas), **Supp. I:** 183

"Child's Calendar, A" (Brown), **Supp. VI:** 71

Child's Garden of Verses, A (Stevenson), **V:** 385, 387, 395; **Retro. Supp. I:** 264

Child's History of England, A (Dickens), **V:** 71

Child's Play: A Tragi–comedy in Three Acts of Violence With a Prologue and an Epilogue (Hill, R.), **Supp. IX:** 115–116

Chimeras, The (Mahon), **Supp. VI:** 173

Chimes, The (Dickens), **V:** 42, 64, 71

"Chimney Sweeper" (Blake), **III:** 297; **Retro. Supp. I:** 36, 42

China. A Revised Reprint of Articles from Titan . . . (DeQuincey), **IV:** 155

China Diary (Spender), **Supp. II:** 493

Chinamen (Frayn), **Supp. VII:** 57–58

"Chinese Button, The" (Brooke-Rose), **Supp. IV:** 103

"Chinese Letters" (Goldsmith), *see Citizen of the World, The*

"Chinese Lobster, The" (Byatt), **Supp. IV:** 155

Chinese Love Pavilion, The (Scott), **Supp. I:** 259, 263

Chinese Pictures (Bird), **Supp. X:** 31

"Chinoiserie" (Reading), **VIII:** 273

"Chip of Glass Ruby, A" (Gordimer), **Supp. II:** 232

Chit–chat (periodical), **III:** 50

Chitty Chitty Bang Bang (film, Dahl), **Supp. IV:** 213

Chitty Chitty Bang Bang (Fleming), **Supp. IV:** 212–213

Chivers, Thomas Holley, **V:** 313

Chloe (Meredith), **V:** 231n, 234

Chloe Marr (Milne), **Supp. V:** 310

Choice of Kipling's Prose, A (Maugham), **VI:** 200, 204

"Choir School" (Murphy), **Supp. V:** 328

Chomei at Toyama (Bunting), **Supp. VII:** 4, 6–7

Chomsky, Noam, **Supp. IV:** 113–114

"Chorale" (Hope), **Supp. VII:** 158

Chorus of Disapproval, A (Ayckbourn), **Supp. V:** 3, 9–10, 14

Christ a Compleat Saviour in His Intercession (Bunyan), **II:** 253

Christ and Satan, **Retro. Supp. II:** 301

Christ in the Cupboard (Powys), **VIII:** 255

Christ Stopped at Eboli (Levi), **VI:** 299

"Christ Surprised" (Jennings), **Supp. V:** 217

"Christ upon the Waters" (Newman), **Supp. VII:** 298

Christabel (Coleridge), **II:** 179; **III:** 338; **IV:** ix, xvii, 29, 44, 48–49, 56, 218, 313; **Retro. Supp. II:** 58–59

Christe's Bloody Sweat (Ford), **II:** 88, 100

"Christening" (Murphy), **Supp. V:** 322

Christian Behaviour (Lewis), **Supp. III:** 248

Christian Behaviour . . . (Bunyan), **II:** 253

Christian Captives, The (Bridges), **VI:** 83

Christian Dialogue, A (Bunyan), **II:** 253

Ezra Pound and His Work (Ackroyd), **Supp. VI:** 4
"Ezra Pound in Pisa" (Davie), **Supp. VI:** 110, 113
Ezra Pound: Poet as Sculptor (Davie), **Supp. VI:** 115

*F*aber Book of Contemporary Irish Poetry, The (ed. Muldoon), **Supp. IV:** 409, 410–411, 422, 424
Faber Book of Sonnets (ed. Nye), **Supp. X:** 193
"Faber Melancholy, A" (Dunn), **Supp. X:** 70
Fabian Essays in Socialism (Shaw), **VI:** 129
Fabian Freeway (Martin), **VI:** 242
Fabian Society, **Supp. IV:** 233
"Fable" (Golding), **Supp. I:** 67, 83
"Fable of the Widow and Her Cat, A" (Swift), **III:** 27, 31
Fables (Dryden), **II:** 293, 301, 304; **III:** 40; **IV:** 287
Fables (Gay), **III:** 59, 67
Fables (Powys). *See No Painted Plumage*
Fables (Stevenson), **V:** 396
Façade (Sitwell and Walton), **VII:** xv, xvii, 128, 130, 131n, 132
"Face of an Old Highland Woman" (Smith, I. C.), **Supp. IX:** 213
Face of the Deep, The (Rossetti), **V:** 260
Face to Face: Short Stories (Gordimer), **Supp. II:** 226
"Faces, The" (James), **VI:** 69
Facial Justice (Hartley), **Supp. VII:** 131
Facilitators, The (Redgrove), **Supp. VI:** 231
Fadiman, Clifton, **Supp. IV:** 460
Faerie Queene, The (Spenser), **I:** 121, 123, 124, **131–141,** 266; **II:** 50; **IV:** 59, 198, 213; **V:** 142
"Faery Song, A" (Yeats), **VI:** 211
"Faeth Fiadha: The Breastplate of Saint Patrick" (Kinsella), **Supp. V:** 264
"Fafaia" (Brooke), **Supp. III:** 55–56
Fagrskinna, **VIII:** 242
"Failed Mystic" (MacCaig), **Supp. VI:** 188, 194
"Failure, A" (Thackeray), **V:** 18
Fair Haven, The (Butler), **Supp. II:** 99, **101–103,** 104, 117
"Fair Ines" (Hood), **IV:** 255
Fair Jilt, The; or, The Amours of Prince Tarquin and Miranda (Behn), **Supp. III:** 29, 31–32
Fair Maid of the Inn, The (Ford, Massinger, Webster), **II:** 66, 69, 83, 85
Fair Margaret (Haggard), **Supp. III:** 214
Fair Quarrel, A (Middleton and Rowley), **II:** 1, 3, 21
"Fair Singer, The" (Marvell), **II:** 211
Fairfield, Cicely, *see* West, Rebecca
Fairly Dangerous Thing, A (Hill, R.), **Supp. IX:** 111, 114
Fairly Honourable Defeat, A (Murdoch), **Supp. I:** 226, 227, 228, 232–233
Fairy and Folk Tales of the Irish Peasantry (ed. Yeats), **VI:** 222

Fairy Caravan, The (Potter), **Supp. III:** 291, 303–304, 305, 306, 307
Fairy Knight, The (Dekker and Ford), **II:** 89, 100
"Faith" (Herbert), **II:** 127
Faith Healer (Friel), **Supp. V:** 123
"Faith Healing" (Larkin), **Supp. I:** 280–281, 282, 285
"Faith on Trial, A" (Meredith), **V:** 222
Faithful Fictions: The Catholic Novel in British Literature (Woodman), **Supp. IV:** 364
Faithful Friends, The, **II:** 67
Faithful Narrative of . . . Habbakkuk Hilding, A (Smollett), **III:** 158
Faithful Shepherdess, The (Fletcher), **II:** 45, 46, 49–52, 53, 62, 65, 82
"Faithfulness of GOD in the Promises, The" (Blake), **III:** 300
"Faithless Nelly Gray" (Hood), **IV:** 257
"Faithless Sally Brown" (Hood), **IV:** 257
Faiz, Faiz Ahmad, **Supp. IV:** 434
"Falk" (Conrad), **VI:** 148
Falkner (Shelley), **Supp. III:** 371
"Fall of a Sparrow" (Stallworthy), **Supp. X:** 294
Fall of Hyperion, The (Keats), **IV:** xi, 211–213, 220, **227–231,** 234, 235
Fall of Kelvin Walker, The (Gray, A.), **Supp. IX:** 80, 85, 89
Fall of Princes, The (Lydgate), **I:** 57, 58, 59, 64
Fall of Robespierre, The (Coleridge and Southey), **IV:** 55
"Fall of Rome, The" (Auden), **Retro. Supp. I:** 11
"Fall of the House of Usher, The" (Poe), **III:** 339
"Fall of the West, The" (Wallace-Crabbe), **VIII:** 321
Fallen Angels (Coward), **Supp. II:** 141, 145
Fallen Leaves, The (Collins), **Supp. VI:** 93, 102
"Fallen Majesty" (Yeats), **VI:** 216
"Fallen Yew, A" (Thompson), **V:** 442
Falling into Language (Wallace-Crabbe), **VIII:** 323
Falling Out of Love and Other Poems, A (Sillitoe), **Supp. V:** 424
"Fallow Deer at the Lonely House, The" (Hardy), **Retro. Supp. I:** 119
Fallowell, Duncan, **Supp. IV:** 173
"Falls" (Ewart), **Supp. VII:** 39
Falls, The (Rankin), **Supp. X:** 245
False Alarm, The (Johnson), **III:** 121
False Friend, The (Vanbrugh), **II:** 325, 333, 336
"False Morality of the Lady Novelists, The" (Greg), **V:** 7
False One, The (Fletcher and Massinger), **II:** 43, 66
"False though she be to me and love" (Congreve), **II:** 269
Falstaff (Nye), **Supp. X:** 193, 195
Fame's Memoriall; or, The Earle of Devonshire Deceased (Ford), **II:** 100
Familiar and Courtly Letters Written by Monsieur Voiture (ed. Boyer), **II:** 352, 364

"Familiar Endeavours" (Wallace-Crabbe), **VIII:** 317
Familiar Letters (Richardson), **III:** 81, 83, 92
Familiar Letters (Rochester), **II:** 270
Familiar Studies of Men and Books (Stevenson), **V:** 395; **Retro. Supp. I:** 262–263
Familiar Tree, A (Stallworthy), **Supp. X:** 294, 297–298, 302
Family (Doyle), **Supp. V:** 78, 91
Family Album (Coward), **Supp. II:** 153
Family and a Fortune, A (Compton-Burnett), **VII:** 60, 61, 62, 63, 66
Family and Friends (Brookner), **Supp. IV:** 127–129
Family Instructor, The (Defoe), **III:** 13, 82; **Retro. Supp. I:** 68
Family Madness, A (Keneally), **Supp. IV:** 346
Family Matters (Mistry), **Supp. X:** 144, 147–148
Family Memories (West), **Supp. III:** 431, 432, 433, 434
Family of Love, The (Dekker and Middleton), **II:** 3, 21
Family of Swift, The (Swift), **Retro. Supp. I:** 274
Family Prayers (Butler), **Supp. II:** 103
Family Reunion, The (Eliot), **VII:** 146, 151, 154, 158, 160; **Retro. Supp. II:** 132
Family Romance, A (Brookner), *see Dolly*
"Family Sagas", *See Íslendinga sögur*
"Family Seat" (Murphy), **Supp. V:** 328
Family Sins (Trevor), **Supp. IV:** 505
"Family Supper, A" (Ishiguro), **Supp. IV:** 304
Family Voices (Pinter), **Supp. I:** 378
Famished Road, The (Okri), **Supp. V:** 347, 348, 349, 350, 351, 352–353, 357–359
Famous for the Creatures (Motion), **Supp. VII:** 252
"Famous Ghost of St. Ives, The" (Redgrove), **Supp. VI:** 235–237
Famous History of Sir Thomas Wyat, The (Webster), **II:** 85
Famous Tragedy of the Queen of Cornwall . . . , The (Hardy), **VI:** 20
Famous Victoria of Henry V, The, **I:** 308–309
Fan, The: A Poem (Gay), **III:** 67
Fanatic Heart, A (O'Brien), **Supp. V:** 339
Fancies, Chaste and Noble, The (Ford), **II:** 89, 91–92, 99, 100
"Fancy" (Keats), **IV:** 221
Fancy and Imagination (Brett), **IV:** 57
Fanfare for Elizabeth (Sitwell), **VII:** 127
"Fanny and Annie" (Lawrence), **VII:** 90, 114, 115
Fanny Brawne: A Biography (Richardson), **IV:** 236
Fanny's First Play (Shaw), **VI:** 115, 116, 117, 129
Fanon, Frantz, **Supp. IV:** 105
"Fanon the Awakener" (Armah), **Supp. X:** 2
Fanshawe, Sir Richard, **II:** 49, 222, 237
Fanshen (Hare), **Supp. IV:** 282, 284

Grænlendinga saga, **VIII:** 240
Grosskurth, Phyllis, **V:** xxvii
Grote, George, **IV:** 289
Group of Noble Dames, A (Hardy), **VI:** 20, 22
"Grove, The" (Muir), **Supp. VI:** 206
"Growing, Flying, Happening" (Reid), **Supp. VII:** 328
"Growing Old" (Arnold), **V:** 203
Growing Pains: The Shaping of a Writer (du Maurier), **Supp. III:** 135, 142, 144
Growing Points (Jennings), **Supp. V:** 217
Growing Rich (Weldon), **Supp. IV:** 531, 533
Growth of Love, The (Bridges), **VI:** 81, 83
Growth of Plato's Ideal Theory, The (Frazer), **Supp. III:** 170–171
"Grub First, Then Ethics" (Auden), **Retro. Supp. I:** 7, 13
Grünewald, Mathias, **Supp. IV:** 85
Gryffydh, Jane, **IV:** 159
Gryll Grange (Peacock), **IV:** xxii, 166–167, 170
Grylls, R. Glynn, **V:** 247, 260; **VII:** xvii, xxxviii
Guardian (periodical), **III:** 46, 49, 50
Guardian, The (Cowley), **II:** 194, 202
Guarini, Guarino, **II:** 49–50
Gubar, Susan, **Retro. Supp. I:** 59–60
"Gude Grey Katt, The" (Hogg), **Supp. X:** 110
"Guerrillas" (Dunn), **Supp. X:** 70–71
Guerrillas (Naipaul), **Supp. I:** 396–397
Guest from the Future, The (Stallworthy), **Supp. X:** 298–302
"Guest from the Future, The" (Stallworthy), **Supp. X:** 298
Guest of Honour, A (Gordimer), **Supp. II:** 229–230, 231
Guide Through the District of the Lakes in the North of England, A (Wordsworth), **IV:** 25
Guide to Kulchur (Pound), **VI:** 333
Guido della Colonna, **I:** 57
Guild of St. George, The, **V:** 182
Guillaume de Deguilleville, **I:** 57
Guillaume de Lorris, **I:** 71
"Guilt and Sorrow" (Wordsworth), **IV:** 5, 45
"Guinevere" (Tennyson), **IV:** 336–337, 338
Guise, The (Marlowe), *see Massacre at Paris, The*
Guise, The (Webster), **II:** 68, 85
"Guitarist Tunes Up, The" (Cornford), **VIII:** 114
Gulliver's Travels (Swift), **II:** 261; **III:** 11, 20, **23–26**, 28, 35; **VI:** 121–122; **Supp. IV:** 502; **Retro. Supp. I:** 274, 275, 276–277, 279–282
Gun for Sale, A (Greene; U.S. title, *This Gun for Hire*), **Supp. I:** 3, 6–7, 10; **Retro. Supp. II:** 153
Guneskera, Romesh, **Supp. X: 85–102**
Gunn, Ander, **Supp. IV:** 265
Gunn, Thom, **Supp. IV: 255–279**
Gunnlaugs saga ormstunga, **VIII:** 239
Guns of Navarone, The (film, Ambler), **Supp. IV:** 3

Gurdjieff, Georges I., **Supp. IV:** 1, 5
Gurney, Ivor, **VI:** 416, **425–427**
Gussow, Mel, **Retro. Supp. I:** 217–218
Gutch, J. M., **IV:** 78, 81
Guthlac, **Retro. Supp. II:** 303
Gutteridge, Bernard, **VII:** 422, 432–433
Guy Domville (James), **VI:** 39
Guy Mannering (Scott), **IV:** xvii, 31–32, 38
Guy of Warwick (Lydgate), **I:** 58
Guy Renton (Waugh), **Supp. VI:** 274–275
Guyana Quartet (Harris), **Supp. V:** 132, 133, 135
Guzman Go Home and Other Stories (Sillitoe), **Supp. V:** 410
Gyðinga saga, **VIII:** 237
Gylfaginning, **VIII:** 243
"Gym"(Murphy), **Supp. V:** 328
Gypsies Metamorphos'd (Jonson), **II:** 111n
"Gyrtt in my giltetesse gowne" (Surrey), **I:** 115
"Healthy Landscape with Dormouse" (Warner), **Supp. VII:** 380
"Hee–Haw" (Warner), **Supp. VII:** 380
"House Grown Silent, The" (Warner), **Supp. VII:** 371

Ha! Ha! Among the Trumpets (Lewis), **VII:** 447, 448
Habeas Corpus (Bennett), **VIII:** 25
Habermas, Jürgen, **Supp. IV:** 112
Habington, William, **II:** 222, 237, 238
Habit of Loving, The (Lessing), **Supp. I:** 244
"Habit of Perfection, The" (Hopkins), **V:** 362, 381
Hadjinicolaou, Nicos, **Supp. IV:** 90
"Hag, The" (Herrick), **II:** 111
Haggard, H. Rider, **Supp. III: 211–228; Supp. IV:** 201, 484
Haight, Gordon, **V:** 199, 200, 201
Hail and Farewell (Moore), **VI:** xii, 85, 88, 97, 99
"Hailstones" (Heaney), **Supp. II:** 280
"Hair, The" (Caudwell), **Supp. IX:** 37
Hakluyt, Richard, **I:** 150, 267; **III:** 7
Halcyon; or, The Future of Monogamy (Brittain), **Supp. X:** 39
Hale, Kathleen, **Supp. IV:** 231
"Hale, sterne superne" (Dunbar), **VIII:** 128–129
"Half–a–Crown's Worth of Cheap Knowledge" (Thackeray), **V:** 22, 37
Half-Mother, The (Tennant), see *Woman Beware Woman*
Halidon Hill (Scott), **IV:** 39
Halifax, marquess of, **III:** 38, 39, 40, 46
Hall, Donald, **Supp. IV:** 256
Hall, Edward, **II:** 43
Hall, Joseph, **II:** 25–26, 81; **IV:** 286
Hall, Radclyffe, **VI:** 411; **Supp. VI: 119–132**
Hall, Samuel (pseud., O'Nolan), **Supp. II:** 322
Hall of Healing (O'Casey), **VII:** 11–12
Hall of the Saurians (Redgrove), **Supp. VI:** 236

Hallam, Arthur, **IV:** 234, 235, 328–336, 338
Hallam, Henry, **IV:** 283
Haller, Albrecht von, **III:** 88
Hallfreðar saga vandræðaskálds, **VIII:** 239
Halloran's Little Boat (Keneally), **Supp. IV:** 348
"Hallowe'en" (Burns), **III:** 315
Hallowe'en Party (Christie), **Supp. II:** 125, 134
"Hallway, The" (Healy), **Supp. IX:** 107
Ham Funeral, The (White), **Supp. I:** 131, 134, 149, 150
"Hamadryad, The" (Landor), **IV:** 96
Hamburger, Michael, **Supp. V:** 199
Hamilton, Sir George Rostrevor, **IV:** xxiv
Hamlet (early version), **I:** 212, 221, 315
Hamlet (Shakespeare), **I:** 188, 280, 313, 315–316; **II:** 29, 36, 71, 75, 84; **III:** 170, 234; **V:** 328; **Supp. IV:** 63, 149, 283, 295
Hamlet in Autumn (Smith, I. C.), **Supp. IX:** 215
"Hamlet, Princess of Denmark" (Beerbohm), **Supp. II:** 55
Hammerton, Sir John, **V:** 393, 397
Hammett, Dashiell, **Supp. II:** 130, 132
Hampden, John, **V:** 393, 395
"Hampstead: the Horse Chestnut Trees" (Gunn), **Supp. IV:** 270–271
Hampton, Christopher, **Supp. IV:** 281
"Hand, The" (Highsmith), **Supp. V:** 179–180
"Hand and Soul" (Rossetti), **V:** 236, 320
Hand in Hand (Stallworthy), **Supp. X:** 294, 296
Hand of Ethelberta, The: A Comedy in Chapters (Hardy), **VI:** 4, 6, 20; **Retro. Supp. I:** 114
"Hand of Solo, A" (Kinsella), **Supp. V:** 267, 274
"Hand that signed the paper, The" (Thomas), **Supp. I:** 174
Handful of Dust, A (Waugh), **VII:** xx, 294, 295–297
"Handful of People, A" (Ewart), **Supp. VII:** 39
"Hands" (Ewart), **Supp. VII:** 39
"Hands" (Hughes), **Retro. Supp. II:** 212
Hands Across the Sea (Coward), **Supp. II:** 153
"Handsome Heart, The" (Hopkins), **V:** 368–369
Handsworth Songs (film), **Supp. IV:** 445
Hanged by the Neck (Koestler), **Supp. I:** 36
"Hanging, A" (Powell), **VII:** 276
Hanging Garden, The (Rankin), **Supp. X:**
Hanging Judge, The (Stevenson), **V:** 396
"Hangover Square" (Mahon), **Supp. VI:** 177
"Hangzhou Garden, A" (Seth), **Supp. X:** 281
Hapgood (Stoppard), **Retro. Supp. II:** 354–355
Happier Life, The (Dunn), **Supp. X:** 70–71

"Happily Ever After" (Huxley), **VII:** 199–200

"Happiness" (Owen), **VI:** 449, 458

"Happinesse to Hospitalitie; or, A Hearty Wish to Good House-keeping" (Herrick), **II:** 111

Happy Days (Beckett), **Supp. I:** 46, 52, 54, 56, 57, 60; **Retro. Supp. I:** 26–27

"Happy Family, A" (Trevor), **Supp. IV:** 503

Happy Haven, The (Arden), **Supp. II:** 29

Happy Hypocrite: A Fairy Tale for Tired Men, The (Beerbohm), **Supp. II:** 45, 46

"Happy Man, The" (Thomson), **Supp. III:** 417

"Happy old man, whose worth all mankind knows" (Flatman), **II:** 133

Happy Pair, The (Sedley), **II:** 266, 271

"Happy Prince, The" (Wilde), **V:** 406, 419; **Retro. Supp. II:** 365; **Retro. Supp. II:** 365

Happy Valley (White), **Supp. I:** 130, 132–133, 136

Haq, Zia ul–, **Supp. IV:** 444

Hárbarðsljóð, **VIII:** 230

Hard Life, The (O'Nolan), **Supp. II:** 336–337

Hard Times (Dickens), **IV:** 247; **V:** viii, xxi, 4, 42, 47, 59, 63–64, 68, 70, 71

Hardie and Baird: The Last Days (Kelman), **Supp. V:** 256–257

Hardie and Baird and Other Plays (Kelman), **Supp. V:** 256–257

"Hardness of Light, The" (Davie), **Supp. VI:** 109

Hardy, Barbara, **V:** ix, xxviii, 39, 73, 201

Hardy, G. H., **VII:** 239–240

Hardy, Thomas, **II:** 69; **III:** 278; **V:** xx–xxvi, 144, 279, 429; **VI:** x, **1–22,** 253, 377; **VII:** xvi; list of short stories, **VI:** 22; **Supp. IV:** 94, 116, 146, 471, 493; **Retro. Supp. I:** 109–122

"Hardy and the Hag" (Fowles), **Supp. I:** 302, 305

Hardy of Wessex (Weber), **VI:** 21

Hare, J. C., **IV:** 54

Hare, David, **Supp. IV:** 182, **281–300**

"Harem Trousers" (McGuckian), **Supp. V:** 286

Harington, Sir John, **I:** 131

"Hark, My Soul! It Is the Lord" (Cowper), **III:** 210

"Hark! the Dog's Howl" (Tennyson), **IV:** 332

Harlequinade (Rattigan), **Supp. VII:** 315–316

Harlot's House, The (Wilde), **V:** 410, 418, 419

Harm Done (Rendell), **Supp. IX:** 189, 196, 198, 199, 201

"Harmonies" (Kinsella), **Supp. V:** 271

"Harmony, The" (Redgrove), **Supp. VI:** 236

"Harmony of the Spheres, The" (Rushdie), **Supp. IV:** 445

Harness Room, The (Hartley), **Supp. VII:** 132

Harold (Tennyson), **IV:** 328, 338

Harold Muggins Is a Martyr (Arden and D'Arcy), **Supp. II:** 31

Harold the Dauntless (Scott), **IV:** 39

Harold's Leap (Smith), **Supp. II:** 462

Haroun and the Sea of Stories (Rushdie), **Supp. IV:** 433, 438, 450–451

Harriet Hume: A London Fantasy (West), **Supp. III:** 441–442

Harrington (Edgeworth), **Supp. III: 161–163**

Harriet Said? (Bainbridge), **Supp. VI:** 17, **19**

Harriot, Thomas, **I:** 277, 278

Harris, Frank, **VI:** 102

Harris, Joseph, **II:** 305

Harris, Wilson, **Supp. V: 131–147**

"Harris East End" (MacCaig), **Supp. VI:** 182

Harrison, Frederic, **V:** 428–429

Harrison, Tony, **Supp. V: 149–165**

Harry Heathcote of Gangoil (Trollope), **V:** 102

"Harry Ploughman" (Hopkins), **V:** 376–377

Harsh Voice, The (West), **Supp. III:** 442

Hartley, David, **IV:** 43, 45, 50, 165

Hartley, L. P., **Supp. VII: 119–133**

Hartmann, Edward von, **Supp. II:** 108

"Harvest Bow, The" (Heaney), **Supp. II:** 276–277

Harvest Festival, The (O'Casey), **VII:** 12

"Harvesting, The" (Hughes), **Supp. II:** 348

Harvey, Christopher, **II:** 138; **Retro. Supp. II:** 172

Harvey, Gabriel, **I:** 122–123, 125; **II:** 25

Harvey, T. W. J., **V:** 63, 199, 201

Harvey, William, **I:** 264

"Has Your Soul Slipped" (Owen), **VI:** 446

Hashemite Kings, The (Morris, J.), **Supp. X:** 175

"Hassock and the Psalter, The" (Powys), **VIII:** 255

Hastings, Warren, **IV:** xv–xvi, 271, 278

Hatfield, C. W., **V:** 133, 151, 152, 153

Háttatal, **VIII:** 243

Haunch of Venison, The (Goldsmith), **III:** 191

Haunted and the Haunters, The (Bulwer-Lytton), **III:** 340, 345

"Haunted House, The" (Graves), **VII:** 263

"Haunted House, The" (Hood), **IV:** 261, 262

Haunted Man and the Ghost's Bargain, The (Dickens), **V:** 71

"Haunter, The" (Hardy), **VI:** 18; **Retro. Supp. I:** 117

Haunter of the Dark, The . . . (Lovecraft), **III:** 345

Hávamál, **VIII:** 230, 232

Have His Carcase (Sayers), **Supp. III:** 345–346

Having a Wonderful Time (Churchill), **Supp. IV:** 180, 181

Haw Lantern, The (Heaney), **Supp. II:** 268, **279–281;** **Retro. Supp. I:** 131–132

Hawaiian Archipelago, The (Bird), **Supp. X:** 19, 24–26, 28

Hawes, Stephen, **I:** 49, 81

"Hawk, The" (Brown), **Supp. VI: 71**

Hawk in the Rain, The (Hughes), **Supp. I:** 343, 345, 363

"Hawk in the Rain, The" (Hughes), **Supp. I:** 345; **Retro. Supp. II:** 200, 202–204

"Hawk Roosting" (Hughes), **Retro. Supp. II:** 204

Hawkfall (Brown), **Supp. VI:** 69

Hawkins, Lewis Weldon, **VI:** 85

Hawkins, Sir John, **II:** 143

Hawksmoor (Ackroyd), **Supp. VI:** 6–7, 10–11

Hawthorne, Nathaniel, **III:** 339, 345; **VI:** 27, 33–34; **Supp. IV:** 116

Hawthorne (James), **VI:** 33–34, 67

Haxton, Gerald, **VI:** 369

Hay Fever (Coward), **Supp. II:** 139, 141, **143–145,** 148, 156

Haydon, Benjamin, **IV:** 214, 227, 312

Hayes, Albert McHarg, **Retro. Supp. II:** 181

"Haymaking" (Thomas), **Supp. III:** 399, 405

"Haystack in the Floods, The" (Morris), **V:** 293

Hayter, Alethea, **III:** 338, 346; **IV:** xxiv–xxv, 57, 322

Hazard, Paul, **III:** 72

"Hazards of the House" (Dunn), **Supp. X:** 68

Hazlitt, William, **I:** 121, 164; **II:** 153, 332, 333, 337, 343, 346, 349, 354, 361, 363, 364; **III:** 68, 70, 76, 78, 165, 276–277; **IV:** ix, xi, xiv, xvii–xix, 38, 39, 41, 50, **125–140,** 217; **Retro. Supp. I:** 147; **Retro. Supp. II:** 51, 52

"He" (Lessing), **Supp. I:** 244

He Came Down from Heaven (Williams, C. W. S.), **Supp. IX:** 284

He Knew He Was Right (Trollope), **V:** 98, 99, 102

"He Revisits His First School" (Hardy), **VI:** 17

"He saw my heart's woe" (Brontë), **V:** 132

"He Says Goodbye in November" (Cornford), **VIII:** 114

He That Will Not When He May (Oliphant), **Supp. X:** 220

"He Thinks of His Past Greatness . . . When a Part of the Constellations of Heaven" (Yeats), **VI:** 211

"He thought he saw a Banker's Clerk" (Carroll), **V:** 270

"He Wonders Whether to Praise or to Blame Her" (Brooke), **Supp. III:** 55

Head to Toe (Orton), **Supp. V:** 363, 365–366

"Head Spider, The" (Murray), **Supp. VII:** 283, 284

Heading Home (Hare), **Supp. IV:** 288, 290–291

Headlong (Frayn), **Supp. VII:** 64, 65

Headlong Hall (Peacock), **IV:** xvii, **160–163,** 164, 165, 168, 169

Hermetical Physick . . . Englished (tr. Vaughan), **II:** 185, 201

Hermit of Marlow, The, pseud. of Percy Bysshe Shelley

"Hero" (Rossetti), **V:** 260

"Hero and Leander" (Hood), **IV:** 255–256, 267

Hero and Leander (Marlowe), **I:** 234, 237–240, 276, 278, 280, 288, **290–291,** 292; **Retro. Supp. I:** 211

Hero and Leander, in Burlesque (Wycherley), **II:** 321

"Hero as King, The" (Carlyle), **IV:** 245, 246

Hero Rises Up, The (Arden and D'Arcy), **Supp. II:** 31

"Heroine, The" (Highsmith), **Supp. V:** 180

Herodotus, **Supp. IV:** 110

Heroes and Hero–Worship (Carlyle), **IV:** xx, 240, 244–246, 249, 250, 341

Heroes and Villains (Carter), **Supp. III:** 81, 84

Heroic Idylls, with Additional Poems (Landor), **IV:** 100

"Heroic Stanzas" (Dryden), **II:** 292

Heroine, The; or, The Adventures of Cherubina (Barrett), **III:** 335

"Heron, The" (Nye), **Supp. X:** 205

Heron Caught in Weeds, A (Roberts, K.), **Supp. X:** 273–275

Herrick, Robert, **II: 102–116,** 121

Herself Surprised (Cary), **VII:** 186, 188, 191–192

"Hertha" (Swinburne), **V:** 325

Hervarar saga, See Heiðreks saga

"Hervé Riel" (Browning), **IV:** 367

Herzog, Werner, **IV:** 180

"Hesperia" (Swinburne), **V:** 320, 321

Hesperides, The (Herrick), **II:** 102, 103, 104, 106, 110, 112, 115, 116

Hester (Oliphant), **Supp. X:** 217–218

"Hester Dominy" (Powys), **VIII:** 250

Heyday of Sir Walter Scott, The (Davie), **Supp. VI:** 114–115

Heylyn, Peter, **I:** 169

Heywood, Jasper, **I:** 215

Heywood, Thomas, **II:** 19, 47, 48, 68, 83

"Hexagon" (Murphy), **Supp. V:** 328

H.G. Wells and His Critics (Raknem), **VI:** 228, 245, 246

H. G. Wells: His Turbulent Life and Times (Dickson), **VI:** 246

H. G. Wells: The Critical Heritage (ed. Parrinder), **VI:** 246

Hibberd, Dominic, **VI:** xvi, xxxiii

Hide, The (Unsworth), **Supp. VII:** 354, 356

"Hide and Seek" (Gunn), **Supp. IV:** 272

Hide and Seek (Collins), **Supp. VI:** 92, 95

Hide and Seek (Rankin), **Supp. X:** 244, 246, 248–250

Hide and Seek (Swinburne), **V:** 334

"Hidden History, A" (Okri), **Supp. V:** 352

Hidden Ireland, The (Corkery), **Supp. V:** 41

"Hidden Law" (MacCaig), **Supp. VI:** 186

Higden, Ranulf, **I:** 22

Higgins, F. R., **Supp. IV:** 411, 413

"Higgler, The" (Coppard), **VIII:** 85, 90, 95

Higgler and Other Tales, The (Coppard), **VIII:** 90

High Island: New and Selected Poems (Murphy), **Supp. V:** 313, 315, 316, 324–325

"High Life in Verdopolis" (Brontë), **V:** 135

"High wavering heather . . . " (Brontë), **V:** 113

High Windows (Larkin), **Supp. I:** 277, 280, **281–284,** 285, 286

Higher Ground (Phillips), **Supp. V:** 380, 386–388

Higher Schools and Universities in Germany (Arnold), **V:** 216

"Higher Standards" (Wilson), **Supp. I:** 155

Highet, Gilbert, **II:** 199

Highland Fling (Mitford), **Supp. X:** 152–154

"Highland Funeral" (MacCaig), **Supp. VI:** 193

Highland Widow, The (Scott), **IV:** 39

Highlander, The (Macpherson), **VIII:** 181–182, 190

Highly Dangerous (Ambler), **Supp. IV:** 3

High–Rise (Ballard), **Supp. V:** 27

High Summer (Rattigan), **Supp. VII:** 315

Highsmith, Patricia, **Supp. IV:** 285; **Supp. V: 167–182**

"Highwayman and the Saint, The" (Friel), **Supp. V:** 118

Hilaire Belloc (Wilson), **Supp. VI:** 301–302

Hilda Lessways (Bennett), **VI:** 258; **Supp. IV:** 238

Hill, G. B., **III:** 233, 234n

Hill, Geoffrey, **Supp. V: 183–203**

"Hill, The" (Brooke), **Supp. III:** 51

Hill of Devi, The (Forster), **VI:** 397, 408, 411

"Hill of Venus, The" (Morris), **V:** 298

Hill, Reginald, **Supp. IX: 109–126**

Hilton, Walter, **Supp. I:** 74

Hind, The, and the Panther (Dryden), **II:** 291, 292, 299–300, 304

Hinge of Faith, The (Churchill), **VI:** 361

Hinman, Charlton, **I:** 326–327

Hinton, William, **Supp. IV:** 284

"Hints" (Reading), **VIII:** 265–266

Hints Towards the Formation of a More Comprehensive Theory of Life (Coleridge), **IV:** 56

Hippolytus (Euripides), **V:** 322, 324

Hips and Haws (Coppard), **VIII:** 89, 98

Hireling, The (Hartley), **Supp. VII:** 129–131

"His Age, Dedicated to his Peculiar Friend, M. John Wickes" (Herrick), **II:** 112

His Arraignment (Jonson), **Retro. Supp. I:** 158

"His Chosen Calling" (Naipaul), **Supp. I:** 385

"His Country" (Hardy), **Retro. Supp. I:** 120–121

His Darling Sin (Braddon), **VIII:** 49

"His Fare–well to Sack" (Herrick), **II:** 111

"His Father's Hands" (Kinsella), **Supp. V:** 268

"His Last Bow" (Doyle), **Supp. II:** 175

"His Letanie, to the Holy Spirit" (Herrick), **II:** 114

His Majesties Declaration Defended (Dryden), **II:** 305

His Majesty Preserved . . . Dictated to Samuel Pepys by the King . . . (ed. Rees–Mogg), **II:** 288

His Noble Numbers (Herrick), **II:** 102, 103, 112, 114, 115, 116

"His Returne to London" (Herrick), **II:** 103

His Second War (Waugh), **Supp. VI:** 274

Historia naturalis et experimentalis (Bacon), **I:** 259, 273

Historia regis Henrici Septimi (André), **I:** 270

Historiae adversum paganos (Orosius), **Retro. Supp. II:** 296

"Historian, The" (Fuller), **Supp. VII:** 74

Historical Account of the Theatre in Europe, An (Riccoboni), **II:** 348

Historical Register, The (Fielding), **III:** 97, 98, 105; **Retro. Supp. I:** 82

Historical Relation of the Island of Ceylon, An (Knox), **III:** 7

"Historical Sketches of the Reign of George Second" (Oliphant), **Supp. X:** 222

"Historical Society" (Murphy), **Supp. V:** 322

"History" (Macaulay), **IV:** 284

History and Adventures of an Atom, The (Smollett), **III:** 149–150, 158

History and Adventures of Joseph Andrews and of His Friend Mr. Abraham Adams (Fielding), **Retro. Supp. I:** 80, 83–86

History and Management of the East India Company (Macpherson), **VIII:** 193

History and Remarkable Life of . . . Col. Jack (Defoe), *see Colonel Jack*

History Maker, A (Gray, A.), **Supp. IX:** 80, 87–88

History of a Good Warm Watch–Coat, The (Sterne), *see Political Romance, A*

History of a Six Weeks' Tour Through a Part of France . . . (Shelley and Shelley), **IV:** 208; **Supp. III:** 355

"History of Angria" (Brontë), **V:** 110–111, 118

History of Antonio and Mellida, The (Marston), *see Antonio and Mellida*

History of Brazil (Southey), **IV:** 68, 71

History of Britain . . . , The (Milton), **II:** 176

History of British India, The, (Mill), **V:** 288

History of Dorastus and Fawni, The (Greene). *See Pandosto: or, The Triumph of Time*

History of England (Hume), **II:** 148; **IV:** 273; **Supp. III:** 229, 238–239

History of England, An (Goldsmith), **III:** 180, 181, 189, 191

239, 243–249; and Collins, **III:** 160, 163, 164, 171, 173; and Crabbe, **III:** 280–282; and Goldsmith, **III:** 177, 180, 181, 189; dictionary, **III:** 113–116; **V:** 281, 434; literary criticism, **I:** 326; **II:** 123, 173, 197, 200, 259, 263, 293, 301, 347; **III:** 11, 88, 94, 139, 257, 275; **IV:** 101; on Addison and Steele, **III:** 39, 42, 44, 49, 51; **Supp. IV:** 271

Johnson, W. E., **Supp. II:** 406

Johnson over Jordan (Priestley), **VII:** 226–227

"Joker, The" (Wallace-Crabbe), **VIII:** 315–316

"Joker as Told" (Murray), **Supp. VII:** 279

Joking Apart (Ayckbourn), **Supp. V:** 3, 9, 13, 14

Jolly Beggars, The (Burns), **III:** 319–320

"Jolly Corner, The" (James), **Retro. Supp. I:** 2

Jonah Who Will Be 25 in the Year 2000 (film), **Supp. IV:** 79

Jonathan Swift (Stephen), **V:** 289

Jonathan Wild (Fielding), **III:** 99, 103, 105, 150; **Retro. Supp. I:** 80–81, 90

Jones, David, **VI:** xvi, 436, 437–439, **Supp. VII:** 167–182

Jones, Henry Arthur, **VI:** 367, 376

Jones, Henry Festing, **Supp. II:** 103–104, 112, 114, 117, 118

Jonestown (Harris), **Supp. V:** 144–145

Jonson, Ben, **I:** 228, 234–235, 270, **335–351; II:** 3, 4, 24, 25, 27, 28, 30, 45, 47, 48, 55, 65, 79, 87, 104, 108, 110, 111n, 115, 118, 141, 199, 221–223; **IV:** 35, 327; **V:** 46, 56; **Supp. IV:** 256; **Retro. Supp. I:** 151–167

Jonsonus Virbius (Digby), **Retro. Supp. I:** 166

Jonsonus Virbius (King), **Supp. VI:** 157

Joseph Andrews (Fielding), **III:** 94, 95, 96, 99–100, 101, 105; **Retro. Supp. I:** 80, 83–86

Joseph Conrad (Baines), **VI:** 133–134

Joseph Conrad (Ford), **VI:** 321, 322

Joseph Conrad (Walpole), **VI:** 149

Joseph Conrad: A Personal Reminiscence (Ford), **VI:** 149

Joseph Conrad: The Modern Imagination (Cox), **VI:** 149

"Joseph Grimaldi" (Hood), **IV:** 267

"Joseph Yates' Temptation" (Gissing), **V:** 437

Journal (Mansfield), **VII:** 181, 182

Journal, 1825–32 (Scott), **IV:** 39

Journal and Letters of Fanny Burney, The (eds. Hemlow et al.), **Supp. III:** 63

Journal of Bridget Hitler, The (Bainbridge), **Supp. VI:** 22

Journal of a Dublin Lady, The (Swift), **III:** 35

Journal of a Landscape Painter in Corsica (Lear), **V:** 87

Journal of a Tour in Scotland in 1819 (Southey), **IV:** 71

Journal of a Tour in the Netherlands in the Autumn of 1815 (Southey), **IV:** 71

Journal of a Tour to the Hebrides, The (Boswell), **III:** 117, 234n, 235, 243, 245, 248, 249

Journal of a Voyage to Lisbon, The (Fielding), **III:** 104, 105

Journal of Beatrix Potter from 1881 to 1897, The (ed. Linder), **Supp. III:** 292–295

"Journal of My Jaunt, Harvest 1762" (Boswell), **III:** 241–242

Journal of Researches into the Geology and Natural History of the various countries visited by HMS Beagle (Darwin), **Supp. VII:** 18–19

Journal of the Plague Year, A (Defoe), **III:** 5–6, 8, 13; **Retro. Supp. I:** 63, 73–74

Journal to Eliza, The (Sterne), **III:** 125, 126, 132, 135

Journal to Stella (Swift), **II:** 335; **III:** 32–33, 34; **Retro. Supp. I:** 274

Journalism (Mahon), **Supp. VI:** 166

Journalism for Women: A Practical Guide (Bennett), **VI:** 264, 266

Journals and Papers of Gerard Manley Hopkins, The (ed. House and Storey), **V:** 362, 363, 371, 378–379, 381

Journals 1939–1983 (Spender), **Supp. II:** 481, 487, 490, 493

Journals of a Landscape Painter in Albania etc. (Lear), **V:** 77, 79–80, 87

Journals of a Landscape Painter in Southern Calabria . . . (Lear), **V:** 77, 79, 87

Journals of a Residence in Portugal, 1800–1801, and a Visit to France, 1838 (Southey), **IV:** 71

Journals of Arnold Bennett (Bennett), **VI:** 265, 267

"Journals of Progress" (Durrell), **Supp. I:** 124

"Journey, The" (Boland), **Supp. V:** 41

"Journey Back, The" (Muir), **Supp. VI:** 207

Journey Continued (Paton), **Supp. II:** 356, 359

Journey from Cornhill to Grand Cairo, A (Thackeray), *see Notes of a Journey from Cornhill to Grand Cairo*

Journey from This World to the Next (Fielding), **Retro. Supp. I:** 80

Journey into Fear (Ambler), **Supp. IV:** 11–12

"Journey of John Gilpin, The" (Cowper), *see AJohn Gilpin"*

"Journey of the Magi, The" (Eliot), **VII:** 152

Journey Through France (Piozzi), **III:** 134

Journey to a War (Auden and Isherwood), **VII:** 312; **Retro. Supp. I:** 9

Journey to Armenia (Mandelstam), **Supp. IV:** 163, 170

"Journey to Bruges, The" (Mansfield), **VII:** 172

Journey to Ithaca (Desai), **Supp. V:** 56, 66, 73–74

Journey to London, A (Vanbrugh), **II:** 326, 333–334, 336

Journey to Oxiana (Byron), **Supp. IV:** 157, 170

Journey to the Hebrides (Johnson), **IV:** 281

Journey to the Western Islands of Scotland, A (Johnson), **III:** 117, 121; **Retro. Supp. I:** 143

Journey Without Maps (Greene), **Supp. I:** 9; **Retro. Supp. II:** 153

Journeys (Morris, J.), **Supp. X:** 172, 183

Journeys and Places (Muir), **Supp. VI:** 204, **205–206**

Journeys in Persia and Kurdistan (Bird), **Supp. X:** 31

Jovial Crew, A (Brome **Supp. X:** 49, 55–59, 62–63

Jowett, Benjamin, **V:** 278, 284, 285, 312, 338, 400

Joy (Galsworthy), **VI:** 269, 285

"Joy Gordon" (Redgrove), **Supp. VI:** 236

Joyce (Oliphant), **Supp. X:** 218

Joyce, James, **IV:** 189; **V:** xxv, 41; **VII:** xii, xiv, 18, **41–58; VII:** 54–58; **Supp. I:** 43, 196–197; **Supp. II:** 74, 88, 327, 332, 338, 420, 525; **Supp. III:** 108; **Supp. IV:** 27, 233, 234, 363, 364, 365, 371, 390, 395, 396, 407, 411, 424, 426, 427, 500, 514; **Retro. Supp. I:** 18, 19, **169–182**

Joyce, Jeremiah, **V:** 174n

"Jubilate Matteo" (Ewart), **Supp. VII:** 44

"Judas Tree, The" (Welch), **Supp. IX:** 269

Jude the Obscure (Hardy), **VI:** 4, 5, 7, 8, 9; **Supp. IV:** 116; **Retro. Supp. I:** 110, 116

Judge, The (West), **Supp. III:** 441, 442

"Judge's House, The" (Stoker), **Supp. III:** 382

"Judge Chutney's Final Summary" (Armitage), **VIII:** 6

Judgement of Martin Bucer . . . , The (Milton), **II:** 175

Judgement of Paris, The (Congreve), **II:** 347, 350

Judgement in Stone, A (Rendell), **Supp. IX:** 192, 194–195

Judge's Wife, The (Churchill), **Supp. IV:** 181

"Judging Distances" (Reed), **VII:** 422

Judgment on Deltchev (Ambler), **Supp. IV:** 4, 12–13, 21

Judith, **Supp. VI:** 29; **Retro. Supp. II:** 305, 306

Judith (Bennett), **VI:** 267

"Judith" (Coppard), **VIII:** 96

Judith (Giraudoux), **Supp. III:** 195

"Judkin of the Parcels" (Saki), **Supp. VI:** 245

Jugement du roi de Behaingne, **I:** 32

"Juggling Jerry" (Meredith), **V:** 220

"Julia" (Brontë), **V:** 122, 151

Julia and the Bazooka and Other Stories (Kavan), **Supp. VII:** 202, 205, 214

"Julia Bride" (James), **VI:** 67, 69

"Julia's Churching; or, Purification" (Herrick), **II:** 112

"Julian and Maddalo" (Shelley), **IV:** 182, 201–202; **Retro. Supp. I:** 251

Marriage A–la–Mode (Dryden), **II:** 293, 296, 305

Marriage of Heaven and Hell, The (Blake), **III:** 289, 297–298, 304, 307; **V:** xv, 329–330, 331; **Supp. IV:** 448; **Retro. Supp. I:** 38–39

Marriage of Mona Lisa, The (Swinburne), **V:** 333

"Marriage of Tirzah and Ahirad, The" (Macaulay), **IV:** 283

Marriages Between Zones Three, Four and Five, The (Lessing), **Supp. I:** 251

Married Life (Bennett), *see Plain Man and His Wife, The*

Married Man, The (Lawrence), **VII:** 120

"Married Man's Story, A" (Mansfield), **VII:** 174

Married to a Spy (Waugh), **Supp. VI:** 276

Marryat, Captain Frederick, **Supp. IV:** 201

Marsh, Charles, **Supp. IV:** 214, 218

Marsh, Edward, **VI:** 416, 419, 420, 425, 430, 432, 452; **VII:** xvi; **Supp. III:** 47, 48, 53, 54, 60, 397

"Marsh of Ages, The" (Cameron), **Supp. IX:** 19

Marshall, William, **II:** 141

Marston, John, **I:** 234, 238, 340; **II:** 4, 24–33, 34–37, 40–41, 47, 68, 72; **Retro. Supp. I:** 160

Marston, Philip, **V:** 245

Marston, R. B., **II:** 131

Martha Quest (Lessing), **Supp. I:** 237, 239, 243–244; **Supp. IV:** 238

Martial, **II:** 104, 265

Martian, The (du Maurier), **Supp. III:** 134, 151

"Martian Sends a Postcard Home, A" (Cope), **VIII:** 74

Martin, John, **V:** 110

Martin, L. C., **II:** 183, 184n, 200

Martin, Martin, **III:** 117

Martin Chuzzlewit (Dickens), **V:** xx, 42, 47, 54–56, 58, 59, 68, 71; **Supp. IV:** 366, 381

Martin Chuzzlewit (teleplay, Lodge), **Supp. IV:** 366, 381

Martin Luther (Lopez and Moore), **VI:** 85, 95, 98

Martineau, Harriet, **IV:** 311; **V:** 125–126, 146

Martyn, Edward, **VI:** 309

Martyrdom of Man (Reade), **Supp. IV:** 2

"Martyrs' Song" (Rossetti), **V:** 256

Martz, Louis, **V:** 366, 382

Marvell, Andrew, **II:** 113, 121, 123, 166, 195–199, **204–220,** 255, 261; **Supp. III:** 51, 56; **Supp. IV:** 271; **Retro. Supp. II: 253–268**

Marvell and the Civic Crown (Patterson), **Retro. Supp. II:** 265

Marwick, A., **IV:** 290, 291

Marwood, Arthur, **VI:** 323, 331

Marxism, **Supp. I:** 24–25, 26, 30, 31, 238

Mary, A Fiction (Wollstonecraft), **Supp. III:** 466, 476

"Mary and Gabriel" (Brooke), **Supp. III:** 55

Mary Anne (du Maurier), **Supp. III:** 137

Mary Barton (Gaskell), **V:** viii, x, xxi, 1, 2, 4–5, 6, 15

"Mary Burnet" (Hogg), **Supp. X:** 110

"'Mary Gloster', The," (Kipling), **VI:** 202

Mary Gresley (Trollope), **V:** 101

"Mary Postgate" (Kipling), **VI:** 197, 206

"Mary Queen of Scots" (Swinburne), **V:** 332

Mary Rose (Barrie), **Supp. III:** 8, 9

Mary Stuart (Swinburne), **V:** 330, 332

"Mary the Cook–Maid's Letter . . . " (Swift), **III:** 31

"Mary's Magnificat" (Jennings), **Supp. V:** 217

"Masculine Birth of Time, The" (Bacon), **I:** 263

Masefield, John, **VI:** 429; **VII:** xii, xiii

Mask of Apollo (Renault), **Supp. IX:** 183–184, 187

Mask of Apollo and Other Stories, The (Russell), **VIII:** 285

Mask of Dimitrios, The (Ambler), **Supp. IV:** 21

"Mask of Love" (Kinsella), **Supp. V:** 262

Mason, William, **III:** 141, 142, 145

"Masque, The" (Auden), **Retro. Supp. I:** 11

"Masque of Anarchy, The" (Shelley), **IV:** xviii, 202–203, 206, 208; **Retro. Supp. I:** 253–254

Masque of Blackness, The (Jonson), **Retro. Supp. I:** 161–162

Masque of Queenes (Jonson), **II:** 111n; **Retro. Supp. I:** 162

Masque of the Manuscript, The (Williams, C. W. S.), **Supp. IX:** 276

Mass and the English Reformers, The (Dugmore), **I:** 177n

Massacre at Paris, The (Marlowe), **I:** 249, 276, 279–280, **285–286; Retro. Supp. I:** 211

Massinger, Philip, **II:** 44, 45, 50, 66–67, 69, 83, 87

Masson, David, **IV:** 212, 235

Masson, Rosaline, **V:** 393, 397

"Mastectomy" (Boland), **Supp. V:** (Boland), **Supp. V:** 49

Master, The (Brontë), *see Professor, The*

"Master, The" (Wilde), **Retro. Supp. II:** 371

Master and Margarita, The (Bulgakov), **Supp. IV:** 448

Master Georgie (Bainbridge), **Supp. VI: 26–27**

Master Humphrey's Clock (Dickens), **V:** 42, 53–54, 71

"Master John Horseleigh, Knight" (Hardy), **VI:** 22

Master of Ballantrae, The (Stevenson), **V:** 383–384, 387, 396; **Retro. Supp. I:** 268–269

Master of Petersburg, The (Coetzee), **Supp. VI:** 75–76, **85–86,** 88

Master of the House, The (Hall), **Supp. VI:** 120, 122, 128

Masterman, C. F. G., **VI:** viii, 320

Masters, John, **Supp. IV:** 440

Masters, The (Snow), **VII:** xxi, 327–328, 330

"Match, The" (Marvell), **II:** 211

Match for the Devil, A (Nicholson), **Supp. VI: 222**

"Match–Maker, The" (Saki), **Supp. VI:** 240

"Mater Dolorosa" (Swinburne), **V:** 325

"Mater Triumphalis" (Swinburne), **V:** 325

Materials for a Description of Capri (Douglas), **VI:** 305

Mathilda (Shelley), **Supp. III: 363–364**

"Mathilda's England" (Trevor), **Supp. IV:** 504

Matigari (Ngũgĩ), **VIII:** 215, 216, 221–222

Matilda (Dahl), **Supp. IV:** 203, 207, 226

Matilda (film), **Supp. IV:** 203

Matisse, Henri, **Supp. IV:** 81, 154

Matisse Stories, The (Byatt), **Supp. IV:** 151, 154–155

Matlock's System (Hill), see *Heart Clock*

"Matres Dolorosae" (Bridges), **VI:** 81

"Matron" (Blackwood), **Supp. IX:** 12

"Mattens" (Herbert), **II:** 127; **Retro. Supp. II:** 179

"Matter of Fact, A" (Kipling), **VI:** 193

Matter of Wales: Epic Views of a Small Country, The (Morris), see *Wales: Epic Views of a Small Country*

Matthew Arnold: A Study in Conflict (Brown), **V:** 211–212, 217

Matthew Arnold: A Symposium (ed. Allott), **V:** 218

Matthews, Geoffrey Maurice, **IV:** x, xxv, 207, 208, 209, 237

Matthews, William, **I:** 68

Matthiessen, F. O., **V:** 204

Matthieu de Vendôme, **I:** 23, 39–40

Maturin, Charles, **III:** 327, 331, 333–334, 336, 345; **VIII: 197–210; Supp. III:** 384

Maud (Tennyson), **IV:** xxi, 325, 328, 330–331, 333–336, 337, 338; **VI:** 420

Maude: A Story for Girls (Rossetti), **V:** 260

"Maud–Evelyn" (James), **VI:** 69

Maugham, Syrie, **VI:** 369

Maugham, W. Somerset, **VI:** xi, xiii, 200, **363–381; VII:** 318–319; list of short stories and sketches, **VI:** 379–381; **Supp. II:** 7, 141, 156–157; **Supp. IV:** 9–10, 21, 500

Maumbury Ring (Hardy), **VI:** 20

Maupassant, Guy de, **III:** 340, **Supp. IV:** 500

Maurice (Forster), **VI:** xii, 397, **407–408,** 412; **Retro. Supp. II:** 145–146

Maurice, Frederick D., **IV:** 54; **V:** xxi, 284, 285

Mavis Belfrage (Gray, A.), **Supp. IX:** 80, 91

Max in Verse (Beerbohm), **Supp. II:** 44

Maxfield, James F., **Supp. IV:** 336

May Day (Chapman), **I:** 244

"May Day, 1937" (Nicholson), **Supp. VI:** 214

"May Day Song for North Oxford" (Betjeman), **VII:** 356

"May 23" (Thomas), **Supp. III:** 405

Maybe Day in Kazakhstan, A (Harrison), **Supp. V:** 164

Morris, Jan, **Supp. X: 171–189**
Morris, Margaret, **VI:** 274
Morris, May, **V:** 298, 301, 305
Morris, William, **IV:** 218; **V:** ix, xi, xii, xix, xxii–xxvi, 236–238, **291–307,** 312, 365, 401, 409; **VI:** 103, 167–168, 283
Morris & Co., **V:** 295, 296, 302
"Morris's Life and Death of Jason" (Swinburne), **V:** 298
Morrison, Arthur, **VI:** 365–366
Mortal Causes (Rankin), **Supp. X:** 244, 251–252
Mortal Coils (Huxley), **VII:** 200
Mortal Consequences (Symons), **Supp. IV:** 3
Morte Arthur, Le, **I:** 72, 73
Morte Darthur, Le (Malory), **I:** 67, 68–79; **V:** 294; **Retro. Supp. II:** 237–239, 240–251
"Morte d'Arthur" (Tennyson), **IV:** xx, 332–334, 336
"Mortier Water–Organ Called Oscar, The" (Redgrove), **Supp. VI:** 236
"Mortification" (Herbert), **II:** 127
Mortimer His Fall (Jonson), **Retro. Supp. I:** 166
Mosada, a Dramatic Poem (Yeats), **VI:** 221
Moseley, Humphrey, **II:** 89
Moses (Rosenberg), **VI:** 433
Moses the Lawgiver (Keneally), **Supp. IV:** 346
"Mosquito" (Lawrence), **VII:** 119
"Most Extraordinary Case, A" (James), **VI:** 69
Most Piteous Tale of the Morte Arthur Saunz Guerdon, The (Malory), **I:** 72, 77
"Mother, The" (Stevenson), **Supp. VI:** 256
Mother and Son (Compton-Burnett), **VII:** 64, 65, 68–69
"Mother and Son" (Stallworthy), **Supp. X:** 297
Mother Bombie (Lyly), **I:** 203–204
"Mother Country" (Rossetti), **V:** 255
Mother Courage (Brecht), **VI:** 123
Mother Hubberd's Tale (Spenser), **I:** 124, 131
Mother Ireland (O'Brien), **Supp. V:** 338
"Mother of the Muses, The" (Harrison), **Supp. V:** 161
"Mother of the World, The" (Powys), **VIII:** 251, 252
Mother, Sing for Me (Ngũgĩ). *See Maitũ njugĩra*
"Mother Speaks, The" (Day Lewis), **Supp. III:** 125
"Mother to Child Asleep" (Cornford), **VIII:** 107
"Mother Tongue" (Stallworthy), **Supp. X:** 298
Mother, What Is Man? (Smith), **Supp. II:** 462
Mother's Day (Storey), **Supp. I:** 420
"Mother's Sense of Fun" (Wilson), **Supp. I:** 153, 157–158
Motion, Andrew, **Supp. VII: 251–267**

"Motions of the Earth, The" (Nicholson), **Supp. VI:** 217
Motteux, Pierre, **II:** 352, 353
"Mount Badon" (Williams, C. W. S.), **Supp. IX:** 282–283
Mount of Olives, The; or, Solitary Devotions . . . (Vaughan), **II:** 185, 201
Mount Zion (Betjeman), **VII:** 364
"Mount Zion" (Hughes), **Supp. I:** 341
Mountain Bard, The (Hogg), **Supp. X:** 106
"Mountain Path" (Cornford), **VIII:** 107
"Mountain Shadow" (Gunesekera), **Supp. X:** 87
Mountain Town in France, A (Stevenson), **V:** 396
Mountains and Molehills (Cornford), **VIII:** 106, 107–108, 109
Mountolive (Durrell), **Supp. I:** 104, 106, 108, 109
"Mourning" (Marvell), **II:** 209, 212
Mourning Bride, The (Congreve), **II:** 338, 347, 350
Mourning Muse of Alexis, The: A Pastoral (Congreve), **II:** 350
Mousetrap, The (Christie), **Supp. II:** 125, 134
Movevent, The, **Supp. IV:** 256
Moving Finger, The (Christie), **Supp. II:** 132
Moving Out (Behan), **Supp. II:** 67, 68, 70
Moving Target, A (Golding), **Supp. I:** 88
Moving the Center: The Struggle for Cultural Freedoms (Ngũgĩ), **VIII:** 217, 225
"Mower to the Glo–Worms, The" (Marvell), **II:** 209
"Mowgli's Brothers" (Kipling), **VI:** 199
Moxon, Edward, **IV:** 83, 86, 252
Much Ado About Nothing (Shakespeare), **I:** 310–311, 327
Much Obliged (Wodehouse), **Supp. III:** 460
"Mud Vision, The" (Heaney), **Supp. II:** 281
Mudlark Poems & Grand Buveur, The (Redgrove), **Supp. VI:** 236
"Mudtower, The" (Stevenson), **Supp. VI:** 253
Muggeridge, Malcolm, **VI:** 356; **VII:** 276; **Supp. II:** 118, 119
"Mugumo" (Ngũgĩ), **VIII:** 220
Muiopotmos (Spenser), **I:** 124
Muir, Edwin, **I:** 247; **IV:** 27, 40; **Supp. V:** 208; **Supp. VI: 197–209**
Muir, K., **IV:** 219, 236
Mulberry Bush, The (Wilson), **Supp. I:** 154–155
Mulberry Garden, The (Sedley), **II:** 263–264, 271
"Mulberry Tree, The" (Bowen), **Supp. II:** 78, 92
Mulberry Tree, The (Bowen), **Supp. II:** 80
Mulcaster, Richard, **I:** 122
Muldoon, Paul, **Supp. IV: 409–432**
Mule on the Minaret, The (Waugh), **Supp. VI:** 274
Mules (Muldoon), **Supp. IV:** 414–415

Mullan, John, **Retro. Supp. I:** 69–70
Müller, Max, **V:** 203
"Mulwhevin" (Dunn), **Supp. X:** 68
Mum and Mr. Armitage (Bainbridge), **Supp. VI:** 23
Mummer's Wife, A (Moore), **VI:** xii, 86, 90, 98
"Mummia" (Brooke), **Supp. III:** 52, 60
"Mummy, The" (Morgan, E.), **Supp. IX:** 163
"Mummy to the Rescue" (Wilson), **Supp. I:** 153
"Mundus and Paulina" (Gower), **I:** 53–54
Mundus Muliebris; or, The Ladies–Dressing Room Unlock'd (Evelyn), **II:** 287
Mundy Scheme, The (Friel), **Supp. V:** 119
Munera Pulveris (Ruskin), **V:** 184
"Municipal Gallery Revisited, The" (Yeats), **VI:** 216; **Retro. Supp. I:** 337–338
Munnings, Sir Alfred, **VI:** 210
"Murad the Unlucky" (Brooke), **Supp. III:** 55
"Murder" (Nye), **Supp. X:** 198
Murder at the Vicarage (Christie), **Supp. II:** 130, 131
"Murder Considered as One of the Fine Arts" (De Quincey), **IV:** 149–150
Murder in the Calais Coach (Christie), *see Murder on the Orient Express*
Murder in the Cathedral (Eliot), **VII:** 153, 157, 159; **Retro. Supp. II:** 132
Murder in Triplicate (James), **Supp. IV:** 320, 327
"Murder, 1986" (James), **Supp. IV:** 340
Murder of John Brewer, The (Kyd), **I:** 218
Murder of Quality, A (le Carré), **Supp. II:** 300, **302–303**
Murder of Roger Ackroyd, The (Christie), **Supp. II:** 124, 128, 135
"Murder of Santa Claus, The" (James), **Supp. IV:** 340
Murder of the Man Who Was Shakespeare, The (Hoffman), **I:** 277
Murder on the Orient Express (Christie; U.S. title, *Murder in the Calais Coach*), **Supp. II:** 128, 130, 134, 135
Murderous Michael, **I:** 218
"Murdered Drinker, The" (Graham), **Supp. VII:** 115
"Murders in the Rue Morgue, The" (Poe), **III:** 339
Murdoch, Iris, **III:** 341, 345; **VI:** 372; **Supp. I: 215–235; Supp. IV:** 100, 139, 145, 234
Murmuring Judges (Hare), **Supp. IV:** 282, 294, 296–297, 298
Murnau, F. W., **III:** 342
Murphy (Beckett), **Supp. I:** 46–47, 48, 51, 62, 220; **Retro. Supp. I:** 19–20
Murphy, Richard, **VI:** 220; **Supp. V: 313–331**
Murray, Gilbert, **VI:** 153, 273, 274
Murray, John, **IV:** 182, 188, 190, 193, 294
Murray, Les, **Supp. VII: 269–288**
Murray, Nicholas, **Supp. IV:** 171
Murray, Sir James, **III:** 113

Nadel, G. H., **I:** 269

Naipaul, V. S., **VII:** xx; **Supp. I: 383–405; Supp. IV:** 302

Naive and Sentimental Lover, The (le Carré), **Supp. II:** 300, **310–311,** 317

Naked Warriors (Read), **VI:** 436

Name and Nature of Poetry, The (Housman), **VI:** 157, 162–164

Name of Action, The (Greene), **Supp. I:** 3

Name of the Rose, The (Eco), **Supp. IV:** 116

"Names" (Cope), **VIII:** 79

"Naming of Offa, The" (Hill), **Supp. V:** 195

"Naming of Parts" (Reed), **VII:** 422

Nannie's Night Out (O'Casey), **VII:** 11–12

Napier, Macvey, **IV:** 272

Napoleon of Notting Hill, The (Chesterton), **VI:** 335, 338, 343–344

Napoleon III in Italy and Other Poems (Browning), *see Poems Before Congress*

Narayan, R. K., **Supp. IV:** 440

"Narcissus" (Gower), **I:** 53–54

"Narcissus Bay" (Welch), **Supp. IX:** 267, 268

Nares, Edward, **IV:** 280

Narrative of All the Robberies, . . . of John Sheppard, A (Defoe), **III:** 13

"Narrative of Jacobus Coetzee, The" (Coetzee), **Supp. VI:** 76, **79–80**

Narrow Corner, The (Maugham), **VI:** 375

Narrow Place, The (Muir), **Supp. VI:** 204, **206**

"Narrow Place, The" (Muir), **Supp. VI:** 206

Narrow Road to the Deep North (Bond), **Supp. I:** 423, 427, 428–429, 430, 435

"Narrow Sea, The" (Graves), **VII:** 270

"Narrow Vessel, A" (Thompson), **V:** 441

Nashe, Thomas, **I:** 114, 123, 171, 199, 221, 278, 279, 281, 288; **II:** 25; **Supp. II:** 188; **Retro. Supp. I:** 156

Nation (periodical), **VI:** 455

Nation Review (publication), **Supp. IV:** 346

National Being, The: Some Thoughts on Irish Polity (Russell), **VIII:** 277, 287, 288, 292

National Observer (periodical), **VI:** 350

National Standard (periodical), **V:** 19

National Tales (Hood), **IV:** 255, 259, 267

"National Trust" (Harrison), **Supp. V:** 153

Native Companions: Essays and Comments on Australian Literature 1936–1966 (Hope), **Supp. VII:** 151, 153, 159, 164

"Native Health" (Dunn), **Supp. X:** 68

"Natura Naturans" (Clough), **V:** 159–160

Natural Causes (Motion), **Supp. VII:** 254, 257–258, 263

Natural Curiosity, A (Drabble), **Supp. IV:** 231, 249–250

Natural History and Antiquities of Selborne, The, (White), **Supp. VI:** 279–284, **285–293**

Natural History of Religion, The (Hume), **Supp. III:** 240–241

"natural man,"**VII:** 94

"Natural Son" (Murphy), **Supp. V:** 327, 329

Naturalist's Calendar, with Observations in Various Branches of Natural History, A (White), **Supp. VI:** 283

Naturalist's Journal (White), **Supp. VI:** 283, 292

"Naturally the Foundation Will Bear Your Expenses" (Larkin), **Supp. I:** 285

"Nature, Language, the Sea: An Essay" (Wallace-Crabbe), **VIII:** 315

Nature of a Crime, The (Conrad), **VI:** 148

Nature of Blood, The (Phillips), **Supp. V:** 380, 391–394

Nature of Cold Weather, The (Redgrove), **Supp. VI: 227–229,** 236

"Nature of Cold Weather, The" (Redgrove), **Supp. VI:** 228,237

"Nature of Gothic, The" (Ruskin), **V:** 176

Nature of History, The (Marwick), **IV:** 290, 291

Nature of Passion, The (Jhabvala), **Supp. V:** 226

"Nature of the Scholar, The" (Fichte), **V:** 348

Nature Poems (Davies), **Supp. III:** 398

"Nature That Washt Her Hands in Milk" (Ralegh), **I:** 149

Natwar–Singh, K., **VI:** 408

Naufragium Joculare (Cowley), **II:** 194, 202

Naulahka (Kipling and Balestier), **VI:** 204

"Naval History" (Kelman), **Supp. V:** 250

"Naval Treaty, The" (Doyle), **Supp. II:** 169, 175

Navigation and Commerce (Evelyn), **II:** 287

"Navy's Here, The" (Redgrove), **Supp. VI:** 234

Naylor, Gillian, **VI:** 168

Nazarene Gospel Restored, The (Graves and Podro), **VII:** 262

Nazism, **VI:** 242

"NB" (Reading), **VIII:** 266

Neal, Patricia, **Supp. IV:** 214, 218, 223

Near and Far (Blunden), **VI:** 428

"Near Lanivet" (Hardy), **VI:** 17

"Near Perigord" (Pound), **V:** 304

"Necessary Blindness, A" (Nye), **Supp. X:** 204

Necessity of Art, The (Fischer), **Supp. II:** 228

Necessity of Atheism, The (Shelley and Hogg), **IV:** xvii, 196, 208; **Retro. Supp. I:** 244

"Necessity of Not Believing, The" (Smith), **Supp. II:** 467

Necessity of Poetry, The (Bridges), **VI:** 75–76, 82, 83

"Necessity's Child" (Wilson), **Supp. I:** 153–154

"Neck" (Dahl), **Supp. IV:** 217

"Ned Bratts" (Browning), **IV:** 370; **Retro. Supp. II:** 29–30

Ned Kelly and the City of the Bees (Keneally), **Supp. IV:** 346

"Ned Skinner" (Muldoon), **Supp. IV:** 415

"Need to Be Versed in Country Things, The" (Frost), **Supp. IV:** 423

Needham, Gwendolyn, **V:** 60

Needle's Eye, The (Drabble), **Supp. IV:** 230, 234, 241, 242–243, 245, 251

"Needlework" (Dunn), **Supp. X:** 68

"Negative Love" (Donne), **Retro. Supp. II:** 93

"Neglected Graveyard, Luskentyre" (MacCaig), **Supp. VI:** 182, 189, 194

"Neighbours" (Cornford), **VIII:** 107

Neizvestny, Ernst, **Supp. IV:** 88

"Nelly Trim" (Warner), **Supp. VII:** 371

Nelson, W., **I:** 86

Nerinda (Douglas), **VI:** 300, 305

Nero Part I (Bridges), **VI:** 83

Nero Part II (Bridges), **VI:** 83

Nesbit, E., **Supp. II:** 140, 144, 149

"Nest in a Wall, A" (Murphy), **Supp. V:** 326

Nest of Tigers, A: Edith, Osbert and Sacheverell in Their Times (Lehmann), **VII:** 141

Nether World, The (Gissing), **V:** 424, 437

Netherwood (White), **Supp. I:** 131, 151

"Netting, The" (Murphy), **Supp. V:** 318

Nettles (Lawrence), **VII:** 118

"Netty Sargent's Copyhold" (Hardy), **VI:** 22

"Neurotic, The" (Day Lewis), **Supp. III:** 129

Neutral Ground (Corke), **VII:** 93

"Neutral Tones" (Hardy), **Retro. Supp. I:** 110, 117

New Age (periodical), **VI:** 247, 265; **VII:** 172

New and Collected Poems 1934–84 (Fuller), **Supp. VII:** 68, 72, 73, 74, 79

New and Collected Poems, 1952–1992 (Hill), **Supp. V:** 184

New and Improved Grammar of the English Tongue, A (Hazlitt), **IV:** 139

New and Selected Poems (Davie), **Supp. VI:** 108

New and Useful Concordance, A (Bunyan), **II:** 253

New Apocalypse, The (MacCaig), **Supp. VI:** 184

New Arabian Nights (Stevenson), **V:** 384n, 386, 395; **Retro. Supp. I:** 263

New Arcadia (Sidney), **Retro. Supp. II:** 332

New Atlantis (Bacon), **I:** 259, 265, 267–269, 273

"New Ballad of Tannhäuser, A" (Davidson), **V:** 318n

New Bath Guide (Anstey), **III:** 155

New Bats in Old Belfries (Betjeman), **VII:** 368–369

New Bearings in English Poetry (Leavis), **V:** 375, 381; **VI:** 21; **VII:** 234, 244–246

"New Beginning, A" (Kinsella), **Supp. V:** 270

New Belfry of Christ Church, The (Carroll), **V:** 274

New Characters . . . of Severall Persons . . . (Webster), **II:** 85

Night–Crossing (Mahon), **Supp. VI: 167–168,** 169

Night Feed (Boland), **Supp. V:** 50

"Night Feed" (Boland), **Supp. V:** 50

Night Mail (Auden), **Retro. Supp. I:** 7

"Night of Frost in May" (Meredith), **V:** 223

Night on Bald Mountain (White), **Supp. I:** 131, 136, **149–151**

"Night Out" (Rhys), **Supp. II:** 402

Night Out, A (Pinter), **Supp. I:** 371–372, 375; **Retro. Supp. I:** 223

"Night Patrol" (West), **VI:** 423

Night School (Pinter), **Supp. I:** 373, 375

"Night Sister" (Jennings), **Supp. V:** 215

"Night Songs" (Kinsella), **Supp. V:** 261

"Night Taxi" (Gunn), **Supp. IV:** 272–273, 274

Night the Prowler, The (White), **Supp. I:** 131, 132

Night Thoughts (Young), **III:** 302, 307; **Retro. Supp. I:** 43

Night to Remember, A (Ambler), **Supp. IV:** 3

Night to Remember, A (film), **Supp. IV:** 2

Night Walker, The (Fletcher and Shirley), **II:** 66

"Night Wind, The" (Brontë), **V:** 133, 142

"Nightclub" (MacNeice), **VII:** 414

Night–Comers, The (Ambler), *see State of Siege*

Night–Comers, The (film), **Supp. IV:** 3

"Nightfall (For an Athlete Dying Young)" (Hollinghurst), **Supp. X:** 121

"Nightingale and the Rose, The" (Wilde), **Retro. Supp. II:** 365

"Nightmare, A" (Rossetti), **V:** 256

Nightmare Abbey (Peacock), **III:** 336, 345; **IV:** xvii, 158, 162, 164–165, 170, 177

"Nightpiece to Julia, The" (Herrick), **II:** lll

Nightrunners of Bengal (film, Ambler), **Supp. IV:** 3

Nights at the Alexandra (Trevor), **Supp. IV:** 514–515

Nights at the Circus (Carter), **Supp. III:** 79, 87, 89–90, 91–92

"Night's Fall Unlocks the Dirge of the Sea" (Graham), **Supp. VII:** 110

Nightfishing, The (Graham), **Supp. VII:** 105, 106, 111–113, 114, 116

"Nightwalker" (Kinsella), **Supp. V:** 263

Nightwalker and Other Poems (Kinsella), **Supp. V:** 262, 263–264

Nin, Anaïs, **Supp. IV:** 110, 111

Nina Balatka (Trollope), **V:** 101

Nine Essays (Housman), **VI:** 164

Nine Experiments (Spender), **Supp. II:** 481, 486

Nine Tailors, The (Sayers), **Supp. III:** 343, 344–345

"Ninemaidens" (Thomas), **Supp. IV:** 494

1985 (Burgess), **Supp. I:** 193

Nineteen Eighty–four (Orwell), **III:** 341; **VII:** xx, 204, 274, 279–280, 284–285

1982 Janine (Gray, A.), **Supp. IX:** 80, 83–85, 86

1914 (Brooke), **Supp. III:** 48, 52, 56–58

"1914" (Owen), **VI:** 444

1914 and Other Poems (Brooke), **VI:** 420; **Supp. III:** 48, 55

1914. Five Sonnets (Brooke), **VI:** 420

1900 (West), **Supp. III:** 432, 445

"Nineteen Hundred and Nineteen" (Yeats), **VI:** 217; **Retro. Supp. I:** 335

"1938" (Kinsella), **Supp. V:** 271

"Nineteenth Century, The" (Thompson), **V:** 442

Nineteenth Century: A Dialogue in Utopia, The (Ellis), **VI:** 241*n*

Nip in the Air, A (Betjeman), **VII:** 357

Niven, Alastair, **VII:** xiv, xxxviii

Njáls saga, **VIII:** 238, 240

"Njamba Nene" stories (Ngũgĩ), **VIII:** 222

No (Ackroyd), **Supp. VI:** 2

No Abolition of Slavery . . . (Boswell), **III:** 248

No Continuing City (Longley), **VIII:** 163, 165, 167–169, 170, 171, 175

No Enemy (Ford), **VI:** 324

No Exit (Sartre), **III:** 329, 345

"No Flowers by Request" (Ewart), **Supp. VII:** 36

No Fond Return of Love (Pym), **Supp. II: 374–375,** 381

No Fool Like an Old Fool (Ewart), **Supp. VII:** 41

"No Immortality?" (Cornford), **VIII:** 105, 109

No Laughing Matter (Wilson), **Supp. I:** 162–163

No Man's Land (Hill, R.), **Supp. IX:** 117–118, 121

No Man's Land (Pinter), **Supp. I:** 377

No More Parades (Ford), **VI:** 319, 329

No Name (Collins), **Supp. VI:** 91, 93–94, **97–98,** 102

No Other Life (Moore, B.), **Supp. IX:** 151, 152–153

No Painted Plumage (Powys), **VIII:** 245, 254–255, 256, 257, 258

No Quarter (Waugh), **Supp. VI:** 275

"No Rest for the Wicked" (Mahon), **Supp. VI:** 167

"No Return" (Smith, I. C.), **Supp. IX:** 218

"No Road" (Larkin), **Supp. I:** 285

"No Room" (Powys), **VIII:** 249, 254, 258

"No Smoking" (Ewart), **Supp. VII:** 47

No Star on the Way Back (Nicholson), **Supp. VI:** 217

"No, Thank You John" (Rossetti), **V:** 256

No Truce with Time (Waugh), **Supp. VI:** 274

No Wit, No Help Like a Woman's (Middleton), **II:** 3, 21

"No Muses" (Smith, I. C.), **Supp. IX:** 222

"No Witchcraft for Sale" (Lessing), **Supp. I:** 241, 242

"No worst, There is none" (Hopkins), **V:** 374

Noah and the Waters (Day Lewis), **Supp. III:** 118, 126, 127

"Noble Child is Born, The" (Dunbar). *See Et Nobis Puer Natus Est*

Noble Jilt, The (Trollope), **V:** 102

Noble Numbers (Herrick), *see His Noble Numbers*

Nobleman, The (Tourneur), **II:** 37

Noblesse Oblige (Mitford), **Supp. X:** 163

"Nocturnal Reverie" (Finch), **Supp. IX:** 76

Nocturnal upon S. Lucy's Day, A (Donne), **I:** 358, 359–360; **II:** 128; **Retro. Supp. II:** 91

"Nocturne" (Coppard), **VIII:** 88

"Nocturne" (Murphy), **Supp. V:** 325

Noh theater, **VI:** 218

Noises Off (Frayn), **Supp. VII:** 61

"Noisy Flushes the Birds" (Pritchett), **Supp. III:** 324–325

"Noisy in the Doghouse" (Pritchett), **Supp. III:** 324, 325

"Noli emulari" (Wyatt), **I:** 102

Nollius, **II:** 185, 201

Nomadic Alternative, The (Chatwin, B.), **Supp. IX:** 52, 58

"Nona Vincent" (James), **VI:** 69

"Nones" (Auden), **Retro. Supp. I:** 2

Nonsense Songs, Stories, Botany and Alphabets (Lear), **V:** 78, 84, 87

Non–Stop Connolly Show, The (Arden and D'Arcy), **Supp. II:** 28, 30, **35–38,** 39

Nooks and Byways of Italy, The (Ramage), **VI:** 298

"Noon at St. Michael's" (Mahon), **Supp. VI:** 174

"Noonday Axeman" (Murray), **Supp. VII:** 272

Norman Douglas (Dawkins), **VI:** 303–304

Norman Conquests, The (Ayckbourn), **Supp. V:** 2, 5, 9, 10, 11, 14

Normyx, pseud. of Norman Douglas

North, Thomas, **I:** 314

North (Heaney), **Supp. II:** 268, **273–275;** **Supp. IV:** 412, 420–421, 427; **Retro. Supp. I:** 124, 125, 129–130

"North Africa" (Morgan, E.), **Supp. IX:** 167

North America (Trollope), **V:** 101

North and South (Gaskell), **V:** xxii, **1–6,** 8, 15

"North and South, The" (Browning), **IV:** 315

North Face (Renault), **Supp. IX:** 175–176

"North London Book of the Dead, The" (Self), **Supp. V:** 400

"North Sea" (Keyes), **VII:** 437

"North Sea off Carnoustie" (Stevenson), **Supp. VI:** 260

North Ship, The (Larkin), **Supp. I:** 276–277

"North Wind, The" (Bridges), **VI:** 80

Northanger Abbey (Austen), **III:** 335–336, 345; **IV:** xvii, 103, 104, 107–110, 112–114, 122; **Retro. Supp. II:** 4–6

Northanger Novels, The (Sadleir), **III:** 335, 346

"Northern Farmer, New Style" (Tennyson), **IV:** 327

"Northern Farmer, Old Style" (Tennyson), **IV:** 327

"Stone and Mr. Thomas, The" (Powys), **VIII:** 258

"Stone Mania" (Murphy), **Supp. V:** 326

Stone Virgin (Unsworth), **Supp. VII:** 355, 356, 357, 360–361, 362, 365

"Stone-In-Oxney" (Longley), **VIII:** 169, 175

Stones of Venice, The (Ruskin), **V:** xxi, 173, 176–177, 180, 184, 292

"Stony Grey Soil "(Kavanagh), **Supp. VII:** 189–190

Stoppard, Tom, **Supp. I: 437–454**; **Retro. Supp. II: 343–358**

Storey, David, **Supp. I: 407–420**

Storey, Graham, **V:** xi, xxviii, 381

Stories, Dreams, and Allegories (Schreiner), **Supp. II:** 450

Stories from ABlack and White" (Hardy), **VI:** 20

Stories of Red Hanrahan (Yeats), **VI:** 222

Stories of the Seen and Unseen (Oliphant), **Supp. X:** 220

Stories, Theories and Things (Brooke-Rose)), **Supp. IV:** 99, 110

"Stories, Theories and Things" (Brooke-Rose)), **Supp. IV:** 116

"Storm" (Nye), **Supp. X:** 204-205

"Storm" (Owen), **VI:** 449

"Storm, The" (Brown), **Supp. VI:** 70–71

"Storm, The" (Donne), **Retro. Supp. II:** 86

Storm, The; or, A Collection of . . . Casualties and Disasters . . . (Defoe), **III:** 13; **Retro. Supp. I:** 68

Storm and Other Poems (Sillitoe), **Supp. V:** 424

"Storm Bird, Storm Dreamer" (Ballard), **Supp. V:** 26

"Storm is over, The land hushes to rest, The" (Bridges), **VI:** 79

"Stormpetrel" (Murphy), **Supp. V:** 315

"Storm–Wind" (Ballard), **Supp. V:** 22

"Story, A" (Smitch, I. C.), **Supp. IX:** 222

"Story, A" (Thomas), **Supp. I:** 183

Story and the Fable, The (Muir), **Supp. VI:** 198

"Story in It, The" (James), **VI:** 69

"Story of a Masterpiece, The" (James), **VI:** 69

Story of a Non–Marrying Man, The (Lessing), **Supp. I:** 253–254

"Story of a Panic, The" (Forster), **VI:** 399

"Story of a Year, The" (James), **VI:** 69

Story of an African Farm, The (Schreiner), **Supp. II:** 435, 438, 439, 440, 441, **445–447**, 449, 451, 453, 456

Story of Fabian Socialism, The (Cole), **VI:** 131

Story of Grettir the strong, The (Morris and Magnusson), **V:** 306

Story of Rimini, The (Hunt), **IV:** 214

Story of San Michele, The (Munthe), **VI:** 265

Story of Sigurd the Volsung and the Fall of the Niblungs, The (Morris), **V:** xxiv, 299–300, 304, 306

Story of the Glittering Plain, The (Morris), **V:** 306

Story of the Injured Lady, The (Swift), **III:** 27

Story of the Malakand Field Force (Churchill), **VI:** 351

Story of the Sundering Flood, The (Morris), **V:** 306

"Story of the Three Bears, The" (Southey), **IV:** 58, 67

"Story of the Unknown Church, The" (Morris), **V:** 293, 303

Story of the Volsungs and . . . Songs from the Elder Edda, The (Morris and Magnusson), **V:** 299, 306

Story So Far, The (Ayckbourn), **Supp. V:** 2

"Storyteller, The" (Berger), **Supp. IV:** 90, 91

Story–Teller, The (Highsmith), **Supp. V:** 174–175

Storyteller, The (Sillitoe), **Supp. V:** 410

Story–Teller's Holiday, A (Moore), **VI:** 88, 95, 99

Stout, Mira, **Supp. IV:** 75

Stovel, Nora Foster, **Supp. IV:** 245, 249

Stowe, Harriet Beecher, **V:** xxi, 3

Strachey, J. St. Loe, **V:** 75, 86, 87

Strachey, Lytton, **III:** 21, 28; **IV:** 292; **V:** 13, 157, 170, 277; **VI:** 155, 247, 372, 407; **VII:** 34, 35; **Supp. II: 497–517**

Strado, Famiano, **II:** 90

Strafford: An Historical Tragedy (Browning), **IV:** 373

Strait Gate, The . . . (Bunyan), **II:** 253

"Strand at Lough Beg, The" (Heaney), **Supp. II:** 278

Strange and the Good, The (Fuller), **Supp. VII:** 81

"Strange and Sometimes Sadness, A" (Ishiguro), **Supp. IV:** 303, 304

Strange Case of Dr. Jekyll and Mr. Hyde, The (Stevenson), **III:** 330, 342, 345; **V:** xxv, 383, 387, 388, 395; **VI:** 106; **Supp. IV:** 61; **Retro. Supp. I:** 263, 264–266

"Strange Comfort Afforded by the Profession" (Lowry), **Supp. III:** 281

Strange Fruit (Phillips), **Supp. V:** 380

"Strange Meeting" (Owen), **VI:** 444, 445, 449, 454, 457–458

Strange Necessity, The (West), **Supp. III:** 438

"Strange Ride of Morrowbie Jukes, The" (Kipling), **VI:** 175–178

Strange Ride of Rudyard Kipling, The (Wilson), **VI:** 165; **Supp. I:** 167

Strange World, A (Braddon), **VIII:** 37

Stranger, The (Kotzebue), **III:** 268

Stranger Still, A (Kavan), **Supp. VII:** 207–208, 209

Stranger With a Bag, A (Warner), **Supp. VII:** 380

Strangers: A Family Romance (Tennant), **Supp. IX:** 239

Strangers and Brothers cycle (Snow), **VII:** xxi, 322, **324–336**

Strangers on a Train (Highsmith), **Supp. V:** 167, 168–169

Strapless (film), **Supp. IV:** 282, 291–292

"Strategist, The" (Saki), **Supp. VI:** 243

"Stratton Water" (Rossetti), **V:** 239

Strauss, Richard, **Supp. IV:** 556

"Strawberry Hill" (Hughes), **Supp. I:** 342

Strayed Reveller, The (Arnold), **V:** xxi, 209, 216

"Street in Cumberland, A" (Nicholson), **Supp. VI:** 216

Street Songs (Sitwell), **VII:** 135

"Streets of the Spirits" (Redgrove), **Supp. VI:** 235

"Strephon and Chloe" (Swift), **III:** 32; **Retro. Supp. I:** 284, 285

Strickland, Agnes, **I:** 84

Strictures on AConingsby" (Disraeli), **IV:** 308

"Strictures on Pictures" (Thackeray), **V:** 37

Striding Folly (Sayers), **Supp. III:** 335

Strife (Galsworthy), **VI:** xiii, 269, 285–286

Strike at Arlingford, The (Moore), **VI:** 95

Strindberg, August, **Supp. III:** 12

Stringham, Charles, **IV:** 372

Strings Are False, The (MacNeice), **VII:** 406

Strip Jack (Rankin), **Supp. X:** 244, 250–251, 253

Strode, Ralph, **I:** 49

Strong, Roy, **I:** 237

Strong Poison (Sayers), **Supp. III:** 339, 342, 343, 345

Stronger Climate, A: Nine Stories (Jhabvala), **Supp. V:** 235

Structure and Distribution of Coral Reefs, On the (Darwin), **Supp. VII:** 19

Structural Analysis of Pound's Usura Canto: Jakobsonand Applied to Free Verse, A (Brooke-Rose)), **Supp. IV:** 99, 114

Structural Transformation of the Public Sphere, The (Habermas), **Supp. IV:** 112

Structure in Four Novels by H. G. Wells (Newell), **VI:** 245, 246

Structure of Complex Words, The (Empson), **Supp. II:** 180, **192–195,** 197

"Studies in a Dying Culture" (Caudwell), **Supp. IX:** 36

Struggle of the Modern, The (Spender), **Supp. II:** 492

Struggles of Brown, Jones and Robinson, The (Trollope), **V:** 102

"Strugnell's Christian Songs" (Cope), **VIII:** 78

"Strugnell's Sonnets" (Cope), **VIII:** 73–74

Strutt, Joseph, **IV:** 31

Strutton, Bill, **Supp. IV:** 346

Struwwelpeter (Hoffman), **I:** 25; **Supp. III:** 296

Stuart, D. M., **V:** 247, 256, 260

"Stubb's Calendar" (Thackeray), *see* AFatal Boots, The"

Studies in a Dying Culture (Caudwell), **Supp. IX:** 33, 43–47

Studies in Classic American Literature (Lawrence), **VII:** 90; **Retro. Supp. II:** 234

Studies in Ezra Pound (Davie), **Supp. VI:** 115

Studies in Prose and Poetry (Swinburne), **II:** 102; **V:** 333

"To the Memory of My Beloved, the Author Mr William Shakespeare" (Jonson), **Retro. Supp. I:** 165

"To the Memorie of My Ever Desired Friend Dr. Donne" (King), **Supp. VI:** 156

"To the Merchants of Edinburgh" (Dunbar), **VIII:** 126

"To the Muses" (Blake), **III:** 289; **Retro. Supp. I:** 34

"To the Name of Jesus" (Crashaw), **II:** 180

"To the Nightingal" (Finch), **Supp. IX:** 68–69

"To the Nightingale" (McGuckian), **Supp. V:** 283

To the North (Bowen), **Supp. II:** 85, 88–89

"To the Pen Shop" (Kinsella), **Supp. V:** 274

"To the Queen" (Tennyson), **IV:** 337

To the Queen, upon Her . . . Birthday (Waller), **II:** 238

"To the Reader" (Jonson), **Retro. Supp. I:** 165

"To the Reader" (Webster), **I:** 246

"To the Reverend Shade of His Religious Father" (Herrick), **II:** 113

"To the Rev. W. H. Brookfield" (Tennyson), **IV:** 329

"To the Royal Society" (Cowley), **II:** 196, 198

"To the Sea" (Larkin), **Supp. I:** 283, 285

"To the Shade of Elliston" (Lamb), **IV:** 82–83

"To the Slow Drum" (Ewart), **Supp. VII:** 42

"To the Small Celandine" (Wordsworth), **IV:** 21

"To the (Supposed) Patron" (Hill), **Supp. V:** 184

"To the Virgins, to Make Much of Time" (Herrick), **II:** 108–109

To the Wedding (Berger), **Supp. IV:** 80

To This Hard House (Friel), **Supp. V:** 115

"To Thom Gunn in Los Altos, California" (Davie), **Supp. VI:** 112

"To Three Irish Poets" (Longley), **VIII:** 167–168

"To True Soldiers" (Jonson), **Retro. Supp. I:** 154

"To Vandyk" (Waller), **II:** 233

"To Virgil" (Tennyson), **IV:** 327

"To wet your eye withouten tear" (Wyatt), **I:** 105–106

"To what serves Mortal Beauty?" (Hopkins), **V:** 372, 373

"To Whom It May Concern" (Motion), **Supp. VII:** 264

To Whom She Will (Jhabvala), **Supp. V:** 224–226

"To William Camden" (Jonson), **Retro. Supp. I:** 152

"To William Godwin" (Coleridge), **IV:** 43

"To X" (Fuller), **Supp. VII:** 74

"To Yvor Winters, 1955" (Gunn), **Supp. IV:** 261

"Toads" (Larkin), **Supp. I:** 277, 278, 281

"Toads Revisited" (Larkin), **Supp. I:** 281

"Toccata of Galuppi's, A" (Browning), **IV:** 357

To–Day (periodical), **VI:** 103

Todhunter, John, **V:** 325

Todorov, Tzvetan, **Supp. IV:** 115–116

Together (Douglas), **VI:** 299–300, 304, 305

Toil & Spin: Two Directions in Modern Poetry (Wallace-Crabbe), **VIII:** 319, 325

Tolkien, J. R. R., **Supp. II: 519–535; Supp. IV:** 116

"Tollund Man, The" (Heaney), **Supp. II:** 273, 274; **Retro. Supp. I:** 128

Tolstoy (Wilson), **Supp. VI:** 304

Tolstoy, Leo, **Supp. IV:** 94, 139

"Tom Brown Question, The" (Wodehouse), **Supp. III:** 449

Tom Brown's Schooldays (Hughes), **V:** xxii, 157, 170; **Supp. IV:** 506

Tom Jones (Fielding), **III:** 95, 96–97, 100–102, 105; **Supp. II:** 194, 195; **Retro. Supp. I:** 81, 86–89, 90–91; **Retro. Supp. I:** 81, 86–89, 90–91

Tom O'Bedlam's Beauties (Reading), **VIII:** 264–265

Tom Thumb (Fielding), **III:** 96, 105

"Tom–Dobbin" (Gunn), **Supp. IV:** 267

Tomlin, Eric Walter Frederick, **VII:** xv, xxxviii

"Tomlinson" (Kipling), **VI:** 202

"Tomorrow" (Conrad), **VI:** 148

"Tomorrow" (Harris), **Supp. V:** 131

"Tomorrow Is a Million Years" (Ballard), **Supp. V:** 26

Tomorrow Morning, Faustus! (Richards), **Supp. II:** 427–428

"Tom's Garland" (Hopkins), **V:** 376

"Tone of Time, The" (James), **VI:** 69

"Tongues of Fire" (Wallace-Crabbe), **VIII:** 325

Tonight at 8:30 (Coward), **Supp. II:** 152–153

Tono–Bungay (Wells), **VI:** xii, 237–238, 244

Tonson, Jacob, **II:** 323; **III:** 69

"Tony Kytes, The Arch–Deceiver" (Hardy), **VI:** 22

"Tony White's Cottage" (Murphy), **Supp. V:** 328

"Too Dearly Bought" (Gissing), **V:** 437

Too Good to Be True (Shaw), **VI:** 125, 127, 129

"Too Late" (Browning), **V:** 366, 369

Too Late the Phalarope (Paton), **Supp. II:** 341, **351–353**

Too Many Husbands (Maugham), **VI:** 368–369

"Too Much" (Muir), **Supp. VI:** 207

"Toot Baldon" (Motion), **Supp. VII:** 253

Tooth and Nail (Rankin), see *Wolfman*

Top Girls (Churchill), **Supp. IV:** 179, 183, 189–191, 198

Topkapi (film), **Supp. IV:** 4

"Torridge" (Trevor), **Supp. IV:** 501

"Tortoise and the Hare, The" (Dahl), **Supp. IV:** 226

Tortoises (Lawrence), **VII:** 118

Tortoises, Terrapins and Turtles (Sowerby and Lear), **V:** 76, 87

"Torturer's Apprenticeship, The" (Murray), **Supp. VII:** 280

"Tory Prime Minister, Maggie May . . . , A" (Rushdie), **Supp. IV:** 456

Totemism (Frazer), **Supp. III:** 171

"Totentanz" (Wilson), **Supp. I:** 155, 156, 157

Tottel's Miscellany, **I:** 97–98, 114

Touch (Gunn), **Supp. IV:** 257, 264, 265–266

"Touch" (Gunn), **Supp. IV:** 265–266

Touch and Go (Lawrence), **VII:** 120, 121

Touch of Love, A (screenplay, Drabble), **Supp. IV:** 230

Touch of Mistletoe, A (Comyns), **VIII:** 54–55, 56, 58–59, 65

Tour Thro' the Whole Island of Great Britain (Defoe), **III:** 5, 13; **Retro. Supp. I:** 75–76

Tour to the Hebrides, A (Boswell), see *Journal of a Tour to the Hebrides*

Tourneur, Cyril, **II:** 24, 33, **36–41,** 70, 72, 85, 97

Toward Reality (Berger), see *Permanent Red: Essays in Seeing*

"Toward the Imminent Days" (Murray), **Supp. VII:** 274

"Towards an Artless Society" (Lewis), **VII:** 76

Towards the End of Morning (Frayn), **Supp. VII:** 53–54, 65

Towards the Human (Smith, I. C.), **Supp. IX:** 209

Towards the Mountain (Paton), **Supp. II:** 346, 347, 351, 359

Towards Zero (Christie), **Supp. II:** 132, 134

Tower, The (Fry), **Supp. III:** 194, 195

Tower, The (Yeats), **VI:** 207, 216, 220; **Retro. Supp. I:** 333–335

Towers of Silence, The (Scott), **Supp. I:** 267–268

Town (periodical), **V:** 22

"Town and Country" (Brooke), **VI:** 420

"Town Betrayed, The" (Muir), **Supp. VI:** 206

Townley plays, **I:** 20

Townsend, Aurelian, **II:** 222, 237

Townsend Warner, George, **VI:** 485

Town–Talk (periodical), **III:** 50, 53

"Trace Elements" (Wallace-Crabbe), **VIII:** 323

"Track 12" (Ballard), **Supp. V:** 21

Trackers of Oxyrhyncus, The (Harrison), **Supp. V:** 163, 164

Tract 90 (Newman), see *Remarks on Certain Passages of the 39 Articles*

"Tractor" (Hughes), **Retro. Supp. II:** 211

Tracts for the Times (Newman), **Supp. VII:** 291, 293

"Traction–Engine, The" (Auden), **Retro. Supp. I:** 3

"Tradition and the Individual Talent" (Eliot), **VII:** 155, 156, 163, 164

"Tradition of Eighteen Hundred and Four, A" (Hardy), **VI:** 22

Tradition of Women's Fiction, The (Drabble), **Supp. IV:** 231

Tradition, the Writer and Society (Harris), **Supp. V:** 145, 146

Wimsatt, M. K., Jr., **III:** 249

Winckelman, Johann, **V:** 341, 343, 344

"Winckelmann" (Pater), **V:** 341, 343, 344

Wind, Edgar, **I:** 237; **V:** 317*n*

"Wind" (Hughes), **Supp. I:** 343–344

Wind Among the Reeds, The (Yeats), **VI:** 211, 222

Wind from Nowhere, The (Ballard), **Supp. V:** 22

"Windhover, The" (Hopkins), **V:** 366, 367; **Retro. Supp. II:** 190, 191, 195–196

Winding Paths: Photographs by Bruce Chatwin (Chatwin, B.), **Supp. IX:** 62

Winding Stair, The (Yeats), **Supp. II:** 84–85; **Retro. Supp. I:** 336–337

Winding Stair, The: Francis Bacon, His Rise and Fall (du Maurier), **Supp. III:** 139

Windom's Way (Ambler), **Supp. IV:** 3

"Window, The" (Moore), **VI:** 93

Window in Thrums, A (Barrie), **V:** 392; **Supp. III:** 3

Windows (Galsworthy), **VI:** 269

"Windows, The" (Herbert), **Retro. Supp. II:** 176

Windows of Night (Williams, C. W. S.), **Supp. IX:** 274

"Wind's on the World, The" (Morris), **V:** 305

"Windscale" (Nicholson), **Supp. VI:** 218

Windsor Forest (Pope), **III:** 70, 77; **Retro. Supp. I:** 231

Wine, A Poem (Gay), **III:** 67

"Wine Fed Tree, The" (Powys), **VIII:** 251

Wine, Water and Song (Chesterton), **VI:** 340

"Wingless" (Kincaid), **Supp. VII:** 220, 221, 226

Wings of the Dove, The (James), **VI:** 32, 55, **59–60,** 320; **Supp. IV:** 243

"Winkie" (Dunn), **Supp. X:** 77

Winkworth, Catherine, **V:** 149

Winnie–the–Pooh (Milne), **Supp. V:** 295, 303–307

"Winning of Etain, The" (Boland), **Supp. V:** 36

"Winnowers, The" (Bridges), **VI:** 78

Winslow Boy, The (Rattigan), **Supp. VII:** 307, 313–315

"Winter" (Blake), **Retro. Supp. I:** 34

"Winter" (Brontë), **V:** 107

"Winter" (Dunn), **Supp. X:** 69

Winter (Thomson), **Supp. III:** 411, 412–413, 417, 418

Winter Apology (Bainbridge), **Supp. VI:** **22–23**

"Winter Field" (Coppard), **VIII:** 98

Winter Fuel (Millais), **V:** 379

Winter Garden (Bainbridge), **Supp. VI:** **22–23,** 24

Winter House and Other Poems, The (Cameron), **Supp. IX:** 17, 22–25

"Winter in Camp" (Fuller), **Supp. VII:** 70

"Winter in England" (Fuller), **Supp. VII:** 70

"Winter in July" (Lessing), **Supp. I:** 240

Winter in the Air (Warner), **Supp. VII:** 380

"Winter Landscape near Ely, A" (Davie), **Supp. VI:** 110

"Winter, My Secret" (Rossetti), **V:** 256

"Winter Night" (Fuller), **Supp. VII:** 72

Winter Pilgrimage, A (Haggard), **Supp. III:** 214

Winter Pollen: Occasional Prose (Hughes), **Retro. Supp. II:** 202

Winter Tales (Brown), **Supp. VI:** 68–70

"Winter with the Gulf Stream" (Hopkins), **V:** 361, 381

Winter Words, in Various Moods and Metres (Hardy), **VI:** 20

Wintering Out (Heaney), **Supp. II:** 268, 272–273; **Retro. Supp. I:** 125, 128

Winters, Yvor, **VI:** 219; **Supp. IV:** 256–257, 261; **Retro. Supp. I:** 335

"Winters and the Palmleys, The" (Hardy), **VI:** 22

"Winter's Tale, A" (Thomas), **Supp. I:** 177, 178

Winter's Tale, The (Chaucer), **I:** 25

Winter's Tale, The (Shakespeare), **I:** 166*n*, 302, 322–323, 327

"Winter's Talents" (Davie), **Supp. VI:** 112

Winterslow: Essays and Characters Written There (Hazlitt), **IV:** 140

Winterson, Jeanette, **Supp. IV:** **541–559**

Winterwood and Other Hauntings (Roberts, K.), **Supp. X:** 273

"Wintry Manifesto, A" (Wallace-Crabbe), **VIII:** 313

"Wires" (Larkin), **Supp. I:** 278, 285

"Wisdom Literature", **Retro. Supp. II:** 304

Wisdom of Father Brown, The (Chesterton), **VI:** 338

"Wisdom of Gautama, The" (Caudwell), **Supp. IX:** 33

Wisdom of Solomon Paraphrased, The (Middleton), **II:** 2

Wisdom of the Ancients (Bacon), *see De sapientia veterum*

Wise, T. J., **V:** 150, 151

Wise Children (Carter), **Supp. III:** 90–91

Wise Virgins (Wilson), **Supp. VI:** 297, **301,** 303

Wise Wound, The (Redgrove), **Supp. VI:** 230, 233

"Wish, The" (Cowley), **II:** 195, 198

"Wish, The" (Dahl), **Supp. IV:** 206, 221

"Wish House, The" (Kipling), **VI:** 169, 193, 196, **197–199**

"Wish in Spring" (Warner), **Supp. VII:** 373

"Wishes to His (Supposed), Mistresse" (Crashaw), **II:** 180

Wit at Several Weapons, **II:** 21, 66

Wit Without Money (Fletcher), **II:** 66

Witch, The (Middleton), **II:** 3, 21; **IV:** 79

Witch, The (Williams, C. W. S.), **Supp. IX:** 276–277

Witch Hunt (Rankin), **Supp. X:** 245, 252

"Witch of Atlas, The" (Shelley), **IV:** 196, 204

Witch of Edmonton, The (Dekker, Ford, Rowley), **II:** 89, 100

"Witch of Fife, The" (Hogg), **Supp. X:** 106–108

Witchcraft (Williams, C. W. S.), **Supp. IX:** 284

Witches, The (Dahl), **Supp. IV:** 204, 213, 215, 225–226

Witches, The (film), **Supp. IV:** 203

Witch's Head, The (Haggard), **Supp. III:** 213

"Witches of Traquair, The" (Hogg), **Supp. X:** 110

With My Little Eye (Fuller), **Supp. VII:** 70–71

"With my Sons at Boarhills" (Stevenson), **Supp. VI:** 260

Wither, George, **IV:** 81

"Withered Arm, The" (Hardy), **VI:** 22; **Retro. Supp. I:** 116

Within the Gates (O'Casey), **VII:** 7

Within the Tides: Tales (Conrad), **VI:** 148

"Without Benefit of Clergy" (Kipling), **VI:** 180–183

"Without Eyes" (Redgrove), **Supp. VI:** 235

"Without the Option" (Wodehouse), **Supp. III:** 456

Witlings, The (Burney), **Supp. III:** 64, 71, 72, 75

"Witness, The" (Lessing), **Supp. I:** **244**

Witness for the Prosecution (Christie), **Supp. II:** 125, 134

Wit's Treasury (Meres), **I:** 296

Wittig, Monique, **Supp. IV:** 558

Wives and Daughters (Gaskell), **V:** xxiii, 1–4, 8, 11–13, 14, 15

Wizard of Oz, The (Baum), **Supp. IV:** 450

Wizard of Oz, The (film), **Supp. IV:** 434, 443, 448, 450, 455

Wizard of Oz, The (Rushdie), **Supp. IV:** 434

Wodehouse, P. G., **Supp. III:** **447–464**

Wodwo (Hughes), **Supp. I:** 343, 346, **348–350,** 363; **Retro. Supp. II:** 205–206

Woefully Arrayed (Skelton), **I:** 84

Wolf and the Lamb, The (Henryson), **Supp. VII:** 136, 141

Wolf and the Wether, The (Henryson), **Supp. VII:** 136, 140–141

Wolf, Friedrich, **IV:** 316–317

Wolf, Lucien, **IV:** 293

Wolf Leader, The (Dumas *père*), **III:** 339

Wolf that gat the Nekhering throw the wrinkis of the Foxe that begylit the Cadgear, The (Henryson), see *Fox, the Wolf, and the Cadger, The*

Wolfe, Tom, **Supp. IV:** 454

Wolff, S. L., **I:** 164

"Wolfhound, The" (Murphy), **Supp. V:** 323

Wolfman (Rankin), **Supp. X:** 244, 246, 248, 250

Wolfwatching (Hughes), **Retro. Supp. II:** 214

Wollstonecraft, Mary, **Supp. III:** **465–482;** **Retro. Supp. I:** 39

Wolves and the Lamb, The (Thackeray), **V:** 35

Woman (periodical), **VI:** 249

Woman, The (Bond), **Supp. I:** 423, 434, 435

ISBN 0-684-31312-X

90000